CYPRUS – Principal Features and Mediterranean Context

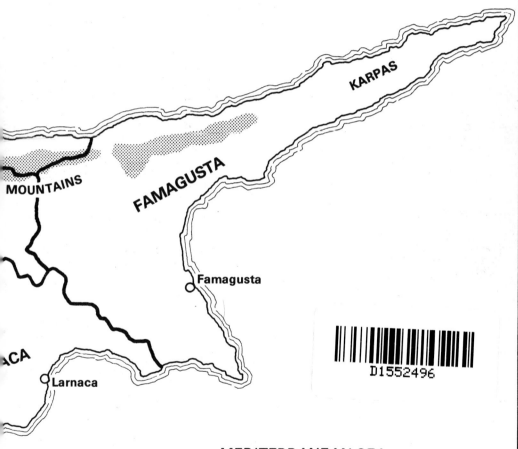

10 5 0 10 20
Miles

—— District boundaries

KARPAS

MOUNTAINS

FAMAGUSTA

Famagusta

ACA

Larnaca

MEDITERRANEAN SEA

The Cyprus Revolt

The
Cyprus Revolt,

An account of the struggle for
union with Greece ,

Nancy Crawshaw

London
GEORGE ALLEN & UNWIN
Boston   Sydney

First published 1978

ISBN 0 04 940053 3

Printed in Great Britain by William Clowes & Sons, Limited
London, Beccles and Colchester

To G. C.
but for whose encouragement
this book would not have
been finished

Contents

PREFACE   *page* 13

NOTE ON TRANSLITERATION   14

I INTRODUCTION   17
Historical Background – British Rule from 1878 to the Outbreak of the Second World War

II THE GROWTH OF THE ENOSIS MOVEMENT IN CYPRUS, 1940–1953   30
Revival of Cypriot Politics during the Second World War – Ascendancy of the Nationalists

   1 Revival of Political Activity, 1940 Onwards
   2 The Labour Government and Abortive Reforms
   3 The Turkish Cypriot Community, 1940–1948
   4 The Plebiscite, 1949–1950
   5 Cypriot Politics after the Rise of Makarios III

III THE YEARS OF WARNING, 1950–1954   57
The Quest for Support Abroad – First Greek Appeal to UN

   1 The Quest for Support Abroad
   2 Rising Pressure in Greece for Enosis, 1950 Onwards
   3 Papagos and the Cyprus Question
   4 The Climax in 1954
   5 Hopkinson's 'Never'
   6 The First Greek Appeal to the United Nations

IV THE ORIGINS OF EOKA, 1948–1955   90
Grivas's Early Subversive Activities – Final Preparations for the Cyprus Revolt

   1 Colonel Grivas ('Dighenis')
   2 Subversive Activities of Grivas, 1948–1954
   3 Psychological Warfare
   4 The Organisation of the Guerrilla Groups

V THE FIRST ROUND, APRIL 1955–
MARCH 1956   *page* 114
Outbreak of Violence – Breakdown of Harding–Makarios Talks

  1 The Outbreak of the Revolt
  2 Political Developments, Summer 1955
  3 International Developments
  4 The Deterioration of Security
  5 Harding's First Five Months
  6 The Harding–Makarios Talks

VI THE INTENSIFICATION OF THE STRUGGLE,
MARCH 1956–MARCH 1957   168
Archbishop's Deportation – His Release

  1 The Deportation
  2 The Intensification of Hostilities
  3 The Rout of the Mountain Gangs
  4 Political Events after the Deportation
  5 The Renewal of Violence
  6 The Radcliffe Plan

VII THE DILEMMA OF THE GREEK GOVERNMENT,
SEPTEMBER 1953–FEBRUARY 1957   210
Anti-Greek riots in Turkey – UN Debate on Cyprus

  1 The Rise of Karamanlis
  2 The Downfall of Theotokis
  3 The Policy of 'Equal Friendship'
  4 The Eleventh Session of the General Assembly

VIII THE CEASE-FIRE, FEBRUARY 1957–OCTOBER 1957 231
Makarios's Return to Greece – Foot's Appointment as Governor

  1 The Intensification of Operations
  2 The Archbishop's Return
  3 The Deadlock
  4 The Atrocity Campaign
  5 Preparations for the Second Round
  6 Strategic and Political Changes in 1957

IX THE SECOND ROUND, DECEMBER 1957–
FEBRUARY 1959   *page* 263
Foot's Governorship – Zurich Agreement

  1 The Appointment of Sir Hugh Foot
  2 The Twelfth Session of the UN General Assembly
  3 The Foot Plan
  4 The Renewal of EOKA Action
  5 The Outbreak of Communal Strife
  6 The Macmillan Plan
  7 Greek Against Greek
  8 Passive Resistance
  9 The Renewal of Violence against the British
 10 Political Developments at the end of 1958
 11 The Bid for Independence at the UN

X THE BIRTH OF THE REPUBLIC, FEBRUARY 1959–
AUGUST 1960   340
Zurich and London Agreements – Independence

  1 The Zurich Agreement
  2 Preparations for Independence
  3 The Negotiations on the British Bases
  4 The Last Stages

XI POSTSCRIPT: THE AFTERMATH, 1960–1976   364
*Breakdown of the Zurich Settlement – Turkey's Military Inter-
vention in 1974*

APPENDICES   397

  1 Abbreviations used in the Text
  2 Important Dates in the History of Cyprus
  3 Procedure for Election of Archbishops of Cyprus
  4 The Eoka Oath
  5 Racial Composition and Strength of the Police Force in
     July 1958
  6 Casualty Tables

BIBLIOGRAPHY   409

INDEX   *page* 427

MAPS

   1 Cyprus – Principal Features and Mediterranean
     Context   endpaper
   2 Cyprus – Principal Places and Roads Mentioned
     in Text   220–221
   3 Distribution of Population and the Turkish
     Occupied Area after 16 August 1974   374–375

Preface

The complicated story of the Greek Cypriot struggle for union with Greece began a long time ago; some Cypriots would say in the fifteenth century BC. A more realistic date is the Greek War of Independence in 1821.

The Cyprus question has taken thousands of people to the island on diplomatic and other special duties. *The Cyprus Revolt* was written in response to demands for a comprehensive study which would deal with the diplomatic and military aspects of the problem. It is intended mainly for the serious general reader who, having served in the island, has acquired a lasting interest and some curiosity about the origins of this most intractable dispute. I also hope the book will be useful to diplomats and officials concerned with the affairs of Cyprus now and in future.

By an accident of history the struggle for union with Greece came to a head during British rule and has remained a blot on Anglo-Greek relations for more than a generation. The EOKA rising against the British was an integrated campaign in which guerrilla warfare played an important but supplementary role and was coordinated with some carefully thought out diplomatic or political move far from the scene of the fighting. I have recorded these events in the form of a narrative history, leaving the reader wherever possible to reach his own conclusions. I was an eyewitness to many of the events described and in the course of reporting in Greece and in Cyprus over a period of fifteen years I interviewed almost all the leading personalities engaged in the Cyprus struggle. Many of them are still prominent today.

The troubles which have befallen Cyprus since Independence lie outside the scope of this work and any attempt to deal with them in depth would be premature at this stage. But since the second crisis arose directly out of the first I have, at the publisher's request, concluded the book with a chapter summarising the main events which led to the final disaster of Turkey's military intervention under the Treaty of Guarantee in 1974.

Extensive use has been made of oral interviews; the majority of the more important are non-attributable. The same applies to collections of documents put at my disposal which threw much light on EOKA. I am specially indebted to numerous officials who went to great trouble to provide background information and documents from sources which were not accessible to myself. Without their help and that of other collaborators in Britain, Cyprus, Greece, Turkey and the USA this book could not have been written. Since Independence I have had much help from Mr Peter Stylianakis, member of the Public Information Office of the Republic of Cyprus, Mr Zafer Zihni, former Director of the Turkish Cypriot information services, Mr George C. Christofides and Mr Kemal Rustem.

I am grateful to the following for help with documents, etc: Mrs Domna Dontas, Chief Librarian, the Greek Ministry of Foreign Affairs; Miss M. McAfee, Librarian, the United Nations Information Centre, London; Miss Dorothy Hammerton, Librarian, Miss Elisabeth Campbell, former Press Librarian, and their staff at Chatham House (RIIA); and for much typing and patient retyping to Mrs N. Golovine, and Miss B. Driver-Holloway who also put in much extra work on the proofs and compilation of the index. I have to thank Mr Geoffrey Chandler for useful comments on the MS. and Mrs Margaret Brooke-Tsatsopoulos for criticising the MS. in detail and helping with the proofs. Responsibility for the text's shortcomings is my own.

Finally I take this opportunity to record my gratitude for the unfailing courtesy and hospitality of the people of Cyprus, both in time of peace and under the stress of war and civil strife.

NANCY CRAWSHAW

Note on Transliteration

The transliteration of Greek words presents many difficulties. Many names, especially in Cyprus, have been anglicised in a form which has long become common usage. I have tried to strike a balance between such spellings and the phonetic rendering of Greek names but inconsistencies are unavoidable.

I know little of the history of Cyprus. I think there was a short while ago some reference to its having belonged to Greece. It was my impression that it had at least some cultural connections with Greece, but that it had never, in fact, been under Greek rule, though it may once have been held to have some allegiance to Turkey.

Georges Bohy, delegate of Belgium, Council of Europe Consultative Assembly, 6th Ordinary Session, 25 May 1954, p. 120.

I

Introduction

Historical Background — British Rule from 1878 to the Outbreak of the Second World War

The troubled history of Cyprus stems from its strategic position on the main routes between Europe and Asia.[1] Too small to exist by itself, Cyprus remained at the mercy of the dominant power in the area; the island was bought and sold, transferred from one ruler to another, without the inhabitants ever being consulted. Poor in resources, apart from rich forests in ancient times and copper through the ages, the Cypriots seldom shared in the prosperity of their conquerors, but were forced to pay revenue to absent rulers, to supply foreign armies with men and foreign fleets with timber. To these perennial hardships were added the ravages of earthquake, drought, and famine.

The defeatist attitude of the Greek Cypriots when it comes to the management of their own affairs is not surprising in the light of the island's turbulent past. But the tendency since Independence to make foreigners the scapegoat for all the island's ills has obscured the real issues at stake. And the political disasters of the last ten years, which culminated in the Turkish invasion of 1974, are largely self-inflicted.

Archaeological and historical evidence indicate that the great majority of the population are of mixed race,[2] but the one element of continuity throughout all the foreign conquests has been the survival of the Greek language and religion. The landscape itself, however, is Middle Eastern rather than Aegean. The burnt up plain of the Mesaoria recalls Syria not Greece. The olive groves of Cyprus are meagre in contrast to the

---

[1] The facts in this introduction are drawn mainly from Sir George Hill's *History of Cyprus*, vols I–IV (Cambridge University Press 1940, 1948 and 1952); Cobham's *Excerpta Cypria Materials for a History of Cyprus* (CUP 1908); R. Gunnis's *Historic Cyprus* (Methuen 1956); H. W. Catlin's *Cypriot Bronzework in the Mycenaean World* (Clarendon Press 1964); Sir Ronald Storr's *Orientations* (Nicholson and Watson, definitive edition 1949); *A Guide to the Cyprus Museum* (Republic of Cyprus Dept of Antiquities 1961), etc.

[2] Hill, op. cit. (CUP) vol. I, pp. 93–4, and vol. IV, pp. 488–9.

rich plantations of Corfu and the Peloponnese. The vast forests of Troodos and Paphos, enhanced by an undergrowth of cistus and sumach, have a quality of their own.

The landscape and architecture are constant reminders of the diversity of influences which have shaped the character of Cyprus. A wilderness of sand-dunes and juniper scrub in the distant Karpas marks the bay where it is said the Phoenicians landed. Hidden by acacia trees the columns of ancient Salamis rise close to the sea; in AD 115–16 thousands of Greeks were massacred here by the Jews, who thereafter were banned from the island. Every Greek Cypriot child learns in school about the destruction of Salamis, considered by some historians to be the greatest single calamity to befall the island. Byzantium is represented by hundreds of small domed churches, often on remote sites. In a quiet garden of orange trees at the edge of the salt lake near Larnaca the Tekke of Umharam provides the link with the Arabs. The splendour of the Renaissance is reflected in the Gothic cathedrals of Nicosia and Famagusta, the military power of the Venetians in massive coastal fortresses. The mosque with its tall minaret indicates the continuing presence of the Turks four hundred years after the Turkish conquest; Turkish houses can usually be identified by their construction round a courtyard and the extensive use of wooden balconies and shutters. The relics of British rule are to be found in solid buildings of sandstone in the colonial style; surrounded by verandahs, these are spacious, cool, austere but dignified. The modern Greek Cypriot's obsession with Ancient Greece is illustrated by a preference for public buildings in neo-Classic form. But it is more in the mind and the emotions that the pervasive sense of Greekness persists than in outward signs.

The fundamental inspiration of the movement for union (Enosis) with Greece is Hellenism; its origins are rooted in the mainland. From childhood the Greek is conditioned in church and school to believe that in the fullness of time all Greek-speaking areas must be united within the frontiers of the Motherland. Greeks outside the narrow circles of the most intellectually sophisticated still day-dream of the return of Constantinople and the 'lost lands of Anatolia' and recall the Treaty of Sèvres with nostalgia. Forced upon a weak and demoralised Turkey in 1920, this agreement provided for territorial changes which brought closer the realisation of 'the Great Idea' (*Megali Idea*). However, the Treaty of Sèvres, a casualty of the Revolution of Mustapha Kemal, was not implemented.

The Greek Cypriot, subject to the same indoctrination as his kinsmen in Greece, claims:

Cyprus is in reality a Greek island inhabited by a European people of the Hellenic nation with a history of Greek civilisation and culture extending over thousands of years . . .[1]

His perennial demand for Enosis springs from the compulsive desire to establish Greek identity beyond all doubt and is the natural reaction to centuries of foreign rule. The concept of a 'Greater Greece' which has inspired the nationalism of the mainland has, nevertheless, made less impact in Cyprus where the advocates of Enosis have in their parochialism shown little concern for the fate of Greek communities elsewhere and pressed their claim to a degree which on occasions seriously embarrassed the Motherland.

The Greek Cypriots claim descent from the early Aegean colonists. The date when they first arrived in Cyprus in significant numbers is disputed by archaeologists. Greek was introduced in the ninth century BC and thereafter became the main language. The Cypriot Greek dialect spoken today shows an affinity with that of Rhodes and contains Homeric words.

Although links between Greece and Cyprus were close in the ninth century, the influence of the Greeks was not exclusive, nor did they at any time control the whole island. Cyprus, in fact, succumbed to a succession of conquerors – the Assyrians, the Egyptians and the Persians. But by the fifth century BC there were eleven Greek kingdoms in the island, the most important being Salamis.

It was during the Roman period that the island was converted to Christianity – in AD 45 – by the Apostles Paul and Barnabas, who was a native of Salamis. After the split in the Roman Empire in 395 the island formed an independent province of Byzantium for nearly 800 years, Byzantine supremacy being broken only by the Arab invasions from the seventh century onwards.

The role played by the Autocephalous Eastern Orthodox Church of Cyprus in keeping alive the Greek tradition throughout its history and in fostering political awareness in modern times has been of major importance. Its resolve and tenacity were first shown in a protracted struggle for autocephaly during the early Byzantine age. The Church of Cyprus successfully resisted the encroachments of the Patriarchs of Antioch who sought for centuries to bring it under their control and in 431 the Council of Ephesus gave qualified recognition to its independence. This was confirmed at Constantinople two hundred years later by

---

[1] A Cypriot Greek spokesman in London in 1954. See Nancy Crawshaw, 'The Cyprus Dilemma', *The Twentieth Century*, November 1954.

the Trullan Council after further struggles with Antioch. Subject to no patriarch, the Church of Cyprus retains to this day the right to elect its own archbishop[1] and ranks fifth in the long hierarchy of Eastern Orthodox Churches.

Two Christian minorities of long standing in Cyprus are the Armenians and the Maronites. Too small to give trouble, they have successfully integrated with the Greek majority while maintaining their separate racial, religious and cultural identities.

Byzantine rule ended when Richard Coeur de Lion seized Cyprus on his way to the Third Crusade. He sold it to the Knights Templars who, after crushing a major rising of the inhabitants, re-sold it to Guy de Lusignan, former King of Jerusalem.

The three centuries of Latin rule, hailed by scholars as the most brilliant epoch in the island's history, were for the local people probably the most wretched. The Latins ruthlessly exploited the peasants and placed the Church of Cyprus under the authority of a Latin archbishop. The Church's survival in the face of these ordeals, the worst in its history, testified to its unfailing resilience. In 1489 Catherine Cornaro, the Venetian widow of the Lusignan King James II, gave Cyprus up to Venice which ruled the island until the Turkish conquest in 1571.

The Greek Cypriots at first welcomed the arrival of the Turks. The Latin clergy were expelled, their cathedrals turned into mosques. Serfdom was abolished. The Orthodox Church regained its rightful place; the Archbishop was recognised by the Turks both in his religious role and in his capacity as Ethnarch, the leader of the Greeks in temporal affairs. The great powers obtained by the Church from now on were to have important implications for the future.

Except for occasional clashes the Greek and Turkish Cypriot communities lived in peace for more than three hundred years, finding at times common ground in their joint hostility to the harsh taxation imposed by the Sultan. Greeks have consequently alleged that the intercommunal friction of recent times came about as the result of Britain's recourse to the tactics of 'divide and rule'. The phenomenon of Greco-Turkish coexistence needs, however, to be put in perspective against the background of the Ottoman Empire. It was the Greeks who were then the subject people. The Turkish Cypriots, although numerically inferior, had little to fear so long as the island belonged to Turkey. The situation was drastically changed by the Greek War of Independence and the rise of the Enosis movement. Alarmed at the power of the

---

[1] See Appendix 3.

Church, the Turks publicly executed the Archbishop of Cyprus and other leading Christians in 1821, although there was little proof that they were helping the mainland Greeks. It was at this stage that Greco-Turkish relations in Cyprus embarked on a course of slow but progressive deterioration which eventually led first to civil strife and then to war. The basic cause was Greek pressure for Enosis.

The Turkish Cypriots are Sunni Muslims. Descended mainly from the immigrants who came from Southern Anatolia after the Turkish conquest, they speak a purer form of Turkish than that spoken on the mainland. Originally a farming community, they settled in most parts of the island, except the Troodos mountains, often on agricultural land confiscated from the Latins. This pattern of scattered Turkish communities over a wide area has persisted until the enforced population removals which followed the Turkish invasion of 1974.

The Turkish Cypriots provide the second element of continuity in the history of Cyprus. Unlike the Greek Cypriots, they were never subjected to foreign rule, except for a brief period of British administration initially by consent of their own Sultan. This essential difference in historical experience has been a significant factor in determining political attitudes.

Separatist trends are deeply rooted in the social structure of Cyprus. The demarcation lines in the village are distinct, with the Turkish quarter close to but separated from the Greek sector. In normal times brawls and disputes are more common between rival factions of the Greek community than between the two races.

Greeks and Turks seldom mix socially; and intermarriage is forbidden except after conversion. The process of voluntary segregation is most obvious in the mixed villages, where the two communities living in proximity lead separate existences. The physical division is informal but conspicuous. Church and mosque occupy prominent sites in each sector; each community patronises its own institutions, coffee shops and clubs. Material differences are not marked. Turkish houses tend to be more spacious but barer; the Ottoman system of land tenure and primitive agricultural practices are common to both communities. Until 1974, on days when nationalist feeling used to run high the one half of the village would be draped in the blue and white flags of Greece, the other in the crimson banner of the Turkish crescent. In some villages it is still possible to distinguish Greek from Turk by differences of dress. In the towns a casual observer would find it difficult to tell them apart. Closer acquaintance, however, is likely to reveal strong differences in temperament and mentality.

Incompatibility is greatest on the subject of the Church and its functions. The Greek Orthodox Church remains the most powerful force in nationalist and local politics. The Turks, on the other hand, attach great importance to the concept of the secular state. Thus the Mufti, unlike the Archbishop, has no nationalist mission, and is required to keep out of party politics. The Greek clergy are anathema to the Turks, who regard their political activities as archaic and sinister; Greek rule in Cyprus is seen as a choice between two evils – the Church or the Communists. The gulf has been widened further by the growth of Greek and Turkish nationalism on rival lines in Cypriot secondary schools. Thanks to the easygoing policy of the British authorities, most secondary schools in Cyprus came under the direct influence, and to some extent the control, of Greece or Turkey. In these countries nationalism is at least tempered by some consideration for broader interests, whereas the Cypriots in their parochialism tend to lose sight of reality. A relatively small number of Greek and Turkish Cypriots, educated together at the English School in Nicosia and the American Academy in Larnaca, escaped much of the racialist and nationalist indoctrination which lies at the root of the friction between the two communities. But most Cypriots think of themselves primarily as Greeks and Turks; Cypriot nationalism containing some element of political cohesion between the two communities has never existed.

Britain's interest in the Cyprus question has always been strategic. The Cyprus Convention concluded between Disraeli and the island's Turkish ruler in 1878 was aimed primarily at checking Russian expansionism. The nature of Western interests in Cyprus has, therefore, not substantially changed. The acquisition of better bases in Egypt a few years later was mainly responsible for the economic neglect of the island up to the end of the Second World War.

The British authorities and the Greek Cypriot bishops were at loggerheads from the start. The Church was engaged in a struggle to recover the wide powers it had enjoyed until the Greek War of Independence in 1821. The British refused to recognise its jurisdiction in secular affairs and for the first time in its history it was required to pay taxes. The title of Ethnarch was treated as an anachronism which had ceased to have either validity or justification since the end of the Ottoman Empire. Nevertheless Greek nationalism was encouraged by the tolerant attitude shown especially by the early British administrators towards the Greek Orthodox Church and Greek secondary education. And the Church continued to exercise as in the past a predominant influence in civil affairs, in contrast to the situation in Greece where Eleftherios

Venizelos had sought during the thirties to restrict its authority to religious matters.

Britain's educational policy appears to have been motivated by considerations of philhellenism and economy. The early English administrators with their own grounding in the classics found little reason to quarrel with a curriculum which was dedicated to the achievements of Ancient Greece no matter how much these might be distorted for the purpose of furthering Greek irredentism. Roughly a third of the teachers came from Greece, their pensions and salaries were paid by the Greek Government and the curriculum was subject to the approval of the Ministry of Education in Athens.

The cession of the Ionian Islands in 1864 was seized upon by the Cypriot nationalists as a precedent for similar action by Britain in Cyprus. The situation was not exactly comparable. The Ionian Islands were less important strategically, did not form part of the Ottoman Empire and had no Turkish minority. When Turkey came into the First World War on the side of Germany in 1914 the Cyprus Convention automatically lapsed and Britain annexed Cyprus. This strengthened the argument for union with Greece since Britain could no longer claim that she was bound by her commitments to the Sultan. Still more important in determining the Greek stand was the British offer of Cyprus to Greece in 1915 on condition that she came to the aid of the Allies in Serbia. Owing to the pro-German attitude of King Constantine the offer was not taken up and never renewed. Thenceforward the Greeks treated it as the recognition on the part of Britain of the rightness of their claim. The circumstances were, however, unique and transitory. Supporters of Enosis also received moral encouragement from British spokesmen. Winston Churchill wrote in 1907:

> I think it only natural that the Cypriot people, who are of Greek descent, should regard their incorporation with what may be called their Motherland as an ideal to be earnestly, devoutly and feverishly cherished . . .[1]

The passage became famous as the result of its selective use by the Cypriot nationalists up to the present time. The subsequent qualifying paragraph in which Churchill makes it clear that the views of the Muslims would also have to be taken into account is always omitted.

The absence of political violence gave the British the impression that

---

[1] Capt. C. W. J. Orr, *Cyprus Under British Rule* (Zeno Publishers, London, 1972), p. 163, quoting Official Records C. 3396 (1908).

the Enosis movement, although tiresome, was no cause for alarm. The colonial administration hoped that by tolerating the sedition which flowed from the pulpit and the press Enosis would burn itself out, and for years the subject was merely academic. Moreover, good relations between Greece and Great Britain ensured that it did not become a source of international friction.

The acceptance by Greece and Turkey of British rule over Cyprus under the treaty of Lausanne in 1923 might have been expected to produce a definitive settlement. But the exponents of Enosis were not deterred. In 1928 the authorities decided to celebrate the anniversary of the British occupation – a decision which in itself was provocative. The Church ordered all Greeks to boycott the ceremonies. The litany was sung in 600 churches, with prayers for Enosis. Noisy demonstrations took place. A further cause of trouble was an ill-timed visit to Sir Ronald Storrs from the Italian Governor of Rhodes.

Even the smallest move in favour of Enosis was guaranteed to provoke reaction on the part of the Turkish Cypriots. Hill's History records no less than twenty examples between 1882 and 1931 of counter-agitation by the Turks. Always strongly opposed to any form of government which would bring them under the domination of the Greek majority, the Turkish Cypriots in 1882 presented a petition to the British Government demanding equality of representation in local affairs and invoking the precedent of the Christians in Asia Minor who, although in the minority, had an equal number of votes with the Muslims on the administrative councils. This demand for parity by the Turkish Cypriots has recurred in subsequent years up to the present time. Uncertainty about the political future of Cyprus led to the formation in 1919 of a small Turkish Cypriot party which advocated the island's return to Turkey. Turkish interests were in effect protected by the Legislative Council since the combined votes of the President, the official members and the Turks exceeded those of the Greeks.

The merits of the colonial regime must be sought mainly in administrative matters such as the establishment of an efficient civil service, a sound system of justice and taxation. The British also did much to check the ravages of erosion and to free the Cypriot peasant from the stranglehold of the moneylender. The outstanding success, however, has been the excellence of the Forestry Department and the foundation of a forestry college which has attracted students from many parts of the Commonwealth. Despite Greek allegations that the British fostered intercommunal tension it was the colonial administrators who took the initiative in bringing representatives of both communities together at the highest level in various spheres of local activities. The main grounds for criticism are economic neglect of the island in the past and the failure, explained by British tolerance and liberalism on the one hand and the meanness of the Treasury on the other, to lay down an enlightened educational policy during the early stages of British rule.

It is in the political field that failure has been most pronounced. In contrast to the indulgent attitude of the first administrators – prompted by a reverence for the classics–has been the insensitivity shown by British statesmen and local officials at a later stage towards Cypriot aspirations. Their insistence that Cyprus has never been part of Greece has been a repeated source of exasperation to the Greek Cypriots since it ignores the historical processes which created Modern Greece and her steady expansion. Ineptitude and expediency have characterised the attitude of all governments, whatever their political colour. The self-righteousness shown by MP critics in opposition has no justification in the light of their own record. Gladstone, a former High Commissioner of the Ionian Islands, who had once expressed warm sympathy for the cause of Enosis, found it desirable to withdraw from this position when he came to power. The great socialist idealist Sidney Webb (Lord Passfield) must take first place amongst the authors of the sharp rebuffs which have typified ministerial statements on the Cyprus question throughout British rule: 'What Cyprus needs at present are fewer occasions for political discussion and more occasions for constructive work.'[1] On the Tory side the Duke of Devonshire caused wide offence for suggesting that since the Cypriots had no tradition behind them of self-governing institutions they could not expect to achieve a measure of democracy quickly.[2] More recently, Lord Winster publicly insulted the municipalities by stating that they were not fit even to run the fire brigade, whose functions he transferred to the police.[3]

The notorious Turkish Tribute also did much to engender lasting bitterness against the British. Originally the annual levy payable to the Sultan for the lease of the island, it continued to be used after the annexation by Britain in 1914 to fund the Ottoman Public Debt and despite the protests of all Governors was not abolished until 1927. This burden on Cypriot revenues always left a budget deficit and had to be met partly by a grant in aid. Had the British Treasury seen fit to make a generous gesture in the shape of a refund, one smouldering grievance

[1] See Hill, op. cit. IV, p. 431, quoting Hansard, 16 December 1929.
[2] See Doros Alastos, *Cyprus – Past and . . . Future* (Committee for Cyprus Affairs, London, 1943), pp. 72–3.
[3] See H.L. Deb., vol. 161, col. 1224.

which was handed down from decade to decade could have been resolved.

The failure to establish self-government had disastrous long-term
consequences for Cyprus and is second only to the Enosis movement as
the basic cause of the present catastrophe. The early attempts to make
even a very restricted constitution work repeatedly came up against the
obstructiveness of the nationalists sponsored by the Church. The rise
of the Cypriot Communist Party in the 1920s constituted a more
serious challenge than did the British to the political monopoly of the
Church, since the authority of the Communists stemmed from the
people. The Communists, moreover, were at variance with the Church
since during the greater part of British rule they were opposed to
Enosis which, in terms of Marxist clichés, they regarded as a substitute
of one form of imperialism for another. Consequently the Church
acquired from 1920 onwards a second vested interest in resisting self-
government which would have undermined its own political monopoly
by opening the door to its rivals.

The first Legislative Council introduced in 1878 was composed of an
equal number of official and non-official members nominated by the
High Commissioner, who held the casting vote. Responsibility for
Cyprus was transferred from the Foreign Office to the Colonial Office
two years later and the Constitution was modified to include twelve
elected and six official members, with the Christians and Muslims
represented by nine to three on the basis of the population census.
When Cyprus became a Crown Colony in March 1925, the Legislative
Council was expanded but the composition remained such that the
Turks and the official members, with the casting vote of the Governor,
could always outnumber the Greeks. Acute controversy arose over the
annual budget which inevitably brought to the fore the whole question
of the Tribute. On the rare occasions when the Turks voted with the
Greeks to reject a Bill it was introduced by Order in Council. To the
Greeks the Constitution was a mockery, a debating society which gave
them no effective power. Sir Ronald Storrs, from the Governor's
angle, described the whole process as 'an exasperating and humiliating
nuisance'.[1] These early experiments in constitutional government
engendered a lasting distrust which made the Greek Cypriots suspicious
of the more advanced formulas of self-government offered to them in
later years.

It was ironic that the first serious outbreak of violence during British
rule should have erupted when Storrs, an impeccable philhellene, was

[1] Storrs, op. cit. p. 472.

Governor. The initial cause was economic rather than political. Cyprus had not escaped the effects of the World slump in the thirties. Under conditions of even greater economic hardship than usual the public mood was ripe for exploitation by agitators. The Tribute, although abolished in 1927, still rankled. Resentment was increased by the Chancellor of the Exchequer's statement on 8 July 1931[1] that the accumulated surplus from Cyprus revenues due to Turkey as tribute under the 1878 Convention had instead been disposed of as the sinking fund for the Turkish Loan guaranteed by Britain and France. Trouble arose yet again over the budget. The elected Greek members refused to agree to additional taxation to meet the substantial deficit. The Bishop of Kition and other members of the Greek Orthodox Church immediately resigned from the Legislative Council. Protest meetings were organised by the Bishop of Kition and disgruntled nationalists at which seditious and inflammatory speeches were made. On 21 October a mob, led by Enosis agitators, surrounded Government House and, after setting cars alight, burnt it to the ground. Rioting subsequently broke out in other towns and some of the villages. With the help of extra troops and the British Navy order was completely restored to Cyprus by early November.

The Bishops of Kition and Kyrenia and other ringleaders, including Savvas Loizides, were deported. Some of the exiles later formed the hard core of the enosist movement in Greece. Alexis Kyrou, the Greek Consul and a fanatical enosist, whom Storrs held partly responsible for the disturbances and whose removal had been requested by him before they broke out, was at last withdrawn. The Constitution was suspended and from then on Cyprus was ruled by decree. Reports of pending clashes between the Church and the Communists prompted the authorities to ban the Communist Party of Cyprus in 1933. Outwardly, Cyprus remained calm for many years. Overseas interest was rare and usually focused on the island's poverty, on the stringent press and anti-sedition laws. How much this peace was due to repression and how much to a general lack of enthusiasm for the nationalist cause is a matter for conjecture. With the decline in public agitation for Enosis, the main reason for the Turkish community's anxieties was removed and the Turkish Cypriots, confident that the British administration was likely to be permanent, now felt secure.

The Cyprus authorities, however, were not spared the problem of ecclesiastical unrest. Archbishop Cyril III, a moderate, died on 16 November. Using this opportunity to agitate for the return of the exiled

[1] Snowden, H.C. Deb., vol. 254, col. 2083 (Oral Answers).

Bishops of Kition and Kyrenia the locum tenens, Leontios of Paphos, refused to elect a successor. In vain did the Cyprus administration claim that according to the Ecumenical Patriarch, the Archbishop of Athens and the Patriarch of Alexandria, the deported bishops could exercise their votes from abroad. In disregarding such opinions the Church of Cyprus could always invoke its independence. New difficulties were created by the death in exile of the Bishop of Kition. The same year the Cyprus administration passed three new laws. The affairs of the Church and monasteries could now be investigated by the Government and their accounts audited; any candidate who had either been deported or convicted of sedition or any offence punishable by imprisonment of more than two years was disqualified from standing as archbishop. A candidate had to be a native of the colony and the Governor had the right in certain circumstances to invalidate the appointment of an archbishop, even though this was made in accordance with Canon Law. History had shown that the Church was irrepressible in the face of far more formidable obstacles than a few minor changes of the law aimed at limiting extremist influence and the usage of its funds for political purposes. The measures, which were probably taken without full regard for their consequences, caused an uproar in ecclesiastical circles. Leontios exceeded the bounds of permissible sedition and on 20 April 1938 proceedings were taken against him and he was confined to the municipal boundaries of Paphos. After his release in May 1939 he was prosecuted again on the renewal of his subversive speeches. No progress was made towards the election of a new archbishop and the British continued to be embarrassed by the problem of the vacant see.

Even if the agitation for union with Greece had been temporarily silenced there was in the late thirties some demand for the restoration of the Constitution. The Committee for Cyprus Autonomy was formed in 1937 and a delegation came to London. Cypriot leftists with vocal contacts among British politicians were responsible for this initiative. But their modest suggestions met with no response from the Colonial Office. Observers of events at the time took the view that a good opportunity was lost for the introduction of self-government and the burial of Enosis. However, when the matter was raised in the House of Commons on 14 June[1] Ormsby-Gore (later Lord Harlech), the Secretary of State for the Colonies, said no changes in the central administration were contemplated and that it was government policy to extend the powers of the municipalities and the village authorities.

[1] See Hill, op. cit. IV, p. 434.

Two years later the Committee presented to the Colonial Office a document representing 200 Cypriots and local organisations. On the basis of information received from the acting Governor, the British Government was suspicious that the signatures had in certain circumstances been obtained under pressure. And on 5 July the Colonial Secretary, Malcolm MacDonald, expressed doubt as to the seriousness of the Cypriot demand for political liberty and Enosis. He was satisfied that the great majority of the people were not discontented under the present administration. Its policy was to work in the direction of more representative government, a process which in his view could not be hurried but 'must proceed first through the gradual increase of responsibility in local government'.[1] MacDonald's speech contained the first hint that a new constitution might be planned for Cyprus. But with the outbreak of the Second World War on 3 September 1939 such plans and Cypriot aspirations were eclipsed by events of greater magnitude outside the island.

[1] See H.C. Deb., vol. 349, cols 1283–5.

II

The Growth of the Enosis Movement in Cyprus 1940-1953

Revival of Cypriot Politics during the Second World War – Ascendancy of the Nationalists

I REVIVAL OF POLITICAL ACTIVITY, 1940 ONWARDS

The war years were marked by an intensive revival of political activity, in which the Communists held the initiative. The Cyprus Regiment was formed in 1940. The response was at first poor, but the entry of Greece into the war brought about a rapid improvement in recruiting. And the local Communists who had initially opposed the military involvement of Cyprus came out in favour of enlistment after the German invasion of Russia in June 1941.

The prospects for constitutional reforms faded on the outbreak of war but schemes for the gradual increase of Cypriot participation in local government went ahead and in 1941 the decision to restore municipal elections was announced. The trade union movement was also given official encouragement by the setting up of the first Labour Department and the enactment of the Trade Unions and Trades Disputes Law on the pattern of legislation in Britain. The same year the Cypriots formed the Pancyprian Trade Union Committee (PTUC).

By far the most important political development was the foundation of the Reform Party of the Working People (AKEL), which was sponsored by moderates as well as by leftists and met for the first time in 1941 at Skarinou.[1] AKEL at this stage was primarily concerned with the immediate task of providing an alternative to the right wing at the

[1] See T. W. Adams, *Akel: The Communist Party of Cyprus* (Hoover Institution Press, Stanford, 1971), p. 23; list of Cypriots attending the Skarinou meeting to found AKEL.

forthcoming municipal elections and was welcomed by the Cyprus authorities as a healthy antidote to the nationalist politicians backed by the Church and obsessed with 'Enosis and Nothing but Enosis'.

After the German invasion of Russia AKEL formed an anti-fascist front, and its subversive character and communist affiliations soon came to light. The Party rapidly became the dominant influence in the trade unions.

The war years were not free from industrial and economic unrest. In December 1942 employees on defence and other works went on strike for higher wages and seven trade unionists were sent to prison after threatening the life of a blackleg. A general strike was planned for 27 August 1943 in protest against the high cost of living but was called off on the grounds that it was illegal. The trade unions and the municipalities refused the Government's invitation to send representatives to the advisory committee dealing with the cost of living unless the Government agreed in advance to accept the Committee's findings, claiming that as popularly elected bodies they should enjoy greater control. The same year craftsmen engaged on military works went on strike for increased wages, but returned after one week on receiving assurances that their grievances would be examined. During a strike in Limassol bombs were thrown at houses and special constables assisted the police in restoring order.

Although economic and social grievances were the primary cause of the wartime unrest, tension was also increased by the revival of the traditional hostility between the Church and the Communists. In 1943 the Greek trade unions split into nationalist and left-wing groups. At its third conference held in Limassol a year later the PTUC declared itself to be an inseparable part of AKEL, 'its guide in the political, social and economic struggle'.[1] A small right-wing union, the Cyprus Workers Confederation (SEK), was eventually formed under the leadership of Michael Pissas, a fanatical enosist. SEK was closely associated with the Church and functioned from the archbishopric.

In the municipal elections, postponed until March 1943 owing to the evacuation of the town dwellers, AKEL scored sweeping victories in Limassol and Famagusta.

During the war Enosis was dormant but not dead and the Labour peer Lord Faringdon angered the Cypriot nationalists with the statement that 'Greece is not truly the mother of the Cypriots . . . and also is a country from which they could obtain no possible advantages'.[2] On his visit to Cyprus in 1944 Sir Cosmo Parkinson, the Permanent

[1] Dept of Labour, *Annual Report, 1944* (Nicosia), p. 10.
[2] H.L. Deb., vol. 126, cols 1023–45.

Under-Secretary of State for the Colonies, met with a flood of petitions demanding union with Greece on her liberation and the abolition of 'all illiberal laws'. Parkinson replied that he was not authorised to discuss in any way a request which amounted to the separation of Cyprus from the British Empire. On 28 August AKEL held a protest strike as a 'day of expression for the people's national feelings'. The strikers had defied the government warning that force might be used to disperse illegal processions. No major clashes took place but there were several prosecutions.

In 1945 force was twice used to deal with disturbances. The authorities had given permission for celebrations on 25 March, Greek Independence Day. At Lefkoniko an Akelist addressed a meeting and a dispute broke out between rival factions of Greek Cypriots. The crowd moved off. But a procession refused to disperse on the village police sergeant's orders whereupon two of his colleagues opened fire. The incident, in which two Cypriots were killed and fourteen injured, was the subject of a local inquiry and strong criticism in England. On 8 October Cypriot soldiers demonstrated against further service overseas. In the attempt by Indian troops at Famagusta to get two Cypriot companies aboard a ship, shots were fired. A sergeant died and four soldiers were wounded.[1]

In December, eighteen left-wing trade unionists, including Ziartides, Secretary-General of the PTUC and a member of AKEL's Central Committee, were tried for seditious conspiracy. The Crown's case was based on documents confiscated during a sudden police raid on trade union and AKEL premises. Opening for the prosecution on 17 December the Attorney-General, Stelios Pavlides KC, submitted that the accused, all of whom were members of the PTUC, an illegal organisation by reason of its activities, had conspired to overthrow the Government by revolution. Pavlides then defined the aims of the PTUC:

> . . . the overthrow of the existing regime and the establishment of a socialistic state by revolution in accordance with Marxist theory. To achieve this, the trade unions are not to be looked upon as labour or trade organisations but as parts of a political party. The accused are next out in search of a party to lead them; it must be a party which is conducted in accordance with the Marxist proletarian formula and the accused had no hesitation in proclaiming that this party should be the AKEL party . . .[2]

[1] See George Kirk, *Survey of International Affairs 1939–1946. The Middle East 1945–1950* (RIIA), p. 167.

[2] Trial documents made available to the author by the courtesy of the late Mr Stelios Pavlides KC.

The accused, Pavlides argued, had exploited popular feeling in presenting their own movement as a genuine desire for union with Greece. Defence counsel, John Klerides KC, pleaded that much of the Crown's evidence was based on quotations from Marxist classics and was essentially theoretical, containing no practical incitement to violence. On 21 January 1946 twelve of the accused were nevertheless sentenced to eighteen months and the remainder to one year's imprisonment. The PTUC was proscribed, but was eventually replaced by the Pancyprian Federation of Labour (PEO).

A communist sympathiser, Leslie Solley,[1] claimed in the House of Commons that the trade unionists were merely engaged in publicising 'the classic works of socialism'. The Secretary of State for the Colonies, Arthur Creech Jones, replied that the main charges against the convicted men were:

> The encouragement of propaganda for the overthrow of the Constitution of Cyprus by revolution, the overthrow by violence of the established Government of Cyprus, and the overthrow by violence of organised government, and there was seditious intention to excite disaffection and to procure the alteration of the law otherwise than by lawful means.[2]

The trial contributed nothing to security and its political value to the authorities was nil. Inevitably it came to be presented to the world at large as the persecution of trade unionism and yet another facet of British tyranny.

After the war unrest increased. Military expenditure was curtailed, the island's economic and strategic development had not yet begun. Markets which had readily absorbed Cypriot produce during the war were now entered by competitors. The detention of illegal Jewish immigrants in camps near Famagusta aroused Cypriot fears that the arrangement might be permanent and intended to reduce the Greek proportion of the population.[3] Their presence, the Mayor of Limassol alleged, was responsible for shortages and rising prices. The detention camps, nevertheless, continued to the dismay of the local British officials burdened with extra administrative problems as well as mounting Cypriot resentment. It was the Akelists who were foremost in voicing the public's discontent.

---

[1] Solley was dismissed from the Labour Party in 1949 for his communist sympathies.

[2] H.C. Deb., vol. 420, col. 304. 5 March 1946.

[3] See Kirk, op. cit. p. 169.

The imprisonment of the eighteen Akelists for seditious conspiracy in no way undermined the strength of the Party which, campaigning under the banner of 'National Cooperation', won the four main towns in the municipal elections on 26 May 1946. By 1946 AKEL had established itself as the only well organised political party in the island. It was, in effect, the new Cypriot communist party. It already had a record of solid achievement in social welfare and other fields. Its growing power, however, created a dilemma for the authorities since the Party was not entirely composed of Communists, having attracted men of influence and moderation. Thousands of workers looked to the trade unions associated with AKEL as the only organisation capable of protecting and advancing their interests. The right-wing unions, sponsored by the Church and obsessed with politics, were mostly ineffectual.

The British administration tended to be criticised at local and international level for its 'toleration' and even 'encouragement' of the Cypriot Communists.[1] The fact was that the average colonial official tended to judge a man by his willingness to cooperate in the day-to-day tasks of running the island, and not by his political affiliations. The Communists worked well in municipal and labour affairs with their opposite numbers in the administration. The problem for the authorities was how to contain communism and preserve law and order without proscribing the only constructive political movement in Cyprus.

2   THE LABOUR GOVERNMENT AND ABORTIVE REFORMS

The Labour Government which came to power at the end of the Second World War proved as reluctant as its predecessors to give up Cyprus. The complexity of the issue, widely misrepresented as a straightforward colonial problem, was elucidated in Creech Jones's introduction to the Fabian Bureau's study 'Strategic Colonies and their Future':

> ... the constitutional history of Malta, Gibraltar and Cyprus illustrates, for example, the difficulty of deciding what limits must be imposed on the people attaining responsible self-government when imperial strategic needs have to be served.[2]

---

[1] Cyrus Sulzberger wrote in the New York Times, 17 May 1949: 'It is understood the Colonial Office has feared that the encouraging of the conservative parties among the island's predominantly Greek population would serve only to build up the idea of *Enosis* . . . As a result communism has been permitted to spread while Greek nationalism has been held in check.'

[2] Fabian Publications and Victor Gollancz, October 1945.

The report recognised the problem of the Turkish Cypriots and the likelihood that Enosis would worsen their position. While accepting that population transfers were a repugnant solution, the authors considered that in the event of Enosis only drastic surgery on these lines would prevent 'the cancer of minority agitation from spreading'. They questioned the value of a plebiscite, stressed the folly of under-rating the current agitation for Enosis and the fact that although emotion could not be ignored 'it was not necessarily wisest to give in to it', and urged the speeding up of constitutional reform since procrastination merely increased nationalist demands.

On 23 October 1946, a year after the publication of the Fabian Survey, the Government announced its intention to introduce 'a liberal and progressive regime in the internal affairs of the island' and to call a consultative assembly in Cyprus to discuss constitutional reforms.[1] A ten-year development programme,[2] dealing with all aspects of the Cypriot economy, was simultaneously released in Nicosia. Lord Winster had already been appointed the next Governor. About the same time the ban on the return to Cyprus of the Cypriots exiled after the 1931 riots was lifted. The 1937 Church Laws, which had impeded the election of a new archbishop, were repealed and the communist trade unionists convicted of sedition freed. The Ethnarchy responded to this gesture of conciliation by cabling the British Government that no plan excluding Enosis was acceptable. AKEL took much the same line. At the end of December a representative delegation, composed of the Bishop of Paphos, the head of the Chamber of Commerce, and John Klerides KC, left for Athens. Their presence was an embarrassment to the Greek Government but a source of enthusiasm to the press and the public.

In London the Prime Minister, Clement Attlee, refused to see them. But on 7 February 1947 they presented the Colonial Secretary, Creech Jones, with a memorandum rejecting the British plan, stating the case for Enosis and suggesting that the Turkish minority could be fully safeguarded and arrangements made with Greece for the protection of Britain's strategic interests. Creech Jones made it clear yet again that no change in the island's status was contemplated. The Turkish Cypriots cabled a protest to Whitehall and were about to send their own delegation, but were dissuaded on assurances from local British officials that their position was in no way endangered.

The Greek Cypriots' visit to Athens bore fruit on 28 February 1947

---

[1] H.C. Deb., vol. 427, cols 396–7 (Written Answers).
[2] *A Ten-Year Programme of Development for Cyprus*, Cyprus Government (Nicosia, 1946).

in the shape of a unanimous resolution[1] adopted by the Greek Parliament. Consequently the Cypriots were encouraged to believe that Enosis had now become a serious possibility. A leakage of information from the State Department, which gave rise to reports that the American Government favoured Enosis, also encouraged the Cypriot nationalists and embarrassed the British.[2]

Winster arrived on 27 March 1947, two days after Greek Independence Day; Greek flags were still flying. The five months delay between the announcement of the constitutional plan and his arrival had given the extremists plenty of time to build up a well organised resistance. The Ethnarchy ordered a boycott of the reception for the new Governor, consequently the only Greeks who attended were officials. Four Greek members of the Advisory Council who stayed away were immediately dismissed by Winster. Within one month the press had become so hostile that the Government thought fit to warn editors of its powers to act against systematic denigration, subversion and incitement to violence.

The possibility of imposing a constitution was dismissed. And the Executive Council (EXCO) decided to convene the Assembly after the archiepiscopal election in the firm belief that the leftists, the moderates and the minorities were eager to take part, and that their participation would eventually force the hand of the right wing which would be loth to see its rivals in power. Official hopes that a more amenable personality than Leontios, Bishop of Paphos, the locum tenens, might be elected were dashed by an overwhelming victory in June for Leontios. The new Archbishop immediately dropped AKEL, whose support was largely responsible for his election, took over the nationalist leadership and reshaped the Ethnarchy Council to include laymen as well as clerics.

On 9 July 1947 the Governor announced that all the various organisations, including the municipalities and the press, were being invited to nominate representatives for a Consultative Assembly which would make recommendations on the type of constitution to be adopted so that the Cypriots might play a greater part in the island's internal affairs.[3] Archbishop Leontios immediately ordered the Greeks to boycott the Assembly. On 26 July he died of scrub typhus. Myriantheus, Bishop of Kyrenia, a fanatical enosist who had been deported for his part in the 1931 riots, became the locum tenens. Unforgiving and unrepentant

---

[1] *Greek Bulletin* (Greek Information Office, London), 3 March 1947.
[2] See Kirk, op. cit. p. 173.
[3] See Kirk, op. cit. p. 175, for detailed account of these events.

after his long exile, he waged a relentless campaign against the British administration for the rest of his life. After some hesitation the British finally decided to go ahead with the plan in the belief that as well as the leftists and the moderates a significant number of rightists wanted to take part but that no public reversal of their policy was possible before the election of the archbishop. In October Myriantheus became Makarios II.

The Assembly was convened on 1 November under the chairmanship of the Chief Justice, Sir Edward Jackson. Owing to the absence of the rightists on the orders of the Church, the members, two of whom were nominated, never exceeded eighteen. Eight out of the ten Greeks were leftists. Seven Turks and a Maronite made up the remainder. The chairman gave a tentative outline of the constitutional plan. The leftists wanted from the start a discussion of full self-government but he ruled that this was outside the Assembly's terms of reference. Against his advice the leftists then sent a memorandum to the Colonial Secretary, Creech Jones, demanding a constitution on the lines of those granted to Malta and Ceylon.[1] They received no reply and in the middle of January they sent the Secretary-General of AKEL, Phifis Ioannou, and the two mayors, Klerides and Servas, to press the claim in London. On Winster's advice Creech Jones refused to see them, but under the pressure of socialist back-benchers he finally agreed to an informal interview. On his return to Cyprus Servas intimated that he had obtained support for a more advanced constitution than the preliminary outline already presented to the Assembly. Prone to wishful thinking, the Cypriots had, as in the past, probably overestimated the influence of the Cyprus lobby in the Labour Party. From now on the Consultative Assembly was doomed.

Meanwhile the British Government, influenced by strategic considerations and the growth of Cypriot communism, could not see its way to meeting the demands of the leftists. And on 7 May 1948 the Constitution[2] was published on the basis of the original outline. In his despatch to the Governor Creech Jones stated that the interests of Cyprus at this stage could best be served by 'the adoption of a form of government which, without entailing any violent break with the existing structure',[3] would facilitate the active participation of the

---

[1] An all-elected Assembly; with Defence, Foreign Affairs, and the protection of minorities reserved to the Governor.

[2] *Cyprus Constitution: Despatch dated 7th May 1948 from the Secretary of State for the Colonies to the Governor of Cyprus* (HMSO), Colonial No. 227.

[3] ibid. p. 2.

Cypriots in their internal affairs. The Constitution[1] provided for universal male suffrage for British subjects over 21; for a Greek majority in the legislature and a quota of seats for the Turks proportionate to their numbers in the population; for a Turkish communal register with the alternative right of individuals to transfer to the general roll. Executive power was vested in the Governor, but representatives of the elected majority in the legislature would be designated by him as unofficial members of the Executive Council and associated with specific government departments. No subject was debarred from discussion except the island's status within the British Commonwealth. Defence, foreign affairs, and the special rights of minorities were reserved to the Governor who was also empowered to implement Bills which he considered expedient, in the interests of public order, good faith and good government, even if they had already been rejected by the legislature. These last provisions, it was stressed, were safeguards which should not be interpreted as the British Government's desire to circumscribe the legislature's freedom of action in normal domestic affairs.

The Archbishop and the Popular Front (EAS) denounced the proposals as wholly unacceptable. Nevertheless the Assembly met on 20 May. In a four-hour debate the chairman defended the Governor's reserve powers, but the leftists renewed their objections to them, voted against the proposals and withdrew, leaving a majority in favour, composed of seven Turks, two Greeks and a Maronite, which was thus completely unrepresentative. The Assembly was adjourned *sine die*. On 12 August it was dissolved by Lord Winster, who stated that the offer remained open should any responsible and fully representative leaders care to take it up in the future. He reaffirmed that no change in the island's sovereignty was intended and that there was no substance in any rumours that negotiations on the subject were planned between Britain and Greece.[2]

The nationalists hailed the event as a double victory – the defeat of the British and the Communists. AKEL protested strongly and continued to press for full self-government.

On the collapse of the Assembly some Cypriots would have welcomed an imposed constitution. They could have disclaimed responsibility for its shortcomings and at the same time seized the opportunity for taking part in the island's affairs. The leftists and the moderates could have been expected to cooperate from the start, the rightists at a later stage, since they could ill afford to lose ground to their rivals. The

[1] ibid.
[2] See Kirk, op. cit. p. 181.

Government, on the other hand, felt that such a move would constitute a breach of faith, that without the goodwill of the two main political groups the immediate proclamation of elections might precipitate serious disorders and that candidates would refuse to stand.

The Labour Government had set itself the impossible task of trying to introduce a more liberal regime and at the same time preclude any risk of either Enosis or communist control of the Legislature. The Cyprus administration was criticised for allowing the archiepiscopal elections to take place before convocation of the Assembly. But earlier experience with Leontios had shown that a locum tenens could be as great a barrier to British aims as an archbishop. The 19 months delay between the first announcement in the House of Commons and the publication of the Constitution was a major tactical error since it enabled the extremists to build up a barrage of opposition which swamped the moderates. Persistently accused of betraying Enosis, the Akelists had no option but to reject the proposals which fell far short of their aims. Their demand for a constitution on the lines of the Maltese legislature was in itself a tacit admission that defence and foreign affairs would remain under British control. In these circumstances it is difficult to conceive that the communist element could, in the last resort, have become a serious danger. A more advanced constitution would have enabled the leftists and the moderates to justify the acceptance of self-government to their critics.

As the result of the fiasco of the Consultative Assembly the nationalists gained great advantages, not through any enlightened policy of their own but because of the mistakes made by their opponents – the British and the Communists. AKEL's recourse to violence after the war had jeopardised the chance for a relatively advanced constitution which would have facilitated the acceptance of self-government by its leaders and the moderates in 1948. Whitehall and the Colonial Government, in their preoccupation with the dangers of communism, had failed to recognise that in the long term the greatest threat to British interests in Cyprus came from the right wing and that the best hope of launching a constitution with the consent of the people lay in concessions to the leftists over the structure of the legislature. From now on the outlook for self-government steadily worsened.

Winster's efforts to introduce self-government had taken place against a background of violence which was not connected with the constitutional question. But the trend was significant in that the authorities could no longer count on a docile population. The chief agitators were the leftists. The causes were again mainly economic and social. Friction also arose between the extremists of the right and the left. Bitterness was intensified during the Greek civil war by AKEL's support for EAM.

Industrial strife reached a climax in 1948 with lost man-days totalling a quarter of a million.[1] On 13 January miners in the American owned Cyprus Mines Corporation, the backbone of the island's economy, went on strike for higher wages and a 48-hour week. Extra police, called out to restore order in the CMC area, opened fire on the rioters. The management negotiated a compromise in March with the Archbishop, who undertook to appeal for the end of violence and a return to work on condition that the CMC granted a moderate rise based on the new cost-of-living index. But the strike went on until May and was only broken then by blackleg labour organised by the Church.[2]

In August miners at Amiandos struck for a month and employees in the building trade for sixteen weeks. Workers dynamited their employers' property and attacked rival trade unionists and blackleg labourers with grenades. The Government introduced heavier penalties for the illegal possession of explosives and instituted forty-eight prosecutions. At the root of the trouble lay the rivalries of the nationalist and the left-wing unions and the hostility of the mining companies, in particular the CMC, to the trade unions. But the British seldom escaped the backwash of any crisis, even if its origins had no connection with the administration. The nationalists blamed the authorities for failing to take stronger measures against the Communists. The Communists alleged that right-wing thugs, sometimes armed, had terrorised the people – especially the trade unionists under the 'almost benevolent toleration of the police'.[3]

These conditions created a suitable outlet for the Cold War. The local Communists carried out the directives of Moscow by seizing every opportunity to embarrass the Western allies. Agitators organised collections for General Markos, commander of the communist guerrillas in Greece, intensified the campaign against the plans for British military bases in Cyprus,[4] and attacked with dynamite the American radio station, which monitored communist broadcasts. The Akelists pressed for self-government by resorting to illegal demonstrations and processions. Now that hopes of their cooperation in launching a constitution were ruled out, the authorities enforced the law more strictly. Adamantos was fined

[1] Unpublished Memorandum on the Cyprus trade unions.

[2] See David Lavender, *The Story of Cyprus Mines Corporation* (The Huntington Library, San Marino, California 1962), pp. 294–9.

[3] See *Annual Report on the Cyprus Police Force* (Nicosia, 1949), p. 24.

[4] See E. Joannides (Foreword by D. N. Pritt KC, MP), *Cyprus Denied Freedom: The Constitution-Making Farce* (Hermes Press, London, 1948), pp. 16 and 30.

for a political speech in November; Servas was sent to prison for three months and thirty-one Akelists were given shorter sentences for lesser offences.

In 1948 the leftists began to lose ground. The bid for self-government had failed. The prestige of AKEL and the Pancyprian Federation of Labour (PEO) had suffered as the result of the miners' and builders' strikes, to the gain of the right-wing unions. The Church, under the leadership of Archbishop Makarios II, a fanatical anti-communist, had intensified its campaign against the left. In September an encyclical from the Holy Synod condemning communism was read out in all the churches.[1] On 13 September the Archbishop ordered that anyone suspected of communist sympathies should lose the right to vote in the election of Church committees.[2]

Before the end of 1948 signs of dissension within AKEL became evident. Phifis Ioannou and Andreas Ziartides, both members of the Central Committee, journeyed behind the Iron Curtain to seek guidance on future policy. The two men saw the Greek Communist Party leader, Zakhariades, who ordered them to drop self-government from AKEL's programme and support Enosis. Ioannou then went to see the Cominform leaders in Bucharest and Ziartides met Markos at the communist stronghold on Mount Vitsi in Northern Greece. That they should have returned with conflicting directives was not surprising. At the highest level of international communism the position was confused and a deep rift had developed between the Greek communist leaders, Zakhariades and Markos.[3]

In March 1949 AKEL's leaders publicly admitted that their support for self-government was a serious error. The Central Committee, with one exception, resigned and a seven-man group was appointed to run the Party until the next congress which was due the following August. Ezekiel Papaioannou, a Moscow-trained Communist who had fought in Spain with the International Brigade, replaced Phifis Ioannou as Secretary-General. The control of AKEL had now passed irrevocably into the hands of the extremists.

Cypriot politics follow no logical pattern and the reasons for this sudden switch in AKEL's policy from self-government to Enosis can only be surmised. The communist revolt in Greece was on the verge of collapse. A row within the Western alliance over the possession of

[1] See François Crouzet, *Le Conflit de Chypre 1946–1959* (Emile Bruylant, Brussels, 1973), pp. 249–50.

[2] Daily Telegraph, 13 December 1948.

[3] See D. George Kousoulas, *Revolution and Defeat: The Story of the Greek Communist Party* (OUP, 1965), 252–4.

Cyprus may well have acquired a greater importance in Soviet aims. In Cyprus AKEL needed to recover lost ground by adopting the slogan most likely to capture votes in the municipal elections to be held in May 1949. For the first time in Cyprus the ominous sign X (*Khi*) had appeared – the emblem of the extreme right-wing terrorist organisation led in Greece by Colonel George Grivas, a fanatical Hellenist and anti-communist. The nationalists and the Akelists campaigned under the banner of Enosis, but a common purpose was no bar to violent clashes between the rival groups. AKEL's belated support for Enosis was of no avail. The Party also suffered from the loss of the moderates, especially John Klerides, whose personal prestige was largely responsible for its previous success in Nicosia. The Akelists, who lost the capital but retained their hold in Limassol, Larnaca and Famagusta with reduced majorities, complained that the Government had discriminated against them. The editor of *Demokratis* was sentenced to three months in prison for publishing communist allegations that the authorities had conspired to falsify the electoral lists by entrusting their revision to the right-wing mukhtars.

3   THE TURKISH CYPRIOT COMMUNITY, 1940–1948

Lord Winster's government coincided with the execution of an important project – the official inquiry[1] into the long-standing grievances of the Turkish community.

It is a popular fallacy that the Turkish Cypriots were highly privileged under the British. Their status and influence, on the contrary, steadily declined during the first sixty years of colonial rule. Some of the limitations imposed on the Turkish community were the legacy of the Ottoman administration and existed by reason of Britain's agreement with the Sultan in 1878. But once the political links between Turkey and Cyprus were finally severed by the treaty of Lausanne[2] in 1923, these anomalies were expected to end. If anything, however, the position of the Turkish Cypriots worsened. In 1928 the colonial administration abolished the high office of Mufti and put Evkaf, the body responsible for the administration of Muslim properties, virtually under govern-

---

[1] *An Investigation into Matters Concerning and Affecting the Turkish Community in Cyprus: Interim Report of the Committee on Turkish Affairs* (Cyprus Government Printing Office, 1949).

[2] The treaty of Lausanne gave the Turkish Cypriots the right to opt for Turkish nationality within two years of its implementation. According to Prof. Beckingham (*Journal of the Central Asian Society*, vol. XLIII, April 1956, Part II, p. 129) after Ataturk's revolution about 8,000 Turkish Cypriots left Cyprus permanently for Turkey where they were attracted by greater opportunities for responsible posts than existed under the British in Cyprus.

ment control. The costs of the Sheri Courts dealing with family law, formerly borne by the Colony's general revenues, were transferred to Evkaf, which was left without adequate funds to carry out its duties. Had the control exercised by the British made for good management it might have been tolerable. But Evkaf properties were often let unprofitably on excessively long leases, sometimes to Greeks and even to foreigners.

The Greek Cypriots, on the other hand, exercised considerable freedom in the management of their ecclesiastical and educational affairs. The position of the Turkish Cypriots also compared unfavourably with that of the Muslims in other territories ceded by the defunct Ottoman Empire, where communal affairs were managed by elected committees drawn from the minorities concerned.

The Turkish Cypriots had played no part in the 1931 riots. But the suspension of the Constitution and the rights that went with it, aimed at containing the seditious activities of the Greeks, equally left the Turkish community without a voice in the island's affairs through elected representatives. The link between the Turks and the Government was from now on maintained by a nominated official belonging to one of the traditional old Turkish families. Though worthy, reliable and highly respected, such men were out of touch with the community as a whole and alien to the processes of modernisation which had taken place in Turkey since the revolution. As a result, Ataturk's religious, social and legal reforms were slow to reach Cyprus and the general progress of the Turkish Cypriot community was held back. The Turkish Cypriots tended to remain silent rather than risk alienating the British administration, their sole protector against the demands of the Greek majority.

Turkey's neutrality and the discontent of the Turkish Cypriots in no way undermined their contribution to the British war effort. The first post-war census[1] recorded that the numbers of Turks serving in the Cyprus Regiment both at home and abroad during the period of the survey exceeded those of the Greeks despite the fact that the latter formed 80 per cent of the total population. The revival during the war of Greek Cypriot demands for Enosis aroused the latent fears of the Turkish Cypriots. The year 1943 was marked by political initiative on their part with the formation of the Turkish Minority Association (KATAK) under Dr Kutchuk and the first exclusively Turkish trade union.

The Turkish Cypriots were, nevertheless, ill organised at the end of

[1] *Census of Population and Agriculture 1946* (Government of Cyprus, Crown Agents), p. 48. It should be noted that Greek Cypriot enlistment declined when the war was over in Greece.

the war to face the rising demand for Enosis. Some of the younger
Turks were deeply concerned at the backward state of the community.
The pressure they exercised eventually resulted in the formation of the
special committee which began work in April 1948 with the blessing of
Lord Winster, who expressed the hope that its report would 'be instrumental in securing a higher standard of living for the Turkish community and pave the way to greater prosperity'.[1]

The Committee, entirely composed of Turkish Cypriots, included the
religious leader and a senior judge among other distinguished personalities. The new generation was represented by a brilliant young advocate
– Rauf Denktash. Sectors of the Turkish community throughout the
island were invited to send representatives to the meetings. In a long
and pungently worded report the Committee recommended that
the Muftiship should be restored; that Evkaf should be managed by an
elected all-Turkish committee; that family law should be modernised
and the cost of the Sheri Courts responsible for its administration borne
by the Colony's general revenues. On the subject of education the
authors wrote:

> We do not wish to claim a wider control over educational affairs
> than is given to the Greek community. On the other hand, we can
> admit of no reason why our control should be less.[2]

They also suggested that the anniversary of the Turkish Republic's
foundation should be celebrated as a national holiday in Turkish
Cypriot schools, that the schools should be run by elected instead of
nominated committees and the lack of text-books made good by books
from Turkey. The report, although devoid of political significance, was
the first step in the gradual reorientation of the Turkish Cypriot
community towards Turkey.

The collapse of the Consultative Assembly created new uncertainties
about the island's future and it was probably no coincidence that the
Turkish Cypriots sought for the first time in August 1948 to interest
Turkey in their political position. They first had to overcome a barrier
of official indifference. Since the treaty of Lausanne, Turkey had disclaimed all responsibility for the Turks outside her frontiers. Good
relations with Greece in the Venizelist–Ataturk tradition were fundamental to Turkey's foreign policy and had acquired a still greater importance against the background of the Cold War. The emigration of

[1] *Committee on Turkish Affairs*, op. cit. pp. 57–8.
[2] op. cit. p. 37.

the Turkish Cypriots to Turkey which deprived the minority of some of its most able citizens was in the long run to have its compensations. It was the Turkish nationals of Cypriot descent who played a major role in diverting the attention of the Turkish Government, press and public to the situation in Cyprus, while Turkish Cypriot university students in Ankara and Istanbul formed small but useful groups of vocal supporters.

From 1948 onwards the press in Turkey showed a growing interest in the Cyprus question. *Hurriyet*, in particular, kept up a barrage of criticism against the Turkish Foreign Minister for his indifference to the fate of the Turkish Cypriots. During November and December *Tasvir* ran a series of articles entitled 'Cyprus must not be given to the Greeks'.

Commentators stressed that the communist danger did not exist solely in Greece, but also in Cyprus where the Greek Cypriot community was sharply split into rightist and extreme leftist factions. Newspapers published rumours of a pending British withdrawal from Cyprus and combined these reports with the demand that in this event the island must be returned to Turkey. Yalman, the distinguished editor of the liberal *Vatan*, saw no reason for changing Turkey's non-expansionist policy, but emphasised that she could not agree to the transfer of an island of such strategic importance to the Greeks.[1]

In November a Turkish Cypriot delegation visited President Inonu and he was reported to have reassured them that Turkey was concerned for the future of Cyprus. Before the end of the year Turkish Cypriots held a large anti-Greek rally in Nicosia and university students in Ankara demonstrated peacefully in favour of the Turkish Cypriot case. Both events were widely covered in Turkey.

4 THE PLEBISCITE, 1949–1950

When the new Governor, Sir Andrew Wright, arrived in Cyprus in August 1949, he was greeted by a barrage of anti-constitution slogans. The Cypriots had anticipated wrongly that his appointment heralded a new attempt to get self-government going. But the authorities were still preoccupied with the communist problem and his first task was the restoration of order.

The idea of holding a plebiscite in Cyprus had been mentioned several times since the war. The Fabian Bureau had dismissed the suggestion as early as 1945. Platts-Mills, a spokesman for the left-wing Cypriots,

---

[1] Summaries of the Turkish Press, compiled by the British Consulate-General, Istanbul, quoting *Vatan*, 13 and 16 December 1948.

had raised the question in the House of Commons on 7 July 1948.[1] Gregorios Kassimatis, a Greek Liberal deputy, had referred to it in the Council of Europe early in November 1949.

One month after Wright's arrival AKEL seized the initiative with an appeal to the Ethnarchy to cooperate in sending a joint memorandum and an all-party delegation to the United Nations. The invitation was rebuffed. The engrained hostility of the Church towards the Communists was in itself sufficient to preclude such a partnership. Moreover it was politically inexpedient; it would have embarrassed the right-wing government in Greece and alienated potential sympathisers in the West, especially in the USA. The Ethnarchy's refusal was a foregone conclusion, but it served as a justification for unilateral action by AKEL, which immediately renewed the demand for a United Front.

On 23 November AKEL sent its memorandum 'The People of Cyprus Accuse Great Britain' to the United Nations. This first public request for a plebiscite took the shape of a historical survey and an indictment of the British.

The British were now faced with a new and able adversary in Michael Mouskos.[2] Born of a peasant family at Pano Panaghia in the Paphos District, Mouskos was educated at the Pancyprian Gymnasium and Kykko Monastery and consecrated a deacon of Phaneromeni Church in 1938 by Bishop Leontios. At the end of the Second World War, which he spent in Greece, the World Council of Churches selected him for a two-year scholarship at Boston Theological College. He was elected Bishop of Kition in 1948, while he was still in America. His studies unfinished, he returned to Cyprus to take up his new duties in the autumn having first spent two months in Greece, where he visited government troops on the Grammos front and praised the morale of the Greek people in their struggle against communism. Before leaving Athens he reaffirmed the Cypriot determination to achieve Enosis. The Bishop of Kition from now on assumed effective control over Church policy in Cyprus.

AKEL's initiative in November had forced the hand of the Church, which decided to hold its own plebiscite. The Bishop of Kition first attracted the attention of the authorities by the prominent part he played in its organisation. On 5 December he presided at an Ethnarchy Council meeting which decided to hold the plebiscite on 15 January 1950 unless the Government in the meantime held its own referendum. On 12 December the Archbishop requested the Governor to do so. He

[1] H.C. Deb., vol. 453, col. 365 (Oral Answers).
[2] Later Archbishop Makarios III, first President of the Republic of Cyprus.

wrote that during seventy-one years of British rule the Cypriots had never stopped demanding the island's national restoration through union with Greece and that Great Britain was disregarding the island's Hellenic character and the principle of self-determination.[1]

EAS (The National Liberation Coalition) immediately offered to support the Church plebiscite on condition that it was a 'genuine' plebiscite for Enosis, but continued to collect signatures for its own petition. The Akelists claimed that they had scored a major victory in forcing the Church to yield to left-wing pressure. Both sides, in their parochialism, were exasperated by the cautious attitude of the Greek Government, which stressed that these activities might have harmful international consequences. Early reports reaching the British authorities indicated that many individuals and possibly whole villages were likely to abstain. The civil servants were precluded from voting under their oath of allegiance to the Crown and, like the moderates, were embarrassed by the whole procedure. Cyprus officials attached little importance to the holding of the plebiscite itself. But they were worried about the risk of serious clashes between the Church and the Communists, who at one time were expected to hold rival plebiscites. The banning of the plan, however, was not considered. Official interference would have been represented as violation of religious rights and would have more tiresome complications for the British Government than the exploitation of the voting results for publicity purposes. The authorities, in any case, had no legal powers to stop people signing an open book.

On 17 December the Governor wrote to the Archbishop commenting on his use of the word 'plebiscite':

Mass petitions of this character have been organised in Cyprus on various occasions in the past, but I know of no instance in which the Government was concerned, except to receive them; and I can conceive of no circumstances in which the Government could be associated with their promotion.[2]

The proposed 'plebiscite', the Governor continued, amounted to no more than an invitation to the public to determine a question which in practice did not exist. He reminded the Archbishop that the subject was closed. No doubt there would be many signatures, he said, because of the people's reluctance to refuse to sign the documents put before them. But such a declaration would be valueless owing to the conditions under

[1] Cyprus Mail, 20 December 1949.
[2] ibid.

which it had been obtained. The Government was solely concerned with the risk of serious disorders. He urged the bishops to reconsider the pursuit of a plan which 'could do no good and might produce the most unfortunate results'. The Archbishop replied that the subject would only be closed after the achievement of Enosis, a claim supported by the entire Greek nation. The letter, written with view to press publication, contained an oblique call for law and order.[1]

The Turkish Cypriots grew increasingly uneasy at these developments. Kassimatis's speech in the Council of Europe was seen as a direct threat to their interests, and in November the two rival Turkish groups merged into one political organisation – the Turkish National Party. The month of December was decisive for the Turkish Cypriots. A sombre warning was given by Dr Kutchuk:

> The bells of danger have begun to toll and in the name of peace and security we call upon the Government to take the strictest measures to check the danger.[2]

The Turkish municipal councillors protested to the communist mayors at their part in signing AKEL's memorandum to the UN. Thousands of Turks held a rally in Nicosia on 12 December and adopted a five-point resolution, vehemently protesting against Enosis. Its authors claimed that Enosis would bring economic ruin, racial and social disorders and civil war to Cyprus. Stressing that a plebiscite was pointless, they reaffirmed that the continuation of the *status quo* was essential for the protection of the minorities and the preservation of peace. If Britain wanted to abandon Cyprus, they added, then it should be returned to Turkey, the ex-suzerain, its nearest neighbour, and the only Near Eastern country capable of defending it. Finally they authorised Dr Kutchuk to submit the resolution to the UN, the British Colonial and Foreign Secretaries, and to the various political parties and associations in Britain and Turkey.[3]

Up to the time of the plebiscite the administration had mainly been concerned with the communist threat to public order. They now turned to the problem of right-wing agitation. Two Greek subjects were obliged to leave Cyprus because the renewal of their residence permits was refused. The first, Pandelis Bitsios, was editor of the fanatically anti-British newspaper *Ethnos*; the second, Socrates Loizides, had long been suspected of using the farmers' union (PEK), of which he was general

[1] Cyprus Mail, 22 December 1949.
[2] ibid. 6 December 1949, quoting *Halkin Sesi*.
[3] ibid. 13 December 1949.

secretary, as cover for subversive activity. Time was to show, however, that such remedies were usually to be short-lived.

The plebiscite was duly held on Sunday, 15 January 1950, its organisation in the end having been completely monopolised by the Church committees, which refused to include the Akelists. This victory for the nationalists was due to the brilliant leadership of the Bishop of Kition. The priests were ordered to end morning service at nine and to arrange for the bells to be peeled and a brief prayer said. An open book was placed in every church and men and women over 18 were required to sign their names. The choice before them was as follows:

We demand union with Greece.
We oppose the union of Cyprus with Greece.[1]

The initial apathy of the public brought forth a sharp reminder from the priests on 17 January that the lists would remain open till the following Sunday. On 29 January an encyclical signed by all the bishops announced a 96 per cent vote in favour of Enosis;[2] the Ethnarchy promptly sent this information to the member states of the United Nations with the exception of the Soviet Union. The Archbishop challenged the Cyprus Government either to accept the results or else conduct its own plebiscite, and received the customary reply that the subject was closed.

On 14 February the Ethnarchy Council announced its intention to promote the cause in Greece, Great Britain and the USA on the basis of the plebiscite results. The Akelists also decided to campaign abroad but their representatives, Adamos Adamantos, Ezekias Papaioannou and Evdoros Joannides, could not as Communists get visas for Greece and the USA, so they were restricted to Britain and countries behind the Iron Curtain.

On 14 May, the eve of the Ethnarchy delegation's departure, the Archbishop of Cyprus held a special service in St John's Cathedral to pray for the success of the mission. The Bishop of Kition, who officiated at Aghia Napa Church, made a rousing political speech after the Te Deum.

At the end of the month interest was aroused by the trial of Polykarpos Ioannides, Secretary to the See of Kyrenia and editor of its religious newspaper *Ephimeris*. He was charged with sedition and incitement to murder. The trial was important as an early attempt by the

---

[1] ibid. 11 January 1950.
[2] ibid. 29 January 1950.

administration to curb the flood of sedition emanating from the extreme right wing, and for the elucidation given by the Attorney-General, Stelios Pavlides KC, of the Government attitude to the Sedition Law in relation to Enosis. Pavlides said that under Section 50(2) of the Criminal Code any attempt to bring about a change of sovereignty was of itself a punishable offence. The Government had refrained so far from interference in manifestations for union with Greece so long as they were conducted with decency, but this had not always been the case. During the trial the Attorney-General attributed to Ioannides 'an effective and venomous style easily calculated to excite extreme hatred and passion, particularly among the half-educated masses'.[1] Defence counsel, George Chrysafinis KC, pleaded that his client had worked for *Enosis* solely within the framework of Anglo-Greek friendship in accordance with the Holy Synod's directive. Pavlides contended that the very nature of the accused's defence proved that his activities lay outside the law. Convicted of an offence arising out of a viciously anti-British article, Ioannides was sentenced to three months' imprisonment and *Ephimeris* suspended.

By 1950 the Communists had abandoned the tactics of violence. Their activities after the plebiscite, although noisy and vexatious, were mostly of a venial character, and they were persecuted for seemingly trivial offences. There was, for instance, the notorious case of a Limassol street named after the former Governor, Sir Richmond Palmer. Palmer was to the Greek Cypriots the symbol of British autocracy at its worst, and the municipal council renamed the street '28 October Street', the date of the Greek people's stand against the Italians in 1941. After refusing to reinstate the original signs the communist mayor and five communist councillors were imprisoned for contempt of court. An outburst of popular resentment led to a general strike. It was incidents such as these which inevitably widened the gulf between the administration and the people upon whose goodwill and cooperation the long-term aims of British policy depended.

5   CYPRIOT POLITICS AFTER THE RISE OF MAKARIOS III

On 18 October 1950 the Bishop of Kition was elected Archbishop Makarios III at the age of 37, four months after his predecessor's death. His rival, the Bishop of Kyrenia, was still campaigning abroad; known Communists had been struck off the voting list by the Church so an easy victory was assured.

[1] *Cyprus Mail*, 31 May 1950.

Even without these advantages, made much of by his opponents, the results would most likely have been the same since none of the other candidates came near his equal in acumen and oratory. Makarios immediately established his position as Ethnarch with the undertaking to work relentlessly for union with Greece; he said, 'No offer of a constitution or any other compromise would be accepted by the people of Cyprus.'[1] In December he called upon all Greek Cypriots not to take part in elections to Village Improvement Boards and other Government schemes.

The authorities reacted to the prospects of militant opposition by strengthening the sedition laws in January 1951. Aliens and members of unlawful organisations could thenceforth be deported on security grounds, and the importation of newspapers published abroad prohibited if the Governor deemed their contents to be prejudicial to peace and good government. The revised press law was directed particularly at the Athenian newspapers which, unhampered by the legal restraints imposed by Cyprus law, could go to any lengths in pursuing their campaign of calumny and vilification against the colonial regime.

The administration was not alone in distrusting the Archbishop. The right-wing extremists, who supported the Bishop of Kyrenia, were openly vindictive about his election. The Akelists did not disguise their displeasure and the conflict between them and the Ethnarchy remained the overriding factor in local politics. AKEL repeatedly branded the Ethnarchy as the tool of Anglo-American imperialism, easing its relentless criticism only when it was opportune to press for a united front. Makarios was well able to withstand the hostility of the Communists, but their offers of cooperation were politically compromising and likely to jeopardise his chances of a sympathetic hearing in Greek Government circles and in the United States. Papaioannou declared a few days later that the Soviet Union was the best ally of the Cypriot people in their struggle for freedom. Nevertheless the Akelists continued to back the nationalists in boycotting the Village Improvement Boards until the end of the year when, in a well publicised bout of self-criticism, they decided the policy was mistaken and joined in the scheme.

Meanwhile the AKEL leaders had made several journeys behind the Iron Curtain.[2] Faithful to the directives of Moscow, they gave ominous warnings about the proposed British military bases. Papaioannou

[1] Cyprus Mail, 20 October 1950.
[2] Ziartides (East Berlin, November 1951); Papaioannou (Prague, August 1951); Protopappas (East Berlin, August 1951); Papaioannou (Moscow, September 1952); Jacovides (Peace Conference, Peking, December 1952).

predicted that they would turn Cyprus into a Nagasaki or a Hiroshima;
Ziartides anticipated that increased military expenditure would worsen
the economic problem by causing inflation.

1951 was a year of quiet consolidation for the nationalists. The Ethnarchy Council was reorganised and the anti-constitution campaign
intensified. New organisations set up under the Archbishop's patronage
for the promotion of Enosis included the militant youth movement
PEON.

The movement steadily gathered momentum throughout 1952.
On 15 January, the second anniversary of the plebiscite, schoolboys
from the Gymnasium rioted in Paphos. April the 25th saw the birth of
the Pancyprian National Assembly which, exclusively composed of
right-wing groups, was much less representative than its name suggested.
Six hundred enthusiasts, many of them from remote villages, gathered
in St John's Cathedral to attend the inaugural meeting. The Bishop of
Kyrenia and Dr Spyridakis, headmaster of the Pancyprian Gymnasium,
accused the British of dehellenising Cypriot education. Zenon Rossides,
Ethnarchy adviser on foreign affairs, spoke on the international aspects
of the Cyprus problem. There were warnings of civil disobedience and
the non-payment of taxes, and hints that if Greece did not take action
the Cypriots might seek help from the Soviet Union. The meeting
adopted a unanimous resolution in favour of Enosis.[1]

In July the nationalists were outraged by an amendment to the
Education Bill making it possible for secondary schools to apply for
extra state aid. The terms were attractive but involved a measure of
Government control over the curriculum and the teacher's appointments. The Church saw the move as a threat to the enosist indoctrination which had pervaded Greek teaching since 1821 and, in the face
of its open hostility, only one Greek school dared to apply for aid. In
trying to introduce this modest, though belated, reform the British
were admittedly not disinterested. But since the scheme was optional
the wild accusations of dehellenisation which it precipitated were ill-
founded. But outside the island, where the facts were not known, the
image of 'British repression' was skilfully exploited by the nationalists.

AKEL in the meantime had kept up the pressure for a popular front.
The leaders sent greetings to Stalin, exhorted their compatriots –
Greek, Turkish and Armenian alike – to rise as one man against
'War'. The Party's 14-point programme published that summer
advocated, amongst other aims, increased propaganda against the
British bases, aid to farmers whose land had been compulsorily pur-

[1] See the Cyprus Mail, 26 April 1952.

chased by the War Department as the site for the Dhekelia cantonment, an end to Greek discrimination against the Turkish minority, and the exposure of the Ethnarchy leadership. The Akelists claimed to represent about 40 per cent of the people but the Archbishop tended to dismiss them as a negligible force in Cypriot politics, and they were incensed by his repeated refusal to see them. In announcing AKEL's decision to boycott a political strike called by the Ethnarchy in July Ziartides gave this warning:

The workers are under the leadership of the Pancyprian Federation of Labour (PEO) and so long as the Archbishop insists on ignoring the largest trade union movement in Cyprus, he will neither be able to organise a strike nor start a battle for Cyprus.[1]

AKEL was by this time weakened by a major upheaval inside the Party leadership. Serious differences had existed for some time between the extremists and the moderates over the Party's sterile policy of 'Enosis and Nothing but Enosis'. The crisis came to a head in the middle of August; prominent Akelists dismissed from the Central Committee two years earlier were now expelled from the Party. The leaders alleged that a group of dissidents, motivated by self-interest, sought to destroy AKEL's unity and work for a constitution. The latest 'purge' included George Cacoyannis, a Limassol lawyer, and Adamantos and Servas, former mayors with a strong popular following. Both men favoured AKEL's cooperation in a constitution as the only sensible course of action at this stage. Adamantos said that AKEL should not take a definite stand on the Enosis question which would not progress so long as the monarcho-fascists ruled Greece and he saw no prospect of change there for the next ten years.[2] Servas advocated that the Cypriots should seize any opportunity, however limited, to extend their political rights and promote the cause. He criticised AKEL for wasting money on overseas campaigns and for organising communist rallies and processions in Cyprus since they merely ended in fines and prison sentences.[3]

AKEL had lost some of its most able members and, in the process, the opportunity to play a decisive role in shaping the country's political future. Its influence in the trade unions, however, progressively increased with the expansion of the island's economy. Opposition to the

---

[1] *Cyprus Mail*, 4 July 1952.
[2] ibid. See 'The Purge of Adamantos', 1 September 1952.
[3] ibid. 13 September 1952, quoting *Neos Demokratis*.

British bases remained AKEL's official policy. But in reality the Party no longer constituted a danger to British strategic interests, for paradoxically the bases came to be built without hindrance by a labour force which was largely communist-controlled through the medium of PEO.

The winter was a period of relative calm. Makarios had been out of the island for five months. It was probably no coincidence that the situation began to change for the worse after his return in March 1953. One of his first actions was to demand the transfer of the island to Greece. The request was not new; in May he received the usual reply that the subject was closed, whereupon he called a protest rally and informed the Governor that the island's fate did not rest exclusively with Britain but was linked to the widely accepted principle of self-determination.

Before May was out the Ethnarchy launched a vigorous attack against two new government projects for marketing agricultural produce. Hadjikharos, General Secretary of PEK, a strong nationalist and a farmer himself, approved of the scheme and disagreed with Makarios who had ordered that it should be boycotted. The Archbishop replaced him by Andreas Azinas, a graduate of Reading University. One effect of this appointment was the early resumption under the cover of PEK of the subversive activities started by Socrates Loizides.

Tension rose in June on the occasion of Queen Elizabeth's coronation. On the Ethnarchy's orders the nationalists, joined by the Akelists, boycotted the celebrations. Serious clashes, again instigated by the Gymnasium boys, broke out in Paphos. PEON, which had initially in belligerent terms declared the celebrations incompatible with the national struggle, now had second thoughts and promptly dissociated itself from the riots. An excess of violence on the part of the nationalists might have damaged their image abroad and prematurely alerted the police to the dangers simmering below the surface. The authorities were not, however, taken in. PEON's clubs were withdrawn from the register before the end of June, and the organisation automatically became illegal. The Ethnarchy called for a demonstration but this was also banned, and instead a protest meeting was held in a Nicosia church. The Communists organised buses, with the help of the Old Trade Unions (PEO), to take demonstrators to the meeting despite the deadly enmity between PEON and the communist youth organisation AON. Such was the desperation of the Akelists in their efforts to sustain the facade of a popular front.

The Turkish Cypriots had watched the situation deteriorate with apprehension. Community relations worsened, friction being greatest in Nicosia, where the nationalist mayor, Dr Dervis, tended to ride roughshod over the Turks with schemes for the demolition of Muslim shrines on the pretext of town planning. The Turks, whose requests for separate municipalities went back several years, complained that the Greek councillors discriminated against them in other ways.

After 1950 the Turkish Cypriot leaders became increasingly critical of the administration's failure to enforce the sedition laws. In a long article, 'The Enosis campaign and the law', the Turkish Cypriot advocate A. M. Berberoglou criticised the Government's continued indifference 'to one unlawful activity in particular' – the Enosis movement. Quoting extracts from the Criminal Code he stressed that the movement was a contravention of the island's laws and prejudicial to the peace and tranquillity of the Turkish community as well as to their economic development. The Enosis movement was treason, he wrote, because it envisaged a change of sovereignty. The Government should therefore either warn the enosists that action would be taken against them or declare officially that agitation for Enosis was not an offence, in which case the Turkish community would consider itself free to demand the cession of Cyprus to the Turkish Republic.[1]

By 1953 the Turkish Cypriots had completely lost confidence in the ability of the Cyprus administration to control the Enosis movement. Their fears led to the formation in many parts of Turkey of the Cyprus Turkish Association for the purpose of bringing the problem to the notice of the Turkish Government and public.

There was certainly concern in official circles towards the end of 1953 at the flow of sedition from the press and the pulpit since this was bound to obstruct any plans for a constitution. On the other hand, the violence of the past few years had been limited to one notoriously troublesome town, and compared with the massive disturbances taking place elsewhere, including Greece, was on a small scale. The political climate alternated between waves of phrenetic excitement and long interludes of uneventful calm. Cypriot politics were essentially parish politics – juvenile, inconsequential and riddled with petty jealousies. Their inherent parochialism made it difficult for an outsider to take them seriously. The trouble-makers, led by Makarios, could be counted on one hand. In the view of the Cyprus administrators the political temperature dropped sharply during the Archbishop's frequent absences from Cyprus. His activities abroad were not their concern. This failure to

[1] See *Halkin Sesi*, 13 May, and Cyprus Mail, 14 May 1952.

assess the significance of the Archbishop's journeys in relation to developments in Cyprus resulted from the division of responsibility between the Colonial Office and the Foreign Office. The Cyprus administration, after seven decades of Enosis, had learned to live with the problem. Thus inured, government officials were unable, even at this late stage, to envisage that it could erupt into rebellion.

III

The Years of Warning
1950-1954

The Quest for Support Abroad—
First Greek Appeal to UN

I   THE QUEST FOR SUPPORT ABROAD

The Cypriot nationalists could achieve nothing without the support of
the mainland Greeks. In Greece the notion that all Greek speaking
areas must in the fullness of time be united with the Motherland is
never far below the surface. At the end of the Second World War the
country's mood was conducive to the revival of irredentist claims. The
people ardently hoped that their sacrifices in the Allied cause would
partly be compensated by the extension of the nation's boundaries.
Disillusionment came swiftly with the Paris Peace Conference in 1946.
The Cyprus question was deliberately avoided by the Greek Government in order not to embarrass Britain. The long-standing Greek
claims against Albania and Bulgaria with their risk of conflict between
the West and the Soviet bloc were not supported by the Allies. The
Dodecanese Islands were the only new territory gained by Greece.

The first to raise the Cyprus issue had been Nikolaos Zakhariades,
the leader of the Greek Communist Party (KKE) on his release from
Dachau at the end of the war.[1] From that time onwards the Communists
relentlessly pursued the cause. By concentrating on Cyprus they were
able to demonstrate their patriotism and stir up trouble in the Western
camp while avoiding a conflict of interests with their new allies, the
communist rulers of Albania and Bulgaria. The message had even
reached the remote villages of western Macedonia, where in March

[1] See C. M. Woodhouse, *The Apple of Discord* (Hutchinson, London, 1948), p. 243.

1947 children who had never heard of the island until their indoctrination by the political Commissars paraded the slogan 'We Want Cyprus'.[1] The occasion was the visit of the first United Nations Special Committee on the Balkans (UNSCOB); the purpose of their investigations Greece's complaint to the Security Council against her northern neighbours for aiding the communist guerrillas. The irrelevance of the demonstrators' demands was significant as an early attempt to interest the UN in the Cyprus question and as a distraction from claims to territories much closer to home and under the control of the Soviet bloc. The Communists having set the pace, the other political leaders could not afford to appear less patriotic. And they soon came to echo the Communists even if only half-heartedly for many years. In March 1947 the Greek Parliament, during the premiership of Demetrios Maximos, unanimously expressed the hope that the union of Cyprus with Greece would be realised.[2] The arrival in Athens of the Cypriot delegation at the end of May was a major embarrassment for the Greek Government. The Cypriots immediately deposited a set of the plebiscite signatures with the Greek Parliament. The friendly reception given to them by King Paul, the enthusiasm of the Church and the press offset to some extent the coolness shown in government circles. The Panhellenic Committee for the Cyprus Struggle for Enosis (PEAEK) formed under the chairmanship of Archbishop Spyridon, Primate of Greece, held a mass meeting in the stadium during July. A six-point resolution was adopted which recognised the results of the Cyprus plebiscite and raised the claim to northern Epirus. Spyridon, himself a northern Epirot, declared that it was the will of the Greek people 'to achieve the freedom of Cyprus after so many bloody struggles', and threatened to take the matter up through PEAEK if the Greek Government failed to do so.

The mobilisation of potential sympathisers in Great Britain, the stronghold of philhellenism, was of vital importance. Classical scholars and Romantics versed in the Byronic tradition could be counted on to put pen to paper in the service of Hellenism. The Cypriot nationalists, furthermore, had a direct link with the British Parliament through the Socialists Kenneth Robinson and Lena Jeger, both members for constituencies with many Cypriots. Other socialist sympathisers included Tom Driberg, Woodrow Wyatt, and Philip Noel-Baker and his son Francis, both dedicated philhellenes though the latter had recently been reported as saying that the time was not yet opportune to press

---

[1] Author's visit with UNSCOB to western Macedonia, March 1947.
[2] See *Greek Bulletin* (Greek Information Office, Greek Embassy, London), 3 March 1947.

the case for Enosis.[1] Amongst these politicians were talented journalists. The Cyprus case was thus assured of press publicity. The possibility of changing Conservative policy by exerting pressure through the Opposition was not overlooked.

The Cyprus delegation, headed by the Bishop of Kyrenia, reached England in August. The Colonial Secretary, James Griffiths, profiting by his predecessor's experience, refused to see them and was strongly criticised in the Greek Cypriot press. A senior official from the Colonial Office informed the delegation that Mr Griffiths would have been pleased to see them in different circumstances, but that he felt no useful purpose would be served by an interview at that time since his Government's attitude had already been defined.

The third line of action lay in the international field, with the USA as a starting point. The USA was important first as a source of funds and secondly for its inherent anti-colonialism, which could be exploited to sway international opinion. As early as 1947 the New York Congressman Emanuel Celler had drawn the attention of Congress to the island's strategic importance.[2]

The Greek Americans, concentrated largely in New York State, Illinois, Massachusetts and Pennsylvania, were geographically well placed to work on American public opinion.[3] Many of them were wealthy and influential; Congressmen needed their votes, but there were no comparable groups of British and Turkish immigrants to redress their influence. Greek Americans held key posts in the administration, in the Attorney-General's Office and the United Nations Secretariat in New York City. The Greek and Cypriot campaigners had a ready-made publicity organisation in the American Hellenic Educational Progressive Association (AHEPA).

The delegation, which arrived in the USA early in September, lost no time in depositing a third set of the plebiscite signatures at the United Nations headquarters. The courteous acknowledgment sent by the Public Information Office was encouraging but misleading. This stated that the volumes would be brought before the Secretary-General for any action which he might consider desirable. The Cypriots worked tirelessly interviewing the delegations of the member states. The

[1] Cyprus Mail, 21 January 1950, quoting the BBC. The Noel-Baker family had been associated with Greece since Byron's day and owned large properties on Euboea. Both Philip Noel-Baker and his son Francis, who tended to see the Cyprus problem through the eyes of dedicated Hellenists, were faithful supporters of Enosis.

[2] See *Congressional Record*, 25 March 1947, vol. 93, p. 2540.

[3] See Francis J. Brown and Joseph Slabey Roucek (Eds.), *Our Racial and National Minorities* (Prentice Hall, New York, 1939).

spokesman for the British delegation gave the customary reply that no change in the island's sovereignty was contemplated. Mr Cabot Lodge, on behalf of the Americans, was reported to have assured them that the documents would have the most careful consideration. Sweden's delegate stated categorically that his country could not support the Cypriot case, giving as a reason the non-intervention clause in the UN Charter. Many delegates paid tribute to the glory that was Greece and proclaimed full support for self-determination. Several of them shifted the responsibility on to the Greek Government stating that their attitude would be determined by the course it adopted. Afghanistan promised help and the anti-colonial powers gave unqualified support. But the outcome of the visit to the United Nations was on the whole disappointing. Ignorant of the procedure, the Cypriots found that without a member state to sponsor them no progress could be made in raising the Cyprus question and, even if a sponsor had been forthcoming, they had already missed the deadline for the General Assembly's agenda.

The Greek bishops in the USA and AHEPA were eager to help. Organisations engaged in the promotion of subversive activities against or on behalf of foreign powers are banned under US Federal Law. But AHEPA, in the category of a cultural society, was able to play a major role in the Cyprus struggle against the British without interference from the US authorities. Its propaganda campaign, at first relatively innocuous, began early in 1950. In September the Cyprus Affairs branch of AHEPA drew the State Department's attention to the plebiscite results, the British Government's refusal to see the Cypriot delegation and the need for US intervention with a view to initiating Anglo-Greek talks on the Cyprus question, should it prove impossible to raise the issue at the UN. Bishop Ezekiel, the Greek Orthodox Metropolitan, also circulated similar petitions from American Greek citizens. The State Department was unsympathetic. The West had its hands full with the war in Korea and other pressing problems. The Nicosia newspaper *Eleftheria* reported on 30 November that Mr Dean Acheson had flatly rejected any idea of UN intervention. The Cypriots, however, were consoled by the undertaking given by seven Senators, including Senator Fulbright, to place a Cyprus resolution before Congress the following year provided that the Korean war was over.

The results of the journey to the USA were not spectacular, but they were by no means fruitless. The Cypriots had left the impression that a genuine plebiscite had been held in Cyprus with appropriate safeguards. A widely used American encyclopaedia went so far as to describe the event as a referendum held by the British authorities. The first hint of serious trouble for Britain did not come until 1951, when Senator McCarran drafted a resolution recommending that in any consideration of the Cyprus question by the United Nations the American delegate should uphold the wishes of the Greek Cypriot majority.[1]

2 RISING PRESSURE IN GREECE FOR ENOSIS, 1950 ONWARDS

In Greece the Communists did not retain the monopoly of enosist agitation for long. The Greek Orthodox Church, in its historical role as the vanguard of Hellenism, was quick to follow suit. And the ecclesiastics seized the chance to re-enter the political arena from which they had been debarred since the thirties when the Venizelist Liberals had restricted their powers to religious affairs. The Church was joined by the Athens bureau of the Ethnarchy Council and the Greek Confederation of Labour. The most fanatical exponents of the cause were usually Cypriot expatriates with lasting grudges against the British who had adopted Greek nationality either out of choice or necessity as the result of deportation from Cyprus after the 1931 riots.

During the first five years after the liberation from the Axis Greek governments were preoccupied with the overriding struggle against the Communists, and the Cyprus question received scant attention despite the efforts of the troublemakers. Towards the end of 1949 the situation changed. The autumn saw the military defeat of the Communists in the Battle of Grammos. Victory had brought northern Epirus within reach of the Greek Army and, in view of its irredentist tradition, its frustration at being ordered to halt at the frontier instead of pursuing the fleeing guerrillas into Albania was understandable. Their immediate task fulfilled and the safety of Greece assured, officers began to speak of that other unredeemed territory – Cyprus. It was seen as a legitimate right which could be realised without complication since the island was controlled by a friendly ally, and the claim to Cyprus slowly gained ground.

The Metaxas dictatorship followed by four years of Axis occupation had brought about the disintegration of parliamentary forces in Greece. This, with the tendency of the electorate to split its vote among a large number of small parties, combined to produce a series of weak coalitions and an unbroken record of political instability during the early postwar years. The military victory at Grammos did not end the danger of communism. And all Greek governments were bound by the same basic foreign policy – close cooperation in the Western alliance and the

[1] *Congressional Record*, vol. 97 (1951), Senate Resolution 104, p. 2733.

revival of Greco-Turkish friendship in the interests of mutual security. These aims were sharply at variance with the Enosis campaign, the mounting pressure of which no political party, whatever its political colour, could withstand indefinitely.

The arrival of the Cypriot delegation in May 1950 had shown that however much the Greek Government might try to disregard the Enosis campaign it could do nothing to curb the press. In October of the same year it was faced with new difficulties in the election of Michael Mouskos as Archbishop Makarios III – an event which heralded an era of brilliant and intensive campaigning for Enosis. In preparation for years of campaigning in the West, Makarios was prompt to make his own attitude to the Cold War clear, and above all to dispel allegations by the Cyprus authorities that he had leftist leanings. As Bishop of Kition he had visited the troops on the Grammos front. A year later, shortly after his election as archbishop, he publicly rejected an invitation from the Orthodox Patriarch in Moscow to join a peace movement calling for a ban on the atom bomb.[1]

Makarios arrived in Athens at the end of March 1951, his first visit since his election as archbishop. Whereas the British diplomats tended to concentrate on the politicians in power, Makarios built up a vast range of contacts throughout the whole strata of the Greek political world. On his return to Nicosia, after three weeks of intensive activity, he spoke of the understanding he had found in Athens but intimated his displeasure with the Greek Government's slowness in pressing the Cyprus issue.[2]

The Greek Government's efforts to pursue a moderate policy over Cyprus were also hampered by the persistent ineptitude shown by politicians and public spokesmen in Britain whenever the subject was raised there. Replying to a parliamentary question, Kenneth Younger, the Labour Minister of State for Foreign Affairs, stated on 14 February that no communication had been received from the Greek Government about Cyprus.[3] This forced the Greek Prime Minister to be more specific than either he or his predecessors had been in the past: 'The union with Mother Greece constitutes an ardent desire on the part of the people of Cyprus and the people of Greece.'[4]

All these developments had aroused the interest of the Turkish Government. The Turks had no wish to jeopardise the rapprochement

[1] See *Cyprus Mail*, 24 November 1950.
[2] ibid. 14 April 1951.
[3] H.C. Deb., vol. 484, col. 380.
[4] *Greek Bulletin* (Greek Information Department, Greek Embassy, London), 20 February 1951.

with Greece by open intervention; so long as they were confident that Britain intended to abide by her undertaking to retain Cyprus they remained silent. However, on 21 April the Turkish Foreign Minister, Fuad Koprulu, stated that Turkey could not allow any change of sovereignty in Cyprus in a manner harmful to Turkish interests, which were best protected by the continuation of British rule.[1] The Greek Cypriots dismissed this timely warning as British inspired.[2]

On 9 September Greece held its third parliamentary election since the war and the second in eighteen months, twenty-four governments having fallen during this period. The desire for stability led to the formation of the Greek Rally under Field-Marshal Papagos. Pacification and economic recovery were the main electoral issues. The party leaders, with the exception of the Socialist Professor Svolos, avoided the Cyprus question. As in previous elections no single group gained an overall majority; the Greek Rally with 114 deputies was the strongest but Papagos refused to join a coalition. And, in the weeks which followed, efforts to form a government were abortive and interest was once again focused on Cyprus.

October began with a flurry of activity on the part of the Greek Confederation of Labour (GCL). In a setting which was cordial, characteristically hospitable, with red wine and sweet cakes in abundance, local and foreign journalists were subjected to a slashing indictment of the Cyprus authorities. The Confederation's complaints concerned restrictions imposed by the Cyprus administration in the interests of security. The authorities refused to allow the Cyprus Workers' Confederation (SEK) to hold its congress if the agenda included Enosis. They also distrusted certain members of the GCL as agitators with no genuine interest in trade unionism. Accordingly, the British Embassy turned down their applications for visas. In the light of the extreme right-wing character of the GCL it was ironic that its spokesmen should have declared that even the Soviet Union was more liberal than the British in these matters. The press conference was the first move in a sustained anti-British campaign in close cooperation with Michael Pissas, the fanatical leader of the Cyprus Workers' Confederation.[3]

Nothing was done to counteract the mounting volume of anti-British propaganda. On the contrary, goodwill visits organised by the Central Office of Information for Greek journalists to visit England

---

[1] See Crouzet, op. cit. p. 389, quoting *Hurriyet*, 21 April 1951.

[2] See Cyprus Mail, 14 and 28 April 1951.

[3] See *Confédération Générale de Travail de Grèce: Press Communiqué*, 6 October 1951; for further activities of the GCL related to Cyprus, its *Monthly Bulletin*, 1951 onwards.

tended to facilitate the aims of the enosists. The repercussions in Greece and Cyprus, for instance, of a cryptic reference made by Anthony Nutting in November on the island's strategic importance were catastrophic. The Cyprus Government tried in vain to damp down local excitement and end confusion by publishing the correct version:

> Whatever may be the long term thoughts and intentions of Greece or Great Britain, the immediate position must be inevitably influenced by the strategic position in the Eastern Mediterranean.[1]

The two months of political uncertainty ended in November with the formation of the EPEK-Liberal coalition under General Plastiras. The new Government's life was bedevilled with the Cyprus question from the start. Loukis Akritas, an EPEK deputy of Cypriot ancestry, made an impassioned criticism of the Government when Parliament opened on 1 November for failing to include Cyprus in its policy statement. He asked how the Government intended to work for Enosis – the only satisfactory solution. Venizelos, the Deputy Prime Minister and Foreign Minister, said that the Cyprus question had only been left out of the policy statement because of its delicate nature and 'relations with our friends and ally, Great Britain'. The Government intended to seek a settlement in accordance with Greek aspirations.[2]

While the Government made every effort to keep the Cyprus question out of the limelight at home, certain political leaders had already begun to make soundings in the international field. The previous year Kassimatis had raised the question in the Council of Europe.[3] In November 1951 John Politis, the permanent Greek representative to the UN, made oblique references to the subject when the General Assembly met in Paris.[4] In addressing the Fourth Committee, George Mavros was outspoken in his criticisms of the British Government for withholding information on the 1950 'plebiscite', with its 95 per cent vote in favour of Enosis.[5] Makarios and the Greek Confederation of Labour also sent communications to the Fourth Committee with a request for representation at its meetings. The first expressed concern about Greek educa-

---

[1] Cyprus Mail, 18 November 1951.

[2] Prime Minister's Office, Information Department, Athens, Daily News Bulletin (DNB), 1 November 1951.

[3] In secret session, and therefore no record exists in the Council's published documents but it was extensively leaked to the press, and mentioned at the UN General Assembly: GAOR (V) 374th Meeting, p. 184.

[4] GAOR (VI) First Committee 340th Plenary Meeting, 12 November 1951, p. 66.

[5] UN doc. A/C 4. S/R 208.

tional facilities in Cyprus; the second complained about conditions for trade unionists.[1]

In the meantime events had taken a more ominous turn with the first outbreak of violence over the Cyprus question. Defying a ban on demonstrations, students clashed with the police on 22 November. The incidents were heatedly debated in Parliament. The Opposition leaders from the extreme right to the extreme left used the opportunity to attack the Government's policy of moderation.[2]

During 1952 the Cyprus question began to dominate Greek political life. The anniversary of the plebiscite on 15 January, now celebrated annually, was marked by student rioting. Early in February King Paul received Zenon Rossides and Savvas Loizides on their return from Paris; the event had more than a mere social significance. The Cypriot leaders, treated as nonentities in the past, could no longer be disregarded. On 16 January the news broke that Greece and Turkey had been formally invited to join the Atlantic alliance, whereupon Makarios cabled the following warning to the Greek Foreign Minister who was attending the meeting of the NATO Council in Lisbon:

Cyprus can form a secure base only after the national aspiration for *Enosis* is realised, when the Cypriot people will wholeheartedly support allied plans.[3]

The deputy Supreme Commander of NATO, Field-Marshal Montgomery, came to Athens in May in connection with the pending Greek and Turkish membership of the Atlantic alliance. Lord Halifax was also in Greece on a private visit to the British Ambassador. Their presence in the capital became the pretext for mass demonstrations under the auspices of Archbishop Spyridon, who berated the Greek Government for failing to deal with the 'enslaved areas'. Serious clashes with the police took place.

The dust had barely settled when Makarios arrived in Athens, his visit coinciding with yet another goodwill tour for Greek journalists sponsored by the Central Office of Information. Between the visits to factories and coalmines the journalists aimed to hit the headlines of the Greek press with a sensational news item on the Cyprus issue. Consequently any ministerial statement was fraught with hazards. This time they reported that Nutting had described the agitation for Enosis as

[1] UN docs A/C 4/194, 27 November, and Add I, 13 December 1951.
[2] Prime Minister's Office, Information Department, Athens, DNB, 24 November 1951.
[3] Cyprus Mail, 28 February 1952, quoting *Ethnos* and *Eleftheria*.

'an organised campaign in Greece and Cyprus by people with a vested interest'.[1]

Calling for a nation-wide protest, Archbishop Spyridon accused the British of trying to gag the Greek Government at the United Nations by unscrupulous manoeuvres on the diplomatic front. The Athens bureau of the Ethnarchy backed Spyridon's statement with plans for a two-hour general strike on 4 July, a day of silent protest. The shops shut, the traffic stopped, bringing the capital to a complete standstill. Spyridon, accompanied by Makarios, placed a wreath on the tomb of the unknown warrior in honour of those who had died for 'self-determination'. Protests against Britain's retention of Cyprus and demands that Greece should appeal to the UN at the next General Assembly formed the substance of various resolutions.

Spyridon's choice of American Independence Day for the silent protest was not fortuitous. The Greeks had on this very day, he wrote to the American Ambassador, turned to that great power which had once held the Americans in bondage and which was now holding 400,000 Cypriots in bondage. The Archbishop anticipated that it would not be long before justice was granted 'not only to our brethren the Cypriots and our enslaved brethren in northern Epirus but also to all other peoples in bondage'.[2]

The Americans, who tended to regard the Cyprus claim as a harmless safety valve for Greek irredentism, must have viewed with disquiet the reference to northern Epirus which, if pressed too far, might trigger off a wider clash between the West and the Soviet bloc.

Venizelos dealt with the mounting agitation by intimating that only if all other courses of action had been exhausted before the deadline for the agenda would such an appeal be made. This left the Greek Government free to shelve an approach to the UN for at least another year. But the Government's difficulties were increased by Makarios's decision to prolong his stay until the end of the month. For as the weeks went by his oratory produced results and he became bolder, veiled criticism finally giving way to outright castigation of the Greek Government's cautiousness in handling the Cyprus question.

The EPEK-Liberal coalition was swamped by problems of pacification and economic recovery. Nevertheless, it had managed to maintain a policy of moderation over Cyprus in the face of rising pressure and a blaze of adverse publicity. But the popular leader, General Plastiras, was failing in health; his weak coalition was largely dependent on the votes

[1] Cyprus Mail, 19 June 1952.
[2] DNB, Athens, 5 July 1952.

of EDA which had replaced the banned Communist Party and held the balance of power in a fragmented Parliament. On 11 October the Plastiras Government resigned after only thirteen months in office to pave the way for new elections.

3   PAPAGOS AND THE CYPRUS QUESTION

On 19 November 1952 Field-Marshal Papagos was swept to power by an overriding majority. On the suggestion of American advisers a majority system was used for the first time; the Rally polled nearly fifty per cent of the votes and gained an overall majority of 178 seats. Greece now had its first strong government since the Second World War, largely thanks to the Field-Marshal's personal prestige. Originally a concentration of right-wing elements, the Rally had gained in strength since the previous year's elections as the result of desertions from the centre.

The Government was largely preoccupied during its first few months with defence and economic problems. The recent progress made by Greece in improving relations with former enemies was in sharp contrast to the waning goodwill towards Britain and the United States. The promise of continuity and strong government gave rise to hopes on all sides of a satisfactory settlement of the Cyprus question. Papagos was determined to continue with the efforts to achieve closer cooperation between Greece and her non-communist neighbours. Greece and Turkey, now members of NATO, had new responsibilities and the Field-Marshal was convinced that with sufficient equipment they could jointly overcome various problems including the defence of Thrace. Apart from manifestations of trouble over Cyprus and fishing rights off the shores of Asia Minor, which were vigorously exploited by the press, outwardly the prospects for Greco-Turkish cooperation were more encouraging than at any time since the era of Kemal Ataturk and the great Venizelos.

On 28 November the Turkish President, Celal Bayar, returned the state visit which had been made by King Paul and Queen Frederika. He arrived at Piraeus in a destroyer to spend six days in Greece. Driving through the streets of Athens he was welcomed by the Greek crowds with a warmth and spontaneity almost without precedent. The trouble brewing over Cyprus was obscured by the glowing speeches of his hosts and his own tributes to Greece in reply.

Stressing the importance of Greco-Turkish friendship when Parliament opened on 17 December, Papagos declared his intention to strengthen relations with Yugoslavia, to work for the security of Greece and Turkey and for peace in the Balkans and the Eastern Mediterranean. Greece would seek to settle the northern Epirus question through international diplomacy and not by force; the Cyprus issue which stirred 'the heart and soul of all Greeks' would be dealt with in the framework of current realities, he said. Finally, Greece would cooperate closely with Great Britain, France and the USA in the free world's defence.[1] The next day an EPEK deputy for the Dodecanese was strongly critical of the Government for not using its large majority to take a more resolute line on the Cyprus question.

The temporary eclipse of the Cyprus question in Greece was more than offset by progress in the United States, where Makarios had now been campaigning for several months. The foundations already existed there; all he had to do was build upon them with the cooperation of the local Orthodox prelates. The Archbishop's assertion that Greek education in Cyprus was in danger of extinction was a certain way of arousing indignation and a generous financial response. The myth of dehellenisation readily gained credence owing to the failure of the British Embassy in Washington to publicise the facts, namely that Greek education was almost entirely controlled by the Ministry of Education in Athens.[2]

The Archbishop's visit eventually bore fruit in the formation of various committees, such as the Justice for Cyprus Association, and in increased American press interest. The committees kept Cyprus in the limelight and worked behind the scenes to get the subject on to the UN General Assembly's agenda. Many Congressmen, some of them very influential, eventually intervened in the Cyprus controversy, usually on lines which were hostile to Britain.

Makarios briefed Papagos on the results of his journey when he arrived in Athens on 24 February 1953. Seizing any opportunity for publicity, he congratulated the Governor of the Dodecanese on the anniversary of its cession to Greece, adding that he was sure that Cyprus would soon achieve Enosis. The Archbishop's presence in Athens was marked by serious clashes on 4 March during a demonstration instigated by the Cypriot Students' Committee. The Minister of Interior had banned the demonstration but had agreed that students should gather quietly in the university grounds. Joined by other trouble

[1] DNB, 18 December 1952.

[2] Many years later Grivas himself unintentionally paid a tribute to British leniency in educational matters. In describing his Cypriot schooldays he wrote that his was a happy childhood 'and happiest of all when I marched behind the blue and white banners on some national day and felt the Hellenic passion for liberty burning in us all'. *The Memoirs of General Grivas*, edited by Charles Foley (Longmans, Green & Co Ltd, London, 1964), p. 3.

makers, they rushed out into the streets nearby and in the clashes which followed 45 policemen and 24 civilians were injured as the result of attacks with stones and iron bars.

After the Archbishop's departure for Cyprus at the end of March the Greek Confederation of Labour managed to keep the issue alive. Its Eleventh Congress on 24 April was attended by representatives of the American Confederation of Labour (ACL) and the International Confederation of Free Trade Unions (ICFTU). The Congress faced a heavy agenda appropriately concerned with labour and economic problems. Nevertheless Michael Pissas, the leader of SEK, insisted on discussing the Enosis question, whereupon the British Labour Attaché, Frederick Hampton, walked out in protest.

The full blaze of publicity was again concentrated on the Cyprus question when on 21 May the Athens bureau of the Ethnarchy released Sir Andrew Wright's reply to the Archbishop's request for a plebiscite. Wright had stated that the subject was closed.[1] This prompted the deputy for the Dodecanese to express grave misgivings. Stephanopoulos, the Minister for Foreign Affairs, commented 'the Cyprus issue has been raised, actually exists, and no one may consider it closed',[2] but he would go no further than the Prime Minister's statement on the opening of parliament.[3]

Gradually the ministers were being dragged into the Cyprus controversy. The Government, however, would not allow itself to be deflected in its determination to consolidate its alliances. As arranged, Papagos visited Ankara and Istanbul in June. In his welcoming speech the Turkish Prime Minister, Adnan Menderes, declared that Greece and Turkey had not joined the Atlantic community 'hand in hand for no reason'. They had together formed a pact with Yugoslavia, a vital link in the defence chain, in the interests of mutual security. While emphasising the military value of the Balkan Pact, Papagos stressed that the economic dangers were no less important. There was scope, he said, for still closer Greco-Turkish cooperation on lines which alone could lead to peace and prosperity.[4] The joint official communiqué issued at the end of the visit was equally hopeful with its message that there was no problem between the two countries which could not be settled on the basis of mutual interest.

Autumn tended to be a season of heightened interest in the calendar

[1] See above, pp. 47–8.
[2] DNB, 21 May 1953.
[3] DNB, 18 June 1953.
[4] ibid.

of the Enosis campaigners. The approach of the deadline for the General Assembly's agenda was one reason. On 10 August Archbishop Makarios sent the United Nations a memorandum requesting that the Organisation should urge Britain to respect the Cypriot people's right to self-determination.[1] He wrote to Papagos on the same day urging the Greek Government to back an appeal to the UN:

> We are entitled to, and demand, such support because what the Cypriots want is not self-government, or autonomy, or independence, but union with Greece.[2]

If Greece failed to help, the Archbishop implied that Cyprus would have to turn to foreign sources, meaning the Soviet Union.

Papagos had not given up hope of bilateral talks with Britain and he decided to raise the matter with Eden who was expected shortly to visit Greece. Alexis Kyrou, the Greek delegate to the UN, had in the meantime returned to Athens for discussions with Papagos, and Makarios was dissuaded from going to the General Assembly in New York.[3] The Archbishop, in fact, had no possibility of presenting an appeal to the United Nations under its rules of procedure. But the move, owing to the publicity given to it by the Ethnarchy, served to exert pressure on the Greek Government. On 21 September Kyrou explained at a plenary meeting of the General Assembly that Greece, despite the heavy pressure of Greek public opinion, had not sponsored the Archbishop's request because she preferred bilateral discussions with Britain. He said the two countries were linked by traditions of friendship. But if the normal processes of talks failed other options remained open to Greece.[4]

Earlier in the month Eden had arrived to spend part of his convalescence in Greece. The visits of Montgomery and Halifax had shown that the mere presence of a British Foreign Secretary in Greece with the Cyprus crisis at fever pitch was in itself sufficient to unleash mass disturbances. His wishes for quiet and privacy were nevertheless observed and, but for a meeting with Papagos at the British Embassy, his visit might have passed off without repercussions. Papagos raised the Cyprus question only to be told in the brusquest of terms that, as far as Britain was concerned, the problem did not exist. The Greek Prime Minister's attitude undoubtedly hardened after this rebuff and

[1] GAOR(VIII) 439th Plenary Meeting, p. 66.

[2] DNB, 9 September 1953.

[3] DNB, Greek Prime Minister's statement, 8 February 1955.

[4] GAOR (VIII) 439th Plenary Meeting, pp. 66–7.

he subsequently turned down an invitation to visit London. Papagos, however, had not finally given up hope of avoiding friction with Britain. On 27 November the Greek Foreign Minister, Stephan Stephanopoulos, said the door to talks had been left open, but that in the event of failure the Greek Government would be free to deal with the Cyprus question in any way it thought fit. The Opposition leaders, on the other hand, pressed increasingly for drastic action. They had nothing to lose by doing so; the likelihood that the Papagos Government would last its full term ensured that they would not have to bear the consequences of a reckless policy over Cyprus.

4   THE CLIMAX IN 1954

The Enosis campaign moved rapidly towards a climax in 1954. In Greece the subject had become a nation-wide obsession. In England it had attracted little interest before this year. From then on it was to figure increasingly in the British Parliament and press. On 2 February the Secretary of State for the Colonies, Henry Hopkinson, was asked whether the Government planned to introduce a constitution for Cyprus in view of the 95 per cent vote for Enosis recorded by the plebiscite. Hopkinson replied that subject to certain conditions the constitutional offer made in 1948 still remained open and that the 'so-called plebiscite' had no relevance.[1]

Lord Winster initiated a full length debate in the House of Lords on 23 February[2] and, taking the Dodecanese as an example, forecast the recession which could be expected to result from the transfer of Cyprus to Greece. He deplored the lack of interest shown by Parliament over the past six years and praised the economic progress made by the Cyprus administration. Winster sought at length to put their Lordships in the picture on conditions generally in the island, its past history, the abortive attempts by Britain to introduce a constitution and the explosive nature of the Greek factor in the problem. Greece had never owned or administered Cyprus, he said. But he thought that they had 'some shadowy claim based on the division of the Roman Empire into East and West'.[3] Winster attached great importance to the interest of Turkey as a partner with Britain in NATO and the bastion of her defence policies in the Near and Middle East. He said Turkish objections and Britain's international obligations ruled out any idea of

[1] H.C. Deb., vol. 523, col. 32 (Written Answers).
[2] H.L. Deb., vol. 185, cols 1068–98.
[3] ibid. col. 1073.

giving up Cyprus. The choice lay in ceding the island to Greece with or without leased bases; in imposing a constitution or in drafting one in cooperation with the Cypriots. In view of the British Government's clean record their Lordships had no need to be kept awake at night by the Archbishop's threatened appeal to the United Nations. There was nothing between the Cypriots and a constitution except the Cypriots themselves.

Lord Ogmore commented on the indifference of the Conservative backbenchers to the Cyprus problem and the curious absence of any mention of Enosis, 'this burning issue', in the Colonial Reports.[1] Lord Listowel advocated new efforts to break the deadlock and an imposed constitution; a friendly population was necessary for strategic reasons, he said.[2] Lord Killearn, who had just returned from Athens, sounded a realistic note with the warning that mounting emotion over Enosis threatened Anglo-Greek friendship.[3] Lord Hankey was against change at the present time, including an imposed constitution.[4]

On behalf of the Government the Under-Secretary of State for the Colonies, the Earl of Munster, said 'Cyprus is today more prosperous than ever before in its history'. Munster's speech, like that of Winster's, reflected the influence of the *Cyprus Annual Report* with its references to the island's current prosperity. It was true that there were no elected representatives at the level of central government but elected local bodies existed throughout the island. The 1948 offer had not been withdrawn and it was up to the Cypriot leaders to come forward and cooperate in constitutional development.

Winster was scornful about the elected bodies. With one or two exceptions, he said, they were not only Communists but completely incompetent. One of his last acts as Governor had been to transfer the control of the fire brigade from the municipalities to the police.[5]

The debate was unfortunate in its timing and content. Certain comments on both sides of the House, reflecting the ignorance and tactlessness prevailing in official circles, were guaranteed to arouse Greek anger even in calmer times. Greece had only recently acquired the Dodecanese. And there was no basis there for comparison with conditions in Cyprus, an island with greater natural resources which had not suffered the ravages of enemy occupation. The debate coincided with

[1] ibid. cols 1080–2.
[2] ibid. cols 1085–8.
[3] ibid. cols 1088–9.
[4] ibid. col. 1091.
[5] ibid. cols 1096–8.

the presence in Athens of Makarios. This, he said, was yet another example of British obstinacy illustrating the futility of the Greek Government's attempts to settle the problem on a friendly basis. Contrary to their Lordships' claims, the administration had reduced Cyprus to economic misery. Greece must take the matter to the United Nations as soon as possible.

The Foreign Minister, Stephan Stephanopoulos, told journalists that Greece would not be influenced by the debate in the Lords. However, an approach on the subject of bilateral talks was made to the British Government which replied that it could not agree to discuss the status of Cyprus.[1] On 17 March Papagos stated that the Greek Government's Cyprus policy, which combined decisiveness with conciliation, was the best way to safeguard the security of the Eastern Mediterranean and was unlikely to lead to anti-British action. Public reaction in contrast was growing increasingly hostile. *Ethnikos Kyrix*, once the mouthpiece of Grivas, called for a campaign of hatred against the British. In Athens hundreds of university students demonstrated outside the Anglo-Hellenic Institute where Donald McLachlan, assistant editor of *The Economist*, was due to give a lecture on NATO. In Rhodes, where Makarios was the guest of the municipality, students expressed their solidarity with him before attacking the British Consulate and nearby shops.

April began with one of the Turkish Government's rare but significant public warnings. It would be improper for Turkey to raise the Cyprus question with Greece and she had not done so, the Foreign Minister, Fuad Koprulu, said. But when the time came to discuss the subject with Britain the Turkish Government, which did not consider a change in the island's status desirable, would expect to have its say.[2] The Greeks were unimpressed. And on 20 April an official spokesman stated that Greece intended to appeal to the United Nations if Britain had not agreed to bilateral talks by 22 August.[3]

Greece sent to friendly foreign states a memorandum giving Britain's repeated refusal to hold bilateral talks as the reason for taking the matter to the United Nations. The note mentioned the strong anti-British feeling which was gathering momentum as the result of the illiberal measures in force in Cyprus; it dismissed Britain's strategic arguments. The value of the bases would, on the contrary, be enhanced by Enosis

---

[1] See Eden's reply to Mrs Lena Jeger, vol. 525, col. 8 (Oral Answers) H.C. Deb., 15 March 1954.

[2] See The Times, 3 April 1954.

[3] *Greek Bulletin* (Greek Information Office, Greek Embassy, London), 22 April 1954.

and the cooperation of the people; a special agreement could be negotiated separately with Greece within the framework of NATO. The memorandum contained the usual pledge about guarantees for the Turkish minority.[1]

Much as the Greek Government might condemn illiberal laws in Cyprus it did not hesitate to clamp down on press criticism which happened to prove embarrassing. And the owner of the *Police Gazette*, which published a pro-British article, was arrested for no worse offence than predicting that the Greek appeal to the UN would be the grave of the Cyprus question and for accusing Makarios of meddling in politics instead of caring for his flock.[2]

The open intervention by Greece and Turkey stimulated renewed interest in the House of Commons. Replying to questions on 28 April Hopkinson referred members to the Turkish Foreign Minister's recent warning. Hopkinson's statement, which was evasive on the subject of bilateral talks and the Greek appeal to the UN, resulted in a marked hardening of attitude on the part of Papagos. He said Greece would appeal to the UN in the autumn if Britain had not agreed in the meantime to bilateral talks. The Greek Government could no longer ignore the just claim of 400,000 Greek Cypriots. Feeling against Britain was rising in Greece to the detriment of Atlantic defence in a vulnerable region. The prudence and moderation shown by Greece in trying to settle the Cyprus question had met with nothing but curt noes from the British Government.[3]

Replying to questions in the House of Commons about these developments the Minister of State, Selwyn Lloyd, was non-committal.[4] However, E. L. Mallalieu was told by Selwyn Lloyd on 12 June that he could not agree that any foreign government, however friendly, had the right to be consulted about the future of one of Her Majesty's possessions,[5] and by Oliver Lyttelton on the same day that no change of sovereignty was contemplated and that the offer of the 1948 constitution, subject to certain conditions, remained open.[6] On 24 June the news broke that the Middle East Headquarters were shortly to be moved from Egypt to Cyprus.

The new Governor, Sir Robert Armitage, had now been in Cyprus four months. He had sounded leading Cypriots on the prospects for a

[1] The Times, 30 April 1954.
[2] DNB, 28 April 1954, and The Times, 30 April 1954.
[3] DNB, 4 May 1954, and *Greek Bulletin* (GIO, London).
[4] See H.C. Deb., vol. 528, col. 830 (Oral Answers).
[5] ibid. col. 1230.
[6] ibid. col. 75 (Written Answers).

constitution. He had also sought the advice of Maurice Cardiff, Director of the British Council, and of Lawrence Durrell, the recently appointed Government Information Officer. Philhellenes and fluent Greek speakers, both men had worked in Greece and were in close touch with Cypriot opinion. Cardiff and Durrell, in common with certain leading Cypriots, saw a faint hope of an end to the dilemma in an offer of self-government with the promise of self-determination at some future even if distant date. The British Government however believed that the uncertainties of such an arrangement would not make for stability.

The Governor and his advisers in Cyprus realised that no constitutional progress was possible so long as the flow of sedition in the shape of rabid Enosis propaganda was not checked. They misjudged the situation, however, in thinking that if the Greek Government could be induced to clamp down on the Enosis campaign Makarios might fall in with British plans for a constitution. The Archbishop was, on the contrary, the inspiration of the campaign, the Greek Government his prisoner.

The possibility of an appeal to the UN had already plunged the Cypriots into a state of exaltation. Although Britain had little to fear on the diplomatic front, a debate was certain to arouse false hopes in Cyprus with the risk of violence. Armitage felt that the British Government needed to make a firm policy statement at the earliest opportunity. And on 28 June he came to London to report on the situation to the Cabinet.

5 HOPKINSON'S 'NEVER'

On 28 July the Minister of State for the Colonies announced a new constitutional plan. In the past six years, he said, no one had taken up the 1948 proposals which offered a wide measure of internal self-government. The British Government had therefore decided to wait no longer. The Governor of Cyprus had been instructed to take the necessary measures for the introduction of a new constitution at an early date. No change of sovereignty was contemplated, Hopkinson emphasised. The new formula was clearly less liberal than the 1948 offer in that it did not provide for an elected majority. Nevertheless there were advantages in that provision was made for unofficial members to serve on the Executive Council and as heads of departments – the first step towards a ministerial system.

Hopkinson mentioned the administration's achievements in bringing prosperity to the island, in safeguarding the rights of all communities and the stability of this vital strategic area. He said the British Government, which recognised the close cultural links of the two main communities with Greece and Turkey, was resolved to continue its policy of vigorous economic development. Without sacrificing these traditional links, the Cypriots now had the opportunity for economic, social and constitutional development.[1]

Replying to James Griffiths, a former Labour Secretary for the Colonies, Hopkinson explained that the nationalist and communist leaders, having refused to cooperate in 1948, had not been consulted. He agreed about the danger of a boycott but hoped that men of good-will and moderation would come forward in sufficient numbers and that in due course the other parties would join them. Under the new plan the majority would be composed of official plus nominated members. The 1948 constitution, with its provision for an elected majority, had been based on the presupposition that all the main parties would cooperate. But in the event this was not the case. The Government was therefore now proposing a constitution which it hoped would work. The rate of progress on this road to self-government would depend on the Cypriots concerned. On the question of Dominion status for Cyprus and the ultimate right of self-determination, which Griffiths had also raised, Hopkinson made the following comment:

> It has always been understood and agreed that there are certain territories in the Commonwealth which, owing to their particular circumstances, can never expect to be fully independent. [Hon. Members: 'Oh!'] I think the right Hon. Gentlemen will agree that there are some territories which cannot expect to be that. I am not going as far as that this afternoon, but I have said that the question of the abrogation of British sovereignty cannot arise – that British sovereignty will remain.[2]

Aneurin Bevan complained that this important statement, which had come on the heels of the Foreign Secretary's announcement about the British departure from Egypt as the direct result of local hostility, should have been made on the eve of the summer recess. The British Government was now going to establish, he said, 'a Middle East Command in the middle of a hostile population made more hostile by the extraordinary language used this afternoon'.[3] Hopkinson dismissed Bevan's

[1] H.C. Deb., vol. 531, cols 504–6.
[2] ibid. col. 508.
[3] ibid. cols 509–10.

allegation that the British plan violated the Statute of Westminster under which newly independent territories enjoyed the right to contract in or out of the Commonwealth. It was not possible to treat all colonies in the same way. The position with Egypt was different. The forces were there under treaty rights. But nothing less than full sovereignty over Cyprus could enable Britain to carry out her strategic commitments in Europe, the Mediterranean and the Middle East.[1]

Opening the full scale debate later that day Tom Driberg attacked the Government's suggestion that certain Commonwealth countries could never expect full independence. This surely meant the abandonment of a principle to which all parties were committed. The Foreign Secretary, he said, had spoken earlier with reference to Egypt on the need for local consent and cooperation in maintaining bases on foreign territory. What cooperation, Driberg said, could the Foreign Secretary expect from the Cypriots over the proposed bases in Cyprus. Ninety per cent of them perhaps ill-advisedly or foolishly wanted Enosis. Self-government was always taken to imply ultimate self-determination.[2]

William Rees-Davies, a Conservative, wanted the sovereignty question clarified. The son of a former judge in Cyprus, he said that there had never been a great demand for Enosis. The present agitation was due to the Orthodox Church leaders and the Communists who saw Britain's negotiations with Egypt as an opportunity to press for Enosis.[3] Challenged by E. L. Mallalieu to name the Cypriots who objected to the present campaign, he replied that the Turks and the considerable European community in Cyprus were strongly opposed to a Greek takeover, whereupon Lena Jeger reminded him that the Cypriots too were Europeans.[4] There was no tradition of Greek sovereignty, Rees-Davies continued. The Orthodox Church leaders were not working for the benefit of the Cypriots but to gain a small island for Greece.[5]

Quoting Churchill's much publicised dictum of 1907, Mrs Jeger regretted the failure of members over the years to take the question of Enosis seriously. There was ample evidence of widespread support for it. The 10,000 Cypriots who had left the sunshine of their native island for the soot and slums of St Pancras, her constituency, were unanimous in their demand for Enosis. And the Ethnarchy referendum (1950) had resulted in a 98 per cent vote in its favour. Mrs Jeger was uneasy about

---

[1] ibid. cols 510–11.
[2] ibid. cols 517–21.
[3] ibid. cols 522–3.
[4] ibid. col. 524.
[5] ibid. cols 524–5.

the Greek decision to appeal to the UN. The island's strategic value would be enhanced, she argued, by respecting the wishes of the majority and cooperating with the Greek Government, which was ready to offer defence facilities to fellow members of NATO. There was, she agreed, a difference between the positions of Egypt and Cyprus, 'but the common denominator was a hostile population'. The cooperation of any Cypriots other than 'purely nominated stooges' must now be less than it was a few years ago.[1]

Reverting to the sensitive issue of sovereignty, Hopkinson stated that 'there were certain territories in which the exact degree of independence which a colony could achieve would depend on its circumstances'. Malta came into this category.[2]

Mallalieu said that however much the British believed that the Cypriots might suffer if they left the Commonwealth he did not think Britain had a right to put a brake on their march towards self-determination.[3] William Aitken thought the Opposition had been stampeded into Enosis by the Ethnarchy in much the same way as the Cypriots had been. Communism might return to Greece, he argued; British sovereignty in Cyprus was important to security. He compared the relative prosperity of the Cypriots with conditions in Rhodes where the people faced 'semi-starvation'. Owing to the Enosis campaign, waged for the past hundred years, the average Cypriot farmer probably did not realise how much worse off he would be under Greece.[4]

In an outburst of impassioned oratory Richard Crossman warned the Government that its policy of locating a base in Cyprus would lead to the same dreary sequence of events which had taken place in Palestine and elsewhere. If the 95 per cent vote for Enosis was suspect then the people should be allowed to decide for themselves. The genuineness of the movement was evident from the fact that the Communists exploited it. He begged the Minister of State, who had made this 'astonishing' announcement, to ask the Cabinet to change its mind. 'May I say that the tragedy of the Middle East', he continued, 'is that there is not a country whose people got their rights from the British without murder.'[5] Jordan, Palestine, Egypt had all learned that British imperialism gave them nothing unless they took it by force or the threat of force. By putting military expediency before political principles over the past

[1] ibid. cols 525–9.
[2] ibid. col. 531.
[3] ibid. cols 533–4.
[4] ibid. cols 537–9.
[5] ibid. col. 546.

eight years Britain had caused enmity over the Middle East. The base in Cyprus would be useless.[1]

Describing Crossman's speech as 'extremely irresponsible and dangerous',[2] the Secretary of State for the Colonies, Oliver Lyttelton, stressed the importance of Turkey in NATO's defence plans and of British sovereignty over Cyprus to security in the Eastern Mediterranean. It was not possible at this stage in the world situation to give Cyprus full control over defence and external affairs any more than it would be to leave such matters to the Greek Government. Driberg noted the discrepancy between the words 'at this stage' and the Minister's 'never'. Denying that 'never' had been used by either the Minister or himself, Lyttelton sidetracked the issue of self-government and concentrated on the refusal of the Cypriots to take up the 1948 constitution. He was doubtful whether the Labour Party would officially endorse Crossman's readiness to surrender Cyprus to Greece. Britain did not admit to the right of any foreign power, however friendly, to interfere with British sovereignty in her colonies and he could imagine 'no more disastrous a policy for Cyprus than to hand it over to an unstable though friendly power'.[3] This would weaken the bastion of NATO and depress living standards for everyone in Cyprus. Once self-government was established the Cypriots would see the idea of Enosis in a very different light.

James Griffiths said that the Labour Party would reserve judgement pending further study of the policy statement. In a balanced speech, in sharp contrast to the emotionalism and distortion shown by certain politicians on both sides of the House, he endorsed a tribute paid by the Minister to the first-rate job done by the Colonial administration in the economic and social field. However he urged the Government to discuss the constitutional plan with the Cypriots rather than try to impose it. Major Legge-Bourke, who had served with the army in Cyprus, said this new agreement with Egypt marked a black day in British history which made the strategic importance of Cyprus infinitely greater.[4]

Aneurin Bevan declared that the Government, in enforcing a base upon the Cypriots after withdrawing from Egypt because of the people's hostility, was guilty of inconsistency and clinging to outdated concepts. The Government's policy was an open invitation to the Cypriots to do whatever they could to make things as difficult as possible for the

[1] ibid. col. 548.
[2] ibid.
[3] ibid. col. 552.
[4] ibid. col. 561.

British once they had established a base there. Woodrow Wyatt deplored the agreement with Egypt. The policy statement, he claimed, was motivated by the Government's wish to placate the 1922 Committee which was strongly opposed to the surrender of the Egyptian base. The proposed constitution, with its majority of nominated and official members, would not provide a democratic outlet – the result would be an increase in communist strength. Cyprus was the only place in the world with a coalition of the Church and the Communists, and the Tories were facilitating its consolidation. Wyatt considered that a base leased from Greece could provide Britain with facilities comparable to those existing in Gibraltar and Hong Kong. He was evasive on the question of Turkish objections to Enosis raised by Reginald Paget, one of the few Socialists to show any interest in this aspect of the problem.

The day after the policy statement the Governor of Cyprus broadcast a special message to the Cypriots:

We have now heard again plainly and unequivocally the long established policy of the British Government that there can be no change in sovereignty over Cyprus. But this statement has this time a difference. It is coupled with the news that a new Constitution is to be introduced.[1]

The Cyprus authorities had anticipated that any efforts to launch a constitution would be swamped by a flood of destructive criticism unless the Sedition Law was strengthened. The sedition laws were less stringent than in Britain in that in Cyprus the prosecution was required to produce evidence of direct incitement to violence. On 2 August the Attorney-General, Criton Tornaritis, gave warning that the existing sedition laws, hitherto leniently interpreted, would in future be strictly enforced. The local Greek newspapers immediately went on strike for a week; in Britain the move, which was seen as an attack on the freedom of the press, created an uproar.

The Governor explained on 6 August that the Sedition Law had not been changed and that so long as it was not broken there was no question of restricting comment on the plan and press freedom. No irrevocable steps would be taken before Parliament assembled in the middle of October, therefore there was ample time to discuss the plan. As for the criticisms that it was more illiberal than earlier constitutions, including the 1948 plan, the present proposals were a marked advance

[1] Cyprus Mail, 29 July 1954, quoting from the Cyprus Broadcasting Station (CBS).

on the existing Executive Council and he urged the Cypriots to consider them in the light of present-day conditions.[1]

The storm did not abate. And on 8 August Tornaritis said the warning had been made necessary by conditions now prevailing in the colony. The enosists had taken increasing licence in pressing their case but no prosecutions had been instigated for their repeated transgressions of the law as long as they did not involve incitement to violence. Propaganda so immoderate, so charged with emotion, had made fair discussion of any proposal, especially a constitution, impossible. Only by enforcing the Sedition Law and containing the flood of Enosis propaganda, amounting at times to intimidation, could 'moderate opinion be given a chance to crystallise and persons who put the interests of Cyprus first be encouraged to come forward and play their part in operating a constitution', Tornaritis concluded.[2]

The Archbishop had been the first to challenge the authorities by preaching several seditious sermons in quick succession. This act of defiance culminated on 22 August with a demonstration in Phaneromeni Church and the square outside. Hundreds arrived in vehicles bedecked with Greek flags to hear him speak. Before a large congregation he declared that the Cypriots would never give way in their struggle for 'Enosis and nothing but Enosis'. 'There is a flame burning in our soul', he said, 'which no power on earth can extinguish.'[3]

The prosecution of Makarios under the Sedition Law might have failed because of the need in Cyprus to prove incitement to violence. A conviction, on the other hand, would have served the cause of the enosists, elevating him to the status of martyrdom. The enforced tolerance of the Archbishop's transgressions made it impossible to take action against the rank and file of the movement. The clumsy attempt to make the Sedition Law effective, far from facilitating the introduction of a constitution, made the authorities look foolish.

Hopkinson's 'never' had at the time made little impact in Cyprus. But it was readily exploited by the extremists and from now on came to be the battle cry of the nationalists as the final negation of Cypriot rights. Nothing any British minister could say or do was capable of eradicating it.[4] The Greek Government embarked on a campaign of full scale political warfare and associated itself with a hostility towards

[1] *Documents and Press Comments on the Cyprus Question* (Press and Information Department, Prime Minister's Office, Athens, 1954).

[2] Undated Press Release, Colonial Office Information Department (COID).

[3] The Times, 23 August 1954.

[4] Churchill stated on 19 October 1954 that the Minister for the Colonies was not aware that he had used the word 'never' in his impromptu speech. H.C. Deb., vol. 531, cols 1033–4.

Britain which was likely to prove as irrevocable in domestic politics as the anti-Westernism of the Arab leaders. The Rector of Athens University, Professor Daskalakis, launched a campaign of hatred against Britain; English was withdrawn from the university curriculum. The Greek Government disregarded diplomatic etiquette and made extensive use of diplomatic channels for the distribution of anti-British propaganda and condoned, even encouraged, the torrent of abuse and invective which flowed daily from the state-controlled Athens Radio in the effort to stir up emotions in Greece and Cyprus.[1]

On 20 August the Greek Government sent the appeal to the UN[2] and simultaneously released the text in Athens. The permanent Greek delegate to the UN, Alexis Kyrou, told the press that Greece did not expect Cyprus to be ceded to her from one day to the next; that no mention of the plebiscite or Enosis had been made. Plebiscites were discredited because of their totalitarian regimes, Enosis was omitted because the Greek case was based on the right to self-determination. He was convinced that America, because of her allegiance to the principle, would favour the Greek appeal which made it clear 'that Cyprus was Greece and Greece was Cyprus'.[3] Holding Britain responsible for the Greek move, the Foreign Minister, Stephan Stephanopoulos, declared on the same day that if the UN proved incapable of securing the rights of a small people its prestige would be irreparably damaged in the eyes of the world.[4]

The event was celebrated all over Greece. Thousands of Greeks filled Constitution Square and the adjoining streets when Archbishop Spyridon, almost drowned in applause, addressed himself to the 'noble and liberal British people', the vast majority of whom, he claimed, did not support their Government's policy on Cyprus.[5] Numerous resolutions were adopted throughout the country expressing approval for the Greek Government's action at the UN. The strangest manifestation of solidarity took place at Pyrgos in the Peloponnese. After the bishop had officiated at the Te Deum and laid a wreath on the war memorial, twenty reservist officers gave samples of their blood. Carrying two bottles of the blood the officers arrived in Athens after a seven-day march; one bottle was intended for Makarios, the other for the British Ambassador to send on to Churchill. This macabre episode was

---

[1] See below, pp. 145–6, 148.
[2] UN doc., GAOR (IX) A/2703.
[3] DNB, Athens, 21 August 1954.
[4] ibid.
[5] ibid.

intended to symbolise the Greek people's determination to sacrifice their blood, if necessary, for the liberation of Cyprus.

6   THE FIRST GREEK APPEAL TO THE UNITED NATIONS

The British Government worked hard to prevent the discussion of the problem at the UN for such publicity was certain to exacerbate the controversy. The General Committee nevertheless met on 23 September to consider whether the Greek item, based on the claim for equal rights and self-determination for the Cypriots under the auspices of the UN, should be included on the agenda.[1]

Opening the discussion, Alexis Kyrou explained that Greece was forced to resort to the United Nations because the British Government had refused to settle the problem by direct talks and had denied the Cypriots the right of self-determination under the UN Charter. The British Minister of State, Selwyn Lloyd, saw a dangerous precedent for the UN in considering demands for the cession of a territory duly recognised by treaty as being under the sovereignty of another member state. The discussion of Cyprus by the UN was, moreover, inadmissible under the terms of Article 2(7) of the Charter. Australia and France voted against the Greek appeal; Colombia, the Netherlands and the USA abstained; the nine delegations which voted in favour included Czechoslovakia, the USSR, Syria and Iceland.[2]

When the General Committee's recommendations came up for endorsement in the plenary meeting the next day, the Iraqi delegate, Al Jamali, suggested that the discussion should be postponed for a few days on the ground that time was needed for further study of the statements made by the Greek and British delegates. This manoeuvre, motivated by the British, was firmly resisted by Kyrou who argued that but for recourse to the United Nations events in Cyprus would have taken a more ominous turn. Selwyn Lloyd summarised the island's history with emphasis on the British connection. The discussion of the Greek item, he repeated, would be an interference by the UN in the sphere of domestic jurisdiction. The fact that Britain was being asked to agree to a plebiscite under UN supervision opened up interesting possibilities elsewhere – for example a Bulgarian request for a UN plebiscite in Macedonia. Possibly this was why the Soviet Union supported the appeal. He urged the Assembly to look where it was going. If the principle was accepted for an ethnic group in a sovereign territory to demand

---

[1] UN doc. A/C 1/L 125 (IX).
[2] GAOR (IX) General Committee, 93rd Meeting, p. 11.

self-determination, then no frontier would be permanent anywhere. Contrary to the picture drawn earlier by the Greek representative of an island under repression and seething with unrest, the only people the British Minister of State knew of who had been sent to prison were two newspaper editors in Athens – this for daring to criticise Greek Government policy in raising the Cyprus issue at the UN.[1] The Turkish Cypriots, who were Muslims, strongly objected to Enosis. Cyprus, he stressed, had fortunately not suffered hitherto from communal strife and Her Majesty's Government would do what it could to keep the peace. Did the Assembly really want to stir up such strife? He begged those states which had known communal troubles to hesitate before taking the risk with Cyprus, reminding them of the social insecurity and the loss of life and property which so often followed.

Cyprus, the British Minister continued, was vital to Britain in the discharge of her treaty obligations to the Arab states, her commitments to the southern flank of the North Atlantic Treaty Organisation, and to the defence of Turkey and Greece itself. There was no alternative to British sovereignty. Full administrative control was necessary 'because leases expire, treaties have a habit of being whittled away and, as I said before, Greek governments, like other governments, change'.[2]

The liberal constitution of 1948 was refused, Selwyn Lloyd continued, because the extremists feared normal constitutional development. He did not believe that any great empire had done so much for the constitutional development of its people. This great endeavour would go on in Cyprus where Her Majesty's Government intended to persevere with another constitution. The traditional friendship between Britain and Greece had been a model relationship in the past, bound by common interests in peace and war. The two nations had fought together, suffered disaster together and triumphed together. Britain's policy towards Cyprus was in the best interests of the countries of the Aegean, the Middle East and the free world. In the interests of peace and stability and of the United Nations he begged the Assembly to reject the Greek item.

The Turkish delegate, Selim Sarper, spoke of Turkey's alliance with Greece and intimated that it would have been wiser not to have created the Cyprus issue. He said that under Article 2(7) of the Charter the question came within the domestic jurisdiction of the United Kingdom and he hoped that the item would not be inscribed. But in

---

[1] See above p. 74.

[2] *Report on the inscription of the Cyprus item on the agenda of the Ninth Session of the General Assembly of the United Nations held at New York on 23/24 September 1954* (Cmd 9300), p. 12.

the event of a debate taking place on the substance he reserved the right to speak. Krishna Menon was concerned that the people of Cyprus – the nationhood of Cyprus as such – had been overlooked. If the issues were freedom and self-government India would have supported the Greek appeal, but there were three claimants to the island; very soon it would become a free-for-all, instead of 'the homeland of the Cyprian nation'. He disagreed with the British Minister's strategic arguments:

> We regard nationhood as territorial; it makes no difference to us whether in any particular territory, people are of one ethnic group or another.[1]

Thirty votes were cast in favour of the Greek appeal, 19 against with 11 abstentions. The main supporters of Greece included the USSR, Czechoslovakia and several Arab states. France, Liberia, Luxembourg, the Netherlands, New Zealand, Norway, Sweden, Turkey and South Africa were amongst those who voted against. The United States and India abstained. This triumph for the Greeks was, however, marred by the deferment of the full discussion in Political Committee until December, right at the end of the agenda.

Despite the trend of events in Greece during the summer and autumn towards a major rift with Turkey, the policy of close cooperation in regional defence went ahead without a hitch and the Second Balkan Pact was signed at Bled on 9 August. Sarper's intervention in the Plenary Committee had been brief, cautiously worded and based ostensibly on the assumption that in the last resort the Cyprus question would not be discussed by the General Assembly. The Greek, Turkish and Yugoslavian Chiefs of Staff were therefore able to hold discussions in Athens at the end of September as originally planned.

The weeks which followed the preliminary success at the United Nations were a period of hopeful expectancy. And full use was made of the time to promote the Cyprus struggle both in Britain and America. The fact that Athens Radio, in its broadcasts to Cyprus, repeatedly attacked the constitutional proposals indicated that the enosists were still haunted by the deep-rooted fear that any form of self-government, however limited, would frustrate all hope of union with Greece. The extremists also feared that Cypriots might be reluctant to sacrifice the recent but growing prosperity of the country under British rule, and the picture they presented was confusing and contradictory. The people were told on the one hand that it was better to be with Liberty, even if

[1] UN/GAOR (IX) 477th Plenary Meeting, 24 September 1954, p. 59.

she came dressed in rags; on the other, they were subjected to the dismal saga of an island in the throes of excruciating poverty. A special exhibition was held in the centre of Athens in which archaeological exhibits were included to prove the 'Greekness' of Cyprus.

Archbishop Makarios arrived in Athens at the end of September en route for New York. Encouraged by the Labour Party's attitude at its annual congress,[1] Makarios thanked Philip Noel-Baker, 'the former Minister and well-known philhellene, for the Party's support which would greatly contribute to a just solution and strengthen Anglo-Greek friendship'.[2] In England the Archbishop was very active. He told journalists at the Waldorf Hotel that the constitution which Britain was about to offer the Cypriots, whatever its format, would be unacceptable. The only solution was the right of the Cypriots to determine their own future, he said.[3] During an interview with The Times he attacked the 'so-called anti-sedition laws', denied that the campaign was in any way anti-British, dismissed the importance of the Communists, putting their numbers at about two hundred, and suggested that the Greek offer of bases in Greece and Cyprus met Britain's strategic arguments. On another occasion, Makarios, at his small hotel in Oxford Street, laughed at the suggestion that perhaps he was intending to lead a revolt in Cyprus on the lines of the recent guerrilla (*andarte*) rising in Greece. He said conditions in Greece were rather different. He did not see the Communists as an obstacle to Enosis. So long as Field-Marshal Papagos was in power the solution was simple; AKEL would be outlawed and the Pancyprian Federation of Labour (PEO) dissolved.[4]

The long-awaited debate opened on 14 December with a draft resolution from the New Zealand delegate, Sir Leslie Munro, who called upon the Assembly not to consider the Greek item any further.[5] At the root of the item, Munro said, was the Greek claim for Enosis which was bound to affect Greco-Turkish relations and the stability of the area. Concerned at the political consequences of further debate, Munro regretted that Greece should have thought fit to raise the matter at all.[6] Alexis Kyrou argued that the postponement could only prolong the deadlock.

The New Zealand text was, after a procedural wrangle, given priority over the Greek draft. Cabot Lodge for the United States supported

---

[1] See *The Labour Party Annual Report 1954*: 'General Debate on Cyprus', pp. 139–41.

[2] DNB, 30 September 1954.

[3] Ethnarchy Press Release, 20 October 1954.

[4] Unpublished interview with the author.

[5] UN doc. A/C 1/L 125 (IX).

[6] GAOR (IX) First Committee, 749th Meeting, 14 December 1954, p. 544.

New Zealand on the grounds that protracted discussion could aggravate tension and embitter national feeling at a time when wider interests were best served by strengthening the existing solidarity among freedom-loving nations.[1]

Anthony Nutting said the Greek and Turkish-speaking people had lived side by side in peace. Agitation for Enosis would hamper orderly progress towards self-government. The Eastern Mediterranean was not a stable region but painstaking diplomacy and political foresight on the part of statesmen like Venizelos and Ataturk had created a happier state of affairs culminating in the present Balkan Pact. 'Impetuous action on the part of the United Nations might now release forces which once out of control could sweep away the endeavours of a generation.'[2]

Kyrou's insistence that a debate should take place on the substance brought the Turkish representative Selim Sarper fully into the controversy for the first time. He attacked the outstanding flaw in the Greek delegate's argument, namely that Greece was not bound by all the provisions of the treaty of Lausanne. Greek propaganda leaflets, he said, disclosed that in this case the principle of self-determination was based on the assumption that Cyprus belonged to Greece. It was, on the contrary, geographically an extension of Anatolia. The people were no more Greek than the island itself. The Greek demand, based on a misinterpretation of historical facts, was 'cloaked in a mist of poetic irredentism'. Turkey deplored the use being made of the moral authority of the Orthodox Church and would not accept any change in the status of Cyprus which did not have its whole-hearted consent.[3]

On 15 December Benites Vinneza stated that the subject was more suitable for discussion in the Fourth Committee. The delegates for Syria and the Yemen disagreed that Britain needed Cyprus for the defence of the Arab world.[4] Syria's delegate moreover objected to a resolution at this stage.

Kyrou, in reply to Sarper, pointed out that several Greek islands were closer to Turkey than Cyprus was. He said Greece did not seek the revision of the treaty of Lausanne – merely self-determination for a colonial people. The Soviet bloc, El Salvador, West Irian and Indonesia were all helpful to the Greek viewpoint. Iraq upheld the New Zealand text. Sweden's delegate was helpful to Turkey in recalling that the

[1] ibid. pp. 544–5.
[2] ibid. p. 545.
[3] ibid. 750th Meeting, 14 December 1954, p. 553.
[4] ibid. 751st Meeting, p. 556; 752nd Meeting, p. 564.

Aaland Islands, despite the fact that 95 per cent of the population was of Swedish descent, had been ceded to Finland. The delegates of Australia and New Zealand exposed the insincerity of the communist bloc's support for Enosis in the light of the USSR's refusal of self-determination to Lithuania and the Balkan States.

The New Zealand resolution was, on the initiative of El Salvador and Colombia, finally amended so that the operative paragraph read '. . . for the time being it does not appear appropriate to adopt a resolution on the question of Cyprus'. The General Assembly on 17 December adopted this text by 50 votes to none, with 8 abstentions. The British and Turkish delegates stressed that their support for the resolution did not imply that they recognised the competence of the UN to deal with Cyprus on any future occasion. Nutting described the outcome as a victory for common sense. Sarper insisted that there could be no just and equitable settlement of the problem without Turkey's full cooperation and consent. Kyrou said Greece had only voted for the amended text because of the insertion 'for the time being'. The Assembly's verdict was for the Greeks simply a postponement.

The outcome was a setback for the Greek Government. Kyrou had been over-optimistic in estimating the support which Greece could expect and had disregarded the historic fact that, however ready statesmen may be in theory to uphold abstract principles, once they are forced into a position of having to take action they put national self-interest first. The Greek Government itself had only two years earlier, out of concern for the Greek minority in Egypt, ignored the right of the Sudanese to self-determination by recognising Farouk as King of the Sudan. The assumption that most former British colonies and nations currently at variance with Britain would automatically support the Greek viewpoint was an over-simplification which had no place in the realities of international politics. Spain, for instance, was not likely to support a plebiscite in Cyprus. Once the precedent was established it would have been difficult to avoid the same procedure in Gibraltar, and the result would have been an overriding vote in favour of the retention of the Rock by Britain – the exact reverse of Spain's objectives. Other nations found themselves in comparable situations. And any antagonism they may have felt towards Britain was secondary to their main interests. That Kyrou, a diplomat of intelligence and distinction, should have made such fundamental mistakes can only be explained by his obsession with Enosis dating from the time of his expulsion as Consul from Cyprus at the request of Storrs in 1931. Shortly after the debate he was posted as Ambassador to Finland.

The debate, described by the French delegate as two days of 'sterile polemics', had only worsened the prospects for a settlement. Britain had with limited success argued her case from the standpoint of strategic priorities and the correctness of her position in international law. But even this victory was to be short-lived. Greece and Turkey had for the first time seriously clashed in public over Cyprus, putting at risk the delicate balance of the alliances they had recently concluded. The Turks had depended mainly on legalistic arguments which were hard to fault; Greece, regardless of existing treaty obligations, on the absolute right of self-determination. The amended resolution gave rise to interpretations which were diametrically opposed and laid the foundations for renewed discord.

The decision to shelve the Cyprus debate and resentment at the American stand set off violent riots in Salonika the next day. Mass meetings, organised by university students, were joined by other demonstrators. After smashing the offices of the United States Information Services they stoned the British Consulate. On 19 December violence broke out in Cyprus in protest against the UN decision. Gangs of schoolboys roamed the streets shouting 'Enosis' and using bottles and stones against the police. Rioting also broke out in Limassol; a mob surrounded the police station and replaced the British flag with the Greek one. Troops opened fire to restore order. Twenty-three people, including eleven policemen, were injured.[1] Reaction to the outcome of the appeal to the UN was delayed in Cyprus. In contrast to the spontaneity of violence over the Cyprus question in Greece, protests in the island had to be organised. This first major outburst ended the period of relative calm, which had hitherto prevailed in the island.

Greece by raising the matter at the UN had embarked on the road of no return. From that moment the Cyprus dispute ceased to be a conflict between a colonial power and its subjects. The Greek action, finally triggered by a series of British blunders in quick succession, was responsible for the direct intervention of Turkey which inevitably complicated the task of reaching a settlement. Thus the progress made by the Greeks in 1954 was illusory; with the internationalisation of the problem the goal of Enosis became more remote than ever and the way was paved for the exploitation of the dispute by third parties.

[1] The Times, 20 December 1954.

IV

The Origins of EOKA
1948-1955

Grivas's Early Subversive Activities — Final
Preparations for the Cyprus Revolt

I COLONEL GRIVAS ('DIGHENIS')

The Church and the politicians were not alone in working for the cause. From 1948 onwards a Greek of Cypriot origin, Colonel Grivas, was engaged in a private conspiracy to unite Cyprus with Greece.

The son of a prosperous corn merchant, George Grivas was born in May 1898 at Trikomo, a bleak village at the eastern end of the treeless Mesaoria. He was educated at the village school and the Pancyprian Gymnasium where he enthusiastically assimilated the doctrines of Hellenic nationalism introduced into the curriculum by teachers from Greece. At 17 he left his native island to become a Greek subject and to enter the Athens Military Academy. His youthful ambition to join the crusade for a 'Greater Greece' (*Megali Ellada*) was realised during the Asia Minor campaign in 1921. His division was, however, forced to retreat from its position within sixty miles of Ankara. After this setback Grivas, according to his own account,[1] was sent to Eastern Thrace to command a company formed for the specific purpose of attacking Constantinople – a plan which never materialised owing to the defeat of the Greek Army.

The successes of Ataturk's irregulars gave the Colonel a lifelong interest in guerrilla warfare. But the political lessons to be learnt from this catastrophic adventure in Greek irredentism were completely lost on him. More Hellenist than the Greeks themselves, Grivas came to pursue the nationalist cause with all the zeal of the expatriate, even on occasions to the extent of endangering the Motherland.

[1] See *Memoirs* (Longmans), op. cit. p. 4.

A captain at 26, Grivas served between the two World Wars in various army units, lectured on tactics at the Athens Staff College and attended advanced courses at French military establishments, including the École de Guerre. When the Italians invaded Greece in 1940 Grivas, now a lieutenant-colonel, was posted to the Pindus region as Chief of Staff to the Second Army Division. After Greece was overrun by the Axis forces he returned to Athens where he spent the war. In 1941 he formed the nucleus of the right-wing terrorist organisation X (*Khi*). The philosophy of the early recruits, mainly royalist officers, was unmistakably irredentist:

Our motto was, is and will always be a GREATER GREECE. . . .

We dreamt of this Greater Greece from the very moment when Mussolini's eight million cardboard bayonets were pointed at us. We dreamt of it when the iron-clad army of the Huns was attacking our army from the rear when it was occupied in Albania.

We dreamt of this Greater Greece when our mighty ally, Great Britain, fought the hard war alone against the dark powers of the AXIS.

We still dreamt of it when the last drop of patriot blood had drained from the wounds inflicted by the conqueror.[1]

At the end of the occupation almost nothing was known about Grivas. But some impression of his character may be formed from the activities of X, which he directed. X first came into the open after the German evacuation and, to quote C. M. Woodhouse, rapidly developed into an organisation of 'reactionary thugs' acquiring 'the sinister significance of a Ku Klux Klan'.[2] The claim that X took part in the resistance is discredited by the leading authorities on the subject and eyewitnesses to the events of the period.[3] Its role during the occupation was, on the contrary, suspect and obscure. Some of its associates were tainted with the stigma of collaboration; and its weapons, on the Colonel's own admission,[4] were obtained from the enemy. For this reason the British refused X's offer to help fight the Communists in 1944.

[1] Unpublished document circulated by X, which came into the hands of the British.
[2] See Woodhouse, op. cit. p. 31 and p. 194.
[3] The myth that X was in the Resistance seems to have arisen as the result of writers on the Cyprus crisis, with little or no first-hand experience of Greek affairs, accepting the Colonel's claim at face value and its repetition without verification.
[4] See *Memoirs* (Longmans), op. cit. p. 7.

During the rising many clashes took place between ELAS and X, which was based on the Theseion area. The Colonel's qualities as a courageous and tenacious fighter came to the fore in December. With about 100 X-ites he held out against the overwhelmingly superior forces of ELAS and was only saved from annihilation by the eventual arrival of British troops.

The excesses of the right-wing bands, of which X was the largest, aggravated security problems in post-war Greece. The Allied Missions in Athens repeatedly urged the Government to disband the right wing as well as the communist irregulars. But X had penetrated large sectors of the gendarmerie, many of whom were recruited from the Peloponnese, the traditional centre of royalism. In January 1946 100 X-ites occupied Kalamata, took prisoners from jail as hostages and executed fourteen of them in the mountains. This outrage led to the declaration of martial law and the closure of X's offices throughout Greece. But since the authorities were still mainly preoccupied with the communist danger, the armed bands of X continued to harass innocent citizens. Through its tactics of violence and intimidation, the organisation had within a matter of months aroused in the general public a hatred almost equal in intensity to its hatred of the Communists.

In the circumstances, the Colonel's decision to enter politics was astonishing. His organisation, now proscribed with the rest of the armed bands, reappeared as the X – Party of National Resistance. The Populists, the most influential of the royalist parties, refused to include X in the large coalition of right-wing groups which won the election in March 1946. Grivas decided that X should run alone; despite the advantages of proportional representation, no X-ites were elected.

2   SUBVERSIVE ACTIVITIES OF GRIVAS, 1948–1954

As the Government's operations against the Communists progressed, the majority of the right-wing bandits were absorbed into the regular forces. The restoration of the monarchy on a firm basis and the approaching defeat of the Communists had moreover considerably reduced the scope of extremist organisations such as X. In 1948 Colonel Grivas turned his attention to the problem of Enosis in the firm conviction that the Cypriots would only gain their freedom through violence. He recognised from the outset that Cyprus was unsuitable for guerrilla warfare. It lacked massive mountain systems to serve as hiding places and bases for operations. Its distance from the Greek mainland and the

Aegean islands was a major obstacle to the importation of arms. Cypriot temperament was also likely to give rise to difficulties, for the people had no tradition of war and were alien to the use of force as a political weapon. But the Colonel decided that these problems were not insuperable.

A nonentity in the Greek political world, Grivas was obliged to seek the contacts he needed at high level through third parties. In 1948 he made his first approach to the influential newspaper editor Achilleus Kyrou through Christodoulos Papadopoulos, the brother of his former aid in X. Kyrou[1] replied that diplomatic negotiations must first be given a chance.

In the Greek parliamentary elections in March 1950 the Colonel made a second bid to enter politics, this time as the leader of the National Agrarian Party X, which polled less than one per cent of the total votes and returned no deputies.[2]

Encouraged by the results of the Cyprus plebiscite at the beginning of the year the Colonel held further discussions with Kyrou and Papadopoulos about the possibilities of starting a revolt in the island. And at his request Papadopoulos went to Cyprus in August to make an assessment of popular reaction. Since the Greek Cypriots could always be counted on to support the nationalist cause provided that they were not required to take practical steps to further its objectives, it was not surprising that Papadopoulos returned with glowing reports of the people's enthusiasm for Enosis. Kyrou's sudden death in September, however, was a setback for the Colonel's plans. A fresh start had to be made, and Papadopoulos was sent to sound General Kosmas, who in May of the following year promised his support. It was decided that Grivas should lead the rebellion and that he should make an early visit to Cyprus in order to study conditions on the spot. In spite of the troubled political situation in the island and the fact that Grivas was blacklisted by at least one British Mission in Athens as a dangerous terrorist and irredentist, he obtained a visa from the British Consulate-General without difficulty.

On his arrival in Cyprus in July Grivas immediately sought out Makarios. But the Archbishop's attitude was discouraging. From the start he was at variance with Grivas on the scope of the armed struggle, its timing and the methods to be used. Grivas favoured a campaign

---

[1] A relative of Alexis Kyrou, the Consul withdrawn from Cyprus at the request of Storrs in 1931.

[2] *Post-War General Elections in Greece* (Prime Minister's Office, Press & Information Dept, Athens, 1964).

combining guerrilla warfare with sabotage. The Archbishop wanted operations limited to sabotage on a small scale; he was strongly opposed to the formation of guerrilla groups and persistently evasive on the all-important question of the starting date. The Colonel feared that undue delay in launching the campaign would give rise to problems of secrecy once the preparations were under way and that conditions were likely to become less favourable since Britain's progressive withdrawal from the Middle East could be expected to increase her determination to retain Cyprus as the last British foothold in the region.

The Archbishop's lack of enthusiasm was reflected in the attitude of the Cypriots as a whole. They were conservative in outlook and haunted by memories of the 1931 rising – a venture which in the opinion of Grivas had failed simply for want of adequate planning. Grivas, however, found a kindred spirit in the Bishop of Kyrenia, a rival of Makarios and dedicated enosist, who preached violence from the pulpit.

During his visit Grivas stayed with his brother, a physician in Nicosia, and toured the mountain areas extensively. After seeing Makarios a second time he finally left the island deeply worried by the Archbishop's scepticism and indecisiveness. But for the Colonel there was no turning back. Once he had made a decision he was pathologically incapable of reconsidering it, however much circumstances might dictate a change of course. And, given the inspired leadership which he was convinced he could provide, no problem was insurmountable.

On his return to Athens Grivas worked to establish the secret Revolutionary Committee. With Makarios in the chair, the Committee met in Athens for the first time in July 1952. Makarios repeated his earlier misgivings: 'Not fifty men will be found to follow you.'[1] Apart from the formation of two special committees under Stratos, a former Minister of War, a second meeting in July must have been equally unsatisfactory for Grivas for it was on this occasion that Makarios ordered the Colonel not to return to Cyprus until he sent for him. Makarios did not send for Grivas, and in exasperation the Colonel turned to Spyridon, the Primate of Greece and junior to Makarios in the hierarchy of the Eastern Orthodox Church. Spyridon authorised the Colonel's return to Cyprus. The concession was significant as the first attempt by Grivas to bypass the authority of Makarios. Grivas for the second time obtained a visa without difficulty from the British Consulate-General in Athens and landed in the island in October. The Archbishop, who was due to leave for the United States, referred

---

[1] *Memoirs* (Longmans), op. cit. p. 18.

Grivas to the Bishop of Kition. During the Archbishop's absence Grivas spent five months in Cyprus, surveying the regions of Penta-daktylos and Olympus and making important local contacts. The priest Papastavros gave much assistance; Azinas called at the house of Dr Michael Grivas to volunteer his services.

On his return to Athens in February 1953 Grivas drew up a general plan[1] and submitted copies to Stratos and Makarios. Disagreeing with the Archbishop's view that the struggle would last about three to six months, he made preparations for a longer campaign. But in the absence of help from the Greek Government he was obliged to rely on small private purchases and on the arms he had retained from the days of X.

The general aim of the plan was to show the world that the Cypriots were not willing to yield until their claims were met and that the British had not got the situation under control. Grivas recognised the impossibility of imposing total defeat on the British. The object of the campaign would be the mobilisation of international opinion on the side of the Cypriots and the ultimate realisation of their claims through diplomatic pressure exercised by the United Nations. A specially constituted Athens Committee would be charged with organising demonstrations throughout Greece in order to expose the British and prove the Greek people's solidarity with the Cypriot cause.

Owing to the difficulties of waging a full-scale guerrilla war and the unsuitability of the terrain, sabotage was to be the main weapon. Sabotage groups would be based on the town and village areas where they operated; only in the case of immediate danger would they be sent to hideouts or to join the mountain guerrillas. The Colonel's decision to form only five guerrilla shock groups initially was determined by the amount of arms available at the time and the fact that a higher number would make concealment and escape more difficult. However, the possibility that they might eventually increase their activities was envisaged and the need to increase arms stocks stressed. The main task of the shock groups would be to assist the saboteurs by harassing the enemy and attacking military targets.

Other points covered by the plan included the organisation of regular food supplies and emergency rations; the formation of execution squads to kill Cypriots considered dangerous to the cause, and the creation of

---

[1] General Grivas, *Guerrilla Warfare and Eoka's Struggle* (Longmans, London, 1964); see Appendix I, pp. 91–5, for the plan in full; also Appendices V, VI and VII, pp. 101–6, for Grivas's directives on ambushes, the manufacture of explosives, detonators, percussion mines and their use.

intelligence centres to amass information about British troop movements.

The plan advocated the immediate despatch to Cyprus of the arms already accumulated and the immediate departure of Grivas for the purpose of further reconnaissance in the island and preliminary preparations for the creation of a rebel movement.

Makarios saw Grivas in Athens in March on his way to Cyprus from the United States and agreed in principle to the use of force but insisted that this should be restricted to sabotage. Similar instructions were repeated in the summer by Azinas on behalf of the Archbishop – but this time with the additional proviso that no one was to be sent to Cyprus at that point. Thus the practical effects of the Archbishop's concession on the use of force were nullified. At this stage certain members of the Revolutionary Committee suggested that the Archbishop should be ignored, thereby showing an extraordinary lack of realism and unawareness of his power and unique authority in Cyprus. Makarios had acquired considerable prestige as a relentless and skilled exponent of Enosis, and was automatically sacrosanct in the role of Archbishop. Grivas, a layman and unknown to the Cypriots, could not hope to oust him or to start a revolution without his full cooperation.

In June, however, Makarios showed signs of yielding to pressure. Dr Grivas wrote that the Archbishop now agreed that Grivas should send one or two men from Greece and more later. Savvas Loizides at the same time advised Grivas that Makarios had authorised funds for the purchase of a small consignment of arms. But when Grivas informed Makarios in Athens that the materials were ready he sensed yet again some hesitancy on the Archbishop's part. However, Grivas and Admiral Sakellarios eventually persuaded him to go ahead with the plan. The Admiral arranged for the materials to be transported to Cyprus by caique and with the help of Azinas they were safely unloaded near Khlorakas on 2 March. Grivas's main concern was now to obtain more arms. But a message on the subject from Savvas Loizides to Makarios was not answered.

The quest for aid in Greece was frustrating. With the exception of General Kosmas, Grivas had failed to obtain the cooperation of anyone in a position of high responsibility. In 1951 he had lost no time in asking Kosmas to sound Papagos – then leader of the Opposition – but the Field-Marshal dismissed the idea as premature. Grivas, who seldom saw beyond the narrow objectives of Greek nationalism in its most extreme form, attributed this indifference to the sentimentality prevailing in Greece about Anglo-Greek friendship and to the personal ambitions of Papagos, whose career might have suffered through the alienation of Britain and America. But the advent of Papagos to power brought no change of official attitude. Early in 1953 the Field-Marshal, now Prime Minister, informed Grivas through General Kosmas that he did not wish to be involved in his plans or for it to be known that he was even aware of his intentions. In May a high-ranking officer, who had previously expressed disapproval of the Colonel's plans, informed him that his efforts to get supplies from military warehouses had been reported to General Ventiris, who subsequently warned Grivas that Papagos was aware of his activities and had taken steps to stop him. The following September a minister in the Papagos Government sent for Grivas and hinted at the possibility of his arrest if he persisted in going against government policy. Grivas was incensed by the warning and urged Makarios to approach the Prime Minister, only to learn from the Archbishop that it was Papagos himself who had dictated the order to the minister. Towards the end of the year Savvas Loizides reported that Stephanopoulos, the Greek Foreign Secretary, and Alexis Kyrou, the Greek delegate to the United Nations, were opposed to armed action before the autumn of 1954 when the Cyprus question was expected to be debated by the General Assembly, since any suggestion that Greece was trying to blackmail the Organisation by the use of violence must at all costs be avoided.

By 1954 the political campaign in Greece was fast gathering momentum. Papagos had announced his intention of raising the Cyprus question in the United Nations if the British persisted in their refusal to participate in bilateral talks on the future of Cyprus. The Greek Government, nevertheless, still refused to sanction the activities of Grivas. In April an official in the Ministry of Foreign Affairs told him that the Cyprus question was going well and that armed action could only cause untold damage. Grivas had always discounted the possibility of a fruitful outcome to the United Nations debate and by midsummer could no longer contain his impatience. On 16 July he met Azinas on the island of Tinos and instructed him to distribute arms in accordance with the General Plan; to find hiding places; to list the dangerous agents and to make preparations for his arrival in the Khlorakas area. In July the British Consulate-General refused Grivas a visa for Cyprus; but this belated precaution was immediately neutralised by the granting of a visa to Zafiris Valvis, the deputy leader of X and its political adviser, who went in the Colonel's place. Grivas now began to make plans for his secret entry into the island, but on receiving no confirmation from the Archbishop suspected him of further vacillation. Azinas, who had been urged by Grivas to impress upon the Archbishop the urgency of his departure for Cyprus, did not return to Greece until September, with the news that Makarios, on his way to New York for the United Nations debate, intended to leave the money in Athens for the hire of the caique which was to transport the materials. The Archbishop, who clearly did not share the Colonel's sense of urgency, told him in Athens on 1 October that he wished him to go to Cyprus and that he had left the money for the caique with Savvas Loizides but that the question of the starting date for the rebellion was shelved. Makarios finally gave instructions that armed action was to start immediately after the Colonel's arrival. The gesture was of no practical significance for the essential preparations still had to be made.

The Archbishop's own story has yet to be told. The motives underlying his reluctance to start the military campaign and his repeated opposition to guerrilla groups can only be surmised. Grivas, who seldom gave Makarios the benefit of the doubt, attributed his hesitancy to fear of deportation from Cyprus. Had this possibility seriously worried Makarios it seems likely that he would have toned down his political activities in the island. His presence was seen by the British authorities as a threat to law and order and a permanent barrier to the acceptance of a constitution. His long absences abroad were marked by an appreciable drop in the political temperature. The strict enforcement of the Sedition Law might at any time from 1951 onwards have led to the Archbishop's prosecution and his subsequent deportation. In fact some of the Cyprus Government's advisers strongly recommended deportation as the first essential remedy for the island's political troubles. The Cypriots frequently drew parallels between the position of the British in Cyprus and in territories which Britain had ceded since the war. Makarios may well have genuinely believed that an intensive political campaign backed by outbreaks of violence on a small scale would be sufficient to secure Greek Cypriot objectives in a matter of months. Further, the Archbishop, who had spent the war under German and Italian occupation in Greece, must have been well aware of the potential dangers of starting guerrilla warfare in Cyprus; of the difficulty of disarming the bands once their mission was over; of the risk that, being Greeks, they would split into rival factions and fight each other; and, above all, of the possibility that they might eventually take up arms against their original sponsors. Even the Archbishop's parting instructions that Grivas was to start violence immediately after his arrival came too late. Thus Makarios paid lip service to the doctrines of the extremists, knowing full well that the campaign could not now possibly be started before the United Nations debate. An astute politician, Makarios was also sufficiently realistic to recognise that the support of the Greek Government was essential to the Cypriot case. His reluctance to authorise an armed revolt lined up with the policy of the Greek Government.

3 PSYCHOLOGICAL WARFARE

The Cypriots' lack of experience in war, mentioned by Grivas as a drawback to the formation of a guerrilla movement, was to a great extent offset by their long record of violence in social relationships and the tendency to take the law into their own hands, especially in the rural areas. The natural separation of the Turks reduced the risk of intercommunal clashes. Brawls and disputes were more common between rival groups of Greeks, the more fractious of the two communities. Even relatively minor occasions – elections to the Legislative Council and the village committees – were apt to precipitate clashes between the supporters of the rival candidates.

In village quarrels the use of knives and firearms was commonplace, and the employment of hired assassins not unknown. The villagers often chose to pay a ransom to get back their stolen livestock rather than report the offence to the police. In the case of the Greeks the inbred reluctance to cooperate with the administration in the interests of law and order could be explained by the fact that the voice of authority at the highest level was always foreign, and at police level it was often Turkish.[1] Fear of reprisals by the criminal and his relatives and dislike of the victim also motivated the silence which protected many a murderer from arrest. And this applied equally to both communities.

The constant concern of the colonial police at the high murder rate was typically reflected in the Commissioner's Report for 1949:

These figures are shocking by any standard. In a primitive community they would be grave enough: in a country with an ancient heritage of culture and law they are a challenge to the public conscience. . . . The great majority of these crimes were the outcome of uncontrolled and unrestrained passions of jealousy and revenge. . . .[2]

[1] Britain took over from the Ottoman administration an all-Turkish police force, and for many decades the Turks tended to predominate partly owing to the Greek preference for better paid work.

[2] *Annual Report on the Cyprus Police Force for the Year 1949* by J. H. Ashmore, Commissioner of Police (Cyprus Government Printing Office, 1950), p. 24.

The sociological background was potentially ideal for the type of guerrilla operations envisaged by Grivas. However, the forces of violence which erupted so spontaneously in domestic life had first to be mobilised in the service of the nationalist struggle. The average Greek Cypriot was emotionally committed to Enosis from early childhood, but emotion had yet to be converted into effective action.

The summer of 1954 saw the start of an intensive Enosis propaganda campaign relayed by Athens Radio regularly to Cyprus. The speakers sought primarily to undermine the authority of the Government, to stir up hatred against the British and to neutralise the Cypriot moderates. The programmes were offensive in style, irresponsible and often childish in substance. Oblique references to violence eventually gave way to direct incitement. Topics ranged from the colonial administration's neglect of the Cypriot farmer to the highly sensational dramatisation of the 1931 rising. The bogey of a possible compromise over self-government and, as a consequence, the final burial of Enosis haunted the extremists like a recurrent nightmare. And in threatening tones speakers warned the Cypriots against the acceptance of any new British constitutional plans. Eminent citizens who worked with the colonial administration, including the Attorney-General and members of EXCO, were branded as traitors. The first phase in the Colonel's war of intimidation had begun.

4   THE ORGANISATION OF THE GUERRILLA GROUPS

Grivas left for Rhodes on 26 October by the regular steamer from Piraeus, accompanied by two assistants, Socrates Loizides and a man who worked for him alternatively under the code names of 'Evaghoras' and 'Notis'.[1] Both men were ex-officers of the Greek Army and of Cypriot origin. In Rhodes Grivas relied on the help of local collaborators. A strong gale was blowing when the three men reached Rhodes and no trace could be found of the caique or its captain. The enforced stay at Rhodes was nerve-racking. Socrates Loizides wanted to return to Greece until a new caique was found; Grivas was haunted by the fear that Papagos had put the police on his trail. Still without news on 3 November, he sent an emissary to Athens to inquire into the possibility of finding another caique. The emissary cabled that nothing would be available for ten days. The Colonel's impatience turned to desperation. Time was short before the United Nations debate; delay was increasing

[1] Grivas made frequent changes of code names for security reasons. In order not to confuse readers I have used the same code name wherever practicable.

the risk of discovery and arrest. He was determined to go ahead with the mission, if need be with a smaller boat, and seems to have been curiously unaware of the seafaring habits of the Greeks. The treacherous Aegean has bred a race of skilled but cautious sailors. Many caiques are family-owned and highly treasured possessions. It was not likely that a captain would be found willing to expose his vessel to the hazards of the weather and the risk of capture. And the Colonel's local advisers immediately turned down his suggestion that a small boat could perhaps be hired in Rhodes. The chartered caique was eventually found in Lindos Bay sheltering from the storm. With the cooperation of the harbour-master it was brought into Rhodes harbour for refuelling. On 8 November the storm abated and Grivas and his companions left for Cyprus from the small bay of Kallithea. A fresh gale blew up the next morning but the captain's decision to hug the shores of Asia Minor was overruled by Grivas, who declared that the dangers of the storm were preferable to the risk of capture by the Turks. After a rough voyage they arrived within sight of Cyprus on 10 November and landed near Khlorakas on Paphos coast at dusk. They were met by local conspirators who took them to the house of the father of Andreas Azinas.

The next morning the automatics, which had arrived from Greece in March, were removed from their hiding places in the nearby fields, and Grivas spent the whole day cleaning them. After keeping back sufficient weapons for the Khlorakas groups he arranged for the remainder to be transferred to the secret locations in different parts of the island. Recruits were drawn from OHEN and PEON. The first, as a religious body, escaped the scrutiny of the police; the second, since its proscription in 1953, had functioned underground.

Grivas's plans provided for the division of the rebel organisation into two main groups; the first was concerned with guerrilla warfare and sabotage, the second with supporting action in the shape of riots and demonstrations. 'Evaghoras' was made responsible for sabotage training; Socrates Loizides for the direction of political sectors in the rural areas. In the middle of November 'Evaghoras' left for Saitta to instruct groups in the Limassol district, and Loizides for Aghios Mamas in the Troodos mountains to form a hard core of completely reliable supporters with a view to expansion later on. Grivas went to Nicosia to start the work of training sabotage groups in that area. He moved freely, making extensive reconnaissance tours and personally supervising the activities of his subordinates. Progress was delayed by the shortage of houses suitable for instruction in the use of firearms, so Grivas decided that the guerrilla warfare training would have to be obtained in battle. The shortage of leaders at intermediary level necessitated the centralisation of the movement and the setting up of a liaison system between Grivas and the groups. He was quick to appreciate the need for unification, for the Greek Cypriot community was riddled with petty jealousies and trifling quarrels. The existence of rival groups within the organisation could easily lead to dissension and the vitiation of the national struggle. He therefore put the fighters from PEON directly under his command; once enrolled as members of the rebel organisation they ceased to have anything further to do with their former leaders. Contact between combatant and political groups was also forbidden for reasons of security.

By the middle of December the distribution of the first consignment of arms and the training of five sabotage groups, three from OHEN and two from PEON, were completed. Socrates Loizides reported that he had enrolled members in eleven villages. The arms, however, did not correspond to the original inventories compiled by Grivas. Magazines were missing and out of nine cases of dynamite only one was usable. Grivas blamed Socrates for the muddle.

Each group was allocated a code name and a target. All members were required to swear a solemn oath of allegiance to the organisation in the name of the Holy Trinity.[1] From the start the Colonel made it clear that he expected hard work and quick results. The leaders were given ten days in which to submit detailed reports on their targets and lists of Cypriots known for their hostility to Enosis. Agents were appointed in the military bases to study the opportunities for sabotage. But progress was held back by a shortage of dynamite. In the main, future plans depended on the arrival from Greece of a further consignment of arms and sabotage material. Towards the end of November Grivas learnt from Azinas that the Cyprus police were on the look-out for a caique which had left Rhodes with a cargo of arms bound for Israel or Cyprus. Early in December the news was received that the caique's captain, on seeing flares off the Cyprus coast, had returned to Greece. It was later revealed that he had jettisoned his cargo rather than risk arrest and the seizure of the vessel. Grivas decided that Azinas must go to Athens immediately to buy a new consignment of arms, and sent him to see the Archbishop's secretary, Nikos Kranidiotis, with a request for £1,000. In the absence of Makarios the matter was handled by the Bishop of Kition who with characteristic caution

[1] See Appendix 4.

authorised a sum of £500. But currency control regulations operating in the Sterling Area had to be circumvented and the necessary arrangements made to transfer the money through an intermediary. The money did not arrive in time, and Azinas was compelled to return to Cyprus without completing the transaction, having obtained the promise of arms and ammunition in ample quantities. He left on a second visit to Athens after securing 150 gold sovereigns. The difficulties of hiring a caique raised fresh uncertainties. Grivas, nevertheless, informed Makarios that subject to the arrival of the arms, the rebels would be in a position to start about the middle of January.

The shortage of arms was not the sole barrier to rapid progress in building up the rebel organisation. From the start Grivas had been at loggerheads with his two assistants from Greece. The Loizides family was mixed up in politics. This in itself was enough to make them extremely suspect in the eyes of the Colonel, to whom all politicians were anathema. It can only be concluded that his sole reason for taking Socrates Loizides to Cyprus was his unique experience as the former general secretary of PEK. Socrates wanted to return to Greece and was, in the opinion of Grivas, inclined to be pessimistic when faced with difficulties. Furthermore, as a former army officer he exasperated Grivas by interfering in military matters instead of sticking to his political work. 'Evaghoras' was considered by Grivas to be a playboy, an absentee who frequently put pleasure before duty. Human shortcomings were intolerable to the Colonel, whose entire emotional and intellectual resources were channelled into the narrow single track of fanatical nationalism. But as former army officers the two men were indispensable, and despite persistent grumbling about their work he continued to employ them while threatening at frequent intervals to dismiss them. But when Azinas went to Greece for the third time he took a message from Grivas to the Archbishop requesting that Socrates Loizides should be sent back to Athens where he could also be useful to the struggle.

Grivas stuck to his opinion that the United Nations debate should be backed up by a display of force to convince the Americans, particularly, that the Cypriots were serious. It was, however, finally left that Makarios would notify the rebels of the starting date which would be determined by the course of events at the United Nations. On 22 November the Archbishop advised Grivas through Kranidiotis that there should be no violence yet and that he would send further instructions by diplomatic courier. On 1 December the Colonel's mounting frustration was increased by the report from Azinas that Alexis Kyrou had cabled the Greek Consul in Nicosia requesting him to tell the rebels to refrain from violence. The political leaders justified the apparent change of plan with the explanation that the illegal presence of Socrates Loizides in Cyprus could jeopardise the Cypriot case at the United Nations, especially as the British regarded him as an accomplice of Makarios. Grivas dismissed the explanation as an excuse. It is questionable whether the Greek Government or Makarios had, in fact, seriously favoured armed action. The Greek political leaders on this and other occasions in dealing with Grivas appear to have adopted the principle that the easiest way to silence a nagging critic is to agree, at least ostensibly. In this way Grivas had come to believe that the politicians approved of his plan to start armed action before the outcome of the UN debate was known.

Although foiled in carrying out his main plan, the Colonel was able to draw some satisfaction from the success of the riots in Limassol and Nicosia which broke out after the UN refusal to debate the Cyprus question at the General Assembly. Nevertheless he spent the New Year alone in a mood of despair. The UN appeal had been rejected, the arms had not yet arrived and in many respects the task of building up a guerrilla force seemed impossible.

The New Year got off to a bad start. On 3 January Grivas received a copy of a report in which an informer had notified the police of his presence in Cyprus. He again felt compelled to move his residence. The trouble with the subordinates was as serious as ever. 'Evaghoras' had been absent without Grivas's permission on Christmas Day and on New Year's Eve, and several of the local collaborators had to be reprimanded for their lack of discipline and discretion; others were called upon to show greater alertness. Much of the Colonel's time was taken up by rudimentary matters such as the need for discipline and secrecy. The fact was that the Cypriots were totally unused to discipline. However oppressive the British regime might seem in terms of its own legislation the average colonial official was on the whole genial, patient and easy-going. The demands made by Grivas with their niggling perfectionism and excessive preoccupation with detail were Teutonic rather than Greek in character and completely alien to a community accustomed to the *laissez-faire* of the Eastern Mediterranean. Progress was also hampered by village tittle-tattle, the lack of loyalty amongst the recruits themselves and the tendency of each man to blame the other when called upon to face the Leader's criticisms.

Immediately after the Archbishop's return the Colonel met him in the presence of the Bishop of Kition at Larnaca. Makarios was inclined to go to great lengths to justify to the extremists any action he might take, which suggests that he greatly underestimated his own strength. In terms of popular support the Archbishop had little to fear from his unimpressive rivals. But the mere creation of armed groups for any purpose whatsoever potentially weakened his physical security, as he himself must have been fully aware – hence his extreme caution in sanctioning the use of violence. Makarios explained that the policy to be followed at the United Nations was decided with Alexis Kyrou in Paris and denied all responsibility for Kyrou's telegram. The Archbishop stated that he agreed with Grivas that the failure of the USA to support the Cypriot case had called for drastic militant action but the Cypriot representatives in New York were not able to communicate with the conspirators in Cyprus in time. The Archbishop reported that Papagos, in view of the impasse at the United Nations, was now in favour of rebel action. The Archbishop proposed Greek Independence Day, 25 March, as the starting date. Grivas and Azinas argued that the delay would increase the risk of discovery and that it was important to take advantage of the darker evenings and the absence of guards on military and government buildings. It was decided to name the organisation EOKA (*Ethniki Organosis Kyprion Agoniston*).[1] The meeting was brought to an abrupt close by the arrival of a police car outside the bishopric and the crucial matter of the starting date was left unsettled. At a later meeting Grivas continued to voice to Azinas his doubts and his fear that Makarios might exploit the Enosis movement for political ends. He was, moreover, deeply concerned at the Archbishop's choice of Savvas Loizides as an intermediary between the Cypriot rebels and the Greek Prime Minister; although an impassioned enosist Savvas Loizides was politically ambitious and could be expected to follow Papagos blindly.

The rebels' plans now depended mainly on the arrival of a new load of arms and explosives to replace the consignment which the captain of the caique had thrown overboard on 24 November. Early in the New Year Grivas made a reconnaissance at Pomas-tou-Khloraka and chose a site for unloading the caique. He decided to supervise the operation himself. After protracted negotiations and several journeys to Athens in the brief space of a few weeks, Azinas was able to report to Grivas on 14 January that the *Aghios Georghios* had left with the essential materials the previous day. But this welcome news was shortly followed by a message from Makarios that a policeman had notified the authorities that the caique was expected to arrive on 19 or 20 January. The

---

[1] See *Terrorism in Cyprus: The Captured Documents* (HMSO), p. 7.

dilemma of the conspirators was further increased by reports of extensive police patrolling in the Xeros area. Grivas did not want to compromise his own small group of saboteurs by open action before the start of the main campaign, and suggested that Makarios should send men to stage a diversion. But the Archbishop refused on the ground that this was too dangerous. The caique had still not arrived on 19 January, and Grivas gave orders for it to be stopped at Rhodes. To save time the letter was sent through one of the pilots employed by a commercial airline. But the Colonel's collaborator in Rhodes cabled Azinas that the caique had left the day before. The Colonel's reaction to this bombshell was coloured by wishful thinking. Clutching at the unlikely theory that the agent possibly meant that the caique had left Greece on 18 January and not on 13 January as stated in the original cable, he went ahead with plans to intercept it at Rhodes. After selecting Perivolia-tou-Trikomou as an alternative landing place, he wanted to send Azinas first to Athens to consult Sakellarios and Ghazouleas about the betrayal, and then on to Rhodes. But Makarios was afraid that the immediate departure of Azinas would arouse the suspicions of the British authorities and he did not leave until 24 January, having been instructed by Grivas to arrange further shipments of materials from Greece or Rhodes and for the replacement of the harbour-master by a loyal supporter of the cause. Azinas took with him sealed orders to be opened by the captain after sailing. Unless signalled to proceed to Perivolia the caique was to make for Khlorakas in accordance with the first plan; immediate danger was to be indicated by a series of green flashes in quick succession from the shore.

Despite the risk Socrates Loizides still wanted to go back to his wife in Greece. The soap-box orator banished by the British from Cyprus fifteen years previously as a serious danger to security had with the passage of time proved a cautious revolutionary. It was reported to Grivas that the Archbishop had written to Socrates telling him that he should decide for himself whether to return to Greece or not. Grivas grudgingly gave him permission to return on the caique, and arranged for a reliable member of the Organisation to escort him to Khlorakas.

Grivas had little confidence in his subordinates. It was almost impossible to convince him that his presence was not essential on every important occasion. He had intended to supervise the unloading of the caique himself, but was finally dissuaded from doing so by Azinas. But for this fateful decision Cyprus might have been spared the catastrophe of the EOKA rising, for Grivas would have fallen into the hands of the British had he gone to Khlorakas.

On 25 January a naval patrol seized the *Aghios Georghios* and arrested three men on board. The remainder of the crew, Socrates Loizides and seven villagers from Khlorakas were caught on the beach. On hearing the news, Grivas immediately left for Kakopetria in the Troodos foot-hills, but after several days he felt sufficiently safe to return to the capital. His host, however, was nervous and requested him to leave straight away with his companions Drousiotis and Papadopoulos. For the fourth time in seven weeks Grivas had been obliged to change his residence. Early in February he moved to a new house in Nicosia, near the Kyrenia Gate, found for him by 'Evaghoras'. Here he started the construction of a secret cellar.

The caique disaster necessitated a drastic change of the original plan, which had provided for combined guerrilla and sabotage operations. The sabotage plans had to be postponed. In spite of this setback Grivas was impatient to start guerrilla action. He informed Makarios that the determination of the rebels to go ahead with the struggle had in no way weakened and he urged him not to delay the start of the campaign beyond 20 February and, in the absence abroad of Azinas, to put the necessary funds at his disposal. The letter ended on a subservient note indicating that for all practical purposes Grivas still accepted the Archbishop's authority as final. Makarios replied on the last day of the month during a meeting with Grivas at the Nicosia annex of Kykko Monastery when he imposed a ban on guerrilla activity for the time being and stipulated that sabotage operations were to be restricted to military targets and that there were to be no casualties. The Arch-bishop's instructions, in effect, amounted to an embargo on all rebel action, since owing to the loss of the dynamite supplies carried by the *Aghios Georghios* Grivas was not yet ready to start the sabotage campaign.

Makarios continued to retain absolute control; every action, every financial grant required his authority. Grivas was constantly in the invidious position of having to remind the Ethnarch that the rebels needed money for their daily subsistence. The full burden of organising the guerrilla and sabotage groups now fell to Grivas alone. Socrates was under arrest; Azinas, a wanted man, could not return to Cyprus; 'Evaghoras' was as unreliable as ever. The period was one of acute anxiety. The possibility that the arrested men might expose the whole movement could not be excluded. Grivas was also haunted by his perennial phobia of communism. His memories of the Greek civil war were seldom far below the surface and he was apt to draw false parallels between the communist rising in Greece and the complex but completely different situation in Cyprus. Obsessed by the fear that AKEL would seize control of the Cypriot liberation struggle, he urged Makarios to buy all the weapons available in the island, including those in poor condition, to prevent them from falling into the hands of the Communists. Oblivious of the horrors and exigencies of revolution, the Cypriots saw the struggle as a romantic adventure. The inability of the recruits to conform to discipline and their tendency to quarrel amongst themselves seriously hampered the task of building up a unified movement. The Colonel, who spent much of his time studying reconnaissance reports drawn up on his instructions by the subordinates, proved to be exacting and critical. One report was returned to its author by Grivas with the sharp comment that it was 'imbued with laziness both moral and physical'. Another, on the Secretariat, was rejected on the ground that it was no more than a copy of earlier documents and the author was ordered to submit a new report within three days.

The general lack of cooperation was discouraging. The villagers of Prodhromos claimed that they were good patriots but their employment as forest rangers and government clerks made it impossible for them to help. One priest said he distrusted his fellow villagers and wished to work alone for EOKA. The witch-hunting for traitors had already begun. An archimandrite,[1] charged with finding hideouts for wanted men, reported that the priests were willing to throw all their resources into the struggle but that they felt their houses were unsuitable. The traditional role of the Church in nationalist activities and the clergy's part in riots and demonstrations made them automatically suspect. The archimandrite suggested that EOKA should rent village houses used by the townspeople as summer residences. The idea was unacceptable to the Colonel. Apart from the security risk, he expected patriotic duties to be carried out on a voluntary basis. It was significant that not even the priests were willing to make undue sacrifices and it is hard not to conclude that however much the Cypriots might want Enosis, they wanted it without trouble.

The Greek secondary schools were hotbeds of Hellenic nationalism, yet progress in the organisation of a militant youth movement was unexpectedly slow. In the spring Grivas had ordered the local leaders to submit reports on individual schoolboys giving particulars of character, age and availability for duty. Rules for the formation of each

---

[1] An archimandrite, a principal official who assists each bishop in the management of his see, has charge of all matters affecting the interior economy of the diocese and the administration of the finances. See J. Hackett, *The Church of Cyprus* (1901. Reprinted in 1972: Burt Franklin, New York), p. 272.

sector were also laid down by him. Each group was to be composed of four or five members, but in important areas likely to produce opposition provision was made for the establishment of larger sectors with the help of reinforcements from outside. The duties covered demonstrations, leaflet and slogan writing, incitement of the population and liaison work with the fighter groups. Grivas adopted the communist procedure of setting up watertight cells; all contact between the sectors was forbidden for security reasons. Several schoolboys refused to accept the responsibilities of group leadership, and a report submitted by the chief organiser in the early spring was disheartening. Only three groups had been formed in the Pancyprian Gymnasium and the Commercial Lyceum. And in the Samuel School, which was regarded by the British authorities as the most unruly in the island, no headway had been made at all apart from the discovery of a keen boy in the fifth form.

Throughout the spring the Archbishop and the Colonel continued to differ over matters of policy. The clandestine bulletin *Enosis* published a report on the capture of the *Aghios Georghios* which Grivas attributed to the pen of Makarios. Grivas had been opposed to the publication of the truth before the start of the armed campaign and had advocated the circulation of false reports giving the impression that the *Aghios Georghios* was engaged on an ordinary commercial smuggling expedition devoid of any political purpose. But Savvas Loizides objected to this version, which would have shown up his brother as a common criminal instead of a national hero. The Archbishop explained that it was impossible to conceal the truth; the British knew from several sources that the caique was carrying arms and explosives and that a revolution was being plotted. Grivas demanded that he should vet the contents of *Enosis* before it went to press. The Archbishop's logic was borne out by evidence submitted by the Crown during the preliminary inquiry into the *Aghios Georghios* case which began at Paphos on 17 March.

Hundreds of schoolboys mobbed the court-house chanting 'Enosis! Enosis!' and 'Englishmen go home!' The police made a baton charge. The demonstrators then threw stones and blocks of wood at the building. Barricades were erected. The Colonel's efforts to stir up the youth had at long last produced results. The hearing started after a two hours delay. Six Greeks and seven Cypriots were charged with conspiracy on the following counts:

(i) Advocating the overthrow of the colony's constitution by revolution or sabotage, and the overthrow by force or violence of its established government.

(ii) Preparing or endeavouring by armed force to produce an alteration in the colony's laws or government.

(iii) Promoting civil war.

A Turkish witness, Police Sergeant Faik, told the court how on 17 January he left Famagusta in HMS *Charity* to patrol the Paphos coast, and how he observed on successive nights green flashes in the direction of the shore. On 25 January he was transferred to the destroyer *Comet*. A caique caught in the beam of the destroyer's searchlight was seen moving out to sea. After the destroyer had fired warning shots, sailors boarded the caique and handed three men, including the captain, over to him and he charged them with dynamite smuggling.

The next witness, Superintendent Alexis Ioannou, stated that on the same night he went with colleagues to Khlorakas. On the way they arrested two men; one of them had a torch. As the police approached the sea he heard the noise of an engine and saw green flashes in the direction of the bay. They crawled on their stomachs to the edge of a precipice. In the distance the silhouette of a man wearing spectacles was visible. Four men stumbled over them and were immediately arrested. Ioannou said he saw the caique heading northwards without lights, a barge operated by oars with a large box on it, a man disembarking and other boxes along the shore. They caught four men on the beach. One of them was Socrates Loizides – the man with spectacles they had seen from the cliff. Loizides had in his possession twenty gold sovereigns and a torch which emitted green and white light. Karadimas, the Greek mechanic, told him that he had only joined the crew because he was destitute and had been misled into believing that the *Aghios Georghios* was on a fishing expedition. Continuing his evidence, Ioannou said that when he searched the caique on 26 January he found maps of Cyprus amongst others and a box containing packets of dynamite bearing the name of a Greek manufacturer. The captain had shown him the spot where the crew dumped the fuses and detonators, but so far the divers had found nothing.

Paphos was quiet on the second day of the inquiry, but the barricades were retained as a precaution. Two naval officers, including the *Comet*'s commander, came specially from England to give evidence on the seizure of the caique. The Court examined a note found by P.C. Kemal Osman in a cave near Khlorakas. Dated 18 November 1954 and signed Azinas, this acknowledged the receipt of 190 gold sovereigns and £220 from Socrates Loizides towards the Cyprus liberation struggle. The most interesting exhibit was a nine-page document taken from

Loizides's brief case. Described by Crown counsel, Mr Rauf Denktash, as 'highly seditious', it proclaimed the existence of EMAK (Cyprus National Liberation Front), a secret revolutionary organisation, well organised and fully armed, which aimed at Enosis and the liberation of the Cypriots from 'intolerable slavery'. It urged the people to leave open revolt to EMAK's trained fighters, and the police and government officials to cooperate without abandoning their jobs. EMAK offered hostility to the British, friendship to the Turks, material as well as moral rewards to patriots, compensation to the victims of the struggle and death to traitors and their relatives. Traitors were few, the statement stressed, but were known to EMAK. Communists, it was explained, were unacceptable mainly for tactical reasons dictated by the need to avoid alienating possible sympathisers at the United Nations.

The proclamation – a mixture of directives, threats and inducements – was clearly intended for distribution at the appropriate time and reflected some uncertainty on the part of its sponsors as to public reaction. The promise of material rewards ran contrary to Grivas's ruling that patriotic duties must be carried out without thought of payment or material gain. Its flamboyant, flowing style recalled the colourful oratory of Socrates Loizides. On the third day the government Inspector of Mines testified as to the highly dangerous nature of the explosive substances in the box on the *Aghios Georghios*. The captain claimed that he had used these same chemicals for thirty years without mishap for starting up caique engines. During the five-day inquiry the Court also considered an article from a Rhodes newspaper found on Karadimas which threatened to brand any Cypriots accepting a constitution as 'traitors', and evidence related to the seditious activities six years earlier of Azinas and Socrates Loizides, both of whom had served as general secretary of PEK, the farmers' union whose members also included the seven Khlorakas prisoners. Counsel for the Cypriots, Mr George Chrysafinis QC, argued that there was no proof that the accused had plotted amongst themselves to commit the offences with which they were charged, or of any link between them and Azinas in connection with the plot, or that it even existed in 1949, and that evidence related to events six years prior to the date of the indictment was inadmissible. Mr Denktash insisted that it contained proof of hostile feelings towards the Government and should therefore be admitted to show the plotters' general aim. The magistrates finally ruled that the evidence was admissible. Counsel for the Greeks, Mr Alexis Tsiros, claimed that even if a conspiracy existed in Cyprus, which he denied, there was no evidence against his clients. Chrysafinis, on behalf of the Cypriots, said it was a basic legal principle that evidence against one of the accused could not be used as evidence against the others unless a conspiracy was proved. The prosecution, aware of this weakness of the Crown's case, had introduced evidence related to events of six years ago. There was no evidence that the seven Cypriots were connected with Socrates Loizides. The fact that they were found near the wooden boxes was not sufficient to prove that they knew the reason for their importation. His remarks applied to all seven men, and most particularly to two who were arrested some distance away from the others. Not one of the three charges could stand. He hoped that the Court would not be prejudiced by the disorders of 16 March.

Winding up for the prosecution, Mr Denktash said the fact that the accused were waiting on the spot giving signals, the subsequent arrival of the caique loaded with dynamite, and the role of each in unloading the cargo had proved that the accused were members of a conspiracy at home and abroad, aimed at the overthrow of the regime by revolution and sabotage. The documents found on Loizides, the receipt on the beach, the fact that one of the accused had volunteered to show the police the place where one of the boxes was dumped in the sea and the fact that the Cypriots were all members of the same organisation (PEK) had proved beyond all doubt that the dynamite was imported for the liberation struggle. The case was referred to the assizes, and the prisoners were refused bail.

The premature disclosure of the rebels' plans as the result of the preliminary inquiry was embarrassing but not disastrous for EOKA. Not one of the accused had given away secrets which would have enabled the Cyprus authorities to nip the rebellion in the bud. If anything, the relative ease with which the plot was discovered and its perpetrators brought to trial may well have induced a sense of false security in British official circles.

The starting date for the armed revolt depended mainly on the replacement of the caique's cargo with dynamite from local sources. Makarios allocated the necessary funds and with the help of Gregoris Afxentiou, a Cypriot and former officer in the Greek Army who had volunteered his services earlier in the year, Grivas built up new supplies. By the middle of March the essential preparations were completed. Sabotage groups of four or five men had been set up in the four main towns and an adequate communications system was functioning. Grivas notified Makarios that he was now ready to start action and that after the first attacks he expected to have about seventy kilos of dynamite left over. He stressed the dangers of delay and renewed his attempts to overcome the Archbishop's resistance to the use of firearms, recommending that pistols should be bought for the sabotage groups because, apart from the possibility that they might need to use them, it was important for the sake of morale that they should be equipped with these weapons. On 29 March the Colonel met the Archbishop who agreed that the campaign should start on the last night of the month. Many weeks of intensive work, however, had not produced the expected results. During a final tour of inspection Grivas decided that the group leaders in Nicosia made a poor impression and lacked self-confidence. One leader admitted that not one of the men in his group knew how to light a fuse. But the fear of discovery while the rebellion was still in embryo and of his own capture was decisive, and he stuck to the decision to go ahead. On the eve of the campaign Grivas felt insecure and moved to a temporary headquarters in the suburb of Strovolos; he wanted to keep in touch with groups and if necessary he could intervene more actively with the Nicosia sector. He waited up to hear the first explosions. After that he went to bed.

V

The First Round
April 1955-March 1956

Outbreak of Violence – Breakdown of
Harding–Makarios Talks

1 THE OUTBREAK OF THE REVOLT

In the early hours of 1 April the underground organisation EOKA made its existence known by a series of explosions in different parts of the island. Leaflets, signed 'The Leader Dighenis',[1] proclaimed that with God's help and the support of all the forces of Hellenism the struggle to throw off the British yoke had now begun. Warnings under the same signature were sent to the police advising them on pain of execution not to interfere with EOKA's activities.

The EOKA Leader was satisfied with the early reports carried by the morning newspapers. The most spectacular success was an attack on the Cyprus Broadcasting Station led by Markos Drakos. His group of four men had gagged the watchmen and planted bombs near the transmitters. Other groups had thrown bombs through the windows of the Secretariat and at Wolseley Barracks. Official quarters estimated the total damage at £60,000. The fuller reports which reached Grivas later were, however, far from encouraging. As he had anticipated, the Nicosia group had achieved very little apart from the attack on the CBS. The Secretariat, with its unguarded buildings, was an easy target; and the bombs aimed at the signals room at the Wolseley Barracks had been thrown across the fence from safe range and fallen short of their objective. Elsewhere the position was worse. The bombs thrown in Famagusta had failed to explode. Afxentiou, the district

---

[1] After Dighenis Akritas, a Byzantine warrior of the twelfth century. See Hill, op. cit., vol. I, p. 261, fn. 2. Greek Cypriots commonly referred to 'Dighenis' as the 'Leader'; to EOKA and its ramifications as the 'Organisation'.

leader, was a wanted man, the police having found a Greek army handbook on sabotage in his home. Modestos Pandelis, one of the newly trained saboteurs, had electrocuted himself by throwing a rope damp with dew over the high tension wires. Several group leaders, including Poskotis, had been arrested. Grivas was also disturbed by the political situation. Neither the Athens nor the Greek Cypriot press had shown much enthusiasm for the first revolutionary exploits. The Cypriot editors were, no doubt, inhibited by the colony's stringent press laws, but the same could not be said of the newspapers in Greece. Athens Radio, instead of bolstering the morale of the Cypriot fighters, had come out in favour of passive resistance and had allowed Savvas Loizides to broadcast a eulogy of his brother, Socrates. The possibility that political opportunists in Greece, especially the Loizides family, might exploit the Cyprus struggle to further their own careers was seldom far from Grivas's mind – an anxiety which was not ill founded in view of the ruthless struggle for power and his own lack of standing in the Athenian political world. These misgivings prompted him to complain strongly to Makarios, who promised to send an envoy to Athens to make the necessary protests.

Alleged communist activities at this time provided Grivas with yet another source of anxiety, and he urged Makarios to republish the proscribed bulletin *Enosis* with a view to waging a journalistic campaign against them. It was rumoured that the Communists were planning to attack Lefka and that they were daily increasing their efforts to obtain arms and paying high prices which EOKA could not afford. One leader informed Grivas that in his area they were even masquerading as members of EOKA. Even in normal times Cyprus tends to seethe with rumours which are often alarmist in character. The wiser inhabitants quickly learn to discount them, and it was not surprising that the Colonel's repeated agitations made little impression on the Archbishop.

The first explosions were followed by a general revulsion against violence. However strongly some sectors of the Greek Cypriot community might desire Enosis, few of them when it came to the point welcomed the prospects of prolonged rebellion, the disruption of normal life and trade. Shortly after the outbreak of violence the Archbishop ordered a cease-fire on the grounds that EOKA needed time to regroup. This appraisal of the military situation, which might more appropriately have come from Grivas, met with his strong disapproval. The EOKA Leader was convinced that any loss of momentum at this stage would be disastrous. But apart from minor incidents violence abated for several weeks.

The *Aghios Georghios*[1] trial opened on 3 May at Paphos before a special assize court composed of the Chief Justice and two senior Greek Cypriot judges. The charge was amended in the first and second counts and as a result now carried heavier penalties, the words 'conspiring to advocate' in the original indictment having been replaced by 'advocating'.

The Attorney-General, Mr Criton Tornaritis QC, described the case as one of 'unprecedented enormity, extreme gravity and of great public importance'.[2] The accused were not being charged for the opinions they held or for the national aspirations which stirred them but for seeking to promote their aim by 'force and violence and armed resistance to lawful authority'.[3] The essence of conspiracy lay in the parties' agreeing and combining to carry out a common criminal or unlawful purpose. There was seldom a witness to such agreement, but proof of this nature was not necessary. It was sufficient to show that the parties had adopted a line of conduct arising from a common intention. In addition to summarising the evidence submitted to the magistrates' court, the Attorney-General referred to the employment of an engine silencer on the caique in order to mislead the Greek Customs into thinking that it was on a fishing expedition when, in fact, the intention was to unload explosives in Cyprus. This suggested that all the accused on board were fully aware of the voyage's true purpose.

On the second day a witness from the Royal Navy's torpedo and anti-submarine section gave new evidence for the Crown. He described how during the second phase of the diving operations frogmen under his command recovered between 4 and 24 April eight boxes from the seabed. Their contents included two rifles, one machine gun, various types of pistols, ammunition and pieces of Greek newspapers. Cross-examined by defence counsel, the witness said that the search took place about 6,000 feet from the shore and that he thought the anchor near one of the boxes was suitable for a vessel of 50 to 100 tons.

On 5 May the Crown sought to connect the recent EOKA outbreak of sabotage with the caique case. But defence counsel argued that the evidence was inadmissible as the charge related to the events of 25 January and not to those of 1 April. The Court ruled that it should be excluded 'for the moment'. A witness for the Crown, the Inspector of Mines, admitted a mistake in his evidence during the preliminary inquiry. At the time he thought that the material in the black box on

---

[1] See above, pp. 109–12.
[2] *Cyprus Mail*, 3 May 1955.
[3] ibid.

the caique was sulphur and potassium nitrate – a highly dangerous explosive. Laboratory tests had since identified it as potassium chloride – a substance freely sold in the market and used (as the caique captain had claimed in his defence) for starting engines. This flaw in the prosecution's evidence was, however, by now of little consequence. The case for the Crown had been greatly strengthened by the divers' finds since the hearing in the magistrates' court – the weapons and ammunition being much harder to explain away than the dynamite. On the following day nine of the accused pleaded guilty to the main charge that on or about the 25th of the previous January they prepared or endeavoured 'by armed force or the show of armed force to procure an alteration in the government or the laws of the colony'.[1] Two Greek seamen, Alevarakis and Christodoulou, pleaded guilty to a new charge – the illegal importation of explosives. The Court discharged the Cypriot villagers Kyriakos Mavronikolaos and Michael Papantoniou who were arrested on the night of the crime some distance away from the boxes.

The Court dealt first with the nine men found guilty of using armed force against the Government.[2] All the accused had stated, the Chief Justice said, that they acted out of 'a sincere love of freedom and their country', and in the case of the Greek subjects as 'a sacred duty' to help their brothers in Cyprus. The Court was not passing sentence for a technical breach of the law. The accused had seriously transgressed the law and a moral principle: 'no doubt blinded by eloquence in newspapers, on the radio and from the pulpit', they had lost touch with the realities of life in Cyprus – a land of peace, prosperity, tolerance and justice. It was wrong to impose political opinions on such a state of society by force. It was useless for the accused to deny that they were morally and criminally liable.

Socrates Loizides had for many years 'engaged in war and revolution'. No doubt the fanatical opinions held by him were sincere but he had tried to introduce armed force and violence into Cypriot politics. It was difficult to know how far he was 'actuated by sincere ideology, and how far by vanity and personal ambition'. But the seriousness of the offence made it the duty of the Court to deter others and impose a serious penalty. Had his crime been against a Government that was not motivated by principles of humanity and mercy he would have paid for his conduct with his life. Anarghyros Melos had sought to import

[1] ibid. 5 May 1955.

[2] Judgement in the Paphos Assize case – Crown v. Evanghelos Louka Koutalianos, of Salamis Island, Greece, and twelve others, 6 May 1955.

secretly by night arms and dynamite into a friendly country. Karadimas had come not solely as a member of the crew but as an agitator and revolutionary. In the case of Koutalianos his services during the Second World War, including the rescue of Allied personnel, had been taken into account.

The branch of the Pancyprian Farmers' Union (PEK) to which the Cypriots belonged, the Chief Justice continued, had apparently long been 'a hotbed of sedition'. No doubt the accused and their fellow villagers were good farmers, good tradesmen and good people. But they had allowed themselves to be led away 'into a course of criminal conduct'. Those who had conditioned their minds bore a grave responsibility.

Loizides was sentenced to 12 years' imprisonment; Karadimas to six; Melos to five; Koutalianos to four years. The Cypriots received sentences varying from four to three years. The two Greeks found guilty of the dynamite charge were sentenced to 12 months' imprisonment, the Court having taken into consideration their youth and the subordinate position they held on the caique.

The shortcomings of the first offensive were inevitably followed by a spate of recriminations and the search for scapegoats – a regular feature of EOKA operations. One of the rebel leaders blamed 'Evaghoras', the sabotage instructor from Greece, for the failures in the Limassol area, alleging that he had not given the orders in time for the Troodos explosions and contrary to Grivas's instructions had used the public road with the result that an EOKA member was arrested. 'Evaghoras', moreover, had committed the unforgivable offence of going into business with a Cypriot firm in Limassol without the Colonel's knowledge. Grivas decided to expel his chief assistant for persistent absenteeism and disobedience. The situation, however, was complicated by the sudden arrest of 'Evaghoras'. As a precaution, Grivas quickly changed his residence. Despite an unconvincing explanation for his presence in Cyprus the police released 'Evaghoras' after questioning. Grivas, who had never become fully attuned to the easy-going mentality of the British authorities, concluded that his assistant had either already betrayed the Organisation or else the police were planning to follow him with the object of identifying his EOKA contacts.

The Colonel was faced with a dilemma. The dismissal of 'Evaghoras' might well have exposed EOKA to betrayal so long as he remained in Cyprus. The plans for the execution of traitors and unreliable members of EOKA had not yet fully matured. In the circumstances it was vitally important to get 'Evaghoras' out of Cyprus. A village mukhtar and a policeman were bribed with £5 each to cooperate in producing faked identity papers. 'Evaghoras' left for Beirut at the end of April. The only difficulties were raised not by the British but unexpectedly by a Greek Consul on the Arab side who demanded full particulars concerning the EOKA man's real identity.

The Archbishop's observation that the rebels needed time to regroup, whatever its underlying motives, had been right. After six months of preparatory work EOKA was still hopelessly amateurish and in no position to wage a sustained campaign. The Colonel's request for two assistants from Greece to replace Socrates Loizides and 'Evaghoras' had not been met, so he was obliged to tackle the Organisation's expansion single-handed. The task was complicated by his ignorance of Greek Cypriot mentality which could possibly be explained by the fact that he had spent by far the greater part of his life in Greece, and as a result certain aspects of Cypriot national character came as a shock. Dedicated to the pursuit of Hellenism and indifferent to financial gain, the EOKA Leader found himself up against the strong trading instincts of the Greek Cypriot community. His stern philosophy that patriots must be satisfied with 'moral rewards' fell on barren soil. And before long some of the saboteurs began to demand payment. One man named his price for putting a bomb in a British cargo boat as £100. Grivas, who seldom abandoned a principle, finally agreed with extreme reluctance on condition that payment would not be made until after the explosion had taken place.

The recruits were not lacking in enthusiasm and ideas but their concept of revolution was apt to be naive. One EOKA leader[1] proposed that the rebels should capture the Chief Justice, Sir Eric Hallinan, who was regarded by the Greek Cypriots as the symbol of British imperialism, and with whom he was acquainted. But the terrorist had second thoughts. The colonial regime had its own paradoxes. It was impossible to reconcile Sir Eric's exalted position in the colony with the fact that he was a native of Southern Ireland, a country which had rebelled against Britain and which could logically be expected to support the cause of Cyprus. The early Cypriot recruits, moreover, when it came to the point shirked the assassination of officials they knew personally. The intimacy of the Cypriot community facilitated on the one hand certain facets of underground warfare, for example penetration and intimidation. On the other hand it was not without its psychological complications. At first few of the rebels were willing to follow EOKA's

---

[1] Polykarpos Georkatzis, a born conspirator who himself became the victim of a conspiracy and was assassinated in 1970.

orders blindly. Most of them had yet to acquire the absolute ruthlessness which their leader demanded of them.

When it came to practical results it seemed, in the eyes of Grivas, that the Cypriots could do nothing right. 'Tselingas', a meddlesome priest, had to be reprimanded for interfering outside his area of duty; 'Dafnis' for his delay in attacking the Nicosia targets. Another saboteur had completely failed in his mission because he had tied the package containing a bomb intended for Government House to his bicycle which he was obliged to leave outside the building. Elsewhere an EOKA group had abandoned its attack because the driver refused to take the men as far as the target when, in the opinion of Grivas, the raid could easily have been made on foot. Even Afxentiou, the boldest and most enterprising of all the EOKA recruits, was unable to convince Grivas that an attack on Boghaz military camp was impracticable owing to the risk that the Turkish shepherds grazing their flocks in nearby fields would report the perpetrators to the police. The EOKA Leader seldom gave his subordinates the benefit of the doubt. Their explanations were usually branded as excuses; their hesitancy and ineptitude as cowardice. Weeks of frustration went by. In despair Grivas staked his hopes on the eventual return from Greece of a group of Cypriot students who, with the assistance of a committee headed by a Cypriot resident there, were receiving elementary training in the use of firearms.

Much of the Colonel's time during the early summer was spent organising the EOKA youth groups. Progress was surprisingly slow. The example of Paphos, with its historical background of lawlessness,[1] had yet to be emulated in other parts of the island. Early in May, Grivas ordered the intensive recruitment of schoolchildren. Their duties were to include demonstrations, the distribution of leaflets and the surveillance of British agents. The most promising and reliable would eventually graduate to the fighter groups, and EOKA would be assured of a constant supply of recruits. The plan came up against many objections on the part of parents and teachers. The first worried about their children's safety; the second about the ultimate effects on discipline and education. The Communists were trying, with some success, to attract children to rival youth groups. Several of the early EOKA youth demonstrations were abortive. Dr Spyridakis, the headmaster of the Pancyprian Gymnasium, an impassioned enosist and author of several anti-British pamphlets, had gone so far as to chase the demonstrators off the streets and back to their classes, thereby defeating the EOKA

---

[1] Remote and inaccessible, the Paphos district had a long record of lawlessness. See Hill, vol. IV, op. cit. p. 265.

Leader's main objective. On the orders of Grivas he was called up before the Greek Consul and required to give an undertaking that such intervention would not be repeated. A few days later, on 24 May, EOKA staged its first major youth demonstration. Five hundred schoolboys, mainly from the Pancyprian Gymnasium, stoned Government House. Troops had to help the police restore order. But this progress was not maintained. Many students informed the local leaders that they would not be able to take part in further demonstrations for the time being owing to the forthcoming examinations. Despite the warning to Dr Spyridakis, the teachers lectured students, recently fined by the courts for leaflet distribution, on discipline. More disturbing for Grivas was the fact that Makarios backed up Spyridakis on the question of school discipline. The Archbishop had justified this apparent lapse in patriotism with the argument that if demonstrations were to obtain international sympathy they must at least appear to be spontaneous.

The Cypriot students returned from Greece during the first week in May and Grivas immediately sent them to different sectors. He set up an extra command at Lefka and ordered the formation of three new mountain guerrilla groups in the areas of Lefka, Kyrenia and Amiandos-Kyperounda. Their training in the use of automatic weapons and explosives was entrusted to Ioannis Katsoulis, a reservist in the Greek Army working as a schoolmaster in the Cypriot village of Evrykhou. The paramount objective of the EOKA Leader at this time was to conserve the Organisation's limited resources and concentrate on dramatic action certain of attracting the world's headlines. An attempt to kill the Governor, Sir Robert Armitage, at the end of May was a failure owing to Cypriot inexperience in the use of time-bombs, detonated at this stage by a primitive and unreliable type of mechanism. The Governor went to a special film performance on Empire Day. Shortly after he left the cinema a coca-cola bottle filled with explosive wrecked several rows of seats. The assassination of General Keightley, the Commander-in-Chief Middle East Land Forces, also ranked high on the EOKA Leader's list of objectives. The General travelled every day between Nicosia and Kyrenia. Grivas, who intended to take part in the operation himself, had personally chosen a site for the ambush at Boghaz. But Makarios vetoed the plan and the rebels had to content themselves with throwing bombs at the General's house. In an order dated 28 June Grivas called upon the area commanders to hold sessions of self-criticism. He declared that even if the material results of the offensive were less than expected, owing to a lack of fire and impetus, its repercussions at international level and on British public opinion were rewarding. The world's attention had been drawn to the agitation in Cyprus against the British regime, with the consequence that Britain was now retracting its policy of 'Never'. He outlined the aims of the next offensive – terrorisation of the police and the paralysis of the administration in the countryside as well as in the towns. The realisation of these aims, he anticipated, would result in the rapid demoralisation of the police force which, even if it did not actually help the rebels, would turn a blind eye to their activities; in the deployment of the army in security duties over a wide area, so that the troops would be exhausted and their morale lowered; and in the eventual intervention of the United Nations. Tactics would include the execution of policemen who were either out of sympathy with EOKA or who tried to hunt the rebels down, raids on country police stations, and ambushes against police patrols in the towns and in the countryside in order to deprive the force of freedom of movement. The EOKA Leader concluded with an appeal for the self-sacrifice and the disregard for danger which a great cause ought to inspire.

On 19 June EOKA opened its second major offensive with attacks on police stations in Nicosia and Kyrenia. Two days later an explosion outside the Nicosia Central Police Station in the Turkish area killed a Greek bystander, the first fatal casualty, and injured thirteen Turks and one Armenian. On 22 June the first mountain guerrilla group to complete its training, led by Renos Kyriakides, shot up Amiandos Police Station killing the sergeant in charge. Bombs were thrown in bars and at army houses and incidents occurred in many parts of the island. The rebels had again relied mainly on bombs. But the use at Amiandos of automatic weapons for the first time was an important development and the first serious indication that the Archbishop's control was dwindling. The second offensive had aroused the wrath of the Turks. Their leaders issued public warnings that a renewal of incidents in the Turkish quarter would lead to intercommunal strife, and to reprisals against the Greeks should any more Turks be injured. The deterioration in the island's security was serious. But Grivas was not yet satisfied. The Nicosia execution group had been guilty of cowardice; so far not a single traitor had been assassinated. Some EOKA members were culpable of negligence and inefficiency. 'Romanos' had failed to cut the telephone wires before attacking Aghios Epiktikos Police Station; 'Kimon' had lost a Sten gun when, without the EOKA Leader's permission, he was arrested trying to move it hidden inside a violin case to a new location. At the end of the month Grivas halted the offensive.

2 POLITICAL DEVELOPMENTS, SUMMER 1955

The summer found the Cypriots in a mood of political confusion. The first wave of terrorism amounted to no more than a token revolt and did not constitute a serious security problem. Nevertheless it had some impact on the attitudes of the Greek Cypriot population and of the Cyprus authorities. The struggle for Enosis in theory was one thing, but now that the rebellion had actually started its consequences were unpredictable. Many Cypriots were apprehensive and would have welcomed a face-saving formula such as an interim period of self-government with the promise of self-determination in the distant future. British officials, for their part, considered that a new political move was urgently needed to halt the deterioration in law and order. In London the Cabinet had been forced to reconsider its position over Cyprus since Greece had raised the question at the United Nations General Assembly in December 1954. But the new constitutional proposals and the Cyprus policy statement were delayed owing to the forthcoming general election. On 26 May the Conservatives were returned to power. The new Foreign Secretary, Mr Harold Macmillan, hitherto uncommitted on the Cyprus question, favoured a new approach.[1] This became public on 30 June when the following invitation was issued:

Her Majesty's Government have been giving further consideration to the strategic and other problems affecting alike the United Kingdom, Greece and Turkey in the Eastern Mediterranean. They consider that the association of the three countries in that area based on mutual confidence is essential to their common interests.

Her Majesty's Government accordingly invite the Greek and Turkish Governments to send representatives to confer with them in London at an early date on political and defence questions which affect the Eastern Mediterranean including Cyprus.[2]

The Foreign Secretary stated in the House of Commons[3] that the discussions would take place without prior commitment or a fixed agenda and would range widely over all the subjects involved. The careful phrasing of the Foreign Minister's statement and of the invitation, the almost casual inclusion of Cyprus as a secondary item within the context of a much broader problem, could not disguise the fact that

[1] See Harold Macmillan, *Tides of Fortune 1945–1955* (Macmillan, London, 1969), pp. 660–77.

[2] *The Tripartite Conference on the Eastern Mediterranean and Cyprus*, Cmd 9594, October 1955.

[3] H.C. Deb., vol. 543, col. 511.

the British Government had made a drastic break with the traditional colonial line that the domestic affairs of territories within the juris- diction of Her Majesty's Government could not be discussed with foreign powers.

The affairs of Cyprus had for centuries been settled over the heads of the people. The fact that the Cypriots were not invited to the conference was in keeping with past history. This time, however, the question of reaction in Cyprus could not be completely overlooked. Shortly after Macmillan's statement Lennox-Boyd left for Cyprus. This was the first visit by a Secretary of State for the Colonies since 1878, and the occasion was marked by the first meeting between a Governor and the head of the Cyprus Church since the 1931 riots. British officials and their advisers alike viewed with concern the possibility that Greece and Turkey might be given a role in future administration. But Lennox- Boyd's primary aim was to convince the Greek Cypriot leaders that the proposed conference was a genuine attempt to break the deadlock. The Colonial Secretary saw Makarios for two hours, met the mayors and Turkish representatives, and received a protest from the secretary of AKEL against a ban on a mass rally planned by the communists.

Turkey immediately accepted the invitation. But Greece was hesitant. The reactions of the Greeks were mixed. In Greece Slavophobia and hostility towards the Turks are endemic. Encircled by neighbours they dislike, the Greeks tend to develop a sense of psychological isolation and physical insecurity if estranged from their Western allies. Bulganin's visit to Yugoslavia in May helped to revive on the one hand the old nostalgia for the traditional friendship with Britain and on the other resentment at the inflexibility and tactlessness recently shown in the face of Greek susceptibilities by British statesmen over Cyprus. The Greek newspapers, almost without exception, criticised the extension of the invitation to Turkey and the omission of the Cypriots and branded the proposals as a trap designed to forestall the forthcoming debate on Cyprus at the United Nations and to procure the indefinite postpone- ment of self-determination. *Kathimerini*, the influential Athenian news- paper, which usually supported the Papagos Government, urged that the presence of Greece at the talks should be contingent on a prior settlement over self-determination. The Athens branch of the Ethnarchy pressed the Greek Government to go ahead with its appeal to the UN on the grounds that it could easily be withdrawn should the outcome of the London conference prove satisfactory to the Greek Cypriots. The British Government's delay in fixing the date, the final decision to hold the conference as late as 29 August confirmed Greek and Cypriot suspicions that the main objective of the British move was to frustrate the Greek appeal to the UN.[1]

The British invitation was from the start an embarrassment for the Greek Government. Acceptance was bound to raise a barrage of criticism at home; rejection would have alienated international opinion and possibly prejudiced future appeals to the UN. Greece finally accepted the invitation on 1 July.[2] This news brought Makarios on a sudden visit to Athens where he denounced the British proposals as a 'trap' and joined the Greek Government's critics in condemning its failure to submit the Cyprus appeal in time for the main agenda. The British Government, although recognising that Greece might be compelled to raise the Cyprus question at UN, hoped that it would be able to withstand the Archbishop's pressure. The idea that a priest from a distant province should in any way direct their country's policy was repugnant to many Greeks. But Greece was entering a new phase of political uncertainty. Papagos was ailing; his Government faced mounting unpopularity. The people had expected much from his Greek Rally and were disillusioned by the party's failure to implement its electoral promises and by the unequal distribution of wealth. With the possibility of elections in the near future the politicians were reluctant to antagonise potential supporters and the press. Its position weakened still further by Britain's choice of dates for the London conference, the Greek Government finally gave way to demands that the appeal should be submitted in time for the supplementary agenda of the UN General Assembly.

The proposals for the conference did nothing to ease tension in Cyprus itself. The attitude of the Greek Cypriots varied from scepticism to indifference. Many of them resented the fact that Cyprus would not be represented. In official British quarters it was contended that the Greek Cypriots had only themselves to blame – that their obstinate refusal to accept a constitution deprived them on this momentous occasion of any means of representation. This argument, designed to highlight the advantages of self-government, impressed no one. On the contrary, it added to the prevailing cynicism. Cyprus was not lacking in elected bodies. The presence at the conference of a small Cypriot delegation headed by the Archbishop was a practical proposition which might well have helped to alleviate a legitimate grievance.

[1] The official British reason for the delay was Mr Lennox-Boyd's prior commitments in the Far East. As Lennox-Boyd only attended the conference on the last day the Greek mistrust of Britain's motives in holding the talks was never removed.

[2] At Strasbourg, on the occasion of a Council of Europe meeting, when the British and the Greek Foreign Secretaries met. See *Tides of Fortune*, op. cit. p. 665.

The first week in August brought forth a general strike organised jointly by the nationalists and the Communists. But for the rest of the month the Tripartite Conference became the main target of the political agitators. Six days before the London talks were due to start the Ethnarchy Council convened an extraordinary general meeting of the Pancyprian National Assembly in the cathedral of St John, a Byzantine building no larger than a very small village church. The cathedral was crammed. The first wave of violence had attracted correspondents from afar. The nationalists came from all over the island, many of them interrupting holidays in the mountains or by the sea to return to the sweltering heat of Nicosia.

The Ethnarchy Council's object in convening the meeting was to obtain public endorsement for the policy of 'immediate self-determination' in the light of the British approach to Greece and Turkey. The meeting was tense, the speakers excitable, and the Archbishop made several appeals for calm. One by one the nationalist representatives – bishops, farmers, trade unionists, citizens from every walk of life – held the floor, their long speeches interrupted only by tumultuous bursts of clapping and cries of 'Enosis'. Any public meeting in Cyprus, whatever its basic purpose, was likely to turn into a forum for grievances against the British administration. This session of the National Assembly was no exception. The Government's educational policy, the curfew at Agros, the lack of a social insurance scheme all came under fire. The future of Cyprus was at stake but the endless digressions from the main issue and the excessive length of the speeches, even by local standards, reflected the inherent parochialism of Cypriot political life.

The Archbishop's speech opened on an optimistic note:

> The wind of freedom blows forcefully from distant Asia to neighbouring Africa, overturning and sweeping away everywhere the effigies of slavery.[1]

If the Tripartite Conference did not result in a settlement which met with their demands the Cypriots would march, he said, their faith undiminished, to the United Nations. The Archbishop called upon Britain to hold bilateral talks with the Cypriots or with Greece and then plunged into a lengthy indictment of British tyranny.

The Bishop of Kyrenia demanded, as usual, 'Enosis and only Enosis', and sent greetings to 'Dighenis' and Socrates Loizides. Polykarpos Ioannides, secretary to the Kyrenia bishopric, opposed all compromise

---

[1] *Cyprus Mail*, 27 August 1955.

and criticised the sedition laws. Michael Pissas, leader of the right-wing trade unions (SEK), called for a more strongly worded resolution than the formula drafted by the Ethnarchy Council. The Abbot of Kykko courageously advocated a compromise. Several speakers urged the Ethnarchy Council to send a telegram warning delegations attending the London talks that any settlement contrary to the wishes of the Greek Cypriots would be rejected by them.

When it came to dealing with the demands of the extremists, the Archbishop showed a cautiousness and moderation which was in sharp contrast to the inflammatory content of his own statement. He resisted suggestions that the Ethnarchy Council's draft resolution on self-determination should be revised to include the word 'unconditional'. He refused to be drawn into a controversy over the military bases, insisting that it was a waste of time to discuss matters which were at present purely hypothetical. The meeting, which ended with the Greek national anthem, went off without disorders, but produced nothing new. The resolution on self-determination was a foregone conclusion. And the door to negotiation and compromise, although not widely open, was at least left ajar.

Two days later the left-wing trade unions (PEO) held a mass rally in the Alhambra Cinema to register a unanimous protest against the Tripartite Conference.

It was not to be expected that the proposed conference would in any way influence the ideas of Grivas. His contempt for political negotiations and his blind faith in violence were too deep-rooted to allow for change. The Colonel went ahead with preparations for the next major offensive, which he intended to launch in support of the second Greek appeal to the UN General Assembly due in the autumn. Early in July he moved to the Troodos area to supervise the training and the expansion of the mountain guerrilla groups. He first stayed at Kakopetria in the house of Ioannis Katsoulis. Throughout the summer the Archbishop continued to oppose the deployment of guerrillas expressing the view that EOKA lacked adequate funds and that he doubted the wisdom of embarking on guerrilla warfare, the outcome of which was unpredictable. Grivas, unimpressed, went ahead with his plans. The timidity shown by the Cypriots in previous operations was, however, a serious obstacle to the creation of a dynamic revolutionary force. Despite the fact that his capture or death would have brought the revolution to a standstill, Grivas decided to take part in future operations and finally based himself on the Pitsilia sector. He was convinced that his personal example of self-sacrifice in the face of extreme danger was necessary to inspire the fighters with courage and enterprise. The fact was that in the presence of the EOKA Leader the guerrillas would find it impossible to shirk their assignments.

By the end of the summer the EOKA Leader's preparations were complete. Guerrilla and sabotage groups had been formed in the countryside and the towns, food storage places arranged in the mountains and plans drawn up for the ambushing of military vehicles. The shortage of dynamite had been overcome mainly through the regular cooperation of workers employed in local mines, which were under Greek ownership and management. But the shortage of arms remained acute, especially as no help was forthcoming from Greece. Makarios had consistently opposed the build-up of arms on any scale in Cyprus and had turned down suggestions that they should be imported from Egypt giving as a reason the British blockade. But it is difficult to decide whether this reflected his considered opinion or was simply an excuse. At the end of August a small consignment of arms from abroad arrived in a suitcase with the connivance of EOKA members in the customs at Limassol.

During the long weeks of preparation general incidents declined, apart from minor bomb explosions in different parts of the island. Grivas, however, put into effect the plan for the terrorisation of the police. In the early stages EOKA had greatly benefited from the weakness of British security. The worst lapses so far had occurred in the British Consulate-General in Athens and the Immigration Department of the Cyprus Government. Their negligence had been responsible for the two legal entries of Grivas into Cyprus, and the one entry of the deputy-leader of X, Zafiris Valvis. It was, however, incredible that the authorities, eight months after the seizure of the *Aghios Georghios*, should have failed to place under observation such an obvious suspect as the schoolmaster Ioannis Katsoulis, with his record of military service in the Greek Army. They were also slow to suspect Azinas. For reasons of climate and geography the Cypriots have little to learn from a study of agricultural conditions in Greece.[1] His numerous journeys to Athens could hardly be explained by his position as Secretary-General of the Panagrarian Union of Cyprus (PEK); its subversive activities were in any case notorious and its links with Greece essentially political. A handful of Greeks in the Cyprus police had, nevertheless, done excellent intelligence work. With the help of information from Greece the *Aghios Georghios* conspiracy was uncovered, and all the participants caught red-handed. On the outbreak of the rebellion most of the key

[1] Israel, only thirty minutes away by air, provided a much more useful basis for comparison.

men in EOKA were quickly identified and many of them arrested. EOKA could not afford to allow these successes to be repeated. In the first week of July selected members of the police force received new leaflets from Grivas censuring them for failing to heed his original warning and threatening them with execution. Attacks against police stations and individual members of the force were intensified. Several attempts on the lives of policemen during July were abortive owing to the hesitancy and inexperience of the execution groups. But in August Zavros, a special constable with three brothers in the regular police force, was shot dead while on duty. The incident was quickly followed up by the murder of Kostopoulos and Poullis, both members of the Special Branch. Poullis was shot dead on the eve of the Tripartite Conference in broad daylight in Ledra Street, which was crowded after the mass rally held by the left-wing trade unions at the Alhambra Cinema.

3 INTERNATIONAL DEVELOPMENTS

The Tripartite Conference on the Eastern Mediterranean and Cyprus[1] opened in London on 29 August. On the second day the British Foreign Secretary, Mr Macmillan, stressed the friendship binding Britain, Greece and Turkey, their common interests in the Eastern Mediterranean, and their membership of the most important alliance perhaps of all history – the North Atlantic Treaty Organisation. In convening the conference Her Majesty's Government was in no way departing from the basic principle that territories within its domestic jurisdiction could not be discussed with foreign powers. The aim of the conference was to try to reconcile the unhappy differences centred on Cyprus which were imperilling the common defence of the three nations in the Eastern Mediterranean and which threatened an ever-widening area far beyond British authority. Macmillan recalled that in 1878 Britain had entered into a defensive alliance with Turkey. It was necessary then for Britain to occupy and administer Cyprus; the need at the present time was still greater, since British responsibilities had multiplied and diversified. He emphasised the importance of Turkey's position in the front line of Western defence and the fact that the treaty of Lausanne,[2] signed by Greece and Turkey, had confirmed Britain's annexation of

[1] See *The Tripartite Conference*, op. cit.
[2] *Treaty of Peace with Turkey and other Instruments, signed at Lausanne on July 24 1923* (Article 20), Cmd 129.

Cyprus. That sovereignty over the island rested exclusively with the British Crown must be recognised from the outset, he said.

Macmillan went on to describe the nature of Britain's present commitments in the Middle East, citing as examples the Baghdad Pact, the Treaty of Alliance with the Hashemite Kingdom of Jordan, and the Tripartite Declaration. These obligations called for a firm position in the Eastern Mediterranean which could only be effected by the possession of Cyprus. He referred to the 'vital and far-reaching obligations' shared by Her Majesty's Government, as a member of NATO, with Greece and Turkey. Each of the three countries was responsible for a naval sub-area in the Eastern Mediterranean; all were interdependent; and all forces were under the Supreme Allied Commander and his deputy. The cooperation essential to joint exercises and manoeuvres was threatened owing to the differences over Cyprus.

He dismissed suggestions that British needs could be met by a leased base. The whole process of defence could not be dissociated from the life of the community. Cyprus was a headquarters as well as a base. This, together with the complexities of modern methods of defence, made it essential 'that the United Kingdom should possess not so much a base in the old sense of the word as a whole complex of interrelated facilities, which ramified over the whole island'.[1] The increase of military forces in Cyprus had contributed significantly to the island's expanding prosperity.

Without naming Greece, Macmillan censured those responsible for terrorism in Cyprus. He denied accusations that Britain was not sincere in her support for the United Nations Charter. But all the relevant circumstances had to be considered. It was in no way the fault of successive British Governments, he said, that the Cypriots had not yet achieved internal self-government. Had they done so, their elected representatives might have participated in the present conference. Finally he spoke of the affection and comradeship felt in Britain for the heroic people of Greece, of the respect and admiration for the sterling qualities of the Turks.

On 31 August the Greek Foreign Minister, Mr Stephanopoulos, welcomed the direct discussions, a procedure long advocated by his country, and went on to describe the Greek contribution to the defence of the Eastern Mediterranean, her resistance to Fascist and Nazi attacks, and later to Communist aggression. Greece had never lost sight of the importance of the common security of the three countries and recognised that Britain must have a base in Cyprus. In sponsoring the

[1] See *The Tripartite Conference*, op. cit.

Cypriot demand for self-determination the Greek Government had never contemplated the withdrawal of British forces from Cyprus.

Stephanopoulos argued that the example of NATO, the existence of American bases in Greece, had shown that problems of mutual security were not affected by questions of sovereignty. The value of the bases, he said, and the island's strategic importance would be strengthened by the formal recognition of the Cypriot people's legitimate right to self-determination. Stephanopoulos denied that the Greek Government sought to unite Cyprus with Greece. The presence of Greece and Turkey at the Conference was only due to the existence of a Greek majority and a Turkish minority: neither had a right to decide the island's future status. He disagreed that the Cyprus question was a domestic matter. Nor could the attitude of the Greek Government, he said, be considered expansionist or imperialist. Greece's frontiers with Turkey were final. All Greece asked was that 'the people of Cyprus be allowed to exercise a fundamental and internationally guaranteed right – the right of self-determination'. [1]

The Greek delegate justified his country's action in placing the Cyprus question before the UN General Assembly as the most peaceable and appropriate means of safeguarding order in the island. Subsequent events had proved the wisdom of this policy, he said. Once the General Assembly had decided to postpone the discussion the matter had passed out of the Greek Government's control into the hands of the extremists.

In granting self-determination to Cyprus the United Kingdom would earn the eternal gratitude of Greece. British military bases in Cyprus would be strengthened and Britain could in due course obtain bases on Greek territory. Turkey would also benefit from this strengthening of their common defences. Greece was determined, moreover, to meet Turkey's requests for safeguards for the Turkish minority.

On 1 September the Turkish Foreign Minister, Mr Zorlu, stated the Treaty of Alliance with Britain in 1878 clearly indicated the importance of Cyprus to the defence of Turkey, and that the fate of the island was the exclusive concern of the British and Turkish Governments. Any demand for a change of status was tantamount to a demand for the revision of the treaty of Lausanne which would not be restricted to Cyprus, but would raise other complex issues. Turkey, he said, had always treated the Cyprus question as a British domestic issue. But in the event of any change of status she would demand the return of Cyprus. The island's importance for Turkey emanated from the 'exigencies of history, geography, economy and military strategy, from the

[1] ibid. p. 17.

right to existence and security . . .'[1] From the military point of view it must belong either to Turkey or to a power as closely interested as Turkey was in the Near East. In war Turkey could only be supplied through her southern ports. Whoever controlled Cyprus was in a position to control these ports.

With reference to self-determination Zorlu reminded the conference that the Aaland Islands, despite the fact that the majority of the population were Swedish, were assigned to Finland, and that western Thrace with its Turkish majority was given to Greece under the treaty of Lausanne. Venizelos himself had said that the principle of self-determination should not always receive prior consideration in the transfer of territories. Though not opposed to self-determination, Turkey was trying to avoid it becoming an element of injustice, insecurity and trouble. Its application to Cyprus clashed with British sovereignty and Turkey's right to protect her own security. Likewise, Turkey was not opposed to self-government but again this must not become a source of trouble. He criticised the Church of Cyprus for exerting local pressure to achieve Enosis. As a result the Greek and Turkish communities were now antagonised. Before the establishment of self-government the Cypriots needed a period of calm. The guiding principle for self-government, when circumstances changed, should be not the consideration of majorities and minorities but that of full equality for both groups.

Zorlu concluded that Turkey was eager to continue her friendship with Greece for the benefit of both countries and for the peace of the world and the Mediterranean. The claims now being raised over Cyprus, however, were creating grave misgivings.

The Tripartite Conference then adjourned to consider the opening statements. Macmillan's undertaking during the adjournment to search for common ground met with no enthusiasm on the part of the Greek and Turkish Foreign Ministers, who expressed the desire to return to pressing duties in their own countries. Meanwhile, serious anti-Greek riots broke out in Istanbul. The Conference was resumed on 6 September, and was attended for the first time by the Secretary of State for the Colonies, Lennox-Boyd, on his return from the Far East.

At a restricted session on 6 September Macmillan made a valiant effort to define the common factor of agreement which ran 'like a vein of gold beneath the great overburden of misunderstanding and confusion'.[2] Agreement existed, he said, on the island's strategic importance; on the vital contribution which the British had to make towards peace

[1] ibid. p. 22.
[2] ibid. p. 29.

and security; on the need for friendship and cooperation between Britain, Greece and Turkey; and on their duty to promote the welfare of the Cypriots. He then outlined a new constitutional plan. This would provide for an assembly with an elected majority; for the progressive transfer of government departments to Cypriot ministers responsible to the assembly; for the appointment of a Cypriot chief minister, chosen by the assembly with the Governor's approval, as head of the new independent administration. A suitable quota of ministerial portfolios and seats in the assembly would be reserved for the Turks and the independence of the public service safeguarded. The British Government hoped to create a true sense of partnership between the Greek and Turkish Cypriot communities, which would be repeated at international level by means of a permanent tripartite committee composed of Britain, Greece and Turkey. The committee's suggestions for improvements to the draft constitution would be welcomed. Nothing was permanent in history, Macmillan said, but Britain could not foresee conditions which would enable her to abandon the trust she had accepted in 1878. He urged the conference to agree to differ over the island's final status but in the meantime to collaborate in the development of self-government. He proposed that once the new constitution was in operation the three nations should meet again with the same terms of reference and expressed the hope that at the next plenary session elected Cypriot representatives would be present.

The text of the plan was then distributed to the Greek and Turkish delegations. Stephanopoulos doubted whether any procedure for the development of self-government could be considered democratic if the Cypriots were not associated with the task. Furthermore, the tripartite committee was bound to conflict with the proper functioning of democracy. Finally Stephanopoulos questioned the British refusal to grant self-determination to Cyprus.

The Turks had detected an ominous note of uncertainty in Macmillan's references to the future. Did the British Government, Zorlu asked, intend to retain in future the right of sovereignty conferred on Britain by the treaty of Lausanne? Macmillan repeated that there was no prospect of any change in the foreseeable future. Still not satisfied, Zorlu pressed the British delegate for a clarification, and finally drew assurances from him that Her Majesty's Government did not accept the principle of self-determination as one of universal application.

In an interim reply on 7 September Stephanopoulos regretted that the British proposals had not taken into account the Greek Government's basic demand – namely that the Cypriots should have the right to choose 'in a democratic manner and within a reasonable period of time' the regime they preferred; that contrary to its policy elsewhere in the Empire the British Government was discriminating against the Cypriots by refusing to concede that internal self-government should lead to self-determination. The Greek delegation, he said, was convinced that the application of self-determination to Cyprus would strengthen the friendship and alliance between the three countries, as well as their collective defence.

In a final rejection Zorlu reflected the hardening of the Turkish attitude towards Greece. The persistence of her demands, he said, despite sincere and friendly warnings from Turkey over the past three years, was responsible for the present impasse. Turkey's calm and prudence in handling the Cyprus question showed the importance which she attached to the friendship and alliance of the three countries. But the safeguarding of Turkey's interest in Cyprus was equally important. Any change in the *status quo* would imperil the equilibrium set up under the treaty of Lausanne and impair Greco-Turkish friendship. Turkey could not accept the British proposal that the three Governments should leave aside the problem of sovereignty and co-operate in the development of self-government. So long as they disagreed over self-determination this would be impossible. Self-government called for the renunciation of self-determination; for the cessation of the present disorders and intercommunal tension.

Zorlu praised the British Government's 'spirit of abnegation and self-sacrifice' in seeking a solution. In fact, Her Majesty's Government had gone so far in this direction that Turkey had some doubts as to Britain's real intentions, but in view of the treaty of Lausanne's clear provisions she did not think that, from the legal and juridical angle, any outside claim to Cyprus could be considered. On the political side, the Greek Government should not raise the Cyprus claim if it valued Turkish friendship. The present troubles in Turkey, which had necessitated the proclamation of martial law, were the direct result of the Cyprus crisis. Zorlu stated that self-government would not be possible in Cyprus until the Greek Government gave up its demands for the annexation of Cyprus, for Enosis, or for the application of self-determination.

The Tripartite Conference was suspended on 7 September but the final Greek rejection came ten days later. This stated that the Greek Government was glad to note that the British Government had departed to some extent from its former inflexible attitude. On the question of self-determination, however, the Greek delegation had met with absolute refusal. And although the British had made certain concessions over self-government the type of constitution proposed could not be considered 'as adequate for so highly developed and civilised a people as the Cypriots',[1] and the proposed establishment of a tripartite committee with the right to intervene in the administration would have rendered self-government 'purely theoretical'.

The Tripartite Conference brought to the surface the deep-seated differences between the three Governments. The British had tried to put the Cyprus dispute into perspective by stressing the overriding need for unity and cooperation in the face of common dangers created by the Cold War. The Greeks relied mainly on theoretical arguments – the absolute right of the Cypriots to self-determination in accordance with Article I of the United Nations Charter – and anticipated difficulties over the tripartite committee's position. The proposal was purely a political move, and its somewhat nebulous functions were clearly intended to be advisory. There was no reason to assume, as Stephanopoulos had done on 6 September, that the Cypriots would not be given a say in constitutional discussions. The Turks, stating their attitude fully for the first time in public, were essentially practical and based their case mainly on legal and strategic arguments, claiming that these must take precedence over vague principles.

The 'common factor of agreement' which the British Foreign Secretary had so painstakingly traced proved to be a mirage – a facet of his perennial optimism. The polite generalisations made by all three countries on the need for friendship and cooperation in Eastern Mediterranean defence failed to disguise the fundamental differences over the vital issues of security, strategy, self-determination and self-government. Britain insisted that her commitments as a member of NATO and in the Middle East necessitated British sovereignty in Cyprus. Greece argued that the value of the bases would be increased by granting the Cypriots self-determination since this would result in a friendly populace. Turkey claimed that her security could only be safeguarded by the continuation of British rule in Cyprus, failing this by the island's return to Turkey. Britain favoured the early introduction of self-government without a time-limit for its duration; Greece approved of self-government solely as a short-term interim measure leading to self-determination; Turkey refused to support self-government unless Greece gave up the demand for self-determination. The gulf was widest on this last issue. Britain proposed that it should be shelved indefinitely. The Greeks argued that it should be granted within a

[1] ibid. p. 43.

reasonable period of time; the Turks that it could never be applied to Cyprus – in view of overriding considerations of geography, strategy and security. The Greek and the Turkish delegates stated that their views were backed by all political parties and public opinion in their countries, in contrast to the position of the British Government which was under constant attack from the Labour Opposition over its Cyprus policy.

The Tripartite Conference was a turning point in that it drastically changed the course of the dispute. The British recognition of the international aspect of the problem encouraged on the one hand the Greek extremists to believe that their tactics would lead to further concessions, and intensified on the other the fears of the Turks, who from now on took a tougher line. Relations between Greece and Turkey sharply deteriorated with serious dangers for the eastern flank of NATO. The first attempt to enlist the help of Greece and Turkey in finding a solution to the Cyprus problem had, in fact, ended in catastrophe.

On 6 September a bomb exploded in the garden of the Turkish Consulate-General in Salonika. The damage turned out to be insignificant and the Greeks subsequently alleged that it was planned by agents of the Turkish Government. But at the time reports that the adjoining house, Ataturk's birthplace, had been destroyed unleashed massive anti-Greek riots in Istanbul and Izmir. Thousands of youths surged up the main centre of Istanbul carrying banners with portraits of Ataturk and 'Cyprus is Turkish' slogans. Rioters hurled the contents of Greek- and Armenian-owned shops into the streets. Greek Orthodox churches were destroyed and pillaged. In Izmir rioters marched on the Greek Consulate, attacked the houses of Greek officers attached to NATO's regional headquarters, and burnt down the Greek pavilion at the International Fair.

After some delay the Turkish authorities brought in troops to restore order. Martial law was declared, the Cyprus Turkish Association was closed down and its president, Hikmet Bil, arrested. The Turkish Prime Minister's explanation that the Communists and other 'foreign' agents were to blame met with scepticism. The timing of the riots and other factors suggested that they were initiated by the Turkish Government in order to demonstrate the strength of feeling in Turkey over the Cyprus question. But once the fury and the latent xenophobia of the mob were aroused the situation got out of control and far exceeded the limited show of force planned by the authorities. Meetings of the World Bank and the Congress of Byzantine Studies had attracted many foreigners to Istanbul at the time. Nothing could have done more to harm Turkey's image in the mid-twentieth century than this spectacle of mass destruction and mob rule directed against an innocent Christian minority.

At the Tenth Session of the UN General Assembly international opinion, influenced by the disturbances in Turkey, swung in favour of the British viewpoint that public debate could only exacerbate the crisis. In the General Committee on 21 September, Nutting stated that his government had already made far-reaching proposals to get Cyprus on the road to self-government. The Greek delegate, George Melas, doubted the value of negotiations. The tragic events in Turkey, he said, were the direct outcome of the Tripartite Conference and the matter should be taken up by the UN. The Turkish delegate, Selim Sarper, stated that the issue did not come within the Organisation's competence. The principle of self-determination should not be lightly pursued without regard to the possible consequences. The Istanbul riots, he stressed, were subject to investigation. If need be counter-charges could be brought against Greece in relation to the treatment of the Turkish minorities in that country. Cabot Lodge, on behalf of the USA, supported direct negotiations while reserving his country's future stand should the situation change. The Greek resolution was rejected by 7 votes to 4 with 4 abstentions.[1] At the Plenary Meeting on 23 September the Greek Foreign Minister, Stephanopoulos, sought to reverse the General Committee's recommendation, on the ground that violence had broken out in Cyprus after the UN had deferred the discussion of the Greek resolution in 1954.[2] No change had since taken place to justify further postponement. Referring to Sarper's speech in the General Committee, Stephanopoulos said the truth was that Kemal Ataturk's birthplace was intact and the Greek quarters in Istanbul were in ruins. In a long, forceful speech Nutting restated the British case and the constitutional proposals outlined at the Tripartite Conference. In considering the Greek resolution the UN, he said, was not confronted with a colonial issue but with 'a straight, if disguised bid for Enosis'.[3] Cabot Lodge stressed that the situation had become more inflamed since 1954 and the considerations which actuated the General Committee to turn down the Greek appeal applied even more strongly now. There were occasions when quiet diplomacy was more effective than public debate and this was one of them. The General Committee's

---

[1] GAOR (X) General Committee, 102nd Meeting, pp. 1–5.
[2] ibid. 521st Plenary Meeting, pp. 53–63.
[3] ibid. p. 57.

recommendation to reject the Greek appeal was upheld by 28 votes to 22 with 10 abstentions. Support for the Greeks came mainly from the Soviet bloc and Latin America.

4   THE DETERIORATION OF SECURITY

During and immediately after the London talks violence in Cyprus was intensified. Bombs exploded at the Cyprus Broadcasting Station and at the RAF signals station at Aghios Nikolaos. Masked men attacked Paralimni Police Station, tied up five policemen, seized rifles and Greener guns. The raid was the work of trained saboteurs and the first rebel operation involving the use of military tactics. Although mainly concerned with British targets in September EOKA also found time to attack the Communists. The month opened with a sensational attempt on the life of Andreas Ziartides, Secretary-General of the Old Trade Unions (PEO). The crime, widely attributed to EOKA, precipitated protest meetings in the main towns.

Political tension was aggravated by the outcome first of the Tripartite Conference and secondly of the Greek Government's appeal to the UN General Assembly. The Communists and nationalists called general strikes in protest against the UN's refusal to include the Cyprus item on the General Assembly agenda. The Communists continued to embarrass the Archbishop by demanding co-ordinated action which, owing to his dependence on the Greek Government, he was not in a position to accept. At Kalopsidha the Archbishop announced his intention to launch in the near future a passive resistance campaign of such intensity that it would disrupt the machinery of government. In view of the failure of the Tripartite Conference and the appeal to the UN the main phase of the struggle would be fought in Cyprus, he said. The British would shortly realise that the Cypriot people would not easily abandon the struggle even if the whole island was converted into a giant prison. On the morning of the Archbishop's visit the troops had removed branches of myrtle bearing anti-British slogans but the villagers managed to replace them in time for his arrival.

The gulf between the British and the Greek Cypriots had begun to widen in accordance with the EOKA Leader's plan. Hitherto, Cypriot hostility towards the administration was largely superficial and confined to a vocal minority. But the new trend could be detected in the attitude of the Government's most staunch supporters. On 20 September Sir Paul Pavlides resigned from the Executive Council giving as his reason the British Government's failure at the Tripartite Conference to recognise self-determination for Cyprus. In the absence of the Attorney-General, Criton Tornaritis, local membership of EXCO was now reduced to one Greek and one Turk. Official links with leading sectors of the Greek community, slender at the best of times, had become almost negligible. Athens Radio had repeatedly branded Pavlides and Tornaritis as 'traitors'.[1]

The deterioration of law and order culminated in the destruction of the British Institute. On the night of 17 September three British soldiers drove into Metaxas Square where a group of young Cypriots overturned their jeep, set it on fire and then made for the Institute. The building, an obvious target, had been attacked before but was seldom guarded. Many officials and correspondents were at Kykko RAF camp outside Nicosia celebrating the anniversary of the Battle of Britain. The police refused three times the offer of military help. Since there was neither a state of emergency nor martial law the army could not intervene except on the request of the Civil Power. The rioters, mainly youths and schoolboys, controlled Metaxas Square for nearly three hours until the police finally called in troops to restore order. But it was too late to save the Institute. Shortly after its destruction the authorities suffered a new setback which seriously undermined the early successes of the Cyprus Police. Sixteen leading members of EOKA escaped from Kyrenia Castle, a medieval fortress normally under the control of the Department of Antiquities. Part of the castle had been hastily converted into an improvised detention centre for EOKA suspects. The detainees' equipment did not include sheets but, after their spokesman complained, these were supplied. British soldiers guarded the castle; Cypriot warders staffed the detention quarters. The EOKA men breached a bricked-up gunport. Using sheets knotted together they slid down the parapet on to a small beach belonging to the English club. Seven men were recaptured. But the remainder rejoined the guerrillas, several eventually became group leaders. Public confidence in the administration was shattered. Leaflets, distributed by *Volkan*, a secret Turkish organisation, strongly criticised recent lapses in security and reflected the growing anxiety of the Turks.

On 25 September 1955, Field-Marshal Sir John Harding (Lord Harding of Petherton), Chief of the Imperial General Staff, was appointed Governor of Cyprus. The choice of a senior service officer was

[1] Manchester Guardian, Reuter, 25 September 1955. Tornaritis, a frequent target for Athens Radio, had been discreetly transferred to London to work at the Colonial Office for an indefinite period.

officially explained by the island's importance as a base for the dis-charge of the British Government's obligations in the Eastern Medi-terranean and as a member of the North Atlantic Treaty Organisation and by the need for concerted action between all the security forces in the island for the maintenance of law and order. The lessons of the British Institute had not been lost. At long last Whitehall had grasped the realities of the situation. Within ten days of the statement Sir Robert Armitage, the patient, imperturbable Wykehamist, was released from his thankless task and left the island, eventually to become Governor of Nyasaland.

5   HARDING'S FIRST FIVE MONTHS

Field-Marshal Sir John Harding arrived in Cyprus on 3 October. His instructions were first and foremost to restore order, to proceed wherever practicable with economic and social development and to leave the door open for discussion with the Cypriot leaders on the basis of the constitu-tional plan put to the Tripartite Conference. Cypriot reaction to the appointment was prompt and vocal. Thirteen mukhtars resigned as the first stage in the Archbishop's passive resistance campaign. The Com-munists sent Harding an ultimatum demanding the abolition of the military regime, of the bases and of 'all dictatorial laws and concentra-tion camps'.[1] Polemics were commonplace in Cypriot life and did not necessarily reflect the true state of local opinion. On 30 September the Archbishop surprised the British authorities by expressing in concilia-tory terms his willingness to meet the new Governor.[2] The two men met the day after Harding's arrival. This political advance was not, however, matched by a corresponding decline in violence. Grivas was determined to show that the rebels were not daunted by the prospects of tougher measures. Terrorism began to gather momentum with the guerrillas showing the signs of discipline and military training hitherto lacking. On 3 October masked men raided Lefkoniko Police Station removing arms and ammunition. Gunmen shot dead a policeman at Famagusta and seriously wounded an English engineer at Amiandos. On the breakdown of the first round of talks between Harding and Makarios, Grivas launched a new offensive. This opened fortuitously with a spectacular success owing to the laxity of the military. At Famagusta docks a newly arrived consignment of guns and ammunition from the Suez base was seized by EOKA. On 28 October, the anniver-

[1] Cyprus Mail, 4 October 1955.
[2] See Manchester Guardian, 1 October 1955 (author's interview with Makarios).

sary of Italy's invasion of Greece in 1940, rioters disregarded the official ban on processions, and mobs of stone-throwing schoolboys were dispersed by troops using truncheons and tear gas.

The new Governor was granted wider powers and greater financial resources than Armitage – advantages to some extent offset by the fact that he faced worse conditions than his predecessor owing to the sharp deterioration in security during the summer. By the autumn EOKA had penetrated most government departments. Three Greeks in the small, overworked Special Branch had been murdered and other Cypriots in a position to expose EOKA silenced by intimidation. Security problems were increased by physical and psychological factors, namely the wide dispersal of government buildings which facilitated the gunman's attacks and subsequent escape through Nicosia's maze of sprawling suburbs; and the public's inborn reluctance to cooperate with the authorities in tracing lawbreakers. After the theft of the Suez consignment Harding became personally responsible for the direction of security operations. Troops were trained in riot-breaking by police methods; outlying police stations protected by the army.

It was unfortunate that Harding's first weeks should have coincided with the trial of Karaolis, who was charged with the murder of P.C. Poullis. Emotions ran high and the public mood was conducive to violence. The trial[1] opened at the Nicosia assizes on 24 October before the Chief Justice, Sir Eric Hallinan, the Greek President of the Nicosia District Court, Mr Pierides, and a district judge, Mr Ekrem. Soldiers from the South Staffordshire Regiment patrolled the veranda outside the court-room. The building was heavily barricaded. And everyone, including the Chief Justice, was subjected to a bodily search on entry.

Prosecuting for the Crown, the acting Solicitor-General, Mr Rauf Denktash, told the Court the story of the Ledra Street incident. P.C. Poullis, who had twice before been threatened by EOKA, was on 28 August surrounded by three men not far from the Alhambra Cinema, one of whom fired at him three times and then escaped on a bicycle which he abandoned after colliding with Christodoulos Michael, a member of the Old Trade Unions (PEO). The gunman fled down a side street off Kykko Avenue. The bicycle was found to be the property of Michael Karaolis, a promising village boy educated at the English School and formerly employed in the Income Tax Office. Karaolis, who did not return to work after the murder, was arrested on 3 September walking across a field near Chatos after getting out of a car which

---

[1] *Cyprus Mail* and *Times of Cyprus*, 24–29 October 1958, and author's notes taken during the trial.

had just gone through a road-block. The driver, a clerk in the arch-bishopric, disappeared. Karaolis, on arrest, gave a false name, a false address and occupation to the police who found on him a note signed 'Zedro' which read:

> I send you the bearer of this note, he is a good boy and a patriot to the point of self-sacrifice. You can trust him. Nobody must learn about his identity.

The prosecution's case relied on the identification of the murderer. The onlookers could only have had a fleeting glimpse of him and no Greek was likely to risk death by identifying the culprit. The most important Greek witness for the Crown was Christodoulos Michael, who had deliberately collided with the fugitive in the belief that a left-wing leader had been attacked. After marked hesitancy, Michael said he was not sure whether the man on the bicycle was Karaolis. Three Turks – Mehmet Ismael, a plain clothes policeman on duty at the time, Fevzi Direkoglou, a special constable and government employee, and Hussein Djenghiz, a taxi driver, swore that they recognised Karaolis as the man on the bicycle. The Crown sought to link the crime with EOKA by producing leaflets threatening the police and signed 'Zedro', the code name of Afxentiou, leader of the Famagusta area.

The defence was ably conducted by a former Attorney-General, Mr Stelios Pavlides QC, and Mr George Chrysafinis QC, with the aid of four distinguished Greek Cypriot attorneys. The defence fell into two parts: the explanations as to how the accused's bicycle got into the murderer's hands and the alibi as to his whereabouts at the time of the crime. Pavlides objected to the inclusion of the EOKA leaflets on the ground that the charge was one of murder and not of conspiracy. The Court ruled that the evidence was admissible as the explanation for the note from 'Zedro' and as an aid to establishing the motive for the crime.

On the fourth day of the trial Karaolis told the Court that he spent the night of 27 August at Strovolos where he shared a room with his two sisters who were at their home in Palekhori. The next morning he ran into his brother-in-law, Phidias Christodoulou, and stayed with him in Votsi's coffee shop until 10.45 a.m. He lent Phidias his bicycle to go to the Old Trade Union meeting at the Alhambra and returned to his lodgings. He then left with his sister's bicycle for the house of his uncle and aunt in Strovolos. He found them with their children listening to the radio. At about noon the current failed and they were joined by their next-door neighbours, the Cherkezos family, for an hour or so in a game of draughts under the shade of the mulberry tree. Then Argyros, the grocer's boy, came with the news that a policeman had been shot in Nicosia. They went on with the game until the arrival of Phidias fifteen minutes later. He told Karaolis that the murderer had gone off on his bicycle.

Karaolis stated that he was afraid that the bicycle incident might be linked with the bomb explosion which had taken place in his office during the summer, that the police might not accept his explanation, and that he would at least be detained in Kyrenia Castle. After leaving his sister's bicycle at his lodging he sought the advice of a friend whose name he could not disclose and hid in his house until 3 September when Andreas Christoudes fetched him and drove him towards Famagusta. During the drive Christoudes put something in his pocket, told him that he would be dropped at a place where a man in a blue shirt would meet him, and that after exchanging passwords he was to give the man the note and follow him. As they drew near Chatos they saw a road-block. Christoudes told him to get out and join the car beyond the road-block. Under cross-examination Karaolis declared that he did not commit the murder of Poullis; that he was not a partner to the crime; that he did not belong to EOKA; that he was not 'a patriot to the point of self-sacrifice'[1] and did not understand the significance of the message from 'Zedro' recommending him in such terms.

Three witnesses testified that the assailant was not Karaolis: Karadonitis, the owner of a kiosk close to the site of the crime; Myriantho-poulos, a schoolmaster and fanatical enosist; and Kallis, a youth of 18, who stated that the murderer was wearing a yellow shirt and that he had chased him up Ledra Street. The key defence witness was Phidias, the accused's brother-in-law. Wavering and inarticulate, he was unable to name any friends at the meeting. The alibi was supported by the accused's uncle, the neighbours and the grocer's boy. The visit to the coffee shop was confirmed by the owner. A Greek Cypriot woman testified that the taxi driver Hussein Djenghiz had been taking her to a wedding at the time he said he was in Ledra Street. A Turkish confectioner corroborated her evidence.

Winding up for the defence, Stelios Pavlides alleged that the evidence of Djenghiz was wholly fabricated and that of Direkoglou and Ismael based on bona-fide mistakes in identification. The conduct of the

[1] *Times of Cyprus*, 28 August 1955.

accused might appear indefensible and incapable of rational explanation. Undoubtedly he had been foolish, lost his head and taken a wrong
turning without realising that he was exposing himself to even greater
suspicions. These were psychological reasons, which even psychologists
might have difficulty in explaining. It was doubtful whether EOKA
would have acted in such a clumsy manner – the use of one bicycle by
three men, the murderer's use of his own bicycle. The accused, Pavlides
pleaded, was an innocent man in a world of prejudice.

Giving judgement, the Chief Justice stated that the prosecution had
established that the bicycle used by the assailant belonged to the
accused and that the note on him was addressed to an EOKA leader.
The defence had introduced evidence to discredit the testimony of
Djenghiz but even without this the Court would have disbelieved him.
Slight discrepancies existed in the evidence of Ismael and Direkoglou
as to whether Karaolis had taken the gun from his shirt or his trouser
pocket. But they were not shaken in cross-examination and had no
doubt that the man they saw was the accused. Christodoulos had shown
great courage in throwing his bicycle in front of the assailant and must
have seen his face, but was unable to identify him. One could understand him saying that the accused was not the man. But it was difficult
to understand why he should say that he did not know.

Sir Eric then dealt with the evidence submitted by the defence.
Karadonitis said that he had seen the men going away with their backs
to him, yet he had sworn in court that not one of the three was the
accused. Myrianthopoulos had admitted that he and his father were
ardent enosists and that even if asked to do so he would not testify
against a nationalist. He gave the impression that he was not without
bias against the Crown. Kallis was an unimpressive witness; his appearance and demeanour indicated that he belonged to the riff-raff of the
town. The story of the bicycle and the alibi were bound up together;
the inability to believe the first was fatal to the second; the weakness of
an alibi was often reflected in small matters. The story of Phidias was
'frankly incredible'. Although within a few feet of the incident, he made
no attempt to stop the man who took the bicycle or to enlist the help
of the bystanders. It was not clear why when amongst friends and
relations he should have told the accused secretly about the bicycle
theft. Counsel for the defence had suggested that EOKA would have
managed things better than to allow the murderer to use his own
bicycle. But it had to be remembered that but for the loss of nerve at
Chatos the accused would have escaped. The Court rejected his
defence and the alibi and found him guilty of murder. Karaolis seemed

unmoved by the pronouncement of the death sentence. The silence of the small court-room was broken only by the anguished cries of his relatives. Asked by the Chief Justice whether he had anything to say he replied: 'Yes. I am innocent.'

On 14 November the Supreme Court of Cyprus dismissed the appeal of Karaolis. The president, Mr Justice Zekia, rejected certain evidence submitted by the Crown, but ruled that even without this the verdict would have been the same.[1] Hundreds of schoolchildren rioted in Nicosia and were dispersed by troops using batons and tear gas, their task hampered by screaming girls.

The Colonel's plan for the deployment of children in militant duties, his ultimate aim that they should act as one person blindly obeying his orders, had at long last materialised, unleashing forces which neither the nationalist leaders nor the parents could contain. In the first half of the autumn term pupils from twenty-one secondary schools had taken part in riots and there were forty-six strikes by schoolchildren. The Director of Education gave several warnings that unruly schools would have to shut. On 14 November Harding ordered the Samuel School to close because of its part in the riots on that day and its long record of disorderly behaviour. Mr Agathokles Samuel, the headmaster and son of the founder, pleaded that his school was no worse than the others and that the staff were doing their best to keep order. Though strongly enosist in their sympathies, the headmasters held discussions with the parents urging them to impress upon their children the dangers of excessive nationalism to the cause and the need for regular school attendance and for patriotism but not riots. Dr Spyridakis, headmaster of the Pancyprian Gymnasium, repeated this advice on 21 November in the second emergency meeting with the parents in two weeks. The Colonel's anger culminated in threats to Spyridakis and his deputy by gunmen seven days later. But on the question of education the nationalist leaders stood firm in the face of terrorist pressure. After the incident the Archbishop, a former pupil of the Pancyprian Gymnasium, ordered the children to return to their classes.[2] The Ethnarchy Council publicly expressed its sympathy with Spyridakis and his deputy in their ordeal with the gunmen.[3] But the insidious doctrine that the state is more sacred than parent or child had taken root. The pupils now obeyed the directives of EOKA and Athens Radio:

[1] Cyprus Mail, 15 November 1955.

[2] Cyprus Mail, 21 and 22 November 1955: Ethnarchy Council urges pupils to return to school.

[3] Cyprus Mail, 23 November 1955 (full text, Ethnarchy Council Statement).

Attention! The Youth is marching by. This is the Youth of Cyprus. . . . It is no small thing that young boys and girls should leave their desks and stand up to the raging lion. . . .

They had seen their fellow-students persecuted and condemned to prison. But instead of hiding in their homes, they filled their pockets with stones and marched against the invaders. . . . Their schools are closed. It is nothing another year is wasted. What are the years worth if they are years of slavery? . . . Even if many years of school are lost, even if the students remain illiterate, nothing is of value compared with the ideal which inspires them. . . . When Cyprus is liberated, a statue of the Unknown Child must be erected side by side with the statue of the Unknown Warrior.[1]

The closure of the Samuel School set off a new wave of mass absenteeism, agitation in one school serving as a signal to the rest.

In the middle of November the Governor announced a £38 million development plan.[2] This included the expansion of technical training and social insurance. The possible construction of a first-rate port which would 'help to make Cyprus the most prosperous island in the Mediterranean'[3] was also mentioned. But Harding stressed that without public security there could be no political progress and that an efficient police force must be the first charge on revenues; a special grant would be allocated for this early in 1956. The move was seen as a belated attempt to make up for past neglect, and an indication of Britain's resolve to retain the island. Its early fulfilment rested with the Cypriots in their readiness to end the revolt. But the people were in no mood to consider its merits. Tension had risen as the result of the dismissal of Karaolis's appeal. EOKA retaliated by stepping up violence. Five servicemen were killed in one week; two of them died in an ambush personally directed by Grivas.

In November a special assize court was set up and extra judges appointed to deal with offences against public order and security. These cases now exceeded the capacity of the existing courts.

The Cypriot judiciary with its traditionally high standards had stood up well to the threats against judges who passed unpopular sentences, but the pressure was bound to increase as the terrorist campaign went on. And the new judges were non-Cypriots brought in mainly from England and Ireland.

---

[1] *Summary of World Broadcasts*, IV (BBC) 625, p. 7, 23 November 1955. See also Daily Supplement.

[2] Cyprus Mail, 17 November 1955, full statement.

[3] ibid.

The term 'Special Court' was widely misrepresented abroad. The Spanish historian Salvador de Madariaga was among the many writers who assumed that the British introduced martial law during the EOKA rising.[1] The civil courts on the contrary continued to function throughout the emergency and the Cypriot terrorists were subject to the same system of justice and the same rules of evidence as the ordinary citizen.

On 26 November the Governor proclaimed a state of emergency.[2] The increase in terrorist outrages and widespread disorders made it necessary, he said, to take further steps to safeguard the normal life of the community.[3] The Governor was thus enabled to act quickly and as he thought fit in the best interests of security without recourse to the slow, cumbersome procedure of legislation by Order in Council.[4] The death penalty, previously in force only for murder, was extended to other offences including the discharge of firearms at the person and the throwing and depositing of bombs with intent to cause death or injury. The unlawful possession of firearms and explosives became subject to the maximum penalty of life imprisonment. The courts were empowered to sentence offenders under 18 to whipping. The regulations covered, as and when circumstances required, deportation, collective punishment and censorship. The extension of the death penalty, the introduction of collective punishment and whipping aroused the greatest anger. The last was considered degrading by the Cypriots – a factor which did not carry much weight with a generation of colonial officials brought up on the dictum 'spare the rod and spoil the child'.

The troops were put on active service, and could now be charged by court martial for serious offences, which eliminated the risk of discrimination on the part of Cypriot judges in an atmosphere potentially hostile to the security forces.

A bomb intended for Harding on the occasion of the Caledonian ball went off in the Ledra Palace the day of the proclamation. Within forty-eight hours a gunman, Andreas Demetriou, tried to kill an Englishman in Famagusta. The Archbishop promptly condemned the emergency measures – first from the pulpit of St Andrew's Church in Nicosia and again in a sermon at Kaimakli. Britain was now imposing a regime comparable to that of the fascists, he said, and was mistaken if she thought

[1] See Salvador de Madariaga, 'World Opinion on Cyprus', Manchester Guardian, 5 April 1956.

[2] *Cyprus Gazette* no. 3891 of 26 November 1955, Subsidiary Legislation no. 730.

[3] Cyprus Mail, 27 November 1955.

[4] See Storrs, op. cit. pp. 500–10, on the trials of administration by means of Orders in Council.

that normality could be restored to Cyprus by the use of force.[1] The Communists described the new measures as worse than anything endured by the Cypriots under Sir Richmond Palmer, and took the opportunity to put in a word for Moscow by demanding that Greece should withdraw from NATO and the Balkan Pact.

The extension of the death penalty did nothing to stop the rising spiral of violence. During the first week in December bombs exploded in the offices of Cyprus Airways and the Nicosia Commissioner. At Lefkoniko the Agricultural Office was destroyed; and mobs of school-children set the post office on fire. An army camp was attacked by terrorists. A Greek Cypriot policeman and a Royal Marine were killed, and seven soldiers seriously wounded in ambushes. The first collective punishment was imposed on 4 December at Lefkoniko. The Governor visited the village, reprimanded the elders for its bad record and informed them that £2,000 would be collected from the inhabitants on the basis of a means test to pay for a new post office. The curfew would remain in force until the fine was paid. Not even the Turks were exempted. There was little delay. The farmers wanted to sow seed while the ground was still soft from the first winter rains. And those working away from home were anxious to avoid any further loss of wages.

In Limassol EOKA met with a reverse. Four cases containing guns, ammunition, limpet mines and grenades were discovered by the port authorities. The cargo, landed from the SS *Aeolia* and packed in Greece, was consigned as 'books'. A Limassol bookseller was arrested.

The schools crisis brought Sir Christopher Cox, the Colonial Office educational adviser, to Cyprus early in December. By this time four schools had lost their 'government' grants and the Larnaca Commercial Lyceum was struck off the register. The Greek state-controlled radio in special programmes directed to Cypriot youth blared out directives daily:

> Fellow-students, Harding is raving . . . The Fatherland asks us to continue our struggle with greater zeal . . . Honour to him who is not intimidated by Harding's bayonets and bullets. The streets of Nicosia are waiting to resound with student demonstrations. Stones are ready to break the Commandos' heads. Pay them as they pay you. Strike them as they strike. Kill them as they kill you. . . . Prepare yourselves for the great struggle so that you may be worthy of great victory. Forward students. . . .[2]

[1] Cyprus Mail, 1 December 1955.
[2] *Summary of World Broadcasts*, IV (BBC) 628, p. 5, 6 December 1955. See also Daily Supplement.

Angered by rumours that Harding and Makarios were about to agree a settlement excluding full self-determination, a deputation of senior boys from the Pancyprian Gymnasium demanded to see the Archbishop. They hotly protested that they had not been consulted and, after demonstrating in the school yard, vented their wrath by ferociously ringing the cathedral bells near the Archbishop's office across the road. They went back to their classes only on receiving the headmaster's promise that Makarios would see them in due course. A few days later the Gymnasium pupils refused to go to school in protest against the arrest of one of the boys. Hundreds of rioting schoolchildren were dispersed by troops. Out of the twenty-nine taken into custody all except three were from the Pancyprian Gymnasium. Dr Spyridakis warned the parents that the school was faced with the choice of orderly conduct or imminent closure. Makarios advised a delegation of boys to avoid incidents and attend school regularly so that it could remain open. Unrest continued in other schools. The relative calm in the Gymnasium was shortlived.

Meanwhile the security forces intensified operations against the guerrillas. On 8 December about a thousand troops surrounded twenty-four monasteries at dawn. In the presence of a padre, wherever possible, they searched the buildings using mine detectors. At the end the monk in charge was asked to certify that the soldiers had carried out their task with respect. The results of this massive operation were modest – two pistols in a box marked with a crucifix, a few sticks of dynamite. But from the Monastery of St Spyridon Makarios lashed out at the British 'barbarians'. At the time of Spyridon's birth in Cyprus, Makarios said, Britons were still pagan. British soldiers, equipped with guns and bayonets, had entered churches and monasteries turning everything upside down looking for weapons and ammunition.[1] The theme was exploited in still more vicious terms by the EOKA propagandists.

The security forces had long suspected that ambushes were being organised from a base in the Troodos mountains. During the early winter Grivas and three groups led by Afxentiou, Renos Kyriakides and Christos Chartas were using a hideout on a ridge overlooking the Adelphi Forest above the villages of Spilia and Kourdhali. Caves reinforced with timber brought up by village donkeys had been converted into living quarters, their entrances ingeniously concealed by boulders and thick bushes. On 11 December units from the Royal Marine Commandos and the Gordon Highlanders moved into the area. According

[1] Cyprus Mail, 13 December 1955.

to the Colonel,[1] the day before the attack Kyriakos Matsis, the chief courier, brought a Nicosia dentist to Spilia to attend to him. It was pouring with rain and the EOKA Leader had a heavy cold. He sent a message asking the dentist to wait another day. Afxentiou then left on a combined hunting and reconnaissance trip in the direction of Kannavia, Chartas for Polystipos to see his family. The next morning Grivas was alone in the hideout. A thick mist veiled the peaks and the forest, but an EOKA guard could just see army lorries moving into Spilia. A tracker dog appeared in the distance and Grivas assumed that this was not a routine patrol but an encirclement operation. He ordered Afxentiou to watch with his men in the direction of Spilia and to fire shots as the security forces moved towards the hide. The warning shots came. After a dangerous march through thick woods Grivas and three guerrillas reached Kakopetria. Kyriakides was wounded and captured in a gun battle while trying to break out of the cordon at Spilia. The British casualties given by Grivas, based on the report of an EOKA man forced at gunpoint to guide the security forces to the caves, were wildly exaggerated. Three commandos in fact were injured slightly from their own mortar fire. The Colonel's version is, nevertheless, interesting for the light it sheds on the daily existence of the guerrillas. The hunting trip, the casual postponement of the dentist's appointment indicated that as yet they felt no real insecurity and that their lives verged on normality.

The Government's action on 14 December in arresting many Communists came as a shock. In the early hours of the morning troops occupied AKEL's headquarters. Roped together in twos and threes, 130 left-wingers, including the Party's Secretary-General, and the mayors of Limassol and Larnaca were hastily removed from their homes to Pyla Detention Camp. AKEL and its satellites were proscribed and *Neos Demokratis* was suspended. An official statement referred to the 'consistently harmful' political role of the Cypriot Communists in recent years:

It was the Communists who since the war led the way in resorting to riot, sabotage and physical intimidation in pursuit of their political aims. It was they who developed the whole paraphernalia of 'struggle' against established authority – the mass demonstrations, political strikes, daubing of slogans, seditious propaganda and monster petitions. That a large number of the public now accepts

---

[1] *Memoirs* (Longmans), op. cit. pp. 55–8.

violence and agitation as a substitute for normal democratic processes is largely their doing.[1]

The statement dismissed AKEL's denunciations of terrorism as 'tactical'. The Communists, it said, had joined the nationalists in recent strikes leading to disorders. Limassol, the centre of the worst disturbances, was a communist stronghold. AKEL had repeatedly served international communism by stirring up hostility to the bases.

The alienation of AKEL was likely in the long term to increase the Government's difficulties. The open hostility of the leftists towards the nationalist extremists, though not motivated by pro-British sympathy, indirectly aided the security forces. The Communists were less easily intimidated than other sectors of the Greek population. In areas where they were strong, incidents were fewer and the need for policing was less. The perpetual slanging of the bases, which Harding found disturbing, was only of academic significance. In reality the bases had been built with the minimum of industrial trouble mainly by a communist-controlled labour force. No newcomer could be expected to unravel the complexities of local politics, the eternal paradox of Cypriot reactions, the misleading sequences of events, the public statements which could seldom be accepted at face value. Dispassionate and impartial, Harding was influenced by strategic priorities and a soldier's concept of loyalty. AKEL had lost ground since the rise of EOKA. Opposed to violence, the Akelists now sought to recover the initiative and preserve a stance of militancy by relentlessly berating Makarios for serving British and American imperialism, for compromising over Enosis behind the scenes and for refusing to form a united front. Misgivings in official circles that they might block a settlement were not surprising. But in the last resort it was the pressure of EOKA which would determine the outcome of the Harding-Makarios talks. The Government hoped by silencing at least one sector of the Archbishop's critics to ease the pressure on him during a delicate phase of political negotiations. The effect was the reverse. In the small, close-knit Cypriot community family loyalties counted for more than political ideologies. The injustice of the arrests precipitated a wave of sympathy for the left wing. The allegations of violence, valid in 1948, could not be sustained in 1955. Most of AKEL's activities came within the law. It was true that communist oratory often bordered on sedition; but in volume and viciousness it came nowhere near that of the ecclesiastics. Makarios, instead of finding his position strengthened, was forced for the first time

[1] Cyprus Government Press Release, 14 December 1955.

to come out in support of a united front. Left-wing trade unionists demonstrated throughout the island. Workers on military construction went on strike.

Grivas was convinced that an operation so patently contrary to British interests could only be explained by Harding's need to balance EOKA by keeping the Communist Party alive. AKEL had no martyrs on the battlefield; therefore they had to be created in the jails. The revival of the communist newspaper under a new name (*Avghi*), the absence of Ziartides at the time of the arrests, his freedom in England although he was on the Cypriot 'Wanted' list helped to endorse the Colonel's theory that the episode was one of collusion between the Cyprus authorities and the AKEL leaders.[1]

The guerrillas grew bolder as the weeks went by. On 15 December Markos Drakos's group ambushed a jeep on the Lefka–Troodos road in daylight killing the driver, Corporal Moran. Major Coombe, of the Royal Engineers, chased the terrorists up a gulley. After emptying his Sten gun he went back to the jeep, fetched his driver's gun, shot dead Kharalambos Mouskos, and captured Zakos and Kharilaos Michael. Drakos escaped wounded. Mouskos, a cousin of the Archbishop, was a native of Paphos. Harding gave special permission for his funeral to take place publicly in Nicosia on condition that the mourners did not exceed fifty. The decision surprised and worried the authorities. Cypriots were easily aroused; processions quickly turned into riots. On this emotional occasion they were unlikely to observe the ban. The day of the funeral the centre of Nicosia was tense; the courtyard of the archbishopric alive with ominous activity. Hundreds of Pancyprian Gymnasium boys were preparing wreaths – white chrysanthemums mixed with myrtle and laurel, tied with blue and white ribbon, the colours of Greece.

After the service held by the Archbishop in Phaneromeni Church, the hearse moved into Metaxas Square followed some way behind by pall-bearers carrying the coffin, the usual procedure for the burial of distinguished citizens. The first death in action of an EOKA fighter was, in the eyes of Greek Cypriots, a landmark in the struggle and merited a hero's funeral. The troops, in understandable ignorance of local customs, thought the empty hearse was a decoy. Crowds broke through the cordon. The officer in charge, faced with an unauthorised procession, ordered the firing of tear gas shells – one of which hit the hearse by chance. The cortège was forced to retreat down a side street. Suddenly the rain came down in torrents and the crowds dispersed. A generous gesture made by Harding in good faith had thus ended in

[1] See *Memoirs* (Longmans), op. cit. pp. 61–2.

catastrophe and given the extremists fresh cause for the vilification of the security forces.

The episode closed on 23 December after the award of the George Medal to Major Coombe. The citation mentioned his total disregard for his own safety, his courage and initiative 'of the very highest order'. In an unusual press conference arranged by the Cyprus authorities, Major Coombe, quoting from 'The Revelation',[1] described his statement as a 'sermon'. Cyprus, he said, was being ravaged by death, pain and fear – its citizens cowed and frightened by a small band of murderers. The tragedy was that the British should now be acclaiming him as a hero and that Cypriots should feel compelled to honour the dead terrorist. There should be no jubilation on either side. He concluded with an appeal for the healing of the rift between the people of Britain and Cyprus.[2]

On 1 January 1956, Harding predicted that EOKA's days were numbered and announced the Government's intention to introduce shortly a social insurance scheme of great advantage to the islanders. The EOKA Leader's New Year message contained a challenge to Cypriot youth:

> The year which has ended has been the beginning of a hard, bloody, and glorious struggle for the overthrow of the repressive yoke of the repugnant tyrant.... We shall continue the New Year with the same decisiveness.... Until the tyrant who desecrates churches, seizes the belongings of bread-winners and rapes virgins (yes, even that has been observed) is driven from the land of our fathers.... Let us continue the struggle that awaits us, harder and bloodier.... On behalf of your fighting EOKA, children, I renew our sacred oath....[3]

On 11 January the situation took a sharp turn for the worse with the first murder of a Turk. Police Sergeant Ali Riza was fatally wounded outside his house in Paphos by four EOKA gunmen. Turkish riots broke out in Nicosia and elsewhere. The crowds heeded Dr Kutchuk's appeal for calm and dispersed quietly. Greek property was damaged.

[1] *The Revelation of St John the Divine*, Chapter XXI, Verse 4:
... and he shall wipe away every tear from their eyes; and death shall be no more; neither shall there be mourning, nor crying, nor pain, any more; the first things are passed away.
[2] Cyprus Mail, 23 December 1955, and author's notes.
[3] *Summary of World Broadcasts*, IV (BBC) 637, 13 January 1956, p. 9.

At the end of January all Cypriots were ordered to hand over their sporting guns to local police stations for safe custody. Owing to EOKA's penetration of the police, a high-ranking priest was able to warn Grivas in advance and terrorists seized quantities of shotguns before the government order came into effect.

Security operations were intensified especially in the suspect areas during the winter. In the course of duty the troops ripped up floor boards, upset sacks of flour, turned out the contents of drawers and cupboards, and seldom had time or inclination to repair the damage afterwards. Hideouts, arms and ammunition were discovered from time to time. But operations were often based on wrong information. The innocent, therefore, suffered equally with the guilty. Curfews stopped the men going to work outside the villages. Loss of wages added to the mounting pile of grievances. New to the hazards of war, villagers did not always stop when challenged.[1] Accidents, such as the occasion at Khandria when the security forces shot dead an elderly Greek who was deaf, increased bitterness and misunderstanding. By late winter prospects for the destruction of the mountain guerrilla network had improved. But the problem of the part-time gangs, absorbed into normal life between combatant activities, remained as intractable as ever.

The crisis in the secondary schools reached its climax in January. The new term in Nicosia started with the distribution of leaflets signed 'Dighenis' ordering the pupils to disobey their teachers. The boys were suspected of producing them on their own initiative with the school duplicator. Before the first week of term was out, the Pancyprian Gymnasium went on strike. Later in the month serious riots broke out in Nicosia on two consecutive days and in Paphos. On 28 January the Government closed the Pancyprian Gymnasium which with its 2,000 pupils constituted a formidable security problem in the heart of the capital. Fourteen schools stopped work in protest. The schools first had to satisfy the authorities that they were able to maintain order before being allowed to reopen. The governing bodies and pupils of several schools gave the necessary written assurances. But disorders broke out again.

On 7 February riots by schoolchildren in Famagusta ended in tragedy and the creation of yet another nationalist martyr. When the security forces opened fire one of the ringleaders, Petros Yiallouros, was fatally wounded. Soldiers often suffered serious injuries from heavy stoning

---

[1] The difficulty of avoiding such accidents was illustrated by the fact that soldiers shot dead a Turkish shepherd who failed to halt on being challenged. See *Greek Irredentism and Cypriot Terrorism* (Cyprus Government, 1956), p. 119.

and were at a disadvantage in defending themselves in that they could only use force as a last resort. By the spring the majority of Greek secondary schools had either been withdrawn from the register by the British authorities or closed down by their own boards.

The almost total stoppage of secondary education was dictated by the overriding needs of security. It deprived the rebels of assembly centres for the organisation of riots and of channels for the dissemination of EOKA doctrines and directives. The risk that idle children would become an easy prey for EOKA was outweighed by the extensive use the Organisation had already made of the schools and the fact that not even the nationalist leaders, much as they wished education to go on, were able to withstand terrorist pressure.

Grivas had not overlooked the possible use of young children. The forcible removal of Greek flags from the elementary schools and other government buildings during the early stages of Harding's administration furthered EOKA's aim. The ubiquitous Greek flag was the least serious of the problems facing the overworked security forces. But Harding regarded the offences as an intolerable affront to the Crown. The onus was eventually shifted on to the school authorities who had the choice either of taking down the flag or of closing the schools. This ended the undignified confrontation between soldiers and small children but led to the virtual suspension of elementary education. Early in 1956, with secondary education at a standstill, Grivas turned to the younger children. Teachers were threatened. At Tsadha dynamite exploded on the doorstep of the headmaster's house. Older boys broke into elementary schools, damaging equipment and sometimes attacking the children in class. More than 200 Greek elementary schoolchildren carrying the Greek flag marched on a Turkish school and stoned the pupils. By the spring all except 81 elementary schools out of a total of 499 had ceased to function. The measures imposed by the authorities were presented abroad as a form of educational persecution. The fact that it was EOKA which caused the total disruption of Greek education was ignored. Years of indoctrination in Hellenic nationalism by Greek nationals and fanatical Cypriot teachers, and highly inflammatory broadcasts from Athens Radio had helped to stir up trouble in the schools. But these factors alone were insufficient to bring about the state of anarchy and violence which existed in the secondary schools nine months after the rise of EOKA. Grivas claimed with pride that the use of children in the front line was his own original idea, a glorious and unique achievement in the history of rebellion.[1] The British looked

---

[1] See *Memoirs* (Longmans), op. cit. p. 28.

upon it as the most diabolical aspect of an inherently evil campaign. Some responsibility must, however, rest with the British for the suspension of elementary educaton. The removal of the Greek flags contributed nothing to the restoration of law and order; on the contrary it served as a stimulus to further agitation. It was impossible for the security forces to protect individual teachers. Faced with the retaliation of EOKA, it was not surprising that the teachers chose to close the schools rather than risk removing the Greek flag.

During the first two months of 1956 fatal army casualties totalled four. A Greek and a Turkish member of the police force and seven Greek civilians were killed. One of the victims, the venerated Abbot of Chrysorroyiatissa, was murdered in his own monastery by masked men armed with shotguns. His funeral service was conducted by Makarios.[1]

6   THE HARDING-MAKARIOS TALKS

The first round of talks was exploratory. When Harding met Makarios on 4 October, two days after his arrival in Cyprus, he stressed the danger of communism, the island's strategic value and the vital role of Turkey in the defence of the free world.

The next day Makarios sent the Governor a three-point plan in which he suggested that the British should first recognise the Cypriot right to self-determination as the essential basis for a final settlement; after this the Archbishop would cooperate in framing a constitution for immediate self-government. The timing of self-determination would be a matter for discussion between Britain and Cypriot representatives elected under the constitution.

The Governor was not authorised to discuss self-determination, and at the second meeting he concentrated on the constitutional plan presented to the Tripartite Conference. The Archbishop was primarily concerned with the island's final status, especially the role of Turkey. But he also expressed misgivings about the question of the Governor's control over security, the necessity for his approval of the Cypriot Prime Minister's appointment and the lack of any indication that the elected majority in the assembly would be Greek.

Harding in a broadcast to the Cypriots on 8 October commented on two important features of the constitutional plan: the promise of freely

[1] A German biographer describes this as one of the most macabre farces in His Beatitude's role as a churchman. See Dr Karl Kerber, *Makarios Kirchenfürst oder ??????* (Im Wolf Frhr, *v.* Tucher Verlag GmbH), p. 36. Note: There is no evidence that Makarios either ordered the murder or that he could have prevented it.

elected representatives taking over the main responsibility for internal affairs and the opportunity, once self-government was firmly established, to express their views on the island's future which lay through these two doors. The first door was already wide open; the second had not been shut. It did not make sense, he said, to shut the first, thereby preventing access to the second.[1]

Three days later Makarios rejected the British plan. The situation, however, was not without hope. The fact that the Ethnarchy Council had been willing to consider a constitution on any basis whatsoever was a marked advance on previous attitudes. Harding had stated that he would always be ready to meet the Archbishop again.

Meanwhile Karamanlis, on the death of Field-Marshal Papagos, had taken over the Greek Government. Spyros Theotokis, an eminent moderate, was appointed Foreign Minister. Seen from Whitehall the chances of a settlement seemed to have improved and on 15 October Eden suggested a second round of talks with Makarios.[2] Harding realised that this could achieve nothing unless he was able to negotiate on a basis which came closer to the Cypriot stand. It was decided to draw up a new policy statement. During the NATO meeting in Paris on 25 October Macmillan raised the Cyprus problem with Theotokis who agreed that a resumption of the talks was desirable.

The Archbishop feared that Karamanlis intended to ease up on the Cyprus campaign and arrived in Athens at the end of October to seek assurances that the new Greek Government would be no less zealous than its predecessor in promoting the Cypriot cause. The visit, which lasted seventeen days, was as usual unpopular in official circles. On his return to Cyprus Makarios claimed that Greece was fully behind the national struggle.

Harding met Makarios secretly in Nicosia on 21 November and showed him the new policy statement:

TOP SECRET

Her Majesty's Government adhere to the principle embodied in the Charter of the United Nations, the Potomac Charter and the Pacific Charter to which they have subscribed. It is not therefore their position that the principle of self-determination can never be applicable to Cyprus. It is their position that it is not now a practical proposition both on account of the present strategical situation and on account of the consequences on the relations between North Atlantic

[1] Cyprus Government Press Release, 9 September 1955.
[2] See *The Memoirs of Sir Anthony Eden: Full Circle* (Cassell, London, 1960), p. 403.

Treaty Organization Powers in the Eastern Mediterranean. They will therefore have to satisfy themselves that any final solution safeguards the strategic interests of the United Kingdom and her allies.

Her Majesty's Government have offered a wide measure of self-government now. If the people of Cyprus participate in constitutional development, it is the intention of Her Majesty's Government to work for a solution which will satisfy the wishes of the people of Cyprus within the framework of the treaties and alliances to which the countries concerned in the defence of the Eastern Mediterranean are parties. Her Majesty's Government will be prepared to discuss the future of the island with the representatives of the people of Cyprus when self-government has proved itself a workable proposition and capable of safeguarding the interests of all sections of the community.

November 21, 1955[1]

The mention of 'treaties and alliances' aroused the Archbishop's suspicions. He rejected the statement out of hand and sent Kranidiotis to Athens to request the Greek Government to exert pressure against Britain by the intensification of Athens Radio broadcasts and by pressing for international action including the intervention of the US Government. According to the British Ambassador, Sir Charles Peake, Theotokis was shaken by the Archbishop's stand but felt that his government was not strong enough to exert pressure on him. The Americans encouraged the Greek Government to support the British move. In Nicosia the US Consul, Mr Courtney, described by Eden as 'consistently helpful', tried several times to persuade Makarios to reconsider his decision. On Peake's advice, Eden sent Karamanlis a personal message as a last resort on 30 November. 'I feel that with your cooperation', he wrote, 'we may have what may be a real chance to find an amicable settlement.' He appealed to the Greek Prime Minister

---

[1] *The Cyprus Question, Negotiations 4 October 1955 to 5 March 1956* (The Royal Ministry for Foreign Affairs, Athens, 1956). The first British statement published in the above differs from the lucid text quoted by Eden which, he writes, was discussed with Harding on 20 October. (See Eden, op. cit. pp. 403–4.) Eden's version does not mention 'treaties and alliances' and states categorically that the Greek and Turkish Governments should be associated with the Anglo-Cypriot talks on the island's future. Eden states that after Macmillan's visit to Paris the formula was gone over again but no change of substance was made. Macmillan must have realised after seeing Theotokis that the Greeks wanted to shift responsibility for a settlement on to the Cypriots. And Harding was fully aware that any plan which provided specifically for Turkey's participation in future talks was certain to be rejected by Makarios. This would explain the major differences in phraseology in the two versions of the first British formula.

'to take a bold initiative in recommending the statement to Makarios'.[1]

The new stand on self-determination became public on 5 December during the long debate in the House of Commons.[2] Macmillan and Lennox-Boyd recognised the validity of the principle but dwelt on the timing difficulties in the case of Cyprus. Eden was determined that the formula should remain secret until it was certain that the Archbishop's agreement could not be obtained.[3] The Government was, accordingly, evasive in dealing with questions on the progress of the talks and gave no indication that Makarios had already broken them off.

The long-awaited debate, dreaded by British officials in Cyprus as a potential stimulus to further trouble, unleashed rumours that Makarios had accepted a compromise which excluded full self-determination. Disturbances broke out in Nicosia shortly after the debate. The Archbishop took steps on 7 December to clarify the position. It was only a year, Makarios told the press, since Mr Hopkinson had stated that Cyprus was one of the territories which could 'never' expect to be independent. Today 'Mr Hopkinson's "never" has been replaced by Mr Macmillan's "sometime"'. The Archbishop then disclosed that he had turned down the latest British offer because it made self-determination in practice unattainable. The Cypriots would continue, he said, to work for a solution which made its realisation 'quick and easy'.[4]

Eden's personal message to Karamanlis evoked a long memorandum dated 5 December,[5] which began on a note of reproach. As a result of the talks between Macmillan and Theotokis in Paris, the Greek Government had evidently expected to be consulted in advance about any new British formula instead of receiving the text about an hour before it was shown to Makarios. The Greek note welcomed the British pronouncement on self-determination but deplored its negative format which was 'so encumbered with considerations of strategic interests and treaty obligations as to render the promise implied therein almost imperceptible . . .'[6]

The Greek Government claimed that Britain's defence obligations in the Eastern Mediterranean, which as a member of NATO Greece was ready to uphold, in no way conflicted with Cypriot aspirations. On the contrary, the island's strategic value would be enhanced by a friendly population. The memorandum criticised the latest security measures in

[1] See Eden, op. cit. p. 405 ff.
[2] H.C. Deb., vol. 547, cols 32–155.
[3] See Eden, op. cit. p. 406.
[4] Cyprus Mail, 8 December 1955.
[5] *The Cyprus Question*, op. cit. pp. 7–11.
[6] ibid. p. 8.

Cyprus. But its overriding purpose was to elicit from the British Government a clear-cut undertaking to grant the island self-determination within a fixed period.

The British Government replied on 9 December that it could not say when self-determination would be practicable since this depended on factors partly outside its control, and drew attention to Macmillan's comments on the subject. The British note explained that the passages on strategic matters in the policy statement had been redrafted at the Greek request and briefly restated the constitutional plan.[1]

The amendments to the formula[2] amounted in fact to no more than minor changes of phraseology. The Greeks made a final effort on 15 December to obtain from the British Government a fixed date for self-determination and in Paris presented Sir Harold Caccia, Deputy Under-Secretary for Foreign Affairs, with two short drafts as possible alternatives to the British formula.[3] Eden's immediate reaction was that the proposals would alienate Turkey[4] and they were ignored in the British reply the next day. The British Government commented that it had already gone a long way to reach 'a sensible compromise', called upon the Greek Government to urge Makarios to resume talks with Harding immediately and stressed that 'a firm courageous lead' from the Greek side might well be decisive in gaining the Archbishop's cooperation.[5]

The Greeks pointed out on 21 December that the formula still lacked 'clarity and simplicity' and that doubts as to its meaning could easily arise out of the references to Macmillan's statement:

> . . . therefore, I say, why cannot we all agree to work together for self-government, while refraining from pressing at this anxious moment in world history too precise a definition of every word and phrase of our different approaches to the problem of the final stages of the argument?[6]

[1] ibid. p. 13, 'Aide Memoire accompanying Second British Draft Statement. 9 December 1955.'

[2] ibid. p. 12, 'Second Draft of British Statement handed to the Greek Foreign Minister on December 9, 1955'.

[3] ibid. p. 14.

[4] See Eden, op. cit. p. 409.

[5] *The Cyprus Question*, op. cit. p. 15, 'Note handed to the Greek Minister for Foreign Affairs by the British Secretary of State for Foreign Affairs on December 16th, 1955, in Paris'.

[6] ibid. p. 16, 'Verbal communication (read from the text) by the Greek Minister for Foreign Affairs to the British Ambassador, on December 21st, 1955', quoting H.C. Deb., vol. 547, cols 41–2.

Although unable to recommend the formula to Makarios, the Greek Government considered that in conjunction with its own memorandum of 5 December it could form a basis for further negotiations. Mr Alexis Liatis, a senior diplomat, arrived unexpectedly in Cyprus on 26 December with instructions from the Greek Government to urge Makarios to resume talks with Harding, despite the formula's shortcomings. Liatis, who found that the Archbishop's attitude had hardened, was pessimistic on his return to Athens. The talks were resumed in January 1956 on the basis of a revised formula but without success, and after the second meeting Harding left for London.

By the end of the month the situation was critical. The Turks, sceptical from the start about the negotiations with the Archbishop, had grown increasingly restive. The Turkish Foreign Minister, Fuad Koprulu, made representations to the British Government on 26 January. Harding met Makarios two days later and reported on the results of his visit to London. The next day he sent the Archbishop the statement of policy which he was willing to issue if Makarios would agree to cooperate in framing a constitution and to use his influence to end violence and disorder. His Beatitude was free, Harding stressed, to reserve his position on constitutional questions since these must be discussed with all sectors of the community. The Governor also enclosed a draft text which provided for a clear undertaking on the part of Makarios that he would 'use all his influence to bring an end to acts of violence and lawlessness'.[1]

The policy statement, shortened and simplified, was in substance unchanged. The sentence on self-determination was still phrased as a double negative; the references to 'treaties and alliances' had survived unimpaired.[2]

On 2 February the Archbishop renewed his objections to the formula. Subject, however, to a clarification of the term 'a wide measure of self-government', he agreed to cooperate with the Governor and representatives of the minority in framing a constitution, in his own words, 'for the transitory regime'. But the general principles of the constitution, Makarios said, should be defined in advance. He then proceeded to do this.[3] The Archbishop's conditions would have provided for a Greek majority in an all-elected assembly, Cypriot control of public security from the start of self-government and the restriction of the Governor's

---

[1] *Cyprus: Correspondence exchanged between the Governor and Archbishop Makarios*, Cmd 9708, March 1956, pp. 4–5.

[2] ibid. p. 3.

[3] ibid. pp. 6–7.

authority (apart from his responsibility for Defence and Foreign Affairs) to that of a constitutional head of state. The Archbishop was willing to assist in pacification but suggested that this could most quickly be achieved by a general amnesty and the repeal of the emergency measures.

The shift in emphasis from self-determination to self-government, the raising of the amnesty and other security matters brought the talks to a grinding halt. The Labour MP Francis Noel-Baker, who had just arrived in Cyprus, offered to intervene. As a fluent Greek speaker and prominent philhellene, Noel-Baker was perhaps better qualified to act as a spokesman for the Greeks than as a mediator in a complex dispute which also involved British and Turkish interests. The Governor was nevertheless impressed by his sincerity and his unshakeable belief that he could influence Makarios, but his tireless efforts, to which Lennox-Boyd paid a tribute,[1] were fruitless. The last phase of the talks degenerated into a repetitive and sterile series of exchanges in which Harding was, for the first time, side-tracked into arguments about the constitution. The amnesty and the security measures figured increasingly in the Archbishop's demands. In the course of the exchanges, Harding informed the Archbishop that the contemplated transfer of power to Cypriot ministers 'by a suitably phased process' did not imply any intention on the part of Her Majesty's Government to delay the procedure; that British control of public security would last as long as the Governor 'deems necessary'; that certain emergency laws would be revoked once Makarios had called for the end of violence and there was evidence of a genuine response to his appeal. The Governor repeated that the Archbishop's constitutional questions must be discussed with all representatives of the community and the Constitutional Commissioner, whose hands could not be tied in advance.[2]

Grivas had viewed the talks with a distrust equal only to that shown by the Turks. In January he gave orders that enlistment and training must go ahead as usual in preparation for a full-scale struggle if Harding and Makarios failed to reach agreement. The instructions were renewed in February. On 15 February he suspended action for a few days in order that he should not be accused of obstructing a settlement.[3]

Throughout the talks Makarios had been in close contact with the Ethnarchy Council. Unlike some of his colleagues, whose parochialism blinded them to the dangers of pressing the Enosis claim too far, the

---

[1] H.C. Deb., vol. 549, col. 1716.

[2] Cmd 9708, op. cit. pp. 8–11.

[3] *Memoirs* (Longmans), op. cit. p. 64.

Archbishop was fully aware of the international complications. He had consistently sought to convince the Council that the situation had drastically changed since the Tripartite Conference, that the wisest course now was to transfer the struggle to Parliament by accepting a constitution as an interim measure. The Cypriots could always with-draw, he argued, if things did not turn out well for them. He even questioned the usefulness of a fixed date for self-determination, which the Greek Government had tentatively suggested to the British. No one could anticipate conditions in Greece a few years ahead, the Arch-bishop reasoned. Without a fixed date the Cypriots would be able to raise the issue when it suited them, if need be immediately. To what extent these arguments were simply the tools of persuasion or the true reflection of His Beatitude's views is unknown, but they certainly indicated the magnitude of the task he faced in trying to wean the nationalists from their traditional policy of 'Enosis and nothing but Enosis'.

The Ethnarchy Council was split on the merits of the Archbishop's advice. Its past policy had been to refuse self-government, thereby eliminating the risk that the political power of the Church would be diminished by the participation of moderates and leftists, including the Communists, in an elected assembly. The new British promise of ulti-mate self-determination was vague, dependent on unpredictable conditions in the remote future. The extremists wanted a firm date within a fixed period of three or five years. The moderates were more realistic. They recognised that the nationalist cause had made consider-able progress since the first abortive appeal to the UN in 1954. They realised that at this stage the best hope of curbing Turkey's mounting involvement in the island's affairs was to reach a quick settlement with Britain. During a meeting held in late February all the councillors, except the Bishop of Kyrenia, agreed with Makarios that expediency dictated the acceptance of a constitution as a means to an end.

Meanwhile Grivas had drawn up his own stringent terms for a settle-ment. They included an immediate amnesty for all fighters and de-tainees, Cypriot control over public security during the interim phase of self-government and the departure of all British troops who had arrived in the island since the outbreak of the EOKA revolt. Carried to its logical conclusion this last condition would have precluded Britain's use of Cyprus as a base in the place of Suez, a paramount aim of British defence policy, for the redeployment of troops withdrawn from the Canal Zone under the 1954 agreement with Egypt was not yet complete.

The long delay in bringing the talks to a conclusion served EOKA's purpose well. Grivas was able to consolidate the guerrilla groups without undue harassment from the security forces. The climax of the negotiations coincided with the parliamentary elections in Greece and consequently official Greek support for a compromise settlement ceased. As the talks drew to a close the EOKA Leader moved into Nicosia to ensure that the Archbishop did not give way to the British.

The return of Francis Noel-Baker, at the Archbishop's request, on 21 February indicated that Makarios still wanted an agreement. But the situation deteriorated on 25 February with the Archbishop's letter to Harding. The Governor had made it clear, Makarios wrote, that the Cypriots should take over responsibility for the functions of government once the constitution came into effect and as soon as order was restored. However, it had not been made clear that all executive, legislative and judicial powers, except Defence and Foreign Affairs, would originate with and be exercised by the people; that representation in the assembly would be proportionate to the population ratio; that the Governor's role in approving the Cypriot Prime Minister's appointment would be purely formal; that the emergency laws would be revoked and an amnesty granted for all political offences. The Archbishop then indicated that no more concessions could be expected from him.[1]

Despite the fact that Makarios had misconstrued the Governor's comments on the timing of the transfer of departmental responsibilities to Cypriot Ministers the gulf on the subject of public security had narrowed slightly. But the second half of the letter left little hope of a settlement and the crisis brought Lennox-Boyd to Cyprus on 29 February. EOKA, on the authority of Grivas, exploded a large number of bombs in Nicosia. The authorities assumed that this outburst was initiated by the Archbishop in order to increase his bargaining power. The more valid explanation is that the Colonel decided to remind Makarios that he would not tolerate any further concessions to the British.

Lennox-Boyd told the Archbishop that the plan for self-government would be based on 'normal, liberal, constitutional doctrine'.[2] The meeting was, however, mainly important for the Colonial Secretary's firm stand on the amnesty which would come into force on the restoration of order. The release of the detainees would begin at the same time, he said, and the emergency laws revoked at a pace commensurate with the return of security. The amnesty excluded violence against the person, the illegal possession of arms, ammunition and explosives. Men

[1] Cmd 9708, op. cit. pp. 11–12.
[2] ibid. p. 12.

convicted of these crimes would have their sentences reviewed by the courts at some future date. The Archbishop wanted the amnesty extended to all offences other than those involving murder and bodily injury. The Government considered that anyone caught with illegal arms and explosives was intent on the use of violence and should pay the full penalty.

In the short term the premature release of the fanatics could have wrecked any settlement before ratification. In the long term the containment of subversion, whether of rightist or communist origin, was essential to the use of the island as a base. These factors lay at the root of the British refusal to relinquish control over security until the Governor considered it safe to do so. The Government was also un-willing to define the composition of the electoral majority at this stage because of assurances given to the Turks that no final decisions would be taken on the constitution's format before they had been consulted. Harding explained the British position to the Cypriots in a special broadcast on 5 March.

The Archbishop confirmed that the three outstanding points were the elected majority, the amnesty and public security. He accused the British of trying to impose a regime which ensured that the colonial power would be able to intervene indefinitely on the pretext of public security. He was not willing to reopen the talks, and in any future negotiations, he said, Britain would have to give way on all three points.[1]

The elected majority was not a serious obstacle to a settlement. The Cypriots could with advantage have taken the final decision on the constitution at the conference table after its details were known and they had exhausted their bargaining capacity. The Archbishop's demands over the amnesty and security, which hardened towards the end of February, were certain to be rejected since they conflicted with British strategic interests. He was thus automatically released from a negotiating position which he may well have felt no longer able to sustain. His decision at the eleventh hour to abandon the policy of cooperation in self-government took place against a background of increasing pressures which ironically were partly of his own making. He had sanctioned the formation of guerrilla groups originally; over the months they had grown sufficiently strong to enable Grivas to challenge his authority. His relentless campaigning in Greece had kept the Cyprus question on the boil there. Much as it might desire settle-ment, the Greek Government, now caught up in the hazards of parlia-mentary elections, was the prisoner of its own impotence. As the election

[1] Cyprus Mail, 3 and 6 March 1956.

drew nearer Makarios was forced into a position of increasing isolation. Shortly before polling day Karamanlis sent him a message, which was widely publicised, telling him to turn down the British offer if he found it unsatisfactory. The prospect of having to shoulder the burden of a compromise without the Greek Government's support must have seemed daunting to Makarios who tended to underestimate the strength of his own following in Cyprus. This, combined with the pressure exerted by Grivas, probably explains the Archbishop's retraction at the eleventh hour from his earlier decision to cooperate for tactical reasons in a constitution.

The explosions on 29 February – the occasion of Lennox-Boyd's visit – were not an isolated incident. The intensive campaign long planned by Grivas had in fact begun. Two Greeks were killed on the same day and a member of the security forces seriously injured. On 3 March a Hermes aircraft was destroyed by a time bomb – the most ambitious sabotage operation yet undertaken by EOKA. But for an unforeseen delay in the scheduled departure time 68 passengers, serving troops and their families, would have died.

The Ethnarchy Council's deliberations remained a close secret during and long after the talks. The erosion of the Archbishop's control over EOKA, slow and insidious, was barely perceptible inside the guerrilla organisation itself, let alone to the colonial administration. The Governor and his advisers formed the impression that Makarios had no serious intention of coming to an agreement, that his offer to cooperate in self-government was a bait to obtain a commitment on self-determination from the British and that this concession, once granted, was simply a stepping-stone for further demands. The talks had begun in a spirit of cordiality and goodwill – a marked contrast to the flow of polemics normally associated with Makarios. But Harding was eventually disturbed, even angered, by the Archbishop's tactics: the shifting position and the equivocation which were the antithesis of the Field-Marshal's own frank and direct approach. Under the impression that Makarios was still in supreme control of all terrorist activities, the authorities saw the renewal of violence towards the end of the talks as a breach of faith on the Archbishop's part. Harding thus came to share the view of his advisers that the isolation of the Archbishop was essential to the restoration of order and as an indication that Britain was determined to resist Enosis.

This was not a sudden decision prompted by a mood of desperation on the part of the authorities on the breakdown of the talks. For many years they had looked upon the deportation of seditious clerics and the proscription of communist organisations as a suitable method of dealing with unrest, believing that such action had contributed to the calm which had lasted more than a decade after the 1931 riots. The Government's advisers had always been strongly divided in their assessment of the Archbishop's character and motives. Some leading Cypriots, on the right and on the left, saw his monopoly of political power as a serious threat to the island's progress and an anachronism in the twentieth century. Others close to the Ethnarchy tried to convince the British that behind the barrage of sedition and vituperation Makarios was at heart a man of peace and compromise. On the other hand it was argued logically enough that however benign a man he might seem behind the scenes it was his public attitude which determined the course of agitation in Cyprus. As early as 1953 certain British officials, convinced that no progress could be made in the establishment of self-government so long as Makarios remained in Cyprus, would have welcomed his removal before the extremists had time to build up a subversive movement. The Archbishop owed his prolonged freedom to his British nationality and to Whitehall's traditional reluctance to sanction the deportation of any colonial citizen from his native land except on a firm charge of incitement to violence. Once the EOKA rebellion had broken out his expulsion was only a matter of time and would have taken place sooner but for the search for a political settlement which began in July 1955 and ended seven months later.

The question of putting Makarios on trial, strongly advocated by the Government's critics, was promptly turned down by the authorities. This would have been calamitous whatever the outcome. The reluctance of Cypriots to testify against the head of the Church would have made his acquittal almost certain. On the other hand, the conviction of the Archbishop on a capital charge when lesser men in EOKA were being executed would have been a major embarrassment. His detention in Cyprus was ruled out on security grounds. The Government could easily have banned his return to the island during one of his many absences abroad, but this would have left him free to work against the British, especially in the USA and Greece, where he enjoyed popular support. The authorities decided that Makarios could only be effectively neutralised by banishing him to a remote territory where he could be held incommunicado.

VI

The Intensification of the Struggle March 1956 - March 1957

Archbishop's Deportation — His Release

I THE DEPORTATION

The failure of the Harding-Makarios talks ended for both sides the phase of limited military action. The first round in the next stage of the conflict, the intensification of hostilities, was opened by EOKA on 3 March with the sabotage of the Hermes aircraft at Nicosia airport. The deportation of Makarios six days later marked the start of an all-out offensive against EOKA. Both events were independent of each other and the direct outcome of the breakdown of the talks which Grivas had anticipated from the outset.

Archbishop Makarios was arrested on 9 March at Nicosia airport, shortly before he was due to take off for Athens, and deported to the Seychelles. The Bishop of Kyrenia, the secretary to the Kyrenia bishopric, Polykarpos Ioannides, the leader of OHEN and priest of the Phaneromeni Church, Papastavros Papathanghelou, were exiled with him.

The same day Sir John Harding described the Archbishop's presence in Cyprus as so detrimental to security that it could no longer be tolerated. This decision had been reached on the strength of information from many sources over recent months. The interests of Cyprus as a whole had compelled him to overlook the Archbishop's shameful record of complicity 'in the bloodshed, intimidation and tyrannous suppression of freedom of opinion', so long as there was hope that he might be induced to use his influence to lead his community back to peace and democratic rule. But Makarios had chosen instead to gain his ends by force and had repeatedly refused to condemn violence:

> He has remained silent while policemen and soldiers have been murdered in cold blood, while women and children have been killed and maimed by bombs, while a Cypriot woman was shot and wounded for the second time as she lay in hospital, recovering from a previous terrorist attack, and even while he stood by the coffin of an Abbot in his own church who was brutally murdered in his own monastery. His silence has understandably been accepted among his community as not merely condoning but even as approving assassination and bomb-throwing.[1]

Harding outlined the Archbishop's past seditious activities, his close contacts with the terrorists, his patronage of PEON, his allocation of church funds for the purchase of arms and explosives, and the use of the archbishopric for their storage – allegations which were beyond dispute. The authorities were, however, on weaker ground when, basing their conclusions mainly on his refusal to condemn violence and on the spate of bomb incidents at the end of the Harding talks, they accused the Archbishop of stepping up terrorism in order to increase his own bargaining power while apparently negotiating in good faith.[2]

The official case against the other three was as follows: the Bishop of Kyrenia, as a leading church dignitary, had 'repeatedly and publicly extolled terrorism, advocated bloodshed and incited the youth of Cyprus to violence' with the encouragement of Polykarpos Ioannides, author of many seditious semons and a persistent advocate of violence. Papastavros Papathanghelou, a leading instigator of the schoolboy riots in the summer 1955, had exercised a pernicious influence over Cypriot youth through OHEN and had frequently preached sedition in recent years.[3] The Bishop of Kyrenia, a more flamboyant exponent of violence than his leader, was an obvious danger to security. The same could be said of Papathanghelou. But Ioannides was a nonentity. Despite his open hostility to the British and an earlier conviction for sedition, his banishment was surprising when other Cypriots, equally guilty and infinitely more influential, remained at large.

Major riots broke out in Greece the next day. The deportation was condemned by the Greek Government as an act of violence incompatible

---

[1] *Terrorism in Cyprus*, op. cit. p. 81.
[2] ibid. p. 80.
[3] See text of official statement as published in the Cyprus Mail, 10 March 1956.

with current civilised standards.[1] In Turkey the news was warmly welcomed. The Prime Minister, Adnan Menderes, said that Britain had already gone too far in making concessions to the Archbishop.[2] The influential Istanbul newspaper *Ulus* commented that the deportation had come four years too late.[3] In Cyprus stringent security precautions forestalled an immediate major outbreak of violence, and local reaction followed the usual pattern of strikes and protests. On 15 March Athens Radio gave the political lead with a warning to the Cypriots that anyone willing to negotiate in the Archbishop's absence would be treated as a traitor,[4] and the Bishop of Kition announced that he would act temporarily for Makarios but would not cooperate with the British so long as his leader was in exile.

In Britain the deportation was, on the whole, well received by the press. 'Arrest and deportation are the mildest of punishments which could be meted out to so bad a shepherd,' wrote the Daily Telegraph. Once the talks had broken down, The Times commented, the deportation was unavoidable and those seeking to exculpate the Archbishop were 'skating on thin ice'. The Sunday Times and the Scotsman considered the measure overdue. The Manchester Guardian, however, in an editorial entitled 'Another Blunder', objected to the circumstantial nature of the evidence and predicted that the Archbishop's removal would make negotiations impossible.[5]

The Labour Party's reaction was one of unqualified hostility. Hugh Gaitskell immediately denounced the deportation as 'an act of folly'.[6] Elwyn Jones QC questioned its legality and urged the Government to put Makarios on trial.[7]

The Liberal Leader, Clement Davies, doubted whether Makarios was a real extremist.[8] The Colonial Secretary, Alan Lennox-Boyd, admitted that it was possible that there were people more extreme than Makarios in Cyprus. It might well be, he said, that the Archbishop had unleashed forces which he was not wholly able to control. But he could not be allowed to remain in the island while murders were being committed which he was in a position to prevent.[9]

[1] *Le Monde*, 12 March 1956.
[2] The Times, 15 March 1956.
[3] *Ulus*, quoted by *News From Turkey*, 22 March 1956.
[4] Daily Telegraph (Reuter), 15 March 1956.
[5] Daily Telegraph, Manchester Guardian, Scotsman, 10 March 1956; Sunday Times, 11 March 1956; The Times, 14 March 1956.
[6] Daily Telegraph, 10 March 1956.
[7] H.C. Deb., vol. 550, col. 447.
[8] ibid. cols 31–2 (Oral Answers).
[9] ibid. col. 32 (Oral Answers).

The House of Commons debated the subject for five hours on 14 March. The Socialists mainly based their attacks on the belief that the remaining three differences between Harding and Makarios could, with patience, have been bridged. The Irish amnesty of 1921 was advocated as a precedent for Cyprus. But the analogy, like many of the politicians' arguments, was false since this did not come into force until after the Dail ratified the peace treaty with Britain, whereas Makarios was making a general amnesty one of the conditions of a settlement with the British.

Aneurin Bevan attacked the Government for failing to inform the House on 5 February of the pending deportations. Kenneth Robinson described the action as 'this last incredible act of insanity' and asserted that Enosis was not a certainty.[1] Francis Noel-Baker praised Makarios: 'a sincere, patriotic, honest, moderate and very remarkable leader of his people.'[2]

The Prime Minister, Anthony Eden, refuted Bevan's suggestion that the Turks would be satisfied with NATO bases in Cyprus and stressed Britain's determination to protect her vital interests: 'The welfare and indeed the lives of our people depend on Cyprus as a protective guard and a staging post to take care of those interests, above all oil.'[3] Lennox-Boyd denied that the issues of public security, the amnesty and the elected majority had caused the breakdown of the talks. The real reason, he said, was the Archbishop's refusal to accept 'a very reasonable statement of policy' and to condemn violence.[4] The Opposition motion of censure on the Government's failure to reach a settlement and, in particular, its discontinuation of the talks about the points outstanding after the major issue of self-determination had been resolved was defeated by 317 to 251 votes.

In ecclesiastical circles the deportation caused an uproar. On 15 March the Archbishop of Canterbury, Dr Fisher, told the House of Lords that Christians everywhere were shocked and uneasy at Britain's action and that Makarios, although a politician, was also the head of a Christian church in which the religious leadership was identified with the struggle for freedom. He sympathised with Francis Noel-Baker's appreciation of the Archbishop's character but added that Makarios had, nonetheless, put himself seriously in the wrong. Fisher disclosed that he had written to Makarios in June expressing concern at the failure

[1] ibid. col. 423.
[2] ibid. col. 475.
[3] ibid. col. 421.
[4] ibid. col. 501.

of the Church authorities, and of the Archbishop in particular as the people's undisputed leader, to make a clear statement on the situation. He feared that this might give the impression that the Church supported the recent outrages. Makarios had replied that an official condemnation on his part was not likely at this stage to meet with the necessary response and would risk exposing himself 'rather unprofitably'. Finally Fisher proposed that a constitution should be drafted on the lines of the correspondence between Makarios and the Governor (in which there was a large amount of common agreement); that the Greek, Turkish and British Governments should appeal for the end of terrorism; and that Makarios should be informed that exile would end when violence ceased.[1] Dr Bell, the Bishop of Chichester, described the deportation as a blunder.[2] Dr Visser't Hooft, chairman of the World Council of Churches, feared that it would delay the unification of the Eastern and Western Churches.[3]

Much of the support for Makarios came from sources which were highly incongruous and can only be explained in the light of expediency and self-interest. Sympathisers of dubious sincerity included the Eastern Orthodox Patriarchs in Moscow and Belgrade,[4] the Roman Catholic minority in Athens,[5] and the Turkish chairman of the union of Muslims in Greece, who was reported to have stated that Makarios was doing no more than his 'patriotic duty'.[6]

Strong criticism from the British Socialists and the clerics was fully expected, but the reaction of the State Department, first made public on 12 March, came as a setback. The official spokesman, Lincoln White, emphasised that the Americans had no advance knowledge of the deportations. Until the present flare-up, he said, the US Government had been encouraged by the steady progress made towards a settlement and had hoped that basic agreements would be reached enabling the Cypriots to realise 'their legitimate desire in the establishment of a government truly representative of the people of the island'. The US Government was confident that a solution could be reached which would 'take into account and safeguard the legitimate interests of all the parties concerned'.[7]

The next day the American Ambassador in Athens, Cavendish

---

[1] H.L. Deb., 15 March 1956, vol. 196, cols 468–73.
[2] ibid. col. 508.
[3] *Le Monde*, 17 March 1956.
[4] ibid. 22 March and The Times, 23 April 1956.
[5] DNB, The Ministry of Foreign Affairs, Athens, 8 May 1956.
[6] ibid. 25 March 1956.
[7] The Times, 13 March 1956.

Cannon, was even blunter. After seeing Spyros Theotokis, the Greek Foreign Minister, Cannon praised the dignity and statesmanship shown by the Greek Government in dealing with the situation and expressed the 'sympathetic concern' of the Americans over recent developments in Cyprus. The progress already made on the lines of self-government had convinced him, he said, that a way could surely be worked out over details and timing, complicated as these might be.[1] Sir Roger Makins, the British Ambassador, requested an explanation. A shorter and milder version of the original statement reasserted that the US was not a party to the dispute and that further progress was possible, once conditions conducive to negotiations were restored.[2] Observers in Washington interpreted the US stand as a tacit appeal for the return of Makarios and a renewal of negotiations, but whatever the motive this public criticism of a close ally could hardly fail to encourage the Greek extremists to seek the reversal of British policy. The American action may be judged in perspective as a clumsy attempt to bolster up the Karamanlis Government rather than as a deliberate rebuff to Britain. The communist danger is likely to have been an overriding factor in the American attitude. Only a few days before the deportation a report was officially distributed in which Senator Armour wrote:

> The defense of Greece is important to the military and naval forces of the USA and Great Britain in that area and also to Turkey and the Straits. Greece in Communist hands would threaten the entire Middle East and would also endanger the security of Western Europe.
>
> The life of the pro-Western Government largely depends on a settlement of the Cyprus issue, and if this Government should fall, the coalition with pro-Communist representation would probably take its place.[3]

2   THE INTENSIFICATION OF HOSTILITIES

Colonel Grivas's reaction to the deportation was, according to his own account,[4] one of renewed determination to continue the struggle and of concern that the full burden, political and military, now fell on his

---

[1] Daily Telegraph and The Daily News Bulletin, Ministry of Foreign Affairs, Athens, 14 March 1956.

[2] Daily Telegraph, 14 March 1956.

[3] USA Senate Special Committee to study the Foreign Aid Programme, *Survey No. 1 Greece, Turkey and Iran* (US Government Printing Office, February 1957), p. 1169.

[4] General George Grivas-Dighenis, *Memoirs: The EOKA Struggle 1955–1959* (Greek edition, Athens, 1961), p. 94.

shoulders. Allowances, however, must be made for the fact that Grivas was prone to moods of martyrdom. The Archbishop's removal undoubtedly had advantages for EOKA. The indignation of the public created conditions conducive to violence. Grivas had a completely free hand in the conduct of operations, except for the tenuous long-range control exercised by the Greek Government through the Consulate-General in Nicosia. More important, the risk of a serious split inside EOKA as a result of the widening rift between the Archbishop and the Colonel was put into cold storage for an indefinite period.

In six months Grivas had transformed EOKA into a relatively efficient and complex underground movement, capable of disciplined and sustained action, in sharp contrast to the amateurishness of the early terrorists. The strength of the guerrillas in March was seven groups in the mountains, forty-seven in the towns and seventy-five village bands, part time and armed with shotguns.[1] EOKA was no longer dependent on explosives smuggled from abroad. Cypriot pharmacies sold without restriction the chemicals used in the manufacture of bombs. Another serious loophole in British security was the failure to close down the Greek-owned mines which became EOKA's main source of dynamite throughout the emergency.[2] But the shortage of arms was still acute.[3] The Greek Government had not given help on the scale Grivas expected. His original plan to make Rhodes a supply centre had fallen through thanks to the vigilance of the British Navy – the one branch of the security forces which was not vulnerable to penetration. The optimism of several EOKA members that arms would be readily forthcoming from the Arab countries, with their perennial hostility towards Britain, proved ill founded. Egypt was too far. Beirut was convenient, but the shipping agents there, so the Cypriots reported, turned out to be uncooperative. Commercial links with Britain presumably took priority over unprofitable national causes.

Shortly after the lifting of the security measures imposed during the deportation, EOKA resumed the offensive with the murder of P.C. Rooney on 14 March. On 22 March Neofytos Sophokleus put a bomb in Harding's bed. The plan was sanctioned by Grivas but Sophokleus, fearing imminent dismissal from Government House, did not wait for

---

[1] See *Memoirs* (Longmans), op. cit. pp. 66–7.

[2] The Manager of the American-owned Cyprus Mines Corporation (CMC) told the author in 1955 that not one stick of dynamite ever got into the hands of EOKA from his mine. The mine's security officer, a naturalised British subject of Yugoslav origin, was shot dead by terrorists in April 1956. See below, p. 175.

[3] Grivas wrote of the situation in January 1956 that '. . . supplies of arms from Greece were reduced to a mere trickle . . .'. See *Memoirs* (Longmans), op. cit. p. 63.

the Colonel's final instructions. He set the mechanism for the bomb to explode at 67°F in the early morning and failed to allow for the sharp drop in night temperatures and the English habit of sleeping with the windows open. When Harding's batman found the bomb the next day Sophokleus was on his way to the mountains, where he faced the wrath of Grivas.[1] In the second half of March fatal army casualties totalled five; several soldiers were seriously wounded. Six Greek Cypriots died. Three were shot dead in coffee shops and one in Kythrea church after masked gunmen had ordered the congregation to face the wall. The goodwill of foreign ecclesiastical circles was important to the struggle and EOKA promptly disclaimed responsibility for the last murder claiming that it was the work of British intelligence.[2] At the end of the month fifteen Turks and two Greeks were injured at Vasilia in the first serious intercommunal clash. A Turkish boy reported a Greek to the authorities for stoning army vehicles.[3] The Greeks attacked the Turkish community in retaliation. The incident set off disturbances in Nicosia in which Greek and Turkish property was damaged.

April began with the murder of the first English civilian. On 2 April Paphos schoolchildren incited by priests hurled bombs at British troops, who dispersed them with tear gas. During the month three soldiers were killed in ambushes. Greek civilian deaths rose to ten. One of the victims, Mr O. Wideson, an elderly anglophile, had survived two earlier attempts on his life. Two Greek Cypriot members of the police force were killed by gunmen. The murder of Assistant Superintendent Aristotelis in the maternity clinic where he had just visited his wife and newborn son angered the public. Cries for vengeance came from the crowds attending his funeral in Nicosia. EOKA's apologia took the form of a warning:

> Police Officer Kyriakos Aristotelis was rightly executed on my instructions . . . Some circles have branded the attack against Aristotelis in hospital as cowardly and immoral. This is foolish sentimentality . . . I have ordered the liquidation of all traitors whoever they may be. The supposed sanctity of places will not save them.[4]

Within forty-eight hours of the warning EOKA shot dead a Greek Cypriot employed by the army, and a naturalised British subject in charge of the CMC's security. On 27 April the weakness of British

[1] ibid. p. 69.
[2] EOKA leaflet, distributed in Kyrenia, 23 March 1956.
[3] *Greek Irredentism and Cypriot Terrorism*, op. cit. p. 120.
[4] EOKA leaflet 'Death to Traitors', distributed in Famagusta, 18 April 1956.

security was shown up for the second time in eight weeks with the destruction of a Dakota at Nicosia airport. A Greek Cypriot policeman working in the immigration office had put a bomb in the cockpit.[1] Towards the end of the month there was a renewal of intercommunal friction after two gunmen had fired at a policeman in Nicosia. A Turkish policeman in mufti who chased the assailants was shot dead. One of the gunmen was dragged off his bicycle by a Turkish girl and held down until the arrival of the security forces. News of the policeman's death spread rapidly through the Turkish quarter. Violent clashes broke out. EOKA killed a Turkish watchman; two Turks wounded a Greek. Much Greek property was damaged by arson. The next day the Turks demonstrated throughout the island but dispersed peacefully in response to their leaders' appeal for calm.

The campaign to crush EOKA called for equally strong action against the Orthodox Church – the inspiration and chief sponsor of the revolt. In the interests of security, religious services needed to be banned and the vast assets of the Church and monasteries impounded. Services were vital as communications and propaganda centres; Church assets assured the terrorists of a steady flow of funds. But in this respect the British authorities were hamstrung by the reactions of Western Christians ever ready to raise the cry of religious persecution. The new British offensive included large-scale military operations against the mountain strongholds, stringent countermeasures and punitive action which embraced an ever-widening circle of the general public. The guilty, the innocent and the indifferent alike paid dearly for each new incident, and citizens who were as yet uncommitted turned increasingly against the British. The traditional reluctance to give the authorities information added to the difficulties of tracing culprits. After Rooney's murder the Nicosia District Commissioner, Martin Clements, during an inquiry in Metaxas Square, condemned the residents for their silence and the bad record of the area, in which twenty-one incidents, classified either as murder or attempted murder, had taken place since November. A four-day curfew was imposed while paratroopers searched the houses one by one. The murder of Aristotelis was followed by the closure of Greek Cypriot restaurants and cinemas for one week; by a ban on all traffic inside the city walls during darkness and the suspension of athletic and race meetings. The same silence overshadowed the countryside. Kalopsidha, the scene of a recent ambush, was fined £1,000; Lapithos, where hooligans set the primary school alight and forced the fire brigade to retreat under a barrage of stones, £7,000. The villagers,

---

[1] See *Memoirs* (Longmans), op. cit. p. 68.

eager to cultivate their fields, usually paid up promptly rather than face indefinite curfews.

Grivas was at first seriously worried about the severity of the counter-measures. He had no confidence in the public's capacity for endurance and was obsessed with the notion that some spectacular action on EOKA's part was essential to bolster morale. Harding's assassination was still top priority, but after the fiasco with Sophokleus the Governor was no longer an easy target. Cypriot servants at Government House had been dismissed and there was a general tightening up of security. The guerrillas discussed in April the possibility of poisoning the milk for Government House before it left Athalassa Farm, and of ambushing Harding on the way to the English church which faced the Greek Consulate-General. But the first plot was likely to be discovered before the milk reached Harding since the kitchen staff used it first and the lethal action of potassium cyanide was instantaneous. The second idea was equally impracticable. Although heavily implicated behind the scenes in EOKA's activities, the Greek Consulate could not afford to be openly compromised by an ambush on its doorstep. The poisoning of the army's reservoirs was also seriously considered. Several plans were submitted to Grivas – some of them involving contraptions of dubious efficacy. The most efficient was drawn up by a high-ranking priest. He reported that he had already started collecting potassium cyanide and was in touch with men at the lithographic works who could provide the large quantities needed for the reservoirs. Alternatively, he could arrange for EOKA agents employed by the NAAFI to dissolve the chemical in the army's drinks or to sprinkle it in powder form over their food. This, he informed Grivas, would only require a small amount of cyanide and the danger to Cypriots and their livestock using the same reservoirs would be avoided. The poisoning of the enemy's water wells was normal practice in Byzantine times. But one of the Colonel's close advisers strongly objected to the use of these medieval tactics by EOKA. Apart from the danger to the Cypriots themselves, there was the question of the Organisation's image in international circles, where support for the cause was vital. Much to the regret of its sponsors the plan was dropped. Proposals that English children should be kidnapped as hostages were rejected for the same reason.

Strong rumours during April that several leading Cypriots were about to seek a compromise with the British increased the Colonel's fear of a possible collapse of public morale owing to the strain of Harding's policy. Grivas wondered whether it might not be safer to execute straight away the two distinguished Greek Cypriot businessmen associated with these reports, but he was dissuaded by an adviser who thought the action premature and likely to strengthen the British claim that EOKA was the sole barrier to a solution. About this time the Nicosia newspaper *Phos* wrote that Harding's policy would rapidly reduce Cyprus to economic ruin. The author called upon the Bishop of Kition to summon the political heads and four senior citizens as advisers to discuss the crisis. Since the British had made law and order a condition for the renewal of negotiations he urged Grivas to call a truce and the Turks to observe Kutchuk's recent appeal for restraint.[1] But the shadow of executions was far-reaching. The Bishop of Kition and the four citizens named by *Phos* promptly repudiated the proposals, two of them expressing surprise that they were mentioned in this connection. The bishop led the way in reasserting the nationalist stand of 'Makarios and only Makarios'.[2] The Ethnarchy Council and the Federation of Trade and Industry did likewise shortly afterwards.[3] And under the pressure of EOKA the doctors and the lawyers eventually made similar declarations. But the last word came from the Seychelles in the Archbishop's pastoral letter which survived the censorship and was posted up in every church in the island:

> We do not hide our grief and sorrow that we have been forcibly separated from the flock but we are sure that they know their shepherd and in the words of Christ, the Good Shepherd, 'the sheep will follow him because they know his voice and will not follow the stranger, but move away from him for they know not his voice'. . . .[4]

The modest move towards compromise was thus strangled at birth. The Colonel's anxieties, however, were not yet over. Papaioannou, the second communist detainee to escape in the past three months, had disappeared from Nicosia General Hospital in April. Other prominent Akelists, including Phantis and Ziartides, were still at large. Suspecting that they owed their freedom to the connivance of the British, Grivas ordered EOKA to keep a strict watch on all leftists. He was also gravely disturbed by the statesmanlike attitude of the Greek Foreign Secretary, Spyros Theotokis, in the handling of the Cyprus question. The Bishop of Kition reassured Grivas that the Ethnarchy was working relentlessly to bring about his downfall and that EOKA's intervention was not necessary.

[1] *Phos*: 'Sound the Alarm', quoted by the Cyprus Mail, 27 April 1956.
[2] Cyprus Mail, 28 April 1956.
[3] ibid. 30 April and 1 May 1956.
[4] Daily Telegraph, 4 May 1956.

Much of the Colonel's time was taken up by routine administration, the authorisation of funds for the purchase of weapons, the sanctioning of executions and the consideration of ideas sent in by the subordinates. Psychological and political warfare was not neglected. EOKA produced two main lines of propaganda – the one intended for its own members, the other for the general public. The object in both was to bolster morale and to sustain the grip of intimidation. Leaflets were written either in the style of a religious tract, likening the struggle to the suffering of Christ and the Resurrection, or in the form of an ultimatum threatening execution and reprisal in the case of any Cypriots daring to defy the Leader's wishes. The repeated demands for sacrifices indicated that by no means all Cypriots were ready to follow EOKA blindly. The people were encouraged to hope for early victory by wildly exaggerated figures for army casualties and fabricated reports on the failure of British operations against the terrorists. The denigration of the security forces fanned local resentment. This campaign was intensified after the trial by court martial of two army officers charged with ill-treatment.[1] In April EOKA ordered all members to collect information on tortures inflicted during interrogation for a 'Black Book' to be used against the British in international circles. The importance of accuracy on the part of the Cypriots making the reports was stressed.

The arrival of reinforcements after Harding's appointment was slow to make an impact on EOKA. The troops needed time to familiarise themselves with local conditions and build up an offensive. Until the late spring the five guerrilla groups based on Kykko Monastery moved freely; the couriers carried mail and messages without interruption; the monastery functioned as the main communications and supply centre. The situation began to change towards the end of April when the security forces launched the first stage in a major drive against the mountain gangs. On 18 April Grivas learnt at Kykko that extensive searches were shortly expected near the monastery. He left immediately on a long march for the district of Stavros Psokos and sent a courier to verify these reports. The courier came back within forty-eight hours

[1] War Office Statement, 11 May 1956: Captain G. O'Driscoll, Intelligence Corps, and Lieutenant (Temporary Captain) R. A. C. Linzee, Gordon Highlanders, were tried by General Court Martial at Nicosia, Cyprus, on 3–7 April 1956, and were found guilty of assault occasioning actual bodily harm and of conspiracy to prevent the course of public justice. Both officers were sentenced to be cashiered. The Commander-in-Chief Middle East Land Forces did not confirm the findings against Captain O'Driscoll on the charge of occasioning actual bodily harm. He commuted the sentence, in the case of each officer, to one of dismissal from Her Majesty's Service.

Each officer had been found not guilty and had been honourably acquitted of another charge or charges against him.

with the news that Kykko was quiet, but that large-scale operations were in progress on the far side of the island, near Pentadaktylos, east of Kyrenia. Twelve villages were under curfew in a cordoned area about ten miles long and four deep. It was likely that the operations would be extended to the Kykko forest. Grivas decided to thin out the Kykko groups before the troops reached the area. He sent two of them to positions near the Kambou river, and one to the north of Ano Panaghia. He himself moved with four men to a site close to the hideout of 'Ipsilantis' where they pitched their tents.

The danger of sudden searches called for greater mobility. Grivas ordered the guerrillas to study forest paths and ways of breaking out of a cordon, and to arrange new food storage hides to replace the monastery. Illness added to EOKA's problems at this time. Several of the guerrillas went down with appendicitis, including Afxentiou who urgently needed an operation, but was immobilised by troop movements. The courier system was upset by the interruption of bus services in the curfewed villages. The guerrillas had enjoyed conditions of relative safety for so long that their initial reaction to the sudden change was one of disarray. But they soon adjusted to the new situation and Grivas still managed to send and receive messages. Amongst his correspondence was a note from the Famagusta group leader reporting the capture of Private Ronald Shilton of the Royal Leicestershire Regiment. Grivas did not normally encourage the holding of hostages. They reduced mobility and were a nuisance to guard and feed. But on this occasion he told the group leader to treat his prisoner well and to keep him away from Famagusta. Throughout the crisis Grivas remained in touch with Nicosia. His link was 'Sebastianos', a woman in whose efficiency and reliability he had the utmost confidence. On 29 April he drove for several hours to a meeting place in the forest to discuss EOKA's immediate problems with her.

The first week in May was calm. The authorities warned the public that a general curfew would be imposed at the first sign of trouble. EOKA, anxious to avoid the disruption of the courier system owing to countermeasures, suspended action. The Orthodox Easter, in the circumstances a potentially explosive festival, was celebrated peacefully. But tension rose in the second week pending the fate of Karaolis and Demetriou. Grivas gave orders that in the event of their execution Shilton was to be killed as a reprisal and that all sectors must be ready to resume militant action. Meanwhile, the Famagusta group had grown fond of their prisoner. In pleading for his life they argued with Grivas that he could be useful to EOKA in propaganda work by means of broadcasts and letters to politicians and trade unionists in England. One of the guerrillas assured Grivas that he would prefer to kill himself rather than see Shilton die. The Colonel was unmoved. The long-awaited opportunity for spectacular action had come and he was determined to use it. After months of waiting, the appeal of Karaolis came up in mid-April before the Privy Council, which upheld the trial court's verdict. The decision over the death sentences could no longer be postponed. Hopes of an early settlement had faded with the collapse of the Harding-Makarios talks and with it the political climate favourable to a reprieve. Violence was now in the ascendancy and the Governor was committed to a strong policy. In the official view an act of mercy at this stage would have weakened the drive against EOKA. The news that the sentences would be carried out brought immediate retaliation from EOKA. An army officer was killed and another seriously wounded near Paphos. At the last minute the US Secretary of State, Foster Dulles, and the British Socialist, Fenner Brockway, tried to stop the executions. Karaolis and Demetriou were hanged in Nicosia Central Prison in the early hours of 10 May. The next day 'Dighenis' announced that EOKA had executed two corporals, Shilton and Hill. The same leaflet, addressed to British soldiers, regretted the necessity for the reprisal and urged them to write to their MPs, relatives and friends with the object of forcing the Tories under the pressure of public opinion to adopt the more sensible policy advocated by the Socialists and the Liberals.[1] The authorities treated the leaflets as a propaganda move. There was no evidence that the missing soldiers had ever been held and murdered by EOKA. The ranks of both men and the date given for Hill's absence from the army were incorrect[2] – a mistake which EOKA later admitted in a second leaflet[3] giving further identification details. But the authorities continued to dispute the authenticity of the claim.[4] In the wave of violence following the executions EOKA murdered a retired English colonel and made an abortive attack on the life of the manager of Barclays Bank in Limassol. At Nicosia airfield an RAF corporal was killed by three youths after he had given them the

[1] EOKA leaflet: 'To British Soldiers', distributed in Nicosia on 11 May 1956.

[2] See the official statements published by the Cyprus Mail, 13 and 30 May 1956, and H.C. Deb., vol. 553, cols 857–8, 5 June 1956.

[3] EOKA leaflet: 'To British Soldiers', distributed in Nicosia, 29 May 1956, and see *Summary of World Broadcasts* IV (BBC), 679, p. 9, 1 June 1956.

[4] Shilton's body was found a few feet below the ground at Prastio near Famagusta on 4 February 1957. The Famagusta group leader, Michael Rossides, was arrested on 22 March 1957, and charged with his murder. In his confession to the police, subsequently retracted in the trial, Rossides claimed close friendship with Shilton. He was found guilty on 5 June 1957 and sentenced to death, but was reprieved after the settlement in 1959.

glass of water they requested. Before the end of May five soldiers died in bomb attacks and one was shot dead in an ambush. Civilian casualties included an Englishman murdered in a Limassol bar and three Greek Cypriots. On 21 May, the day of island-wide memorial services for Karaolis and Demetriou, pandemonium broke out near Phaneromeni Church. Troops were faced by screaming schoolgirls, used by EOKA as a decoy. As the security forces tried to disperse the demonstrators a terrorist on a roof in Ledra Street threw a bomb into a Land-Rover, injuring two members of the police force. Forty-one incidents had taken place in the Old City during the past twelve weeks. Residents in the main trouble centre were given two days to remove their baggage before the security forces closed down thirty-five shops and eighteen houses – the most severe penalty yet imposed.

As the struggle between EOKA and the British worsened, the Turks became increasingly involved in strife with the Greeks. During the last week in May two Turkish policemen were killed in Paphos. In a clash at Larnaca six Greeks and seven Turks were injured. Armed with iron bars, sticks and stones, eighteen Greeks were stopped by the security forces on their way by bus from other villages to join the fight. At Aphania a pitched battle took place after the Turks had shot at Greeks in a coffee shop. The Greeks then attacked the Turkish sector. A Turkish auxiliary in the RAF police was killed; the security forces opened fire to restore order. After the funeral in Nicosia of P.C. Irfan Ali, who had died the night before from injuries suffered in the Ledra Street bomb attack on 21 May, serious rioting broke out in the Old City. The Turks set a Greek factory alight; a watchman on the premises was found battered to death. The Nicosia District Commissioner estimated the damage to Greek property at £4,400.[1] The authorities decided to separate the communities by a barbed wire barricade with five gates which could be closed at the start of intercommunal trouble.

3   THE ROUT OF THE MOUNTAIN GANGS

Early in May the security forces extended operations to the Troodos and Paphos Forests. These were directed by Brigadier Butler of the Parachute Regiment and based on preparatory work by the Royal Marine Commandos and the Gordon Highlanders permanently stationed in the area. They were joined by all branches of the security forces in a campaign to drive the guerrillas into a smaller area and to

[1] Cyprus Mail, 29 May 1956.

cut them off from the villages and other sources of supply. Use was made of helicopters and tracker dogs. Sea escape routes were patrolled by the Navy. The respite enjoyed by the guerrillas after the first scare at the end of April was, in consequence, short-lived. In May Grivas set up a command post at Mavros Gremnos in the heart of the Paphos Forest. The guerrillas were under growing pressure and constantly on the move, yet EOKA's courier system remained intact. During this period Grivas exchanged correspondence with the subordinates on arrangements for the importation of arms in suitcases through the Limassol customs.[1] He dealt with requests for fuses of long duration and a compensation claim for £10 by a youth who lost his bicycle on an EOKA errand, and authorised the payment of £5 10s to a terrorist as expenses for the execution of a traitor.

In the middle of the month Grivas was warned that extensive searches were expected in the areas of Lysi, Lefka and Vretcha. The guerrillas' sense of insecurity grew daily with reports of new searches and the imminent arrival of troops in the vicinity of the hides. Grivas gave orders that the sector leaders were to stage demonstrations in the towns and villages in order to pin down soldiers who might otherwise be sent as reinforcements to the mountains. On 16 May he saw 'Ipsilantis' for an hour and told him how to get out of encirclement. The next day the courier reported that there were twelve stationary army trucks on the road leading to Kykko and Panaghia. Troops were heading for the hideouts and had occupied the monastery; the delivery of letters was impossible. Many guerrillas were stuck in their hides.

During the third week the security forces changed tactics and concentrated on a smaller area; even dung heaps were uncovered. Foot patrols moved into the forest by night, often marching many miles across thickly wooded, steep terrain to reach their objectives. The news grew worse daily. Three guerrillas had been captured with their weapons; several monks at Kykko had been arrested. The nightmare of betrayal inside EOKA itself had become a reality. On 22 May 'Asklypios', the Kykko agent, reported that one of the captives had pointed out all the hides to the security forces from a helicopter. 'Asklypios' asked Grivas to arrange a new forwarding centre for mail since it was impossible to use Kykko. The next day a courier from the monastery informed Grivas that intensive searches were taking place near the EOKA camps north of Kykko and that 'Asklypios' feared they

---

[1] A total of 43 light automatics, 12 pistols, bullets, grenades, time pencils, etc. were imported up to October 1956 in suitcases through Limassol with the connivance of the customs. See *Memoirs* (Longmans), op. cit. p. 108.

would soon reach the EOKA Leader's area. Grivas considered the possibility of avoiding encirclement by moving south via the secondary road out of Panaghia but he decided to obtain information on the local position from 'Athanatos' and 'Ipsilantis' before finalising his own plans. But Styllis reported that 'Ipsilantis' had deserted his camp in haste without even notifying the intermediary at Panaghia responsible for informing 'Athanatos'. On his return, Styllis was injured in the leg by an army patrol. Grivas cleaned the wound and Markos Drakos came to inject him with penicillin. This day Grivas described as the worst so far in the struggle.[1] He was cut off from all the sections and without information. The next day 'Asklypios' and 'Sebastianos' were arrested. After re-establishing the link with Nicosia and the food suppliers on 27 May, Grivas decided to break out of the cordon and sent for Antonis Georghiades, the Milikouri leader, who knew the countryside well. He arranged to move that night with Georghiades and Pavlis. Yiangos, 'Akritas' and Styllis, who was still lame, were to follow the next morning. Rough, uneven terrain, covered in thick undergrowth broken by steep precipices, added to the hazards of the long march through the night. The least sound, a falling stone or a lump of earth, could have given their position away to a patrol lying in ambush. After seventeen hours across country they reached Diplis exhausted and camped there for two weeks. Originally the Colonel hoped to set up a new hideout at Aghia Arkha and then move on to the Limassol district. On 3 June Georghiades, after inspecting the site, reported that it was unsuitable. The Colonel spent the next few days looking for other hideouts without success.

On 8 June Grivas was woken at 2 a.m. by the barking of a police dog near the hide. His group immediately left for a nearby hill. From here they saw soldiers on the Milikouri road and with them the traitors 'Botsaris' and 'Bouboulis'. After a long march the guerrillas reached the heights above the junction of the Kykko–Ano Panaghia and the Milikouri–Peravassa roads.[2] Grivas decided to strike out in the direction of Limassol. The group crossed the road at dusk and spent the night in the hills south of the road having first made sure that the area was free of large-scale operations. Disturbed by heavy gunfire from the Kykko direction, they moved to a new position early next day. At sunset they crossed out of the cordoned area and stayed overnight in the relative safety of the wooded country to the east. On 10 June they left at dawn in the direction of Aghia Arkha. Early in the afternoon they stopped in

[1] See *Terrorism in Cyprus*, op. cit. p. 30.
[2] ibid. p. 40.

a well wooded valley to fill their water bottles and rest in the shade. At this moment a patrol from the Parachute Regiment and a tracker dog came up along the bed of the stream. The six guerrillas vanished through the bushes under heavy automatic fire, leaving behind all their weapons and some of the Colonel's personal belongings including his binoculars and spectacles. On reaching the heights above the stream the guerrillas saw soldiers coming from all directions. The group split into pairs and hid in the undergrowth all day. They had no food. Grivas decided to take a chance at dusk on finding a gap in the cordon. When they arrived on the slopes above the river Platys the next day they found that the road along the river was unguarded. They crossed over and arrived in the hills south-west of Kaminaria before dawn. Georghiades fetched food from the village and they spent the night and the next day hiding on the outskirts. On the evening of 12 June Georghiades and Nikitas went to get food for the onward journey, but were fired on by a patrol outside the village. After a lengthy detour they rejoined the group unharmed but empty-handed. They left immediately for Trooditissa, five miles away, and arrived there the following afternoon. There was a patrol near the monastery, but no troops inside. Georghiades and his companion got into the building by a back door. A monk set out at once for Nicosia with a message from Grivas for Lefkosiades only to learn from the radio in a village that the archimandrite had been arrested. The abbot gave the two guerrillas clothes and food and they returned to pick up the Colonel and the rest of the group, who awaited them at a safe distance. In the evening they crossed the main Troodos–Platres road. Early the next morning they reached the southern slopes of Troodos where they rested in the forest until nightfall, when they left for Saitta. Here they met the Limassol District leader, Hadjimiltis, who undertook to find Grivas and Georghiades a hideout in Limassol. On 17 June Grivas disbanded the group. Yiangos and Styllis went to join the Xeros guerrillas. Nikitas eventually returned to Limassol, Kafkallides to his village, Agros. That evening Grivas and Georghiades left for Yerasa via Aghios Mamas. At midnight on 18 June they approached the outskirts of Palodhia, where an EOKA man was ready to organise their move to Limassol. But the possibility of betrayal weighed heavily on the Colonel's mind. Afraid that the persistent barking of the village dogs would give their presence away, he returned with Georghiades to Yerasa for the night. The following evening they were driven to Limassol by a Greek Cypriot police inspector.

The search for Grivas and the escaped guerrillas went on inside the cordon for several weeks. On 12 June 'Ipsilantis' and his gang of six were captured. A few days later a fire broke out in the Paphos Forest. With a sudden change of wind, the flames swept up the valley where army vehicles were parked. Many soldiers were trapped within range of exploding petrol tanks. Twenty died and sixteen were seriously burnt. The reluctance of the army, for security reasons, to allow the villagers to help at the start contributed to the rapid spread of the flames and the delay in bringing them under control. Brigadier Baker (later Field-Marshal Sir Geoffrey Baker), the Chief of Staff, accused the guerrillas of starting the fire to facilitate their own escape.[1] EOKA made counter-accusations that British troops were responsible for the disaster.[2] Malicious rumours circulated in the villages that the soldiers set the forest alight in order to smoke the guerrillas out of their hides. The use of mortars must certainly have added to the seasonal hazards of fire during the driest months of the year. But the report of the official inquiry was inconclusive and stated that there was no definite evidence to show whether the fire was deliberately started by EOKA to create a diversion or accidentally by the troops in the pursuit of their duties.[3]

The Troodos operation finished at the end of June. Searches on a reduced scale continued throughout the summer and were extended to the northern Kyrenia Range and the Karpas but without spectacular results. In the main offensive about 2,000[4] troops had taken part in a cordoned area of 400 square miles. Most of the mountain gangs were broken up and their network disrupted beyond recovery as a central base for the direction of EOKA operations. The security forces captured seventeen leading guerrillas and recovered large quantities of weapons. Thousands of documents had fallen into the hands of the British which exposed the Organisation's plans and the identities of its members and numerous collaborators. The EOKA Leader was driven into permanent hiding, immobilised and unable ever again to take part in combatant duties. His narrow escape was unfortunate in that it gave a boost to Cypriot morale by helping to perpetuate the legend of invincibility. But it is questionable whether his capture in the summer of 1956 would have substantially altered the course of the struggle. At the start Grivas was indispensable. Without his dogged persistence, his utter ruthlessness, the revolt would never have got off the ground. But once the

[1] Cyprus Mail, 18 June 1956.
[2] EOKA leaflet: 'The Incendiaries', distributed in Nicosia, 24 July 1956.
[3] Cyprus Mail, 19 July 1956.
[4] In addition to those mentioned on p. 182, units from the following took part: The King's Own Yorkshire Light Infantry, the South Staffordshire Regiment, the Royal Norfolk Regiment, the Royal Horse Guards, the RAF Regiment and a small naval landing party from HMS *Diamond*.

machinery of terrorism had been set in motion it could freewheel under the force of its own momentum. The pressure of the security forces in the spring had already forced Grivas to delegate responsibility to the sector leaders, who were now capable of acting on their own initiative. Grivas had recognised that Cyprus was unsuitable for guerrilla warfare based on the countryside. The mountain groups had nevertheless served their purpose. They bestowed upon the revolt the aura of 'Resistance' and conjured up in the Cypriot mind the heroic epic of the Greek War of Independence in a way in which urban terrorism, more generally associated with gangsterism and common crime, could never have done.

Meanwhile Grivas had set up headquarters in the house of a Limassol businessman, Dafnis Panaghides. By the end of June he was in correspondence with Nicosia and able to direct EOKA's affairs through the courier system from his host's house.

The arrest of 'Sebastianos' and other leading members of EOKA caused chaos in the guerrilla administration. Grivas was once again obliged to deal with routine matters which fell far outside the scope of a military leader's normal duties. When the pregnant wife of an EOKA prisoner needed to go into a maternity clinic it was the Colonel who granted the request. When a large sum of money was lost in transit it was he who investigated the loss and reprimanded those concerned for their carelessness in failing to seal letters up correctly. The worst muddles had arisen in EOKA's finances owing to the replacement of 'Sebastianos' by a woman in Nicosia with no flair for accountancy. Exasperated by her lack of method, Grivas took over the accounts himself, to find that family allowances had been paid out of the EOKA central fund instead of from a special fund set aside for the purpose. The failure of the subordinates to send in their claims on the 15th of each month, in accordance with his orders, had resulted in a huge backlog of arrears. Grivas, who bitterly resented such digressions from the all-important work of military planning, persevered for two months in trying to train the new assistant by correspondence. She was arrested by the British just in time to be spared the humiliation of dismissal from her post by the Colonel.

On the military side, the first task was the reorganisation of the escaped guerrillas into new mountain groups. Drakos, who had fled from Lefka, was joined at his old site near Kykko by men from the disbanded groups of Antonis Georghiades. The others were based on the Tylliria, Pakhna and Omodhos.

The sectors obeyed the Leader's orders to carry out diversionary action. The collapse of the mountain gangs was not followed by an early decline in violence in the rest of the island. In June the funeral of a Turkish auxiliary policeman in Famagusta set off a fresh wave of intercommunal unrest in which the Turks set Greek Cypriot property on fire. Two Englishmen, a schoolteacher and a police officer, were shot dead and Mr Justice Shaw was seriously wounded by gunmen. Six soldiers died, three of them from injuries caused by an electrically detonated mine. Two Greeks were killed by grenades and one by an axe. Six were shot dead. On 16 June EOKA threw a bomb into a restaurant, killing the American Vice-Consul. 'Dighenis' apologised for this 'tragic mistake'[1] and advised foreigners to keep away from places frequented by the British, since it was difficult to distinguish between them. More than seventy bomb explosions were recorded – mainly in the towns and near army camps. During July three British servicemen and a Maltese policeman were killed. An English customs official and his wife were murdered in an ambush on the lonely Kantara pass. Eleven Greek Cypriots lost their lives.

In the first two weeks of August, gunmen killed a British police sergeant, twelve Greek Cypriots and a Turkish civilian. Zakos, Michael and Patatsos were under sentence of death. It was consistent with the EOKA Leader's adherence to the dictum 'an eye for an eye, a tooth for a tooth'[2] that he should have ordered the abduction of three soldiers as hostages. But the plan failed.[3] For want of military victims the Kyrenia group seized a retired British official, Mr Cremer, on his way to the Turkish hamlet of Temblos where he sometimes taught English, and bundled him into the boot of a car. Grivas threatened to execute him unless the convicted men were reprieved.[4] Zakos, however, made a dramatic appeal from prison for the old man's release and he was dumped on a deserted stretch of road near Karavas. The three terrorists were hanged on 9 August. But the expected reprisals against the British did not take place. Instead, on 16 August, Grivas declared the suspension of operations, giving as a reason his wish to create an atmosphere of peace in which negotiations for a political settlement could be resumed with Makarios.

[1] See *Memoirs* (Longmans), op. cit. p. 72, text of leaflet.
[2] EOKA leaflet: 'Communiqué', distributed at Kalavassos, 16/17 May 1956: 'Moderate measures are of no use in a Liberation struggle. Corporals Gordon Hill and Ronnie Shilton paid for the dishonesty of the English leadership and of the murderer Harding....'
[3] See *Memoirs* (Longmans), op. cit. p. 85.
[4] EOKA leaflet: 'Announcement', distributed in Nicosia on 3 August 1956. This described Cremer as a high-ranking agent of British military intelligence. (This elderly citizen had never served in Cyprus but his friendship with some of the Turks living near his home was sufficient to arouse Grivas's suspicions.)

The public was weary of curfews, made almost unbearable by the intense summer heat, and the guerrillas needed a breathing space. Faced with a gesture on the part of EOKA, which was certain to be seen as conciliatory by the world outside, it was difficult for the Cyprus authorities to continue full-scale operations.

4 POLITICAL EVENTS AFTER THE DEPORTATION

The controversy over the deportation persisted for weeks, and at the end of April brought the Government into open conflict with the Archbishop of Canterbury. At a meeting of the British Council of Churches he complained that six weeks had lapsed since his proposals[1] to the House of Lords and that, as far as was known, the Government had not come forth with any constructive plan. He had direct evidence, he said, that the moderates in Cyprus welcomed his suggestions.[2] The Council adopted a resolution supporting Dr Fisher's plan but came closer to the official view in appealing for the end of violence and in regretting the Cypriot Church leaders' failure to condemn terrorism.[3]

R. A. Butler and John Boyd-Carpenter reproved Dr Fisher for his 'unhelpful' intervention with a sharp reminder that no one was willing to come forward while terrorism lasted. Boyd-Carpenter added that if Dr Fisher knew of such moderates, he should encourage them to contact the Governor who was only too ready to discuss the problem with responsible Cypriots.[4]

At the end of May, from the pulpit of St Paul's Cathedral, Canon Collins called upon the congregation to support Fisher's proposals, to unite for the purpose of obtaining Makarios's unconditional release and, if necessary, to use their political rights to force an election to be fought mainly on this issue.[5]

The volume of ecclesiastical protest made little impact on the Government. On the contrary its attitude towards the Orthodox clergy progressively hardened. Early in June the Prime Minister, Anthony Eden, prompted by the discovery of pistols in the Paphos bishopric, condemned the Cypriot clergy for their complicity in violence.[6] The Minister of Defence, Duncan Sandys, blamed the island's troubles on 'a campaign of hate inspired and inflamed by a body of

[1] See above, p. 172.
[2] The Times, 25 April 1956.
[3] Full text supplied by courtesy of the British Council of Churches.
[4] The Times, 28 April 1956.
[5] ibid. 28 May 1956.
[6] ibid. 2 June 1956.

priests' who did not shrink from 'aiding and abetting deliberate murder to promote their political aims'.[1]

On 12 June Archimandrite Makhereotis, priest of the Greek Orthodox church in Camden Town, was arrested and put on an aeroplane for Athens. A naturalised Greek subject of Cypriot birth, Makhereotis had served as a Greek army chaplain during the communist rising in Greece at the end of the Second World War. Unlike his parishioners, he had little to lose by expulsion from Britain. The London Cypriots, though ready to pay lip-service to Enosis when occasion demanded, were primarily anxious to avoid action likely to damage their trade[2] and their rights as British citizens. Nevertheless, by the summer pamphlets aimed at whipping up Enosis agitation and published by the Greek Ministry of Foreign Affairs were to be found in the dustbins of Soho. And the possibility of EOKA action in England was strongly rumoured. The police had reason to suspect that the Cypriot community was being subjected to severe pressure.

The Home Secretary, Major Lloyd George, stated that Makarios had authorised the archimandrite to form a committee to collect funds in aid of 'the national struggle' and that the Cypriot church had been used as a centre for anti-British propaganda.[3] Heated exchanges took place between the Home Secretary and Archbishop Athenagoras, head of the Greek Church in Western Europe. Accusing the police of totalitarian methods, Athenagoras claimed that, as the priest's superior, he should have been informed of his arrest and deportation. Lloyd George expressed surprise at Athenagoras's comments on the English police. They merely carried out the orders of the Home Secretary, who alone was responsible. He disagreed, moreover, that action of this kind could not be taken against a person in holy orders without reference to his superiors. Foreign priests had no diplomatic privileges or special status, Major Lloyd George added, and like any other foreigners they could not expect to be allowed to indulge in activities inimical to the country whose hospitality they enjoyed.[4]

On arrival in Athens the archimandrite played on the Anglican bishops' fears that relations between the Orthodox Church and the Church of England would deteriorate and claimed that the funds were solely for the 'victims of the struggle'. He never expected, he said, that a liberal country like Britain would treat a priest as a criminal.[5]

[1] ibid. 11 June 1956.
[2] Some Cypriots, fearing a boycott, went so far as to change the Greek names of restaurants.
[3] H.C. Deb., vol. 554, cols 578–80.
[4] See H.C. Deb., vol. 554, col. 1606 (Oral Answers), Lloyd George's letter to Athenagoras.
[5] *Cyprus Mail*, 13 June 1956.

Aneurin Bevan and Kenneth Robinson upheld the archimandrite's complaints of arbitrary arrest and totalitarian methods.[1] Francis Noel-Baker challenged the Government to produce evidence that Makhereotis was connected with the murder of British soldiers in Cyprus.[2] The Bishop of Chichester expressed uneasiness at the lack of proof that the funds were in aid of anything other than relief.[3] Lena Jeger was worried about the hardships of the families.[4] The difference in the position of the detainees' families and those of captured or dead terrorists was not understood in England. The first category was entitled to government aid, the second depended on EOKA funds. From the security angle any action which struck at EOKA's financial resources was sound. Charitable donations used to ease civilian hardship merely reduced EOKA's liabilities towards its own dependants and supporters, thus leaving the Organisation with more money for military projects. Grivas, in fact, decided about this time to stop payments to the detainees' families because their needs were adequately met by the Cyprus welfare department. The Government finally placed in the Library of the House of Commons two Cypriot documents which can have left little doubt as to the true aim of the archimandrite's activities. And except for renewed protests on the part of Francis Noel-Baker,[5] the subject was dropped.

On the political front the situation was one of total deadlock. Both sides were entrenched in rigid positions – the British adamant that the renewal of negotiations with Makarios could serve no useful purpose, the Ethnarchy insistent that no talks could take place in his absence.

The clergy were not alone in urging a change of government policy. In lay circles it was the Labour Opposition which exerted the greatest pressure. The debate[6] on 14 May, the second since the deportation, was again initiated by the Socialists. They condemned the executions and criticised the Government for breaking off the talks when, as they claimed, agreement was near. They underrated, as usual, the Turkish factor. The one exception was Reginald Paget. 'I am convinced', he said, 'that Enosis – that is what is meant by "self-determination" in this context . . . will be resisted by armed force by the local Turks, and the local Turks will be supported by the Turks from the mainland

---

[1] H.C. Deb., vol. 554, cols 579–81.
[2] ibid. col. 581.
[3] H.L. Deb., vol. 197, cols 1115–17.
[4] H.C. Deb., vol. 554, cols 1602–3.
[5] ibid. vol. 556, col. 1434, 19 July 1956.
[6] ibid. vol. 552, cols 1653–1750.

with sufficient force to enable them to win.'[1] James Griffiths, the Party's deputy leader, urged the Government to give the Cypriots a clear promise of self-determination; to bring Makarios to London and to invite Ethnarchy's representatives to come there.[2]

The most significant statement to come out of the debate was the undertaking given by Griffiths that Labour on its return to power would grant the Cypriots self-determination five years after the adoption of a constitution whatever the circumstances prevailing at the time.[3]

The Government was faced with a plethora of formulas, both in and outside Parliament. Most of them were either impracticable in the circumstances or merely amounted to measures that had already been tried without success. The Cyprus Conciliation Committee, composed mainly of Socialists,[4] advocated that an all-Parliamentary Commission should seek ways of reopening the talks. Violence would not cease, the Committee believed, until the Government declared its intention to resume negotiations only on the basis of self-government and guaranteed self-determination. Francis Noel-Baker was more realistic. His plan provided for an elected Greek majority in a liberal constitution, a fixed date for self-determination, strong safeguards for the Turkish minority and the concentration of the military bases in one enclave to remain indefinitely under British sovereignty whatever the final status of the island.[5]

The controversy in England over the deportation was encouraging for the Cypriot leaders. They were anxious to forestall the new constitutional plan which Britain was shortly expected to announce. And in June they stepped up the campaign for the Archbishop's release and the renewal of the talks. Nikos Kranidiotis, the Ethnarchy secretary, suddenly arrived in London at the invitation of Francis Noel-Baker. A few days later the Ethnarchy released the text of a letter[6] from Makarios to Noel-Baker. His Beatitude wrote that when the talks collapsed the gulf between himself and Harding was not wide and that the breakdown was due to the British refusal to guarantee an overall Greek majority in the legislative assembly. The letter, though characteristically vague, was generally taken to mean that Makarios was willing to resume the talks at the point where they had been broken off. Kranidiotis claimed

[1] ibid. cols 1668–9.

[2] ibid. cols 1666 and 1668.

[3] ibid. col. 1733.

[4] The Committee included several Liberals and one Conservative, William Yates.

[5] Cyprus Mail, 18 June 1956.

[6] Dated the Seychelles, 13 May 1956; see Cyprus Mail 14 June and Manchester Guardian 15 June 1956.

that there were no longer any serious differences between the Ethnarchy and the British Government. The only substantial disagreement at the time of the breakdown of the talks with Harding – the question of the elected majority – had in the meantime been resolved. Any settlement, however, must be reached through the Archbishop, who could not under any circumstances negotiate in exile. Cyprus was preferable, but London might be acceptable as a compromise. The Noel-Baker proposals were a basis for discussion, he said, but he did not believe that the military installations should remain under British sovereignty forever.[1] His optimism was not endorsed by Greek Government circles. It was significant that the amnesty and public security, which had proved such thorny issues during the Harding-Makarios talks, were barely mentioned. This shift in emphasis on the part of the Cypriot nationalists was a shrewd tactical move which brought their views into alignment with those of socialist sympathisers in Britain. The impression of reasonableness and moderation was, however, to some extent marred by a letter in The Times on 20 June in which Kranidiotis wrote that the Cyprus question was one of self-determination. And his mission came to an abrupt end.

The British Government ignored the Cypriot move and remained unshaken in its view that any negotiations with Makarios were useless so long as EOKA had the upper hand. Harding, with full Cabinet approval, had repeatedly opposed the renewal of talks with the Archbishop. It was much better to negotiate with a representative group, he said early in June, and more in keeping with modern democratic procedure, than to confine oneself to one individual no matter how wise and experienced he might be.[2]

After the deportation it was the military struggle which dominated the headlines. The political and diplomatic activity that went on behind the scenes tended to escape notice. And the Government was frequently accused of political inertia.

Harding returned to London in June for consultations, having reached the conclusion that no lasting solution was possible so long as the final status of Cyprus was uncertain. For the first time since 1915 the surrender of British sovereignty was seriously contemplated by the Cabinet. This bold departure from previous policy took the form of a plan for a settlement based on self-determination. The proposals, which were submitted to Turkey, provided for ten years of limited self-government under British rule; for a national referendum at the end of

[1] Cyprus Mail, 18 and 22 June 1956, and Manchester Guardian, 21 June 1956.
[2] Daily Telegraph and Cyprus Mail, 19 June 1956.

this period, subject to NATO's approval, to determine the island's final status by a two-thirds majority; and for the permanent retention of military bases under the sovereignty of Britain which would be responsible for the defence of Cyprus. Anglo-Turkish relations had been severely strained as the result of the Harding-Makarios talks. The Turks considered that concessions to the Greeks had already gone too far, and that the current plan went still further in meeting their demands. It left the door open to Enosis; the involvement of NATO was an inadequate safeguard since no one could envisage that organisation's position so far ahead; a permanent British presence was by no means a certainty in view of Britain's post-war record of progressive retrenchment from her overseas commitments;[1] and finally the Turks did not trust the Greeks to honour any treaty arrangements related to Cyprus. The finality of Turkey's rejection, which came at the end of June, made it pointless to show the plan to Greece. The details were never officially disclosed. But the essentials were extensively reported by the international press,[2] and it was assumed that the overall majority in the assembly would be Greek.

The Turkish Cypriot leader, Dr Kutchuk, told the press in Istanbul on 21 June that the Turkish minority was absolutely opposed to self-determination and only willing to accept self-government on a basis of equality with the Greeks.[3] Any plan for Greek majority representation, he said a few days later in Nicosia, was 'a hangman's noose around the neck of the Turks'.[4]

The rejection of the plan was immediately followed up by two important official Turkish statements. The surrender of Cyprus either now or in future, the Foreign Minister, Etem Menderes, said on 29 June, would jeopardise the treaty of Lausanne. The Turks were content that British rule should continue but could not countenance the island's annexation by a power not noted for its stability and which might not be able to resist the encroachment of communism.[5] On 2 July the Prime Minister, Adnan Menderes, gave this warning:

Britain must remain firm and strong. We look to her to maintain her position in the Mediterranean and the Middle East. If she relinquishes

[1] Professor Ahmet Esmer had recently drawn attention to British precedents for giving up the Empire, pointing out that Britain could easily give up Cyprus. *The Week*, 20 April 1956.
[2] Daily Telegraph, 18 June 1956; The Times, 19 June 1956; Christian Science Monitor, 20 June 1956.
[3] Daily Telegraph, 22 June 1956.
[4] The Times, 27 June 1956.
[5] Daily Telegraph, 30 June 1956.

positions she holds, chaos will ensue not only for Turkey but
for the whole Western World. After that, Soviet penetration of the
whole vast area will be an accomplished fact.

Greece had never exercised sovereignty over Cyprus, Menderes added.
She had not hesitated to endanger the future of NATO or the Balkan
Pact, and was not alone in having a public opinion. Turkey was un-
willing to discuss any plans for self-government while terrorism supported by Greece continued.[1]

The sharpness of Turkey's reaction came as a shock to the British
Government. From now on Conservative ministers were at pains to
emphasise the importance of the Turkish alliance and the island's
strategic value. On 7 July Selwyn Lloyd stressed Turkey's vital interest
in Cyprus which lay only forty miles from her coast and covered her
southern ports, and he repeated Eden's recent warning that the indus-
tries of Britain and Western Europe depended on Middle East oil.[2]
There must be no doubt as to the availability of the Cyprus bases for
their defence, Selwyn Lloyd said.[3]

The Prime Minister told the House of Commons on 12 July that
Britain in a new approach had accepted the principle of self-determination, but that its application raised far wider issues for Turkey as a
signatory of the treaty of Lausanne. Since international agreement had
proved impossible, the British Government was going ahead with plans
for self-government and Lord Radcliffe would leave for Cyprus the
next day to start work on a constitution, but this would not be introduced until terrorism was defeated.[4]

Hugh Gaitskell, in a confused assessment of the situation, recognised
that the failure of the negotiations with Turkey made international
agreement impossible. But he blamed terrorist activity in Cyprus on
the Government's refusal to give a firm undertaking to implement self-
determination.[5] Clement Davies condemned the Government for
yielding to 'Turkish blackmail'.[6]

Lord Radcliffe arrived in Cyprus on 13 July to make a preliminary
survey. The Greek Cypriot leaders, on orders from the Ethnarchy and
EOKA, stated that they were not willing to meet him or to take part in

[1] ibid. 2 July 1956 (interview with Anthony Mann).
[2] Eden's speech, Norwich: 'No oil, unemployment and hunger in Britain. It is as simple as that today.' The Times, 2 June 1956.
[3] Observer, 8 July, and Manchester Guardian, 9 July 1956.
[4] Policy Statement. H.C. Deb. vol. 556, cols 595–602.
[5] ibid. cols 598–9.
[6] ibid. col. 600.

constitutional discussions as long as Makarios was in exile. The restriction must have been irksome in the extreme. Sociable and naturally hospitable, the Cypriots like nothing better than an opportunity to air their grievances with distinguished visitors. Despite the pressure of EOKA, the mayors finally agreed to see Radcliffe on condition that only municipal problems were discussed.

At the Opposition's request the Cyprus question was debated on 19 July – the fourth time in four months.[1] The Socialists vigorously attacked the Government for abandoning self-determination under pressure from Turkey. Aneurin Bevan advised the Cypriots to stop violence because it was both the proper and 'the most ingenious thing to do', since the Government would then be deprived of all excuses for not pressing ahead with a settlement.[2] On the Government side, two significant new trends were perceptible: Selwyn Lloyd's indication that any Greek proposals acceptable to Turkey and Greece would be sympathetically received by Britain;[3] and the first British official references to partition, a study of which, Walter Elliot stated, should come within Radcliffe's terms of reference.[4] Julian Amery warned the House that a rigid adherence to the doctrine of self-determination could only lead to the division of the island.[5]

In the House of Lords on 25 July Attlee scorned the idea that Cyprus had any strategic value in the hydrogen bomb era or was a potential threat to the Turks: 'It would be utter madness for anyone who wanted to attack Turkey to do it from Cyprus.'[6] He begged the Government to make a fresh approach through NATO, failing that to bring back Makarios. Lord Lloyd, the Under-Secretary of State for the Colonies, reminded the Socialists that they had not yielded to the demand of self-determination, even when there was no problem of violence. It was still more important not to do so now.[7] The Archbishop of Canterbury, for once constructive, said it was essential for the time being to drop all references to this explosive term.[8] Listowel's exposition of Labour's attitude to self-determination[9] must have seemed disconcertingly vague

[1] ibid. cols 1395–1532.
[2] ibid. col. 1512.
[3] ibid. col. 1414.
[4] ibid. col. 1426. Elliot had mentioned partition in a letter to The Times, 17 July 1956. A Turkish deputy had advocated it in the Turkish Parliament on 25 February 1956. See *Summary of World Broadcasts* IV (BBC) 651, p. 14, 25 February 1956.
[5] H.C. Deb., vol. 556, cols 1453–4.
[6] H.L. Deb., vol. 199, cols 205–10.
[7] ibid. cols 210–21.
[8] ibid. cols 221–5.
[9] ibid. col. 285.

to Cypriots, who had placed their confidence in James Griffiths's assurances on 15 May.[1]

The Cyprus question was debated in Parliament with monotonous frequency. The level of discussion was seldom high. Speeches tended to be partisan and ill informed. Although they passed largely unnoticed in England, their repercussions were far-reaching in that they influenced the protagonists in Greece, Turkey and Cyprus. Eden's statement[2] of 12 July evoked warm praise from Dr Kutchuk, who commented that self-determination should be the subject of a treaty between Britain and Turkey with a British guarantee that it would not be implemented without Turkish consent.[3] But Clement Davies's reference to 'Turkish blackmail' outraged the Istanbul paper *Ulus*:

> The Liberal Party is still in the grip of the traditional hatred for Turkey fostered by men like Gladstone and Lloyd George. . . .

Hugh Gaitskell caused greater offence. His words made it clear, *Ulus* wrote, that if the Labour Party was returned to power it would be ready to sacrifice Turkish friendship.[4] Attlee's indictment of the Tories, on the other hand, delighted official circles in Athens.[5]

5   THE RENEWAL OF VIOLENCE

The second half of August was unusually eventful. On 22 August the British authorities responded to EOKA's proclamation by calling upon the guerrillas to surrender. Thousands of leaflets, dropped from the air, offered an amnesty. The fighters were given two choices. They could go to Greece, provided that country accepted them, in which case they would be required to apply for Greek nationality and would lose the right to return to Cyprus. Alternatively they could stay in the island and would only be prosecuted for crimes involving violence against the person. Describing the terms as 'generous', an official spokesman stated that EOKA was now in a cul-de-sac and the next move would be to speed up the Radcliffe constitution. Meanwhile anti-terrorist operations would go on.[6] Grivas replied that unless the surrender terms were withdrawn immediately and political negotiations started he would resume 'freedom of action' as from midnight on 27 August.

[1] See above, p. 192.
[2] See above, p. 195.
[3] The Times, 12 July 1956.
[4] *News from Turkey*, 6 August 1956, quoting from *Ulus*.
[5] The Greek Daily News Bulletin, 28 July 1956.
[6] Cyprus Mail, 23 August 1956.

Shortly before the expiry of EOKA's time-limit the British Government published in London and Nicosia extracts from the Grivas diary, which the security forces had found six days earlier in screw-top jars buried near Lysi, the birthplace of Afxentiou. EOKA's directives were, of necessity, communicated mainly by correspondence. Its members were under strict orders to destroy all documents once they had served their immediate purpose. The Colonel was perhaps the worst offender in disregarding this security rule. A compulsive writer with an eye to posterity, he had entrusted his diary for safe keeping on the eve of the rebellion to his bodyguard Gregoris Louka, a cousin of Afxentiou. The Colonial Secretary, Lennox-Boyd, stated that the published extracts established beyond all doubt that Makarios had played a leading role in the foundation of EOKA and in financing the purchase of arms smuggled into Cyprus for its terrorist activities.[1] The Colonial Secretary promised a full report on the diary and the publication of other documents when the translations were completed.

An EOKA leaflet, entitled 'The Forgers' and partly phrased as a challenging questionnaire, gave the impression that Grivas was desperate to find out exactly which documents had fallen into British hands. The Greek Government also alleged that the diary was faked, and accused the British Embassy in Athens of trying to bribe a Greek to obtain specimens of the Colonel's handwriting. But in fact the British authorities already had this evidence on visa forms held by the Consulate-General in connection with his earlier visits to Cyprus, as well as examples from local sources.

The crisis precipitated by Egypt's nationalisation of the Suez Canal had now come closer to the island. Towards the end of the month plans for the arrival of French troops in Cyprus were well under way. Grivas treated the event with cautious neutrality. In due course he welcomed them as a Francophil, and assured them that they would be left unharmed. The message, however, contained a veiled warning that they should keep clear of any involvement on the side of the British in EOKA's struggle for freedom and concluded by wishing them a speedy return to France.[2]

A bomb explosion at Larnaca on 29 August ended the truce. On the last day of the month a gun battle took place in Nicosia General Hospital where Polykarpos Georkatzis, after feigning illness in the Central Prison, had been taken for X-ray examination. In an attempt to foil his escape a British police sergeant was killed. Two of the four

---

[1] See Colonial Office Statement, 27 August 1956.

[2] EOKA leaflet: 'French Soldiers', distributed in Nicosia, 11 September 1956.

guerrillas engaged in the rescue operation and a hospital orderly also lost their lives.

The Greek Consul's choice of this moment of triumph to suggest another truce to Grivas was in some respects surprising. But the first instalment of the diary had already gravely embarrassed the Greek Government and the prospect of further disclosures was disquieting. A cease-fire ostensibly initiated by EOKA might have prompted the British Government to hold up the next publication in the interests of diplomacy. But Grivas argued that the British would misinterpret a new truce as a sign of weakness and before such a move could be made the constitution, since it shelved self-determination, must be dropped and the question of the amnesty and internal security settled on EOKA's terms.[1]

The diary unleashed a heated controversy in Parliament. The Socialists, notably Aneurin Bevan and Philip Noel-Baker, were quick to question its authenticity.[2] On the Government side Bernard Brain commented that the theory hitherto advanced that Makarios was a sincere moderate man had now been 'revealed as dangerously false'. Patrick Maitland, more in sorrow than anger, expressed disappointment on learning how heavily committed the Archbishop was to violence.[3]

The next instalment of the diary and other documents were released on 26 September.[4] An official spolesman explained that for security reasons certain passages in the Colonel's daily record of operations had to be suppressed and only a fraction of the incriminating material recovered by the security forces could be published, so great was the volume. It was claimed in the communiqué that the documents showed the Archbishop's overriding responsibility for bloodshed in Cyprus, and that he could have ended it at any time. This conclusion was supported by a quotation from a letter written by Grivas to Makarios on 29 January 1955, during the period of the Colonel's short-lived sub-servience to the Archbishop: 'I will not lay down my arms unless you yourself ask me to do so.'[5]

The myth of forgery could no longer be upheld despite one final effort on the part of Grivas to do so.[6] The documents corroborated beyond doubt the fact that Makarios was the central figure of the rebel

[1] *Memoirs* (Greek edition), op. cit. p. 131.
[2] See H.C. Deb., vol. 558, cols 365–6 and 436.
[3] ibid. cols 395 and 428.
[4] See *Terrorism in Cyprus*, op. cit.
[5] ibid. p. 42. Note: The official communiqué cut the end of the sentence – '. . . because it will mean that our object has been fulfilled.'
[6] EOKA leaflet: 'The Forgers', distributed at Trakhonas on 4 October 1956.

movement, and as presented they revealed almost nothing of his relatively moderate views on violence and his frequent differences with Grivas over its use. As a diplomatic exercise the disclosures had produced the desired result. They helped to justify British action in deporting the Archbishop which had aroused widespread criticism both in England and abroad. Sympathy for Makarios began to wane, especially in the USA where the head of the Church of Cyprus was now seen in a new light.

Grivas had, in the meantime, stepped up action. The Greek Cypriots were the first to suffer. Before the end of September, eight civilians were shot dead and one fatally wounded. During the second half of the month ten members of the security forces died. On 28 September alone a soldier and a woman welfare officer were killed in an ambush on the Kyrenia Pass; gunmen shot dead a soldier in Larnaca and two police sergeants in Ledra Street.

After the murder of the police sergeants in Ledra Street the security forces imposed a total curfew on the Greek sector of the Old City. Residents were given two hours to leave, but about 12,000 people, including English families and Turkish Cypriots, were caught in the security network. At dawn on the Saturday police warned householders through loudspeakers that they would be shot if they came out into the streets. The curfew was lifted at noon for an hour to allow the women to shop, but bread supplies quickly ran out. A few people reached the Municipal Market on the Turkish side and did not return to the curfewed area. Householders were confined to their homes for the whole of the Sunday. During an hour's break on the Monday crowds of women found access to the Municipal Market barred by armed police and troops with fixed bayonets. On the Greek side crush barriers were broken and the windows of the city's small shops smashed in the stampede to get food. Many shoppers came away empty-handed. The situation grew tense when no food was brought in from outside. There were threats to defy the curfew, which had to be extended to allow vans to bring in supplies past the barricade at the Metaxas Square end of Ledra Street. For the remainder of the curfew vans were allowed in during a two-hour break. The police organised teeming crowds into queues to ensure fair distribution. Thousands of workers, dependent on jobs outside the Old City, and paid by the day, ran out of money. By the fifth day the authorities had to distribute food free to the needy. The curfew did not end until 6 October – eight days after the death of the police sergeants.

Early in October the security forces launched Operation Sparrowhawk, named after the migrant birds which frequent the crags of

Pentadaktylos in spring and autumn. The guerrillas, suspected of carrying out the ambushes near Kantara in July and on the Kyrenia pass in September, were known to be based on the eastern Kyrenia Range. Many villages in an area of about 200 square miles were placed under curfew during exhaustive searches for wanted men, arms and explosives. Interest was concentrated mainly on an isolated farm-house about a mile from the Turkish hamlet of Trapeza below Penta-daktylos. It was here that one of the paratroopers, after stumbling over a hole, found oil drums containing arms and ammunition buried below ground. The area was immediately cordoned off. The troops began to search the whole slope and the farmhouse. A second paratrooper saw a piece of corrugated iron sticking up through layers of pine needles on top of the entrance to another hideout in which a machine gun, bombs, ammunition, bedding and food were stored.

Inside the house the farmer, his family and visitors appeared to be leading a normal life. But the paratroopers' suspicions were aroused on finding two wireless sets and new clothes which were not the peasant garb usually worn by Cypriot farmers. Further searches of the house that day were unproductive. Still suspicious, the troops maintained the cordon overnight. At dawn on 5 October a soldier searched the farm-house again. In a dark corner where the fodder was kept, he removed a coat concealing a hole in the wall. He flashed his torch and saw a man's head. When he put his gun inside someone shouted in English 'Don't shoot, we surrender'. A second paratrooper, left on guard while the first went to consult his officer, realised on seeing the men through the hole that they had not surrendered. Unable to understand what they were saying he fired through it. Shortly afterwards soldiers watching another part of the building saw straw moving on the floor. A trapdoor lifted and six men, only partly clad and one of them injured on the ear, came out and gave themselves up.

The gang included Photis Christofi, a group leader with £5,000 on his head, and Hadji Kharalambous, an escaped EOKA prisoner. The six men had crouched in a cavity eight feet by three feet between two rooms. The coat had covered the only air-hole. The hide was typical of many used by the guerrillas in emergencies. EOKA's ingenuity in their construction meant that a house could be searched time and again without showing the slightest abnormality. Short of a chance discovery of a minor clue or a lead from an informer, wanted men could remain hidden even in the most suspect building almost indefinitely. The farmer said he was unaware of the existence of the secret place in his house and that he had never seen any of the prisoners before except one who was a native of his home village. After interrogating the prisoners the troops found several more hideouts within a close radius of the farmhouse.

The operation lasted eight days. Before leaving the area the security forces blew up the empty farmhouse. By doing so they ensured that the building could not be used again by EOKA and that any secret places, weapons and explosives which had survived the search were destroyed. The authorities, moreover, viewed the practice as a fitting punishment for harbouring terrorists and as a possible deterrent to other house-owners who might, either out of fear or sympathy, be ready to act as hosts to wanted men in future.

All six men were sent for trial. The Court accepted the evidence of a forensic expert that one of the machine-guns recovered had been used in the Kyrenia ambush and other murders. But the prosecution was unable to prove that any one of the gang had committed these crimes.[1] They were, however, all sentenced to life imprisonment, the maximum penalty for the illegal possession of arms.

Operation Sparrow-hawk paralysed EOKA in the Kyrenia Range for a long time to come. During October the Organisation kept up the pressure by means of sporadic incidents in other parts of the island concentrating mainly on the Cypriot civilians. Fourteen were killed by gunmen in three weeks. Five of the murders took place in coffee shops, two in barbers' shops and one at a wedding reception. The presence of spectators helped to further the process of intimidation, so whenever possible EOKA chose public places for its executions.

Six servicemen were killed during the month. The worst incident took place at Lefkoniko on 23 October. After a game of football soldiers from the Highland Light Infantry went straight to a drinking fountain at the edge of the field. One soldier was killed instantaneously, another died later and four were seriously wounded by a bomb explosion. The bomb, buried in the ground nearby, was electrically detonated by means of a flex attached to a mechanism more than 300 yards away. When rounding up more than a hundred people for questioning, the troops did not conceal their anger. The incident culminated in the familiar pattern of complaints of ill-treatment and claims for damages on the part of the villagers.

Towards the end of October Anghelos Vlakhos, the Greek Consul-General, suggested once again that Grivas should declare a truce – this time immediately after the UN General Assembly's acceptance of the

---

[1] Grivas subsequently acclaimed Sofokleus and Petronas, two members of the gang, as the heroes who perpetrated the Kyrenia ambush. See *Memoirs* (Longmans), op. cit. p. 95.

Greek appeal. The Greek Government's motives in making this approach to the Colonel may well be explained by the fact that restraint on EOKA's part would have strengthened its position in presenting the Cyprus case. But Grivas argued that the British delegate would exploit the truce as a reason for holding Anglo-Cypriot talks and for avoiding any decision being taken by the UN on the substance of the appeal. The Colonel added that in any case it might be impossible for him to call off hostilities at short notice.[1]

The nationalisation of the Suez Canal in July 1956 was to have an immediate and long-term impact on the course of events in Cyprus. On 31 October British and French aeroplanes stationed at Akrotiri began bombing Egyptian airfields. The political prophets had always forecast that the Cyprus bases, surrounded by a hostile population, would be unusable. But EOKA's activities did not, in fact, upset the functioning of the bases. The British campaign against EOKA, on the other hand, was drastically slowed down. Troops normally available for local operations were either on 48-hour stand-by or else engaged in loading up supplies in preparation for the landing in Egypt. The absence of certain units, particularly the paratroopers with special experience of guerrilla warfare, enabled EOKA to recover the initiative. Fatal casualties due to EOKA action during the first three weeks in November totalled thirty-three – the highest figure for any comparable period in the four-year emergency. Fifteen servicemen, four British civilians, one Turkish and eleven Greek Cypriots died. Six deaths were caused by road mines, one by an ambush in the Troodos Mountains, five by bombs placed in army quarters by Cypriot employees of the NAAFI. Three soldiers and three special constables were either shot dead or fatally wounded. Alan Grice, a local resident, was killed by an explosion under a Land-Rover; Douglas Williamson, the Assistant Commissioner at Platres, by a parcel bomb; Angus Macdonald, a journalist on assignment for the *Spectator*, by gunmen shortly after his arrival in Cyprus. Dr Bevan, who had dedicated much of his medical career to the Cypriots, was the victim of a ruse in the sick bay of the Amiandos Mining Company. While examining a man who came ostensibly to consult him, he was shot dead by the 'patient's' escort. Defamation of character was one of EOKA's most dangerous weapons and thrived, especially at village level, on the Cypriot inability to reject hearsay and falsehood. Before Dr Bevan's death the EOKA grape-vine vibrated with rumours that he was using truth drugs on captured terrorists. In a more sophisticated society totally false allegations such as these would

[1] *Memoirs* (Greek ed.), op. cit. p. 140.

have met with the scepticism they deserved. In Cyprus they endangered lives. The Greek Cypriots were, with one exception, shot dead either in Nicosia or Famagusta.

On 22 November, the Cyprus Government made the death sentence mandatory and extended it to the illegal possession of firearms and explosives and to consorting with anyone carrying these weapons. The maximum penalty of life imprisonment was introduced for possessing incendiary materials and assisting in their manufacture. Expressing his regret at the need for sterner measures Harding stated that recent outrages had shown even more clearly than before that EOKA's policy was one of 'wanton, senseless killing'. EOKA, he said, had shot down civilians going about their normal business, and killed ever increasing numbers of their own countrymen. His only option in these circumstances was to impose stronger penalties in the interests of the Cyprus people and of a lasting, peaceful settlement.

Harding's action aroused a storm of protest in both Houses of Parliament.[1] The sharp decline in violence which began the day after Harding's statement made the critics look foolish. During the remaining forty days of 1956 British casualties dropped to two servicemen and one civilian. The introduction of stronger penalties was not, however, the main factor in the steady improvement in security. The respite enjoyed by EOKA during the Suez crisis had ended; the security forces were now back to full strength. In late December several guerrillas long wanted for their activities in the Paphos district were captured. A small mixed patrol of men from the Royal Artillery and the police force captured the group leader, George Raftis, and his two companions in a river-bed. Soon afterwards, a patrol driving without lights in the Paphos Forest suddenly came upon Evaghoras Pallikarides on a sharp bend. Bound for new winter quarters, Pallikarides was carrying a Bren gun and leading two donkeys loaded with equipment. The two guerrillas with him escaped in the darkness through the undergrowth. A rabid enosist as a schoolboy, Pallikarides took part in the Coronation riots in 1953 organised by the Paphos Gymnasium where he was educated, and in the demonstrations[2] during the *Aghios Georghios* case in March 1955. While still at school he joined EOKA. On return from a long holiday in Greece, at the request of the Paphos group leader, he organised the distribution of EOKA leaflets among his schoolmates. After a spell of subversive activity in Nicosia, he joined a mountain group based on a hide near Lysso.

[1] See H.L. Deb., vol. 200, cols 813–39, 6 Dec.; H.C. Deb., vol. 562, cols 1610–40, 21 Dec.
[2] See above, pp. 54 and 109.

The growing success of the security forces increased the Colonel's obsession with treachery. It was the first explanation that came to his mind whenever EOKA suffered a defeat; it was the haunting fear that determined EOKA's escape policy. The efficiency of the guerrillas' courier system, combined with frequent lapses in prison security, enabled Grivas to keep in touch with prisoners. This he did mainly through 'Sebastianos', his former contact with Nicosia, who was able to get messages from the women's block to the men. Once an EOKA member had fallen into British hands he was seldom trusted again by Grivas. Permission to escape, which had to be sanctioned by the EOKA Leader, was restricted to a handful of key men in whom he still had complete confidence. Unauthorised escapes, the Colonel suspected, were due to connivance on the part of the authorities. He was equally suspicious of acts of clemency, the release of prisoners and detainees. When Nitsa Hadjigeorghiou, who had lured an RAF corporal to his death, was let out of prison, Grivas ordered EOKA to ostracise her in case she was working for the British. After Harding commuted the death sentence on Nikos Xenophontas to life imprisonment, EOKA immediately circulated a warning that he might reappear in the service of the security forces, disguised as a masked guerrilla.

The hunt for traitors, despite the general improvement in security, resulted in the death of eleven Cypriots during December. All were shot dead. Most of the incidents had again taken place in the coffee shop, the centre of village social life. Even men known to be at risk were unable to resist its simple pleasures. Amongst EOKA's victims were men who had never cooperated with the security forces at any time. Some informers, on the other hand, could not be reached by the Organisation. They were either protected or absent from the island. Grivas eventually overcame this obstacle to his policy of reprisals by ordering the execution of their innocent relatives.

6 THE RADCLIFFE PLAN

Lord Radcliffe completed his report[1] early in the winter after a second visit to Cyprus. The question of the island's final status lay outside his terms of reference which were exclusively concerned with self-government. He was instructed to draft a constitution which would leave Cyprus under the sovereignty of Britain, provide for the use of the

[1] *Proposals for Cyprus: Report submitted to the Secretary of State for the Colonies by the Rt. Hon. Lord Radcliffe, GBE*, December 1956, Cmnd 42.

island as a base, and for the retention of British control over Foreign
Affairs, Defence and Internal Security. Subject to this the constitution
was to be drawn up on the principles of 'liberal democracy'; to confer a
wide measure of responsibility on elected Cypriot representatives, while
simultaneously providing any guarantees necessary for the protection
of the island's various communities, religions and races.

Radcliffe recommended a diarchy in which the Governor would
exercise absolute authority in his reserved field; the local legislature
would correspondingly be master in its field. The proposals provided for
an assembly of thirty-six seats with a Greek majority; for a cabinet
composed of ministers drawn from the assembly; and for universal
franchise. It would be the Governor's duty, in his capacity as constitutional head of state, to appoint as Chief Minister the member who
appeared to have the most support in the assembly. Rights guaranteed
under the constitution would be safeguarded by the Supreme Court and
a special tribunal set up to examine complaints. Both would be composed of an equal number of Greek and Turkish Cypriots, and headed
by a non-Cypriot.

Radcliffe stressed that the proposed constitution was 'appropriate
to the state of affairs in which men may express their will by voting and
their views by speaking without fear of terrorism or intimidation ...'.[1]
Commenting on the cultural traditions and the advanced educational
and professional standards of the Cypriots, he said it was a curiosity of
their history that their political development had remained 'comparatively immature'.[2] In these circumstances no qualification or restriction
should be imposed which was not 'honestly required by the condition
of the problem'.[3] He had accordingly pared away a number of features
often present in advanced colonial constitutions. He had not included
any official members. The six members nominated by the Governor
served mainly to represent the small minority without the need to set
up separate rolls. Bills in which the Governor was free to reserve
assent were reduced to four categories of legislation; those affecting the
constitution, the Royal prerogative, the currency and the trustee status
of Cyprus Government stock.

Words such as 'defence' and 'internal security' could not be precisely
defined. The overriding consideration was that very large military and
air installations depended on some measure of coordination with the
rest of Cyprus. It would be difficult to draw up an exhaustive list of

[1] ibid. p. 5.
[2] ibid. p. 8.
[3] ibid. p. 9.

matters with which the authority responsible for defence and internal security might, in exceptional circumstances, be concerned without restricting the range of self-government under normal conditions. Defence and internal security could not suitably be exposed to the public proceedings of an independent authority such as the Supreme Court. He therefore proposed that the Governor should be the final judge in determining which matters came within his reserved field and that an advisory council should be set up at the highest level to promote the smooth functioning of the diarchy. Finally, even in respect of the reserved subjects, the Governor would be empowered to delegate to the assembly any particular piece of legislation he considered suitable.

Radcliffe noted that the influences which separated the communities were strong: religion, language, education, tradition and custom. He questioned the ability of the Greek and Turkish Cypriots to work together politically. Their representatives had cooperated in the past in various activities. In some cases the combination seemed 'happy and unresentful';[1] in others it was marred by recurrent suspicions and complaints of discrimination against the Turks. The events of the past eighteen months, the Greek campaign for Enosis, had without doubt done much to sharpen the alienation of the two communities – a factor which would have to be recognised in any constitutional plan now and in the future.

Radcliffe did not consider that the Turkish claim for equal representation with the Greek Cypriots in the legislative assembly was either consistent with the concept of the 'liberal and democratic constitution' or the sole means of giving the Turkish minority effective protection. Equal representation embodied the idea of federation which was associated with territorial separation. No such pattern existed in Cyprus. And a constitution based on an equal division of power between 18 per cent and 80 per cent of the population was not in the interests of the island as a whole.

Six seats would be reserved in the assembly for Turks elected on a separate roll and a place for a Turkish minister in the cabinet. Any changes in the laws regulating their domestic, religious and educational affairs would require the consent of two-thirds of the Turkish members. If the assembly failed to act, the Governor would be empowered to adopt amendments at the request of the minority through their representatives in the assembly and on the Evkaf council.

Since the political field was small it was desirable, Lord Radcliffe

[1] ibid. p. 12.

added, to concentrate all the available talent into one assembly. Minority rights could be better protected by a competent, independent tribunal than by a second chamber. Accepting the necessity for a Turkish Cypriot roll, with its disadvantages of perpetuating racial segregation, Radcliffe had considered the possibility of mitigating the drawbacks by introducing a common roll for a limited number of candidates. Elected by mixed constituencies, such candidates would be less likely to pursue strictly communal policies. There was, however, little evidence as to how such schemes worked out in practice. Although the idea, given sufficient support, might commend itself to future Cypriot statesmen, he decided that the simplest form of franchise was preferable at this stage. For similar reasons he was against giving the Turkish Cypriots the option to transfer to the general roll.

Whitehall hesitated at first to release the report. The disclosure of plans which could not immediately be put into effect had proved consistently disastrous in the past. But the Government was under constant pressure to make a political move. And Harding had never had any illusions that the problem could be settled by military measures alone. Radcliffe had made an outstanding contribution to the search for a compromise – his conclusions were of lasting significance. The publication of the plan was likely to strengthen the British position in defending its case abroad and to some extent disarm critics in England who complained of political inactivity.

The Colonial Secretary, Alan Lennox-Boyd, made a brief visit to Athens and Ankara in the middle of December. The Radcliffe proposals were published on the 19th. Lennox-Boyd, on the same day, restated the British Government's position on self-determination but added that when the time came to exercise this right it must apply equally to the two main communities and include partition among the eventual options.[1] This first official reference to partition, even as a remote possibility, came as a bombshell to the Greeks.

In Cyprus, Harding warned the people that despite Britain's acceptance of the principle of self-determination it would be sheer folly to assume that it could be implemented without the cooperation of the Greek and Turkish Governments. He urged them therefore to leave this vexed question aside for the time being and to concentrate on self-government. It was particularly important, he said, that everyone should study closely both Radcliffe's constitutional proposals and his covering note setting out the reasons for each recommendation. Harding stated that Makarios had been shown the proposals, and that

[1] See H.C. Deb., vol. 562, col. 1268.

the British Government was willing to facilitate a visit by a representative group of Cypriots to the Seychelles so that they might discuss them with the Archbishop. It could not, however, allow him to return to Cyprus before order was restored.[1]

As a gesture of goodwill the Governor released a number of detainees and relaxed a few minor emergency laws. But the most stringent penalties involving the death sentence remained in force.

The Greek Government had made up its mind to reject the proposals at the time of Lennox-Boyd's visit and announced its decision immediately after publication, before the Cypriots had even had a chance to study the report. The Greek official spokesman's misrepresentation of certain recommendations prompted a sharply worded correction from Lord Radcliffe which The Times published on 24 December. Turkey, which attached great importance to the reference to partition, eventually accepted the proposals as 'a basis for discussion', but advocated stronger safeguards for the Turkish minority.

Before the end of the year the former Attorney-General, Criton Tornaritis, and an official from the Colonial Office, Derek Pearson, left for the Seychelles to discuss the proposals with Makarios.

[1] See *Your Questions Answered. Lord Radcliffe's Constitutional Proposals for Cyprus* (Government of Cyprus, January 1957), Governor's broadcast, 19 December 1956.

VII

The Dilemma of the Greek Government September 1953- February 1957

Anti-Greek riots in Turkey — UN Debate on Cyprus

I   THE RISE OF KARAMANLIS

The Greek Government's difficulties as the result of the Cyprus crisis grew increasingly from the autumn of 1955 onwards. The climax came in September with the anti-Greek riots in Istanbul and Smyrna, which were quickly followed by the rejection of the Greek appeal to the UN. The policy of better relations with Turkey pursued by all Greek Governments since the end of the Second World War had now collapsed; the future of Greece in the Western alliance was precarious, for anti-NATO feeling and the trend towards neutralism had grown. The communist contention that the excessive fiscal burden of Greek defence was responsible for the country's basic poverty thrived on popular misconceptions as to the true purpose of the alliance and on the general frustration over Cyprus.

Despite the inflammatory state of public opinion the death of Papagos on 6 October raised hopes that a fresh start might be made in tackling the Cyprus problem. The new Prime Minister, Constantine Karamanlis, and his close associates recognised that Greece would have to make concessions. Moreover, they took a less pessimistic view of Makarios's character than the British authorities, seeing him as a potential moderate, unique in that he alone was capable of carrying the vast majority of the Cypriots with him in any compromise. But the

Greek Government had to contend with the Archbishop's unpredictability, his tendency to alternate reasonableness in private discussion with public outbursts of belligerency. His sudden arrival in Athens in December was an embarrassment; his presence in Crete on the anniversary of a Turkish massacre of Christians in 1866 could only exacerbate the situation.

The Foreign Minister, Spyros Theotokis, nevertheless still thought that conditions were generally favourable to a Greek initiative; international opinion, owing to the anti-Greek riots, was out of sympathy with Turkey at least for the time being. The NATO Council meeting in Paris had given him the opportunity to discuss the Cyprus problem privately with the British and Turkish Foreign Ministers. The unexpected visit of Alexis Liatis to Cyprus at the end of December indicated that the Greek Government had still not given up hope of a settlement.[1]

Karamanlis tried to steer a narrow course between loyalty to the Western alliance and concessions to his rivals of the centre and the left who were ready to exploit the Cyprus issue to the full in order to regain power. Opening the electoral campaign at Salonika on 24 January, he dwelt on the dangers of 'equal friendship' – now synonymous in Greece with neutralism. The frontiers of Greece could not, he warned, be safeguarded by friendship alone.[2]

On 4 January 1956 Karamanlis formed the National Radical Union in answer to the demand for change and in preparation for new elections. The Government at the same time exposed an alleged communist plot in a timely attempt to discredit EDA before the electoral struggle began and to impress upon the Americans that Greece was still a reliable ally worthy of aid.

It was unfortunate that the last phase of the Harding-Makarios talks should have coincided with the Greek parliamentary elections, which Karamanlis had hoped to avoid until there was a settlement. The opposition parties ignored appeals made by Karamanlis and Pipinellis that the Cyprus struggle should not become a factor in the campaign which was, in the event, waged almost exclusively on this issue. The main centre parties joined with the right-wing Populist Party and the extreme left-wing EDA to form the Democratic Union for the purpose of the election.

This incongruous alliance campaigned for immediate self-determination which it accused the Government of having abandoned. Even

[1] See above, p. 161.
[2] See *DNB*, Foreign Press Division. The Prime Minister's Office (Information Department), Athens, 24 January 1956.

Tsaldaris, the Populist leader and a hardened reactionary, gave qualified approval for the policy of 'equal friendship'. The test of the Soviet Union's good faith would, he said, be the extension of its present backing for the Cyprus cause to the Greek claim for the return of northern Epirus. The leader of the Progressive Party, Spyros Markezinis, the dynamic force behind the Greek Rally until his quarrel with Papagos, also joined in the attack on the Prime Minister's Cyprus policy. As the campaign gathered momentum, the Greek Government succumbed to the pressure of its rivals, with Karamanlis increasingly shifting the onus for any settlement on to Makarios. Theotokis, who at one stage had reported substantial progress towards a solution, said that the Greeks had no reason to be *plus royaliste que le roi*. EPEK's leader, Papapolitis, denounced the appointment of Karamanlis as head of the National Radical Union as a plot to bury the Cyprus question and the agreement rumoured to have been reached by Harding and Makarios as the abandonment of self-determination and a sop to the Turks.

The National Radical Union was elected on 19 February with a majority of only thirty seats. Ten days later, the breakdown of the Harding-Makarios talks precipitated a fresh wave of criticism against Karamanlis. The EPEK leader called for a national policy in foreign affairs, Tsaldaris for a broad coalition, EDA's chairman, Passalides, for new elections. Karamanlis blamed the inability of the Western allies to understand the significance of the Cyprus question for the failure of his policy.

2   THE DOWNFALL OF THEOTOKIS

The deportation of Makarios on 9 March plunged the Karamanlis Government into a new crisis. Mobs defied the emergency measures; serious riots broke out in Salonika and Athens; and at Heraklion in Crete the British Consulate was destroyed by students. The Communists were made the scapegoat. Mass rallies planned under the chairmanship of Archbishop Spyridon were cancelled. It was officially explained that 'dark forces intended to turn the mass meeting into a true carnage'; that the KKE had ordered its followers to attack the security forces with clubs, iron bars, stones and bottles of petrol if they obstructed the demonstrators on the way to foreign embassies.

The Greek Government consistently played upon the American obsession with the dangers of communism in Greece, and from now on the Americans were brought more and more into the dispute. Karamanlis told journalists from the USA that Greece now expected decisive intervention on the part of their Government. The Communists were certain, he said, to take advantage of the ineptitude of the West in handling the Cyprus controversy; their strength in Greece, although not as great as it might seem at first sight, was rising owing to poverty and disillusionment with the Western allies. The balance was delicate: Karamanlis tried to maintain on the one hand that Greece could be relied upon as a military partner; on the other that she might succumb to communist domination if American aid was not forthcoming. On the whole these tactics worked.

In an attempt to bolster up the Karamanlis Government the American Ambassador hastened to express to Theotokis the US Government's sympathetic concern over recent developments in Cyprus and congratulated the Greek Government 'on the dignity and statesmanship' it had shown in dealing with the crisis.[1] Mr Irving Brown, the representative of the American Labour unions and the International Confederation of Free Trade Unions, was reported as saying in Athens that the British Government's arrest of Makarios constituted 'a gift on a silver platter' to the Communists which not only endangered the Cyprus cause but that of the entire free world.

The new Government got off to a difficult start in Parliament with a post-mortem lasting several days on the Cyprus crisis. The Opposition leaders again accused Karamanlis of abandoning the Cypriots; Venizelos berated him for delegating the responsibility for a settlement to Makarios. The Communists pressed the case for neutrality. Clinging to the policy of moderation, Theotokis spoke for two hours on 7 April in defence of the Greek Government role in the Harding-Makarios negotiations; the British recognition of self-determination was the direct outcome of the Greek stand, he said.

Greek governments were used to hanging on to office by a thread. Karamanlis was faced with a formidable opposition: Venizelos, Papandreou, Kartalis, Passalidis, Papapolitis and Tsaldaris – all eminent men endowed with political acumen and the gift of oratory. In addition Karamanlis was confronted with the persistent agitation of the Athens branch of the Ethnarchy, which had grown in power out of all proportion to its importance since the deportation of Makarios. EOKA, acting through the Ethnarchy, was determined to oust Theotokis from office.[2] A scurrilous press campaign was organised against him. And a deputation headed by Savvas Loizides complained to the Prime Minister that he lacked the necessary fighting spirit to conduct the

[1] See above, pp. 172–3.
[2] See above, p. 178.

Cyprus struggle. Karamanlis refused to allow the Foreign Minister to resign.

Papandreou called for a second debate for the express purpose of dealing with the Ethnarchy's complaints. And on 26 April Theotokis was for the second time in ten days called upon to justify the Government's policy. He reproved the Ethnarchy for its use of the press instead of raising the issue in Parliament. Savvas Loizides, now a deputy for the Radical Union, argued that *Ethnos* was only doing its duty in publicising the need for a Foreign Minister of greater militancy. The next day Karamanlis stated that endless discussion was only damaging the Cyprus cause; the debate was now over; the time had come to drop the subject.

The first executions of EOKA fighters on 9 May precipitated a new wave of violence. Mobs clashed with the police and tried to wreck premises belonging to the British and Western allies. The mayor of Piraeus smashed in front of a jeering crowd a plaque commemorating the visit of Princess Elizabeth and the Duke of Edinburgh. Averoff sent back his OBE awarded for wartime services with the British. The Greek Ambassador in Washington condemned the executions and urged Greeks to refrain from indiscriminate attacks against Americans. The American Government cancelled the Sixth Fleet's visit to Crete.

The campaign against Theotokis was stepped up. Venizelos had already made a scathing attack on him. The Foreign Minister's talks with Macmillan in Paris, he had said, were supposed to have reduced tension; instead they had resulted in the execution of the two Cypriot patriots. The Opposition's motion of censure was defeated by only five votes. Theotokis resigned at the end of May. He said he had stayed at his post as long as he felt there was any hope of influencing the British. Thus the Athens branch of the Ethnarchy, a small, insignificant association composed mainly of extremists exiled by the British after the 1931 riots and banned by Metaxas for activities considered harmful by the dictator to the broader interests of Greece, had scored yet another victory. The setback was humiliating, symptomatic of the inherent weaknesses which bedevilled government in post-war Greece. The thankless task of piloting his country through the international complications of the Cyprus dispute now fell to Evanghelos Averoff,[1] who became Foreign Minister.

3 THE POLICY OF 'EQUAL FRIENDSHIP'

Zenon Rossides, the chief Ethnarchy spokesman abroad, declared that the Cypriot leaders and the Greek Government were now in complete

---

[1] Averoff-Tossizza, more generally known in Greece as Averoff.

agreement that an appeal should be made to the UN on the basis of immediate self-determination. At a press conference in Athens the Indian Ambassador was evasive on the subject of self-determination for Cyprus. And, as part of a new enlightenment campaign arranged by the Ethnarchy in places as far apart as India and Central America, Pandit Nehru was presented with a silver box engraved with the word 'Cyprus' and containing documents setting out the Cypriot case. The Indian Government's distrust of the Cypriot claim for self-determination remained unchanged, however, throughout the course of the dispute.

Eden's statement on oil in Norwich[1] prompted Karamanlis to describe the British attitude as 'a crude projection of material interests'. The prolonged debate in the House of Commons on 12 July[2] also aroused embittered comment. A spokesman for the Ministry of Foreign Affairs, however, saw redeeming features, even grounds for hope, in Attlee's 'wonderful speech in the House of Lords'.[3]

The policy of 'equal friendship' found practical expression in a rapprochement with the Soviet Union. It was the Soviet Embassy which replaced the British as the social centre of the rich Athenian elite. But the boycott was not complete. King Paul, a loyal friend of Sir Charles Peake, used to make discreet visits to the British Ambassador's house in Kavouri. The flirtation with the Russians culminated in the visit of the Russian Foreign Minister, Dimitri Shepilov, to Athens in July – an event which the more responsible statesmen found disquieting. With a foot in both camps, Averoff stated that Greece, while remaining loyal to her existing alliances, wanted to improve relations with the Soviet Union. Pipinellis, renowned for his prudence in the handling of sensitive issues of foreign policy, declared that Shepilov's visit should not be interpreted as the prelude to anti-Turkish action on the part of Greece.

EOKA's truce on 16 August might have been expected to provide a respite from the constant polemics which kept the issue at boiling point in Greece. But it became instead a bone of contention. The Opposition leaders were flexible in their attacks, thus ensuring that whatever the Government did it was bound to be in the wrong. Venizelos stated that EOKA must have either proclaimed the truce under pressure from the Greek Government or else acted in desperation for want of its support. Papandreou argued that if the Government knew about the truce in advance it must be held responsible for an error in timing. If, on the

[1] See above, p. 195, fn. 2.
[2] See above, p. 195.
[3] See above, p. 196.

other hand, it was unaware of the move, this showed that it was out of touch with the struggle and therefore it was useless for it to stay in power. The controversy came to an abrupt end with the publication of Harding's surrender terms for EOKA,[1] their immediate rejection by Grivas and his subsequent call for a united front and the reconsideration by Greece of her military alliances. Members of the Government were frequently exasperated by their own impotence to act decisively in the dispute. And Averoff sharply retorted that the Cypriots could not expect Greek foreign policy to be laid down in Cyprus.

Public reaction that autumn vacillated hysterically between indignation and false optimism. Incidents in Cyprus, especially the executions of the EOKA fighters Michael, Patatsos and Zakos, fanned the first; the second was stimulated by the progress in the diplomatic field. The Greeks over the past four years had taken up much time in the Council of Europe, despite their failure to obtain a formal debate. Most delegates saw the Council as an instrument for forging European unity and objected to its use for savage controversy which could only have the opposite effect. Theotokis and Kassimatis had both spoken on the Cyprus question eloquently and with restraint. But the persistent, intemperate speeches of Mr Droulia,[2] who was asked several times by the President to avoid the subject, did nothing to advance his country's reputation.

Nevertheless the Greeks found the distinguished Belgian international lawyer Professor Rollin and the Irish delegates ready to back their case. They were also indirectly encouraged by British Socialists, who used the meetings to criticise the Conservative Government's policy. And in September 1956 the European Commission on Human Rights, set up under the Treaty of Rome, decided to carry out an inquiry in Cyprus to ascertain firstly whether the state of emergency was justified in accordance with article 15, namely that a threat existed to the life of the state; and secondly the circumstances in which the curfew was being applied. Progress had also been made at UNESCO. But after years of failure the outstanding success was the inscription of the Greek Government's appeal on the UN General Assembly's agenda. The Prime Minister's warning that the UN was unable to enforce the principles of the Charter since the great Powers ignored them whenever they conflicted with their interests was lost in the mood of public euphoria.

[1] See above, p. 197.
[2] See Council of Europe Consultative Assembly Official Reports of Debates: 7th Ord. Session, Twentieth Sitting, 20 October 1955, p. 552; 8th Ord. Session, Sixth Sitting, 18 April 1956, p. 139; 8th Ord. Session, Thirty-second Sitting, 9 January 1957, p. 1031.

The decision taken by the NATO Council in December to extend its terms of reference to political disputes between member states created in the ranks of the Opposition a fresh uproar concerning Greek membership of the alliance. Averoff gave assurances that Greece had reserved her position over Cyprus and that nothing would be allowed to stand in the way of the forthcoming appeal to the UN.

The genial but offhand manner in which Lennox-Boyd had presented the Radcliffe plan to the Greek Prime Minister was ill received in Athens. But the main factor in the rejection was that, like previous constitutional offers, the move was mistimed. Any British political initiative made before the UN debate was inevitably interpreted as a device to forestall full discussion by the General Assembly. With the Greek item on the agenda for the first time but not due for consideration until the following February, Karamanlis was not in a position to make concessions when at long last Greek diplomacy appeared to be achieving results.

4   THE ELEVENTH SESSION OF THE GENERAL ASSEMBLY

When the Political Committee met on 18 February 1957 it had before it two draft resolutions: the Greek appeal for the granting of equal rights and self-determination for Cyprus and the British complaint against Greece for supporting terrorism in the island.

Speaking for more than two hours, the Greek Foreign Minister, Averoff, stressed the essentially Greek character of Cyprus throughout history and refuted suggestions that the treaty of Lausanne was an obstacle to self-determination. The Cypriots, he said, had seen the steady emancipation of former British colonies at the end of the Second World War and awaited their turn. But efforts by Greece to negotiate a friendly settlement consistently met with 'Never'. In an allusion to the Soviet Union, he told the Assembly that Greece had only decided to appeal to the UN because the Cypriots were about to seek the support of another power.

His country's sole aim, Averoff declared, was to liberate the Cypriots from the colonial yoke: 'Cyprus the concentration camp, the scene of torture and human degradation must disappear.'[1] The Cypriot nationalist movement was essentially spontaneous; even before the rise of Makarios the Greek Cypriots had rejected a colonial constitution; their will was truly represented by the plebiscite in 1948 with its overwhelming vote in favour of Enosis. During the Harding-Makarios

[1] UN doc. A/C.1/PV 847 (XI), p. 22.

talks, conducted on the basis of a master-to-servant relationship, Averoff claimed, the Archbishop had made one concession after another. His refusal to fall into the trap 'of allegedly liberal formulas designed to conceal and guarantee the permanency of British domination in the island' had terminated in deportation to the 'rocky shores of another British colony'.[1] Averoff argued that freedom of speech precluded government intervention in the state-owned radio which, in broadcasting passages from the press, was carrying out a legitimate activity in echoing the voice of public opinion.

Excerpts from the works of well-known writers were frequently used to support the Cyprus case. *A History of the English-Speaking Peoples* by Winston Churchill had proved invaluable right from the time Grivas had ordered his liaison officer to borrow the book in Nicosia so that he could study it in his Limassol hideout. Characteristically Averoff defended terrorism in Cyprus first by quoting Churchill:

> It is the primary right of men to die and kill for the land they live in and to punish with exceptional severity those of their compatriots who have warmed their hands at the invader's hearth.

And then De Valera:

> It is we who taught the Greeks that the civilian is entitled to murder soldiers and policemen if his country is denied its freedom.

Averoff denied that the Greeks had sent the Cypriot fighters arms; their support for them was solely political. He pressed for the Archbishop's early return on the ground that his presence was essential to a settlement. After attacking the British security measures and Britain's neglect of the Cypriot economy he claimed that the current boom was limited to the military bases.

The Greeks and Turks had lived peacefully together for centuries; the trouble between the communities was fomented by the Cyprus authorities, the Greek Foreign Minister continued. The police, which included many Turks, and the auxiliary force,[2] which was composed exclusively of them, condoned Turkish attacks against the Greeks.

Referring to recent statements by Eden and Selwyn Lloyd on the importance of the island for the protection of British oil supplies, he reminded the Committee that Greece had warned the United Nations

---

[1] ibid. p. 27.

[2] The Auxiliaries were a mixed force: the Mobile Reserve, which Averoff may have had in mind, exclusively Turkish.

before the Suez crisis about the underlying dangers of these pronounce-
ments. Cyprus had become a springboard of aggression instead of
defence, he said.

The dispute could not be settled on a tripartite basis, he said. The
whole Assembly was aware of the tragic consequences of this policy.
The help of the United Nations was essential to a settlement. He
promised full guarantees for the Turks, and finally, in arguing the case
for self-determination, he quoted President Eisenhower:

> Our country supports without reservation the full sovereignty and
> independence of each and every nation of the Middle East.[1]

The Cypriots saw themselves as an essential part of Europe. It was
interesting that Averoff, when pleading their case at the UN, should
have thought fit by implication to include them in the Middle East.

The British delegate, Commander Noble, sought to convince the
Assembly that the EOKA rising was encouraged, guided and financed
with the help of the Greek Government. The British complaint, he said,
was not about the terrorism in the island. Major outbreaks of violence
had been timed to coincide with the UN debate. Greece was not in a
position to claim annexation, therefore the aim of Enosis was cloaked in
the demand for self-determination. UN involvement in such a claim
could be dangerous and was contrary to Article 2(7) of the UN
Charter. Realising the legal flaw in her case, Greece was now talking
increasingly about independence and trying to overthrow the treaty of
Lausanne.

Outlining the terrorist campaign since its start on 1 April, Noble
described some of the grimmer incidents, including the murder of the
Abbot of Chrysorroyiatissa, and stressed that Greek Cypriot civilians
formed nearly half the total fatal casualties. He complained of the
persistent encouragement given to the terrorists by the Greek state radio
which had broadcast subversive proclamations even before they reached
Cyprus and which had been used to direct EOKA to its targets by
singling out individuals for attack. The Greek Government had
subsidised the Panhellenic Committee for the Union of Cyprus with
Greece, surely a very significant name, Noble said. This organisation,
according to its own account, had issued over 3 million anti-British
pamphlets printed by departments of the Greek Army and Government.
Other offensive material, also distributed by the Greek Government
through the press and the UN, had accused British troops of 'sacrilege

[1] ibid. p. 53.

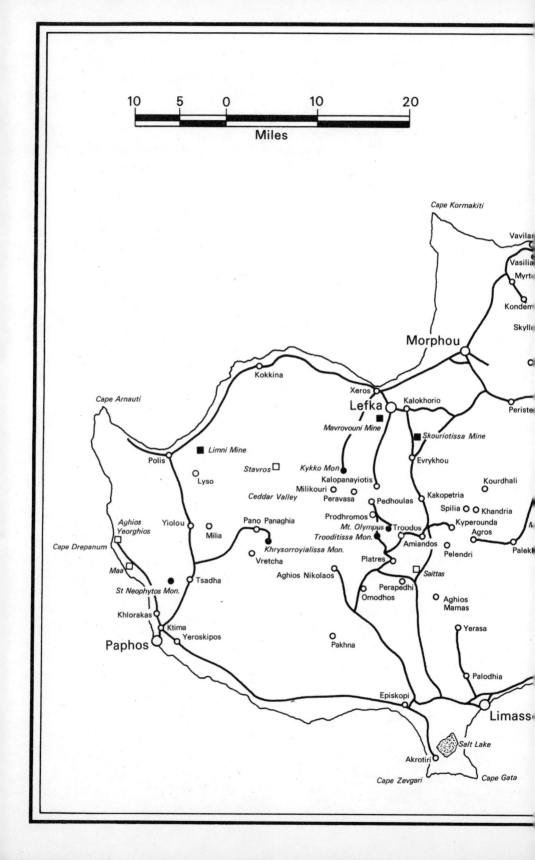

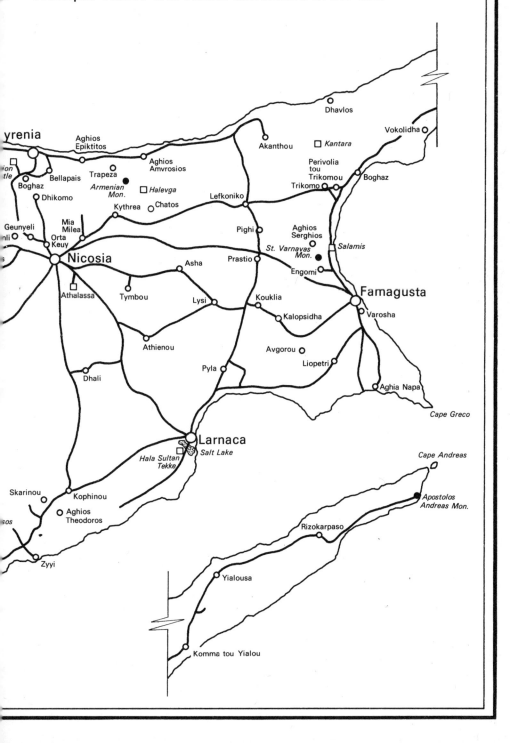

S – Principal Places and Roads mentioned in the text

and outrageous profanation'[1] in searching a graveyard. These were 'harsh words', Noble said, from the pen of a representative who saw nothing wrong in the murder of a Greek Cypriot in the middle of a church service, of an abbot in his own monastery. Undoubtedly Greece was subject to strong pressure, but all member states must accept responsibility for their government's activities.

Blaming Makarios for the breakdown of the talks with Harding, the British delegate strongly criticised Greece for her summary rejection of the Radcliffe proposals and disagreed that they did not provide for ultimate self-determination. Turkey had generally approved of the plan; had Greece also been willing to discuss it, the British Government would have agreed to do likewise, but so long as Greece insisted on Enosis there could be no solution, he said.

Concentrating largely on the historical and legalistic aspects of the dispute, Mr Sarper, for Turkey, challenged the competence of the UN to deal with the Cyprus question. The forces behind the campaign, he said, were promoting their own selfish interests. The treaty of Lausanne excluded for all time any possibility of subjecting Cyprus to Greek rule. Self-determination was not applicable in all circumstances. Greece, for instance, had refused Turkey this right when she invaded Asia Minor in 1921. And western Thrace, where the Turks were in the majority, was ceded to Greece as part of the Lausanne settlement.

Sarper had no time for the thesis beloved of Hellenists that Cyprus was Greek since it had once formed part of Byzantium. Other countries had shared this common destiny one thousand years ago; this could not make them the 'sole heir of the Eastern Roman Empire', he said.[2] As for the 'amusing incident' of the plebiscite, he marvelled at the courage of the 5 per cent who voted against Enosis. He had known other countries where the result in similar circumstances would have been a 98 per cent vote in favour. Turkey's inaction early on in the dispute, Sarper explained, was due to his Government's desire to avoid the deterioration of friendly relationships between three allied countries. Turkey did not favour colonialism; she was not opposed to constitutional advance but wanted to stop self-government becoming a stepping-stone to Enosis. Her intervention in the Cyprus dispute was not motivated solely by her friendship with the United Kingdom; Cyprus was attached to Anatolia 'not by virtue of any friendship or alliance but as the result of geological and geographical phenomena'.[3] The Turkish delegate made it clear

[1] UN doc. A/C.1/PV 847 (XI), p. 78.
[2] UN doc. A/C.1/PV 848 (XI), p. 42.
[3] ibid. p. 87.

that in accepting Lennox-Boyd's policy statement as a basis for negotiation his Government attached great importance to the ultimate right of the Turkish Cypriots to opt for partition when the time came to implement self-determination.

Averoff denied that Greece was sending arms to EOKA; the diplomatic bag was too small, he said. Instead of making these accusations Commander Noble ought to have congratulated the Greek Government on its effective vigilance over thousands of miles of coastline. Only one vessel so far had got through – the *Aghios Georghios*.

The Grivas documents, the basis of the British charges, were highly embarrassing to the Greek Government. No one could anticipate the next disclosure. The Colonel's capacity for producing reams of heady prose under adverse conditions – a leaking tent in the Troodos Forest, a cramped hideout within easy range of the security forces – was virtually unknown except to the Special Branch and his immediate companions in Cyprus. This helped Averoff to cast doubts upon the authenticity of the documents. It was surprising, he said, that a man engaged in guerrilla warfare on a beach-head, hunted by troops, helicopters and police dogs, should find the time and means to write a long diary. After two-score years or more no one was allowed, for instance, to see Sir Roger Casement's diaries. Was it not possible that they were forged?

Averoff accused the British intelligence service of trying to incriminate the Greek Government and presented the Political Committee with a long memorandum giving four instances in which it was alleged that British agents had tried to stage arms shipments to Cyprus.[1] The document mentioned offers of high payment as inducements to caique captains to transport arms close to the shores of Cyprus where they would be seized by the Royal Navy and the promise of their speedy release after a token period of imprisonment for the sake of appearances in Kyrenia Castle. Averoff had, in the meantime, amended[2] the original Greek text to provide for an independent inquiry by the UN into the British charges. He also suggested that the UN should investigate Cypriot complaints of ill-treatment by the security forces and he placed with the Secretariat a confidential file containing 237 signed depositions from ex-detainees. In a misleading interpretation of Lennox-Boyd's statement of 19 December[3] Averoff declared that Britain's intention to partition Cyprus was first disclosed on that day. He dismissed criticism that Greece had shown undue haste in turning down the Radcliffe

[1] UN doc. A/C.1/589 (XI), 19 February 1957.
[2] UN doc. A/C.1/L. 170 (XI), 18 February 1957.
[3] See above, p. 210.

plan; the proposed constitution, he said, gave far too wide powers to the Governor.

Noble demanded that the dossiers on ill-treatment should either be published or withdrawn.[1] He refuted the charges that the British Government had tried to fake evidence in order to prove that Greece had sent the Cypriot terrorists arms and ammunition. The first two allegations, he said, were completely fabricated. The third and fourth allegations, mentioning members of the British Embassy in Athens, depended on the evidence of a Greek subject – a left-wing journalist who had called at the Embassy saying that he had valuable information about arms smuggling from Greece to Cyprus. Like other callers on similar missions he was advised to inform the Greek authorities but said he did not want to because they were involved. Nevertheless he was reported to them – a point which the Greek Foreign Minister might have mentioned. Highly sensational articles written by this same man on the lines of the current allegations had been the subject of a strong protest by the British Chargé d'Affaires to the Greek Foreign Minister the previous September, Noble continued. Possibly put off by the complexity of the subject, many delegations took no part in the general debate. The main support for Britain and Turkey came from members of the Commonwealth, NATO and the Baghdad Pact. Greece had to rely chiefly on the USSR, the Soviet satellites and the Arab states.

The Australian delegate, Sir Percy Spender, deplored terrorism and the role played by the Church under Makarios:

We are acquainted with the idea of a Church militant, but the idea of a Church combatant is alien to us.[2]

Greece wanted to assimilate Cyprus, he said. A case based on the argument that the Greek Cypriots were in the majority could become a dangerous precedent which might prompt countries like China to claim Malaya. Turkey had already experienced Greek attempts to acquire Turkish territory. Mr Bryn, for Norway, saw no validity in Averoff's comparison of the EOKA revolt against British rule to Greek resistance to the Axis during the Second World War. Mr Picot, for France, observed that if all ethnic and religious groups were to be granted self-

---

[1] See Stephen G. Xydis, *Cyprus: Conflict and Conciliation 1954–1958* (Ohio State University Press, 1967), p. 52. Xydis, who had access to Averoff's private papers, wrote that the Greek Foreign Minister considered that these documents were more useful if their secrecy was maintained.

[2] UN doc. A/C.1/PV 849 (XI), pp. 33–5.

determination the national entity of most of the states represented in the Committee would collapse. Belgium, France and Portugal were strongly opposed to UN intervention. Spain supported the NATO countries in recognising the strategic importance of Cyprus. Defence considerations also influenced Iraq and Pakistan; they upheld the viewpoint of Turkey, their partner in the Baghdad Pact. Ceylon's delegate, Mr Gunewarden, praised the British record in granting independence and was sceptical about the Greek Government's charges. The desire of Greece to make the Cypriots feel that she wanted them to be part of the Greek Kingdom was understandable, he said. But Ceylon could never approve Enosis any more than she could agree to India taking over Ceylon just because it was only thirty miles away and its inhabitants came from that continent 2,500 years ago. Turkey equally had no right to Cyprus on the grounds of distance and security. A member of NATO and the Balkan Pact, she had little to fear from an island where 20 per cent of the people were of Turkish origin. The Assembly, he said, should call upon Greece to use its influence to stop terrorism. However, he agreed with Averoff that the Governor's powers under the Radcliffe plan were too great. Mr Khoman, for Thailand, expressed sympathy for the Greek Cypriots; concern for the rights of the Turkish minority and confidence in the United Kingdom's undertaking to satisfy the islanders' legitimate aspirations. His Government was against UN intervention in the affairs of a member state.

The terse statement made by the American delegate, Mr Wadsworth, indicated his Government's impatience at the failure of the three Western allies to resolve their dispute. Commenting that little progress had been made, despite American efforts to facilitate negotiations, he urged the UN to avoid aggravating the crisis by formulating specific proposals and was critical of all three draft resolutions.[1]

Mr Boland, for Ireland, spoke of the use British politicians made in the past of the Orange Order to arouse the fears and passions of the Protestant minority. A similar situation, he suggested, might explain the present anxieties of the Turks. On the question of possible solutions, he pleaded, 'Not partition, anything but that.' He recognised that the extension of Soviet power in Europe would mean the end to all liberty, Greek and Cypriot alike. The need for a settlement which did not weaken the free world was met, in his opinion, by the Greek offer in the event of Enosis to grant bases in Cyprus under NATO control. He deplored the impotence of the UN in handling problems such as the invasion of Hungary when 'this Assembly was little more than a kind of

[1] See above, pp. 219 and 223, fn. 2.

chorus commenting on the unfolding of a doom which it was powerless to avert'.[1] Mr Quiroga-Galdo of Bolivia praised Greece as the source of eternal civilisation, Turkey as the symbol of nobility and chivalry embodied in the figure of Kemal Ataturk. But he disagreed with the Turks that the treaty of Lausanne could not be revised. The Bolivian delegate and his Venezuelan colleague, Mr Perez-Perez, found both the British and Greek draft resolutions too controversial. Mr Illueca, for Panama, drafted a resolution providing for an on-the-spot study of the situation by a special UN team which would report back at the next annual General Assembly.

The Soviet Union's delegate, Mr Tzarapkin, outdid the Greek Foreign Minister in denouncing British oppression, the lamentable state of Cypriot education and the efforts to eradicate Greek influence. The indictment was simply the preliminary to the main purpose of his speech – an all-out attack on the USA and the American oil companies which, he alleged, were trying to establish control over the Middle East. As for the self-government plan, this was nothing more than 'a transition from the domination of Cyprus by the United Kingdom to domination by the United States', Tzarapkin said.[2] The Byelo-Russian and the Ukrainian delegates repeated these charges almost verbatim; the substance of the statements made by the representatives of Czechoslovakia, Poland and Yugoslavia was much the same, the tone less vitriolic.

Egypt, Syria, Jordan and the Sudan condemned the use of Cyprus as a base for the recent Anglo-French attack on Egypt. Syria's delegate, Mr Zeinidine, reminded the Committee that Cyprus had once been part of the Syrian Empire, but gave assurances that his country no longer claimed the island. Sceptical about Britain's charges against Greece, Mr Loufti, on behalf of Egypt, thought a UN investigation team might help the Committee to establish the truth. Mr Maghoub, for the Sudan, while generally endorsing the Greek stand, spoke of Britain's excellent record in granting self-determination and self-government to its former colonies. Cyprus must not be the exception, he said.

The general debate, which dragged on until 22 February, was prolonged towards the end by renewed exchanges between Averoff and Sarper. The Greek case had one obvious flaw and the Turks had made the most of it. In practice there were certain exceptions to the right of self-determination. The most relevant to the current dispute was the precedent of western Thrace, which was ceded to Greece in 1923 under

[1] UN doc. A/C.1/PV 853 (XI), p. 61.
[2] UN doc. A/C.1/PV 854 (XI), pp. 23-5.

the treaty of Lausanne although the population was predominantly Turkish. Predicting correctly that the result would be a large Greek majority, Averoff declared that the Greek Government was willing at the present time to hold a plebiscite in the province. He went on to read out a telegram from the Mufti of Xanthi testifying to the perfect freedom and equality enjoyed by the Turkish community under Greek administration. Averoff had deliberately ignored the large influx of Greeks into the area and the migration of the Turks since 1923. Describing the Greek Foreign Minister's statement as a 'perfect example of confusion',[1] Sarper, who as a young diplomat had served as Consul in Komotiní, recorded the historical facts of the population exchanges in detail and was sceptical about the spontaneity of the Mufti's telegram. Both speakers had strayed far from the Cyprus problem and the general debate came to an abrupt end when the Peruvian chairman, Victor Belaunde, asked Sarper to stick to the subject.

The draft texts had no chance of obtaining the two-thirds majority required in the Plenary Meeting. The UN disliked above all else a negative result which only heightened the Organisation's public image of ineffectuality. Mr Entezam of Iran and Mr Khoman of Thailand made tireless efforts behind the scenes to find a way out of the deadlock. With the backing of the USA, Khoman drafted a formula expressing the hope that through the resumption of negotiations in an atmosphere of peace and tranquillity a solution might be found acceptable to all concerned in accordance with the Charter of the United Nations. But the text was not tabled as a resolution; Greece feared that the words 'all concerned' might open the door to a Turkish veto on any settlement.[2] American support at the UN was not to be underrated; the Greeks made a tactical error in rejecting the Thai proposal.

The Committee had witnessed a sordid wrangle between three allies – a war of allegations and recriminations in a dispute which, if it got out of hand, had potential dangers extending far beyond the territories directly involved. When the members came to discuss the resolutions they were in a sombre mood. The trend was towards moderation and the lowering of the temperature.

The intervention of Krishna Menon at this late stage was decisive. India, he said, saw the problem largely as one of nationality. An advocate of independence, he dismissed arguments based on Greek mythology, Greek gods and religion:

---

[1] UN doc. A/C.1/PV 855 (XI), p. 26.
[2] See Xydis, op. cit. pp. 40–1, for details of these backstage manoeuvres.

Supposing my country were to claim Japan and China because Buddhism originated in India that would be a very sorry position – and not a position we would like to take.[1]

The problem was not a purely domestic issue. Britain had occupied India for 300 years but that did not give her the right to remain there. This also applied to Turkey's occupation of Cyprus. Treaties were not necessarily sacrosanct; the Cyprus problem could not be assessed on the basis of distance. The relevant factors were the island's traditions, its economic life and the evolution of national feelings there. Recriminations about violence could achieve very little, he continued. Everyone knew that it was 'six of one and half a dozen of the other'. The Black and Tans had not been able to subdue Ireland; the use of force would not solve the problem of Malaya. National independence, the affiliation of one country with another, could not be based upon affinity of race or religion. India had no sympathy whatsoever with the intrusion of religion into political agitation, believing that self-government could only be achieved in conditions of comparative tranquillity. This would be forthcoming once the parties concerned resumed negotiations. In these days of guided missiles, atomic bombs and fast transportation, he questioned whether strategic arguments had the same value as they did in the days of sailing ships and steamers. But even if still valid, they could not be allowed to affect the rights of the Cypriots in relation to their homeland.

Menon then introduced the following draft resolution:

The General Assembly,
Having considered the question of Cyprus,
Believing that the solution of this problem requires an atmosphere of peace and freedom of expression,
Expresses the earnest desire that. a peaceful, democratic and just solution will be found in accord with the principles and purposes of the Charter of the United Nations, and the hope that negotiations will be resumed and continued to this end.[2]

Not one of the other draft resolutions, Menon said, was likely to reconcile the conflicting wishes of the contestants. The term 'good neighbours' in the British text needed to be defined not only geographically but in other ways. The Greek claim created serious difficulties since self-

---

[1] ibid. p. 41.
[2] UN doc. A/C.1/L. 172 (XI).

determination could not be separated from the concept of annexation or *Anschlüss*. Panama's resolution was unacceptable, for the problem was not merely one of fact finding but of nationhood and reconciliation: 'Therefore the idea of trying to churn things up and come to a head-on collision with the British on the question of domestic jurisdiction does not appeal to us.'[1] The Committee as a whole was strongly in favour of the Indian formula and agreed to give it priority. Even the Soviet delegate grudgingly promised his support on the understanding that Cypriot participation was implicit in any 'negotiations'. The Indian text was accepted by 76 votes to nil with two abstentions.[2]

When the delegates came to explain their votes it was evident from the outset that Menon's seemingly innocuous proposal contained the seeds of controversy. Noble and Sarper interpreted the terms as meaning that negotiations were to be resumed by all the parties to the dispute. Averoff took the view that the resolution provided for bilateral talks between the British Government and Cypriot representatives. Menon was evasive when pressed for a clarification. The debate had shown, he said, that fifty states or more were interested in the Cyprus issue. The prime responsibility rested with the United Kingdom, which wielded the power; once the problem of self-government was tackled, the interests of other parties would fall into place.

The Greek Government faced strong criticism in Parliament for its handling of the UN appeal. Krishna Menon's concept of a Cypriot nationality, which cut right across the doctrines of Hellenism, was detested by the Greek Cypriots. In a debate which began on 11 March and lasted five days Averoff said that Menon's resolution had taken the Political Committee by surprise: Greece had voted for it because her opponents were ready to use the veto if she did not do so; the Indian delegate, whose views carried weight in the Assembly, did not believe in Enosis but in independence; the Greek Cypriots should be grateful to him. For anyone who refused 'to accept independence as a transitional stage in order to achieve Enosis'[3] deserved to be criticised. Averoff's comment left a legacy of suspicion in the minds of the Turks, and to a lesser extent of the British, concerning the true motives of the Greeks when they eventually came to demand independence.[4] The UN debate had been useful, the Foreign Minister continued, in informing

[1] UN doc. A/C.1/PV 855 (XI), p. 53.

[2] General Assembly Resolution 1013 (IX); adopted at the 66oth Plenary Meeting on 26 February 1957 by 55 votes to nil (one abstention).

[3] *Summary of World Broadcasts* IV (BBC) 195, p. 6, 11 March 1957.

[4] See below, p. 260.

international opinion; and, as the result of the Greek stand, the idea of partition was now discredited. Kartalis preferred Thailand's text.[1] Menon's resolution, he said, would enable the British, if they wanted to quibble, to seek a new one. Kassimatis recognised the lack of support for Enosis in the UN Assembly, but considered that the abstention of the Americans, who had in previous years voted against the discussion of the dispute by the UN, was a marked advance. Papapolitis accused the Government of having abandoned self-determination; Tsaldaris and Venizelos were also highly critical. Themistocles Tsatsos found Menon's resolution much closer to the British viewpoint than the Greek. The Karamanlis Government's continuation in office, he said, was an obstacle to a settlement which could only be achieved by a plebiscite leading to Enosis. Constantine Tsatsos, a minister in the Government, saw merits in the formula as a compromise which paved the way for Anglo-Cypriot talks.

Whenever possible the Greek Government tried to shift the responsibility on to the Cypriots; Averoff thus claimed that Menon's proposal had the approval of the Ethnarchy and the mayors in Cyprus. Karamanlis stated that Greece faced the struggle alone and it had to be waged within the framework of her alliances. Papandreou denounced the Government for pulling down the flag of self-determination and pledged the Opposition to keep it flying.

The Government survived a motion of censure by 26 votes. Ironically some of the Prime Minister's most ruthless critics were prominent men of the centre reared in the Venizelist tradition. But the temptation of the Opposition to use the Cyprus crisis, even at the nation's peril, to try to regain power was overriding. Any Greek Government, whatever its political complexion, would have been faced with the same dilemma.

---

[1] Thailand's text did not greatly differ from Menon's except that the latter left the question of which parties should participate in negotiations completely vague.

VIII

The Cease-Fire
February 1957-October 1957

Makarios's Return to Greece — Foot's Appointment as Governor

1 THE INTENSIFICATION OF OPERATIONS

The improvement in general security which began in January 1957 was not matched by a decline in racial tension. On 18 January four Turkish auxiliaries, on guard at a power station near the archbishopric, were injured in a bomb attack, one of them fatally. Crowds of young Turks crossed the 'Mason-Dixon Line' and took their revenge, ransacking shops at the end of Ledra Street. Many fires, started on Greek property in the Turkish quarter, blazed through the night. The bells of the Orthodox Churches rang out in warning. The security forces put both sectors of the Old City under curfew for a few days. The Greek and Turkish Cypriot trade unions issued a joint appeal for calm, but disturbances broke out again on 22 January and the curfew had to be reimposed. All was quiet by the 24th. The Greek shops, however, remained closed. Merchants, headed by the deputy mayor, complained that the Government's security measures were insufficient to prevent new Turkish attacks. Angry telegrams were sent to Dag Hammarskjold and the Archbishop of Canterbury, among other world figures, in which the local leaders protested against the 'vandalism of the Turkish mobs' and the attitude of the Cyprus Government and demanded self-determination.

Ten days later Greeks threw bombs at a police patrol in Famagusta. A Turkish police constable died. After his funeral Turkish demonstrators stoned bicycles and a doctor's car in a hospital yard. They also damaged the Orthodox Church of Aghios Georghios and the only Greek shop in the walled city. The whole town was put under curfew. Turkish workers went on strike in protest against the bomb incidents, bringing the port of Famagusta to a standstill; one Greek died and several were seriously injured during the disturbances.

From January onwards the security forces, having recovered the momentum they lost during the Suez crisis, went from strength to strength. During the month Markos Drakos was shot dead in the Troodos Mountains after one of his men had attacked a patrol of the First Suffolk Regiment. Many arrests were made throughout the island. Key men caught in their hideouts included Nikos Sampson at Dhali and the two escaped prisoners Polykarpos Georkatzis and Karademas at Omodhos.

The Chief of Staff, Brigadier Baker, summarising on 31 January the progress of the security forces, stated that sixteen EOKA gangs had been reduced to five in the past year. Rioting and bomb throwing had virtually ceased. Few assassins remained at large but there were many in the detention camps. EOKA's main victims were now so-called 'traitors' and soft targets – defenceless civilians, whose deaths enabled the Organisation to hit the headlines.

The security forces kept up the pressure for the rest of the winter. Evanghelos Evanghelakis and Andreas Chartas were arrested in Nicosia early in February. In the Troodos Mountains leading EOKA men, long on the 'wanted' list, were captured and guerrilla groups disrupted. Demetrakis Christodoulou was shot dead trying to escape from the security forces; Sotiris Tsangaris was killed in a gun battle near his native village, Pelendria. Stylianos Lenas was seriously injured by a Marine patrol and captured later. Known as 'Krupps' to the Cypriots for his expertise in making bombs, he had taken refuge in the mountains, the authorities having offered a £5,000 reward for his arrest. During these operations an officer in the Royal Marines lost his life.

The offensive reached its climax with the epic resistance of Gregoris Afxentiou, who defied a cordon of troops for more than ten hours. He was based with his group on a forest hideout half a mile away from the Monastery of Makheras on the slopes of Mount Kinonia. A friend of Abbot Irineos, he had convalesced in the monastery, disguised as a monk, after his operation during the previous summer when the security forces had the Troodos guerrillas on the run. At dawn on 3 March a patrol from the Duke of Wellington's Regiment started searching the monastery area. After finding an oil-drum, a 2-inch mortar and a haversack under some bushes, they came upon a hole in the ground. An officer gave an order in Greek, telling the men to come out. Four of them did so; Afxentiou, they said, was still there.

The troops next shouted to Afxentiou to surrender. Seconds later a burst of automatic fire, which killed Corporal Brown, was followed by a shower of grenades from the hide. Captain Newton then threw a grenade into the hide. Next the security forces sent one of the four men, Efstathiou, to fetch Afxentiou. But when he did not return the troops took up firing positions. Grenades started to pour out of the hide forcing the soldiers to move back fifty yards. At one stage a smoke screen formed around the entrance and the troops fired to prevent the men escaping. The exchanges lasted several hours. The hide was too dangerous to approach. The security forces, having already lost one soldier, decided to blow it up. The Royal Engineers poured petrol down the slope in a steady trickle towards the entrance hole. The first beehive charge did not achieve its objective and a burst of fire came from the hideout. Captain Shuttleworth came down dangerously close to the hole in order to lower a second charge into the exact position. Trailing a long length of fuse, he crawled back up the track.

As the explosion reverberated through the mountains, Efstathiou rushed out of the flames. He said that on returning to the hideout he found Afxentiou slightly wounded by the first grenade but he refused to give any information on his leader's condition when he left him. The intensity of the flames made it impossible for the troops to get inside the hideout before the next morning. They found, near Afxentiou's charred body, a sub-machine-gun, a loaded magazine, revolvers, grenades, and ammunition of a different calibre from that used by the security forces. Close to his head were empty cartridges.

The pathologist at the British Military Hospital and the Coroner, Mr Justice Ellison, were satisfied beyond any doubt that Afxentiou died from a gunshot wound through the skull; that death was instantaneous and had occurred before the body was burnt. There was strong evidence that the bullet had been fired directly at the head, but the possibility could not be excluded that the wound might have been caused by exploding ammunition due to intense heat. Efstathiou testified that Afxentiou was alive when he last saw him and that no bullets had exploded before he left the hide. Cross-examined by counsel for Afxentiou's parents, he said that his leader had never expressed any intention to commit suicide. The Coroner's verdict[1] was that Afxentiou died from a gunshot wound caused by a bullet explosion due to the intense heat in the hideout.

Military action against EOKA was combined with the stringent enforcement of the emergency laws. Pallikarides was executed on 13 March. Aged 18, he was the first terrorist to be convicted of carrying

[1] *Cyprus Mail*, 29 March 1957.

firearms since November, when the death sentence was made mandatory for this and other offences. The precedent caused dismay. Many more Cypriots had subsequently been convicted on the same count. The Pallikarides case created an uproar in England and abroad. Forty Labour MPs, headed by Fenner Brockway, tried to secure a stay of execution. A Congressman, Mr Fulton,[1] telephoned Harding from America to plead for the condemned youth's life a few hours before he was hanged.

The Cyprus authorities were certain that Pallikarides had killed an elderly villager from Lysso, but were unable to produce the witnesses necessary to try him for murder.[2] A belief in the deterrent effect of the death sentence is also likely to have been a factor in Harding's decision that the law must take its course.

Towards the end of the winter, EOKA's defeat seemed imminent. During January and February fatal casualties inflicted by the Organisation totalled 20 compared with 49 in the last two months of 1956. Harding considered that in view of the great improvement in security the Archbishop's continuing detention in the Seychelles could no longer be justified. The time had come to follow up the spectacular successes of the security forces with a fresh political initiative on the part of the British which would incorporate terms for the Archbishop's release.

The Cabinet was, however, preoccupied at the time with Lord Ismay's offer of mediation which had arisen out of the recent extension of NATO's terms of reference to cover political disputes between its members. But weeks went by without a decision being taken. The importance attached at this stage to the NATO offer is hard to understand; Greece had contracted out of the arrangement as far as Cyprus was concerned. And it was not likely that Ismay, as an Englishman, would obtain the cooperation of the Greeks who, in any case, distrusted NATO as a group of 'colonial powers'.

The Greek Government had in the meantime renewed its efforts with Grivas to declare a cease-fire, this time using the argument that it was politically expedient in the light of the recent UN Resolution on Cyprus. Immediately after the UN debate the Bishop of Kition suggested to Grivas that he should call off operations straight away on a temporary basis and at a later stage declare a formal truce.[3] On 24 February Kition's suggestion was backed up by a warning to Grivas from the

---

[1] See *Congressional Record – House*, pp. 3701–3, 21 March 1957.

[2] See *Corruption of Youth in Support of Terrorism in Cyprus* (Government of Cyprus, August 1957), Appendix pp. 28–30.

[3] See *Memoirs* (Greek ed.), op. cit. pp. 158–9.

Greek Consul-General in Nicosia that if EOKA delayed the proclamation the British would seize the initiative with the inevitable result that
Turkey would be included in any negotiations with Greece. Despite
EOKA's heavy losses, Grivas wanted to continue fighting. After much
hesitation he agreed to issue a cease-fire order on 14 March. This
declared that in order to facilitate the resumption of negotiations
between the British Government and the only representative of the
people, the Ethnarch, Archbishop Makarios, EOKA was willing to
suspend operations as soon as he was released.[1]

The new situation created a dilemma for the British Government.
The EOKA offer was certain to be taken at its face value by the world
at large; its outright rejection would have aroused strong criticism at
home and abroad. The British Government, moreover, had a moral
obligation to back up Ismay's offer of mediation, and on 20 March
Lennox-Boyd said that it had been accepted in principle and that the
EOKA Leader's offer had been noted. The Archbishop was being
asked if he was willing in the circumstances to make a statement
calling for the end of violence.[2]

Makarios said the resolution was a starting-point which expressed,
as he understood it, the desire for Anglo-Cypriot talks. EOKA had
offered in the spirit of the resolution to suspend operations subject to his
release. But the British Government was dissatisfied because EOKA had
referred to the suspension and not the cessation of hostilities. He did not
want to see the road blocked by this argument and he had therefore
asked EOKA to cease all operations provided that the Government
showed a spirit of understanding and lifted the state of emergency. He
then quoted his letter of 2 February 1956 to the Governor suggesting
that in the interests of pacification the emergency measures should be
revoked and an amnesty granted for all political offences.

Makarios stressed that as the spiritual and national leader of his
people their interests would always be his first concern, and he could
not agree to his personal release becoming the subject of political
bargaining. He supported the Greek refusal to take part in Cyprus
talks within the framework of NATO, intimating that it would be a
waste of time for the British Government to try to find other Cypriots
willing to negotiate in his absence. The Archbishop's statement,
containing as it did elements of controversy and equivocation, came as a
grave disappointment, yet it would have been difficult for the British
Government to ignore the general trend in international circles

[1] ibid. p. 165.
[2] H.C. Deb., vol. 567, col. 392.

towards conciliation. On 28 March the Colonial Secretary, Lennox-Boyd, announced that Makarios and his compatriots would be released from the Seychelles. Lennox-Boyd mentioned Ismay's offer to mediate and regretted that the Archbishop's statement was not the clear appeal for an end to violence that the Government had requested. Nevertheless it no longer considered his detention essential to security. He was therefore free to come to London, to see anyone and discuss anything, and as head of the Ethnarchy he would be accepted as one of the representatives of the Greek Cypriots. The Governor was prepared to grant a safe-conduct to Colonel Grivas and any other members of EOKA, whether British or foreign, in order to promote a rapid return to peaceful conditions. Lennox-Boyd refuted the Greek Government's interpretation of the UN Resolution adopted by the Archbishop in his statement. There was nothing inconsistent, he said, between the Resolution's terms and the concept of NATO conciliation. The Colonial Secretary emphasised that any relaxation of security measures could only be made when the Governor considered that it was safe to do so.

On 29 March Lord Salisbury resigned in protest against the Archbishop's release. He said the release would have been justified had Makarios made an unconditional appeal to EOKA to halt terrorism instead of deliberately refraining from doing so and that 'a close and confident relationship with Turkey' should be the basis of British policy in the Middle East at the present time.[1]

The British failure to grasp the political initiative owing to vacillation in Whitehall at a time when the guerrillas were on the verge of collapse was disastrous for the prospects of an early settlement. EOKA rapidly recovered its lost prestige by being the first in the field to offer a cease-fire and benefited by the opportunity to rebuild its forces. The Archbishop's release, strongly advocated by Harding, was misrepresented by the Greek Cypriots as a move forced upon the British by the pressure of EOKA and world public opinion. EOKA immediately claimed that just as the Organisation had forced Harding to free Makarios, so it would force him to liberate Cyprus.[2] No greater encouragement could have been given to the latent belief that the Cyprus question could still be settled on the lines demanded by the extremists. Cypriots who, with the turn of the tide against EOKA, had begun to cooperate with the British, were baffled and afraid, and information which until then had been readily forthcoming ceased to reach the security forces.

---

[1] Daily Telegraph, 30 March 1957.
[2] EOKA leaflet: 'The Second Anniversary of EOKA', distributed at Evrykhou, 30 March 1957.

2 THE ARCHBISHOP'S RETURN

The immediate consequences of the Archbishop's release were disquieting. At his first press conference in the Seychelles, which by chance took place on the day of Lord Salisbury's resignation, Makarios accused the British Government of intransigence. At various stages on the journey from Mahé to Athens he dismissed the Radcliffe plan, the NATO offer of mediation and the right of the Turks to a say in the future of Cyprus.

The Greek Government quickly followed up the British decision to free the Archbishop with a move to end the fighting in Cyprus. And the Greek Consul tentatively suggested to Grivas that he should proclaim the end of hostilities the day Makarios arrived in Athens and hinted at the possibility of the EOKA Leader's early departure from the island.[1] The Colonel reacted indignantly. He said he had never expressed any intention of abandoning the struggle and of leaving Cyprus. This would be possible only on the condition that any talks were based on self-determination.[2] Hastily retracting his proposal, the Consul explained that the Greek Government's message was presumably inspired by concern for the EOKA Leader's safety.[3] Grivas replied that this must be discounted; he had enough resources to continue action until the next UN General Assembly.[4] Averoff wrote that no decision would be taken before he met Makarios, but that the loss of Grivas would be a great blow to the cause.[5] The Colonel had in the meantime sent a letter to await the Archbishop's arrival complaining about the Government's insincerity and the Consul's cease-fire proposal which, he said, simply aimed at presenting the Archbishop with a *fait accompli*.[6]

Makarios reached Athens on 17 April, his power and authority enhanced by exile. More than 200 foreign correspondents had come specially for the event. Greek and Cypriot officials headed by the Archbishop of Athens welcomed him at the airport where he was received with military honours. The suburban mayors greeted him en route; a special ceremony at Hadrian's Arch, the gateway to ancient Athens, marked his arrival in the capital. The procession was headed by a motorised column. The Archbishop and the Bishop of Kyrenia, standing up in a white cadillac, their black robes billowing in the wind,

---

[1] *Memoirs* (Greek ed.), op. cit. Greek Consul to Grivas, 2 April 1957, p. 168.

[2] ibid. Grivas to the Consul, 3 April, p. 168.

[3] ibid. the Consul to Grivas, 8 April, p. 169.

[4] ibid. Grivas to the Consul (no date), p. 169.

[5] ibid. Averoff to Grivas, 12 April, p. 170.

[6] ibid. pp. 169–70.

drove past the tomb of the unknown warrior. Students displayed the slogans 'Down with colonialism!' and 'NATO – hands off Cyprus!' and climbed trees and lamp-posts to get a glimpse of the Archbishop. Crowds broke the police cordon when he appeared on the balcony of the Hotel Grande Bretagne to address the masses in Constitution Square. His speech was frequently interrupted by wild outbursts of applause and cries of 'EOKA!', 'Enosis!', 'Dighenis!', 'Self-determination!'

The Greek Cypriots were jubilant at the release of Makarios. Relief that the ordeal of violence and countermeasures was over greatly added to their rejoicings. Restrictions on movement and on the sale of publications were eased; soldiers no longer carried guns; their relations with the local community rapidly improved. Trade revived and outwardly life returned to normal. The Bishop of Kition and the Ethnarchy secretary were freed from house arrest and some detainees released. The death sentence was lifted except for crimes of violence against the person, the carrying of firearms and the use of bombs with intent to kill or injure. The cases of men already convicted on capital charges were subject to review.

The British move in freeing Makarios led to a rapid improvement in Anglo-Greek relations but this was outweighed by a sharp rise in tension between Greece and Turkey. The Archbishop's speeches after leaving the Seychelles had incensed the Turks. Dr Kutchuk claimed during April that Makarios's release had aggravated EOKA's hostility towards the Turkish Cypriots, that owing to the strength of intercommunal tension partition[1] was now the only solution and that any discussion of the Radcliffe proposals would amount to digging the graves of 120,000 Cypriot Turks.[2]

Accusing the Greek Government of planning the Archbishop's reception weeks ahead, the Turkish Prime Minister, Adnan Menderes, said that there could be no clearer proof of 'Greek partnership with Makarios in every respect than this'. The speeches at the ceremony were calculated to incite terrorism and reflected 'the well-worn Greek aspiration for conquest and the annexation of Cyprus'. Events had proved, Menderes said, that the British Government had taken an injudicious step 'in releasing this priest'.[3] The Greek Government no doubt saw the celebrations as a safety-valve for emotions generated by the Archbishop's return. The Greeks nevertheless failed to convince the

---

[1] *Summary of World Broadcasts* IV (BBC) 215, pp. 15–16, 11 April 1957.
[2] ibid. 224, p. 11, 18 April 1957.
[3] ibid. 227, p. 22, 23 April 1957.

Turks that responsibility for the arrangements rested with Archbishop Dorotheos; that the Prime Minister's absence from the airport on the arrival of Makarios was in itself a clear indication that they had no official character. It was not likely that celebrations on the scale of the reception and the use of Constitution Square for mass meetings – banned since the EAM riots of 1944 – could have taken place without permission from the authorities at the highest level.

Apprehensive about the possibility of new talks between the British Government and the 'Red Priest', the Turkish war veterans cabled President Bayar that they were ready, if necessary, to shed their blood for 'Cyprus and our Dodecanese'.[1] Turkish anger culminated in 40,000 protests to Governor Harriman after his invitation to Makarios to be the guest of New York City. On 18 April Ankara Radio commented:

We remember: Mr Harriman is the Governor who refused to meet King Saud, and who by acting in this manner almost jeopardised his Government's policy. In acting thus, he argued, he was acting on behalf of civilisation; he would not greet a tribal chief who represented a feudal regime. Yet today he is preparing to shake hands with a coward who is an obvious murderer and terrorist and whose hands are stained with the blood of thousands of innocent people. We thought everything possible; but we never imagined that a foe of the Moslems would come forward in this century and organise a kind of crusade against the comrades-in-arms of the USA in Korea. . . .[2]

The cooperation of Greece was essential to the promotion of the Cyprus case. Grivas's attempt to drive a wedge between Makarios and the Greek Government inevitably failed. On 22 April the Consul gave Grivas two messages. The first, from Averoff, conceded that the EOKA Leader's presence in Cyprus had some advantages, but repeated that his loss would be a great blow to future progress. The second, from Makarios, contained firm orders that there must be no deviation from the truce.[3] The Archbishop wrote again to Grivas, this time praising the EOKA Leader's 'magnificent' efforts and stressing the importance of the truce and the need to pave the way for Anglo-Cypriot talks by creating a peaceful climate in accordance with the UN resolution. Questioning the usefulness of going on with the armed struggle, the

[1] ibid. 227, p. 22, 23 April 1957.
[2] ibid. 228, p. 15, 24 April 1957.
[3] *Memoirs* (Greek ed.), op. cit. p. 173.

Archbishop undertook to send Grivas his views on the ways of ending it without diminishing the EOKA Leader's prestige.[1]

The Colonel, without waiting for the Archbishop's suggestions, wrote straight away criticising the Greek Government's failure to exploit EOKA's military successes and the Archbishop's sources of information – the 'so-called' leading classes who grumbled at the loss of prosperity due to curfews. A final cease-fire would only make sense if the pre-conditions for a favourable settlement were assured. AKEL and international communism would benefit by the end of hostilities. EOKA had weakened AKEL, which no longer need be considered a political power in Cyprus. But if EOKA gave up the struggle many nationalists might well turn to the left wing, and there was the risk that the Turks, incited by the British, might resort to militant tactics and terrorisation of the Greeks.[2]

The Colonel's letter was typical of his capacity for twisted arguments and lack of consistency. On the one hand he had dismissed AKEL as of no significance in local politics, yet in the same letter he was at pains to convince Makarios that it might supplant the Ethnarchy in the pursuit of the armed struggle.

There could be no guarantee of peace so long as Grivas was in Cyprus and Averoff returned to the subject of his departure, intimating that it might constitute the prerequisite for a relatively satisfactory settlement.[3] The Greek Consul-General, Mr Vlakhos, informed Grivas on 30 April that arrangements could probably be made for the departure of the fighters awaiting trial or execution and for the wanted men to be given the choice of leaving or staying in Cyprus on condition that they reported to the police once a week. The Consul's help would be available to Grivas for the implementation of these plans in accordance with any ideas the EOKA Leader might have about the fighters' prestige and safety. Vlakhos also suggested that the end of military action by EOKA would rob the British of any claim to victory and that the Greeks, by being the first to observe the UN resolution, would win international approval.[4] But the Colonel's faith in the use of force, or the threat of it, as an aid to diplomacy was not to be shaken, and all attempts to expedite his removal by logic and cajolery failed.

The security forces had in the meantime launched a major operation over an area of about 60 square miles in the Paphos Forest in an

[1] ibid. p. 170.
[2] ibid. pp. 170–1.
[3] ibid. Averoff to Grivas (no date), p. 173.
[4] ibid. Greek Consul-General to Grivas, p. 173.

abortive search for the EOKA Leader. The 'martyrdom' of Milikouri, the centre of the search, made sensational news for weeks, especially in Greece where it was reported that the villagers, the victims of 'unspeakable tortures', were dying in scores with their animals from disease and starvation.

The villagers, it was true, suffered hardship and loss of earnings in the early stages. Every house was thoroughly searched. EOKA's ingenuity in the construction of hideouts often made their discovery impossible without damaging walls and floors. And the farmers were not able to cultivate their crops until sufficient troops became available to escort them to their fields and grazing lands. The wild reports of starvation prompted a flood of food parcels from sympathisers. Supplies were also supplemented by the Government. The villagers cheerfully bartered fresh eggs and vegetables with the troops for bully beef and storable rations. The ailing took the opportunity to obtain treatment from the army doctors based in the area.

The allegations against the troops thrived on the Government's refusal, on security grounds, to allow journalists into the area. When the ban was finally lifted on the last day of the operation, correspondents found that relations between the villagers and the 'occupying army' seemed remarkably good; soldiers were surrounded by children clamouring for chocolates; the Royal Engineers were busy repairing houses damaged by the search. Naturally the villagers had complaints: the curfew had disrupted the collection of petals for rose water – a task which needed to be done at dawn when the flowers were in full bloom with the dew still on them. Some of the vines could not be pruned because the vineyards were outside the range of the working parties escorted by the military; the troops, bitterly cold at night in their bivouacs, had picked up loose firewood normally used by the villagers.

The curfew, which had lasted 54 days, was lifted on 13 May and culminated in a mass protest addressed by the people of Milikouri to Dag Hammarskjold.

3 THE DEADLOCK

The euphoria which swept Cyprus after the Archbishop's release rapidly faded once it became clear that the island faced a new political deadlock. In a letter to the British Prime Minister Harold Macmillan on 28 May, Makarios accused the British of ignoring the UN resolution[1] and the Cyprus authorities of enforcing the emergency laws in full and

[1] UN General Assembly Resolution No. 1013, 26 February 1957.

resorting to 'unspeakable torture'. He was, however, willing to negotiate with the British on the basis of self-determination.

The British Government replied that in releasing the Archbishop, in relaxing the emergency laws, in accepting the Radcliffe plan and the NATO Secretary-General's offer of mediation it had helped to create a calmer atmosphere. The Archbishop, on the contrary, had made no corresponding contribution, and so long as the threat of terrorism existed, security operations would have to continue. Makarios by his persistent refusal to denounce violence would bear a heavy responsibility for any loss of life in the event of a renewal of terrorism.[1] The note, which rejected the Archbishop's proposal for bilateral talks, stressed that wider interests had to be considered and that the British Government's position on self-determination was as stated by the Colonial Secretary on 19 December 1956.

Entrenched in Athens and surrounded by extremists, Makarios from now on exerted long-range control over Cypriot politics. Mayors, trade unionists, teachers, lawyers and even the leftists came out in full support of the nationalist line that only the Ethnarch, Archbishop Makarios, was entitled to negotiate a settlement. Local Cypriot advisers urged the Government to allow him back to Cyprus as the first step towards ending the deadlock. But the authorities considered the security risk was too great: Grivas and other terrorists remained at large; Turkish anger was rising with the danger that the Archbishop's premature return might well set off new clashes between the Greek and Turkish Cypriots.

EOKA's directives to the public were mainly communicated in the name of PEKA, its political wing. The aims of the nationalists centred on the Archbishop's return and the end of the emergency laws and the detention camps. The mayors were prominent in exerting pressure on the Government. On 24 May, the Administrative Secretary, John Reddaway, challenged them to denounce violence publicly and to undertake to support the security forces in any new outbreak of terrorism. Reddaway's letter marked the start of a series of acrimonious exchanges on the subject of violence which dragged on for weeks, widening still further the gulf between the Cyprus Government and the local leaders. The leftists had lost much ground owing to their passive attitude to the militant struggle. Two of the mayors were Communists and in no position to adopt an anti-terrorist line. EOKA was basking in the aura of 'resistance'. The denunciation of violence would have been tantamount to the denunciation of the guerrilla movement itself. All the

[1] See above, pp. 235-6.

mayors, the rightists and the leftists, evaded the issue in their reply, only to be censured by the Cyprus Government for condoning the use of terrorism as a political weapon. And on 25 May PEKA called a general strike to protest against the Government's refusal to meet the nationalists' demands. The majority of Cypriots wanted to make up for time and money lost when terrorism was at its height; it was a glum population which shut its shops in Nicosia, Limassol and elsewhere. Since political strikes were illegal the participants ran the risk of prosecution, but this was seen as a lesser evil than the reprisals which could be expected to follow the flouting of EOKA's orders.

EOKA refrained from militant action. This would have been unpopular with the public, which had already suffered enough in the past years from the disruption of trade and prolonged curfews in the heat of summer. The Organisation sought instead to foment friction between the Cypriots and the administration without actual recourse to violence. The issue was kept alive by regular memorial services in the villages for the guerrillas who had lost their lives in the struggle. Portraits of the dead were paraded at the gravesides where boys and girls recited patriotic poems extolling the glories of EOKA. Attendance was compulsory. Troops were sent to cordon off the villages involved in these emotional ceremonies, which led to fresh grievances and the risk of clashes between the people and the security forces.

EOKA sustained the grip of intimidation by means of leaflets, aggressive in tone and often threatening reprisals. The Organisation viewed any improvement in relations between the Cypriots and the authorities as a major danger to the cause. A ban was promptly imposed on the Government's new technical schools with their welcome opportunities for higher education:

NOTE CIRCULATED TO PARENTS IN NICOSIA

With regret we have observed your anti-national behaviour in sending your child to the Technical School where our enemies may corrupt his spirit with their propaganda. There exist our own proper schools which offer Greek culture and education.

If you do not decide to transfer your child to a Greek school then you and your child will be branded as common traitors. Your own name and that of your child will be published so that you will be despised by the people and condemned wherever you may be.

There is still time.

EOKA. 14 July, 1957.

Political agitation inevitably spread to the Turkish Cypriots. Backed by Ankara, Dr Kutchuk declared in May that partition at an early date was the only solution. Fears that a Labour Government might be returned at the next British election, which would give way to Enosis, were responsible for the new sense of urgency underlying the Turkish stand. The Turks did not at this stage envisage compulsory population exchanges, but in the absence of territorial divisions between the communities they believed that many families from both races would want to move. The problems of demarcation lines and compensation had now become regular topics for discussion in Turkish Cypriot circles. Economically the Turks were likely to suffer more than the Greek community but they insisted that anything was preferable to Greek rule. In the summer all the Turkish councillors in the main towns resigned. They complained that because Turkish citizens were inadequately protected the Greek majority was turning the councils 'into political organisations in order to further their own political ambitions'. Turkish discontent in the municipalities, especially Nicosia, had been festering for nearly ten years.[1] A British expert, in the throes of investigating the problem, was shortly expected to recommend greater safeguards for the Turks. The choice of this moment for their resignation appeared to be inspired by the desire to illustrate the impracticability of cooperating with the Greeks in any form of self-government, including the Radcliffe plan, where they had the majority.

At the end of the summer, Dr Kutchuk, fortified by a second visit to Ankara, stated in Nicosia that Turkey would claim all the sector north of the 35th Parallel – roughly half of Cyprus. Privately, the Turkish leaders intimated that they would only give up partition provided the Greeks dropped the demand for self-determination, which the Turks interpreted as 'just another word for Enosis'.

4   THE ATROCITY CAMPAIGN

EOKA's main weapon against the administration during the cease-fire was the atrocity campaign. This reached its peak in the summer and was coordinated with the intensification of the Greek Government's efforts to discredit Britain in the United Nations and the Council of Europe.

EOKA adopted two lines of attack. The first dealt with the conduct of the army after operations involving arrests and searches, the second with specific allegations of torture against interrogators and intelligence

[1] See above, p. 55.

officers. The Cypriot capacity for exaggeration was recognised even by EOKA, which repeatedly stressed in its orders the need for accuracy in compiling dossiers on ill-treatment. The allegations against the troops met with considerable scepticism in British and international circles.

About 36,000 troops were stationed in Cyprus at any one time. In the days of National Service the army inevitably had its quota of toughs from the Gorbals and ex-Borstal boys. Reputations varied with different regiments. The South Staffordshires were noted for the gentleness of their tactics in dispersing riots; the Royal Marine Commandos for their ability to get on with the villagers. The paratroopers, usually called upon to deal with the most critical situations, were associated with roughness in carrying out searches. The soldiers' reactions in any given incident were apt to be influenced by the degree of provocation and the number of casualties suffered by their units. The great majority of British soldiers carried out their duties under conditions of strain with exemplary patience and restraint. The security forces needed information quickly from a captured terrorist before the rest of the gang had time to get away.[1] That rough handling took place when armed men were arrested was officially admitted as unavoidable, especially if they put up any defence. 'What do you expect us to do with them? Sit them down and give them all cups of tea?'[2] was the comment of a young corporal to a British correspondent at the height of the emergency.

The troops did not entirely escape the volume of abuse which flowed from EOKA. But the main targets during the cease-fire were individual interrogators and intelligence officers. Some military experts believed that the campaign actually aided the security forces in that it terrorised EOKA's members to the extent that when captured they readily told all they knew. In dealing with the more resistant prisoners, on occasions when the time factor was important, the exponents of coercion justified its use in the interests of defeating terrorism and saving lives.

Good intelligence was essential to the defeat of EOKA. Information was also vital for the collation of evidence which would enable the Crown to bring the prisoners to trial. Interrogation in depth took place in special centres. Platres and Omorphita became notorious. The names of the same interrogators appeared time and again in Cypriot complaints. Suspicions that these, although often either exaggerated or fabricated, might contain a strong element of truth were increased by

[1] See *Report on the inquiry into allegations against the Security Forces of physical brutality in Northern Ireland arising out of events on the 9th August 1971*. (Compton) Cmnd 4823, p. vi. Note: Maudling's Introduction refers to the need for speed in all anti-terrorist operations.

[2] See 'Justice in Cyprus: I – An Inquiry Needed', *Manchester Guardian*, 1 July 1957.

the deaths of two prisoners. Andreas Panaghiotou was injured in the Troodos Mountains when he tried to escape from his army escort; the latter was completely vindicated by the Coroner. Panaghiotou's death in a cell at Platres the next day, however, was never fully explained. Nikos Georghiou was suddenly taken seriously ill while in custody at Platres. Attempts were made to save his life at Akrotiri RAF hospital, but he died two days later after a brain operation. Mr Justice Morgan, the Coroner at Limassol, stated that death was probably caused by intracranial haemorrhage and purulent bronchitis occasioned by some unknown external agency of which there was no direct evidence.

The terrorists captured during the late winter and spring came up for trial in the summer. The fact that some of them faced capital charges and that EOKA made full use of the courts as a forum for the atrocity campaign added to the uneasiness of the cease-fire. The long-drawn-out process of public inquiry, trial and appeal ensured that the allegations got maximum publicity. The death of a fighter in battle, a rare event since the security forces were ordered at considerable risk to themselves to take prisoners, was by comparison quickly forgotten.

A liberal system of justice had functioned throughout the emergency. Against the background of violence and reprisals the guerrilla benefits even more than the peacetime criminal from the concept that a man is innocent until proved guilty. The intimidation of witnesses obliged the Crown to rely very largely on confessions and statements made by the accused. It automatically followed that defence counsel would seek to get such evidence rejected as inadmissible on the ground that it was obtained under duress or in breach of Judges' Rules. Many of EOKA's defeats were due to betrayal. And it was natural that those responsible should seek to justify their actions to the Organisation by pleading torture. The atrocity campaign served a legal as well as a political purpose.

EOKA's use of the courts for propaganda resulted in 'the trial within a trial'. Members of the security forces giving evidence for the Crown were subjected to lengthy allegations of brutality when cross-examined by defence counsel. The judges often ruled that the allegations were irrelevant without necessarily indicating whether they were true or not. In addition to the Crown's witnesses, certain interrogators who were not present were named time and again in defence counsels' indictment. The irrelevancy of the submission meant that evidence of rebuttal was not allowed. The security forces were thus deprived of an opportunity to clear their reputation.

On 23 May Sampson was acquitted of the murder of a British police officer. Mr Justice Shaw found that all allegations of torture were untrue but severely censured the police for failing to provide him, on arrival in Nicosia, with dry clothes and immediate medical attention for injuries sustained in his struggle with them on arrest. Sampson had been made to travel face downwards from Dhali to Nicosia in a truck in drenching rain, with no covering other than his shirt, trousers and two pullovers. This 'unconscionable' treatment, Mr Shaw stated, raised a doubt as to whether his confession, a vital part of the Crown's evidence, was free and voluntary.[1]

Michael Thrassyvoulides, the leader of the Limassol killer group, was tried by Mr Justice Shaw in May for discharging a firearm at Vassos Karapattas. The Crown's case was based on a confession. Defence counsel objected to the production of the statement in court. He contended that the accused was not at the time in lawful custody; that he had already suffered ill-treatment at Platres interrogation centre prior to making his statement; that he was induced to make the statement by certain promises, in particular that he would be sent to Camp K and that this would end his ill-treatment which would otherwise continue.

Shaw entirely disbelieved the accused's evidence regarding the manner in which his statement was recorded and there was no corroboration at all of his allegations of ill-treatment apart from the testimony of his mother and her friend who said they had seen blood on his underpants. The allegation that force and violence were used had not been substantiated, but there was some truth in the allegation concerning the promise over Camp K. He was, in fact, sent there. Shaw ruled that the evidence was insufficient to prove the case against the accused beyond all reasonable doubt and he was acquitted.[2]

Mr Shaw, a courageous judge, who had not hesitated to pass the death sentence in the past, was seriously wounded by EOKA in the early stages of the emergency. After this incident he lost the confidence of the security forces, who felt that he tended to lean too far in favour of the terrorists in an overconscientious effort to ensure that his experience had in no way affected his impartiality. Sampson was immediately re-arrested on a charge of carrying a Sten gun and subsequently sentenced to death by Mr Justice John.

George Sphongaras was convicted by Mr Justice John of depositing

---

[1] Official Judgement (Registrar of the Supreme Court, Nicosia).

[2] See *Cyprus Mail*, 5 June 1957. Note: The Limassol group headed by Thrassyvoulides was acclaimed years later by Grivas to have killed 5 soldiers and 1 British special constable. See *Memoirs* (Longmans), pp. 77 and 103.

a bomb which exploded in the salt store of the Kyrenia customs house. The Crown's case was based solely on his statement to the police and evidence of opportunity. In court he made serious allegations of ill-treatment against a Turkish police constable who, in his absence abroad, was not called as a witness. The Supreme Court of Cyprus upheld Sphongaras's appeal. The Chief Justice disagreed with the trial judge's conclusion that the whole story of ill-treatment was an invention based on the actual amount of rough handling likely to take place on the arrest of suspects. The Chief Justice subsequently censured a Greek Cypriot newspaper for misinterpreting his judgement. The appeal was upheld on the grounds that the trial judge had misdirected himself on a point of law and because, as suggested by the newspaper, the Supreme Court had believed the allegations of ill-treatment. Despite this clarification one passage in particular in the Supreme Court's findings could hardly fail to strengthen the atrocity campaign:

> Now because we are bound by findings of fact we will omit all references to allegations of ill-treatment which were disbelieved. But it is apparent that the learned Judge did not disbelieve all the allegations that were made ... But though he (the trial judge) rejected the uncontradicted evidence going to the more serious allegations of ill-treatment, the learned Judge has accepted that the appellant was kept in custody for questioning over a period of twelve days and, it seems, that there was physical interference with him when he was arrested which is described as 'rough-handling' ... It was also accepted that at any rate over the early stages of his detention he was forced to endure the discomfiture, to say no more about it, of wearing a sack over his head.[1]

The Supreme Court dismissed the appeal of Michael Rossides who was convicted of the murder of Private Shilton and sentenced to death. The case against Rossides was based on a confession twice made to the police. He told them that he was forced to shoot his friend on the orders of Grivas by the group leader 'Zaimis'; that he shot him three or four times with an automatic pistol. Deeply moved, Rossides said, he fell to the ground before seeing whether Shilton was shot dead or simply wounded. This was the whole truth which he had told the police in order to ease his conscience:

> Be sure that as from that day I continually lost my sleep and I used to see Ronnie's ghost in front of me.[2]

[1] Official Judgement (The Registrar, Supreme Court of Nicosia).
[2] Cyprus Mail, 3 June 1957.

Defence counsel pleaded that the confession was not valid on the ground that it was dictated by the police and Rossides's signature obtained under pressure.

The Appeal Court found that the two confessions were substantiated by a number of factors – Shilton's disappearance on 17 April 1956 tallied with Rossides's statement that the soldier was brought to him late in that month. The condition of the body dug up in February 1957[1] was consistent with the burial date given in the confession. The body was found $4\frac{1}{2}$ miles from Lysi. Rossides had estimated that the place of the killing and burial was about 2 miles from Lysi. The discrepancy was understandable. Rossides had confessed to the shooting of Shilton and mentioned that he was wearing civilian clothes and that he was hit by a shovel. Bullets were found in the body which was in civilian clothes; the head showed a severe injury caused by a heavy blow from a large instrument. The Supreme Court therefore upheld the trial judge's conclusion that Rossides's two confessions were voluntary and admissible in evidence. In the lengthy indictments of British brutality circulated abroad by the Cypriots it is significant that Rossides does not figure in the list of alleged victims.

The Cyprus Government replied on 11 June in a White Paper. Harding accused EOKA of organising 'a campaign of denigration designed to foster hatred'[2] against the security forces and to sow doubt and misgiving outside the island. Grivas had at his disposal, Harding said, the whole propaganda machinery of a Church engaged in political subversion, the Greek Government's publicity organs and the Greek Cypriot press for the promotion of the campaign.

Harding conceded the unavoidability of rough handling in capturing terrorists, but stressed that in no cases had the courts accepted allegations of torture or systematic ill-treatment apart from the court martial which found two army officers guilty of assaulting a prisoner.[3]

Harding recalled the Lefkoniko incident,[4] in which a soldier was disembowelled after a game of football by an explosion at the village drinking fountain. Despite wild allegations of ill-treatment and malicious damage during the search which immediately followed the incident, a very thorough inquiry had shown that these were ill founded. 'The people of Lefkoniko', Harding concluded, 'had reason to be thankful that it was British troops with whom they had to deal on that day.'

[1] During Operation Sparrow-hawk.
[2] *Allegations of Brutality in Cyprus* (Cyprus Government White Paper), p. 3.
[3] See above, p. 179.
[4] See above, p. 204.

The White Paper outlined the history of the ill-treatment campaign, the importance attached to it by Grivas as a propaganda weapon and its marked intensification since the serious defeats suffered by the guerrillas in recent months. It accused the Cypriot lawyers of abusing for political ends the legitimate concern of their profession for human rights and gave examples of Cypriots who had complained of ill-treatment, usually at the instigation of their lawyers, and had then retracted when asked by the authorities to substantiate them. It was significant that the Cypriots imprisoned in Wormwood Scrubs for many months should have chosen this moment to complain of ill-treatment alleged to have taken place before they left Cyprus.

The lawyers replied that the White Paper was a serious attack on the integrity of the Cyprus Bar and especially on the lawyers who formed the local 'Committee on Human Rights' and were engaged in defending the cases before the Special Court. Since they were either members of or closely associated with EOKA the complaint carried little weight. The lawyers' main aim was, however, to prove that the ill-treatment allegations had not been satisfactorily disposed of in the White Paper and to stress the urgency of an independent inquiry.

They denied that the Special Court was being used for propaganda. The fact that allegations of ill-treatment were allowed to be aired extensively in evidence was clear proof of their relevance. It was a strange coincidence that at a time when the prosecution had to rely on statements made by the accused without supporting evidence many of the defendants should have been overcome by the desire to show 'penitence and remorse'. This in itself was a justification for a full inquiry into the methods of the police and investigating officers. The lawyers claimed that one of the Cypriots in Wormwood Scrubs had, in fact, formally complained about ill-treatment while he was still in Cyprus. This omission from the White Paper cast serious doubts on its accuracy.

The White Paper's statement that only nine private prosecutions had been filed in connection with ill-treatment had no significance, the lawyers argued, since the Government refused to disclose the names of the investigators against whom the prisoners and detainees had made complaints of torture. The lawyers' reply also commented on the failure of the prosecution to call certain witnesses in recent trials.

Recalling the White Paper's references to the high standards of the UK police, the lawyers pointed out that the complaints were mainly directed against intelligence officers, members of the armed forces and the Special Branch – many of them of 'dubious national extraction' although of British nationality. The lawyers noted that Cypriot judges had for some considerable time been precluded from adjudicating in cases against the security forces. Dissatisfied with the Governor's assurances that when ill-treatment was proved the offenders were punished, the report observed that the two officers court-martialled for assault were subsequently given reduced sentences and that this particular case had come to light mainly owing to the fact that the prisoner in question came up before the court on remand and was able to complain of ill-treatment. The Turkish magistrate, Mr Fuad, had ordered an investigation and a medical examination. But since this case the procedure had been changed and a suspect no longer needed to be brought before the court after his arrest. He could be detained for four days under a police remand. And after this period his appearance in court could be further postponed and even completely avoided by the service of a detention-without-trial order. The detection and proper investigation of ill-treatment complaints was accordingly extremely difficult.

In conclusion the lawyers stressed that the reasons they had given illustrated beyond all doubt the need for an independent public inquiry. Since they were fully aware of the uselessness of this procedure under the conditions then prevailing in Cyprus, their reaction seems to have been motivated by political aims rather than a desire to establish the truth and to ensure humane treatment for their clients.

The allegations were taken up by Makarios on 19 July[1] at a conference organised by the Greek Press Union in Athens. Accusing the British of trying to conceal the atrocities instead of stopping them, he said that he had 317 signed statements from victims of torture and knew of many others who had only confided their sufferings to relatives, lawyers and doctors. The Archbishop dealt in some detail with alleged sexual abuses during interrogation and much of his indictment was not published in England.[2] He also dealt at length with the strange case of Abbot Irineos of Makheras whose tortures were said to have taken place shortly after the gun battle near the monastery between the security forces and Afxentiou.[3] The abbot's complaint had been thoroughly investigated by the British authorities and refuted without specific mention of his name in the White Paper. He first complained

[1] Statement by the Archbishop of Cyprus on 'The Tortures Practised in Cyprus by British Security Forces', 19 July 1957.
[2] *Summary of World Broadcasts* IV (BBC) records several gaps marked 'obscene passage' in the version broadcast by Athens Radio.
[3] See above, pp. 232–3.

about torture when he was visited by a Nicosia lawyer three weeks after Afxentiou's death. When requested to substantiate the allegations, he told a senior police officer that he had not asked the lawyer to visit him and that he had had no intention of complaining beforehand. But the Church was powerful and had sent the lawyer. He could not forget what had happened to the Abbot of Chrysorroyiatissa who was murdered by EOKA.[1] The abbot subsequently stated that he had only withdrawn his complaint for fear of further torture.

Irineos began his remarkable career as a clerk in the RAF. After studying theology he became abbot at 24. The Brotherhood of Makheras is an exclusive order; and the removal in June of twelve priests from detention camps to the monastery raised a storm of protest. The abbot threatened to cut off the food of his unwelcome guests unless the Government's belated cheque for their maintenance was sent without further delay. Tales of hunger and hardship, much on the lines of the allegations made about Milikouri, filled the newspapers and food parcels flowed in from all parts of the island. A shrewd businessman, the abbot had successfully negotiated with the Cyprus Government a monthly subsistence allowance of £10 for each priest, compensation for the loss of revenue due to the ban on pilgrims and tourists, and the installation of showers and latrines.

The monks and the priests and the soldiers guarding the monastery lived in the main building and enjoyed the spacious grounds. After the hot dusty camps in Nicosia the monastery on the cool, wooded slopes of Mount Kinonia formed a pleasant billet for soldiers and priests alike. The rumours had, as always, thrived on the ban on journalists. A British journalist who was finally able to visit the monastery found the Grenadier Guards on duty; the tact of the young officer in command was partly responsible for their good relations with the inmates. The abbot, who at 32 had the presence of a much older man, did however complain that the presence of troops upset the routine of monastic life. As a former employee of the RAF he was used to soldiers but the elderly monks were shocked by the sight of guardsmen in shorts. He made general references to the people's sufferings under the emergency and to the Church's traditional role in furthering a national struggle. But at no time did he mention his own much publicised complaint of torture at the hands of the British security forces.[2]

The question of atrocities was extensively discussed in the House of Commons, which was exactly what the Cypriots hoped for. Jennie Lee

[1] See above, pp. 156 and 169.
[2] *Manchester Guardian*, 5 August 1957 (author's report).

and Fenner Brockway persistently questioned the Secretary of State for the Colonies about complaints made by the hardened Cypriot prisoners in Wormwood Scrubs. The subject of brutality took up much of the full debate on the Cyprus question on 15 July.[1] It was raised by Callaghan on behalf of the Opposition. Profumo replied that these allegations came from EOKA and that one could not expect them to pay attention to accuracy. Makarios was obsessed with 'atrocities', he said, but had no means of verifying his information since he was not in Cyprus. Jennie Lee and Fenner Brockway were still not satisfied with the situation concerning the Wormwood Scrubs prisoners. Jennie Lee read out a gruesome complaint made by one of them against a Greek and a Turk, both allegedly British agents, and against an RMP of the Parachute Regiment.

Lennox-Boyd said the principal prison medical officer's report showed that no scars or bruises were noted at the time of their arrival. The slight scar on the prisoner's wrist could conceivably have been caused by a rope some time ago. These people led very rough lives and there had been a tremendous amount of fighting between the prisoners themselves before they arrived in England. He could not accept that these wounds were caused by British troops. Geoffrey Hirst and Frederic Gough, a former member of the Parachute Regiment, came out firmly in its defence.

Kenneth Robinson also expressed strong dissatisfaction at the Government's handling of the ill-treatment question, and with other Socialists pressed for an independent inquiry. He found the White Paper inexplicit on the subject of the seven prosecutions brought against members of the security forces between September 1955 and June 1956. The really serious charges only began to be made about November 1956. Since that date it had been impossible under the amended emergency regulations to bring a private prosecution against any of the security forces without the authority of the Attorney-General. The Cypriot allegations were almost exclusively levelled against Special Branch officers and interrogators. If these men were innocent, it was totally unfair to deny them the opportunity of clearing their names by means of an independent inquiry.

Lena Jeger found it shameful that Britain should have to be arraigned by the Human Rights Sub-Committee of the Council of Europe and that the Governor, supported by the Colonial Secretary, had refused to allow the judicial inquiry requested by the Council.

Lennox-Boyd anticipated that certain atrocity charges made by the

[1] H.C. Deb., vol. 573, cols 771–898.

Greek Government and Makarios would be raised at the forthcoming UN debate. He reminded the House that during the previous year the Greek Government had cabled a list of accusations against British troops. The UK representative had asked that this should either be published or withdrawn.[1] The Colonial Secretary hoped that members, when listening to current stories on atrocities, would remember that it was withdrawn. In order to deal with two sets of charges, those made by Makarios and those made by certain Members of the House of Commons, he had placed an interim statement in the Library. A full statement would take a long time, since many of the troops had left the island and the descriptions were so vague that the men might be unidentifiable. There could be no question of an inquiry, he said, involving witnesses whose lives would be endangered if they gave evidence.

The Colonial Secretary stated that a more misleading statement could not be imagined than the Archbishop's claim that the death of Nikos Georghiou was due to torture. As for His Beatitude's strictures relating to the delay in holding the inquest, this was due to the request for an adjournment by the lawyer Glavkos Klerides who needed time to call additional evidence.

Lennox-Boyd challenged the veracity of Lena Jeger's assertion that Britain had been arraigned before the Council of Europe. These reports had originated in Athens. The British Government had respected its obligations to maintain the secrecy of the proceedings of the Sub-Committee. It was unfortunate, he said, 'that this confidence should not only have been violated but that the violation should be inaccurate'. Lennox-Boyd thanked Jennie Lee for admitting her error in confusing Renos Kyriakides with Athanasios Sophokleous – one of the two Wormwood Scrubs prisoners whom she had seen that day. In such grave charges it was essential to be accurate in every detail, he said.

Michael Pissas, the leader of the right-wing trade unions, was chiefly responsible for publicising in the USA the campaign alleging atrocities.[2] Under the persistent pressure of the International Confederation of Free Trade Unions (ICFTU), the Cyprus Government had,

---

[1] According to Xydis, op. cit. p. 42, Averoff advised Dag Hammarskjold on 23 February 1957 that he was withdrawing the file on atrocities from the UN Secretariat as a goodwill gesture towards the British Delegation. The truth was never established either one way or the other; five atrocity allegations were due to come up before the Human Rights Commission of the Council of Europe, but the Zurich settlement came before the hearing.

[2] See Michael Pissas, *The Truth About Concentration Camps in Cyprus* (New York, December 1957) and *Violation of Human Rights in Cyprus – A Factual Documentation* (printed by the Ethnarchy of Cyprus, of which Pissas was a member). Both booklets, which deal with torture allegations, were distributed by the Cyprus Federation of America.

against its better judgement, released him from detention on condition that he confined his activities to trade union work in the Belgian mines. The Cyprus authorities had failed to take the precaution of giving him a passport which was valid for Europe only and it was not long before he left Brussels to work up the vilification campaign in America. It was not politically realistic to expect that Pissas would honour his undertaking, but the ICFTU's record in this affair amounted to a breach of faith.

The allegations gained ground with the Government's refusal to hold an independent inquiry. This would almost certainly have revealed some abuses. But it would have put the campaign into perspective. Instead of which many of the allegations came to be accepted at their face value and recorded as fact.

5 PREPARATIONS FOR THE SECOND ROUND

During the cease-fire security operations were aimed mainly at keeping the troops occupied and at containing rather then eliminating EOKA which seized the opportunity to re-form the guerrilla groups. In preparation for the second round, ANE (The Valiant Youth of EOKA) was founded in the summer with the object of enlisting and training recruits. ANE's commanders were instructed to draw upon three categories of young men: nationalist sympathisers who had not yet had an opportunity to join EOKA; the uncommitted who, although they had not succumbed to communism, had equally shown no enthusiasm for the nationalist struggle; and finally communist supporters hitherto opposed to the cause. The inclusion of this last category was characteristic of the Colonel's doctrinaire approach to politics.

The initial selection was entrusted to priests and schoolteachers; final membership had to be sanctioned either by EOKA or PEKA; ages ranged from 14 to 25; married men were not eligible. ANE functioned on the communist system, with each member knowing only the identities of the men in his own group. Communications between one cell and another were forbidden. ANE's wide range of duties included surveillance and intimidation. Children began with leaflet distribution and slogan painting. Later, on demonstrating proficiency as gunmen, they were promoted to full membership of EOKA.

During the summer EOKA also formed the first anti-Turkish groups and drew up elaborate plans for the defence of the Greek villages against possible Turkish attacks.[1] Sector leaders were ordered to submit

[1] See *Guerrilla Warfare* op. cit., Appendices II, III & IV, pp. 96-9, for the anti-Turkish plans in full.

detailed reports on their villages, the race ratio and the number of arms available. The mixed villages were instructed to concentrate their defences inside and not to expect reinforcements; the all-Greek communities were told to base their defences on the edge of the villages on the side most vulnerable to attack. A reprisals system was worked out to take place on the same or on the next night.

The Turks soon heard about these preparations. They did not believe that the Greeks, once organised on anti-Turkish lines, would limit their activities to defence. And a new Turkish underground movement was formed, which eventually became the TMT (Turk Mudafa Teskilat – Turkish Defence Organisation). Four Turks were fatally injured in an explosion at the end of August. The accident led to the discovery of explosives in a Turkish house – the first indication that the Turks were contemplating militant action in the event of EOKA launching a second round.

After the formation of ANE, recruiting for the guerrilla groups increased rapidly. By the end of the summer EOKA had rearmed and refilled all the important gaps in its ranks, and had at its disposal an efficient force with a potentially greater striking power than ever before. But the time was not yet politically ripe for militant action against the British. An open breach of the cease-fire would have conflicted with the line that the Greek Government intended to adopt at the forthcoming UN debate, namely that whereas EOKA had acted in the spirit of the last Assembly's resolution Britain had disregarded it by continuing security operations. Outwardly the situation remained calm and the authorities eased the emergency laws by stages. The death sentence ceased to be mandatory for throwing bombs, for discharging and carrying firearms. Life imprisonment became the maximum penalty for these crimes.

In the meantime EOKA had renewed violence. Its first target was the left wing. AKEL, by its passive attitude to the struggle, had lost ground to the nationalists. Nevertheless, with its admirable record in social welfare, labour and municipal affairs, it still constituted the only serious challenge to the Church politicians in the long term. All the leading Akelists formerly held by the British in detention camps were now free and Ziartides, the Secretary-General of PEO, had recently returned from England. The timing of the Colonel's sudden outbursts against the leftists usually defied rational explanation. But on this occasion he may well have calculated that the time was opportune to weaken the leftists before they had a chance to rebuild their strength, and to impress again upon the Americans the inherently anti-communist character of

EOKA before the Archbishop's forthcoming campaign in the United States.

The attacks against the leftists took the form of isolated incidents mainly in villages. Most of the victims were trade unionists. Four men were thrashed by an EOKA group at Vokolida. At Avgorou masked men tied a villager to a post at night, leaving a warning notice that he was not to be released until daylight. The attacks continued into the late autumn. The Central Committee of AKEL had from the first urged all parties to set aside their differences and continue the struggle for Enosis. Abusive and indecent attacks against the left, AKEL maintained, merely undermined the national effort and the provocation of the villagers by the right wing assisted the colonialists in their policy of 'divide and rule'.

EOKA then turned to the few remaining village mukhtars. Although their services were essential to the villagers, EOKA looked upon them as the tools of the administration and many had resigned under pressure.

In September the new Mukhtar of Asha was marched to the church by an EOKA gang, tied to the door and a placard bearing the word 'traitor' tied round his neck. At Karavas three armed masked men forced the mukhtar to leave his house and go to the coffee shop where they removed his seal from him. Next they tied him to an electric pole and gave orders that he was to be left there until dawn. Other mukhtars were either threatened or assaulted. On 14 October the Mukhtar of Dhali, a respected citizen well known for his moderation, was shot dead by gunmen.

Despite the general deterioration in security, British policy remained conciliatory. The emergency measures were eased by stages. Sampson and Rossides, amongst others facing execution, had their sentences commuted to life imprisonment.

By the late autumn ANE's preparations were complete. Its own periodical, *Reveille*, was in circulation. Inflammatory, abusive, fanatically pro-Enosis, the first issue contained an appeal for members, Hellenic poems and slashing attacks on the Communists and the British.[1] The second was chiefly devoted to the glorification of the Greek Army's heroic stand against the Italians in 1941 'when the Great Powers were aroused from the lethargy of their pessimism to courage by the example of Greece'.[2] ANE's authors saw Turkey as the spoilt child of Britain.

---

[1] *Reveille: A Periodical Publication for the Guidance of ANE*, Issue 1, 10 October 1957.

[2] ibid. Issue 2, *The Trilogy of the Greek Drama* (Undated, recovered on 22 Nov. 1957 at Aghios Theodoros, Famagusta District).

Carried away in their extremism, they expounded a philosophy which ironically matched that of the Communists with its lapses into hostility towards the Americans and the West.

EOKA decided that the people – and even some of its own members – needed to be reminded that the struggle was not over. The date chosen as a suitable occasion for a display of strength was 28 October, the anniversary of the Greek stand against the Italians in 1941. Citizens were called upon to cooperate fully with EOKA and ANE in demonstrations; to hoist large Greek flags at sunrise on churches, houses, shops and clubs; to use small paper flags inside coffee shops and clubs and for the decoration of streets and squares. Country dwellers were ordered to paint Enosis slogans in conspicuous positions in their villages. Nationalistic texts to be learnt by heart were widely distributed for use over loudspeakers. Attendance at church, the closure of schools and coffee shops were compulsory. The programme provided for the chanting of national songs and patriotic speeches at the end of the doxology. ANE now came into its own. Its orders were to march in formation shouting Enosis slogans, to sing the Greek national anthem and to stand up to the British troops if they intervened to stop the demonstrations.

Violent clashes broke out between the security forces and the Cypriots for the first time since the cease-fire and many people were injured. EOKA had achieved its objective.

6 STRATEGIC AND POLITICAL CHANGES IN 1957

By mid-1957 Britain's strategic requirements had substantially changed. The Suez fiasco the previous year had brought to the surface the latent misgivings in military circles about the merits of Cyprus as a base.[1] Britain no longer needed the island in conjunction with a complex of Middle East bases and treaties, many of which had ceased to exist. In the short term the direct link with Aden and the Persian Gulf had been disrupted by a ban on military aircraft flying over the intervening Arab territory. In the long term the security of Britain's oil supplies was likely to depend on mutual commercial interests and the cooperation of the producer states and not on the use of force.

Harding himself considered that the time had passed when 'friends and allies' needed to be supported by land forces as well as air power.

[1] *Despatch by General Sir Charles F. Keightley, GCB, CBE, DSO, Commander in Chief, Allied Forces, 12 September, 1957: Supplement to The London Gazette, 10 September, 1957. See p. 5328.*

He envisaged that the island's future strategic importance would lie chiefly in air support for NATO and the Baghdad Pact.[1]

The first public hint of change came in the Defence White Paper of April 1957, which announced the British Government's decision to reduce its overseas military commitments.[2] Harding foresaw that it would not be possible to deploy sufficient troops to control the whole island indefinitely against the wishes of the Cypriots and he was satisfied that Britain's future requirements could be met by the retention of two or three enclaves combined with the use of certain ancillary facilities. On the political side he had, after several months' experience of the island, reached the conclusion that no solution was possible so long as the issue of sovereignty remained outstanding. This view was eventually endorsed by the Cabinet and thereafter Britain's role in Cyprus was treated as a 'holding operation' pending a settlement which was acceptable to Greece, Turkey and the Cypriots.

In Greece the situation had also changed. The Cyprus issue, once a useful distraction from internal problems, had now become a millstone for the Government. Faced with a growing sense of isolation, Greece urgently needed to restore relations with Turkey and play her full part in NATO. The expulsion of the Ecumenical Patriarch, threatened by the Turks, would have constituted a far greater blow to Hellenism than the failure to acquire Cyprus. When it came to the persecution of minorities as a weapon, Greece had more to lose than Turkey. The empty spaces of Anatolia could have comparatively easily absorbed the Turkish peasants living in Greek Thrace; but the resettlement in Greece of the highly urbanised Greeks in large numbers from Istanbul and Smyrna, as the result of either their flight or enforced evacuation, would have created major economic and social problems. The spectre of partition was also growing. Britain's lukewarm support for the idea was rightly interpreted as nothing more dangerous than a diplomatic manoeuvre to induce the Cypriots to accept self-government as the lesser evil. But the tenacity with which the Turks had recently adopted partition as their official policy could not be ignored. The Greek Government was inevitably compelled in 1957 to view the Cyprus question from a less parochial angle than the Ethnarchy and Colonel Grivas. Steps were taken during the summer with the object of placating the Turks. Alexis Kyrou, probably the most fanatical advocate of Enosis in the Greek Foreign Office, was appointed Ambassador to

[1] See Field-Marshal the Lord Harding of Petherton, 'The Cyprus Problem in Relation to the Middle East', *International Affairs* (RIIA, July 1958), vol. 34, no. 3, pp. 291–6.
[2] *Defence: Outline of Future Policy, April 1957*, Cmnd 124, pp. 4–5.

Finland and George Pezmazoglou, a member of a distinguished Istanbul family, Ambassador to Turkey.

The summer was marked by a series of confused political initiatives at international level. The United States sounded the Turkish Government without success on the possibility of a solution based on guaranteed independence. Paul-Henri Spaak, the new NATO Secretary-General, shortly after taking up his appointment in May, made an unofficial approach to Turkey, proposing an independent state on the lines of Belgium or Austria. The question of Cyprus was not analogous, however, and Spaak's proposals were in any case premature. The Turks were infuriated, which was not surprising since the Greek Foreign Secretary had recently described independence as a transitional stage in the struggle for Enosis.[1] Spaak was debarred from playing the role of mediator for months to come and even had to exclude Turkey from the routine visit made by each new Secretary-General to all the NATO countries.

Britain tried to organise a tripartite conference. Backed by the USA and NATO, this new initiative excluded any settlement based on Enosis or partition and provided for an open agenda and for the attendance of Spaak and an American representative. Although the British Government still believed that its strategic interests could best be met by full control of the island, it was willing to consider any solution which was acceptable to Greece and Turkey. Turkey accepted the invitation, but the Greek Government refused it. So the conference was not held.

The pursuit of self-determination had over the years proved costly and fruitless. Privately Greek statesmen were, in the summer of 1957, ready to consider the independence of Cyprus under an international guarantee. And Averoff sounded Grivas on the subject in August. After dwelling on the bogey of partition, the Greek Foreign Minister intimated that he did not expect spectacular results from the forthcoming UN debate. The Colonel responded by calling for a more vigorous policy on the part of the Greek Government and insisted that self-determination must not be abandoned. Conditions would become more favourable with time, he argued, as the result either of a change of government in England or developments in the Balkans and the Middle East.[2] The Greek decision to raise the question again at the UN

---

[1] 'But anyone who, in order to realize Enosis, is not willing to accept independence as a transitional stage deserves to be criticised. . . .' *Summary of World Broadcasts* IV (BBC) op. cit. See above, p. 229.

[2] See *Memoirs* (Greek ed.), op. cit. pp. 196–7.

General Assembly brought to an end for the time being efforts to solve the problem within the framework of the Western alliance. Faced with the constant pressure of the extremists it was difficult for the Greek Government to avoid a further appeal to the UN, especially in the light of the over-optimistic interpretation of Resolution 1013 of the previous Assembly.

The demands of the extremists were also encouraged by the Labour Party, whose representatives gave the impression that the Socialists would grant Cyprus self-determination shortly after it returned to power. Every British by-election was watched by the Cypriots with keen interest.

Tom Driberg made a speech to the Cypriot mayors in which he was quoted as saying:

> Whatever the present British Government does or fails to do, you have the right to expect of the British Labour Party that it will apply in Cyprus the principle of self-determination when it comes to power – I hope that this will take place during the coming elections.

Ta Nea commented:

> Everyone understands, of course, the exceptional importance of this most clear statement by a British Labourite who occupies the position Driberg occupies in the Labour Party.[1]

More damaging to the chances of an early compromise was a statement on 4 October by Barbara Castle, deputy chairman of the National Executive, at the Party's annual conference in Brighton. She assured Lena Jeger that the Party had no intention of dragging the island through 'the tragedy of partitioned Ireland' and, referring to self-determination, she said it would endeavour 'to complete this freedom operation for the people of Cyprus during the lifetime of the next Labour Government'.[2] C. M. Woodhouse, the Conservative MP for South Oxford and an expert on Greek affairs, was viciously attacked by Athens Radio after he had tried in a broadcast to put the promises of the Socialists into perspective.[3] Desmond Donnelly, the Labour MP for Haverfordwest, warned the Cypriots during a visit to the island against wishful thinking. He said too much emphasis had been given

---

[1] *Summary of World Broadcasts* IV (BBC) 358, 25 September 1957, p. 13.
[2] *The Annual Conference Report of the Labour Party 1957*, p. 196.
[3] *Summary of World Broadcasts* IV (BBC) 377, 15 October 1957, p. 16.

to comments by people who had only a very limited influence in the Party or no influence at all, and that there had been complete misunderstanding over Barbara Castle's recent statement.[1] At the highest level the Greek political leaders and Makarios were sceptical about the sincerity of the Opposition's promises. Such misgivings were not shared by the extremists and the public. And the rash undertakings given by some of the Party's spokesmen greatly contributed to the anxieties of the Turks and the hardening of Turkey's demands for partition.

In the autumn of 1957 Harding's two-year appointment drew to a close. The main object of his mission, the restoration of law and order, had been achieved. The fact that the security forces had been halted at the height of their successful drive against EOKA was due to political factors beyond his control. Outwardly the island had been calm for six months. The time was approaching when political contact would have to be renewed with Makarios. At international level the prospects for a political solution had slightly improved. The question of British sovereignty was no longer an insuperable obstacle. The Greek Government was trying, even if feebly, to shift from the stand of hostility to that of détente in her relations with Turkey. But several factors had to be weighed against this progress. The moderation privately expressed at ministerial level in Athens had yet to become effective in actual policy. The growing ascendancy of the Turks and their demand for partition had created new problems. The most ominous portent for the future was the reorganisation of EOKA. Trained in more advanced techniques, better equipped than their predecessors, the new guerrilla groups were ready to strike at any time.

---

[1] See Cyprus Mail, 26 October 1957.

IX

The Second Round
December 1957-
February 1959

Foot's Governorship — Zurich Agreement

I THE APPOINTMENT OF SIR HUGH FOOT

Sir Hugh Foot (later Lord Caradon) was in many respects an obvious choice for the governorship of Cyprus. He had a reputation for liberal and impartial administration, he had seen terrorism at work in Palestine and had previously served in the island as Colonial Secretary. Urbane, quick-witted, impetuous and approachable, he possessed qualities which could be expected to impress the Greek Cypriots. His close links with British Socialists, moreover, put him in a good position to exercise a restraining influence over Opposition members whose stand on the Cyprus question was one of the serious barriers to a settlement.

In Greece the appointment met with mixed reaction. The cynics dismissed it as a typically British manoeuvre intended to influence the forthcoming debate[1] at the United Nations, but some commentators welcomed it as a conciliatory gesture. In Turkey, where the historic associations between philhellenism and British liberalism have never been forgotten, the appointment aroused grave misgivings; the Turkish Cypriots were also apprehensive. Dr Kutchuk was worried about the possible relaxation of the emergency measures. Nevertheless he suggested that Sir Hugh, as a former Colonial Secretary, understood the intercommunal problem and could be instrumental in promoting a settlement on the basis of partition which, Kutchuk said, he was sure

---

[1] The British delegate, Commander Noble, during the meeting of the First Committee on 9 December 1957, referred to Foot's reputation 'for wise, liberal and progressive administration'. UN doc. A/C.1/PV 927 (XII), pp. 13–15.

he would do. Kutchuk went on to pay a warm tribute to Sir John Harding, 'the only Governor who really understood the problem'.[1]

Several prominent Greek Cypriots, including the Bishop of Kition, welcomed the change so long as it heralded a change of policy. An important exception was Colonel Grivas, who distrusted the new Governor from the outset.[2] The political associations of the Foot family had not been overlooked by the EOKA Leader, for whom all politicians were charlatans given to infinite duplicity – none more so than those who came in the guise of colonial administrators. A speech made by Foot in Jamaica to the United Nations Association, in which he denounced violence, 'the servant of tyranny',[3] enraged the EOKA extremists and aroused all the latent fears of the nationalists that some day the influences for compromise and moderation might triumph in Cypriot politics. Grivas was especially afraid that Foot might persuade old friends amongst the Cypriots to negotiate a compromise settlement. Shortly before the new Governor's arrival, Grivas circulated a warning that he was certain to try and seek out moderates and might well try to impose the Radcliffe constitution.[4] At the same time the mayors, on the Colonel's instructions, declared that they were not willing to have any contact with representatives of the British Government until the return of the Archbishop and the end of the state of emergency.[5]

The Governor's arrival in Cyprus on 3 December coincided with two unfortunate events. In Cyprus PEKA proclaimed a general strike for the opening day of the United Nations debate. In the House of Commons, the Secretary of State for the Colonies tersely rejected Mr Kenneth Robinson's ill-timed suggestion that the moment was now opportune to allow the Archbishop's return to the island. 'I think that a new chapter', Mr Lennox-Boyd stated, 'could well be opened if the Archbishop himself would take the initiative in calling for the end of terrorism for which, in the past, his utterances have been largely responsible.'[6]

Foot told journalists shortly after his arrival that he came with an open mind and without prejudice and that he would be accessible at all times to any Cypriots who wanted to see him: 'We can together find a

---

[1] Cyprus Mail, 22 October 1957.

[2] Grivas wrote: 'From the outset of our conflict I lacked respect for Foot and regarded the self-created aura of "liberalism" surrounding him with distaste. I was sure it was fraudulent.' *Memoirs* (Longmans), op. cit. p. 129.

[3] Daily Telegraph, 26 October 1957, and 'Colonial Violence', *Aspect*, February 1963.

[4] PEKA leaflet 'Attention. . . . Cohesion and no Separation', distributed at Engomi 1 December 1957.

[5] Cyprus Mail, 1 December 1957.

[6] H.C. Deb., vol. 579, cols 183–4 (Oral Answers).

way out of our anxieties.'[1] The next day during a rapid tour of the Limassol area he stopped at a small monastery near Curium where he lit a candle with a 'prayer for a December of goodwill'.[2] The Governor's first week in the island, however, was marked by the worst outbreak of violence for eight months. On 7 December Greek secondary school-children in Nicosia left their classes, armed with sticks and stones, for Phaneromeni Church to pray for the success of the UN debate which they mistakenly believed was due to start that day. Demonstrators clashed with the security forces, who finally broke up the riots with batons and tear gas. The Governor appealed for peace and stressed the need for law and order during the UN proceedings. But on 9 December, the first day of the debate, serious disturbances broke out again in all the main towns except Larnaca. Twenty members of the security forces and eleven Cypriots were injured.[3] The next day pupils of the Pancyprian Gymnasium barricaded themselves inside the school and pelted the security forces with bottles and stones. A Turkish police-man was wounded by a Greek. Rumours that he had been killed set off a wave of intercommunal rioting in which the Turks wrecked Greek property. The security forces put the Old City under curfew and re-manned the 'Mason-Dixon' line separating the Greek and Turkish communities. The Governor broadcast a new warning on the dangers of further violence. The next day, in the face of considerable criticism from the British and the Turks, he ignored protocol and called on Dr Dervis, the Mayor of Nicosia. The mayors had persisted in their boycott of the Governor, and Dr Dervis later made it clear that there had been no breach of this undertaking on his part since only questions of security were discussed.[4] Grivas in the meantime had reluctantly ordered EOKA to cease operations but to be ready to resume action on a larger scale than ever before should the Governor's promises turn out to be traps.[5] Either the order did not reach the local leaders in time or else it was never intended to stop the UN demonstrations. The disturbances were consistent with the Colonel's philosophy that if diplomatic action is to be effective it must be backed by force. The Cypriots had long realised that without violence they could not hope to capture the world's headlines.

[1] Cyprus Mail, 5 December 1957.

[2] Cyprus Mail, 9 December 1957.

[3] *Truce? Diary of Principal Security Incidents in Cyprus from 14th March, 1957 to 31st March, 1958*, pp. 11–12. Government of Cyprus and Cyprus Mail, 8 and 11 December 1957.

[4] Cyprus Mail, 12 December 1957.

[5] These instructions are referred to in a PEKA leaflet entitled: 'Who is to blame', first distributed in Varosha on 9 December 1957.

2   THE TWELFTH SESSION OF THE UN GENERAL ASSEMBLY[1]

The diplomatic struggle at the United Nations had begun well before Foot's appointment. On 13 July Greece had inscribed on the provisional agenda of the Twelfth General Assembly an item entitled:

(a) Application under the auspices of the UN of the principle of equal rights and self-determination of peoples etc. in the case of Cyprus.

(b) Violation of Human Rights and atrocities by the British Colonial Administration against the Cypriots.[2]

An explanatory memorandum submitted by the permanent representative of Greece two months later noted that no progress had been made since the adoption of Resolution 1013. The Cypriots' compliance with the UN decision had merely resulted in unilateral violence against the inhabitants. On 18 September, before the General Committee, the Greek Foreign Minister Mr Averoff argued that Britain had not complied with Resolution 1013 adopted by the General Assembly the previous February. Negotiations had not been resumed with the Cypriots and prisoners were still being tortured. Mr Selwyn Lloyd, the British Foreign Secretary, replied that his delegation would vote against the Greek item in its present form (sub-item b) not because of any difficulty in refuting the charges but because under Article 2 (7) the UN was not competent to consider complaints against the internal administration of a member state. Each charge had been examined. Selwyn Lloyd stated: 'In one or two cases in which prisoners had been ill-treated disciplinary action had been taken. The charge of atrocities, however, was ridiculous.' The Turkish delegate, Mr Esin, stated that the wording of the item reflected the Greek desire to use the UN for propaganda purposes. Several countries supported Norway's proposal that the item should be included for discussion provided the wording was neutral. Russia and Czechoslovakia strongly supported the original Greek wording. After a renewed effort by Averoff to get the subject of human rights included, which was overruled, the item was finally accepted for discussion under the heading of 'The Cyprus question'.

On 5 December the permanent Greek delegate to the United Nations sent a letter and a memorandum to the Secretary-General listing examples of repressive measures taken by the British authorities before and after the February resolution. The second category included

[1] UN doc. 1st Committee (XII), A/C.1/PV 927 – A/C.1/PV 934 and GAOR(XII), 731st Plenary Meeting, pp. 618–22.
[2] UN doc. A/3616 (XII).

the creation of a new detention camp at Pyroi, the ill-treatment of priests and new allegations of torture. The debate in the Political Committee opened on 9 December. The draft resolution submitted by Greece called for self-determination in Cyprus and claimed that no progress had been made towards a settlement since the February resolution (1013), that the situation was still fraught with danger and that a solution in conformity with the UN Charter was urgently required to preserve peace and stability in the area.

The British delegate, Commander Noble, stressed the ties between Britain, Greece and Turkey. Their Prime Ministers were shortly due to meet in Paris. The best way to resolve a dispute between friends was to discuss it amongst themselves. Some progress had been made on the lines of the resolution adopted in February but further talks were needed. Noble then made an oblique but important reference to partition. The Greek campaign for Enosis, he said, was being conducted in the name of self-determination. The British Government had always upheld self-determination and in December 1956 had thought it right to reaffirm its support for this principle which must be applied equally to the Greek and Turkish communities. He summarised the various steps taken by the British Government in the search for a settlement, including the intensive but abortive efforts made by Britain in the summer to arrange a meeting between the three powers at which all aspects of the problem would be freely discussed. Turkey had accepted the suggestion but Greece insisted that the outlines of any solution must first be agreed through diplomatic channels. Noble referred to the renewal of violence and to the possibility that speeches made in the Committee might affect the course of events in the island, and to the new Governor's reputation for 'wise, liberal and progressive administration'. It would be tragic, he said, if wide-scale violence should intervene at a time when the British Government believed that progress was possible.

The Greek Foreign Minister argued that the object of the Assembly's previous resolution was bilateral talks between the British and the Cypriots. The improvement in local conditions was solely due to EOKA's cease-fire; any hopes that Britain would comply with the resolution had withered on the execution of Pallikarides. Averoff spoke at length on the objections to partition and the subject of British atrocities, which he alleged had continued since the previous General Assembly resolution was adopted. In a gruesome account of the Milikouri curfew, he stated that the sick, the children, the old people were completely isolated from the outside world for fifty-four days. Fifty-four days of 'sadism,' he added. He scorned the idea of new tripartite talks as tactics designed to create confusion and shift the responsibility of the British Government on to the shoulders of others – a method 'dear to and almost traditional in British policy'.[1] He praised the liberal attitude of the British Labour Party in contrast to the rigid policy of the Conservative Government. The Brighton resolution had evoked great rejoicings in Greece and Cyprus. In the circumstances, the Greek Government could do no less than recognise the right of self-determination which the Labour Party itself had accepted. But the evil of colonialism had to be rooted out. Tyranny still reigned in Cyprus. Greece therefore had to revive her resolution for self-determination.

The Turkish delegate, Mr Selim Sarper, spoke of the need to strip the Cyprus problem down to bare essentials and to avoid irrelevant slogans. Turkey supported the lofty principle of self-determination but was opposed to its use as a cloak for annexation. Separatism was inherent in the social structure of Cyprus, Sarper said, but as the result of terrorism organised by extremists from Greece the two communities had reached the point of hostility which made cooperation between them impossible. Without specifically mentioning partition, he emphasised the importance of Lennox-Boyd's statement in December 1956, deplored the Greek Government's refusal in recent months to cooperate in negotiations and urged further progress within the framework of the General Assembly's resolution of the previous February. With reference to the Greek allegations of atrocities, Sarper stated that his country had not always been a friend of Britain, and Turkish officers and men could testify to the honourable manner in which British soldiers carried out their duties. Greek terrorism was responsible for crimes against the Turkish community. The true objective of the Greek campaign was Enosis, Sarper repeated. The formula of self-determination had first been introduced by Mr Sophokles Venizelos for tactical reasons. Sarper supported his arguments by references to history and quotations from Greek official and independent sources. Finally he questioned whether the devastation of Turkey in 1921 by the Greek Army was motivated by the desire to prove the sanctity of the principle of self-determination.

Averoff blamed the Allies for the war in Asia Minor and contended that the Greeks and Turks of Cyprus had lived side by side for centuries without a single incident. The next day he sought to prove at greater length the falsity of the Turkish arguments. Commander Noble refuted the charge of atrocities.

On 11 December the Greek case was restated by Savvas Loizides, a

[1] UN doc. A/C.1/PV 927, p. 51.

Cypriot nationalist and Greek subject. Speaking with great emotion, Loizides traced the efforts made by the Cypriots from 1950 onwards to obtain the support of the UN and reproached the Committee for its lack of response which, combined with British indifference to the wishes of the Cypriots, had finally driven them to armed resistance. He had heard of quiet diplomacy since boyhood. But the patience of the Cypriots was exhausted. Loizides claimed that two communities had lived in brotherhood – the Turkish minority enjoyed the closest social and professional cooperation with the Greek majority; Greek schoolboys played games with Turkish schoolboys and that this ideal state of communal relations had existed until the British and the Turks decided in 1955 to cooperate in opposition to Greek Cypriot national aspirations. The Greek Cypriots were determined to live again in friendly cooperation with the minority.

On the subject of torture, Loizides said that he knew many of the victims personally and he would break down if he had to describe these atrocities in detail. Indeed he begged the Committee to read the *Violation of Human Rights in Cyprus*, recently published by the Ethnarchy. Loizides then quoted in full as supporting evidence an article from the Sunday Dispatch and concluded by appealing to the Committee to support self-determination for Cyprus: every hesitation on the part of the UN, he said, would mean 'more bloodshed, more pain and horror in prison and concentration camps and interrogation rooms'.[1] Loizides twice had to be reminded by the chairman, once on the objections of the Turkish representative, that he was only entitled to speak as a member of the Greek delegation and not on behalf of Cyprus.

Twenty-eight nations in addition to those directly concerned in the dispute took part in the general debate which lasted nearly four days. Mr Cabot Lodge, on behalf of the USA, reaffirmed his Government's view that a settlement must be worked out by those directly concerned. It would be a mistake, Lodge said, for the Assembly at this time to adopt any specific solution. Pakistan supported the British line calling for further progress on the basis of the Assembly's previous resolution. France, Belgium and Portugal asserted that the UN was not competent to intervene in the Cyprus problem. Malaya favoured independence and urged the protagonists to avoid complicating the problem by looking to outside powers. Afghanistan supported the right to self-determination provided it was exercised by both communities. Iran's delegate proclaimed support for self-determination but said that the Assembly's first task was to adopt a new resolution on lines similar to last year's.

[1] UN doc. A/C.1/PV 931, p. 21.

The main support for the Greek draft resolution came from the Soviet bloc and the Arab and Afro-Asian states. The delegate for the Soviet Union, Mr Peive, called for the end of military bases. With special reference to the threat which Cyprus constituted to the security of his country, the Syrian delegate noted with satisfaction that Greece favoured the demilitarisation of the island. The Latin American states were less united in their attitude. Bolivia advocated that a UN plebiscite should be held in Cyprus to enable the Cypriots to determine the future. Guatemala declared she would vote for the Greek draft resolution and urged other Latin American countries to do likewise. Panama deplored the failure of the parties concerned to implement the Assembly's previous resolution and announced her intention to vote for any resolution which safeguarded 'the inalienable and sacrosanct rights of self-determination'. Uruguay wanted no words of rancour, hatred or acrimony to be included, but otherwise supported the resolution. Colombia's delegate, Mr Zuleta Angel, doubted whether the Assembly's previous resolution indicated three-power talks as the procedure to be followed and agreed to vote for any resolution upholding self-determination.

The general debate was brought to a close on the evening of 11 December. The delegate for the USA moved an adjournment on the ground that members would be better able to make sound decisions on the draft resolution after a night's sleep. The Greeks understandably wanted to press ahead with the vote. The whole trend of a UN debate could be changed overnight. And there were obvious advantages in bringing the matter to a conclusion before the Committee was still further confused by a complex of sub-amendments and even an alternative resolution. Averoff pleaded that since the Committee had been in session since 10 a.m. the few extra minutes needed to vote on the draft resolution would not make much difference. And all would sleep better for having disposed of the Cyprus problem. Averoff's interjection before the vote was ruled out of order and the motion was carried by a small majority.

When the Committee met on the following day to vote on the draft resolution it was confronted by a renewed dialogue between the Greek and Turkish delegates. Sarper announced that his earlier forecast had already come true – namely that the mere presentation of the draft resolution was in itself sufficient to encourage EOKA to resort to violence and bloodshed on a scale hitherto unparalleled. He could now confirm that the recent murders of four Turks and the wounding of a Turkish woman were the work of EOKA. He implored the Assembly not to encourage the extremists and therefore to vote against the Greek resolution. Averoff avoided the issue of the murdered Turks but made a countercharge based on the alleged destruction of Greek property by Turkish Cypriots. The Greek and Turkish delegates tended to exploit day-to-day events in the island in developing their arguments. The occasion of Foot's visit to the Mayor of Nicosia to discuss security matters became the subject of conflicting interpretations. Averoff claimed that its purpose was to thank the mayor for his role in urging the population to keep calm. Sarper took the opposite view that the Governor's aim was to persuade the mayor to use his influence with the Greek population and EOKA in favour of moderation.

In an eleventh-hour attempt to avert a vote on self-determination, Chile, Canada, Norway and Denmark drew up during the adjournment four amendments to the Greek resolution. The first three made the preamble less contentious and were accepted by the Greek delegate. The fourth and only crucial change sought to replace the operative paragraph on self-determination by the proviso that 'further negotiations and discussions be promptly undertaken in the spirit of cooperation'. This was immediately rejected by Averoff, who claimed that it did not constitute an amendment under UN Rules of Procedure since it completely altered the substance of the resolution. Averoff said such tactics were 'a manoeuvre designed to block resolutions by modifying their sense', whereupon the Greek delegate introduced a sub-amendment which added to the four-power draft the words 'with a view to applying the right of self-determination in the case of the people of Cyprus'.[1]

The Norwegian representative, Mr Engen, defended the right to modify a resolution. But he questioned the validity of the Greek sub-amendment on the ground that it was the reintroduction of the operative paragraph which the four powers had sought to amend. If Greece was entitled to do this then it was also the privilege of the four powers to reintroduce their amendment as a new sub-amendment, and the whole procedure could go on indefinitely. He did not, however, intend to take advantage of this position out of respect for the Committee and in the interests of orderly procedure.

The discussion degenerated into a confused and protracted wrangle over procedure. Averoff, strongly supported by Egypt, Syria, Haiti, Guatemala, Tunisia and Lebanon, persuaded the Committee to vote first on the Greek sub-amendment. Thirty-three delegations voted in favour, eighteen against and twenty-seven abstained. The resolution as a whole was adopted by 33 votes to 20 with 25 abstentions.

[1] A/C.1/PV 933, p. 12.

The delegate of Mexico expressed the hope that a slightly amended text, acceptable to the majority, might be drawn up before the Plenary Meeting. This wish was shared by Krishna Menon, who explained that his delegation had not taken part in the debate or the voting because it was clear that no decision taken at that time would secure the overwhelming support of the UN. Lodge stated the abstention of the US was in line with his earlier speech, namely that the Cyprus problem could not be solved by deliberation at the UN in the absence of agreement between the parties concerned. Ceylon's delegate expressed confidence in the British Government and favoured a Royal Commission.

At the Plenary Meeting on 14 December the voting followed the same pattern as in the Political Committee, with the exception of Iraq and Morocco which abstained, having previously voted in favour of the draft resolution. Ghana had second thoughts about supporting the motion but finally did so on receiving an assurance from the Greek Foreign Secretary that self-determination would give the Cypriots the right to opt for independence. Noble had stated that Greece was invoking the principle solely to achieve Enosis. With 31 votes in favour, 23 against and 25 abstentions, the draft resolution failed to obtain the necessary two-thirds majority and the previous Assembly's resolution remained in effect.

In spite of the Greek Government's need of an early settlement its performance at the UN General Assembly had shown that it was still the prisoner of the extremists. The Foreign Secretary's preoccupation with atrocities, the inclusion of Savvas Loizides in the Greek delegation pointed to this fact. The British had scored a technical victory but no more. The abstention of the American delegation, the successful press campaign conducted by Archbishop Makarios during the course of the debate had militated against the British. The Greek Cypriots were triumphant. Seen from their angle, it was only a matter of time before Afro-Asian states joined the UN after independence and the two-thirds majority came within their grasp. Grivas claimed that 'the majority of the member states of UNO have recognised our just demand and condemned colonialism'.[1] Months later, Makarios, speaking at Kalamai in Greece, declared that the implementation of self-determination had been promised by the British Labour Party and approved by the overwhelming majority of the members of the United Nations.[2] AKEL, more realistic in treating the outcome as a defeat for self-determination, exploited the issue on the usual communist lines with the claim that the

[1] EOKA leaflet: 'To All Members of EOKA, PEKA and ANE', Ktima, 1 January 1958.
[2] *Summary of World Broadcasts* IV (BBC) 508, 25 March 1958, pp. 9–10.

Soviet Union and the Peoples' Democracies were the only real supporters of the Cypriot cause.[1]

3   THE FOOT PLAN

The UN debate was followed by a short period of calm. The Governor
went ahead with his goodwill mission and was impressed time and again
by the courtesy and friendliness of the ordinary people. On 21 December he declared that he had set himself the task of building two bridges:
'a bridge of trust with the Greek community and a bridge of trust with
the Turkish community'.[2] As a Christian gesture, he announced the
decision to release one hundred detainees and lift the restrictions on six
hundred Cypriots confined to their villages and the ban on the Larnaca
Gymnasium, one of the island's most disorderly schools. Within an hour
of the Governor's broadcast, large crowds gathered around Phaneromeni Church to celebrate the event to the wild pealing of church bells.
On Christmas day Foot made a surprise visit to Pyla Detention Camp.
In a talk on the Forces' Broadcasting Service he urged the troops to
pursue a policy of positive friendship with the Cypriots. He recognised
the dangers. But, he said, 'we are not going to get out of the mess we
are in without taking risks'. The Governor refuted suggestions that his
concessions to the Greeks had been made at the expense of the Turkish
community:

> For myself I would rather get in an aeroplane and leave the island
> and never come back than do anything to harm the Turks I know
> here. We have a firm and long-standing friendship with the Turkish
> community of Cyprus and our country is in close alliance with the
> Turkish Republic.[3]

Foot's policy of conciliation did much to ease tension on the Greek side.
The Greek Government and Archbishop Makarios were favourably
impressed by him. Athens Radio temporarily abandoned its customary
hostility towards Britain combining qualified praise for the new Governor's actions with the demand that all the detainees should now be set
free. Grivas alone remained deeply suspicious of his motives.

The improvement in Anglo-Greek relations was outweighed by the
rising hostility of the Turks. The Turks had from the start suspected
Foot of philhellenism. The concessions to the Greeks confirmed the

[1] Central Committee of AKEL leaflet: 'United in the Struggle for Self-Determination',
Nicosia, 15 December 1957.
[2] Cyprus Mail, 22 December 1957.
[3] ibid. 27 December 1957.

worst fears of the Turks, who faced the New Year in a mood of grim determination. Towards the end of December the TMT sent a personal warning to Foot accusing him of favouring the Greeks and stressing the futility of trying to 'build bridges of trust'. TMT leaflets proclaimed in alarmist tones that Enosis was about to be staged in a new form; that the proposals for new talks indicated that Britain was working hand in glove with Greece; that the Turks would never accept any solution other than partition; and that any Turks who came forward to co-operate with the British in plans for a change of regime would be exterminated and their property destroyed.

The Greeks, on the other hand, faced the New Year in a buoyant mood. Colonel Grivas sent a rousing message to all members of EOKA, ANE and PEKA claiming that 1957 had been a year of great achievement for the fighters; the Empire of the Tories and an army of 36,000 men had been shaken; a Field-Marshal defeated, humiliated and recalled. The message concluded with a reminder of the hard struggle ahead. The results of the United Nations debate and the imminent visit of a sub-commission of the European Human Rights Committee, which marked a turning point in a protracted campaign to secure an international inquiry into British actions, were both guaranteed to give rise to wild optimism on the part of the Greek Cypriots.

The Human Rights Sub-Committee arrived in Cyprus on 13 January 1958 and stayed sixteen days for the purpose of determining whether the situation justified the emergency measures imposed by the British and of investigating conditions in which the curfew was imposed. In the attempt to create an impression of normality, EOKA, for the first time since the outbreak of the rebellion, banned all celebrations on the anniversary of the plebiscite. But the British authorities had little reason to fear the outcome of the Sub-Committee's visit, which took place against a background of violence, Greek and Turkish.

Before taking up his appointment Foot had decided that unitary self-government and the shelving of the sovereignty question offered the best chance of a settlement, and that given peace and freedom from outside intervention the two communities were capable of working out their own salvation. This view was not substantially changed by his study of conditions in the island during December. On New Year's Day he arrived in London having drafted the proposals which came to be informally known as the Foot plan.[1]

---

[1] The substance of the Foot plan was never officially disclosed by the British but its essentials were leaked through Greek and Turkish sources. See *Memoirs* (Greek ed.), op. cit. p. 230, and *Summary of World Broadcasts* IV (BBC) 447, 11 January 1958, p. 5.

Harding, in the light of experience, had reached the conclusion that no settlement was possible without the agreement of Greece and Turkey and so long as the sovereignty problem was unresolved.[1] The Foot plan marked a sharp departure from the line followed since May 1957, which concentrated on the international approach and a final settlement excluding Enosis and partition.[2] Foot's enthusiasm seems to have influenced the Cabinet. Within ten days his proposals were accepted in full. It now remained to convince Turkey, Greece and Archbishop Makarios of the plan's merits. The Governor hoped to announce the proposals and the end of the emergency in Cyprus at the end of the month and had even gone so far as to prepare his speech for the occasion. The British Ambassador in Ankara Sir James Bowker was instructed to explain the position to the Turkish Government and seek approval for the arrival of Foot. The British Government had not heeded Bowker's warnings and seriously misjudged the Turkish attitude, which had been progressively hardening since the Archbishop's release from the Seychelles, the process having been rapidly accelerated during recent months first by Mrs Castle's statement at Brighton, secondly by Harding's departure from the island, and finally by his successor's overtures to the Greeks. Turkish distrust of Britain had now sunk to its nadir. Publicly committed to partition but privately willing to consider a solution based on a federal constitution and the establishment of a Turkish military base, Turkey was determined to work for an early settlement which in certain contingencies would give her direct control over part of the island.

By 1958 almost every constitutional formula within the range of the human intellect had been discussed time and again by the parties concerned, amended, and finally rejected by at least one of them; there was little new to suggest. The Turks had anticipated important provisions in the Foot plan before its official disclosure. The worst feature of the plan, which might have been acceptable at an earlier stage, was the postponement of the sovereignty issue. The Turkish Government was not prepared to take chances on the possibility that a Labour Government in Britain might during the long interim period yield to Greek pressure and back out of the provisions giving both communities the eventual right to opt for self-determination separately. As far as the Turks were concerned the Foot proposals were dead even before the discussions had begun.

[1] See Harding, op. cit.
[2] See Sir Hugh Foot, GCMG, KCMG, OBE, *A Start In Freedom* (Hodder & Stoughton 1964), pp. 158-9.

Bowker nevertheless duly saw Mr Zorlu, the Turkish Foreign Minister, on 9 January. The same day Zorlu made an important statement on Ankara Radio. Asked to comment on recent newspaper reports that Britain was about to grant Cyprus self-government and self-determination at the end of a ten-year period, he replied:

> ... in the face of the existing and growing animosity between the two communities the Turkish Government has on several occasions pointed out that there is no longer any question of self-government on the island and because of this increasingly grave situation the only possible decision to be taken immediately is a decision for partition.[1]

The official Turkish reply to the British Government contained strong objections to the plan and the request that Foot should visit Ankara. The British Foreign Secretary, Selwyn Lloyd, however, was not yet fully convinced that the Turkish refusal was final, and when in Ankara at the end of January for the Baghdad Pact conference he took the opportunity of raising the Cyprus question again. Foot joined him in Ankara on 28 January. The Governor by this time had become second only to Makarios as a target for Turkish hostility; and the reason for his inclusion on a mission of such delicacy has never been adequately explained. His advice[2] could have been safely conveyed to the Foreign Secretary in London, but his presence in Turkey – where, according to the Ankara correspondent of the New York Times,[3] he was the focal point of Turkish resentment – could hardly fail to aggravate the crisis. The Turks believed his visit indicated Britain's intention to impose the plan. It was probably no coincidence that the Turks in Nicosia chose this moment to riot against the British.

On 27 January thousands of Turkish youths, hurling bottles and stones, besieged Ataturk Square for several hours. The security forces failed to restore order with tear gas. In the afternoon the Turkish leader, Rauf Denktash, appealed to the demonstrators to go home 'for the day'. As the crowds began to leave the square an army truck which was being heavily stoned drove at speed through the mob, knocking down several people and killing a man and a woman. The incident precipitated a new wave of rioting which culminated in a pitched battle

---

[1] *Summary of World Broadcasts* IV (BBC) 447, p. 5.

[2] 'I was greatly helped in Ankara and Athens by the presence and advice of the Governor of Cyprus.' Selwyn Lloyd, H.C. Deb., vol. 582, col. 1049.

[3] New York Times, 29 January 1958.

between the British forces and the Turks. Rioting broke out again the next day. Seven Turks were killed in two days in clashes with the security forces. Twelve soldiers, 28 police and 14 members of the fire service were injured in the first incident.

It may be concluded that when Selwyn Lloyd saw the Turkish Prime Minister, Adnan Menderes, on 28 January, he urged him to call off the riots. Menderes's statement to the Anatolia Agency the next day contained a veiled appeal for calm. After expressing his sympathy with the Turkish Cypriots for their 'tragic losses', he assured them that the current talks with the British Government need not give rise to anxiety, and requested them to await the outcome with patience and confidence. The Turkish disturbances abated, having served their purpose; for the second time in three years Turkey had demonstrated to the world by acts of violence the strength of Turkish opposition. Relations between the British and the Turkish Cypriots, however, remained tense. The TMT immediately banned all contact between the Turks and the British and called upon the Turkish mukhtars to resign. The cooperation of the Turkish community was vital to the struggle against EOKA. The Mobile Reserve was entirely composed of Cypriot Turks. Turks also served in large numbers in the regular police force and as auxiliary and special constables. As guards and escorts they were irreplaceable. The British were now faced with the prospect of armed hostility on two fronts. Foot returned to Cyprus on 30 January showing signs of strain. He told journalists at Nicosia airport that the talks had been most valuable in helping him to appreciate the Turkish Government's view, but before embarking on the next stage in tackling the problem ahead, the first task must be to re-establish 'the long and close friendship between the Government of Cyprus and the Turkish community and to work in confidence together'.[1]

Meanwhile reports of EOKA's plans to renew violence in the near future had reached the Cyprus authorities. On 2 February Foot broadcast an urgent appeal for the continuation of peace. He condemned the prolonged attempts in Cyprus to force a conclusion by violence and stressed his determination to take the necessary steps to restore order in the event of renewed disturbances.[2] Grivas, whose exasperation at the course of events in Turkey had been growing, treated the appeal as the first public attack on EOKA to be made by the new Governor, and replied that his patience and the credit of time had run out and that the fight must go on because there was no other

[1] Cyprus Mail, 31 January 1958.
[2] ibid. 3 February 1958.

way of dealing with British intransigence.[1] Foot's brief respite from EOKA's vilification campaign came to an abrupt end. On 7 February PEKA accused him of partiality towards the Turks;[2] three days later ANE denounced him as 'the Trojan Horse created by the fascist government of Britain'.[3]

In spite of the setback over the Turks, Selwyn Lloyd and Foot went to Athens as planned. Talks with the Greek Government began on 11 February. The Greeks raised the question of independence. The British were reported to have sounded the Greek Government on the idea of a Turkish military base in Cyprus as an alternative to partition.[4] Foot's wish to meet Archbishop Makarios, strongly opposed by his military and civil advisers in Cyprus, was sympathetically received by the British and Greek Foreign Ministers, and a meeting took place in the Hotel Grande Bretagne on 13 February.

The Athens talks ended cordially but without agreement on the basic points. The dependence of the security forces on the Cypriot Turks, in any case, made it useless to persist with the Foot proposals in the face of Turkey's opposition. And this phase in the crisis finally ended with Selwyn Lloyd's cryptic statement to the House of Commons on 18 February. He had sought in Athens and Ankara, the Foreign Secretary said, to find common ground upon which to base a settlement and was confident that this was possible, but further discussion was necessary and this would be undertaken with extreme urgency.[5]

The failure of Foot's conciliatory mission can partly be explained by the fact that his appointment was premature. After the long respite enjoyed by the rebels during the cease-fire EOKA was stronger than ever before; the Turks had moved into the field of militant action; conditions were ripe for a major outbreak of violence, this time on two fronts. In these circumstances the policy of pacification had little chance of survival. Foot had brought courage and enthusiasm to his task. But he had prejudged the situation before his arrival in the island in the light of an earlier experience which had little relevance to the current problem and had failed to profit from certain valuable conclusions reached by his predecessor. But blame for the fiasco of the Foot plan must also rest at the door of the British Government, which was in a position to understand the extent of Turkish reaction and which had

[1] See *Memoirs* (Longmans), op. cit. p. 133.

[2] PEKA leaflet: distributed in Nicosia, 7 February 1958.

[3] ANE leaflet: 10 February 1958, recovered from pupil of the English School.

[4] See *Memoirs* (Greek ed.), op. cit., letters to Grivas from the Greek Consul and Makarios, p. 230.

[5] H.C. Deb., vol. 582, cols 1049–50.

given the new Governor a free hand to seek a settlement on lines likely to exacerbate the crisis with Turkey. It was a fact that Foot's activities had helped to ease Anglo-Greek tension and to gain the goodwill of Archbishop Makarios.[1] But during the greater part of 1958 the course of events was neither determined by the Greek Government nor by Makarios but by Turkey and the extremists of EOKA. Both, for different reasons, viewed the new Governor's actions with the deepest distrust.

4 THE RENEWAL OF EOKA ACTION

The rebel movement which faced the Foot administration in 1958 was stronger and even more fanatical than the earlier guerrilla groups which had been largely subdued under Harding. The long respite of the cease-fire had enabled EOKA to build up its military strength. The political extremists at the core of the movement had also gained ground. Confined to his hideout in Limassol, Colonel Grivas was more than ever before the prisoner of his own prejudices and theories. The year 1958 was for EOKA essentially one of isolation in which the Organisation remained largely out of touch with trends in Cyprus and in Greece, and its worst blunders – the war against the Communists and the passive resistance campaign – reached a climax during this period.

The disillusionment with Greece and her allies became more pronounced. EOKA propaganda assumed an increasingly anti-Western and anti-American character, differing little in substance from that of communist origin. The Western powers were attacked for their imperialism; Dulles and Eisenhower for denying the small nations their rights.[2] The glories of Ancient Greece and the Greek War of Independence figured less in EOKA manifestos. Instead the rebellion was presented as a religious crusade to be waged with a bible in one hand and the sword in the other, the rebels as Christian warriors headed by Christ, the new Champion of Liberty:

> Christ is the leader of all fighters. He is the leader of all heroes because he himself became the greatest hero during his terrestrial life. Our captain Jesus is championing our struggle. He is inspiring, strengthening and fortifying us . . . Where can we turn our eyes now that all

---

[1] On 28 February Archbishop Makarios stated that Mr Selwyn Lloyd's visit to Athens had contributed nothing to the solution of the Cyprus question but that his own meeting with Sir Hugh Foot had been useful. *Summary of World Broadcasts* IV (BBC) 490, 3 March 1958, p. 20.

[2] PEKA leaflet distributed at Ktima on 23 February 1958.

our erstwhile Allies have closed their doors to us and have kicked us out into the four winds. We can only look to our eternal and real friend the Saviour Jesus for help . . .[1]

New recruits were urged to take the EOKA and PEKA oaths in the same spirit as they would take Holy Communion. Religion and Greek History were prescribed as the perfect curriculum for the education of Greek Cypriot youth.

By 1958 ANE's hold over the secondary schools was formidable. EOKA now worked to bring the younger children under its control, with the revival of catechism in schools where the absolute loyalty of the staff was assured and the setting up of special groups – the *Akritopoula* – for the small children. Teachers were ordered to foster nationalism by means of patriotic songs and to allow their pupils to take part in political processions and strikes. Those who put education and discipline before politics were at first censured by EOKA and later threatened with dire penalties.

The duty of every Christian, as envisaged by EOKA, involved a relentless war against communism. The campaign against the left wing which Grivas had started the previous autumn was intensified in January. During the first two weeks violent clashes took place between the right and the left at Akhna and Pighi. On 21 January a carpenter was murdered in a coffee shop at Komma tou Yialou; at Lysi three men were wounded, one fatally. All the victims were members of the left-wing trade unions. The next day the Pancyprian Federation of Labour (PEO) called for a 48-hour strike:

The working class must in a body express its indignation over the brutal crimes which resulted in the murder of leading members of our trade union movement.[2]

Demonstrators carried placards in the main towns denouncing the right-wing terrorists as fascists and murderers. The Larnaca branch of PEO cabled Archbishop Makarios warning him of the dangers of civil war and protesting against the 'criminal murder of a trade union leader and a democratic patriot'.[3] On 1 February PEO claimed that civil war had only been narrowly averted thanks to the patriotism and restraining

[1] Enlightenment Bureau of ANE, addressed by the Women's League of Famagusta to 'Cypriot Mothers Whose Heroic Sons Died in the Struggle', Famagusta, 22 December 1958.
[2] PEO leaflet, Nicosia, 21 and 23 January 1958.
[3] The Times, 23 January 1958.

influence of the trade union leaders, and urged the workers to avoid reprisals and concentrate on the struggle for self-determination.[1]

Under the auspices of PEO the widows of the two murdered men addressed an impassioned appeal to the press, the mayors, the Ethnarchy and the local politicians:

> We, the death stricken widows whose husbands were murdered by the masked men on the night of 21st January, we who shed bitter tears for the loss of our protectors consider it necessary to forward an appeal to every Greek Cypriot, and generally to the responsible political leaders of the country.
>
> The death of our beloved ones fell upon us like a heavy block of stones. Our eyes are still wet with bitter tears. We never thought that murderers would be so cowardly and without any reason make us dress in black, and deprive our children of their father.

The widows declared that their husbands were not criminals but affectionate fathers and husbands and honest patriots 'working tire-lessly in the ranks of the Trade Unions and the people's movement for the achievement of self-determination, for the return of the Archbishop and the solution of all the problems which subject our country to hard-ships', and that their husbands had been killed solely because of their membership of the left-wing party:

> Do the murderers not understand that the method of political murders is fratricide? Do they not realise that to achieve the exter-mination of the Left-wing party and the Trade Union Movement thousands of women will be dressed in black, and that thousands of innocent children will be deprived of their fathers? Do they not realise that such madness will lead us to civil war?[2]

The murders set in motion the cycle of recriminations. Faced with the rising hostility of the people, EOKA tried to justify the incidents by alleging that the EOKA men were forced to open fire in self-defence, that EOKA's blows were aimed at traitors irrespective of political ideologies, and that no plan existed to exterminate the left wing as a whole. The apologies concluded with the familiar accusation of AKEL's

---

[1] PEO leaflet: 'To the Governor. An answer to Colonialism', Nicosia, 1 February 1958.

[2] Circular: 'Fratricide Must Cease', 5 February 1958, published by Arshi Press, distributed in Nicosia, 12 February 1958.

cooperation with the British.[1] But the volume of left-wing protests continued to rise. AKEL challenged EOKA to accept the verdict of an independent commission set up by the people to investigate the allegations against the left, and offered to discredit and publicly expel from the Party any Akelist found guilty of treason. At the same time AKEL stressed the danger of partition, the need for unity and the avoidance of incidents likely to spark off civil war.[2]

The diversity of EOKA's actions in 1958 was one indication of its increased strength. In the spring Grivas turned his attention to passive resistance. The campaign was first initiated in October 1955 by Archbishop Makarios with an appeal for the resignation of village headmen. On subsequent occasions EOKA had made abortive attempts to impose a ban on lotteries, football pools, British cigarettes and footwear. During the long months of inaction Grivas had given much thought to the possibility of intensifying the campaign and the adaptation of Gandhi's methods to the needs of Cyprus. In February he warned the merchants to stop importing cigarettes, confectionery and footwear from Britain as these were shortly due to be boycotted. On 2 March he inaugurated a new campaign of passive resistance in order to show the world that the Cypriots were ready to sacrifice everything for their freedom and that the struggle was not, as the British contended, limited to a few hotheads.[3]

Two weeks later, almost one year after the cease-fire, Grivas renewed armed action against the British with an intensive sabotage campaign directed mainly at military installations and water pumps. Fifty bombs exploded during the first ten days of April. On 15 April a British interrogator was fatally wounded in Nicosia. PEKA intensified its agitation for the closure of the detention camps; protest strikes were organised and leaflets alleging ill-treatment circulated; special prayer meetings were held by relatives. On 10 April detainees tried to break out of Camp K having first set many of the huts on fire. Troops were brought in to restore order; their presence in the camp after the disturbances became the object of agitation.

The conflict between political expediency and the needs of security was always present during the Cyprus crisis. But the gulf between the civil administration and the armed forces was now greater than at any

---

[1] EOKA leaflet, Nicosia, 3 February 1958.

[2] Central Committee of AKEL, leaflet: 'Keep away from the road of cutting each others' throats', Nicosia, 8 February 1958.

[3] EOKA leaflet: 'Forward all to the new Battle', distributed in Nicosia and Varosha, 2 March 1958.

time before. The army and the police, responsible in the last resort for law and order, could see little merit in the new Governor's policy of conciliation, especially in the face of rising disorders. The Governor hesitated to adopt strong measures at this stage for fear of jeopardising a political settlement. Immediately after the setback to the Foot plan the British Government began discussions in the search for a new political formula. Whitehall's prolonged delay in making a policy statement increased speculation and tension in the island. In the hope of curbing the sabotage campaign which now showed every sign of ending in bloodshed and communal strife, Sir Hugh Foot in the middle of April took the drastic decision to make a direct approach to Grivas. The optimism of newly arrived officials in Cyprus was irrepressible and the one characteristic most governors had in common. The Colonel's uncompromising personality, his deep-rooted mistrust and dislike of Sir Hugh Foot, which had been expressed time and again in EOKA and PEKA leaflets, precluded all possibility of a successful outcome to the new Governor's highly controversial and hazardous venture. Two young Cypriot lawyers, Glavkos Klerides and Michael Triandafyllides, were involved in Foot's attempts to communicate with Grivas. The Triandafyllides family had long been suspected of close links with EOKA. Glavkos Klerides, a key man in the Organisation, had managed to retain the confidence of senior British officials throughout the whole of the rebellion. His ability, his influential position in the community, his usefulness as a go-between, his moderation and courtesy when dealing with the British may well explain his escape from arrest and detention, long after the security forces suspected his activities.

On 16 April Foot asked Glavkos Klerides to arrange the delivery of a personal letter to Grivas in which he appealed to him to save the people of Cyprus from disaster by suspending the campaign of sabotage and violence. The Governor undertook to meet the EOKA Leader 'alone and unarmed' at any place of his own choice, and gave his word that on that day he would be in no danger of arrest. EOKA's side of the story is told in detail by Grivas.[1] Klerides promptly reported the interview to Grivas; Foot had stressed the secrecy of this proposed mission, taken on his own initiative and without the authority of the British Government, and his fears that the renewal of full-scale EOKA action would seriously damage the prospects of a solution in strengthening the opposition of the army and the Turks to the policy of conciliation. The truce must continue for another two or three months to enable him to facilitate the Archbishop's early return. At the end of the report

[1] *Memoirs* (Greek ed.), op. cit. pp. 243-9.

Klerides wrote that on no account must Grivas agree to a meeting but it was important that the text of the letter should be got into the hands of EOKA. He suggested that he should ask for it, get it photographed and then return the original as undeliverable. On 17 April Foot tried for the second time to get the letter to Grivas through Glavkos Klerides. Ten days later the Governor heard that he had received it on 20 April. The next day Grivas ordered a temporary cease-fire but threatened a major offensive unless the British took prompt action to settle the question and reopen negotiations. But the peace was precarious. On 22 April Glavkos Klerides sent Grivas a further report on his discussions with the Governor. The report amounted to a veiled plea for the maintenance of the truce. The Governor's aim, wrote Klerides, was to ensure two or three months quiet until the British were in a position to negotiate with the new Greek Government.

Klerides dwelt on the difficulties known to exist between Foot and General Kendrew over policy: the fact that the army, using EOKA activity as an argument, was strongly opposed to the return of Makarios and the release of the detainees, and favoured a stricter enforcement of the emergency regulations, whereas the Governor believed that the Archbishop's return was essential. In their attempts to reason with Grivas the Cypriot leaders seldom committed themselves. But on this occasion Klerides went so far as to express the view that Sir Hugh Foot was sincere in his assessment of the difficulties, and that his desire to placate Greek opinion was motivated by his need for support from at least the Greek faction in view of the mounting antagonism of the army and the Turks towards him. In his reply to Foot, Klerides suggested, the EOKA Leader might consider making the truce dependent on the willingness of the British Government to expedite the final settlement, possibly within a fixed time-limit, and not merely on the Archbishop's return. But it was necessary to leave the door open for Foot to work in official circles to this end.[1]

On 24 April, a second Cypriot lawyer, Michael Triandafyllides, reported[2] on an interview with the Governor which was arranged through the American Consulate. According to Triandafyllides, Foot asked him to inform Grivas that hopeful developments were taking place; the stabilisation of the political situation in Greece was expected with the possibility of progress over the Cyprus question; that if Grivas abstained from violence he undertook to abolish the state of emergency in stages. Grivas did not reply to the Governor. He suspected that the

[1] *Memoirs* (Greek ed.), op. cit. p. 245.
[2] ibid. p. 246.

Cyprus authorities wanted a letter from him as an aid to tracing his hideout; and he dismissed the guarantee of one day's immunity from arrest with scorn. The EOKA Leader's next move was to issue a 'final' warning that unless the troops ceased ill-treating the detainees he would start attacks against the British.

Foot visited Camp K the same day and sent for Glavkos Klerides in the evening. Klerides reported[1] to Grivas that the Governor had assured him that the troops would be withdrawn as soon as the damage was repaired; that relatives would soon be allowed to visit the camp; and that the complaints of the detainees would be investigated. The Governor had deplored the possibility that the troubles at Camp K might become a reason for Grivas to renew violence. The consequences were bound to be harmful for the forthcoming Cyprus discussions in London. He concluded by expressing his appreciation to Grivas for having kept the truce up to now. But it was useless to reason with Grivas, and the campaign over the detainees was now in full swing and was not likely to stop in midstream. On 4 May two British soldiers were shot dead by EOKA as a reprisal for the alleged ill-treatment of the detainees. Grivas had dealt a final blow to the policy of conciliation. Foot could no longer stand out against the army's demand for tougher measures and the death penalty was restored for carrying arms.

Averoff, the Greek Foreign Secretary, had in the meantime stressed to Grivas the grave consequences which would result from a renewal of a general conflict, the dangers to the Greek community in Istanbul, the sharp worsening of Greco-Turkish relations, the exploitation of the situation by EDA, and the even greater risk of enforced partition.[2] EOKA suspended violence against the British pending the outcome of a policy statement. The length of the truce, Grivas stated, would be determined by the nature of the plan.

The Turkish Cypriots, fearing that the plan would exclude partition, stepped up their activities in close cooperation with the Turkish Government; events in Cyprus reflected official policy in Turkey. As in 1955, the Turkish Government was determined to show the world the strength of Turkish feeling on the Cyprus question. And the methods which had successfully promoted the Greek case were faithfully copied by the Turks. Huge demonstrations were held during the early summer throughout the country in favour of partition. In Istanbul a wax effigy of Makarios was burnt in front of a vast crowd. The main targets for attack were the British and the Patriarchate. Britain was censured

[1] ibid. p. 249.
[2] ibid. pp. 276–7.

for her perfidy in the past, and her assistance to Greek imperialism in the time of Lloyd George. A law student at the Konya rally on 22 June accused the Patriarchate of committing every form of treason despite the fact that it owed its freedom to the Sultan Mohammed:

> ... Curses be upon you! Patriarchate and the devils residing there, you are now aiding EOKA, which is murdering innocent people and unfortunate women. What an irony of fate that 26,000,000 Muslim Turks gave the Patriarchate the right to live in this beloved homeland![1]

Many assurances were given that troops would be sent from Turkey to Cyprus.[2] A woman commentator announced that if necessary the women would go with the Turkish soldiers.[3] The danger of communism was stressed time and again.[4] It was reported that a member of a newly formed youth army had presented a sword to Dr Kutchuk.[5] In spite of the massive scale of the rallies and the enthusiasm they generated no serious incidents were reported in Turkey. On every occasion troops were brought out in strength as a precaution against riots. But they had a disastrous effect in whipping up agitation in Cyprus and providing the Turkish Cypriot leaders with a forum in Turkey for speeches which would have exposed them to arrest under the emergency laws had they been made in the island. The Turkish Cypriots listened daily to these broadcasts.

The Turkish community had been greatly strengthened by the addition of Rauf Denktash, an able lawyer who had completed his education in England on a British Council scholarship and who had recently resigned from the Government legal service. Kutchuk and Denktash announced over Ankara Radio on 31 May that the British were planning to enforce a settlement which would be unsatisfactory to the Turks.[6] During a press conference held on 3 June at the Hilton Hotel in Istanbul, Kutchuk said the British Government was about to grant self-determination to Cyprus, which would mean the extinction of the Turkish Cypriots.[7] A week later the Turkish Government reaffirmed its determination to introduce partition.[8] In Cyprus the TMT, though

---

[1] *Summary of World Broadcasts* IV (BBC) 583, 22 June 1958, p. 12.
[2] ibid. 594, 4 July 1958, p. iii.
[3] ibid. 575, 12 June 1958, p. 8.
[4] ibid. 551, 14 May 1958, p. iii.
[5] ibid. 575, 12 June 1958, p. 8.
[6] ibid. 564, 31 May 1958, p. 11.
[7] ibid. 567, 3 June 1958, p. 6.
[8] ibid. 570, 9 June 1958, p. 9.

smaller and less well organised, modelled itself on the pattern of EOKA and grew increasingly aggressive. The boycott of British goods initiated by EOKA was now applied by the Turks to Greek goods. Turks caught smoking Greek cigarettes or using Greek shops were beaten up by gangs of Turkish youths. Turks known to have deviated from the national line that coexistence between the communities was impossible were liable to be denounced as traitors. The TMT warned all Turkish members of Greek trade unions that they must resign, and shot dead two Turkish Communists ostensibly for ideological reasons, but the true motive is likely to have been their membership of PEO, which essentially involved cooperation with Greeks. On 18 May the TMT, in anticipation of the British policy statement, declared that the hour of total action had come: 'The island would be drowned in blood and fire the very day self-government is announced.' The same leaflet instructed the Turkish Cypriots to complete their preparations and hold themselves in readiness for action within the next fifteen days.[1]

The Turkish Cypriots, despite their belligerency, were clearly at a serious disadvantage in that the TMT as yet had only very limited access to firearms. But Turkish orators set out to bolster morale by comparing the campaign with the struggle for Islam and by urging the Turks not to be discouraged by the lack of arms: 'Anatolia's war was fought with sticks and axes.'[2] The local leaders advised householders to accumulate in their homes knives, axes, sledges, pointed tools, large stones, boiling water and petrol. Convinced that Turkey would send troops to their aid, the Turkish Cypriots were in no way daunted by the fact that Greeks outnumbered them by four to one. Turkish houses displayed posters showing the island partitioned beneath the figure of a helmeted Turkish soldier. The fanaticism which was associated with EOKA now permeated the TMT, which called for 'PARTITION OR DEATH!':

Oh Turkish Youth!

The day is near when you will be called upon to sacrifice your life and blood in the 'PARTITION' struggle – to the struggle for freedom. . . .

You are a brave Turk. You are faithful to your country and nation and are entrusted with the task of demonstrating Turkish might. Be ready to break the chains of slavery with your determination and willpower and with your love of freedom.

[1] TMT leaflet, Pyla, 18 May 1958.
[2] TMT leaflet, Nicosia, 20 May 1958.

All Turkdom, right and justice and God are with you. PARTITION OR DEATH![1]

5   THE OUTBREAK OF COMMUNAL STRIFE

On the night of 7 June shortly after 10 p.m. a bomb explosion outside the Turkish Press Office in Nicosia set off the worst outbreak of racial strife which the island had seen since British rule. The explosion served as a time signal and an excuse for Turkish rioters to invade the Greek sector of the old town. The Greeks sounded the alarm by pealing the church bells; in the violent clashes which took place, two Greeks were killed and much Greek property was ransacked or destroyed by fire. Shortly before midnight the troops were called out to assist the police to restore order and to man the 'Mason-Dixon' Line, the rough boundary separating the Greek and Turkish sectors. The Old City was placed under curfew but the fighting went on until 3 a.m. The original explosion did little material damage. And circumstantial evidence strongly pointed to the fact that the bomb was of Turkish origin. This, however, did not deter Turkey from making a formal protest to Britain the next day alleging that the Cyprus administration had failed to give the Turkish minority adequate protection.

The crisis reached a climax on 12 June when eight Greeks were massacred in a cornfield near the Turkish village of Geunyeli.[2] Communal feeling had been running high in the neighbouring villages. The day before the massacre Police Sergeant Gill, who was responsible for the area, found Greek and Turkish villagers at Skylloura standing around armed with sticks and stones. The Turks were greatly alarmed, fearing an imminent attack by the Greeks. Close to the village, on the road to Philia, the sergeant found nearly two hundred Greeks crouching in the dried-up bed of a stream. The men, who mostly came from Philia, carried clubs, knives and pitchforks amongst other weapons. About fifty of them were able to escape before the arrival of a military patrol which enabled the police sergeant to arrest and disarm the remainder. The offenders were later released. Several hours later, in the small hours of the morning, Sergeant Gill returned to Skylloura where two Turks informed him that the Greeks were about to attack the Turkish community at Aghios Vasilios. As he approached the village he saw two buses turn round and make off in the direction of Mammari.

---

[1] TMT leaflet, Larnaca, 7 May 1958.
[2] See *The Findings of the Commission of Inquiry into the Incidents at Geunyeli, Cyprus on 12 June 1958* (Cyprus Government, 1958).

The patrol which pursued them eventually rounded up five vehicles carrying a total of 250 Greeks. The men were disarmed and made to walk back to Mammari.

On the afternoon of 12 June Turks reported to Sergeant Gill at Yerolakkos Police Station that their community at Skylloura had been attacked by Greeks. Sergeant Gill found that the report was a false alarm but that Greek and Turkish villagers faced each other with sticks in hostile confrontation from their respective sectors. The Turkish mukhtar feared an attack from Philia or Kondemenos. Meanwhile a troop of the Royal Horse Guards had arrived with two armoured scout cars and taken over control of the village. And Sergeant Gill left to investigate the situation in the direction of Kondemenos.

A short distance outside Skylloura Sergeant Gill found thirty-five armed Greeks entrenched in a dried-up river bed, and lined up in formation in a concealed position close to the Turkish quarter. The mood of the Greeks was aggressive and the sergeant did not accept their explanation that they were there solely to protect Greek workers returning home to Kondemenos. With the help of a passing RAF officer, he arrested them. The Royal Horse Guards escorted the prisoners to Yerolakkos Police Station where Gill intended to charge them under the Offensive Weapons (Prohibition) Law, 1955. While he was talking to Assistant Superintendent Trusler, who had come to Yerolakkos from Nicosia, a hostile crowd began to gather, and it was decided to take the prisoners to Nicosia Central Police Station.

In the meantime the Central Police Station had become the centre of commotion as the result of serious rioting by Turkish men and women nearby. On reaching the outskirts of Nicosia, the army officer in charge of the convoy with the prisoners received a message ordering him not to bring the prisoners into the town. The convoy returned to Geunyeli. The Greeks were eventually released at a place to the north of the Turkish village and, having been disarmed, ordered to walk across country to their own village of Kondemenos. A troop of the Royal Horse Guards escorted them for about 400 yards away from the main road and withdrew after the last Greek had disappeared over the horizon. The army then took steps to maintain security in the immediate vicinity of Geunyeli.

A few minutes after the Greeks were out of sight, army watchers saw smoke and flames coming from the crest of the hill. It was assumed at first that the Greeks had set fire to Turkish crops. And an angry crowd of Turks armed with primitive weapons began to swarm out of Geunyeli. Lieutenant Baring of the Royal Horse Guards overtook the crowd, having ordered the Grenadiers to follow him and set up a road block to hold back the Turks. Baring went ahead to investigate the fire. On the way he arrested two Turks, a motor cyclist and his pillion passenger. He then came upon the mutilated body of a Greek. A group of men came towards him; some of them were wounded. The thirty-five Greeks had run into a Turkish ambush. Four were killed on the spot and four died later of their injuries. The remainder owed their survival to the arrival of Baring in the armoured car.

The massacre was quickly followed up by a flood of Greek allegations that the security forces had deliberately exposed the prisoners to a Turkish attack. Considerable disquiet also prevailed in British circles. The Cyprus Mail, noted for its moderation in criticising the Government, demanded an explanation for the fact that the thirty-five Greeks had been dumped near a Turkish village.[1] On 16 June the Governor appointed a Commission of Inquiry and entrusted the task to the Chief Justice, Sir Paget Bourke, who decided in the public interest to hold the inquiry in private. His decision had been influenced by several considerations: the risk that public proceedings might accelerate the high degree of tension already prevailing in the island, with the possibility of further disturbances and loss of life; the probability that witnesses, in danger of reprisals, would be afraid to speak the truth, thereby defeating the object of the inquiry. The inquiry opened at the end of June and lasted eight days. The Governor expressed his intention to publish its findings in due course. During the hearing thirty-seven witnesses, representing the security forces, the Turks and the Greek survivors, gave evidence before the Commission.

The inquiry threw light on the events which had led to the abandonment of the Greek prisoners near Geunyeli. The primary concern of the police and army officers in Nicosia on the day of the massacre had been to stop the convoy with the prisoners from driving into the centre of the Turkish disturbances which were taking place outside the Central Police Station. Assistant Superintendent Trusler, the police officer in charge of Nicosia Rural Sub-Division, had given specific instructions that the convoy was to be stopped and the Greeks taken to Aghios Dhometios Police Station. But the message never reached the convoy. Instead Major Redgrave of the Royal Horse Guards, who was controlling the convoy by radio, understood that his orders were to send the Greeks back to the country and let them walk home.

According to army witnesses the prisoners were diverted to Geunyeli because the road to this village was the first turning into the country in

[1] Cyprus Mail, 16 June 1958 (editorial).

relation to the position of the convoy at the time of the message; a diversion via Geunyeli was the right direction for their own homes to the north of Skylloura; once clear of Geunyeli, which was under military surveillance, no other sources of trouble were to be expected on their route; since the Royal Horse Guards had taken over the security of the rural area no incidents had occurred apart from a minor stone-throwing attack by Greeks; the Royal Horse Guards were on patrol in the district and all was quiet. The choice for the exact site for the release of the prisoners had been left to the discretion of the officers on the spot.

The Commissioner questioned the legality and the propriety of sending prisoners home on foot without an escort. Two senior police witnesses also regarded the practice as an irregularity. The army officers, however, clearly accepted it as a salutary measure in dealing with excitable trouble-makers and as a practical alternative on the occasions when the police were not able to take the offenders into custody. It had the effect of tiring them so that they gave no more trouble the same day. The officers giving evidence were agreed that it would have been unreasonable to send the Greeks back the way they had come; that it would have involved a loss of face for the security forces and would not have led to any improvement in the attitude of the offenders who would, if anything, have been liable to cause more trouble once they realised that nothing was to be done about them.

The Greek survivors described how, in their haste to get home, they had run up the slope, leaving behind the field of crops which later went up in flames. As they descended the slope on the other side they saw two motor cyclists and a pillion rider coming along the village road from Geunyeli. The motor cyclists opened fire and two of the Greeks were wounded. When the Greeks tried to go back they suddenly found themselves surrounded by a large group of Turks armed with axes, pieces of wood and knives. The Greeks scattered in the attempt to escape. And those who tried to go back the way that they had come saw that the crops were alight.

Much of the evidence produced at the inquiry was conflicting, and in several respects the Commissioner's findings were inconclusive.[1] They nevertheless threw some light on the events which had led to the release of the Greeks north of Geunyeli. The Commissioner was satisfied that the arrest of the Greek party outside Skylloura on 12 June was lawful and that they were there either to launch an attack on the Turkish quarter or else go to the assistance of their compatriots in the event of renewed communal clashes.

[1] *Findings of the Commission of Inquiry*, op. cit. pp. 19–21.

The Commissioner stressed the difficulties prevailing in the operations room at the Central Police Station at the time. Herein might lie some explanation as to why Superintendent Trusler's specific instructions were not conveyed to Sergeant Gill who was in charge of the prisoners. A blunder had occurred causing some confusion but he was unable to say to what extent if any it was due to the lack of liaison between the police and military. The report was critical of the fact that no message was sent to inform the operations room that the convoy was proceeding to Geunyeli. Had this been done, the Commissioner commented, the senior police officers concerned would have been informed and, in the light of their evidence, would have intervened to prevent the diversion.

The Commissioner completely rejected the submission that the security forces had shown a reckless indifference to the fate of the Greeks. He was fully satisfied that all concerned with their release had acted with the utmost good faith; that they had appreciated that some trouble might be expected in the vicinity of Geunyeli and had taken steps to secure the area. It was the view of the officers in charge on the ground that, once clear of Geunyeli, no other source of trouble lay on the route. In this assessment, however, the Turkish hamlet of Kanli appeared to have been overlooked. The Commissioner rejected allegations that Sergeant Gill had issued ominous threats to the Greeks at the start of their walk and that two Turkish members of the security forces on duty that day had engineered or assisted the ambush.

The report failed to establish with any degree of certainty the place from which the attackers came and to solve the mystery of the two motor cyclists. It was clear that the ambush was planned by Turks who had surmised from earlier events at Geunyeli that the Greeks were about to be sent across the fields. The Commissioner did not accept the evidence of survivors who testified that the Turks in the fields were joined by others who came by trucks and cars from Geunyeli. It was possible that the Greeks after their ordeal were confused in their recollection. The Grenadiers, for instance, had left the village in vehicles, described as trucks at the hearing. If the assailants came from Geunyeli this would have meant that either the vigil kept by the security forces was defective or that a route hidden to the security forces led to the site of the ambush. But the dirt track from Geunyeli was visible from the convoy's position. It was possible that the Turks went to their positions before Baring arrived and that they were reinforced from Kanli. The report paid a tribute to the 'magnificent work'[1] carried out in the

[1] ibid. p. 5.

Nicosia District countryside and to the prompt action taken by Lieutenant Baring which had averted a worse tragedy.[1]

Eight Turks were eventually tried for murder in connection with the Geunyeli incident. But all were acquitted for want of sufficient evidence. The Greek Cypriots, in their highly emotional state, were quick to suggest that even British justice which had long stood the test of conditions in Cyprus was now corrupt, despite the fact that Greek terrorists had time and again been acquitted for the same reasons.

In 1958 EOKA's ill-treatment campaign dwindled. The allegations of atrocities by the security forces had ceased to make much impact on international opinion; the campaign had, moreover, achieved its objective in securing the intervention of the Council of Europe; criticism had been aroused in circles where it could gravely embarrass the Conservative Government. The atrocity campaign was largely replaced during the communal fighting by allegations of British partiality towards the Turks.[2] In the summer, PEKA ordered its members to cultivate hatred of the British, making favouritism towards the Turks an important facet of its propaganda.[3] The campaign rapidly gained ground after the Geunyeli massacre. The Geunyeli Report, which vindicated the troops of the main charge, was not published for many months owing to an explosive situation during the summer.

The burden of keeping the two communities apart fell to the British troops. Despite the presence of 30,000 or more troops incidents could not be avoided. Installations such as the oxygen factory required many guards in order to persuade the Greeks to go on working there. Large areas had to be policed by mobile patrols and units permanently stationed in the worst trouble spots. Much of the time the troops were seriously overworked and carried out their duties in an atmosphere of constant criticism. British soldiers helped to extinguish hundreds of fires, usually started by the Turks, but were accused by the Greeks of deliberate negligence in the case of every house or church which was burnt down. When the security forces searched the suburb of Omorphita they found lethal weapons in the houses of both communities; yet the Greeks insisted that the Turks had been warned of the search in advance.

[1] ibid. p. 18.

Stelios Pavlides QC, a former Attorney-General who appeared for the victims, criticised certain conclusions reached by the Chief Justice. See Cyprus Mail, 11 December 1958.

[2] See Archbishop Makarios, Indictment alleging partiality, Athens, 28 August 1958 (press release).

[3] EOKA leaflets: 'NEWS BULLETIN, Anglo-Turkish Front', distributed in Ktima, 12 July 1958 and 'Bulletin of Anglo-Turkish Collaboration', distributed in Varosha, 31 July 1958.

Partiality where it existed was dictated by political expediency and operational necessity. At policy level it could be traced to the importance which Britain and the US attached to Turkey as the last reliable bastion of Western defence in the Middle East. In the island, psychological and practical reasons entered into the question. Apart from periods of truce, the Greek Cypriots had for three years been shooting British soldiers in the back. The natural sympathies of the army as a whole were inevitably with the Turks, who were seen as loyal, courageous allies, sharing the same dangers in pursuit of the common enemy – EOKA. The British forces had their hands full; in need of Turkish cooperation, they tried wherever possible to avoid conflict with the Turks. The January riots had been a disastrous exception. It was at times difficult to keep the balance. The Turkish police who formed a vital component of the security forces as a whole favoured their compatriots, just as the Greek police turned a blind eye to EOKA's activities.

The Greek complaints soon found their way to the House of Commons through members of the Labour Opposition who attacked the Government for failing to carry out the emergency regulations with impartiality. A few of the complaints were valid. A Turkish Cypriot suspected of terrorist activity was granted bail; and escaped to Turkey before trial; whereas Greek terrorists were always held in custody. Ankara Radio broadcast its inflammatory propaganda unhindered when Athens was jammed.

On 15 July Mr Profumo recalled that Athens Radio had not been banned until repeated protests had failed; EOKA not until five months after its first acts of violence. On the 29th Mr Lennox-Boyd stated that the granting of bail to the Turkish police sergeant was within the discretion of the judge, but admitted that his escape was 'highly unfortunate'.[1]

6 THE MACMILLAN PLAN[2]

The shock of the Geunyeli incident left the Cypriots in a daze; the violence abated for a brief interlude. The situation nevertheless remained tense pending the forthcoming policy statement. The Greek mayors informed Foot that they had no confidence in the security forces and protested against Turkish vandalism, accusing the admini-

---

[1] H.C. Deb., vol. 591, col. 79 (Written Answers), and vol. 592, col. 1137.

[2] Harold Macmillan, *Riding The Storm* (Macmillan, London, 1971), p. 667 ff.

stration of leniency towards the Turkish minority. The Geunyeli tragedy was kept alive; Greeks wore black armbands for the victims. The Turks went ahead with plans for setting up separate municipalities. In the middle of June paratroopers were sent to Cyprus – a move which indicated the seriousness with which the British took the security problem. After the first wave of violence normal life was paralysed. Many Greeks had fled during the initial panic and were living in conditions of squalor; in one week alone 600 Greek families had abandoned their homes. Empty houses were immediately seized by Turkish squatters. The hastily drawn demarcation line separating the Greek and Turkish sectors in Nicosia left Greeks and Turks on the wrong side – each community at the mercy of the majority. The sunset-to-sunrise curfew had disrupted marketing arrangements. Restaurant and café life, a vital source of income in the towns, had come to a standstill. In the extreme summer heat of the Nicosia plain Cypriots were deprived of their sole means of relief and relaxation – the long cool hours after dusk spent outside. Tension and tempers rose as a result; in spite of the dangers the Greek Cypriots began to press the administration to lift the night curfew.

During the outbreak of communal fighting the Turks had ransacked the Municipal Market, looting the property of the Greeks. After several weeks of chaos the administration took over the market with the object of 'maintaining supplies and services essential to the life of the community'.[1] But the chances of any return to normality were blocked by political motives. The Greek Cypriot Mayor of Nicosia was informed by the Commissioner's Office that with troops and police on guard the Greeks could safely return to their stalls. The mayor, however, stated that no Greeks would go back unless the 'Mason-Dixon' line was adjusted to bring the market into the Greek sector. And at the expense of their financial interests the Greeks continued to boycott the market, claiming that Turkish threats made their return too dangerous.

Outside Cyprus events moved quickly. The NATO powers had watched the deteriorating situation with mounting anxiety. On 12 June the Turks held a mass rally for partition in Ankara. Two days later Turkey rejected the British proposals in advance of their publication; the same day Greece withdrew her forces from NATO's Eastern Mediterranean headquarters at Izmir. This new setback to the Western alliance resulted in the sudden intervention of Paul-Henri Spaak, the Secretary-General of NATO. On 17 June the British Prime

[1] Cyprus Mail, 26 June 1958.

Minister announced that the British Government had agreed to the NATO Council's request to postpone the policy statement by forty-eight hours.

On 19 June the British Government stated[1] that in view of the disagreement between Greece and Turkey and between the two communities it had decided to give a firm lead out of the deadlock. The new plan provided for separate Greek and Turkish houses of representatives and a council of ministers which would be presided over by the British Governor and include four Greek Cypriot and two Turkish Cypriot ministers. Defence, internal security, and external affairs would be reserved to the Governor. Greece and Turkey would each be invited to appoint one representative to cooperate with the Governor. The international status of the island was to remain unchanged for seven years. But if the Greek and Turkish Governments were willing to extend this 'experiment in partnership' the British Government might, at the appropriate time, be willing to share the sovereignty of the island with Greece and Turkey.[2]

In the absence of the Turkish leader Dr Kutchuk, Denktash immediately branded the plan as 'a stepping-stone towards Enosis'. The Greek Cypriots waited, as usual, for a lead from Archbishop Makarios, who dismissed the plan as 'wholly unacceptable' because it precluded 'the fundamental and inalienable right of the people of Cyprus to self-determination, and would create a permanent focus of unrest and a threat to the peace of the whole region'. But, the Archbishop added, the Greek Cypriots did not reject a transitory phase of self-government and were always ready for bilateral talks. PEO came out in full support of the Archbishop. The plan, PEO's spokesman commented, while giving more democratic rights to the people than its predecessors, brought partition closer than ever before. And the road of partnership did not lead to self-determination demanded by the people but instead to the partition of the island into three parts – British, Greek and Turkish.

On 20 July the Greek Government rejected the proposals but gave qualified support for a temporary solution on a basis of democratic self-government under British rule, leaving the settlement of the sovereignty question until 'a more appropriate time'. The matter was one between the British and the Cypriots. Both Makarios and the Greek Government, despite their opposition to the plan as it stood, had modified their positions to some extent in the direction of a compromise. The time-limit for self-determination was shelved, and the need for

[1] *Cyprus: Statement of Policy, June 1958*, see Cmnd 455.
[2] ibid.

continuing British rule recognised. But Greek tactics were still designed to exclude Turkey from any negotiations.

The Turkish Prime Minister declared his Government's willingness to take part in talks but its inability to consider any settlement which excluded partition. The British press, including the socialist newspapers, were almost unanimous in their approval for the plan. The Manchester Guardian, which from time immemorial had constantly found fault with British policy in Cyprus, went so far as to describe it as 'a good plan – as good a plan as can be devised'.[1]

In spite of the attitude of the socialist and liberal newspapers in Britain, the Greek Cypriots still hoped for the support of the Labour Party. The lull continued pending the outcome of the debate due to take place in the House of Commons on the Cyprus plan. But tension rose again when on the eve of his departure for London Foot released the text of his letter sent to Grivas in April, with the explanation that he had decided to make the disclosure because of reports that the local press was about to publish the letter.[2] Grivas branded Foot's action as a publicity stunt and as a breach of confidence which he had scrupulously observed, although under no obligation to do so.[3] The fast-diminishing confidence of the army and the Turks in Foot's methods was undermined still further by the news of his attempt to make a direct approach to the EOKA leader.

The debate opened on 26 June.[4] The Secretary of State for the Colonies, Alan Lennox-Boyd, reminded the House that the legal sovereignty of Cyprus was vested in the British Crown under Article 20 of the treaty of Lausanne. This gave Her Majesty's Government the legal right to do whatever it considered best in and with the island and to decide what other countries should be consulted about its status.

Lennox-Boyd summarised the efforts made by the British Government over the past year to reach a settlement through diplomatic channels; the abortive attempts to organise a conference between Britain, Greece and Turkey the previous autumn; the Foreign Secretary's negotiations in Ankara and Athens at the beginning of 1958. In the interests of secret diplomacy, he threw no light on these discussions but, he said, it became unmistakably clear that no agreement on Cyprus policy was possible. Meanwhile the situation in the island was deteriorating rapidly. The British Government therefore abandoned

---

[1] Manchester Guardian, editorial, 20 June 1958.
[2] See *Memoirs* (Longmans), op. cit. p. 139.
[3] ibid. pp. 138 and 141.
[4] See H.C. Deb., vol. 590, cols 615–735.

the search for a course of action which had been agreed by all three governments in advance and set to work on a plan to be put forward on a British responsibility. The two lessons to be learnt from the dangerous developments of the past few months were firstly that Cyprus was on the brink of civil war which could not be limited to the island, secondly that there was no possibility of agreement between the Greek and Turkish Governments, and that the only hope of avoiding disaster was for Her Majesty's Government to take a new initiative.

The British Government, which based its new policy on two main principles – partnership and communal autonomy – had always taken the view that Cypriot interests must come first. The policy of communal autonomy provided for an undivided Cyprus and took into account the separatist activities already practised in religious, educational and social affairs. The exact scope of the plan was a matter for discussion, but this separatism might be extended to aspects of local government. Lennox-Boyd had little to add to the policy statement of 19 June apart from drawing attention to the arrangements for dual nationality and Greco-Turkish participation in the future government of the island. He said these provisions were of special importance to the two Cypriot communities. The plan assured the Greek Cypriots of a unified Cyprus and representation on the Governor's Council in proportion to their numbers in the population, the Turks of communal autonomy and an impartial tribunal to examine complaints of discriminatory legislation. The plan, moreover, held out hopes of an early end to the emergency. Britain's NATO allies had shown great understanding; the twelve countries not directly involved and the Secretary-General regarded this policy as a basis for discussion. The British Government was willing to start talks with Greece and Turkey and representative Cypriots as soon as they were ready.

Nearly a year had elapsed since the last debate on Cyprus and it was the first to take place since the appointment of Foot as Governor. The unusual restraint shown by the Opposition may well be explained by Foot's influence with the Labour Party, by the threat of war between Greece and Turkey, and the possibility that the Socialists might shortly find themselves in power after the general election and be called upon to honour their pledge to grant Cyprus self-determination.

No debate on Cyprus was complete without an indictment of the Conservative Government's past errors and the monotonous references to Hopkinson's 'Never'. But having disposed of this preliminary, James Callaghan, the Labour Party's spokesman on colonial affairs, gave a balanced assessment of the Government's proposals. Callaghan recognised the plan's advantages: the early end to the emergency, the return of the exiles and the resumption of a form of normal government. But he criticised the extent of the concessions made by the British Government to the Turks, and the fact that the plan emphasised separation of the Greek and Turkish communities rather than their unity. He wanted to see a legislative assembly based on a common electoral roll. When Labour came to power it was likely that changes would have to be made to the constitution. Permanent solutions should not be based on what might be 'a temporary and passing quarrel'.[1]

Callaghan's speech was chiefly significant for his comments on self-determination. He said the Labour Party did not intend to depart from the doctrine that all peoples of the Commonwealth were entitled to decide their own destiny. But self-determination must come with the consent of the people. It would be wrong to impose it by force and the Socialists did not intend to do so. It was impossible to apply the doctrine in an atmosphere of civil war; the consent of the minority was essential if self-determination was to be lasting. Most of the opposition speakers expressed concern at the proposals for dual nationality and the participation of Greece and Turkey in the Governor's Council. The lack of provisions for a legislative assembly based on a common roll was also widely criticised. Desmond Donnelly was, in addition, dissatisfied with the arbitrary time-limit of seven years and thought that the Archbishop's return within the next few weeks should be made a corollary to the plan. Subject to these reservations he believed that, provided the government was sufficiently courageous and flexible, the plan had a reasonable chance of success as a basis for discussion. Donnelly warned of the grave consequences likely to follow the total collapse of the plan: including the possible withdrawal of Britain from the island; in this case the Greek Cypriots would suffer the most, since the alternative would be annexation by Turkey or partition. If the Turks pushed their claim too far the result might well be political chaos in Greece, even communist government. In this situation Turkey would be the most vulnerable and have the most to lose.

Paget was pessimistic and urged the Government not to go ahead with the proposals once they were finally rejected, and to put a term to the negotiations and, failing agreement, to declare a period of colonial rule for seven years. Kenneth Robinson stated that he could not support the plan, which in his view seemed to perpetuate the present wide gulf between the Greeks and the Turks, making 'self-determination virtually

[1] ibid. col. 628.

impossible and partition of the island almost inevitable'.[1] Crossman described the plan as a very 'desperate'[2] one. When the Tory Government came to power the idea of self-government for a specific period leading to eventual self-determination was reasonable and practicable. But owing to the sharp deterioration of conditions in Cyprus over the last six years this concept would have to be temporarily abandoned. He concluded with an appeal for flexibility on the part of the Greeks, the Turks and the British Government. Aneurin Bevan, winding up for the Opposition, spoke with unprecedented moderation. It had always been the position of the Labour Party, he said, that full self-government was the same thing as self-determination. But self-determination was the last phase in the process. He could not commend the proposals, but he advised the Greeks and the Turks not to reject them out of hand.

The Socialists differed mainly on the question of whether the Cyprus problem should be treated as a colonial or an international dispute. The two members for St Pancras, with its large Cypriot population, regretted the association of Greece and Turkey with the island's administration. Callaghan welcomed the international approach as a 'belated concession to common sense'.[3] Crossman also approved of the decision. But Bevan believed that the Greek and Turkish High Commissioners should act solely as midwives, leaving after the birth of the new state.

Summing up for the Government, the Prime Minister, Harold Macmillan, stated that early agreement was not to be expected, but that he saw grounds for cautious optimism in the Turkish Foreign Minister's statement on 19 June that the British plan was reconcilable with Turkey's objectives.[4] But in the event of failure to introduce the plan the British Government would stand by its policy statement of 19 December 1956. Macmillan had, in effect, given the Cypriots the choice of cooperation or ultimate partition, whilst carefully avoiding all direct reference to the word.

The debate did nothing to improve the situation in Cyprus, where events were working up to a new clash between the communities. The assurances given the Turks by the Socialists had come too late; and Callaghan's hint that a Labour Government would change the constitutional plan was in itself sufficient to deepen Turkish misgivings. The Greeks were bitterly disillusioned by the new element of uncertainty which now obscured Labour's real intentions on the exercise of self-

[1] ibid. col. 687.
[2] ibid. col. 701.
[3] ibid. col. 623.
[4] ibid. col. 727-35.

determination. Foot returned to Cyprus on 29 June and immediately lifted the night curfews. Violence broke out within a few hours. At Peristerona-Pighi the security forces clashed with the villagers; in the Paphos district, Turks armed with knives and pickaxes fatally wounded a Greek Cypriot; in Nicosia Turks set alight the Greek Orthodox Church of Aghios Loukas for the second time in two weeks.

On 30 June serious clashes broke out between Greeks and Turks at Omorphita, a new suburb on the outskirts of Nicosia. Troops quelled the initial outbreak. But the suburb, with its neighbour Kaimakli, continued to be the centre of intermittent communal friction for many weeks. The sight of a Turkish youth brandishing a knife over the garden wall was sufficient to set off a new wave of panic. Early in July Greek householders were still leaving Omorphita in considerable numbers by lorry. The Turks, convinced that military help from Turkey was imminent and partition a certainty, became very bold. Many of them moved into Greek houses and hoisted the Turkish flag. Troops at the time blamed the authorities for their delay in authorising the curfew. The security forces were now faced with the problem of a head-on clash with the Turks in the attempt to evict them or the virtual toleration of the illegal seizure of Greek houses. The removal of the flags led to fresh incidents; and in the circumstances troops were ordered to leave them.

The new wave of violence reached its climax on 5 July at Avgorou, a village between Famagusta and Larnaca. A routine patrol of the Royal Horse Guards found a slogan prominently displayed outside the coffee shop and ordered a youth standing nearby to remove it. He refused and when the patrol tried to arrest him they were attacked by men and women armed with large stones and bottles. Hopelessly outnumbered by the angry crowd a riot squad was unable to break up the disturbances with batons. An officer forced his way into an armoured car which was already surrounded. Under heavy attack from large rocks thrown from the crowd he elevated the gun to its maximum and fired fifteen shots; a farmer and a pregnant woman were killed outright.

Thirteen Cypriots and twenty-two members of the security forces were injured in the clash. The towns of Famagusta and Larnaca went into mourning; their mayors demanded an inquiry and the punishment of those responsible for the Greek Cypriot casualties. Three days later two British soldiers were shot dead in a Famagusta shop by EOKA gunmen as a reprisal for the Avgorou incident. The attempted removal of a slogan had thus ended in catastrophe. Operations such as these contributed little to security. The price paid at Avgorou was indeed heavy both in casualties and the aftermath of human bitterness and served only to strengthen the hands of the EOKA extremists.

The formation of anti-Turkish groups by EOKA had begun in 1957. In the opinion of Grivas, the success of the Turkish attacks the following summer was due to carelessness and delay in the execution of the defence plan for Nicosia.[1] Early in June EOKA gave orders that all citizens, rightists and leftists, were to be summoned to attend Church for the formation of mass defence groups under the banner of EAEM (The Solid United National Front). Ostensibly non-political, EAEM was, in fact, controlled by EOKA and its leaders were experienced men drawn from the Vigilance Groups; their affiliations remained secret. EAEM claimed to be the only authorised defence organisation. In spite of the magnitude of the dangers facing the Greek Cypriots, EOKA could not put aside its struggle for dominance in local politics. EAEM became heavily involved in the war against the left wing and was in effect the instrument of EOKA's attempts to extend its stranglehold over the populace by exploiting the Greek fear of the Turks. Efforts to set up defence groups within the framework of a united front were short-lived. The organisation soon started to splinter off into rival factions of left and right. The fear of the Turks was so great by midsummer that even some of EOKA's own supporters wanted to seek the British Army's help in defending the villages. But the proposal was rejected by the leaders on the ground that it would hamper the activities of the fighters, the writing of slogans and the distribution of leaflets.

The steady flight of the Greek Cypriots from Turkish areas was the first step in the direction of partition. EOKA was determined to stop the evacuations, and circulated orders that no Greek Cypriot was to leave his home, office or shop; and that those who had already done so were to return. The Greek community was urged to avoid provocation but in the event of attack to fight back rather than succumb to a coward's death and lock themselves up in their houses to be slain like rats. The EOKA scribes deplored the fact that during the initial out-break of communal violence not one single Turk had been attacked or threatened despite the overwhelming superiority of the Greeks. It was lamentable, one leader wrote, that a people who had stood up to thou-sands of soldiers should be afraid of a handful of Turks. This uninten-tional tribute to the army was a strange contrast to the perpetual allegations of British brutality.

The crisis gave wide scope for Grivas's mania for planning. He gave orders that the Greeks must not attack first. Whenever possible the

[1] *Memoirs* (Greek ed.), op. cit. p. 257.

Turks should be drawn on to Greek property so as to show them up as the aggressors. All reprisals – the execution of Turks and the destruction of their crops – were to take place only in accordance with a careful, pre-arranged plan. Certain villages were allocated the task of sending small groups to the assistance of others in distress once it had been established that no troops were in the area.

During the month of June two Turks had lost their lives at the hands of EOKA. The brief respite which followed the Geunyeli incident was broken by the Turks at the end of June. EOKA hit back with the murder of three Turks on 1 July. On the 10th four Greeks were killed by the Turks. The next day, EOKA embarked on full scale retaliation. Five Turkish workers returning to the village of Sinda were fatally wounded when their bus was ambushed by gunmen from a concealed site in an orange grove close to the road. The gulf between the communities was wider than ever before. Nevertheless the Greek mayor of Nicosia, Dervis, and the acting Turkish leader, Denktash, joined Foot in calling upon everyone in Cyprus to stop violence between Greeks and Turks at once: 'If this goes on there is no end to the suffering it may bring. Let bloodshed cease here and now.'[1] A few days later Archbishop Makarios endorsed the appeal from Athens but qualified his statement by strong recriminations against the British and the Turks.

Violence continued to gather momentum. On 17 July, EOKA gunmen killed five Turks. On 22 July the Governor ordered an island-wide standstill. Civilian movements and communications were completely restricted. The TMT was proscribed; 50 Turks and more than 1,500 Greeks were arrested, among them many men and women who had recently been released after careful screening. The Governor announced that the new measures had been taken to save lives and property and to prevent civil war. Since the beginning of June, 95 people had been killed and more than 170 wounded; most of the victims were unarmed and many of the killings and woundings had been carried out with horrible brutality. Had it not been for the ceaseless activities of the security forces, the Governor stressed, 'the slaughter and destruction would have been multiplied and many hundreds of people would have lost their lives'.[2]

The measures were the most drastic yet enforced. But violence did not abate. EOKA was now in the ascendancy, and Turkish casualties were nearly double those of the Greeks. In the towns the Turks could hold

---

[1] Cyprus Government News Release, 12 July 1958, no. 7, and Sunday Times, 13 July 1958.
[2] 'Governor's Statement on Action to Save Lives and Prevent Civil War' (Cyprus Government Press Release, 22 July 1958).

their own in spite of the numerical superiority of the Greek community. And here Turkish reprisals mainly took the form of arson. The chief Turkish victims were shepherds and farmers engaged in lonely occupations and living in remote hamlets encircled by Greek villages. Many Turkish villagers, afraid to go out to harvest their crops, were facing acute shortages.

At the end of July the Turkish community of Aghoursos in the Paphos district moved more than a hundred miles to the mixed village of Skylloura in the Nicosia plain, taking their furniture and livestock with them and leaving behind fields and property owned by their families for generations. A British official flew by helicopter in an eleventh-hour attempt to dissuade them from uprooting. This was the first time that the Turks had moved in organised groups. Other villages were ready to follow. Some were motivated by genuine fear of the Greeks on the basis of experience; others succumbed to the pressures of the TMT which aimed at reinforcing the Turkish communities in the northern sector of the island in order to facilitate partition. At Skylloura the new arrivals camped in tents provided by the Turkish Government. Shepherds grazed their flocks on the corn stubble in sight of the Greek sector across the road. Troops based on a small mosque kept the peace.

The Greek and Turkish communities now faced serious hardship. Commercial life, which normally functioned on an island-wide basis, was drastically curtailed by prolonged curfews and by the refusal of the Greeks to go through Turkish villages. Andreas Ziartides, the Secretary-General of the Pancyprian Federation of Labour, estimated that £600,000[1] was lost in wages in the building and contracting industry alone during this period of communal strife. Many Greeks were living in conditions of squalor and deprivation. Greek factories in the habit of employing Turkish workers were short of labour. The Turkish community, which was far from self-sufficient and depended on the Greeks for much of its trade, was confronted with food shortages and black market prices. Greek lawyers refused to attend the courts because they were located in the Turkish quarter of Nicosia. Doctors and dentists of both communities lost many patients.

At the end of July the British Prime Minister, Harold Macmillan, appealed for the end of violence, and was backed up by the Greek and Turkish Prime Ministers.[2] As the weeks went by Archbishop Makarios was visited in Athens by increasing numbers of Cypriots, among them

---

[1] See Nancy Crawshaw 'Cyprus: Conflict and Reconciliation', *The World Today* (RIIA April 1959), p. 141.

[2] Cyprus Government Press Release, 22 July 1958.

former extremists, who urged him to exert his influence in favour of a compromise settlement before final catastrophe descended upon the island. On 4 August Colonel Grivas issued a cryptic leaflet declaring a five-day cease-fire against the British and the Turks, but reserving the right to future action in the event of 'provocation'. The TMT immediately gave orders that all armed groups should stop action until further notice; that no Greek property should be touched unless Turkish property was touched; that no pressure should be brought to bear on Greeks in the minority unless pressure was brought to bear on Turks in the minority.

Communal strife did not break out again for the remainder of British rule. The Greeks had at last realised that the vicious circle of attack and reprisal, followed by the flight of the Greeks and the migration of the Turks to the north of the island, could only hasten the dreaded day of partition. The Turks themselves now had misgivings about partition. Eight weeks of communal strife had forcibly shown up many of the practical difficulties involved. It was estimated that the creation of a homogeneous Turkish sector would necessitate the resettlement of some 60,000 people, and that, of the two communities, the Turks would suffer more. The Turks had also realised that, short of grave international complications, the help which Turkey could send them was strictly limited, and that the promises of military reinforcements were worth no more than the rhetoric of opportunist politicians.

The summer's crisis had alarmed NATO and the new Secretary-General, Paul-Henri Spaak, took the initiative in holding informal discussions with the Greek and Turkish delegates in the alliance. Harold Macmillan left England on 6 August to visit Greece, Turkey and Cyprus. The visit was notable for the cordiality shown by the British Prime Minister's hosts but little of substance was achieved. Macmillan felt that there was nothing to be gained, either by further talks with the Governments concerned in the dispute or within the framework of NATO, and therefore decided to go ahead with the partnership plan subject to minor changes. Spaak had already told him that Turkish membership of the Governor's Council was the main stumbling block for the Greeks. Under the modified plan the proposals for dual nationality were dropped; the Greek and Turkish representatives were to be given the status of ambassadors and would not be members of the Governor's Council. On 19 August the Greek Government rejected the plan, which was accepted a week later by the Turks.[1]

[1] See *Riding The Storm*, op. cit. pp. 674–87 (an interesting and amusing record from the government angle of Macmillan's attempts to get the plan accepted).

7   GREEK AGAINST GREEK

The dangers of Turkish militancy in 1958 might have been expected to absorb all EOKA's resources and to have generated a sense of unity. But the Greek Cypriots were more divided than ever before. At the top level, serious disagreement existed between Makarios and Grivas over EOKA's attacks on the Communists, the passive resistance campaign and the military tactics to be used against the Turks.[1] The ranks of EOKA were, as usual, riddled with dissension, petty rivalry and betrayals. The brief period in the summer of closer cooperation between the left and the right against the Turks in the villages had provided added opportunities for friction.

The two new organisations, the Left-wing Nationalists (OAE) and the Left-wing Patriots (OAP), which had first appeared in the early spring, sought to capture the loyalties of the moderate leftists and claimed to represent Akelists who had defected from the party. EOKA had at last recognised the futility of trying to discredit the left-wing movement as a whole. The OAP and the OAE renewed the attacks against Ziartides, comparing his return to Cyprus with that of the exiled politicians to Greece at the end of the Second World War,[2] and urged all citizens irrespective of their political beliefs to form a new united front:

> Let us form our own LEFT-WING NATIONAL FRONT, and hand-in-hand with PEKA and EOKA increase the strength of the Cyprus people. We know that they will welcome us, if we isolate the national traitors and suspects.
>
> Do not hold back for a moment from joining the ranks of the fighting Cyprus people.
>
> LONG LIVE UNITY
>
> LONG LIVE THE ALLIANCE PEKA-EOKA-OAE

The chorus of vilification was joined by PEKA and ANE with renewed allegations of treachery and collaboration with the British and the lack of patriotism shown by the communist youth:

> They glorify Mother Russia and forget all about Mother Greece.[3]

---

[1] See *Memoirs* (Greek ed.), op. cit. p. 273.
[2] OAE leaflet, 13 February 1958.
[3] ANE leaflet, 23 February 1958.

AKEL had little difficulty in exposing the 'Left-wing Nationalists' and the 'Left-wing Patriots' as instruments of the extreme right; their tracts came from the same presses as those which printed EOKA's directives and were phrased in the same threatening style.

The left wing at this time upheld the main aims of the nationalists – the return of the Archbishop, the release of the detainees and the end of the emergency – and came into open conflict with EOKA on the subject of education. EOKA's war against the left wing had rapidly spread to the schools, where the Organisation had persistently worked for anarchy, treating education as one of the sacrifices every good patriot must be willing to make in the interests of the nationalist cause. The communist youth movement PEOM,[1] while deploring the horrors of school life under colonialism, repeatedly stressed the importance of school attendance, hard work and good marks in examinations.[2] The disruption of education was unpopular with the majority of Greek parents and AKEL's opposition to EOKA in this case could be sure of strong but silent support.

During the early stages the wooing of the moderate left took place against a background of minor incidents and village quarrels. A bomb was found in the office of the communist newspaper *Haravghi* and the nationalists accused the left of having put it there themselves. The word 'AKEL' was splashed in red paint across the statue of Archbishop Makarios II at Kyrenia. The left wing denied all responsibility accusing EOKA of provocation.

From the middle of May EOKA's attacks against the left were marked by increased brutality. In the village of Lefkoniko on 23 May a left-wing trade unionist, Savvas Menakas, was tied to a tree and beaten to death, his muscles reduced to pulp. When his wife tried to reach his body she was threatened with the same treatment. At the inquest the Coroner, Mr Trainor, commented, 'One would not hear of a more disgraceful piece of brutality from the depths of the jungle.'[3] Immediately after the murders of Menakas and Yiasoumi the Pancyprian Federation of Labour called upon all workers to strike and to attend mass meetings in protest against these crimes.[4] On 25 May the murders were forcefully denounced by AKEL, which appealed to all responsible political circles, the Archbishop, the Ethnarchy and the press to raise their voices in demanding the end to political murders and the prevention of

[1] Pancyprian National Organisation of Pupils (*Pankyprios Ethniki Organosis Mathiton*).
[2] PEOM Administrative Council leaflet: 'National Duty', Larnaca, 23 May 1958.
[3] See Manchester Guardian, 6 October 1958.
[4] Leaflet issued by the Executive Bureau of PEO, Nicosia, 24 May 1958.

civil war.[1] A third left-wing trade unionist, Andreas Sakkas, was shot dead in a Nicosia coffee shop the same day.

The nationalist organisations renewed their campaign against Ziartides and dismissed the protests of the left wing as hysterical and theatrical.[2] Alleging that the two men were traitors, PEKA condemned the workers for representing them as innocent victims.[3] EOKA threatened yet again to strike down traitors without distinction between left and right.[4] The people in their anger cried out for retaliation, and the catastrophe of civil war between the Greek Cypriots was only narrowly averted thanks to the restraining influence of AKEL and PEO. AKEL's manifesto emphasised the overriding need for unity in view of the new dangers facing the Greek Cypriots – the possibility of partition and the establishment of Turkish troops in the island. On 12 June AKEL aligned itself with the policy of Makarios, recognising him as the sole representative in future negotiations and concluded with an appeal for the avoidance of civil strife:

Keep away from Civil War (between Greeks)
Keep away from Civil War (between Greeks and Turks)...[5]

AKEL's recognition of Archbishop Makarios as the sole representative of the Cypriots marked a significant change in left-wing policy and indicated the urgency with which the left-wing leaders viewed the latest developments on the political front. Hitherto the left wing had insisted that any discussions on the island's future status must include members of all parties. EOKA reacted to the appeal for unity by murdering three more left-wingers in rapid succession: Evanghelos Avghousti, Nikodemos Ioannou and Antonis Paraskeva.[6] When an execution had taken place angry villagers were apt to demand an explanation from EOKA's agents. And as the result of this pressure EOKA would eventually publish an indictment, sometimes after several weeks' delay. Unable to destroy the left by violence alone, the Organisation resorted to trumped up charges of treachery based on hearsay and malicious gossip; in fact, some of the offences attributed to the leftists were of a comparatively trivial nature.[7] But the least inter-

---

[1] Central Committee of AKEL, 'Horrible New Murders', 25 May 1958.
[2] PEKA leaflet, Nicosia, 26 May 1958.
[3] ibid.
[4] EOKA leaflet, Varosha, 29 May 1958.
[5] Declaration of the Central Committee of AKEL, Nicosia, 12 June 1958.
[6] On 14 June at Aghios Ambrosios, 20 and 21 June at Aghios Theodoros.
[7] The Times and Cyprus Mail, 27 August 1958.

ference with EOKA's objectives was, in the eyes of the extremists, sufficient to justify arbitrary execution, and the Organisation's refusal to accept AKEL's challenge to allow an independent investigation was not surprising. The presence of large numbers of mourners at the victim's funerals hampered EOKA's attempts to create an image of public disgrace and considerable pressure was finally exerted by the terrorists to keep the people away.

The struggle between the left and the right continued in the shape of threats and recriminations throughout the summer. But the next major clash did not take place until 25 August, three weeks after the truce with the Turks, when fighting broke out at Milia in the Famagusta district. Trouble was reported to have begun when members of the local branch of the Building Workers Union started a heated discussion on the effects of the passive resistance campaign. Three masked men threw bombs at the Union's premises. The next day, left-wingers visited the homes of nationalists demanding to know why the bombs had been thrown. The villagers began to assemble in the square. The EOKA men opened fire with automatic guns on the crowd. A young mother, Maria Varnava, and a schoolgirl, Despoullia Katsouri, were killed. Intermittent fighting lasted for three hours and twenty people were injured. The police finally arrived and placed the village under curfew. At Famagusta workers went on strike in protest against the brutality of the right; police had to break up a demonstration near the left-wing trade union headquarters at Varosha and prevent leftists from setting fire to the premises of the nationalists. Angry left-wing demonstrations also took place elsewhere. Ziartides went first to Milia and later addressed workers' meetings in Famagusta and Nicosia. Stressing the need for unity, he urged trade unionists to safeguard their organisations and their rights against the attacks of the masked men. It was more than ever important to stand united behind Archbishop Makarios in his rejection of the British plan and in view of a unilateral enforcement of the plan by the British. The local organisations, the mayors and the political leaders headed by the Ethnarch had the duty to work for unity, he said. Resolutions were adopted calling upon the Archbishop, the Bishop of Kition and the Mayor of Nicosia to use their influence to stop Greek killing Greek.

EOKA immediately blamed the left wing for the tragedy at Milia, alleging that they had provoked the nationalists, who had been obliged to defend themselves.[1]

[1] EOKA leaflet: 'The Incorrigibles', Aghios Omologhitadhes, 31 August 1958. Compare with EOKA's version of the incident published by the Milia branch of EAEM at Varosha, 24

8 PASSIVE RESISTANCE

The passive resistance campaign brought EOKA into sharp conflict with the nationalists as well as with the left wing. The new policy was strongly influenced by the Colonel's puritan outlook and his belief that the Cypriots had a weakness for luxury and ostentation which needed to be curbed. The boycott campaign was accordingly combined with a crusade against gambling and ostentation, frivolity and vanity. EOKA ordered men and women to pray in church for the liberation of Cyprus instead of meeting in gambling dens, and coffee shops to close during the hours of religious services. Women were urged to give up cosmetics and to dress in the coarse cloth woven in the villages. But religious and moral considerations were not the sole reason for such directives. Most of them had a practical significance as well – the Colonel's constant fear that gamblers who got into debt might be tempted to betray EOKA for the high rewards offered by the security forces; the use of the Church as a channel for communications and propaganda; and the risk that a decline in church-going would slacken EOKA's hold over the general public. The enforcement of the boycott was largely entrusted to the Valiant Youth of EOKA (ANE). EAEM ran island-wide competitions to encourage the production of local cloth, and special tasks were allocated to a political committee headed by the Bishop of Kition; but this, according to Grivas,[1] failed in its duties which had to be taken over by the EOKA sectors.

The Colonel's intervention in the economic field, made without expert advice and on his own initiative, was based on conclusions which were doctrinaire and dangerously oversimplified. His theory that Cypriot needs could be fully met by increased local production and imports from countries outside the Commonwealth ignored the fact that long-established patterns of trade cannot be changed overnight and that the prosperity of Cyprus was bound up with special tariff arrangements and membership of the Sterling Area. The idea that a substantial drop in revenues would seriously embarrass the British administration was also a major error of judgement. It was the Cypriots who were certain to suffer from these tactics.

September 1958, one month after the incident. This claimed that a group of seven or eight Communists carrying sticks and a shotgun went past the village religious club. A party of unknown men flashed torches to identify the Communists who ordered the men to put their torches out. Fearing an attack the men threw bombs to disperse the Communists who then fired back. In the early hours of the 26th the Communists started gathering in the square and attacked three nationalists. The masked men (EOKA) fired on them killing two women.

[1] *Memoirs* (Greek ed.), op. cit. p. 371.

In the circumstances, the possible economic effects of the boycott gave the authorities little cause for anxiety. Britain's trade with Cyprus was almost negligible. Some reduction in imports and the expansion of local industry were desirable objectives in line with government planning policy. The higher rate of duty on goods from countries outside the Commonwealth was expected to offset partially the loss of revenues from other sources. In that it was turning many nationalists against EOKA, the boycott actually served the purpose of the British. The impact of the campaign on security, however, was disturbing. Passive resistance as practised by EOKA bore little resemblance to Ghandi's methods and rapidly developed into a highly organised form of blackmail backed by force.

The Greek Cypriots were opposed to the boycott from the outset. Almost half of Cypriot exports were absorbed by the British market; the possibility that people in England might refuse to buy Cypriot produce could not be overlooked; troops in the island had spontaneously boycotted local beer as a reprisal. The left wing paid lip-service to the principle of passive resistance and the expansion of local industry and the boycott of British goods in protest against the Government's inflexibility over self-determination. At the same time they hinted at the likelihood of exploitation of the people by unscrupulous merchants under the cover of passive resistance, and stressed the need to go ahead with development projects. The people could not remain 'with crossed hands while hunger and unemployment knock at the door . . .'[1] The prospects of unemployment arising out of the boycott aroused serious misgivings in trade union circles. PEO owed much of its influence to the good wages and conditions of the average Cypriot worker. Nationalists engaged in commerce also shared these anxieties and sought to restrain Grivas through the Archbishop and the Greek Consul, both of whom had grave doubts about the wisdom of the EOKA Leader's policy. Towards the end of April, Makarios appealed to Grivas to reconsider the boycott, which he considered was damaging Cypriot rather than British interests.[2] The reactions of AKEL could not be expected to make any impact on Grivas, and he dismissed the objections of the nationalists on the grounds that the Archbishop, the Greek Consul and the Bishop of Kition were misinformed. The campaign continued to gather momentum.

Almost every aspect of Cypriot life came within the scope of the passive resistance campaign. The boycott was promoted by simple

[1] AKEL leaflet distributed by the Nicosia/Kyrenia District Committee, 1 May 1958.
[2] *Memoirs* (Greek ed.), op. cit. p. 365.

312 The Second Round

advertising techniques combined with intimidation, and touched upon such humdrum subjects as nutrition:

> Use Cyprus raisins for yourselves and your children. The raisin is not a fruit. It is a food. A handful of raisins cannot be replaced either by condensed milk or by chocolates or other luxuries. Raisins for food mean health. In this way we shall be protecting the Cypriot vine grower and we shall export less money for various unhealthy luxuries, which we import from abroad. If the mother knew how good the raisin was for her children she would never give them anything else . . . The same thing can be said of dried figs.[1]

The teaching of English was restricted as a countermeasure against dehellenisation and Greek Cypriots were forbidden to attend government schools, including the new technical training institutes. The most sinister aspect of the campaign was EOKA's attempt to undermine the authority of the judiciary by setting up its own 'arbitration committees' on the pretext of saving legal expenses and reducing British revenues from court fees. The poor response of the people was reflected in the flood of propaganda and warnings to the uncooperative:

> We have observed that a number of Greek women have not participated in the earnest and enthusiastic response to the orders of Dighenis concerning Passive Resistance . . . We do not want to believe that these ladies have no Greek feelings . . . We believe that these ladies have simply failed to attach the necessary importance to the boycott campaign against all British goods . . .

> We are very certain that in future we shall see these very same ladies in the front line as fervent preachers of Passive Resistance.[2]

General warnings were shortly replaced by leaflets which identified the traders who ignored the boycott and the Cypriots who continued to patronise banned shops.

Having failed to obtain public cooperation by persuasion, it was not long before EOKA finally resorted to force. Gangs smashed television sets in the homes of their owners and beat up Greeks caught smoking English cigarettes. Shopkeepers were warned by anonymous telephone calls to close for several weeks as a penalty for selling British produce, or

[1] PEKA leaflet, Nicosia, 12 May 1958.
[2] PEKA leaflet: 'To the Greek Women of the Cyprus Towns', Nicosia, 4 June 1958.

else face the destruction of their premises. Cypriot women had their cotton dresses torn off by hooligans, smeared with ink or lipstick and their make-up removed in public.

With the lapse into hooliganism the campaign got completely out of hand. EOKA itself was finally obliged to call for restraint. The smearing of women's faces with paint and the damaging of cotton dresses in church were denounced as senseless puritanism,[1] and future offenders were threatened with a beating.

The inauguration leaflet which Grivas had circulated in March was swiftly followed up by long lists of banned goods, ranging from tractors to Kleenex; the ban, originally limited to goods with a local counterpart, was eventually extended to all imports from Britain and the Commonwealth. By midsummer passive resistance had brought Cyprus to the brink of economic ruin. The warning notices sent out by Grivas to the merchants in February had not taken into account orders already in the pipeline and goods worth millions of pounds had piled up in the warehouses. Merchants faced with bankruptcy and unable to meet their overheads were forced to dismiss their employees. The boycott had benefited a small number of manufacturers with a vested interest in the exclusion of specific imports. Some traders paid EOKA to add rival products to the lists of banned goods. The monopolies thus set up led to black-marketeering, corruption and high prices. The leftists lost no time in attacking the profiteers:

> Monopolistic capital spreads everywhere its voracious claws beneath the transparent cloak of Patriotism to strangle the whole economy of the island regardless of whether it will have to step over the corpses of the commercial as well as the agrarian and working classes.[2]

The same leaflet proclaimed that the Cypriots were suffering more from the monopolies set up by prominent local industrialists than from the colonial regime. The complaints of profiteering were corroborated by the nationalists who reported the matter to Grivas.

Grivas was also informed that many of the merchants objected to the ban on importing from British and Commonwealth countries because of the economic consequences, and that they intended to ask Makarios to intervene. According to Grivas, the Mayor of Nicosia stated on his return from Athens that he was obliged on the Archbishop's orders to report to the press that he disagreed with EOKA's concept of passive

[1] Document recovered from a terrorist.
[2] Leaflet signed 'United Anti-Monopolistic Front', distributed in Larnaca, 1 May 1958.

resistance. When a member of his audience objected, Dervis added that if he was not allowed to speak he would spread the Archbishop's message by some other means.[1] Makarios could criticise EOKA more freely from the relative safety of Athens. But there is little doubt that the views expressed by him were inspired by responsible Greek Cypriots. At the end of June the Archbishop protested to Grivas for the second time about the boycott and suggested that without openly admitting its mistake EOKA should relax the campaign, and that the Colonel's informers were not telling him the truth because they did not want to disagree with him.[2] The suggestion that he was misinformed offended Grivas, who decided that he wanted no further contact with Makarios on the subject of passive resistance. The Bishop of Kition was reluctant to pass this message on. He wrote to Grivas mentioning the great esteem which the Archbishop had for the EOKA Leader; this was why he had spoken so plainly. Makarios believed that because of the Turkish campaign against the British plan the Greek Cypriots faced a period of protracted struggle and needed to conserve their resources. He had never wanted to stop passive resistance but was merely critical of the methods used.[3] The Greek Consul, Mr Frydas, supported the bishop's apologia in similar vein. But Grivas was adamant. The Archbishop's mistakes over passive resistance, he wrote, made him doubt his ability to handle the campaign as a whole.[4] In future any decisions taken by the Archbishop would have to be endorsed by himself.

Grivas agreed to one concession only – the lifting of the ban on old stocks for six months to allow for their clearance from the warehouses. Envisaging the permanent reorientation of the Cypriot economy on a basis which excluded trade with Britain, he considered that the financial losses suffered by the Greeks as the result of British agencies being taken over by the Turks was of no importance. Grivas had at first been puzzled, even disturbed, by the reports that some of EOKA's own supporters were profiteering, and he gave orders that they should be punished by heavy fines and a ban on further trading. But the EOKA Leader's misgivings seem to have been a passing phase. In assessing the effects of the boycott, he continued to be guided by the progress reports of his subordinates which, for the reasons given by the Archbishop, were grossly misleading. But Grivas remained convinced to the last that passive resistance had been enthusiastically taken up by

[1] *Memoirs* (Greek ed.), op. cit. p. 366.
[2] ibid. p. 367.
[3] ibid. p. 369.
[4] ibid. p. 368.

the population as a whole and that hostility to the campaign was limited to the Archbishop, the Communists, and a few unscrupulous capitalists acting together in a sinister alliance.[1]

9   THE RENEWAL OF VIOLENCE AGAINST THE BRITISH

The decline in racial strife by the late summer enabled EOKA to concentrate on the security forces and Greek civilians. During the first week in August gunmen killed Colonel Collier at his home in Limassol and Sergeant Hammond as he walked through the market of Aghios Dhometios holding the hand of his small son. Before the month was out seven Greek civilians and four policemen – one Greek and three Turkish – also lost their lives. Two Greek women had died in a clash between the right and the left.

September began with the battle of Liopetri. Grivas had sent three experienced men under the leadership of Xanthos Samaras to train EOKA members there in the laying of ambushes. Soon after they arrived soldiers came to the village, imposed a curfew and took away suspects for questioning. The four men and Elias Samaras, the brother of Xanthos, tried to escape by car. Unable to get through the cordon, they returned to the village on foot. Their driver, who went on alone, was arrested. They first sought refuge in the house of an EOKA member who was afraid to take them in. Finally a farmer hid them in his barn. Elias was later sent away by the others; he first went home to change his clothes but shortly afterwards was caught and taken to Famagusta for interrogation.[2]

In the early hours of 2 September an army patrol approached the barn. When a soldier shouted out the surrender order in Greek a burst of gunfire came from the building. The soldiers withdrew and watched the barn until daylight, when they approached it again repeating the surrender order. The only response was a sharp burst of gunfire which hit one of the patrol.

After the arrival of reinforcements the troops surrounded the adjoining house and a second soldier was injured by shots from the barn. They next fired incendiary bombs and grenades into the barn, but these failed to set the hay alight. A man rushed out firing a gun and was shot dead by the army. In an attempt to get into the house, the officer leading the charge and two of his men were wounded. While a soldier was trying to bring the casualties inside the house he was shot at, but

[1] ibid. p. 367.
[2] ibid. Addendum, p. 61.

the gunman was killed when the soldier returned fire. Finally the soldiers forced an entry through a wall at the back of the house. They were then able to remove the wounded from the verandah and get on to the roof of the barn. After boring a hole through the roof a soldier poured petrol down it and set the hay alight. The last two men came out of the blazing building firing their guns and were shot dead by the army. The gun battle, which had lasted more than three hours, was now over. The Cypriots had fought to the last. One soldier died and several were wounded.

Elias Samaras, who betrayed the hideout, had at the time been assured that his brother would come to no harm. The promise was probably given in all sincerity but without due regard in the heat of the moment to the practicability of its implementation. EOKA's weapons were mostly stored in secret places until needed for some specific operation. Very few fighters were allowed to carry arms all the time, so that wanted men, when cornered by the security forces, usually had no option but to surrender without a struggle. The struggle had cost Xanthos his life.

Samaras was sent to England for his own safety. After seventeen days, overcome by guilt and remorse, he returned home against advice and placed himself at the mercy of EOKA.

In a long letter to his district leader, Samaras told the story of the events which led to his capture – how he was first tortured at Famagusta Old Police Station and how he tried to mislead his interrogators by taking them to places where he knew there was nothing to find. Finally he broke down under torture and guided his interrogator to the house with the barn. He hoped that the wanted men would no longer be there, for when he left them they said that they would leave shortly after him.

He did not want to go to England and he told his wife to refuse the offer. When they refused a second time he was threatened with detention at Pyla Camp. He still knew much about EOKA. Fearing he would be tortured again, he decided that he must at all costs get away from his interrogators, so he agreed to go to London.

Samaras pleaded that if death were to be his fate he should be allowed to see his family and the graves of the four men. If he should die without seeing his young children again he implored the district leader to 'protect them and speak to them like a father'.

This grim description of the ordeals suffered under interrogation, this catharsis of a tormented man, ended on a religious note:

Leader, I pray that God may protect you from all evil and lay his hand upon you, so that you may guide our shattered ship into the haven of eternal freedom. I also wish all members the peace and protection of God our Father. And one thing more. Rather than fall into the hands of the enemy let them fall glorious and honoured. Enlighten them to do their duty, and especially to do God's will, so that he won't punish them like me. I await your instructions. Your unworthy child, Elias Samaras.[1]

There was sympathy for the defector who, stricken with remorse, had the courage to return. But his fate did not rest with the district leader, who sent the confession to Grivas, enclosing a letter from the parents of Elias with a plea that his life should be spared. Without hesitation Grivas ordered his execution.

The subject of ill-treatment was seldom dormant for long. The latest allegations arose out of an incident in the Paphos district. On 13 September Private Morrison from the Argyll and Sutherland Highlanders was killed and another soldier wounded in an ambush at Yiolou. When the news of Morrison's death reached his battalion at Polis, troops went out at once to search for the killers. The speed of the operation resulted in damage to property. Doors were forced open and floors pulled up. Villagers sustained minor injuries. Those who resisted arrest were roughly treated, especially after two soldiers were stabbed at Kathikas.

The Mayor of Kyrenia sent a telegram to the Governor complaining about the 'brutality' of the troops. This met with a sharp rebuff. When the battalion heard about the death of their comrade they were naturally furious, the Governor replied. It was not surprising that roughness did on occasions take place in the heat of the pursuit of murderers. And it was indeed impossible to find arms in cleverly concealed hides without doing some damage. He was satisfied that the injuries and damage incurred were only minor. The Governor deplored the mayor's failure to express either regret for the young soldier's death or compassion for his parents. Concerned solely with minor injuries, the mayor by his silence appeared to condone murder. British troops, the Governor concluded, had come to Cyprus 'to stop killing, violence and intimidation'. More than one hundred had already died in the course of this duty, which they would continue to do despite organised abuse.[2]

The deputy chairman of the National Executive of the Labour

---

[1] ibid. p. 62.
[2] See The Times, Daily Telegraph, Manchester Guardian (Reuter), 22 September 1958.

Party, Mrs Barbara Castle, who was in Cyprus for a few days, accused the authorities of permitting, even encouraging, the troops to use unnecessarily tough measures in anti-EOKA operations.[1] Praising the restraint shown· by the security forces, the Chief of Staff, Brigadier Gleadell, denied that there was any indiscriminate toughness. He said firmness was essential in dealing with violence but the security forces combined this with courtesy.[2]

The Conservative Government's term was drawing to a close. Thousands of troops had served in Cyprus during the emergency, either in the bases or with the security forces. The impact of Mrs Castle's reported comments on their political loyalties, less than a week before the Party's annual conference, caused consternation in socialist circles. Jim Matthews, an ex-soldier and a trade union member of the National Executive, publicly dissociated himself from her criticisms. He said he could well understand the feelings of the troops when their comrades were shot in the back and stabbed by the very people they were trying to help. It would be better if Mrs Castle tried to do likewise. Some people might prefer to see Mr Aneurin Bevan as the next chairman of the National Executive.[3]

At London Airport Mrs Castle told the press that she stood by her comments on the rough methods used in anti-terrorist operations. But she blamed the authorities rather than the soldiers and said that the Cyprus Government's investigations were inadquate.[4]

On 23 September Gaitskell made it clear that Mrs Castle's visits to Turkey, Cyprus and Greece had been made in a purely personal capacity and not as a representative of the Labour Party. The same applied to her statements. Gaitskell spoke of the horror and disgust, repeatedly expressed by himself and his colleagues, at the brutal murders committed by Cypriots against their own countrymen and British troops, and of the 'intolerable provocation' to which the troops were subjected.

Mrs Castle's remarks had been quoted without variation by leading correspondents. Nevertheless Gaitskell said that it appeared that she had not been fully and accurately reported, and that she would elucidate her comments that evening on BBC and Independent Television News.[5] In the interviews she repeated that her allegations were not against the

---

[1] ibid.
[2] See Daily Telegraph, 22 September 1958.
[3] See The Times, 23 September 1958.
[4] See The Times, Daily Telegraph, Manchester Guardian, 24 September 1958.
[5] ibid.

troops but against the policy of the authorities.[1] Her performance did little to reassure her critics. However, the Executive patched up its quarrel in time for the Scarborough conference and Mrs Castle was duly elected chairman. Although Gaitskell claimed that there was virtually no disagreement over the Party's Cyprus policy, he urged members to exercise the greatest care in what they said on the subject since this could influence the Greeks, the Turks and the Cypriots.

On 3 October the restraint usually shown by the security forces in the face of acute provocation broke down. On that day Mrs Cutliffe was shot dead in Varosha and her companion, Mrs Robinson, was seriously wounded. The wives of sergeants in the 29th Field Regiment, Royal Artillery, they had just come out of a shop with Mrs Cutliffe's daughter. The attack came shortly after a threat from EOKA to 'hit indiscriminately at <u>every</u> English person' wherever they might be found.[2] A wave of recent incidents directed against English women included the burning of prams. The afternoon of the crime no Greek women were about in the streets. Some shops closed earlier than usual and Greeks were seen hurriedly leaving the area before the gunmen opened fire.

The military police arrived on the spot first. The sirens were sounded. All traffic and pedestrians were halted at the road blocks inside the town and workers bound for their villages were stopped on the outskirts. On the basis of a description by Mrs Cutliffe's daughter, a search for the killer was immediately set in motion and the troops ordered to round up all Greek males between the ages of 14 and 26. The troops searched all houses within the immediate area of the crime, which was cordoned off, and detained many of the owners.

The authorities at a high level were apprehensive about the possible reaction of the troops once they realised the reason for the search. Shortly after the incident Hugh Foot and General Kendrew left Nicosia by helicopter for Famagusta. The brigade commander sent a signal with the warning that the shooting of the army wives could well be a deliberate attempt by EOKA to provoke the security forces at the time of the NATO and UN talks. It was imperative that all ranks should clearly understand that there must be no retaliation or excesses. This could only harm the army and would be no help in solving 'this dastardly crime'.[3] By the time the message was on the air the operation was already well under way. In less than two hours about 1,000

[1] The Times, Daily Telegraph, 24 September. *The Annual Conference Report of the Labour Party 1958*, p. 223.

[2] 'To the Cromwell-Volkanites', leaflet distributed in the Nicosia area, September 1958.

[3] Manchester Guardian, 5 December 1958.

Cypriots had been rounded up by the security forces and taken in some forty trucks and Land-Rovers to four main centres for identification and questioning. Panayotis Chrysostomos was found dead, with seven broken ribs, by an army chaplain at brigade headquarters. Arrested at home, the father of six children, he was at 37 well over the age-limit of the suspect group. Andreas Loukas, a student of 19, lay seriously ill at Karaolis Camp. The number of Cypriots injured was estimated at 256.

Asked by the Labour member for St Pancras Kenneth Robinson to what extent the troops were responsible for the death of the two civilians, the Colonial Secretary replied that in circumstances of 'almost un-exampled provocation' they had shown exemplary restraint. The speed of the operation and the fact that many Cypriots had sought to resist or escape arrest made some use of force necessary. The Government and the military commanders had repeatedly given explicit orders against any form of ill-treatment, 'but after this particularly horrible crime the security forces in Famagusta were disgusted', which was hardly surprising.[1]

At the inquest the government pathologist, Dr Nedjat Sanerkin, testified that Chrysostomos suffered from a chronic lung disease but that despite this condition he could probably have lived another ten or twenty years had his ribs not been broken.

A Greek Cypriot worker told the court that there were already about 25 to 30 people in the truck when Chrysostomos was picked up. Chryso-stomos was placed face downwards and beaten when he groaned. On arrival at brigade headquarters he was beaten again. One member of the security forces had pulled him out of the truck, another had struck him. A second Greek witness, a solicitor's clerk, said that there were three or four men lying face downwards in the truck. One of them cried out that he was dying, he could not breathe.

The first army witness, a sergeant in the RAC, was walking to take up position at one of the road blocks, and had accepted a lift in the truck in which Chrysostomos made his journey. He denied that the truck was grossly overcrowded. And no one had been hit, he said, while he was in it. Some of the men were kneeling, some sitting, some lying down and some sprawling. When the truck arrived at brigade head-quarters, apart from soldiers, there were only about 14 or 15 people in it. He said that when Chrysostomos was lifted off at brigade headquarters he looked ill, but showed no sign of injury.

The second army witness, a private in the Royal Ulster Rifles and the

[1] H.C. Deb., vol. 594, cols 745–7.

driver of the truck, also denied that it was overcrowded. Including the soldiers, there were about 17 people in the back. He had not seen any Cypriots struck and he did not know the reason for their arrest. At brigade headquarters all the detainees got out except one, who seemed to be asleep or to have fainted.

The third army witness denied that the Cypriots had been packed into the truck like sardines and that they had been beaten or kicked. He heard some muttering but no groaning. At brigade headquarters he thought Chrysostomos might have fainted. He lifted him out but had not dragged or dumped him on the ground.

The Coroner found that Chrysostomos had died of heart failure while suffering from respiratory complications caused by the fracture of seven ribs. He was unable to determine how his ribs came to be broken. The evidence given by the army and the Greek witnesses conflicted. There were also discrepancies in the evidence of the Greeks.

The 29th Field Regiment, to which Mrs Cutliffe's husband belonged, was based on Karaolis Camp. The soldier in charge of the improvised interrogation cage in a disused quarry told the Court that all the detainees brought to the camp, about 400 he thought, were able to get out of their vehicles unaided. But some had head wounds and he took a man who was bleeding and a blind man to the cage. Later he saw the injured man, still on the ground, in a very bad condition. He could not identify him from the photograph of the deceased produced at the inquest.

A captain in the Royal Military Police said that he had hit Loukas before they got to the camp. The Coroner stressed that whether or not this was the blow which fractured his skull was of the greatest importance. If he was of the opinion that Loukas and two other boys advanced to attack the officer, as he had stated, then the officer would have been justified in striking first. If on the other hand he believed that the boys were beaten up for no reason at all, the Coroner said, he would have to find that Loukas met his death in circumstances amounting to murder. He had to rely on medical evidence. According to this the blow which fractured the deceased's skull would have been immediately followed by unconsciousness. But the witnesses had not spoken of this. He could not, therefore, say with any certainty that the captain's blow had fractured the deceased's skull.

There was also the possibility that the fatal blow might have been dealt by one of the soldiers in the cage, Mr Justice Trainor continued. Had he been certain that this was so, he would have had to bring in a verdict of murder by persons unknown. He recorded that Loukas had died from a cerebral haemorrhage as a result of a blow from a blunt instrument but that there was insufficient evidence to enable him to conclude when or by whom the blow was struck.

He felt in the case of Loukas, as he had done in other cases, that some witnesses were more anxious to inculpate the security forces than to help the Court with unbiased evidence. Nevertheless, he considered that the degree of force used on the day of the round-up appeared to be entirely unjustified:

> People were so assaulted and beaten that doctors were fully occupied at Karaolis Camp and the hospital tending the wounded that evening. One can fully understand the horror, disgust and anger that filled the hearts of everyone on that day, but nothing can justify the assaults on persons who had done nothing to warrant them.[1]

Mrs Cutliffe's killer was never found. The crime damaged the Cypriot cause by alienating sympathisers in England and abroad. EOKA was quick to deny responsibility for the murder, and a Greek Government spokesman tried to explain it away by making allegations which were both slanderous and totally lacking in credibility.

10   POLITICAL DEVELOPMENTS AT THE END OF 1958

The idea of independence for Cyprus was not new. In the corridors of the United Nations it was known to be the favourite thesis of Krishna Menon. And as early as the spring of 1957 Greek statesmen were discussing it privately as a possible alternative to the sterile policy of self-determination. Political expediency dictated that this drastic change of tactics should appear to emanate from Makarios rather than from the Greek Government, which by the autumn had convinced the Archbishop of the need for a new formula precluding both Enosis and partition. The Archbishop's acceptance of an interim period of self-government leading to independence, a status which would not be changed without the sanction of the United Nations, was made public by Barbara Castle immediately after her return from Cyprus and Greece. The news came as a shock to Grivas who was deeply affronted that EOKA had not first been consulted.[2]

The Archbishop was now faced with the task of selling the idea to Grivas. In a letter dated 28 September he told the EOKA Leader that

---

[1] Cyprus Mail, 4 December 1958.
[2] See *Memoirs* (Greek ed.), op. cit. p. 305.

the news reaching him was disheartening. The British public and press had turned against the Cypriots; the socialist newspapers had ceased to criticise the security forces and were emphasising the importance of protecting the interests of the Turkish Cypriots. Mrs Castle and other Socialists had explained that they could not oppose the British plan unless he put forward a new proposal. Greece's position within the Western alliance was an immense obstacle to any substantial backing for the Cypriot case, but the Greek Government was resolutely opposed to her withdrawal from NATO. The Archbishop also painted a black picture about the prospects for the forthcoming UN debate. America was now in complete agreement with the British on the question of self-determination. The Cypriots could not expect as much success as in the previous year. The only hope, the Archbishop said, was to base the next appeal on independence, to face reality and reach a decision before the British imposed the partnership plan which must inevitably end up in partition. Grivas promptly rejected this suggestion.[1]

The Archbishop's choice of emissary was mistaken since Mrs Castle was under a cloud even with her socialist colleagues.[2] When on 28 September he formally submitted his independence proposal to the British Government through the Embassy in Athens, he met with a firm refusal. The British Government was no longer opposed in principle to ultimate independence but believed that premature attempts to press the issue would intensify racial tension in the island. The phrase 'without the sanction of the United Nations' was in itself sufficient to arouse Turkish suspicions that the Archbishop's new approach was yet another camouflaged attempt to achieve Enosis. Any vacillation in British policy might well precipitate a fresh setback in Anglo-Turkish relations, which had narrowly survived the summer's crisis. And in the face of renewed attacks by EOKA the British Government decided to go ahead with its plan, if need be without Greek cooperation in the early stages.

In the meantime, Spaak was engaged in intensive efforts to organise a new conference between Britain, Greece and Turkey. The Greek Prime Minister, on 20 September, informed Spaak that Britain's decision to go ahead alone with the partnership plan would undermine Greece's position in NATO.[3] The British and Turkish Governments believed that NATO tended to take too seriously the veiled threats of

---

[1] ibid.

[2] See above, pp. 317–19.

[3] See *The Cyprus Question: Discussion in the North Atlantic Treaty Organisation September–October, 1958* (Athens, 1958), p. 7, Document 1.

the Greeks to leave the alliance. But no one could overlook the gravity of the dispute and since the withdrawal of the Greek army units from Izmir in the summer NATO had viewed it with mounting concern. By the autumn the climate inside NATO was more favourable to Spaak's intervention. The Turks' initial distrust of the Secretary-General had to some extent been overcome. There was less sympathy for the Greeks than in the past and greater understanding of the Turkish case. Privately Turkey showed some willingness to abandon partition and of the two main protagonists now seemed the more reasonable.

Spaak visited Athens on 23 September. The Greek Government told him that the British plan had created serious dangers and that it ought to be postponed. The next day Spaak outlined his own proposals to the NATO Council in Paris. These provided for separate assemblies for each of the communities, a representative body with competence over questions of joint interest; a governmental council with a Greek Cypriot majority to deal with internal affairs under the presidency of a British Governor. The heads of the two houses of representatives would assist the Governor in his executive duties. Each house would be able to submit any measures it considered discriminatory to an impartial tribunal.

Spaak's formula met most of the conditions of the British partnership plan. It concentrated solely on a provisional solution, stressing that this must guarantee the Turkish minority's position and the British military bases.[1] The main difference in Spaak's proposal was the introduction of two assemblies and a governmental council. Spaak suggested that the plan should be postponed until after the NATO talks. But this would have left a political vacuum and, having obtained the qualified support of the Turks for the plan, the British Government wanted to avoid any weakening in resolve, which was almost certain to undermine the delicately balanced improvement in Anglo-Turkish relations. That Spaak had accepted the British Government's reasons was evident from the fact that on 30 September the NATO Council issued a statement which encouraged the holding of a conference. Dealing first with the controversial issue of the appointment of the Turkish representative, the Council noted that the Greek Government's misgivings arose out of its rejection of the right of Greece and Turkey to exercise sovereign or administrative power in Cyprus. By way of reassurance to the Greeks, it recalled the British Government's statement on 15 August that it would not be appropriate for members of other states to sit on the

---

[1] *Discussion of Cyprus in the North Atlantic Treaty Organisation*, Cmnd 566, October 1958, pp. 4 and 5.

Governor's Council. Nevertheless the functions of the Greek and Turkish representatives were defined only in general terms in the British proposals and a certain misunderstanding had arisen. But since Turkey had designated the Consul-General in Nicosia as its representative under the plan there was no question of a senior Turkish official arriving in Cyprus on 1 October exclusively for this purpose. In the circumstances the NATO Council took the view that this appointment in no way undermined the Greek Government's position or prejudiced the outcome of the conference and that no obstacles stood in the way of its convocation.[1]

On 4 October the Greek Prime Minister Mr Karamanlis wrote to Spaak reminding him of the Greek Government's misgivings in accepting his first formula. Now Greece was being asked to compromise still further. She would, however, agree to take part provided the Council adopted two amendments to Spaak's latest text. Blood continued to flow in Cyprus, Karamanlis said, and the state of public opinion in Greece and Turkey was highly excited. An interim solution could at best only give a few years' peace. Advantage should therefore be taken of the forthcoming conference to pave the way for a final settlement on the basis of the Archbishop's independence proposals.

In view of the severe strains to which NATO was subjected as the result of this 'quarrel', the Prime Minister wrote, the participation of Spaak was indispensable. He welcomed America's offer to attend, but also wanted the inclusion of France and Italy. Greece was willing that the discussion of her appeal should come at the end of the UN agenda, but she could not agree to withdraw it so long as a settlement inside NATO was not in sight.[2]

The permanent Greek delegate to NATO, Mr Melas, presented the two amendments to the Council on 6 October. Three things had happened, Melas said, since the Greek Government had accepted Spaak's first formula. The British and Turkish Governments had rejected it and produced a new one in which Greece was required to make further concessions. The British Government, contrary to the Greek request, had begun to apply its plan in Cyprus. Finally Archbishop Makarios had only made public his proposals for a final settlement on the eve of Spaak's visit to Athens. Consequently the Greek Government had not then determined the attitude which it later adopted towards the plan. Since the initiative for the independence plan had come from Greece, the explanation given by Melas for the

[1] *The Cyprus Question*, op. cit. pp. 10 and 11, Document 3.
[2] ibid. p. 13, Document 4.

failure to raise the issue with Spaak in Athens was singularly transparent. The true reason lay in the pressure which Makarios was exerting behind the scenes.

On the day of Melas's speech to the NATO Council, the Archbishop wrote to Grivas explaining how he had objected to the restriction of the conference to the three main powers and representatives of the Cypriot communities. Greece, he had insisted, should only take part if his own independence plan was discussed in conjunction with the British plan and the Spaak proposals. And the Greek delegate's statement to NATO had been drafted in accordance with his views.[1] The Bishop of Kition also wrote to Grivas discrediting the conference. Describing the move as a British manoeuvre to mislead public opinion and to avoid a debate in the United Nations so that the 'satanic plan' could be enforced, Kition told the Colonel that he had urged Makarios to persuade the Greek Government to take a tougher line. The EOKA Leader's reaction was unusually negative. He decided not to obstruct the NATO talks because he did not want to be held responsible for their failure. He intended, however, to dissociate himself completely from this diplomatic initiative if it led Makarios and the Greek Government into a trap. The Colonel's concept of a trap in this context was any solution which ruled out Enosis.[2]

The hardening of the Archbishop's attitude was reflected in a new note of hostility which marked the Greek delegate's speech on 6 October. Accusing the British of trying to foment discord between the two Cypriot communities, he declared that the traditional affection felt by Greece for Britain had been replaced by strong animosity and that the Greco-Turkish entente was seriously endangered. Melas hinted that Greece might leave NATO if Britain went on with the plan. Turning to the sensitive issue of the British military bases, he said so long as these concerned only Britain, Greece and Turkey there were no complications, but since the Suez affair the Arabs had been claiming that they too had an interest for much the same geographical and strategic reasons as those put forward by Turkey.

The conference was probably doomed from this moment. Nevertheless the negotiations dragged on. And on 13 October Spaak submitted a third draft. Its main changes of substance concerned a Turkish request that amendments to the British plan could be raised at the conference, and the extension of the agenda to cover a final settlement. The presence of a NATO observer was made optional. A fourth formula,

[1] See *Memoirs* (Greek ed.), op. cit. p. 309.
[2] ibid. p. 310.

produced on 17 October, did not specifically name which countries outside the dispute should take part and included two Turkish amendments. The first stipulated that the inclusion of the final settlement on the agenda should not be made a prior condition for the discussion of the interim solution. The second indicated that the Turkish Government would agree to discuss the interim solution solely on condition that it did not prejudice the final settlement.

Spaak met the British, Greek and Turkish representatives on 19 October in a final attempt to resolve the major difficulties which had arisen over the composition of the conference and other matters. Britain was strongly opposed to the inclusion of France. The crisis with de Gaulle meant that the French stand on any given issue was unpredictable. The Turks feared that Italy and France would be biased by their immediate Mediterranean interests. The United States and Norway were acceptable both to Great Britain and Turkey. But Greece demanded that their functions should not be limited to those of observers and she rejected the Turkish amendments. Her conditions were not accepted and on 25 October the Greek delegate notified the NATO Council that his Government would not proceed further.

The immediate cause of the breakdown, Melas told the Council on 29 October, was the refusal of Britain and Turkey to include the countries proposed by Greece.[1] His Government, moreover, had taken strong exception to Lennox-Boyd's description of Cyprus as 'an off-shore island of Turkey'. And the Turkish Government had destroyed any illusions about a successful outcome of the conference. Quoting the New York Times of 22 October, he referred to the Turkish Foreign Minister's recent denial that his Government had abandoned the right to partition. The Greeks had made a great sacrifice in giving up Enosis, but there was no sign of conciliation on the part of Britain and Turkey.

Melas said neutralist propaganda had successfully exploited the Cyprus question by turning the Greeks against the alliance. But since Spaak's visit to Athens there had been a public reaction in NATO's favour. This was, however, likely to be reversed in the event of the collapse of the conference under its auspices. Failure would be worse than no conference at all.[2]

The NATO Council as a whole had reached the conclusion that a conference could usefully be held. The Greek Government, having succumbed to the Archbishop's pressure, had to find face-saving excuses. The Colonial Secretary's comment at Blackpool early in

[1] Italy and France.
[2] *The Cyprus Question*, op. cit. pp. 24–6.

October, although unfortunate, had little bearing on the breakdown. The same could be said of the Turkish Foreign Minister's denial that his Government had given up partition. Time was needed in Turkey, as in Greece, before the public could be won over to a policy of moderation. The Greeks like the rest of NATO knew that the Turkish Government was willing to forgo partition in favour of a compromise settlement.

Karamanlis accused the British and Turkish Governments of wrecking the NATO Council's mediation effort by taking up extremist positions.[1] Next came a long official communiqué. A twisted account of the negotiations, this tirade, with its blatant errors of fact and misleading half-truths, sought to convey the reasonableness of the Greek stand in contrast to the 'incomprehensible and unacceptable intransigence' shown by Britain.[2]

The British Government had agreed that the conference should be held under Spaak's chairmanship and that, in addition to the main contestants, the USA and Norway should attend. This was in itself a major concession. No colonial power had previously allowed a majority of foreign states to discuss matters within its domestic jurisdiction. The British Government was willing to consider Spaak's formula and other amendments in conjunction with its own plan. The Turks saw the plan as an alternative to early partition. Its postponement, in the British view, could only weaken the chances of a peaceful settlement. It was also agreed that the subject of a final as well as an interim solution should be on the agenda and that Archbishop Makarios should, if desired, represent the Greek Cypriots.

The British version of the negotiations was presented in a short White Paper.[3] This was slightly tendentious in that it left the impression that there were no dissenting voices apart from the Turkish reservations about the discussion of a final settlement. The Socialists initiated a post mortem in the House of Commons on the breakdown. Apart from refuting the Greek allegations of British intransigence the Foreign Secretary Selwyn Lloyd had little to add in the way of clarification.[4]

II THE BID FOR INDEPENDENCE AT THE UN

EOKA kept up its attacks throughout the autumn and early winter. Casualties were high; bomb explosions in NAAFI quarters rose sharply.

[1] Greek Information Office, Press Release (Greek Embassy, London), 29 October 1958.
[2] ibid.
[3] See Cmnd 566, op. cit.
[4] See H.C. Deb., vol. 594, cols 324–6.

After the death of two RAF men on 11 November all Greek Cypriot employees were replaced by volunteers from Britain. Greek diplomatists, charged with presenting the Cypriot case abroad, were on occasions embarrassed by EOKA's excesses. And disagreement arose between Grivas and the Greek Government about the tactics to be followed during the forthcoming appeal to the United Nations. The Colonel was pessimistic about the outcome and made plans for a long military struggle. In the middle of November, however, he reluctantly agreed to suspend operations for a short time in order to make a good impression on foreign opinion. The Archbishop later urged him to keep the truce until the spring in the hope that a Labour Government would be elected in Britain. Although dubious about the reliability of the promises made by the Socialists once they got into power, the Archbishop believed it would be easier for the Cypriots to negotiate with a Labour Government because it would have no commitments to the Turks.[1]

The independence proposal, taken at its face value, was expected to go down well in the USA and the United Nations. Success for a Greek resolution, although unenforceable, would have constituted a moral victory for the extremists and endangered the precarious peace in the island.

The British Government's policy was to obtain the Assembly's endorsement for the resumption of talks between Britain, Greece and Turkey without any commitment to specific terms for a solution at this stage. Turkey's objectives were roughly the same except that she left the door open to partition. The Greeks were working for the implementation of independence by means of a good offices committee composed of five countries. The draft resolutions[2] submitted by Britain, Greece and Turkey before the opening of the UN debate on 25 November 1958 covered these basic aims.

The first speaker, the Greek Foreign Secretary, Evanghelos Averoff, launched a sharp attack on Britain and Turkey. Britain had disregarded resolution 1013 (XI).[3] The Macmillan plan, he said, was 'the murderous knife of partition'.[4] British talk of conferences and negotiations was simply a manoeuvre to block action by the UN. Accusing Turkey of trying to revive the Ottoman Empire and of ignoring the treaty of Lausanne, he contended that 'the idea of the partition of

[1] See *Memoirs* (Greek ed.), op. cit. pp. 334, 335 and 339.
[2] UN doc. A/C.1/L.221 (XIII), A/C.1/L.222 (XIII) and A/C.1/L.223 (XIII).
[3] See above, p. 228.
[4] UN doc. A/C.1/PV 996 (XIII), p. 26.

Cyprus is a Turkish territorial claim reflecting expansionist ambitions . . .'.[1]

The British delegate, Commander Noble, stressed the international aspects of the Cyprus problem and Britain's efforts, including the abortive NATO initiative, to find a solution. Prolonged discussions with Greece and Turkey had failed. It was now the British Government's duty, he said, to break the deadlock by pressing on with the partnership plan. Britain's willingness to share sovereignty with Greece and Turkey at the end of seven years was in itself an indication that her retention of the island on the present basis need be no obstacle to a final settlement. Denying that Britain favoured partition, Noble explained that the plan's separatist character was a practical necessity dictated by the present intercommunal tension. Independence was a noble principle, but any attempt to endorse a final settlement in advance of general agreement could only lead to civil war or worse – the danger of partition and international conflict in the Mediterranean.

The Turkish Foreign Minister Fatim Zorlu condemned the Greek Government's independence proposal as 'a tactical move and a procedural rewording of its demand for Enosis'.[2] Accusing the Greek Cypriots of trying to wipe out the Turkish minority, he dwelt at length on the intercommunal strife of the summer. Independence or self-determination, if granted to Cyprus, must be given equally to both communities, he said. British and Turkish policy had changed since 1955. Whereas Turkey now accepted partition [as the alternative to the Turkish annexation of Cyprus], the British plan left the door open to any settlement at the end of seven years – Enosis or partition.

The proceedings on 26 November were largely dominated by a dialogue between the Greek and Turkish Foreign Ministers on the legalistic aspects of the dispute.

When the Assembly resumed on 28 November, Colombia, the first of the third parties to table a draft resolution, called for the renewal of talks and the deployment of a UN observer team in Cyprus.[3] Later in the day Noble expressed gratitude to Colombia's delegate, Mr Araujo, for his efforts to find a compromise. But the problem, he said, was too complicated, too explosive for the United Nations.

On 1 December, Iran's delegate, Dr Abdoh, introduced a draft resolution calling upon the three states involved in the dispute to resume

---

[1] ibid. p. 23.
[2] UN doc. A/C.1/PV 997 (XIII), pp. 23–5.
[3] UN doc. A/C.1/L.225 (XIII).

negotiations which would include Cypriot representatives.[1] At the end of the day Ceylon submitted a draft resolution which was also sponsored by Haiti, Iceland, India, Ireland, Nepal, Panama and the United Arab Republic.[2] The preamble welcomed the British delegate's statements that he did not 'favour the partition of Cyprus' and that his Government sought 'to preserve the united personality of Cyprus'. The operative paragraphs called for the continuation of negotiations with a view to 'promoting self-government for Cyprus in accordance with the provisions of the Charter of the United Nations and the preservation of its integrity'.[3] Equivocal and potentially explosive, this move, inspired by Krishna Menon, was immediately attacked by the British delegate, who stressed the dangers of requiring the Turks formally to abandon partition at this stage. Noble claimed that the resolution had misquoted him. He had not said that the British Government did not consider partition to be a solution, merely that it was not in favour of it. One must above all else avoid prejudicing the future, the British delegate emphasised.[4] Iceland's delegate commented that it was unusual to see a resolution so vehemently attacked before it had even been presented for discussion.

Abdoh's role throughout the debate was consistently constructive in his tireless efforts to find a compromise acceptable to the three main parties, and on 2 December he submitted a revision which laid down a more specific line of action than his original text and covered the final as well as the interim settlement.[5] Next came the Belgian draft resolution, calling for the end of terrorism and renewed efforts on the part of those concerned to reach a friendly settlement.[6] Commendably brief, Mr Nisot made it clear that Belgium, which did not believe the problem could be solved through the UN, favoured direct talks.

The main event of the day was a speech by Krishna Menon lasting more than an hour. Attacking the British plan and partition, India's delegate elaborated on the thesis that Cyprus had always been a single entity. Separatist trends were of very recent date, he said, and it was inappropriate to compare the position of the Commonwealth Nations, as Commander Noble had done, with the proposal to share 'imperial power' between Britain, Greece and Turkey. The Commonwealth States

[1] UN doc. A/C.1/L.226 (XIII).
[2] UN doc. A/C.1/L.228 (XIII).
[3] ibid.
[4] See UN doc. A/C.1/PV 1003 (XIII), pp. 93–5.
[5] UN doc. A/C.1/L.226 (XIII).
[6] UN doc. A/C.1/L.229 (XIII).

were linked on a voluntary basis, not by means of an imposed partnership. India had repeatedly opposed self-determination for Cyprus.

In a lengthy indictment of British imperial policy from the time of the American Colonies, Menon stressed the dangers of encouraging separatist tendencies. Nevertheless he praised the United Kingdom's search for a peaceful and democratic solution of the Cyprus dispute at the cost of sacrificing its own authority. He objected to the idea of a conference limited to Britain, Greece and Turkey. The exclusion of the Cypriots, the main party to the dispute, was, he said, an unwarranted interference in the affairs of others. It was evident from Menon's statement that his formula aimed at independence. As the result of Ethiopia's decision to join the nine original sponsors, it now became the ten-power draft resolution.[1]

Zorlu accused Menon of endorsing the Greek Government's tactics in using the independence proposal as a manoeuvre which would quickly result in Enosis. The Indian delegate must have done a lot of work on the island's past history in order to prove that a Cypriot nation had existed from time immemorial. Had his researches taken him far enough, he would have found that 3,000 or 4,000 years ago there were about a dozen separate kingdoms on Cyprus, Zorlu said.[2]

On 3 December, Noble refuted Averoff's charge that Britain was exploiting the threat of war. As the power responsible for the island's safety she was, on the contrary, doing everything possible to avert civil strife and a wider conflict. Describing Krishna Menon's speech as a novel presentation of the history of Cyprus through the ages, he denied that he had made any comparison between the British plan for Cyprus and the partnership existing in the Commonwealth, or that he had implied that there was any limitation on the absolute freedom and sovereignty of India and these nations. The Indian delegate's speech was a sustained and fundamental criticism of the policy Britain was pursuing in the interests of the Cypriots. Mr Menon was entitled to that opinion, but it disqualified him from serving as an impartial mediator in the current dispute. Satisfactory formulas were not produced by men who had already decided in advance that one of the parties was wholly at fault. In contrast to Mr Menon's text, the Iranian draft resolution had all the elements of a genuine compromise, Noble concluded.[3]

Menon's theories of a Cypriot identity were intensely disliked by the Greeks because they cut right across the philosophy of Enosis. But this

[1] UN doc. A/C.1/L.228 Rev I (XIII).
[2] UN doc. A/C.1/PV 1005 (XIII), pp. 54–5.
[3] UN doc. A/C.1/PV 1006 (XIII), p. 27.

time the Greek and the Indian delegates found common ground on the subject of independence. And Averoff agreed to give the ten-power draft resolution priority, while reserving the right in the event of its rejection to put the Greek text to the vote. Unlike Mr Menon's speech, Averoff said, the ten-power draft did not specifically mention independence and it omitted the formation of a good offices committee. In the circumstances its acceptance by Greece was a major concession.[1]

Menon answered the criticisms made by the Turkish and British delegates. After a renewed attack on the Indian delegate by Zorlu and a short intervention from Averoff, the general debate was closed. Mr de La Colina, on behalf of Mexico, suggested that a working group composed of the sponsors of the seven draft resolutions should try to produce one text acceptable to the main parties. Some of the resolutions were favourable to Greece. Averoff, understandably enough, wanted them put to the test first. The Committee accepted his view that the Mexican proposal was premature.

Colombia considered that only its own draft met the need for direct UN intervention. Accusing Abdoh of backing the Turkish line, Averoff dismised the Iranian text and urged the Committee to vote for the ten-power draft resolution. Mr Belaunde, of Peru, who found merits and shortcomings in all seven formulas, wanted the Assembly's authority affirmed in any text and was willing to cooperate in drawing up one acceptable to all. Menon was at pains to deny that India's approach was partisan and in order to meet Noble's criticism offered to delete certain passages from the ten-power draft. India's objections to partition, he said, should not be seen as a plea for a unitary state. Australia and the USA did not have unitary government. And in countries like Switzerland different linguistic and ethnic groups lived as one nation under one administrative system. Menon's words must have had some consolation for the Turks since they opened up possibilities of federations and cantons. Time was running out. The thirteenth General Assembly was shortly due to end; the Chairman urged the delegates to speed up their work.

Zorlu, on 4 December, claimed that whereas the differences between the British and Turkish texts were mainly procedural, the formulas of Greece and Turkey were diametrically opposed. All that the Greeks wanted was to dominate the Turkish community. Makarios had publicly acclaimed independence as a stepping stone to Enosis. The lofty word independence must not be allowed to conceal other ambitions. The Indian delegate, Zorlu alleged, had espoused the claim of

[1] ibid. pp. 43–5.

Greece even more assiduously than that country itself. The Greek and Indian resolutions were aiming at the same thing. Colombia's proposal for a UN Commission was unacceptable, Zorlu said. Turkey would only support a formula based on tripartite negotiations; Iran's text had this merit but it outlined the scope of the negotiations thereby binding the conference to conclusions even before the discussions had begun.

Ireland's delegate criticised the British, Iranian, Belgian and Colombian drafts for failing to indicate the broad objectives of any Cyprus policy. He said the Turkish formula, on the other hand, had laid down guidelines but was essentially partitionist. Ireland favoured the ten-power draft. Mr Herrarte, on behalf of Guatemala, condemned the British and Turkish drafts in hostile tones. The first, he said, tended to perpetuate colonialism indefinitely; the second provided for partition. Guatemala would support the draft resolutions formulated by Greece and the ten powers. Austria approved of Iran's text subject to a minor change to cover self-government.

Averoff wanted partition, not mentioned in any of the texts, categorically excluded on the ground that the Turks would otherwise work for it during the period of self-government with the inevitable revival of the counter-demand for Enosis. The Greek Foreign Minister's speech, long but less extremist than on previous occasions, contained the first faint hint of detente with Turkey. He had even seen 'a ray of light',[1] Averoff said, in his Turkish colleague's recent statements.

Abdoh made yet another effort to produce an acceptable compromise with a second revision which mentioned 'the development of self-government and free institutions to meet the legitimate aspirations of the Cypriots in accordance with the Charter'.[2] The revised text, which met Belaunde's wish to see the UN's position acknowledged, gained Peru's support. Dr Abdoh then reproved the Greek Foreign Minister for misrepresenting Iran's stand by alleging that it was partisan and pro-partition.

In a short conciliatory reply to Averoff, the Turkish Foreign Minister stated that his Government's main aim was that the parties to the dispute should go to a conference without prejudicing the future.

Noble, in an attempt to reassure the Greek Government, then said that there was no possibility of Greece and Turkey acquiring sovereign rights in Cyprus under the British plan. The cooling-off period of seven years offered the best hope of averting extremist demands when

[1] UN doc. A/C.1/PV 1008 (XIII), p. 36.
[2] UN doc. A/C.1/L.221/Rev (2) (XIII).

the time came for a final settlement. He welcomed Menon's deletions of certain passages in the ten-power draft, but found that the operative paragraphs still prejudiced the future. Britain, he repeated, was against partition. But premature efforts to steer the island away from partition might well precipitate this catastrophe. This was why his delegation had strongly opposed the ten-power draft. The British Government had little affection for the activities of Archbishop Makarios. Nevertheless, it was willing that he should attend a conference on the basis of Iran's latest proposal. It would now be appropriate, he said, if the three 'protagonists' Britain, Greece and Turkey withdrew their draft resolutions. His delegation was willing to do so if the other two did likewise.

The overriding aim of the Greek Government was to eliminate Turkey from any settlement even at the cost of losing its own power to intervene in the affairs of Cyprus. Averoff, still suspicious of both the British plan and the Iranian formula, refused to withdraw the Greek draft. The Turkish delegation, however, agreed to support Iran's text and not to press its own to the vote.

Cabot Lodge was brief. His delegation regarded the last Iranian text as a procedural resolution leading to negotiations and the USA would vote for it. The American stand tended to influence other voters; stronger backing would have been helpful to Britain's efforts to settle the problem within the framework of the Western alliance. But Cabot Lodge had little sympathy for the British; the antipathy had, if anything, increased since the Suez crisis.

The Mexican delegate, Mr de La Colina, requested a recess of 45 minutes to explore the possibilities of trying to reach an agreement. The British delegate was uneasy about this suggestion. Iran's final draft was well supported; the introduction of fresh arguments could well jeopardise its chances. But a motion in favour of a recess was adopted. Averoff used the opportunity to reshape the Iranian draft on Greek lines. Zorlu argued that confusion was now likely to arise over the substance of the new Iranian draft owing to the Greek delegate's deletion of the phrase 'the three governments concerned and representatives of the Cypriots'. And he sub-amended the Greek amendments so that in essentials the Iranian text reverted to the original.

The debate degenerated into a tedious controversy over discrepancies in translation. Zorlu noted that the Greek delegate used the word 'autonomie' instead of the exact phraseology of the Charter as translated from the French: 'to develop self-government'. Averoff replied that an element of vagueness was useful in a resolution and that the 'three governments' were omitted because it was the Cypriots who were involved. The Greek Foreign Minister then launched into a long discourse on the precise meaning of 'autonomie' and 'territoire autonome'. The first, he said, corresponded exactly to 'self-government'.

Abdoh pointed out that his original draft should be treated as authentic and any subsequent changes harmonised with this text which was in English. Zorlu persisted with his objections to the word 'autonomie'. The British delegate was working on the English texts of both the draft resolution and the amendments. Self-government meant to him self-government, he said, and 'not autonomy or anything else'.[1] He much regretted that he was unable to listen to himself at that moment in French and wondered how what he had said was being interpreted. The Turkish sub-amendment was necessary in the interest of clarity, he said.[2]

The sponsors of the six other draft resolutions agreed to give voting priority to the Iranian text. But a new procedural wrangle developed over the Greek amendments and the Turkish sub-amendments. On the chairman's ruling the Turkish sub-amendments were voted on first and adopted. Averoff's subsequent attempt to withdraw the Greek amendments was ruled out of order. He then voted against his own amendments, as revised by the Turks, and the Iranian draft resolution as a whole. The confusion which prevailed in the Committee was partly responsible for some surprising results. After renewed arguments, Iran's text was adopted by 31 votes to 22, with 28 abstentions.

The Greek Foreign Minister, who had earlier criticised the Colombian draft, now spoke in its favour. Mr Ramos, on behalf of the Argentine, declared his intervention at this stage to be out of order, and Noble tried to block further action by invoking rule 132. The Colombian text was, however, put to the vote. The result was tied: 17 in favour and 17 against, with 47 abstentions.

Menon's formula, sponsored by the ten powers, was now withdrawn. Had they pressed it to the vote it might well have obtained a substantial majority. The fact that Menon gave in when success seemed at hand was surprising. But the efforts to promote the Greek case in the face of Averoff's opportunism and vacillation had proved a thankless task. The collapse of the Indian resolution was probably due as much to the erratic tactics of the Greek Foreign Minister as to the diplomatic skill exercised by the UK delegation behind the scenes. The latent distrust between India and Greece had in the end undermined their short-lived cooperation in the common cause of independence for Cyprus.

[1] UN doc. A/C.1/PV 1010 (XIII), pp. 18–20.
[2] ibid. p. 21.

The premature endorsement of independence by the General Assembly, which in the British view would have been a major disaster, was thus narrowly avoided. The Greek bid for independence had met with a resounding defeat. The Iranian resolution, on the other hand, was a hollow victory for Britain and Turkey since it was not likely to obtain the two-thirds majority necessary in the Plenary Session. The delegates of Mexico and Spain appealed for renewed efforts to draw up a common text. Late that night, Averoff and Zorlu were brought together on the initiative of the British delegation. In agreeing to the meeting the Greek Foreign Minister had shown political courage and a face-saving formula was now needed. The talks continued the next morning when a compromise resolution was reached. In order to ease the position of the Greeks this text was presented as a Mexican initiative and simply stated:

The General Assembly,
Having considered the question of Cyprus,
Recalling its resolution 1013 (XI),
Expresses its confidence that continued efforts will be made by the parties to reach a peaceful, democratic and just solution in accordance with the Charter of the United Nations.[1]

The delegations had from the start been divided into those who wanted to avoid prejudicing the future and into those who believed that the UN's duty was to prescribe specific action for a settlement. With the exception of Iceland, the British viewpoint was backed mainly by the European members of the Western alliance, by Iran, Liberia, Malaya, Pakistan and the old Commonwealth countries. American support for the British stand was lukewarm to the degree of being almost ineffectual. Nevertheless, the American delegation's vote for the Iranian resolution antagonised the Greek Foreign Minister, who regarded it as an intolerable surrender of its previous neutrality.

The Latin American States mostly favoured UN intervention, which they tended to see as a panacea for the world's problems. The United Arab Republic concentrated on recriminations about the Suez campaign and accused Britain of building up Cyprus as a base for further aggression against the Arabs. The Soviet bloc, as usual, took the opportunity to castigate the Western powers, especially the United States.

The debate had taken place against a background of mounting indifference in the USA. Makarios's campaigns, which had made a

[1] UN Resolution 1287 (XIII).

major impact the previous year, were no longer news. Tales of terrorism
and torture in Cyprus were eclipsed by violence on a far greater scale
in Algeria. This declining interest was also reflected in the General
Assembly. The French delegate regretted that the intractable problem of
Cyprus had come up before the UN yet again; the New Zealand
delegate commented that never had any subject been debated at such
length for so little purpose; the Spanish delegate was exasperated by the
time taken to clear up so many small points and the splitting of hairs
over which parties should be invited to the conference. The outstanding
feature of the fifteen sessions devoted by the Political Committee to the
subject of Cyprus was the controversy between Averoff and Zorlu, a
brilliant exponent of his country's interests in this particular dispute.
The Assembly by this time must have been in no doubt that the Cyprus
issue was, as the British delegation had argued, an international and
not a straightforward colonial problem. Averoff had fought hard to put
across the Cypriot cause. But, an able politican, he was sufficiently
realistic to recognise that any possibility of settling the problem through
the United Nations had now been exhausted. The setback for the
Greeks had, in fact, strengthened his hand in persuading the Greek
Government to accept the policy of reconciliation with Turkey as the
only course left open to Greece.

The Greek Foreign Minister broke the news to Grivas. He tried to
present the situation in a favourable light, claiming a great success
for Greece. No settlement could be expected through the UN, Averoff
wrote, and the Cypriots were not likely to obtain the help of the USA
and 'perfidious Albion' in achieving their objectives. Averoff's letter
amounted to an apologia for the rapprochement between Greece and
Turkey. This new contact, he stressed, was a ray of hope. Endorsing
the conclusions reached earlier by the former Governor of Cyprus,
Sir John Harding, Averoff explained that it would be difficult for the
British to object to a settlement agreed by Greece and Turkey.[1]

The results of the debate had greatly displeased the EOKA Leader
and he was in no way convinced by Averoff's arguments. He distrusted
the proposal for guaranteed independence, fearing that it would lead
to shared sovereignty. He disagreed about Turkey's strategic importance, postulating the unusual view for a military man that Turkey
and NATO needed Greece more than she needed them. Confined to a
hideout in Limassol, cut off from the realities of world politics, the
EOKA Leader deplored the Motherland's half-heartedness in handling
the Cyprus struggle and urged that a tougher line should be taken with

[1] See *Memoirs* (Greek ed.), op. cit. p. 337.

the United States. Ignoring Averoff's recommendations for the end of armed action, Grivas ordered reprisals because the security forces were carrying out operations in the villages. The Consul wrote to Grivas implying that EOKA's activities merely facilitated the security forces in their attempts to isolate the Organisation from the public, which would find it difficult to justify mine explosions at such a time.[1]

A dedicated enosist and one of EOKA's earliest recruits, Andreas Azinas[2], also tried to convince Grivas of the need for compromise. The Greek Foreign Minister had told him, Azinas wrote, that the Turks were now politically committed to the slogan: 'Partition or Death!' The concessions made to them were seen by the Greek politicians as a way out of the deadlock. The British, who alone had power to impose partition, would now be replaced by an administration in which the Greek Cypriots would be predominant owing to their dynamism and superior numbers. Azinas intimated that Enosis would have to wait until the international climate was more favourable and that the alternative to a compromise now was a long abortive struggle with the risk of partition. Grivas, however, who had already expressed his intention to go on with the armed struggle until victory was achieved, still remained an obstacle to peace.

[1] ibid. pp. 340–1.
[2] See above, pp. 54, 95, 101–3, 105–7.

X

The Birth of the Republic
February 1959-August 1960

Zurich and London Agreements – Independence

1   THE ZURICH AGREEMENT

The reconciliation which began between Averoff and Zorlu at the end of the United Nations debate was consolidated when the two men met in Paris on 18 December at the NATO Conference. They had further talks in Paris during the third week in January 1959. These negotiations were tacitly encouraged by the British Government, which for the past eighteen months had treated its role in Cyprus as a holding operation, pending a political settlement. In these changed circumstances any plan agreed by Greece and Turkey was likely to be acceptable to Britain subject to safeguards for the military bases.

With Britain's interest in the island on the wane and the indifference of the United Nations after a series of tedious and inconclusive debates, the problem of Enosis now passed for all practical purposes into the hands of Greece and Turkey, which by tradition was where it belonged. Averoff and Zorlu had already prepared the ground for a summit conference in Zurich. Before leaving for Switzerland, Averoff had told Makarios about the proposed settlement and had the impression that he accepted it unconditionally. But apart from this gesture it was in keeping with the island's history that the Cypriots, whose fate was to be decided, were not represented at Zurich.

The conference, which opened at the Dolder Hotel on 6 February 1959, was attended by the Prime Ministers of Greece and Turkey, Karamanlis and Menderes. Their Foreign Ministers and a team of distinguished experts were also present. The talks ran into serious difficulties over the Turkish demand for a military base and at one stage seemed on the verge of collapse. However, on 11 February, it was announced in a joint Greco-Turkish communiqué that agreement had been reached on a general plan for a settlement. Averoff immediately left for London to inform the British Government of the details.

The Zurich agreement provided for a presidential regime, with a Greek President and a Turkish Vice-President; a Supreme Constitutional Court and a High Court composed of Greek and Turkish judges, to be presided over in each case by a neutral; the creation of separate Greek and Turkish municipalities in the five largest towns, with the condition that the President and Vice-President should examine within five years whether this arrangement should continue; a Cypriot army of 2,000, which must be composed of 60 per cent Greeks and 40 per cent Turks; security forces with a complement of 2,000 men in a ratio of 70 per cent Greek to 30 per cent Turkish.

Executive authority was vested in the President and Vice-President, who were empowered to appoint a Council of Ministers, composed of 7 Greeks and 3 Turks. Candidates could be drawn from outside the House of Representatives. One key ministry, Defence, Finance and Foreign Affairs, was reserved for a Turk. Legislative authority was vested in the House of Representatives, to be elected every five years by universal suffrage in a ratio of 70 per cent Greek to 30 per cent Turkish members, and posts in the Civil Service allocated in the same proportions. Separate Greek and Turkish communal chambers would be responsible for religious, educational and cultural affairs. The President and Vice-President retained the right to veto either jointly or separately any law related to defence, security or foreign affairs. Legislation concerned with changes in the electoral law and the enactment of laws related to municipal and fiscal matters, required a simple majority on the basis of a separate vote from both the Greek and Turkish members of the House of Representatives.

The judges of the Supreme Constitutional Court and the High Court of Justice were to be appointed jointly by the President and Vice-President, whose agreement was also necessary to introduce conscription or any change in the size of the Cypriot army.

Two treaties were to be concluded with the new republic. In the first Britain, Greece and Turkey guaranteed its independence; the second, a defensive alliance between Greece, Turkey and Cyprus, provided for the stationing of small contingents of Greek and Turkish troops in the island and the training of a Cypriot army. The settlement precluded Enosis and partition as well as the division of Cyprus into two independent states and any change in the twenty-seven basic articles agreed by Greece and Turkey at Zurich.[1]

The basic articles covered major concessions to the Turks. At Zurich they had dropped the demand for a military base, accepting instead the Treaty of Guarantee and the Treaty of Alliance which met the Turkish Government's desire for a military presence in Cyprus and, in its view, the right to direct military intervention in certain circumstances. The Turkish insistence on the separate vote in the House of Representatives was prompted by the deep-rooted fear of discrimination at the hands of the Greeks in the light of past experience mainly in the field of local government. This concession amounted in theory to a veto which could be applied equally by either community, but in practice was of far greater importance to the Turkish minority.

Britain's acceptance of the agreement was a foregone conclusion. But one major obstacle to its implementation still had to be overcome. The EOKA Leader distrusted from the start the meetings between Averoff and Zorlu, although they had taken place under the cloak of the activities of NATO and the OEEC. Averoff telephoned a message to the Greek Consul on 12 February, which was conveyed to Grivas by the Bishop of Kition. The Greek Foreign Minister stressed that the maximum success possible had been achieved in the pursuit of the Cyprus struggle. It would, therefore, be helpful if EOKA and the various Cypriot organisations came out in public support of Makarios. Such an acclamation, Averoff felt, would forestall any disruptive action on the part of the Communists. The Foreign Minister confirmed that the British bases would be retained, but dismissed reports that either a Turkish or a NATO base would be established in Cyprus.[2]

The Archbishop backed up the Greek Foreign Minister's appeal. In the present circumstances no better solution was possible, Makarios wrote. The Turkish problem, which Britain had created, would remain a permanent barrier to Enosis, even if the Socialists came to power. The birth of Cyprus as an independent sovereign state meant the end to centuries of slavery. The Archbishop had some reservations on the arrangements for a Greek-Turkish-Cypriot military headquarters. But the Turkish Vice-President's veto, he stressed, would apply solely to defence and foreign policy. Subject to Britain's acceptance of the agreement, a conference would shortly be held in London and the Cypriots would try to improve the terms. Makarios felt that it would be

---

[1] See *Conference on Cyprus: Documents signed and initialled at Lancaster House on February 19, 1959.*

[2] *Memoirs* (Greek ed.), p. 374.

useful if Grivas, in the meantime, issued a proclamation indicating EOKA's support.[1]

Grivas wrote to the Bishop of Kition on 13 February. He was not in favour of the proclamation requested by Averoff and Makarios. EOKA's silence, he believed, would mystify the British to the advantage of the Cyprus struggle. He was not in any case able to take up a definite position as he did not know the full terms of the settlement. One aspect of it, however, which had attracted wide publicity, was the provision for the stationing of Turkish troops in Cyprus. He was strongly against this on any basis whatsoever.[2] On 16 February the EOKA Leader received two notes from the Consul. The first warned him that any signs of discord in the Greek Cypriot front could weaken the Archbishop's position when he was brought into negotiations at a later stage. The Consul admitted that the settlement was likely to fall short of the nationalist aim, but by way of consolation implied that it might only be an interim measure.

The second note contained a message from Averoff in which the Greek Foreign Minister tried to overcome the Colonel's objections to the presence of Turkish troops in Cyprus. This arrangement Averoff described as comparable to the NATO Commands in Smyrna and Naples, which in no way diminished Turkish and Italian sovereignty.[3] Appealing to the Colonel's deep-rooted anti-communism, the Consul commented on the significance of the Soviet Union's hostility to the approaching end of the Cyprus problem. Had EOKA supported Makarios, Moscow would have hesitated to organise agitation against the agreement. Russia wanted, the Consul continued, to perpetuate the split in the Western alliance by sabotaging any settlement. There was still time for Grivas to support the Archbishop if he wished.[4]

The Bishop of Kition now joined in the concerted effort to obtain the Colonel's cooperation. He began by completely agreeing with the views expressed by the EOKA Leader on 13 February. But the main purpose of his letter was to persuade Grivas, in the event of the British Government's endorsement of the settlement, to declare immediately his confidence in the political leadership and EOKA's acceptance of the Zurich agreement. Soft-pedalling the thorny issue of the Turkish troops, the Bishop wrote that the presence of a few units was unfortunately linked to the proposed alliance between Greece and Turkey.

[1] ibid. p. 377.
[2] ibid. p. 376.
[3] ibid. pp. 383-4.
[4] ibid. p. 384.

As an independent state Cyprus might, at some future date, be able to change this and other unsatisfactory aspects of the settlement.[1]

The London Conference opened at Lancaster House on 17 February. Britain, Greece and Turkey were represented by their Foreign Ministers; the two Cypriot communities by Archbishop Makarios and Dr Fazil Kutchuk. Selwyn Lloyd, on behalf of Britain, accepted the Zurich agreement, subject to the retention of two areas under British sovereignty for use as military bases. The Greek Prime Minister, Constantine Karamanlis, arrived the next day. The aircraft bringing the Turkish Prime Minister, Adnan Menderes, crashed near Gatwick. One of fifteen survivors, Menderes was not well enough to attend the talks.

Archbishop Makarios had invited leading Greek Cypriots, drawn from all sectors of the community, to meet him in London. Others joined the group on their own initiative. Grivas was incensed that Makarios had not asked him personally to send someone. However, contrary to the EOKA Leader's complaint that EOKA was not represented, the Archbishop's party included some of the Organisation's most prominent and influential members. The settlement was unpopular with the Greek Cypriots and after lengthy discussions with his unofficial advisers, the Archbishop on 18 February raised objections to the Vice-President's veto, Turkey's right of intervention, the defence alliance which gave Greece and Turkey the right to station troops in Cyprus, and the number of seats allocated in the National Assembly to the Turkish Cypriots which, at 30 per cent of the total, was nearly twice as great as their ratio to the whole population. A serious rift between the Government on the one hand and Makarios and his unofficial advisers on the other thus developed the day before the documents were due to be signed and initialled.

In a tense interview with Makarios the Greek Prime Minister told him that he must accept the settlement as it stood and that if he retracted now no further help could be expected from Greece. Selwyn Lloyd gave the Archbishop until the next morning to reach a decision. If the Conference collapsed as the result of the Archbishop's rejection of the agreement, the consequences for Cyprus, he said, would be unpredictable.[2]

The Archbishop met the Cypriot delegates at the Dorchester Hotel, where he was staying, at 8 a.m. the next morning. He told them that he had in Athens accepted the principles of the agreement, believing that the details would be subject to negotiations when he came

[1] ibid. pp. 378-9.
[2] See *Riding the Storm*, op. cit. pp. 695-6.

to London and he still hoped that modifications would be allowed.

The prospect of continuing the struggle without Greece was in itself daunting; the certainty that Britain would go ahead with the partnership plan and the overriding fear of partition were decisive factors underlying the Archbishop's reply. Embittered but resigned to the realities of the situation, most of the group pledged their support, and the Archbishop accepted the Zurich and London agreements unconditionally. The decision had been reached, Makarios said, after a 'night's prayer and reflection on the agonising dilemma' which faced him.[1] Finally he urged the Greek Cypriot leaders to work for unity and to cooperate sincerely with the Turks.

The relevant documents for the final settlement of the Cyprus dispute were duly signed and initialled at Lancaster House on the same day, 19 February 1959.[2]

The three Prime Ministers and their Foreign Secretaries were next confronted with the task of presenting the settlement to their respective Parliaments. Macmillan's statement was greeted on the whole with relief by the House of Commons, although some of the right-wing members of the Conservative Party thought the Government's concessions had gone too far, especially in relation to the military bases.[3] Averoff bore the brunt of the storm in the Greek Parliament. The Liberal Leader, Sophokles Venizelos, described the Zurich and London agreements as 'a national humiliation' and his party, he said, would not be bound by them. The Karamanlis Government nevertheless obtained the necessary vote of confidence, thus removing at least one danger to the eventual ratification of the settlement. The Turks were able to present the solution to the Grand National Assembly as a major triumph for Turkish diplomacy.

The day after the Conference at Lancaster House ended, Grivas received a letter from Averoff. Trying to justify the settlement, Averoff hinted that, had the Greeks rejected the agreements, partition might have become a certainty. The Greek Foreign Minister claimed considerable diplomatic success for his Government in obtaining major concessions from Turkey which, for instance, had dropped the demand for a base in Cyprus. Turkish troops would form, side by side with the Greek contingent, part of a joint Greco-Turkish-Cypriot headquarters. The Greek Army's presence on this basis was a safeguard against partition, he wrote. Cyprus, for the first time in 3,000 years, Averoff

---

[1] Daily Telegraph, 20 February 1959.
[2] Cmnd 679, op. cit.
[3] See H.C. Deb., vol. 600, cols 618–30.

continued, would be independent; the dominant position of the Greek Cypriots in the administration ensured that the influence of Greece was likely to grow; the rapprochement between Greece and Turkey held out better prospects for Hellenism in Constantinople. Turning to one of the most controversial features of the settlement – the provision for separate municipalities – Averoff envisaged that after the trial period of four years the Turks would opt for financial reasons to merge with the Greeks.

Grivas refused to issue a leaflet supporting the settlement until the fate of the EOKA prisoners was decided. Averoff assured him that this question would be solved. The Turks at Zurich had agreed to a general amnesty, but this created difficulties for the British.[1] The Greek Foreign Minister was fully aware of the problem facing the Cyprus authorities. The free movement of the extremists in the island could have wrecked the settlement before its ratification during the difficult year of transition which lay ahead. The Greek Government agreed that 23 hard-core prisoners, including the 14 held in England, should go to Greece. They were released subject to the condition that they did not return to the island without the Cyprus Government's permission before the date on which their sentences would have expired.

The Archbishop returned to Cyprus on 1 March, almost three years after his banishment to the Seychelles. Enthusiastic crowds lined the roads from the airport, but Grivas, angered by the terms of the amnesty, ordered EOKA not to take part in the reception. Two days after the Archbishop's return, ANE, the extremist youth organisation, paved the way for the settlement in an ominous manifesto. This mentioned the Greek War of Independence and the underlying aim of the Greater Greece movement to re-establish the Byzantine Empire with Constantinople as its capital. The writer implied that in the light of historical precedent the present settlement could well be temporary:

His Beatitude has most certainly acted very correctly in accepting the settlement of our question by Independence. This is what present-day conditions give us. It does not follow that things will remain thus for ever. Our country will in other historical circumstances achieve step by step union with the rest of Hellenism now that it has rid itself of slavery and embarked on the path of freedom. Whoever thinks, that because we began the campaign with the slogan of *Enosis*, we should carry on with it until death does not know history, nor does he know

[1] See *Memoirs* (Greek ed.), op. cit. pp. 388–90.

that the people possess the sense of existence and self-preservation and that in order that they should unite with the rest of Hellenism it is imperative that the people should first exist.[1]

It is a matter of conjecture whether the declaration was simply intended to soften the blow or whether it reflected the true intentions of the nationalists for future action in circumstances more favourable to Enosis.

Makarios, soon after his return, asked Grivas to meet him in Nicosia. Instead, the EOKA Leader sent Antonis Georghiades to see the Archbishop. Georghiades came back with the Archbishop's explanation that the general outline of the Zurich agreement was agreed by him with Karamanlis before he left for Switzerland. Makarios did not know its exact contents until after it was signed; it was only in London that he first realised the Greek Prime Minister had gone beyond the original terms. Tassos Papadopoulos, amongst other important EOKA members, had tactfully tried to convince Grivas that the Archbishop had no alternative to accepting the settlement.

The Colonel's delay in ordering the cease-fire and the uncertainty surrounding the date of his departure became a source of mounting anxiety. With the consent of the Greek Government, the Cyprus authorities had intended to send prisoners awaiting trial and wanted men with Grivas to Greece. But the Colonel refused to go unless they were released and allowed to stay in Cyprus. And the Governor finally yielded to this pressure.

The EOKA Leader has recorded how he considered the possibility of continuing the struggle alone.[2] But he could not count on the backing of other states to replace the aid formerly given by Greece and there was the risk of civil strife between the Archbishop's supporters and his own. On 9 March he reluctantly ordered the cease-fire. The original text contained three provocative passages which were not likely to inspire public confidence in the agreements. At the Archbishop's request the EOKA Leader deleted them. The leaflet nevertheless indicated that Grivas held the political leadership solely responsible for the end of the armed struggle and the settlement. In a second proclamation, addressed to EOKA, he expressed his disapproval still more clearly.

The Colonel's departure from Cyprus on 17 March was unobtrusive. Escorted by two senior Greek army officers he was flown to Greece by the Royal Hellenic Air Force. Looking wan and emaciated, still clad in

---

[1] ANE leaflet: 'Independence', distributed at Athienou on 5 March 1959.
[2] *Memoirs* (Greek ed.), op. cit. pp. 401–3.

his guerrilla's outfit, he was given a national hero's reception at the airport, where Archbishop Theoklitos and the Greek Foreign Minister awaited him. The following evening the Greek army colonel, whose military career had ended more than twenty years earlier, was promoted to Lieutenant-General in retirement with full pay in the form of a pension for the rest of his life.

Success had come late in life to the EOKA Leader. The Cyprus struggle was his great opportunity. The smallness of the terrain, the limited miltary scope of the campaign, were well suited to the Colonel's personality. His inability to delegate, which would have been a major handicap in a full-scale guerrilla war, was no problem during the formative stages of EOKA since he was able to supervise personally every facet of the Organisation's evolution. In different circumstances his irascibility, his intolerance, his carping criticism, his tendency to distrust even close colleagues would have created insuperable obstacles. He quarrelled with his two assistants long before the campaign had started and was soon at variance with Makarios and Afxentiou, the most able of the guerrilla recruits. Apart from a few associates, who worked closely with him from the start, and his hosts when he was in hiding, the Colonel had little direct contact with the Cypriots. The problems of human relationships, made more exacting by the stress of battle conditions, were thus reduced to the minimum in a campaign which was almost exclusively directed by correspondence. Grivas was able to inspire awe but not affection. But this was no barrier under conditions in which the heroic image of a guerrilla leader could be built up on a basis of fantasy, worshipped at long range and glorified by the cause he represented.

The Greek Communists disclosed the identity of Grivas early in 1955. But the supporters of the Enosis campaign, both in Greece and Cyprus, were reluctant to accept the unpalatable truth that 'Dighenis', the military leader of the 'noble struggle', was none other than the notorious Greek army officer who created and led the right-wing terrorist organisation X and they tended to dismiss the reports as either communist mischief-making or British propaganda aimed at discrediting EOKA. By the early summer of 1957 the time for anonymity was over. After the Archbishop's return, pamphlets in Greek on EOKA, which eulogised George Grivas as 'Dighenis', the military leader of the Cyprus struggle, could be bought in Athens at newspaper kiosks for 3 drachmas. The Colonel's exploits as a national hero in Cyprus had redeemed his past activities, at least in the eyes of those who found it convenient to forget them.

Almost single-handed the Colonel managed to dragoon groups of enthusiastic but incompetent amateurs into a compact and effective guerrilla organisation. Punctilious about money, he was quick to spot the smallest discrepancy in EOKA's accounts and the merest hint of commercial exploitation in the form of some minor excess in payment for weapons and other materials needed by the guerrillas. Thrifty by choice, attuned to a spartan way of life, Grivas was highly skilled in making the best use of limited resources. He imposed the same stringent conditions on his subordinates. As a result, EOKA's running costs were reliably estimated at less than £100 a year. This modest expenditure was in marked contrast to the billions of dollars spent on the supporting campaign abroad, especially in the USA. Grivas used terrorist tactics as an adjunct to diplomacy, timing EOKA's attacks so that they were certain to make headline news. A meticulous planner, he left nothing to chance down to the smallest detail. His organisation of hideouts and storage places for weapons and, above all, his courier system were brilliantly conceived.

He was dispirited by the shortage of arms – in contrast to Mao Tse Tung and Che Guevara, who treated the problem as a challenge to be met by raiding the enemy's arsenals. But, apart from a few bold raids on police stations before the colonial administration was alerted, EOKA deliberately avoided operations likely to bring the guerrillas into full confrontation with the British Army. By limiting military action mainly to sabotage and ambushes, by concentrating on soft targets, he was thus able to conserve his forces.

Within the concept of his own narrow philosophy Grivas tried to be just both to members of EOKA and the ordinary Greek Cypriot public. But he lacked compassion and his campaign will be remembered for its ruthlessness in dealing with Cypriot defectors. By the standards of Che Guevara he relied to excess on intimidation and reprisal. Because the theatre of operations was small and the community close-knit, the Greek Cypriots were especially vulnerable to this weapon. Fear probably played as great a part as loyalty in keeping EOKA under control. Greek Cypriots suspected of betrayal were, in almost every case, executed without trial even by guerrilla tribunal. The vast majority of citizens branded as 'traitors' by EOKA had never given information to the British. The EOKA struggle was a rising against the British and 156 members of the security forces lost their lives. Yet out of 238 civilian casualties 203 were Greek Cypriots.

The security forces deployed in anti-terrorist operations numbered about 40,000, and the EOKA Leader's avoidance of capture has been widely acclaimed. This feat, although remarkable, was not without precedent. In the 1940s, a feared and detested brigand remained at large in the Paphos district for four years. The successful evasion of the authorities is, moreover, a familiar pattern of life in Mediterranean islands which are even smaller than Cyprus.

The greatest danger to the Colonel's survival was his own suspicious nature. But for the influence of Azinas, he would have fallen into the hands of the British before the EOKA rising began because he did not trust his subordinates to carry out the unloading of the *Aghios Georghios* on their own. His narrow escape in the mountains was due on the one hand to a combination of luck and mistaken British tactics, and on the other to his tenacity and capacity for endurance.

In order to survive Grivas had to remain immobilised and house-bound for the greater part of the struggle – a frustrating experience for a man of action and courage. Nevertheless, aided by his constant companion Antonis Georghiades, he was able through the courier network to direct EOKA's policy and operations. But he had no means of checking misleading information. Impervious to the ideas of others at the best of times, the Colonel, now cut off completely from the outside world, was more than ever prone to errors of judgement.

His neurotic obsession with the dangers of local communism tended to distract him from the main purpose of the struggle. His retaliation against the Turkish Cypriots in 1958, resulting in heavy casualties on both sides, created a conflict within a conflict, which also harmed the long-term aims of the EOKA campaign and paved the way for recurrent strife between the two communities.

In terms of political aims the Colonel achieved very little. It was ironic that a man haunted by the phobia of communism should have played into Soviet hands by weakening the Western alliance. It was still more ironic that as the result of his activities the realisation of Enosis ceased to be a possibility within a foreseeable time, if not for ever.

The EOKA rising, however, backed by an intensive political campaign abroad, played a part in forcing the British to look at the Cyprus problem in a new light. The changing strategic needs brought about by the development of faster aircraft, by the lapse of treaty obligations in the Middle East and by the aftermath of the Suez crisis would have forced them to do this sooner or later. At best it can be said that Grivas helped to bring colonial rule to an end a few years earlier than the British intended. Against this achievement the EOKA campaign left in its wake a bitter division of loyalties between the Greek Cypriots

and intensified the animosity of the Turks – both factors which have
bedevilled the island's politics for more than a decade.

2 PREPARATIONS FOR INDEPENDENCE

The early preparations for independence took place against a background of lawlessness. The free circulation of EOKA prisoners and
wanted men in March 1959 proved premature in the interests of
security, even if politically expedient. Many gunmen kept their arms
after the voluntary surrender called for by Archbishop Makarios and
the authorities. Incidents occurred between Greek Cypriots and British
soldiers, also among the Greek Cypriots themselves; two Greeks were
murdered by EOKA as a reprisal in circumstances of great brutality.
Friction between the Greek and Turkish Cypriots persisted. Archbishop Makarios and Dr Kutchuk made several appeals to their respective communities. They urged them to avoid clashes. They called upon
the press, a perennial source of mischief making, to cooperate in restoring friendly relations. And a special committee was set up to investigate
incidents in mixed villages.

In spite of the disturbed political situation, preparations for independence went ahead. But the Transitional Committee, which held its
first meeting on 4 March 1959, was alone in making rapid progress.
During the transitional period, responsibility for administration was,
wherever possible, shared with the Cypriots; and the Joint Council,
composed of the Governor's Executive Council and the Transitional
Council, functioned as the main governing body. The first hurdle in
setting up a ministerial system was cleared at the end of March when
Archbishop Makarios and Dr Kutchuk reached agreement over the
allocation of duties between the Greeks and Turks. Early in April the
Governor accepted the two Cypriot leaders' recommendations for
appointments to the Transitional Committee; seven Greek and four
Turkish members of the Committee were later invited to take up ministerial posts. Arrangements were made for the new ministers to study
the work of the departments they would eventually control.

The Joint Constitutional Commission also began its work in April.
The team, charged with drafting a constitution within the framework
of the basic structure agreed at Zurich, was distinguished. Professor
Bridel, the Swiss expert on constitutional law, was appointed the neutral
adviser. The Greek and Turkish delegations included Themistocles
Tsatsos, the eminent Athenian lawyer and former Minister of Justice,
Professor Nihat Erim, an expert on international law and former

Minister of State, and Dr Suat Bilge, legal adviser to the Turkish Foreign Office. Several eminent lawyers, Rauf Denktash, Glafkos Klerides and Michael Triantafyllides represented the Cypriots. The British, having failed on so many previous occasions, had no hand in drafting the constitution and sent only an observer.

In the late spring, tension was aggravated by renewed political activity by the Greeks. EDMA, the political successor to EOKA, was formed out of ex-fighters in support of Makarios and the settlement. During a three-day rally held at the end of May, EDMA publicised its first policy statement, promising wealth for the farmer and opportunity for youth. But the occasion was chiefly significant for the militant Hellenism preached by some of the former EOKA leaders, with its inevitable provocation of the Turks.

The Greek mayors, nationalist and communist, came into open conflict with Archbishop Makarios over Article 20 of the Zurich agreement, which provided for separate Greek and Turkish municipalities. Dr Dervis, the nationalist Mayor of Nicosia and a former supporter of Makarios, publicly denied an Athens newspaper report that he had approved Article 20 during the London Conference. He also made a vigorous attack on the Archbishop and the Greek Government, claiming that the agreement was signed by Makarios under pressure. Demanding that Article 20 should be amended, the mayors severely criticised the Archbishop's preliminary proposals for its implementation on the ground that they would transfer certain functions hitherto exercised by the municipalities to the central Government. The mayors, the only important elected representatives in Cyprus, constituted a formidable body united in opposition. The Archbishop nevertheless re-asserted his determination to stand by the agreements. The Communists were also active. They had recently formed the new youth movement EDON, and at a mass rally in Nicosia on 28 June the left-wing leaders attacked the agreements and the right wing's monopolisation of political life.

The trouble with the mayors subsided temporarily, but was soon replaced by a new threat to the settlement in the shape of a rift between Archbishop Makarios and the former Leader of EOKA, General Grivas. The rivalries of the ex-fighters in the struggle for power in Cyprus and the General's personal political ambitions in Greece lay at the root of the crisis. At the end of July, Grivas warned Cypriots against the ratification of the London agreement, stating that the signatories had entered into verbal commitments of which he had no knowledge at the time. Dr Kutchuk promptly faced this new danger to Turkish interests by supporting Makarios and urging the Greek Government to curb the harmful activities of Grivas. Senior EDMA officials journeyed to Athens, but failed to bring about a reconciliation between Grivas and Makarios.

In August, the Cyprus Enosis Front (KEM), a subversive organisation which had first appeared in May, circulated leaflets attacking Makarios and threatening to resort to violence in a renewed campaign for Enosis. The Bishop of Kyrenia stated from the pulpit that Cyprus would achieve Enosis once Grivas became Prime Minister of Greece. These developments coincided with gun-running activities on the part of the Greeks; and at the end of the month the British authorities decided to rearm sectors of the police. The atmosphere of conspiracy was heightened in September by reports of a plot by KEM to assassinate Makarios and start civil war in the island. A leading EDMA official was dismissed on the Archbishop's instructions in this connection. The editor of *Ethniki*, which had criticised the dismissal, was beaten up by armed gangs. September was marked by widespread outbreaks of violence in both communities. Makarios and Kutchuk jointly urged the public to help fight the current crime wave. AKEL, the communist party, although still banned officially, called upon all groups to surrender their arms.

General Grivas, in the meantime, denounced the reports of an assassination plot as a pretext devised by Makarios to justify further concessions to the British and the Turks. The rift was superficially patched up when the two men met in strict secrecy in Rhodes in October. The facade of unity was precarious; the rivalries which sharply divided the right wing had merely been pushed below the surface.

Shortly after Makarios returned from Rhodes, the Greek mayors of the six main towns resumed their offensive and submitted a memorandum to the Archbishop calling for the replacement of his Advisory Council by a Pancyprian Congress and for the revision of the Zurich and London agreements. At the end of October Dr Dervis announced that the mayors had decided to boycott the Council, which he claimed represented no one except the Archbishop himself.

Serious trouble arose over the Turks when on 18 October a British naval patrol boarded and searched the *Deniz* off the coast of Cyprus and seized two cases of ammunition before the vessel was scuttled by its crew. Registered in Izmir, the *Deniz* was manned by three Turkish subjects. The crisis intensified suspicions in Cyprus that the Turkish underground, TMT, was still active and that the Turks were stockpiling arms and ammunition as a precaution against future trouble with the Greeks or a breakdown of the agreements. Public confidence was severely shaken. The Government of Cyprus, supported by Archbishop Makarios and Dr Kutchuk, appealed to Greeks and Turks to hand in illegal arms and ammunition to their leaders by 4 November, on the understanding that no offenders would be prosecuted until after that date. The response was poor and the deadline was extended for a short period.

After the *Deniz* episode, Archbishop Makarios suspended the work of the Greek team on the Joint Constitutional Commission. This action dismayed the Turks, who viewed every delay as a threat to the survival of the settlement and the numerous advantages they had gained under it. Immediately denouncing the smuggling activities, Dr Kutchuk questioned whether the *Deniz* was bound for Cyprus. The Turkish leader, Mr Denktash, in Athens at the time for the signing of the Treaty of Alliance, publicly criticised the Archbishop for breaking off the constitutional discussions and dismissed the incident as no worse than the gun-running activities of the Greek Cypriot extremists. The Turkish Government formally denied that it had ever approved arms smuggling to Cyprus; and Ankara Radio claimed that the *Deniz* was hunting dolphins. But on 11 November its crew was found guilty by a Famagusta court of the illegal possession of ammunition in Cypriot territorial waters and sentenced to one year's imprisonment. In view of wider interests the Governor commuted the sentences and the three men were immediately deported.

Criticism of Makarios had meanwhile grown on many fronts. His transitional Cabinet consisted almost exclusively of former EOKA men and their close associates – mostly young and inexperienced. Older men of influence, rightists and leftists equally, were ignored. With the approach of the presidential elections, the main targets for attack were the Archbishop's alleged 'dictatorial methods' and the terms of the settlement. The appearance in November of a new weekly newspaper, *Epalxis*, reflecting the views of the Bishop of Kyrenia, marked the start of a campaign for the overthrow of the Zurich and London agreements and the removal of Makarios as the island's political leader.

On 15 November, John Klerides, a distinguished citizen of moderate views, and his former political rival Dr Dervis organised a large meeting in Nicosia, at which it was unanimously decided to form a new party, the Democratic Union, with the object of opposing Makarios in the presidential elections. Dr Dervis attacked the Greek Government and the United States for their part in the Cyprus settlement and the Archbishop for failing to use the *Deniz* episode as an argument against the clauses related to the stationing of Greek and Turkish troops in Cyprus. Klerides described the agreements as worse than the Macmillan plan of 1958 and stated that the policy of the Democratic Union should be to support a presidential candidate who would avoid dictatorial actions and appoint ministers solely on the recommendation of the elected representatives and parliamentary candidates opposed to expenditure on a Cypriot army. At the end of the month Klerides was nominated the Democratic Union's candidate for the presidency.

The ban on the communist-led AKEL, imposed during the first few months of Harding's governorship, was not lifted until early December 1959, and the Party's attitude was at first uncertain. But after the Archbishop's offer of seven seats in the House of Representatives had been rejected by AKEL, whose terms for cooperation in the presidential contest were also unacceptable to him, the Party, backed by the powerful leftist labour federation, PEO, came out in full support of Klerides. Thus the Democratic Union had rallied to its side right-wing extremists who were determined to overthrow the agreements at any price, Communists who were sufficiently realistic to accept the settlement as an interim necessity, and many men of ability and moderation. EDMA, as a concession to its numerous critics, had reappeared as the Patriotic Front and its members resorted to a smear campaign of extreme viciousness. Mass meetings were held by both groups; fighting broke out between the right and the left in several districts. Makarios and Klerides appealed for order.

Apart from sporadic outbursts of violence, polling day on 13 December went off peacefully. Registered electors numbered 238,879; abstentions were negligible. Makarios gained 144,501 votes, Klerides 71,753.[1] The ban on AKEL and the belated formation of the Democratic Union had given the Archbishop's opponents little time to organise. Moreover, local observers considered that he partly owed his victory to the conservativeness of the women, who in Cyprus tend to follow blindly the lead given by the Church irrespective of their husbands' political views. Nevertheless it was significant that a third of the electorate had voted against the Archbishop, who less than a year earlier had figured as the sole political spokesman for the Greek population.

Dr Kutchuk, unopposed, automatically became Turkish Vice-President elect on nomination day.

By the end of 1959 the ministerial system had already been in operation for several months. And outside the spheres reserved to the

[1] *Cyprus: The Transitional Year* (Cyprus Government, 1959), vol. III, pp. 6–7.

Governor, the Chief Justice, the Financial Secretary and the Accountant-General, Cypriot ministers had been able to submit policy proposals to the Joint Council and take responsibility for the execution of its decisions in relation to their own departments. Government services had been reorganised and Cypriots promoted to the highest posts. Most British officials had left the island, which for all political purposes was by now self-governing. The fact that the administration continued to function relatively smoothly through the difficult transitional period was mainly due to the high quality of the Cypriot civil service.

3   THE NEGOTIATIONS ON THE BRITISH BASES

The Greek Cypriots bitterly resented the fact that the political fate of their island, apart from the question of British bases, was largely settled over their heads by Greece and Turkey at Zurich. After the settlement, Archbishop Makarios tried to mitigate this resentment by extracting as many concessions as possible from the British, whose military requirements were only vaguely outlined during the hasty proceedings of the London Conference. The London documents which provided 'the agreed foundation for the final settlement of the problem of Cyprus'[1] left ample scope for interpretation and manoeuvre.

Negotiations centred on two issues: the size of the areas to remain under British sovereignty and the ancillary facilities to be granted in the territory of the future republic. The broad aim of the Greek Cypriot negotiators was to eliminate any lingering vestiges of 'colonialism' and to secure the maximum financial advantages out of Britain. Sharp differences arose from the start over the practical and political implications of sovereignty and the size of the base areas. In February 1960 the British Foreign Secretary mentioned that the area required by Britain would cover 150 to 170 square miles and include 16,000 inhabitants.[2] For administrative reasons the British Government of its own accord subsequently reduced this preliminary assessment to 4,500 inhabitants. The Cypriot delegation was the first to make a specific proposal for the delineation of the bases, in the shape of a rough sketch shown to the Defence Minister, Duncan Sandys, in Cyprus in April 1959. The proposed area of 36 square miles excluded all villages and was totally inadequate to meet British military needs. Nevertheless Mr Sandys assured Archbishop Makarios that full weight would be given to the Cypriot view that no villages should be included in the base areas.[3]

---

[1] Cmnd 679, p. 4.
[2] H.C. Deb., vol. 616, cols 636–44, 1 February 1960.
[3] *Transitional Year*, op. cit. vol. I, p. 26, Press Release 3, 24 April 1959.

The first British proposals for the bases were presented to the London Committee in May. These provided for an area of 160 square miles and included seven villages. The Cypriot delegation responded in June with detailed counter-proposals based on their earlier suggestion informally raised with Mr Duncan Sandys. In October the British Government made its first major concession in proposing an area of 120 square miles and the exclusion of all villages except Akrotiri, which could not be left outside the base area owing to its proximity to the runway.

While Cyprus was a British colony, the bases operated in conjunction with a large number of military sites located throughout the island. It was now necessary to reduce their number and concentrate as many facilities as possible inside the bases. During the spring and summer of 1959 the British delegation was engaged in extensive surveys, mainly of a technical nature, and the first British proposals for sites and facilities to be retained in the Republic were not tabled until August. By December few final decisions had been taken; almost every other line of the voluminous draft treaty was bracketed to indicate an objection or a reservation. Nevertheless British officials at high level in Cyprus expressed the view that the Republic could still be established by 19 February 1960; and early in the New Year advance contingents of Greek and Turkish troops arrived in the island according to schedule.

In the middle of January 1960 the British, Greek and Turkish Foreign Ministers and the two Cypriot leaders met in London to review the work of the London Committee. After a short conference it was unanimously decided on 18 January to postpone independence by one month. Discussions continued through working committees. By the end of January the second edition of the draft treaty was printed. This progress was facilitated by the presence of Archbishop Makarios in London and by further important concessions on the part of the British. The British Government stated in a policy declaration that it did not intend to set up 'colonies', to develop the bases for anything other than military purposes, or to set up civilian commercial and industrial enterprises in competition with those of the Republic. It was agreed that Dhekelia power station, despite its key position in the heart of the base, should remain under Republican sovereignty, and that traffic control at Nicosia airfield, a right clearly reserved to Britain in the London agreement, should be taken over once Cypriots qualified for the work became available. The Republican Government was invited to provide certain public services for Cypriots in the base areas; and an offer was made to rehouse in the Republic, at British expense, any villagers wishing to leave Akrotiri. On 1 February the British Foreign Secretary stated that British requirements had now been reduced to the absolute minimum.

Four days later the Under-Secretary of State for the Colonies, Julian Amery, arrived in Cyprus. During his visit the Cypriots made new proposals, and on the British side aid was increased to £10 million over a five-year period, but no agreement was reached. On 8 February the Cyprus Government announced that the necessary legislation could not be adopted by the British Parliament in time for the new independence date, 19 March 1960. Archbishop Makarios immediately criticised the postponement and was supported by Dr Kutchuk, who had made an attempt at mediation before Amery's departure from the island. On 9 February Mr Selwyn Lloyd repeated that British requirements were the minimum. Nevertheless the return of Amery to Cyprus at the end of the month encouraged the belief that the British were about to make new concessions.

The work of the London Committee was transferred to Cyprus, and the negotiations entered their final and most difficult stage. Five weeks of tedious bargaining, in which Greek Cypriot mistrust of the British reached its climax, destroyed all hopes of a speedy settlement. The Turks, exasperated by the niggling tactics of the Greeks, finally boycotted the negotiations on details concerning the NAAFI's position within the bases; but the talks ended in agreement on 17 March. Towards the end of the month the negotiators returned to the questions of financial aid and the size and administration of the bases. Amery, who was due to leave on an official visit for the West Indies, had meanwhile received fresh instructions to stay in Cyprus until agreement was reached.

The Greek leaders now adopted tougher tactics. On 1 April, the fifth anniversary of the start of the EOKA rising, Makarios threatened to launch a civil disobedience campaign and to implement the Zurich and London agreements on his own should the British persist in postponing independence. This outburst, with its references to the glories of EOKA and hints of a renewed struggle, antagonised the Turkish leaders. Dr Kutchuk reminded the Archbishop that the Turks would revert to their former stand on partition should the Greeks revive the demand for Enosis; he pointed out the futility of any attempt on the part of the Archbishop to enforce the agreements alone, since the Constitution had no legal validity unless the Treaties of Guarantee and Alliance were signed at the same time, and stressed the extent of the concessions already made by the British. On 2 April, Dr Kutchuk made a new proposal for a base area of 100 square miles. Twelve days later Amery stated that differences on the question of size had been substantially narrowed.[1]

Meanwhile the problems created by the postponement of independence had grown. The island's economy was stagnant; both communities faced serious unemployment. Relations between the Greeks and Turks were exacerbated by Turkish fears that the collapse of the agreements was imminent. On the other hand the delay encouraged Greek critics of the agreements. But the methods used by the Archbishop's followers in the attempt to silence opposition gave cause for grave concern. On 26 April Mr Pharmakides, the editor of *Ethniki*, which had continuously attacked Makarios and the settlement, was kidnapped by gunmen. After widespread agitation, in which left-wing activity played an important part, he was released a sick man, having been held blindfold for eleven days under sentence of execution.

By mid-April much of the text of the Treaty of Establishment had been agreed, but the size and administration of the bases and the question of financial aid were still outstanding. Moreover, new difficulties had come to the fore. Greek anxieties about the future of the bases in the event of a British withdrawal had persisted since the London Conference in 1959. Legal experts held the view that the existence of British sovereign bases formed an integral part of the London agreement; any undertaking concerning their future disposal would therefore require the consent of all the parties. But the Greek Government and the Greek Cypriot leaders were not content to leave well alone, and the problem of finding a formula acceptable to both Greece and Turkey introduced new hazards for the survival of the settlement. The Cypriot Greek leaders, furthermore, were now insisting that the undertaking given in the British policy declaration on the bases[2] should be made legally binding. On 16 May Archbishop Makarios accused Britain of using the argument of unemployment to force the Cypriots into unacceptable concessions. Amery denied the Archbishop's claim that a deadlock existed, and was supported by Dr Kutchuk. The Governor authorised measures to alleviate unemployment but warned the public that economic catastrophe could only be prevented by a prompt settlement of the political question and the establishment of the Republic by the summer.[3]

On 18 May Archbishop Makarios refused Amery's invitation to

---

[1] *Transitional Year*, op. cit. vol. IV, p. 14, Press Release 8, 14 April 1960.
[2] See CYPRUS, Cmnd 1093, pp. 201–5.
[3] *Transitional Year*, op. cit. vol. IV, p. 23. Press Release 5, 18 May 1960.

resume talks. The overthrow of the Menderes Government in Turkey at the end of the month interrupted negotiations with Greece and Turkey over the cession formula and aggravated the atmosphere of uncertainty in Cyprus. The Archbishop reacted to the event by re-asserting his determination to stand by the agreements. At this stage two courses lay open to him. Unless the British Parliament passed the necessary legislation before the summer recess, independence was certain to be delayed until the winter. The Archbishop might have gambled on obtaining still better terms, but the potential advantages were offset by the dangers inherent in the local situation – economic hardship, communal strife and an intensification of the campaign for the abrogation of the agreements. Negotiations were resumed on 23 June after an adjournment of seven weeks. The cession issue was resolved in an exchange of Notes between the British Government and the two Cypriot leaders.[1] Aid was increased from £10 million to £12 million over the five-year period. On 1 July the British and Cypriot delegations announced that agreement had been reached on all outstanding questions.

Under the final settlement Britain retained a total area of 99 square miles which formed the two Sovereign Bases of Akrotiri and Dhekelia. Administration was subject to the control of Air Officer Commanding-in-Chief, Middle East Air Force, RAF, the cost being borne on the air estimates. No frontiers were set up between the Sovereign Base Areas and the Republic; and two pockets of Republican territory remained at the centre of the Dhekelia base. Specially constructed bypasses ensured unbroken communications under British control inside both areas.

Eighteen essential sites, which for geographical or technical reasons could not be moved, including the radar installations on Mount Troodos, remained under the sovereignty of the Republic. The loss of two large training areas originally allocated to the British necessitated alternative facilities in the Republic. The British authorities were empowered to fit suppressors to any apparatus in nearby villages which interfered with the Dhekelia base installations, and to assume exclusive control of Nicosia airfield in the event of any emergency determined by Britain. They also retained special facilities in the ports and the right to meet from British resources any deficiencies of staff, labour or equipment at Famagusta port and Dhekelia power station.

Subject to the 'military requirements and security needs of the British Government', the Cypriots were granted freedom of movement

[1] Cmnd 1093, p. 207.

across the boundaries, extensive rights in relation to administration, employment and cultivation inside the bases, and freedom to fish and navigate in the adjacent territorial waters.[1] British jurisdiction over Cypriots in the bases was restricted to security offences. These concessions, which met the Cypriot demand that the island should remain a single, economic and administrative unit, were made at the expense of security.

In theory British and Cypriot interests were fully protected by the numerous legal safeguards written into the Treaty of Establishment. But the fact that the bases were not self-contained made them vulnerable to outside conditions, and the success of the arrangements was bound to depend largely on political stability in the island and the goodwill and cooperation of the Republican authorities.

4   THE LAST STAGES

The end of the Anglo-Cypriot talks in July 1960 cleared the way for independence. The Constitution,[2] after more than a year's intensive work, had now been ready for several months. In drafting it, the outstandingly able team, which had sought to find a lasting compromise, came up against many problems. The neutral adviser was French-speaking; the working document was in English; the authentic versions in final form had to be in Greek and Turkish, languages which do not easily translate from the one to the other. This may account for some of the anomalies in the final draft, which had serious legal defects.[3] The Constitution was in reality the legacy of intercommunal strife rather than a model for sound government based on democratic lines. Composed of 199 Articles, it left in its wake a trail of dissension over the 30:70 per cent ratio of Turks to Greeks in the civil service. The Turks wanted this condition implemented before the end of British rule. And had it been possible to meet their request much trouble might have been avoided later on. But without either dismissing Greeks or creating extra posts it was not practicable at the time. The Constitution was not without bias in relation to local politics. It precluded the break-up of the extensive fertile land owned by the Church, a reform long overdue, without the permission of the ecclesiastical authorities. The

---

[1] Cmnd 1093, p. 201.

[2] ibid. pp. 91–172.

[3] See Stanley Kyriakides, for an excellent analysis of the Constitution, *Cyprus: Constitutionalism and Crisis Government* (University of Pennsylvania Press, 1968), Chapter III, 'Major features of the 1960 Constitution'.

power of the Church was thus written into the settlement on an even firmer basis than it had been under colonial rule.

The Electoral Law, although introduced by the colonial Government, was based on the Constitutional Commission's recommendations. It provided for universal suffrage; for six multi-member constituencies; and for the election of 35 Greeks and 15 Turks to the House of Representatives. Electors were entitled to vote for the candidates of more than one party so long as the number of votes cast on any single ballot sheet did not exceed the number of candidates in any one constituency. Highly complex, the Law was the subject of acute controversy. The main ground for criticism was the size of the constituencies which made a victory for the Patriotic Front a certainty and the election of opposition candidates virtually impossible.

AKEL, which had tested its strength in the presidential elections, agreed to cooperate with the Patriotic Front in exchange for five seats in the House of Representatives offered by the Archbishop. This switch in allegiance was prompted by tactical considerations rather than by a change of ideology. The Democratic Union took no part owing to the discriminatory character of the electoral system.

Polling day, on 1 August, resulted in an easy win for the Patriotic Front, which gained 30 seats out of 35 allocated to Greek members. All five AKEL candidates were elected. But the three ex-EOKA fighters belonging to the extreme rightist anti-Makarios front obtained only an insignificant number of votes and 36 per cent of the Greek electorate abstained. In Larnaca, where AKEL was not represented, abstentions rose to 59 per cent. The most likely explanation for the apathy of Greek voters was the conviction that a victory for the Patriotic Front was inevitable. It was perhaps significant that although the Archbishop's supporters had the benefit this time of AKEL's votes in three large constituencies, abstentions corresponded approximately in number to the votes cast against the Archbishop in the presidential elections. Dr Kutchuk's Turkish National Party was also returned with little opposition. Elections for the Communal Chambers were held a week later and completed the preparations for independence.

The Republic came into being on 16 August 1960, eighteen months after the signing of the Zurich and London agreements. The event was greeted with relief and jubilation by the Turks but met with little enthusiasm on the part of the Greeks, whose reactions to the settlement from the time of Zurich had ranged from open hostility to cynicism and disillusion.

Eighty-two years of British rule was thus brought to an end. The

Cyprus revolt against the British had been waged in the name of self-determination and anti-colonialism, for this was in keeping with the trend of the day and the easiest way to obtain international support. But its real purpose was Enosis and the term 'settlement', with its implication of permanency, was deceptive. For the struggle for Enosis was soon to be renewed, this time bringing both Greece and Greek Cypriots into direct conflict with the Turks, only to culminate in the Turkish invasion and occupation of the northern sector of the island – the greatest single calamity to befall Cyprus in modern times.

XI

Postscript: The Aftermath 1960-1976

Breakdown of the Zurich Settlement — Turkey's
Military Intervention in 1974

The second Cyprus dispute arose out of the first but differed greatly in character and dimension. The first was a revolt against a colonial power and as such was contained within a narrower arena. The second, potentially more dangerous, arose out of a clash between two ethnic groups. At the root of the trouble in each case lay the perennial problem of Enosis. The aims of the Greek nationalists had not changed, only the nature of the opposition. The involvement of Greece and Turkey became more complex after Independence because of their responsibilities under the Zurich settlement and the presence of their own troops in the island. In relations with each other they blew hot and cold over the Cyprus problem, alternating between a united front and outright hostility which brought them to the brink of war. The danger of war between these two NATO allies, the struggle to keep Cyprus from succumbing totally either to the West or to the Communists led to the direct inter-vention of the USA and the USSR. Within this framework Makarios was able to pursue the policy of non-alignment, sometimes with ques-tionable advantage for the interests of Cyprus. Great Britain, from whom decisive action might have been expected, played a negative role even to the extent of disregarding her obligations to safeguard 'the indepen-dence, territorial integrity and security of the Republic, and also the state of affairs established by the Basic Articles of its Constitution'.[1] It was as if inhibited by her former position as colonial ruler she was determined to stand aside.

In the island itself the rise of Turkish Cypriot nationalism, barely perceptible under British rule, came to equal that of the Greeks in

[1] Cmnd 1093, pp. 86-7.

fanaticism, thus increasing the risk of local conflict. With the end of the colonial administration, a buffer between the two communities was removed; the way was now open to direct confrontation between them. The prospects for stability were also undermined by the fact that the Cypriots had embarked on independence without prior self-government owing to their past refusals to accept a constitution. Decolonisation was limited to the civil service, which had been extensively Cypriotised, but there had been no devolution of executive power. The absence of proven politicians had created a vacuum which made it inevitable that the Church and guerrilla elements would play a greater part than was desirable in the interests of sound government. The dangers of strife, moreover, were enhanced by the embittered split between the rival followers of Makarios and Grivas.

In 1959 many Cypriots were relieved that the emergency had ended and did not inquire closely into the Zurich settlement. But a small group, the followers of General Grivas, was strongly opposed to Makarios for having accepted the agreements, which they regarded as an interim arrangement to be overthrown at the first opportunity.

The inherent complexity of the Constitution gave rise to difficulties from the outset but the main reason for the breakdown of the settlement was the lack of goodwill which had persisted between the Greek and Turkish Cypriots since the intercommunal fighting of 1958. The Greeks discriminated from time to time against the Turks; President Makarios and some of the Greek Cypriot ministers were tactless in their treatment of the Turkish Vice-President, Dr Kutchuk. The Turks, for their part, made excessive use of their constitutional powers. The Greek Cypriots came increasingly to resent the fact that the 27 Basic Articles laid down at Zurich gave the Turks powers which were disproportionate to their numbers in the population. The allocation of 30 per cent of the posts in the civil service to the Turks caused genuine difficulties. Turks were not always available to take up specific posts, but in some cases the Greeks obstructed their appointment to posts which they were qualified to fill. Controversy also arose over the Cyprus army, which in accordance with the settlement should have numbered 2,000 in a ratio of 60 per cent Greek to 40 per cent Turkish. The Turks wanted separate units and Dr Kutchuk vetoed a law passed by the House of Representatives for the formation of mixed units.

The first major crisis came in December 1961 when the Turks refused to vote for the budget as a reprisal for the Greek failure to fulfil certain obligations affecting Turkish interests in other spheres. Thereafter the Republic was obliged to operate three separate tax systems, to the detriment of the economy. The second major crisis came a year later. Separate Turkish municipalities had existed *de facto* since 1958. Provision was made at Zurich for their eventual legalisation. But in December 1962 the Mixed Municipal Commission still could not agree on the final boundaries. The Greek deputies refused to renew the municipal law, abolished the municipalities and introduced a special law to cover local government. The Turks, through the Turkish Communal Chamber, immediately enacted a law setting up their own municipalities. The Greek and Turkish actions were both declared illegal by the Supreme Constitutional Court.

Whereas the Greeks had welcomed the deadlock over the army plan, which they disliked on account of cost and the high percentage of Turks, they were exasperated by the difficulties over the budget. After Independence, striking progress was made in the economic field. The Greeks nevertheless believed that they could have achieved still greater success but for the lack of a coordinated fiscal policy under central direction. And by 1963 they were almost unanimous in their demands for a revision of the Constitution. In November Makarios submitted thirteen amendments[1] to Dr Kutchuk for his consideration. Some of the suggestions were technical, a few had advantages for the Turks, others affected Turkish security. Nothing at this stage impinged upon the wider interests of Turkey under the Treaties of Guarantee and Alliance but the Turkish Government saw the attempt to change the basic articles as a dangerous precedent and rejected the proposals. Nevertheless some modification of the Constitution was indicated. Responsible Greek Cypriots have claimed that the British High Commissioner supported the idea.

The Archbishop had made his move at a time when intercommunal tension was high. Both sides had been stockpiling arms since Zurich and a clash was expected sooner or later. In December the Greeks launched a major attack on the Nicosia Turks, the first stage in a campaign to settle the problem by force. This recourse to aggression, in disregard of the Republic's treaty obligations and the international consequences, and their ruthless persecution of Turkish civilians led to a decline in public sympathy for the Greek case. The Greeks aimed at the subjugation of the Nicosia Turks by a swift knockout blow and, in consequence, the automatic surrender of the smaller Turkish communities in the rest of the island. The Turks were largely defenceless, the Turkish police having been disarmed as the result of a ruse on the part of the Greek

---

[1] *Cyprus Today, November–December 1963* (Greek Communal Chamber), vol. I, no. 6, Supplement.

Cypriot Minister for the Interior, Polykarpos Georkatzis, the day before the fighting started. Former EOKA members and other irregulars in groups of a hundred, usually led by the police, took part. Turks were murdered in their homes; 700 Turkish hostages, including women and children, were seized in the northern suburbs. The offensive was sanctioned by Makarios and the Cabinet but, according to the testimony of diplomats in the capital at the time, the Archbishop and some of the ministers were genuinely taken aback by the excesses committed; Makarios himself went to the hospital, the scene of atrocities. On Christmas day Turkish fighters from the mainland flew low over Nicosia, and the Turkish army contingent, stationed in Cyprus under the Treaty of Alliance, left its normal barracks to take up strategic positions in the Turkish villages of Ortakeuy and Geunyeli. The Nicosia–Kyrenia road, except for the last few miles south of the coast, now came under Turkish control. The Greek Cypriot leaders who had initially discounted the possibility of strong reaction from Turkey now feared that she might invade Cyprus. After some hesitation Makarios agreed that a joint truce force composed of British troops and liaison officers from the Greek and Turkish contingents should be set up under Major-General Young. The first British patrol became operational on 27 December. A permanent cease-fire line (known as the 'Green Line') was established in Nicosia and Larnaca and by the end of the year British troops had taken over all the tactical positions formerly held by Greek and Turkish Cypriots. This speedy action, made possible by the presence of the troops in the Sovereign Bases, averted much bloodshed and further intervention from Turkey.

On 1 January 1964 Makarios said he wished to terminate the Cyprus agreements. But a new crisis was temporarily averted pending the outcome of the London conference called by Britain for 15 January. The deadlock at this meeting was complete. The Greek Cypriots, backed by Greece, demanded 'unfettered independence' on the ground that the Zurich settlement was unworkable. The Turkish Cypriots wanted a separatist solution. Turkey's Foreign Minister, Mr Erkin, later described the Republic as a form of federal state without the geographical separation usually associated with this form of government.[1] The British urged the participation of other NATO powers in the peace force – a proposal which was rejected by Makarios.

In the meantime no further serious fighting had broken out in Cyprus, largely thanks to the effective manning of the 'Green Line' by British troops. However, once the danger of Turkish intervention had

[1] BBC Home Service, 29 January 1964.

passed, the Greek Cypriots regarded the British troops as defenders of the Turks and an obstacle to a total Greek victory. They alleged, moreover, that the 'Green Line' was facilitating partition by preventing normal contacts between the two communities. Both were, in fact, free to cross from one sector to the other. It was the fear of attack, abduction and reprisal which stopped them. Significantly, in places where no cease-fire line existed, each community remained in its own sector.

The Greeks used the January lull to import large quantities of arms. On 4 February they opened the second round of violence with the battle of Ghaziveran. In the same month a massive attack dislodged the Turks in Limassol from positions dominating the port and was followed by wanton destruction of Turkish property. The Turkish quarter of Ktima was also destroyed in retaliation for an incident believed to have been started by a Turk. Although hopelessly outnumbered, the Turks sometimes provoked incidents in the hope of obtaining Turkey's aid. Greek operations divided into those with some military aim and those of a punitive nature designed to reduce the morale of Turkish civilians. Greek police and irregulars in overwhelming strength would attack a Turkish village with large weapons from safe range, finally occupy it and carry out mopping-up operations. The British peace force, by this time completely at variance with the Greek Cypriot authorities, was obliged to stand aside at Limassol and elsewhere rather than openly clash with the police in the attempt to protect the Turks. The Turks saw their position as a struggle for survival. They were deprived of normal postal and telegraphic facilities, unable to enter or leave Cyprus without the risk of arrest or abduction, since the Greeks controlled the main communications. Nearly 20,000 had left their homes after the Christmas fighting; sixty per cent were refugees living in congested conditions in the Nicosia and Kyrenia districts; approximately 55,000 Turkish Cypriots relied mainly on food and medical supplies shipped from Turkey. The withdrawal of the Turks early in the New Year from the Government, on the ground that they no longer recognised its legality, facilitated Greek efforts to eliminate them from positions of importance.

During February Makarios, who was committed to the policy of non-alignment, rejected an American proposal for an enlarged peace force, possibly composed of troops from Western Europe in addition to members of NATO. The left wing, with its rooted objections to the extension of Western power, had to be placated. The Greek Cypriot leaders, moreover, believed that their aim could best be realised through the UN. On 15 February Britain, backed by Turkey, seized the initiative from the Greeks and appealed to the Security Council, which in a unanimous resolution[1] set up the United Nations Force in Cyprus (UNFICYP). It urged member states to refrain from 'any action or threat of action likely to worsen the situation ... or to endanger international peace'. It recommended that the function of the force should be to prevent a recurrence of fighting and contribute to the maintenance and restoration of law and order and a return to normal conditions. Britain provided the logistic support and the largest contingent but the force did not become operational until 27 March. Turkey in the meantime had threatened to intervene unless all fighting stopped forthwith.

By the time the UN arrived much of the fighting was over. The British force had contained the situation in Nicosia. The Turks, having suffered serious defeats elsewhere, had uprooted themselves either spontaneously or on orders from the TMT. Sporadic incidents were reduced by the lack of contact between the communities. UNFICYP, like the British, functioned on the principle of minimum force and by the consent of the Makarios Government. Without powers of search, arrest and disarmament, the contribution it was able to make to law and order was very limited, and in the last resort its effectiveness was determined by the small size of its own force compared with the vast numbers of armed men circulating in the Republic. The Greek Cypriots became rapidly disillusioned with the UN when they found it was neither prepared to disarm the Turks nor to take over the Nicosia–Kyrenia road from them by force. It soon became evident that they intended to cooperate with the UN only when it suited them. The day after the arrival of the mediator, Mr Tuomioja, a former Finnish Foreign Secretary, Makarios abrogated the Treaty of Alliance and hinted at the possibility of the mediator's failure even before he had a chance to start work. At the end of the month, while the Commander of UNFICYP, General Gyani, was negotiating a cease-fire on the eastern side of the Kyrenia Pass, Greek Cypriots, led personally by the Minister of Interior, launched a surprise attack against Hilarion, the Turkish stronghold to the west. The Secretary-General of the United Nations, U Thant, condemned their attack as 'a planned and organised military effort'.[2]

Many of the UN's propositions would have been feasible had the two communities been equal in numbers and military resources. But the failure to take sufficiently into account the population ratio of four

[1] UN doc. S/5575.
[2] UN doc. S/5671.

Greeks to one Turk led to a faulty assessment of the intercommunal problem. And the UN lost the confidence of the Turks from the outset. Its approach at the highest levels, doctrinaire, bureaucratic and bound by protocol, militated against them. For instance Greece was willing, in response to U Thant's appeal, to place her contingent under UNFICYP provided Turkey did likewise. The Greek Cypriots had nothing to lose by such a move. But for the Turks, who refused, it would have meant the withdrawal of troops from Geunyeli and a loss of protection for the Turkish sector of Nicosia. The UN accepted the massive importation of arms by the Cyprus Government as a legitimate right in defence of the state; Turkish efforts to bring in arms were stigmatised as 'smuggling'. UN plans for dismantling the fortifications of both sides, although theoretically impartial, would in practice have put the Turkish Cypriots at risk, since UNFICYP could not guarantee their safety from renewed attack by 30,000 Greek Cypriots armed and out of control. In day-to-day matters the UN got off to a bad start by withdrawing escorts for Turkish convoys, despite the fact that abductions were of recent date – 483 Turks were still missing in 1964 compared with 32 Greeks.

The first Turkish demonstration against the UN came early in April when Dr Bunche visited Paphos, the second at the end of the month when angry Turkish women confronted General Gyani with accusations of partiality towards the Greeks and demands for the return of Turkish hostages. Nevertheless the Turkish Cypriots would have been worse off without UNFICYP, despite its limitations. The soldiers on the ground were not unsympathetic to their plight and often more realistic than the political experts at headquarters.

Except for the Hilarion attack there were no major outbreaks of fighting during the first three months of the UN mandate; local incidents, however, continued. In May Turks attacked a Finnish patrol, mistaking it at night for Greeks. Two Greek army officers who ventured into the Turkish walled city at Famagusta were shot dead. Thirty-two Turks were immediately seized by the Greeks as a reprisal. The Greek Cypriots intensified warlike preparations with the purchase of heavy arms and the introduction of conscription. They insisted that these measures were solely for the defence of the island against Turkey and not for use against the Turkish Cypriots. Turkish arms and reinforcements were landed secretly. In June a new threat of intervention by Turkey prompted President Johnson to invite the Turkish Prime Minister, Ismet Inonu, to Washington to discuss the Cyprus problem. On his return, he was assured by the British Government that it still upheld the Zurich settlement. Diplomatic efforts to bring Greece and Turkey together for talks were hampered, however, by the fact that Greece had aligned herself with Makarios in no longer recognising its validity.

The Archbishop's contacts with Nasser and the USSR were disturbing to the American Government, which now favoured bringing Cyprus under the umbrella of NATO by means of some form of Enosis. During July, Greek and Turkish representatives met the mediator separately in Geneva to consider a proposal initiated by Dean Acheson, a former Secretary of State. Acheson's plan provided for union with Greece; for a military base under Turkish sovereignty and two Turkish cantons exercising local autonomy; for the compensation of Turkish Cypriots wanting to leave Cyprus and the cession of the small Greek island, Kastellorizon, to Turkey. The Greeks rejected the plan; the Turks wanted a canton large enough to contain the great majority of the Turkish Cypriots.

During August, General Grivas, who had returned to Cyprus earlier in the summer, launched a major attack on his own initiative against Turkish villages in the Mansoura area. The operation, which was in breach of an assurance given by Makarios to the UN Commander,[1] was intended to neutralise the Kokkina beach-head, the nearest point to Turkey and a centre for smuggling arms and men. The Greek Cypriots quickly overran several Turkish coastal villages. Turkey prevented the fall of Kokkina, which was imminent, by attacking Greek villages with high explosives and napalm bombs from the air. Inonu's critics at home who had long advocated a tougher policy on Cyprus were placated, but Greece and Turkey were again close to war. When the talks were resumed in Geneva on 15 August the Turks rejected a revised version of the Acheson plan which was less favourable to them than the first plan.[2] In the meantime the prospects of a political settlement were further undermined by the sudden death of the mediator, Mr Tuomioja, who was respected and trusted by both sides. Mr Galo Plaza Lasso, an ex-President of Ecuador, was appointed his successor.

By the end of 1964 the conditions which the Zurich settlement had sought to maintain ceased to exist. The island was in the throes of becoming a huge arsenal; the illegal forces circulating in the Republic on the Greek side alone included the National Guard, Greek army officers who were arriving in large numbers, various private armies and

---

[1] H. D. Purcell, *Cyprus* (Benn Ltd, London), p. 351.
[2] See Robert Stephens, *Cyprus: A Place of Arms* (Pall Mall Press, London, 1966), p. 201.

the rump of the EOKA extremists. On the Turkish side were the army officers from the mainland, who directed security in the enclaves and trained the TMT irregulars who later became the disciplined, uniformed force known as the Turkish Fighters. At international level the agreements had failed. Greece and Turkey were wide apart. The nearest the guarantors had been able to get to the implementation of the Treaty of Guarantee was the formation of the Joint Force. Britain had borne the brunt of the operation with Greek and Turkish officers playing but a token part; the exercise was never repeated. From now on Britain's role as the main guarantor became increasingly negative.

The years 1965–1967 were a period of military expansion by the forces of both sides; as the years went by demobilised National Guardsmen formed an ever-expanding reserve which could be called into action at short notice. Greek officers and NCOs who landed secretly eventually totalled 10,000. The burden of mobilisation fell most heavily on the Turks who, as a small community, could ill spare the manpower. The Turks served for four years in contrast to the National Guardsmen's maximum period of two. The danger of a major flare-up was constantly present in the manned confrontation areas. The Government, at the risk of provoking serious incidents with the Turks, sought to reassert its control over the whole of the Republic. As far as the Turks were concerned, the Government had ceased to exist as a legal entity after the 1963 fighting and they refused to recognise its jurisdiction. Conflict also arose over social issues – harvesting rights, the movement of one community across the territory of the other.

In these difficult conditions the UN functioned by persuasion. The turnover in troops was rapid and performance varied from unit to unit. The personality of a single officer in handling a delicate problem could make the difference between success and failure. UNFICYP wherever possible interposed its forces between the combatants. In the political field the outlook for UN mediation was discouraging. The two communities remained diametrically opposed. The Greeks were determined to create a unitary state in which the Turks had only minority rights and returned to their own villages. The Turks were convinced that short of partition only federal government could give them security. The traumatic experiences they had suffered at the hands of the Greeks in 1963, the years of restriction and deprivation which followed were not likely to be forgotten in living memory and were decisive in moulding current Turkish attitudes and their demands for the future. The Turkish rejection of a plan produced by Galo Plaza in March 1965 was therefore not surprising. The report,[1] which specifically excluded Enosis and partition, supported independence and suggested that Turkish minority rights could be guaranteed by the UN under the supervision of a commissioner on the spot. Since the Turks had seen the ease with which the Greeks brushed aside the UN's authority, the suggestion that they could be protected by a UN commissioner was derisory and they refused to accept Galo Plaza as mediator from then on. Makarios, however, would accept none other. Mediation at high level was brought to an end by the deadlock and Galo Plaza's resignation.

Life in Cyprus after Independence was characterised by long spells of uneasy calm broken by a major intercommunal crisis every few years; each new crisis brought the island closer to disaster. From 1966 onwards the Cyprus Government's extension of coastal defences aggravated local strife. The UN recognised the right of the state to defend its territory, but in the words of its own representative defence requirements were 'so far-reaching as to cover virtually any military measures it [the Government] might choose to take'.[2] Such operations, which could stretch far inland, encroached upon the positions of the Turks, who retaliated with a crop of new fortifications. In 1967 tension increased when the Cyprus Government formed a new para-military unit in the police and imported large quantities of Czech arms. Furthermore, the National Guard increasingly identified itself with the Greek army; its barracks displayed their slogans. And the doctrine of Enosis was extensively propagated by Greek officers from the mainland.

Paradoxically, the Greeks, in their determination to resist any move which took the island a step nearer to partition, resorted to tactics which only made the Turks more insistent on a separatist solution. The main weapon of the Greek Cypriots was the blockade. This could be permanent as in the case of Kokkina, which existed under siege for nearly four years, or temporary as in the case of the Nicosia enclave, which was shut off by the Greeks for two days on one occasion and two weeks on another. A stringent ban on strategic materials, which included many essential commodities used in daily life, was applied to all the Turkish communities. The economy suffered drastically in consequence. The two communities were caught up in the cycle of reprisals. The Turks took their revenge wherever they had sufficient strength to do so even though this put at risk their kinsmen who were at the mercy of the Greeks. The tactics of retaliation came to a climax in the Larnaca district when the Turkish strategic stronghold of Kophinou again

---

[1] *Report of the United Nations Mediator on Cyprus to the Secretary-General,* UN doc. S/6253.

[2] UN doc. S/6426, para. 15.

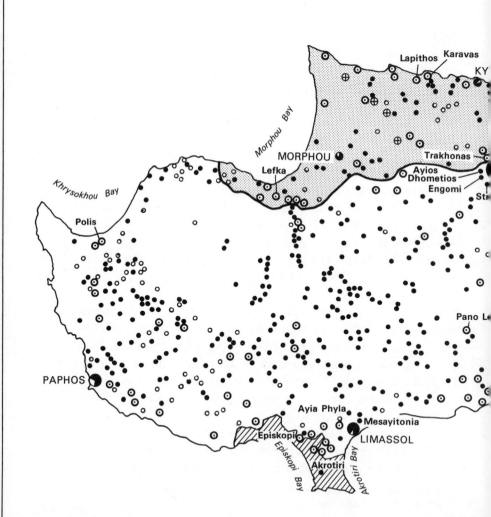

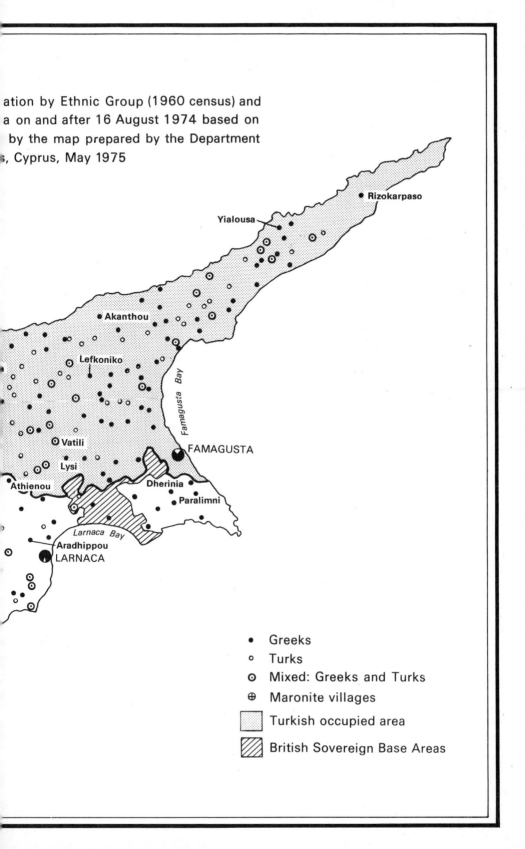

ation by Ethnic Group (1960 census) and
a on and after 16 August 1974 based on
by the map prepared by the Department
, Cyprus, May 1975

Rizokarpaso

Yialousa

Akanthou

Lefkoniko

Famagusta Bay

Vatili

FAMAGUSTA

Lysi

Athienou

Dherinia

Paralimni

Larnaca Bay

Aradhippou
LARNACA

- • Greeks
- ○ Turks
- ◉ Mixed: Greeks and Turks
- ⊕ Maronite villages
- Turkish occupied area
- British Sovereign Base Areas

became the centre of serious unrest. The Turks frequently held up Greek cars on the main road. On 26 January Grivas ordered a battalion supported by armoured cars to advance on Kophinou. UNFICYP obtained from the local Turkish commander an undertaking not to hold up the traffic and the National Guard stopped short of Kophinou. Serious incidents nevertheless continued in the area and culminated in a four-hour gun battle near Mari on 8 April.

On 21 April 1967 Papandreou's Government in Greece was overthrown in the bloodless *coup d'état* which brought the colonels, Papadopoulos, Makarezos and Pattakos to power. From the moment that Papandreou, in collaboration with Makarios, decided to send large numbers of Greek troops to Cyprus the fate of the island became as inextricably bound up with politics in Greece as if Enosis had taken place. Colonel Papadopoulos, the new Prime Minister, had himself served with Greek intelligence in Cyprus and the rise of the Greek Army to political power was bound to have far-reaching repercussions on developments in the island. The summit talks with Turkey, planned by the previous Government, went ahead in September on the Evros frontier but ended in failure, the military leaders of Greece having underestimated the extent of Turkish objections to Enosis.

At the end of September, Rauf Denktash, President of the Turkish Cypriot Communal Chamber, landed secretly in the Karpas and was arrested, his legal entry having been prevented by the Cyprus Government's threat to prosecute him in connection with the 1963 troubles. His release was strongly urged by Turkey, the Western embassies and the UN. After a visit from his former colleague, Glavkos Klerides, Denktash adopted a conciliatory tone in place of his former militancy. Makarios resisted local pressure for his trial and on 12 November he was sent back to Turkey on the undertaking not to return to Cyprus illegally. The Archbishop's prudence was, however, nullified shortly afterwards by reckless action on the part of Grivas, who on 15 November mounted a strong attack against the Turks at Kophinou.[1] The area had remained in a state of constant unrest and the new crisis followed a spate of violence in which the Turks were the chief victims. The dispute centred on the Cyprus Government's right to send police patrols via the direct route to Aghios Theodoros, a mixed village where the Turks came under the control of the Turkish Fighters in Kophinou. Because of serious incidents during the summer, patrols via the direct route had been temporarily suspended but the Greeks were now impatient to resume them. The presence of armed police, Greek or Turkish, in a mixed

---

[1] See UN doc. S/8248, 16 November 1967, for details of the Kophinou incident.

village was a provocative arrangement. However, the UN, which at top level was often more concerned with academic considerations of protocol than with the realities of civil war, gave the Greek Cypriots moral encouragement by upholding their viewpoint while trying at the same time to discourage them from reinstating the patrols by force. The day before the attack, UNFICYP notified the Cyprus authorities that since Denktash's release the Turkish Government was ready to reconsider its stand on the patrols. Nevertheless three Greek Cypriot police patrols escorted by the National Guard were sent along the direct route to Aghios Theodoros. The Turks warned UNFICYP that further patrols would be resisted. Fighting broke out in the village after National Guardsmen escorting a fourth patrol removed a Turkish road-block. About the same time, the Greeks launched the attack against Kophinou. Fatal casualties included twenty-seven Turks and two Greeks. Nine Turkish Cypriots were seriously wounded. At Kophinou many houses were gutted. The UN British contingent (First Battalion of the Royal Green Jackets), which had recently taken over the area from the Swedes, came under heavy fire. The National Guard, under the command of Greek officers, tried to drive the soldiers away so that there would be no UN witnesses to the battle. However, they fought back with fists and rifle butts; not one left his post. The British troops received but scant recognition for their firm stand apart from some passing concern for their safety expressed in the House of Commons.[1]

The fighting did not end until early the next morning, when the Greek Government under pressure from Turkey ordered Grivas to withdraw all forces from the area of operations. The question of the patrols, however, had become a matter of national pride. Further armed patrols were sent to Aghios Theodoros in defiance of UNFICYP's advice and a sharp warning from Turkey. Greece tried to placate the Turkish Government by recalling Grivas and appointing the experienced diplomat and politician, Panayotis Pipinellis, Foreign Minister. But Turkish preparations for war went ahead and on 24 November President Sunay notified several Western states and the Soviet Union that Turkey was determined to settle the problem 'once and for all'. The same day U Thant reported, 'Greece and Turkey are now on the brink of war'.[2] The Turks were expected to land in Cyprus that week-end but freak storms in the Eastern Mediterranean upset the timetable. During the delay an intensive peace drive got under way, in

[1] 16 November 1967, H.C. Deb., vol. 754, cols 635–7.
[2] UN doc. S/8248 add. 5.

which President Johnson's special envoy, Cyrus Vance, the Canadian Prime Minister, Lester Pearson, the NATO Secretary-General, Manlio Brosio, and U Thant took part. Turkey's terms for calling off the invasion included the permanent removal of Grivas and all illegal forces in Cyprus and the disbandment of the National Guard. Vance left for home at the end of the month, having finally obtained agreement between Greece and Turkey. But the danger of war was renewed when Makarios expressed reservations on the disbandment of the National Guard, prior to a final settlement, and Vance was suddenly recalled to Nicosia. U Thant, who put his good offices at the disposal of the contestants, suggested that peace could best be served by the withdrawal of the illegal forces from Cyprus and the extension of UNFICYP's mandate to cover the supervision of disarmament and special security measures. The Greek Cypriots were against any increase in UNFICYP's powers and their stand was supported by the USSR and France in the Security Council, which on 22 December renewed UNFICYP's mandate without change.[1]

In the course of the next few weeks some 10,000 Greek troops left Cyprus – their departure watched by the Turks from the ramparts of the Old City in Famagusta. About 1,000 Greek officers remained behind with the National Guard. The Turks made no complaint since this would have weakened their position in retaining the Turkish officers who controlled security in the enclaves.

A new crisis broke out a week later when the Turkish Cypriots formed the Provisional Cyprus Turkish Administration, which had the semblance of a ready-made government capable of taking over on a separatist basis in the event of a final settlement. The Turkish Foreign Minister, Mr Kuneralp, in Cyprus at the time, told the UN representative that the change was intended to facilitate administration and not to promote partition or the creation of a separate state. U Thant, however, was strongly critical of the action.

The Kophinou crisis was a turning-point in the island's post-colonial history. It had demonstrated the folly of trying to press for Enosis in the teeth of Turkey's opposition and forced the Cypriot nationalist leaders to reverse their stand and to favour a compromise. Makarios found himself in a stronger position to pursue a policy of moderation. The shelving of Enosis could reasonably be attributed to factors outside his control. Grivas, the most dangerous of his opponents, was held incommunicado by the colonels in Athens. At the end of 1967 Makarios said that in view of the failure of the Greco-Turkish dialogue and the

[1] UN docs S/PV 1385 (20 Dec. 1967); S/PV 1386 (22 Dec. 1967).

evacuation of the Greek forces from Cyprus a solution must be sought 'within the limits of what is feasible which does not always coincide with what is desirable'.[1] His re-election as President on 25 February 1968, with a 95 per cent vote in his favour and few abstentions, marked public acceptance of the new policy. The Turks, however, were not convinced. His sole opponent, the Nicosia psychiatrist Dr Evdokas, had based his campaign on Enosis. The Archbishop denied that his defeat meant the death of Enosis, thereby confirming the perennial suspicions of the Turks that whatever the Greeks might say their ultimate objectives were the same.

On 7 March Makarios lifted the last restrictions on the Turks. The move was highly praised by U Thant, who criticised the Turkish leaders for still refusing to allow Greeks into their enclaves. The Turks, as the minority, were at a permanent disadvantage and wary of concessions which could either weaken their defences or their negotiating power pending a final settlement, and they had yet to be convinced that the peace move was genuine. In the event the pacification policy got off to a bad start in April with the demolition by the Greeks of empty Turkish houses at Omorphita and the militant display of the Czech weapons at the EOKA day parade. Intercommunal tension rose in May. A Turkish lorry carrying seven machine-guns was intercepted by Greek Cypriot policemen. Shortly afterwards two Turks were killed, the one by the police and the other by the National Guard. But in June the outlook improved. The patient efforts of the UN representative, Osorio Tafall, resulted in the start of talks between the two Cypriot leaders, Klerides and Denktash. For the first time in five years the intercommunal problem entered a phase of detente.

After Independence, Makarios acquired a wide reputation for political astuteness. It was therefore surprising, even allowing for human fallibility, that he should have embarked on a course of action in 1964 which had obvious dangers from the outset. He introduced conscription and agreed to the stationing of large numbers of Greek officers in the island. The purpose was twofold: the defence of Cyprus against Turkey and the assimilation of the irregular bands which threatened internal security into a disciplined army under government control. In reality there was little Cyprus could do to prevent an invasion by so powerful a neighbour as Turkey except avoid provocation. Conscription armed the Archbishop's enemies as well as his supporters. And the assimilation of irregulars was only partially successful, for in the long term the National

[1] *Cyprus Mail,* 1 January 1968.

Guard and the reserve provided trained recruits for future dissident groups. At the end of British rule EOKA was still a small close-knit organisation, split into the supporters of Makarios who advocated independence and the extremist followers of Grivas who were determined to stake everything on Enosis. The dissident group, although capable of harassment, intimidation and sporadic outbursts of violence, could not have begun to mount a *coup d'état* or an effective opposition to the legal government. Cyprus after 1964 became a vast arsenal; far larger forces than ever before were drawn into the conflict between Makarios and Grivas; the island was at the mercy of the intrigues and uncertainties of mainland politics, and eventually the ambitions of the military dictatorship. The Greek officers were politically an unknown quantity, but in view of the army's irredentist tradition there was the inherent risk that individual officers far from home would use their position to propagate the doctrines of Enosis. The Archbishop therefore put at risk his own safety and the policy of independence without any compensatory advantages in the sphere of national security. The significance of these mistakes did not become fully apparent until early 1969 when terrorism revived on the Greek side with the rise of the National Front.

The toleration of a police force split into political factions since the time of EOKA, the appointment of militant ex-guerrillas to positions of power, the massive importation of arms and their indiscriminate distribution created conditions in which subversion flourished. The National Front was formed by EOKA extremists and based on Limassol. Its early attacks were directed against police officers and individuals known to be loyal to Makarios. It seized arms, raided villages and assaulted a branch secretary of the Unified Party, which supported Enosis. Like its predecessor EOKA it was pro-Enosis and anti-communist; its links with Greek army officers were soon suspected. Makarios was slow to act against the National Front; its existence strengthened his arguments against concessions to the Turks; it was potentially useful as a counterweight in certain contingencies to the newly-formed political parties which constituted the first serious challenge to his monopoly of political power. Consequently the Front was not proscribed until August 1969. The following January, measures were taken to provide for the detention of suspects for up to three months but the day the Bill was debated in the House of Representatives the Front announced a temporary 'suspension' of action. The Government, reluctant to enforce a law which recalled colonial repression, decided to invoke it only if the Front struck again.

The local Communists were, as always, well informed and not reassured. They had never had the same easy access to arms as the right wing and stood to lose most in a show of force between the political parties. Strong rumours that Greece and Turkey, exasperated by the lack of progress in the intercommunal talks, were about to impose a settlement gave rise to further anxiety. The time was ripe for Soviet intervention. Makarios, as the exponent of the policy of non-alignment, was adept at manipulating the delicate balance between East and West, and with his approval AKEL approached the Russians. On 17 February the official Soviet News Agency, Tass, accused the imperialist powers of plotting against the independence of Cyprus, and the National Front and other reactionary forces, allegedly associated with the Greek regime, of spreading Enosis propaganda with the aim of setting up in Cyprus a NATO base and a military dictatorship.

On 8 March the President's helicopter was attacked by gunmen from the roof of the Pancyprian Gymnasium, just after he had taken off to attend an EOKA memorial service for Afxentiou at Makheras Monastery. Makarios escaped unhurt. After escorting the pilot, who was seriously wounded, to hospital he went by road to Makheras and conducted the service as planned. The National Front disclaimed liability and was later exculpated by Makarios. The authorities, who immediately focused attention on Polykarpos Georkatzis as the possible instigator of the attack, stopped him at the airport from leaving Cyprus. Two days later, one week after the helicopter incident, he was found dead near Kythrea. Georkatzis had lost his post as Minister for the Interior the previous year as the result of pressure from the Greek junta, which linked him with a plot to kill the Greek Prime Minister, Colonel Papadopoulos. For years he had exercised power and control over the police, which was largely composed of ex-EOKA members and his own supporters. He operated his own private army and set up an intelligence network which was reputed to have penetrated every security and political organisation in the island, except AKEL. It is probable that the murderers of Georkatzis wanted him eliminated before he had a chance to make embarrassing disclosures. The Cyprus Government strongly denied that Greek army officers were responsible for his murder. At the helicopter trial he was named as a conspirator on two counts, but the Court refused to allow his widow to call witnesses to clear his name and to eradicate it from the indictment. In the long-drawn-out proceedings, locally known as 'the Trial of Georkatzis', four men – a student, a businessman, and two members of the police – were eventually found guilty of trying to kill Makarios and the helicopter pilot, and of conspiracy. All had pleaded not guilty. Polykarpos Polykarpou, a police constable, and Kostas Ioannides, director of the opposition paper *Gnomi* and son of Polykarpos Ioannides, whom the British had exiled to the Seychelles in 1956, were acquitted for want of evidence. Kostas Ioannides was deported to Greece in defiance of a Supreme Court interim order banning this action. This clash between the executive and the judiciary was yet one more indication of the breakdown of law and order in the Republic.

The part-fulfilment of the Tass prophecy enabled the Communists to revert to the theme of a Western plot with renewed authority and to stir up Turkey's anxieties with warnings of a forthcoming Greek-sponsored coup in Cyprus. On 19 March the Turkish Foreign Minister stated that any attempt to carry out a coup would be resisted by Turkey with all her forces and strength.[1] Relations between Greece and Turkey were seriously endangered for the first time since the Kophinou incident in 1967. The possibility of drastic action by the Turks unleashed a wave of diplomatic activity in Western capitals. And the authorities in Greece went to great lengths to persuade the Turks that the Soviet action was aimed at the disruption of NATO's eastern flank and that Ankara's fears were groundless.

The junta was not alone in seeing Makarios as an obstacle to a settlement with the Turks, but whatever its true role in the recent Cypriot conspiracies it was determined to dissociate itself from the abortive attempt to remove Makarios.

On 23 May the National Front struck again. Twenty gunmen captured Limassol Central Police Station, escaping with arms and ammunition valued at £15,000. The raid exceeded in scope and military skill anything ever attempted by EOKA against the British. Twenty-one men were in due course given prison sentences varying from four to five years. They included Michael Rossides, whom the British had sentenced to death[2] and now reputed to be the head of the National Front, a National Guard officer, and two members of the police.

Parliamentary elections, already long overdue owing to the intercommunal troubles, went ahead on 5 July without incident. Thirty-five seats were contested by five parties, none of which won an absolute majority, and the Communists substantially increased their strength.[3]

---

[1] Cyprus Mail, 20 March 1970.

[2] See above, pp. 248–9.

[3] The Unified Party (Klerides) 15; AKEL (Papaioannou) 9; the Progressive Front (Ioannides) 7; the Democratic Centre Union (Lyssarides) 2; Independents 2. The National Democratic Party (Evdokas) gained no seats.

The politicians had in the main endorsed the policy of independence and the continuation of the intercommunal talks. However, Dr Ioannides, the surgeon and Mayor of Nicosia, qualified his stand with an appeal for self-determination which to most Cypriots meant the sure route to Enosis. Dr Evdokas, who openly campaigned for Enosis, gained no seats. Shortly before the election he was imprisoned as the author of an article, 'Machievelli to Makarios', published by *Gnomi*. The Turks elected fifteen members to the Turkish Communal Chambers and Denktash was returned as chairman.

The dramatic events on the Greek side obscured the fact that a settlement of the intercommunal problem upon which the island's future depended was as remote as ever. As the years went by the expansion of the confrontation areas was matched by widening psychological barriers; both sides became more entrenched in their attitude of mutual hostility and a whole generation was growing up which had never known personally any member of the other community.

The intercommunal talks were now in their third year without any real progress having been made. The main obstacle was the Archbishop's refusal to yield to the Turkish demand for complete authority in their own areas. His stand was not surprising. *De facto* partition already existed; with the passing of time its roots grew deeper. Having borne the brunt of the Zurich agreement Makarios found it difficult to endorse a settlement which would make the division *de jure* and expose himself to accusations of a second sell-out. The Greek Cypriots, moreover, were not dissatisfied with the stalemate. Striking economic progress on their side had generated a euphoria which made it easy to forget the long-term problem and the serious risk inherent in delaying a solution. It was the Turkish Cypriots who suffered from the continuing uncertainty about the island's future status. Their preoccupation with security left them in a state of economic stagnation and dependent on a large annual subsidy from Turkey, which was absorbed by defence and administrative costs. The contrast with the affluence of the Greek Cypriots was disturbing.

The Turks were convinced that the rival groups of Greeks were all working for Enosis, that the differences between them centred solely on the matter of timing. The Greeks contributed to this belief by flagrant inconsistencies between official policy and public utterances on the subject. Open support for Enosis was not, for instance, limited to patriotic outbursts behind the closed doors of the junior officers' mess. Only that year General Yerakinis, Commander of the National Guard, had made a strong nationalistic speech in Paphos. The campaign also found outlets in the statements of ministers and government officials. Even Makarios, upon whom the survival of the independence policy depended, lapsed into oblique references to Enosis, giving the impression that any settlement short of this was but an interim expedient. In the circumstances, the conciliatory gestures he made from time to time, the offers to rehouse Turkish refugees at Government expense, were lost in a welter of distrust.

In August 1970, after a long period of peace, intercommunal incidents were renewed. The most serious was at Trikomo, where a National Guardsman killed a Turk and wounded two others when they drove into a restricted area. The Turks retaliated by holding up traffic on the north coast where they controlled a stretch of the road. In 1971 the situation remained tense. Both sides over the years had improved their military capacity so that the risk of large-scale confrontation was greater than in the past. The situation worsened in September. The intercommunal talks reached a complete deadlock. General Grivas returned secretly to Cyprus; in November ESEA (the Co-ordination Committee for the Enosis Struggle) was formed as a front organisation for his activities. Pledged to self-determination and Enosis, its members included eminent and reputable citizens such as the former President of the Supreme Court, Mr Justice Vassiliades. A new crisis broke in January 1972 with the disclosure by a pro-Enosis Athens newspaper that the Cyprus Government had been secretly importing additional arms and ammunition from Czechoslovakia. The cargo, consigned as explosives for industrial use and transported in a Danish freighter from Yugoslavia via Syria to the small mining port of Xeros, was moved shortly after its arrival from a disused mine to the greater seclusion of the archbishopric and Athalassa Police Head-quarters. The original order was believed to have been placed the previous summer in response to a request from Greek Cypriot villagers who complained that Turkish Fighters in the Chattos area were blocking the access to their fields. Certain left-wing politicians close to Makarios, anxious to redress the balance of the right wing's overriding superiority in arms, favoured the formation of a militia to assist the police. And with the return of Grivas the plan acquired a new impetus and purpose, which explained the cargo's delayed arrival, the purchase of heavy weapons more suitable for war than police work, and the large quantities imported – far in excess of anything needed for dealing with inter-communal unrest.

The Archbishop's relations with the Greek junta, uneasy at the best of times, flared into open rift. The imprudent choice of Czechoslovakia was probably dictated by nothing more sinister than considerations of cost and availability. However, the junta's fear that the arms might get into the hands of the Cypriot Communists and fellow-travellers was well-founded. The incident, moreover, put Greco-Turkish relations at risk once again. The Kophinou disaster had taught the junta the danger of antagonising the Turks and during the second week in February Greece made a *démarche* to the United Nations which brought her into alignment with the Turkish Government, which had also protested to the Secretary-General the same week. The Cyprus authorities, having denied all knowledge of the arms, now claimed that the Greek Government had been aware of the plan all along and that the heavy arms were for the National Guard, the personal weapons for the police. Makarios refused the junta's request to surrender the arms to the National Guard, which would have enabled Greek army officers in Cyprus to control their use. In a stiff note to the Archbishop on 11 February, which stressed that Athens, not Nicosia, was 'the national centre of Hellenism', the Greek Ambassador, Mr Panayotakos, called upon him to hand over all the imported arms to UNFICYP and to form a government of national unity. Makarios, however much he might dislike it, was a prisoner of the Greek dictatorship, since he could not get rid of the Greek officers he had invited in 1964 to form and train the National Guard. He eventually reshuffled the Council of Ministers and replaced members who had been consistently hostile to the military regime by others who were at least neutral in their attitude. After protracted negotiations between the UN special representative and the Cyprus Government the arms were placed inside the fortified perimeter of UNFICYP's base camp, under the supervision of unarmed Greek Cypriot police. The explosives were too dangerous to move.

The situation nevertheless remained unstable. The Greek Government had lost control over Grivas; his presence, a breach of the undertaking given to the Turks after the Kophinou incident, was a constant threat to security. Grivas, who had at his disposal a number of well trained guerrilla groups, was also in collusion with the Greek Cypriot bishops, Kition, Kyrenia and Paphos. Members of the Holy Synod of the Orthodox Church in Cyprus, they demanded Makarios's resignation as President on the ground that his exercise of temporal and political power conflicted with his religious duties and was a violation of Canon Law. Since the Archbishop's political role had never been challenged by the Greek Cypriots before, this belated introduction of Canon Law as a weapon indicated the desperation felt by his rivals in their efforts to precipitate his downfall.

Clashes between the pro-Government elements and the Grivas supporters continued for the rest of the year. The Grivas groups vigorously opposed the intercommunal talks and demanded a referendum on Enosis. In November the existence of EOKA B, a right-wing guerrilla movement formed by Grivas, came to light; the same month, four men were detained in connection with a suspected plot against Makarios after an arms cache was found near the archbishopric. Makarios nevertheless remained confident that the Government was able to control the illegal groups.

The year 1973 was a turbulent one for the Greek Cypriots. Violence increased; the confrontation between Makarios and the bishops reached a climax. Makarios who, twenty years earlier, had been repeatedly urged by the colonial regime to make an outright condemnation of violence now did so. But condemnation came too late to save Cyprus. The year began with renewed demands from the bishops for Makarios's resignation. The bishops had shown themselves to be essentially naïve and parochial in thinking that they could oust Makarios in a long and relentless campaign, and they were out-manoeuvred by him. He enjoyed popular support at home; his estrangement from the junta assured him of respect abroad. The Communists, the best organised and the only cohesive political group in the island, backed him to the hilt, partly out of motives of self-interest and partly in compliance with Moscow's directives. The Soviet Union had a vested interest in his survival, which was a safeguard against Enosis and the extension of NATO's influence. His adamant refusal to give way to the Turks helped to perpetuate a dispute which was damaging to the Western alliance. Only recently the Soviet Ambassador had come out publicly in his favour. The enemies of Makarios were to be found amongst the intelligentsia and the security forces. In terms of numbers this was but a small minority – a minority which none the less showed signs of getting out of control because it was backed by force. The chances of dislodging Makarios by lawful means were slender. Since no one dared to stand against him in the presidential elections he was automatically re-elected in February.

After the election violence increased. Raids on police stations, the theft of arms, sometimes in collusion with members of the force, and bomb explosions became commonplace events. The British had learnt to their cost that the creation of a reliable police force could prove impossible once the rot of political corruption had set in and Makarios was now faced with the same problem. In March he formed the Tactical Reserve Force to help deal with the disorders. Its five hundred recruits were handpicked for their loyalty and trained on para-military lines. The Turks were alarmed; any increase in Greek Cypriot military strength was always seen as a potential threat to themselves.

During April EOKA B murdered a member of the socialist party EDEK, and pro-Government irregulars killed one of Grivas's supporters in Limassol. In July the Minister of Justice was kidnapped and held in captivity for a month. Grivas demanded an amnesty for all political prisoners as a condition of his release. A plan to abduct the Minister of the Interior was foiled. In August an ambush intended for Makarios was discovered on the Nicosia–Troodos road in time; in October bombs exploded near Aghios Serghios shortly before he was due to pass on his way to take a church service. Security operations were intensified throughout the year. Complaints of ill-treatment, made by both sides, were the subject of controversy.

On 25 November the junta in Greece was overthrown by a *coup d'état* and replaced by a military regime which was still more authoritarian in character. Its official policy towards Cyprus, however, remained unchanged – the pursuit of a settlement based on independence through intercommunal talks.

In January 1974 two prominent members of the Government, Glavkos Klerides and Tassos Papadopoulos, publicly criticised Grivas whose presence had become a serious embarrassment to the Government which, however, did not want to elevate him to martyrdom with his arrest. He was known to be in ill health and the probability of an early death from natural causes seemed to offer the best way out of the dilemma. On 27 January Grivas died from a heart attack. Two days later EOKA B announced a suspension of its activities and Makarios declared an amnesty. The move was premature, and before the month was out violent clashes took place between the rival factions. A large quantity of arms was stolen from a National Guard camp. Although a rallying point for the extremists, Grivas was not the sole motivating force behind EOKA B as he had been in the first guerrilla movement during British rule. EOKA B overlapped with the National Guard thereby coming under the influence of Greek army officers. On 25 April, after two village raids in which the inhabitants and a priest were beaten up, the Government made EOKA B an illegal organisation. Makarios explained that the policy of leniency had been abused by the subversive groups and gave their members forty-eight hours to surrender.

The proscription of EOKA B made little difference to the wave of violence. At the end of April Makarios saw the Greek Ambassador in connection with the disorders. By the early summer it was widely known that he planned to reduce the number of Greek officers attached to the National Guard. On 2 July he wrote to President Ghizikis of Greece alleging that the junta was hatching plots against him:

> More than once I have sensed and on occasion almost felt, the invisible hand stretched out from Athens seeking to destroy my human existence.[1]

Makarios also accused the junta of complicity in Grivas's return to Cyprus, in the political murders and many other crimes committed in the name of Enosis by EOKA B which he had formed. The National Guard, staffed by Greek officers from the start, had been the chief source of EOKA B's men and materials, he wrote. The opposition press which backed its criminal activities was financed from Athens; even the three bishops who demanded his deposition were controlled from Athens. The National Guard as constituted and officered had become a centre of conspiracy against the state. The Greek Government, he continued, could end this situation, and the violence and terror exercised by EOKA B. Makarios requested the replacement of the Greek officers by one hundred military instructors to help reorganise the Cyprus armed forces. Makarios ensured that this ultimatum was not confined to the archives of secret diplomacy by informing local journalists[2] a week later that relations with Greece had not been harmonious for a long time, that his letter to Ghizikis would soon be released for publication, and that the National Guard was in future to be manned by Cypriot officers. Makarios dismissed reports of a coup, but said if one should take place he felt it had no chance of success. The Greek Cypriots had been lured into complacency by the plethora of rumours; only the left wing took them seriously. Warnings had come from the Soviet Union and from the Americans: it was surprising that Makarios should have disregarded the latter.

The Ghizikis dictatorship probably did not differ from the first Greek junta in seeing Makarios as an obstacle to a settlement of the Cyprus question and in disliking his fraternisation with local and international communism. But whereas the Papadopoulos regime had learned caution after the Kophinou incident, the new dictators were more fanatical in their nationalistic ambitions, more reckless in their methods and incredibly blind to the possible reactions of Turkey. The Archbishop's boldness in challenging the junta was a risky manoeuvre. His letter, however, is likely to have been a decisive factor only in the

[1] *Sunday Times*, 21 July 1974.
[2] *Cyprus Bulletin* (PIO. Republic of Cyprus), 10 July 1974.

timing of the coup. The idea of eliminating Makarios by force as a last resort was not new, but once he showed his determination to purge the National Guard without delay the junta needed to act quickly. And on 15 July the National Guard, led by Greek officers, overthrew the Cyprus Government. The Nicosia broadcasting station was seized at dawn, the archbishopric was severely damaged and the presidential palace destroyed. Serious fighting broke out between the National Guard on the one hand and the Tactical Reserve and the various groups loyal to Makarios on the other. Casualties were heavy. Before the end of the day Nikos Sampson, an ex-EOKA leader whom the British had sentenced to death, was proclaimed President of the Republic. Makarios, who was at first reported dead, escaped to Paphos via the Troodos mountains. At his request he was taken by RAF helicopter from Paphos to the safety of the British Sovereign Base at Akrotiri. On 16 July the RAF flew him to London.

On the day of the coup the Turkish Cypriots withdrew into the relative safety of the enclaves. The Turkish Prime Minister, Bulent Ecevit, flew to London on 17 July to seek British cooperation under the Treaty of Guarantee. But the British Government was not prepared to send troops to Cyprus for this purpose. Turkish intervention had only been narrowly averted in the past; diplomatic observers regarded it as inevitable in the event of any new attack upon the Turkish Cypriots; the surprising factor was that it should have been triggered by an all-Greek conflict. It was not certain whether the junta would have ordered the National Guard in due course either to attack the Turks or to seize the whole island. But Turkey was not prepared to take a chance. On 20 July the Turkish armed forces launched a sea- and airborne operation against the island. Troops came ashore west of Kyrenia and paratroopers were dropped in the central plain near Geunyeli. The objective was to establish a bridgehead in the Kyrenia area and link up with the large Turkish enclave in Nicosia by a corridor from the sea. Heavy fighting took place on the outskirts of Nicosia for the control of the airport. That evening the Security Council in New York discussed the emergency and adopted a resolution[1] deploring the outbreak of conflict and continuing bloodshed and expressing concern at the threat to international peace and security and the explosive situation in the Eastern Mediterranean. It called upon all states to respect the sovereignty of Cyprus; upon the belligerents to cease fire; for the end of foreign military intervention; for the withdrawal without delay of foreign military personnel, apart from those covered by international

[1] Security Council Resolution 353 (1974).

agreement; for the early start of negotiations between Greece and Turkey for the restoration of peace and constitutional government.

Despite years of planning and the availability of local information the Turks underestimated the difficulties of the operation; the initial force was too small and met with unexpected resistance. The National Guard, although many units were exhausted after the coup, made a counter-attack inflicting heavy Turkish casualties. The Turks also received a setback in the death of the battalion commander who was killed early on. The Greek and Turkish contingents, legally stationed in Cyprus under the Treaty of Alliance, clashed when the former made an abortive attempt to break through to the Nicosia–Kyrenia road and cut off the invading troops before they reached the main Turkish enclave of Nicosia. Only Nicosia was adequately defended, elsewhere the Turkish enclaves – Famagusta, Limassol, Paphos and many small villages – quickly surrendered to the Greeks, who greatly outnumbered the Turks.

Kyrenia did not come under Turkish control until 22 July, the third day of the invasion. The surrender was preceded by a sea and air bombardment which set large areas of the Kyrenia Range alight; the town itself suffered little damage. The Turks accepted a cease-fire. Fighting, however, continued in the vicinity of the airport and the British High Commission. The Turks feared that the Greeks might land troops by air. UNFICYP, strongly reinforced by British troops, took over the control of the airport and immobilised the runways.

The Greek junta had misjudged the situation in interpreting the Turkish threat to invade as bluff. On the day of the invasion it ordered general mobilisation in Greece. Without air cover it was powerless to send direct aid to Cyprus; in certain quarters the possibility of attacking Turkey across the Evros River was considered, but the Chiefs of Staff advised that the Greek Army was in no position to make a counter attack. The threat of war between Greece and Turkey lasted several more days. However, on 22 July the junta ordered a cease-fire in Cyprus and Glavkos Klerides, in accordance with the Constitution of 1960, took over the presidency from its illegal incumbent, Nikos Sampson. The next day, after a meeting between President Ghizikis and the four heads of the armed forces in Greece, the military junta decided to hand power over to a civilian government. Karamanlis left France for Greece to become Prime Minister after an absence of eleven years.

The collapse of the Greek military regime after seven years had ironi-cally come about as the direct consequence of the Turkish intervention in Cyprus. The return of democratic government in Greece was warmly welcomed by the Turkish Prime Minister, Bulent Ecevit, and the prospects for a settlement of the Cyprus question looked encouraging. In the meantime the Turks continued landing men, arms and supplies and extending their control westwards in breach of the cease-fire. They claimed that their purpose was not to take more territory but to flush out the remaining irregulars who, entrenched as snipers, threatened the Turkish positions. On 25 July a conference was called at Geneva in accordance with Security Council Resolution 353 and the Treaty of Guarantee. This, attended by the Foreign Ministers of the three guarantor powers, Britain, Greece and Turkey, ran into difficulties on the second day owing to conflicting interpretations of the UN resolution. Turkey refused to consider any constitutional plan unless her forces remained in Cyprus. The Turks believed, not unreasonably, that if their forces were withdrawn the situation would revert to that existing before the coup. Greece took the line that the opposing forces must be withdrawn prior to any constitutional discussions. The Greek Cypriots, embittered by past experiences of their affairs being settled by other states, objected to the discussion of constitutional matters which they deemed to be outside the guarantor powers' terms of reference. Despite difficulties the cease-fire was finally agreed on 30 July. The declaration, signed by the three Foreign Ministers, decreed that the areas controlled by the armed forces should not be extended, that all Turkish enclaves occupied by Greek and Greek Cypriot forces should be immediately evacuated and that military and civilian detainees should be exchanged as soon as possible. The Foreign Ministers noted the existence of two autonomous administrations, called for the creation of a security zone between the opposing forces and for early negotiations, in which Greek and Turkish Cypriot representatives would participate for the purpose of re-establishing peace and constitutional government. The agreement was seen by the Greeks as a capitulation to the Turks, who remained free to retain all the occupied territory without any commitment on the withdrawal of their troops.

The undertakings at Geneva remained academic. The Turkish enclaves were not immediately evacuated by the National Guard. The Turks moved into new military positions and maintained a daily build-up of troops, armour and supplies in the region of the Kyrenia bridgehead. On 31 July they seized Lapithos and Karavas on the north coast, heavy fighting broke out in the Famagusta area on 5 August. Ecevit in the meantime threatened to boycott the next round of talks on the ground that the Turkish Cypriots were still prisoners in the enclaves. By

9 August, the opening day of the second Geneva conference, the Turks dominated the east and west approach roads to Nicosia; they still threatened the airport and were in position to relieve the Turks of Famagusta and cut off the whole of the north in the process. The cease-fire lines were not finally agreed by Britain, Greece and Turkey until this date, only then was UNFICYP able to start work on setting up buffer zones. As recently as twenty hours before the signing of the local agreement, the Turks had mopped up two more important villages.

The second Geneva conference opened in an atmosphere of mutual recriminations. The Greek representative threatened to walk out unless the Turks withdrew to the cease-fire line of 30 July. On 11 August, however, the Greek Government made several concessions to the Turks in ordering the immediate withdrawal of the National Guard from the enclaves and the release of Turkish and Turkish Cypriot prisoners, which should have taken place earlier. The Turks were thus deprived of any possible pretext for extending their territory still further. Greece also gave way over her request for the withdrawal of the Turks to the cease-fire line of 30 July. Disagreement arose on the future constitutional arrangements for Cyprus. George Mavros and Glavkos Klerides pressed for a unified Cyprus on the basis of the 1960 Constitution. The Turks demanded new constitutional arrangements which would provide for autonomous areas within a federal state. Tension was aggravated by Turkey's threat to use force if her demands were not met.

The Turks produced two plans.[1] Denktash submitted a formula which provided for a bizonal federation with the demarcation line running from the west of Lefka in an almost straight line, which would take in the Turkish quarters of Nicosia and Famagusta, leaving all the area to the north of the line under Turkish control. The Turkish Foreign Minister, Mr Gunes, submitted a plan for six autonomous Turkish cantons. The Nicosia enclave would have been enlarged to take in all the northern coast from Vavilas to Davlos, part of the Mesaoria, and the Turkish quarters of Nicosia and Famagusta. The Karpas, except for one small Turkish enclave, would have remained under Greek control but geographically isolated from the rest of Greek Cyprus. Both plans, which would have brought about thirty per cent of the island under Turkish control, were strongly objected to by the Greek Cypriots. Nevertheless the Gunes plan, subject to negotiation, might have formed the basis of a satisfactory settlement since, unlike the Denktash plan, it did not involve partition and could be implemented without large

[1] Polyvios G. Polyviou, *Cyprus: the Tragedy and the Challenge* (John Swain & Son, 1975), Appendices 3, 4, 5 and 6.

displacements of the population. Mr Callaghan supported the request made by the representatives of Greece and Cyprus for an adjournment of thirty-six hours to consult with their governments about the proposals. The Turks refused to extend the deadline and were strongly rebuked by Callaghan for their intransigence and bad faith. A few hours later the Turks, who had maintained that the cease-fire only held good for the duration of negotiations, began bombing Nicosia.

On 13 August the war was resumed in full. The next day Turkish tanks reached the outskirts of Nicosia. On 15 August the suburbs of Famagusta were occupied. The advance brought the Turkish troops to the edge of the British sovereign base at Dhekelia, well to the south of the Denktash line. All hopes of aid from the mainland were finally removed with an announcement by Karamanlis that Greece was unable to make war on Turkey in Cyprus. Ecevit had declared that the operation would be short. And on 16 August Turkey ordered a cease-fire, having occupied the greater part of northern Cyprus so that forty per cent of the island was now under her control. The foundations for a federal state, with two autonomous administrations, had been laid, the Turkish Prime Minister stated. Thousands of Greek villagers, alarmed by reports of atrocities during the first invasion, had fled ahead of the advancing army which was able to occupy unhindered hundreds of deserted villages and to isolate the Karpas by its advance. The number of Greeks displaced totalled about 200,000, roughly a third of the Cyprus population. The vast majority were forced to live in the open until camps and improvised accommodation could be organised. Both Greek and Turkish Cypriots took refuge in the British bases.

The Greek Cypriots were seized by an upsurge of anti-Western feeling. The guarantor powers and the UN had failed them. Mob violence on 19 August turned against the Americans in an attack on the Embassy; the new Ambassador, Rodger Davies, and his secretary were killed by an unknown assassin, firing from a nearby building site. The murder was attributed to EOKA B.

Turkey's action during the first invasion had attracted international sympathy. The independence of Cyprus was threatened by the Greek junta and its local collaborators, EOKA, and the safety of the Turkish community was placed in jeopardy for the third time in fourteen years. The Turks had exercised their legal rights by intervening under the Treaty of Guarantee to restore the independence of Cyprus and safeguard the security of their own people.

The second invasion was an outright contravention of the Zurich settlement upon which they had consistently based their case in the past and it must be seen as a turning point in Turkish policy and tactics. From now on considerations of strategy took priority over the obligations imposed by the Zurich treaties, which specifically precluded partition and the division of Cyprus into separate states. Hopes that the Turks had occupied an area greatly in excess of their needs and rights, in order to safeguard the original bridgehead and corridor to Nicosia pending a settlement, faded as the months went by when increasing numbers of Turks from the south and immigrants from the mainland were settled in northern Cyprus in order to form an all-Turkish zone. At the end of January 1975 the British Government allowed 9,390[1] Turkish Cypriot refugees, who had been camping in the base of Episkopi, to leave for Turkey from Akrotiri airfield. The refugees were ultimately bound for northern Cyprus, where they were to be settled on Greek property. The Greek Cypriots were incensed by the British action, which was taken under strong pressure from the Turkish Government and never fully explained. And in Athens mob violence led to an attack on the British Embassy which the police did little to prevent. The danger presented by the refugees to security and the possibility that Turkey might try to evacuate them by force are likely to have influenced the decision, in addition to the humanitarian considerations given as the official reason.

Since the Turkish Cypriots formed only 18 per cent of the total population the occupied zone was too large for them to manage and the administration broke down. The destructiveness of the Turkish Army militated against the Turkish Cypriots whose interests it had come to protect. With the connivance of the officers, Greek houses intended for Turkish Cypriots from the south were stripped bare. The Turkish Cypriots, long resentful of the economic deprivation they had suffered at the hands of the Greeks, joined in the looting, in some instances to replace equipment removed by their kinsmen from the mainland. Absent British residents were also victims of extensive looting. All Greek property was confiscated and taken over by the Turkish Cypriot administration. The Turkish Cypriots regarded this outright expropriation as the compensation due to them for the looting and destruction of Turkish property by the Greeks between 1963 and 1968 and for their exclusion by the Cyprus Government from all development aid over the past eleven years.

Despite their overwhelming military superiority, the Turks continued

---

[1] *Report from the Select Committee on Cyprus.* Session 1975–6 (HMSO), 'Appendix 3. Memorandum submitted by the British High Commissioner in Nicosia', p. 77.

long after the invasion to suffer from the psychosis of a people on the defensive: intransigence, an obsession with security and exaggerated territorial claims. The Turkish Government, a weak coalition under the pressure of extremists, missed the opportunity to negotiate a settlement during the first three months after the cease-fire. At that time Turkey could have given up territory without loss of face; the Greek refugee problem had not yet become an issue of local politics. Makarios was still abroad. After his triumphant return in December the attitudes of both sides hardened and the situation froze into a dangerous stalemate. In the meantime Turkish Cypriots from the south and immigrants from the mainland were settled in districts which Turkey was originally expected to give up, thus adding practical to political difficulties in future negotiations.

Military conquest was followed by economic stagnation and the iso-lation of the Turkish Cypriots from the rest of the island, which drove them into ever-increasing dependence on Turkey. Partition existed in its most drastic form, for the boundary which divided the two communities was almost impenetrable and the freedom of movement associated with a normal frontier non-existent. Both sides imposed restrictions and suffered economically as the result, for the island as a single geographic and economic entity could only realise its full potential by the pooling of resources and the interchange of produce between the regions. Two years after the invasion the Turkish zone was still on a semi-war footing with martial law in force; the 10,000 remaining Greeks, most of whom were in the Karpas, lived under strict surveillance.

The greatest single problem still facing the Government of the Republic was the 180,000 refugees. Population density in the south had doubled; pressure on water supplies and sewerage was acute. The pattern of agriculture and population distribution which had existed for centuries was totally dislocated and nearly a third of the total population uprooted. The majority of those displaced were agricul-turalists faced with eking out a living either in new occupations or in the cultivation of unfamiliar crops. The Turkish Cypriots, like the Greeks, had experienced a major social upheaval. The difference was that the Turks accepted the situation as permanent and the sacrifices entailed as essential to future peace. The Greeks, on the other hand, were encouraged by their leaders and the UN to believe that their plight was temporary and that in due course all would return to their villages in the Turkish-occupied area – an objective which was not likely to be realised without a new war and one in which the Greeks were victorious.

The Turkish invasion had drastic consequences for the West. The Soviet Union had the satisfaction of seeing NATO troops clash with each other instead of cooperating under the Treaties of Alliance and Guarantee. In the short term Western defence in a sensitive area was undermined by a temporary ban on all American military aid to Turkey forced upon Congress by the Greek lobby; in the long term, by the Greek Government's withdrawal, as a sop to an outraged public opinion, from military participation in NATO.

In Cyprus itself the Turkish invasion marked the climax of the struggle for union with Greece which had begun more than one hundred years earlier. The Greek Cypriots had paid dearly in the cause of Enosis: in terms of human suffering the cost to both communities was beyond calculation.

Appendices

1   Abbreviations used in the Text   *page* 399
2   Important Dates in the History of Cyprus   401
3   Procedure for Election of Archbishops of Cyprus   403
4   The EOKA Oath   404
5   Racial Composition and Strength of the Police Force in
     July 1958   405
6   Casualty Tables   406

Abbreviations used in Text

ACL	American Confederation of Labour
AHEPA	American Hellenic Educational Progressive Association
BIS	British Information Services
CBS	Cyprus Broadcasting Station
CMC	Cyprus Mines Corporation
EXCO	Executive Council
GAOR	General Assembly Official Records [UN]
H.C. Deb.	House of Commons Debates
H.L. Deb.	House of Lords Debates
ICFTU	International Confederation of Free Trade Unions
JCC	Joint Constitutional Commission
MELF	Middle East Land Forces
NATO	North Atlantic Treaty Organisation
PTUC	Pancyprian Trade Union Committee
UNDP	United Nations Development Programme
UNFICYP	United Nations Force in Cyprus
UNSCOB	United Nations Special Commission on the Balkans
USIS	United States Information Services

GREEK AND TURKISH

AKEL	*Anorthotikon Komma Ergazomenou Laou* Reform Party of the Working People
ANE	*Alkimos Neolaia Tis EOKA* Valiant Youth of EOKA
AON	*Anorthotiki Organosis Neolaias* Reform Youth Organisation
EAM	*Ethnikon Apeleftherotikon Metopon* National Liberation Front
EAS	*Ethnikos Apeleftherotikos Synaspismos* National Liberation Coalition
EDEK	*Ethniki Dimokratiki Enosis Kyprou* National Democratic Union of Cyprus
EDMA	*Eniaion Dimokratikon Metopon Anadimiurgias* United Democratic Reconstruction Front

ELAS	*Ethnikos Laikos Apeleftherotikos Stratos*	
	People's National Liberation Army	
EMAK	*Ethnikon Metopon Apeleftheroseos Kyprou*	
	Cyprus National Liberation Front	
EOKA	*Ethniki Organosis Kyprion Agoniston*	
	National Organisation of Cypriot Fighters	
EPEK	*Ethniki Proodeftiki Enosis Kentrou*	
	National Progressive Union of the Centre (Greece)	
GSEE	*Yeniki Synomospondia Ergaton Ellados*	
GGCL	Greek General Confederation of Labour	
KATAK	*Kibris Adasi Türk Azinligi Kuruma*	
	Association of the Turkish Cypriot Minority	
KEM	*Kypriakon Enotikon Metapon*	
	Cyprus Enosis Front	
KEM	*Kypriaki Etairia Metaphoron*	
CTC	Cyprus Transport Company	
KKE	*Kommunistikon Komma Tis Ellados*	
	The Communist Party of Greece	
KTP	*Kibris Türktur Partisi*	
	Cyprus is Turkish Party	
OAE	*Organosis Aristeron Ethnikophronon*	
	Left-wing Nationalists' Organisation	
OAP	*Organosis Aristeron Patrioton*	
	Left-wing Patriots' Organisation	
OHEN	*Orthodoxos Christianiki Enosis Neon*	
	Orthodox Christian Union of Youth	
PEAEK	*Panellinikos Epitropi Agonos Enoseos Kyprou*	
	Panhellenic Committee for the Struggle for the Union of Cyprus	
PEK	*Panagrotiki Enosis Kyprou*	
	Panagrarian Union of Cyprus	
PEKA	*Politiki Epitropi Kypriakou Agonos*	
	Political Committee of the Cyprus Struggle	
PEO	*Pankyprios Ergatiki Omospondia*	
	Pancyprian Federation of Labour (Old Trade Unions)	
PEOM	*Pankyprios Ethniki Organosis Mathiton*	
	Pancyprian National Organisation of Pupils	
PEON	*Pankyprios Ethniki Organosis Neolaias*	
	Pancyprian National Organisation of Youth	
SEK	*Synomospondia Ergaton Kyprou*	
	Confederation of Cypriot Workers (New Trade Unions)	
SEKA	*Syndonistiki Epitropi Kypriakos Agonos*	
	Coordination Committee for the Cyprus Struggle	
TMT	*Türk Mukavemet Teshkilati*	
	Turkish Resistance Organisation	

Important Dates in
the History of Cyprus

BC

c. 4000	Neolithic Age
3000–1000	Bronze Age
1400–1200	Influx of Mycenaean peoples from the Greek mainland
1450	Conquest of Cyprus by Pharaoh Thothmes III
End of 13th century	Arrival of new Achaeans and others, mostly from Asia Minor, including the first Greek colonisers
800	Arrival of the Phoenicians
707	Surrender of Cyprus to the Assyrian, Sargon II
525	Fall of Cyprus to Persia
392	Rise of Evaghoras, who later relinquished claim to all the Cypriot kingdoms except Salamis
386	Cyprus revolt against Persia
336	Birth of the Stoic, Zeno of Kition
320	Egyptian conquest – Ptolemy I
58	Cyprus becomes a Roman province of Cilicia

AD

45	Conversion of Cyprus to Christianity
115	Destruction of Salamis by the Jews
395	Division of the Roman Empire
647	Muslim invasion
1184–91	Isaac Comnenus the despot – ruler of Cyprus
1191	Richard Coeur de Lion's occupation of Cyprus and its subsequent sale to the Knights Templars
1192	The Cyprus rising against the Templars
	Restoration to Coeur de Lion and subsequent sale to Guy de Lusignan
1489	Caterina Cornaro's surrender of Cyprus to the Venetians
1571	Turkish conquest
1572	Expulsion of the Latin hierarchy
	Restoration of the Orthodox Prelates
1821	Execution of the Cyprus Orthodox archbishops and other Christians for alleged complicity in the Greek War of Independence

1878	British occupation under the Cyprus Convention
1914	Lapse of the Cyprus Convention with Turkey's entry into the First World War on the side of the Germans
1915	Offer of Cyprus to Greece which the latter refused
1923	Treaty of Lausanne (Treaty of Peace with Greece and Turkey)
1925	Cyprus designated a British Crown Colony
1931	Greek Cypriot riots for Enosis
	Burning of Government House
	Suspension of the Cyprus Constitution
1933	Banning of the Cypriot Communist Party
1941	Formation of AKEL
	Restoration of municipal elections
1948	Rejection of the Winster constitutional offer
1955–8	EOKA revolt against the British
1959	Zurich and London Agreements
1960	Birth of the Republic of Cyprus
1963	Civil war between Greeks and Turks
1964	Arrival of the United Nations Force in Cyprus (UNFICYP) in March
1967–8	Renewal of Greco-Turkish strife
1974	Turkish invasion and occupation of northern Cyprus

3

Procedure for Election of Archbishops of Cyprus

Although the archbishops are generally considered to be popularly elected, the people exercise their choice through intermediaries.

The archbishop is elected by an assembly composed of the bishops, suffragan bishops, the abbots or their representatives, other leading ecclesiastics, and 66 elected general representatives, of whom 22 are priests and 44 laymen. The general representatives in their turn are elected by special representatives drawn from the Orthodox community throughout the island. The lists of the special representatives are compiled by the priests and the mukhtar of each Christian community and have to be ratified by the bishop of the diocese. The general and special representatives must not have been deprived of their religious rights by the competent ecclesiastical authority.

If all those present at the assembly, which must form a quorum, agree to the election of the same candidate there are no further proceedings. In the event of disagreement the voting is carried out by secret ballot and the candidate who receives most votes becomes the Archbishop of Cyprus.

Candidates for the archbishopric must be members of the clergy and possess a diploma from an orthodox theological college, and must not be younger than thirty years. The office is for life and the incumbent can only be dismissed on a ruling from the Holy Synod.

Source: 'The Charter of the Church of Cyprus, 1914.'

4

The EOKA Oath

I swear in the name of the Holy Trinity that:

I shall work with all my power for the liberation of Cyprus from the British yoke, sacrificing for this even my life.

I shall perform without question all the instructions of the Organisation which may be given to me and I shall not bring any objection, however difficult or dangerous these may be.

I shall not abandon the struggle unless I receive instructions from the Leader of the Organisation, and after our aim has been accomplished.

I shall never reveal to anyone any secret of our Organisation, neither the names of my chiefs nor those of any other members, even if I am captured and tortured.

I shall not reveal any of the instructions which may be given me, even to my fellow combatants.

If I disobey this oath I shall be worthy of every punishment as a traitor, and may eternal contempt cover me.

Source: Leaflet distributed in Cyprus between April and October 1955.

5

Racial Composition and Strength of the Police Force in July 1958

The Regular Police Force
United Kingdom   462
Greek Cypriots   932
Turkish Cypriots   891
Others   39

_____

2,324

Auxiliary Police and Special Constables
Greeks   70
Turks   1,700

_____

1,770 (Approx.)

The Mobile Reserve
All Turkish   542

Source: The Government of Cyprus (July 1958).

6

Casualty Tables

A SUMMARY OF CASUALTIES 1 April 1955 – 30 March 1959

	Services	Police	Civilians*	Greco-Turkish Clashes (June–Aug. 1958)	Greco-Turkish Clashes	Totals
Fatal	105	51	238	109	6	509†
Wounded	603	185	288	79	103	1,258

* Out of 238 Civilians killed 203 were Greek Cypriots.

† 1 Turkish and 4 Greek civilians, and 1 Turkish RAF Auxiliary policeman were killed during intercommunal rioting prior to June 1968.

Source: Official Casualty List

B Breakdown

Date	Services	Police			Civilians			Totals
		UK	Greek	Turkish	UK	Greek	Turkish	
1955								
Apr.	–	–	–	–	–	–	–	0
May	–	–	–	–	–	–	–	0
June	–	–	1	–	–	1	–	2
July	–	–	–	–	–	–	–	0
Aug.	–	–	2	–	–	1	–	3
Sept.	–	–	–	–	–	–	–	0
Oct.	1	–	1	–	–	–	–	2
Nov.	5	–	–	–	–	1	–	6
Dec.	6	–	1	–	–	4	–	11
TOTALS	12	–	5	–	–	7	–	24

B Breakdown—continued

Date	Services	Police			Civilians			Totals
		UK	Greek	Turkish	UK	Greek	Turkish	
1956								
Jan.	3	–	–	I	–	4	–	8
Feb.	2	–	–	–	–	7	–	9
Mar.	5	I	I	–	–	8	–	15
Apr.	3	–	3	I	2	10	I	20
May	8	–	–	3	2	5	I	19 (+ I*)
June	6	I	–	2	I	9	I	20 (+ I†)
July	3	I	–	–	I	11	–	16 (+ 2‡)
Aug.	–	I	–	–	–	12	I	14
Sept.	7	2	–	–	I	8	–	18 (+ I§)
Oct.	6	–	–	–	–	14	–	20
Nov.	16	3	I	–	4	9	I	34
Dec.	I	–	I	–	I	12	–	15
TOTALS	60	9	6	7	12	109	5	213
1957								
Jan.	I	–	I	I	4	8	–	15
Feb.	4	–	–	I	–	3	–	8
Mar.	I	–	–	–	–	3	–	4
Apr.	–	–	–	–	–	–	–	0
May	–	–	–	–	–	–	–	0
June	–	–	–	–	–	–	–	0
July	–	–	–	–	–	–	–	0
Aug.	–	–	–	–	–	–	–	0
Sept.	–	–	–	–	–	–	–	0
Oct.	–	–	–	–	–	4	–	4
Nov.	–	–	–	I	–	2	–	3
Dec.	–	–	–	–	–	–	–	0
TOTALS	6	0	I	3	4	20	0	34

* Auxiliary RAF Turkish Policeman
† I USA.   ‡ I Armenian and I Maltese.   § I Maronite.

B   *Breakdown*—continued

Date	Services	Police			Civilians			Totals
		UK	*Greek*	*Turkish*	*UK*	*Greek*	*Turkish*	
1958								
Jan.	–	–	–	–	–	2	–	2
Feb.	–	–	–	–	–	–	–	0
Mar.	–	–	–	–	–	1	–	1
Apr.	–	1	–	–	–	1	–	2
May	2	–	–	–	–	11	2	15
June	–	–	–	1	–	5	–	6
July	3	–	–	4	–	11	–	18
Aug.	2	–	1	3	–	9	–	15
Sept.	4	1	–	–	–	14	1	20
Oct.	9	1	1	3	6	11	–	31
Nov.	5	–	1	1	4	4	–	15
Dec.	2	–	–	–	–	2	–	4
TOTALS	27	3	3	12	10	71	3	129

Source: Official Casualty List.

C   *Greek and Turkish Fatal Casualties*

Intercommunal Fighting June to August 1958

	Greeks*	Turks†
June	16	2
July	28	44
August	12	5
September	–	2
TOTALS	56	53

* 16 were shot, 4 were killed in riots, 8 in the Geunyeli incident, 8 were stabbed and the rest died from injuries caused by other means – beatings, etc.

† 32 were shot, 9 were killed in three ambushes, 8 were beaten and the rest died from injuries caused by other means.

Source: Official Casualty List.

Bibliography*

Background and Colonial Period

NOTE ON THE BIBLIOGRAPHY

The documentation on the contemporary Cyprus question is massive, but full-length works of merit and distinction are few. *Bitter Lemons* (Lawrence Durrell, 1957) is outstanding for its brilliance in conveying the paradoxical and elusive atmosphere of Cyprus; so, for an earlier period, are the Cyprus chapters in *Orientations* (Storrs, 1937). In the academic field a much neglected standard work, *A History of the Orthodox Church of Cyprus* (Hackett, 1901), contains information of importance to the present day; Professor Crouzet's *Le Conflit de Chypre* (2 vols, 1973) is unlikely to be surpassed in its scope, depth and impartiality; Stanley Kyriakides has contributed a valuable work on the breakdown of the Constitution, *Cyprus Constitutionalism and Crisis Government* (1968); and a recent study by a young Greek Cypriot lawyer, Polyvios G. Polyviou, *Cyprus: the Tragedy and the Challenge* (1975), deserves special consideration for the constructiveness and moderation of its approach – an approach which, had it prevailed earlier, might have averted the tragedy. There are some excellent studies on Greek nationalism and irredentism which throw light on the Cyprus question and I have therefore included them. I have also felt it right to include a number of highly partisan works, since entrenched attitudes of mind have contributed as much as any other factor to the insolubility of the Cyprus problem. A bibliographer can only hope to ensure that all the characteristic viewpoints are represented. This I have tried to do without in any way implying agreement with the stand taken or that such texts are necessarily reliable.

UNOFFICAL SOURCES

Adams, T. W., *Akel: The Communist Party of Cyprus* (Hoover Institution Press, Stanford University, 1971).
Adams, T. W. and Cotterill, Alvin J., *Cyprus Between East and West* (Johns Hopkins Press, Baltimore, 1968).
Alastos, Doros:
    Cyprus: Past . . . Future (Committee For Cyprus Affairs, London, 1943).
    Cyprus in History (Zeno, London, 1955).
Anonymous, *The Communist Leadership in the Cyprus Struggle* (EOKA, 1958).

* Note: Greek titles have been translated into English.

Anthem, Thomas:
   'The Cyprus Challenge', *Contemporary Review* (London, July 1954), pp. 1–6.
   'The Economic Future of Cyprus', *Middle Eastern Affairs* (November 1959), pp. 350–5.
Argyropoulos, P. A., 'Chypre: problème international?', *Politique Étrangère* (Paris, December 1956), pp. 523–32.
Arnold, Percy, *Cyprus Challenge* (Hogarth Press, London, 1956).
Atabinen, R. S.:
   The Cyprus Question (tr. D. Young, 1957).
   Révisions Historiques (Hachette, Istanbul, January 1958).
Athens University, *Cyprus* (tract setting out the Greek attitude to Enosis, August 1974).
Balfour, Patrick, *The Orphaned Realm* (P. Marshall, 1951).
Batey, Charles, 'Enosis and its Background', *The Round Table* (March 1957), pp. 129–40.
Bayar, Celal, Speech at Konya, *Summary of World Broadcasts* IV (BBC), Daily Series 380, 21 October 1957.
Beckingham, C. F.:
   'The Cypriot Turks' (Historical Note), *Journal of the Royal Central Asian Society* (April 1956), pp. 126–30.
   'The Turks of Cyprus', *Journal of the Royal Anthropological Institute* (London, vol. 87 July–December 1957).
Bedevi, Vergi H., *Cyprus Has Never Been A Greek Island* (Cypriot Turkish Historical Association, Nicosia, 1964).
Bell, Coral, *Survey of International Affairs 1954* (RIIA/OUP, 1957), pp. 173–84.
Benenson, Peter [author of Introduction], *Gangrene* (Calder, London, 1959), pp. 31–5.
Brewer, Sam Pope, 'Communist Party Disturbs Cyprus', New York Times, 4 January 1949.
British Council of Churches, *The Resolutions passed in April 1956 and October 1958 on the Crisis in Cyprus*. Typescript.
Calogeropoulos-Stratis, S., *La Grèce et les Nations Unies* (Manhattan Publishing Co., New York, 1957).
CBS Commentator, *After the News, Selection of Commentaries from the Cyprus Broadcasting Service* (Rustem Bookshop, Nicosia, 1957).
Churchill, Winston, *The Second World War* (6 vols, 1948–1954) (Cassell, London), vols I, III, IV and V.
Cobham, C. D., *Excerpta Cypria: Materials for a History of Cyprus* (CUP, 1908).
Crawshaw, Nancy:
   'Political Changes in Greece', *The World Today* (RIIA, January 1952), pp. 26–38.
   'The Future of Cyprus' (2 articles), Manchester Guardian, 9 and 11 July 1952.
   'The Cyprus Dilemma', *The Twentieth Century*, November 1954, pp. 413–21.
   'Cyprus and Its Crisis' (5 articles), Manchester Guardian, 20, 21, 24 January and 6 and 7 February 1956.
   'The Republic of Cyprus', *The World Today* (RIIA, December 1960), pp. 526–40.
Crouzet, François, *Le Conflit de Chypre 1946–49* (2 vols) (Bruylant, Brussels, 1973).
Crozier, Brian, *The Rebels* (Chatto & Windus, London, 1960).
Cyprus Affairs Committee, London, *Cyprus Presents Its Case to the World* (circa 1950).
Cyprus Greek Alumni Associations (ESEAK), *Appeal of the Cyprus Youth to all People of the Freedon-Loving World: 'We want nothing but Liberty through Union with Greece'* (Nicosia. Undated).
Dikaios, P., *A Guide to the Cyprus Museum* (Nicosia, 1961).
Durrell, Lawrence, *Bitter Lemons* (Faber, London, 1957).
Economides, M., *The Case for Enosis* (The Committee For Cyprus Affairs, London, circa 1954).
Eden, Sir Anthony, *Full Circle* (Cassell, London, 1960).
Emilianides, Achille, *Histoire de Chypre* (Presses Universitaires de France, 1962).
EOKA, Leaflets distributed in Cyprus throughout the emergency, 1955–1959 (also PEKA and ANE leaflets, 1957–1959).

Ethnarchy of Cyprus:
  'What's Happening in Cyprus' (5 articles reprinted from *Tribune*, May–June 1957).
  Violation of Human Rights in Cyprus (October 1957).
  Cyprus Bulletin (years: 1956–1958).
Fabian Colonial Bureau, *Strategic Colonies and Their Future* (London, 1945).
Fletcher-Cooke, John, CMG, 'Communism and Nationalism in Cyprus'. Lecture to Colonial Office, Overseas Service Conference, Rhodes House, Oxford, 13 April 1956. Stencilled.
Foley, Charles, *Island in Revolt* (Longmans, London, 1962).
Foot, Hugh (Lord Caradon):
  'Colonial Violence', *Aspect* (1963).
  A Start in Freedom (Hodder & Stoughton, London, 1964).
Foot, Sylvia, *Emergency Exit* (Chatto & Windus, London, 1960).
Georghiades, Antonis, *Die Zypernfrage* (Bonn, 1963).
Greek Communal Chamber:
  The Greek Heritage of Cyprus (Nicosia, 1963).
  Cyprus: A Handbook on the Island's Past and Present (Nicosia, 1964).
Greek Communist Party, 'Statement on Cyprus', *Summary of World Broadcasts* IV (BBC), Daily Series 592, 4 July 1958.
Greek General Confederation of Labour (GGCL):
  Press Communiqué on Cyprus (Athens, 6 October 1951).
  Letter to British Ambassador (3 October 1951). Stencilled.
  Newsletter (1954 onwards).
Grivas-Dighenis, General George:
  Memoirs: The EOKA Struggle 1955–1959 (Greek) (Athens, 1961).
  The Memoirs of General Grivas, ed. by Charles Foley (Longmans, 1964).
  Guerrilla Warfare and EOKA's Struggle (Longmans, 1964).
Gunnis, Rupert, *Historic Cyprus* (Methuen, London, 1936).
Hackett, J., *A History of the Orthodox Church of Cyprus* [1901] (Burt Franklin, New York. Reprinted 1972).
Halkin Sesi:
  'Mr. J. Huizinga you are terribly mistaken' (23 February 1956).
  'Cyprus: A Likely Election Issue in the next British General Elections' (20 May 1957).
Harding, Field-Marshal Sir John (Lord Harding of Petherton):
  'Terrorism in Cyprus', Daily Telegraph, 7, 8 and 9 January 1958.
  'Tragic Cyprus: Triple Dilemma', *Life* (31 March 1958), pp. 74–9.
  'The Cyprus Problem in Relation to the Middle East', *International Affairs* (RIIA, July 1958), pp. 291–6.
  'Beware this Grivas Trick', Daily Express, 6 August 1958.
Hill, Sir George, *History of Cyprus*, vols I–IV (CUP, 1940, 1948 and 1952).
Hinde, Wendy, 'Cyprus: An Anglo-Greek Problem', *The New Commonwealth*, vol. 28, no. 5 (2 September 1954), pp. 227–9.
Home, Gordon, *Cyprus Then and Now* (Dent, 1960).
Ierodiakonou, Leontios, *The Cyprus Question* (Almqvist & Wiskell, Stockholm, 1971).
Jeffery, George, *Cyprus Under Richard I* (Zeno, London, 1975).
Jenkins, Romilly, *The Dilessi Murders* (Longmans, 1961).
Joannides, E., *Cyprus Denied Freedom* (Hermes Press Ltd, London, October 1948).
Kerber, Karl, *Makarios Kirchenfürst Oder ??????* (Verlag GmbH, Diessen/Ammersee, 1964).
Kirk, George, *The Middle East, 1945–50* (OUP for RIIA, London, 1954).
Klerides, Glavkos, letter to the Colonial Secretary, Nicosia, containing statement by the Abbot of Makheras alleging ill-treatment (21 March 1957). Stencilled.
Koumoulides, John, *Cyprus and the Greek War of Independence 1821–1829* (Zeno, London, 1974).
Kranidiotis, Nikos, *The Cyprus Struggle for Freedom* (Greek) (Athens, 1958).

Kraniotakis (President of the Union of Athens Journalists), 'Address to Makarios', 16 July 1955.

Kutchuk, Dr Fazil, 'The Turkish Community in Cyprus and Enosis', *Halkin Sesi*, 17 August 1954.

Kyprianou, Spyros A., *The Cyprus Question* (The Ethnarchy of Cyprus, London, July 1956).

Labour Party (British), Annual Reports for the Years 1954–1958.

Lavender, David, *The Story of the Cyprus Mines Corporation* (The Huntington Library, San Marino, California, 1962).

Lee, Dwight E., *Great Britain and the Cyprus Convention Policy of 1878* (Harvard, 1934).

Le Geyt, Capt. P. S., *Makarios in Exile* (Anagennisis Press, Nicosia, 1961).

Lewis, Bernard, *The Emergence of Modern Turkey* (OUP for RIIA, London, 1961).

Loizides, Savvas:

   The Cyprus Question (Nicosia, 1950).

   The Cyprus Question and the Law of the United Nations (Nicosia, 1951).

   Cyprus Demands Self-Determination (Athens, 1956).

Luke, Sir Harry:

   Cyprus Under The Turks 1571–1878 (Hurst, London, 1921).

   'Present-Day Cyprus', *United Empire* (November–December 1955).

   Cyprus: A Portrait and an Appreciation (Harrap, London, and K. Rustem Bros, Nicosia, 1973).

Maccas, Leon, *European Life* [Cyprus issue] (Athens, 30 September 1954).

Mackenzie, Compton, 'Sidelight', *Spectator* (28 May 1954).

Macmillan, Harold:

   Tides of Fortune, 1945–1955 (Macmillan, 1969).

   Riding the Storm 1956–1959 (Macmillan, 1971).

Madariaga, Salvador de, 'World Opinion on Cyprus', Manchester Guardian, 5 April 1956.

Makarios:

   Statement by the Archbishop of Cyprus on the Tortures Practised in Cyprus by the British Security Forces (19 June 1957). Stencilled.

   Reasons for Rejecting the Partnership Plan (13 September 1958). Stencilled.

Manchester Guardian:

   The Record on Suez, A Chronology of Events (November 1956).

   'The Search at Famagusta – What Happened on 3 October' (5 December 1958).

Mathews, J. E., *Cyprus – An Economic and Geographic Outline* (Zavallis Press, Nicosia, 1964).

Mayes, Stanley, *Cyprus and Makarios* (Putnam, London, 1960).

Menderes, Adnan, Speech on return of Makarios to Athens from the Seychelles. *Summary of World Broadcasts* IV (BBC), Daily Series 227, 23 April 1957.

Meyer, A. J. with Simos Vassiliou, *The Economy of Cyprus* (Harvard, 1962).

Meynaud, Jean, *Les Forces Politiques en Grèce* (Études de Science Politique, no. 10. Lausanne, 1965).

National Committee for Self-Determination of Cyprus, Athens, 'One of the Greatest Crimes of This Century' [Execution of Karaolis] (circa 1956).

National Council for Public Enlightenment, Athens:

   The Tripartite Conference (Great Britain–Greece–Turkey) and the Cyprus Question (July 1955).

   The Anti-Greek Riots of September 6 1955 in Constantinople and Smyrna and their Aftermath (January 1956).

New Commonwealth, 'Constitution for Cyprus?' (28 April 1952).

Newman, Philip, *A Short History of Cyprus* (Longmans, London, 1953).

Noel-Baker, Philip, 'Philhellenism: The Cyprus Problem' (London undated).

Orr, Capt. C. W. J., *Cyprus under British Rule* (Zeno, London, 1972).

Papadopoulos, Theodore, *Social and Historical Data on Population (1570–1881)* (Cyprus Research Centre, Nicosia, 1965).

Pavlides, Sir Paul, An open letter to London Newspapers, 22 May 1956 and postscript for June 1956 (unpublished).

Peristiany, J. G. (editor; also author of Chapter on Cyprus), *Honour and Shame: The Values of Mediterranean Society* (Weidenfeld & Nicolson, London, 1965).

Philips Price, M., 'Turkey's Twin Anxieties', Manchester Guardian, 9 November 1956.

Pissas, Michael:
The Truth About Concentration Camps in Cyprus (New York, December 1957).
Constitutional Offers and Other Facts About Cyprus (Ethnarchy, London, October 1958).

Purcell, H. D., *Cyprus* (Benn, London, 1969).

Rapp, Sir Thomas, 'The Real Problem of Cyprus', *The Listener* (22 September 1955), pp. 449–50.

Richardson, William, 'Dachau in Cyprus' I & II, New York Post, 18 and 19 September 1956.

Rossides, Zenon, *The Problem of Cyprus* (Athens, 1957).

Royal Institute of International Affairs:
Cyprus Background to Enosis (London, 1955). Stencilled.
Background Note on Cyprus 1957 (OUP). Stencilled.
Middle East. A Political and Economic Survey (OUP, 1958), 3, pp. 147–78.
Background Note on Cyprus 1959. Stencilled.

St Clair, William, *That Greece Might Still be Free: The Philhellenes in the War of Independence* (OUP, 1972).

Spaak, Paul-Henri, *Combats Inachevés: De L'Espoir aux déceptions*, vol. 2 (Fayard, 1959).

Spyridakis, Dr C.:
Educational Policy of the English Government in Cyprus 1878–1954 (Nicosia, 1954).
A Brief History of the Cyprus Question (Nicosia, 1954).
A Brief History of Cyprus (Nicosia, 1963).

Spyridakis, Dr C. and Others, *A Report of the Cyprus Greek Secondary School Teachers' Organisation on the Educational Policy of the Government of Cyprus* (Nicosia, 1965).

Stephens, Robert, *Cyprus: A Place of Arms* (Pall Mall Press, London, 1966).

Storrs, Sir Ronald, *Orientations* (Nicholson & Watson, London, 1949).

Sulzberger, C. L., 'Strength of the Communists Poses Problem in Cyprus', New York Times, 17 May 1949.

Sweet-Escott, Bickham, *Greece: A Political and Economic Survey 1939–1953* (OUP for RIIA, 1954).

Tachau, Frank, 'The Face of Turkish Nationalism as Reflected in the Cyprus Dispute'. *The Middle East Journal*, vol. XIII, no. 3 (Washington, 1959), pp. 262–72.

Toynbee, Arnold J.:
The Western Question in Greece and Turkey (Constable, London, 1922).
Survey of International Affairs 1931 (OUP for RIIA, 1932).

Tremayne, Penelope, *Below the Tide* (Hutchinson, London, 1958).

Vanezis, Dr P. N., *Makarios: Faith & Power* (Abelard-Schuman, London, 1971).

Vassiliou, Vassos:
International Relations (Special Issue on Cyprus) (Athens, August 1964).
'The Ecumenical Patriarch of Constantinople', *International Relations* (Athens, December 1964–April 1965).

Weir, W., *Education in Cyprus* (Cosmos Press, Nicosia, 1952).

Wilkinson, George (G. W.), 'Cyprus: The Closed Issue?', *The World Today* (RIIA, 9 September 1954).

Winster, Lord, 'Cyprus: Tactics that ruined a Governor's Mission', Daily Telegraph, 28 April 1949.

Woodhouse, C. M:
Apple of Discord (Hutchinson, 1949).
'Cyprus and The Middle Eastern Crisis', *International Journal*, vol. XI, I (Canadian Institute of International Affairs, Toronto, Winter 1955–56).
'Greece's Great Idea', *Spectator* (27 January 1950).

X, *Account of the National Aims and National Work of the Organisation X.* Stencilled.

Xydis, Stephen G.:
  Cyprus Conflict and Conciliation 1954–1958 (Ohio State University Press, 1967).
  Cyprus Reluctant Republic (Mouton, The Hague–Paris, 1973).
Ziartides, A., 'Statement to the Foreign Press representatives' (Nicosia, 13 May 1957).

PRESS AND RADIO SOURCES

Cyprus	Greece	Turkey
Bozkurt	*Akropolis*	*Cumhuriyet*
Cyprus Mail	*Avghi*	*Hurriyet*
Eleftheria	*Eleftheria*	*Journal d'Orient*
Ethniki	*Estia*	*Milliyet*
Ethnos	*Ethnikos Kiryx*	*Tasvir*
Halkin Sesi	*Ethnos*	*Ulus*
Haravghi	*Kathimerini*	*Vatan*
Neos Dimokratis	*Vima*	*Zafer*
Phileleftheros		
Phos		

International

BBC Summary of World Broadcasts, IV, 1954–1959 (verbatim and summarised reports of broadcasts by Athens Radio and Ankara Radio).
The Christian Science Monitor
The Daily Telegraph
The Daily Worker
The Economist
Le Figaro
The Financial Times
Frankfurter Allgemeine Zeitung
The Manchester Guardian
Le Monde
Neue Zürcher Zeitung
New Statesman
New York Herald Tribune
The New York Times
Spectator
The Times
Tribune
The Washington Post
etc.

OFFICIAL SOURCES

British

Central Office of Information (COI):
  Briefing for Officials on Cyprus (8 April 1954 and 3 September 1956).
  Cyprus, EOKA's Campaign of Terror [For distribution in the USA]. (undated).
  'Facts about Cyprus' (3 May 1954). Stencilled.
  'Harding's Appointment' (26 September 1955). Stencilled.

Colonial Office Information Department (COID):
  'Amnesty Terms for EOKA' (22 August 1956). Press Release.
  'Colonial Secretary's Statement on Cyprus' (28 July 1954). Stencilled.
  'Cyprus Constitution: Summary of Lord Radcliffe's Proposals' (19 December 1956). Press Release.
  'Cyprus. Emergency Measures Relaxed' (18 December 1956). Stencilled.
  'Enosis' (London, 17 September 1954). Stencilled.

'EOKA and Archbishop Makarios' (26 August 1956). Stencilled.
'Cyprus: Governor's Statement' (Appeal for the end of violence, 25 April. Broadcast to H.M. Forces, 19 June 1958). Stencilled.
'Interim Statement on Allegations of Ill-Treatment made by Greek Cypriot Prisoners in Wormwood Scrubs' (1 August 1957). Stencilled.
'Further Comments on the Above' (undated).
'Third Statement on the Allegations of Ill-Treatment of Greek Cypriots made by Archbishop Makarios during a Press Conference in Athens on 19 July 1957' (1 August 1957). Stencilled.
'Terrorism in Cyprus. The Grivas Diaries and Captured Documents' (28 September 1956). Stencilled.

Cyprus Government:
Address by the Governor to the Executive Council 28 December 1954.
Address by the Governor to the Executive Council 9 February 1957.
Address by the Governor to the Executive Council 26 April 1958.
Allegations of Brutality in Cyprus (Nicosia. 11 June 1957 [Date of Harding's foreword]).
'Allegations of Ill-Treatment' (27 June 1957). Press Release.
'Allegations of Ill-Treatment. Government's Reply' (22 June 1957). Press Release.
'Allegations of Ill-Treatment in the Sampson Case.' Press Release.
'Allegations of Maltreatment of Persons held in Custody by the Security Forces' (undated). Stencilled.
Annual Report for the Department of Agriculture (years 1950–1960).
Annual Report for the Department of Education (years 1950–1960).
Annual Report for the Department of Labour (years 1950–1960).
Annual Report on the Cyprus Police (years 1922–1958).
Background Notes on Attempts to Reach a Settlement in Cyprus 1947–1948.
'The Campaign against EOKA' by Brigadier Geoffrey Baker, CB, CMG, CBE, MC (6 February 1957). Stencilled.
Census of Population and Agriculture, 1946 (D. A. Percival, 1949).
Church and Terrorism in Cyprus 1956.
Corruption of Youth in Support of Terrorism (Nicosia, August 1957).
Cyprus: A Review of Events in 1956.
Cyprus Gazette, no. 3891 of 26 November 1955, Subsidiary Legislation [Emergency Laws].
Cyprus: The Transitional Year (1959). Stencilled.
Department of Cooperative Development. 1956 (Nicosia, 1957).
Digest of The Cyprus Vernacular Press (years 1955–1960).
'Economic Development Programme' (Harding, CBS Broadcast, 16 November 1955).
Economic Survey 1954 (Nicosia, 1955).
Economic Review 1955–1956 (Nicosia, 1957).
Economic Review 1957 (Nicosia, 1958).
Economic Review 1958 (Nicosia, 1959).
Explosive Incidents, April–October 1955. Stencilled.
Findings of the Commission of inquiry into the Incidents at Geunyeli, Cyprus on 12 June 1958.
Gazetteer of Cyprus (Nicosia, 1956).
The Greek Cypriot Press and the Constitution (undated).
Greek Irredentism and Cypriot Terrorism (Nicosia, 1956).
International Communism and the Cyprus Question (Nicosia). Stencilled.
Labour Conditions in Cyprus during the War Years, 1939–1945 (C. H. Ashiotis).
Mischief in the Air: A Selection of Extracts from Athens Radio Broadcasts to Cyprus – March to August 1955.
The Monopoly of Enosis (undated).
The Myth of Dehellenisation (undated).

Cyprus Government—*contd.*

'Sir John Harding's New Year's Broadcast to the People' (1 January 1956). Stencilled.

Official Casualty List, 1 April 1955–30 March 1959. Stencilled.

Political Influence of the Greek-Orthodox Church in Cyprus (undated).

Propaganda Leaflets in Greek (printed).

Your Questions Answered [Radcliffe's Constitutional Proposals].

Report of the Cyprus Police Commission (Nicosia, 1956).

Visit to Cyprus of Duncan Sandys (25 April 1957). Stencilled.

A Chronological Record of the Part Played by Students of Cypriot Schools in Acts of Violence and Disorder between 18th August 1954 and the 31st January 1956 (Governor to Secretary of State for the Colonies, 26 March 1956). Stencilled.

'School Disorders' (Director of Education, 15 June 1957). Stencilled.

Statement of Government Decisions on the Recommendations of the Cyprus Police Commission 1956 (Nicosia, 1956).

A Ten-Year Programme of Development for Cyprus, 1946 (Nicosia, 1946).

Ten Years of Development in Cyprus 1949–1959.

Terrorism in Cyprus: The Captured Documents.

An Investigation into Matters Concerning and Affecting the Turkish Community in Cyprus: Interim Report of the Committee on Turkish Affairs (1949).

Ministry of Defence:

Strategic Importance of Cyprus (18 September 1954). Stencilled.

Foreign Office:

Propaganda Campaign by Archbishop Makarios (30 August 1957). Stencilled.

Hansard:

Parliamentary Debates, 1930–1960 (Commons & Lords).

Her Majesty's Stationery Office (HMSO):

Conference on Cyprus (London, February 1959), Cmnd 680.

Correspondence exchanged between the Governor and Archbishop Makarios March 1956, Cmnd 9708.

Cyprus Annual Report (years 1948–1959).

Cyprus, Cmnd 1093 (July 1960).

Cyprus Constitution: Despatch dated 7 May 1948 from the Secretary of State for the Colonies to the Governor of Cyprus, Colonial no. 227.

Cyprus: Statement of Policy, Cmnd 455 (June 1958).

Defence – Outline of Future Policy, Cmnd 124 (April 1957).

Despatch by General Sir Charles F. Keightley, GCB, GBE, DSO, Commander-in-Chief Allied Forces (Supplement to the London Gazette, 10 September 1957).

Lord Radcliffe, *Constitutional Proposals for Cyprus* (December 1956), Cmnd 42.

Annual Report on the Social and Economic Progress of the People of Cyprus 1932, and for the years 1933–7.

Treaty Concerning the Establishment of the Republic of Cyprus, Nicosia, 1960, Cmnd 1252 [This treaty gives effect to the London and Zurich agreements.]

Treaty of Peace with Turkey signed at Sèvres August 10, 1920, Cmnd 1964.

Treaty of Peace with Turkey and Other Instruments signed at Lausanne on July 24 1923 [superseded the treaty of Sèvres which was not implemented].

Miscellaneous:

Lecture on Cyprus to the British Lions Club, Syracuse, N.Y., by John Peck, Director of the BIS, New York (20 November 1958).

Cyprus: A Review of Events in 1956. Stencilled.

Colonel George Grivas – A short background Note (1 February 1957). Stencilled.
Enosis and only Enosis: A briefing paper on the politics of Archbishop Makarios (August 1957). Stencilled.
Know your Cyprus.
The Threat to Peace and Freedom of Expression in Cyprus (after 1957).
Why we are in Cyprus: Background Notes for British Servicemen (May 1956).

Press Summaries:
Istanbul Press Review, 1948–1950; May–July 1958 (British Consulate-General, Inf. Dept, Istanbul).
Outlines of the Daily Press, 1950–1960 (British Embassy, Inf. Dept, Athens).

Greek

Ministry of Foreign Affairs (MFA), Athens:
Antonopoulos, Anastassios (Director of NATO Division, MFA), *The Political Position of Greece* (21 May 1955).
The Cyprus Question: Negotiations 4 October 1955–5 March 1956.
The Cyprus Question – Discussion at the North Atlantic Treaty Organisation, September–October 1958.
The Cyprus Question: Correspondence exchanged between Mr Konstantin Karamanlis and the Right Honourable Harold Macmillan, Prime Minister of the United Kingdom (10 June 1958–19 August 1958).

Prime Minister's Office, Information Dept and Foreign Press Division (FPD):
Brown, Irving (European Representative of the AFL and Member of the Executive Committee of the ICFTU), extract from speech, 12th Congress of the General Confederation of Greek Workers, 16 October 1955 [On the arrest of Makarios] (DNB 15 March 1956).
Cavounides, George (Director, FPD), *Cyprus* (21 May 1955). Stencilled.
Declaration of Policy (4 April 1956).
Documents and Press Comments on the Cyprus Question (PID, Athens, 1954).
Foster, Cedric, anti-British broadcast over Boston Radio (DNB, 27 July 1956).
Karamanlis, statement on release of Makarios, 28 March 1957. Cable to Makarios, 28 March 1957.
Karamanlis, policy statement (DNB, 5 April 1956).
Makarios, statement on failure of talks with Harding (DNB, 6 March 1956).
'Statement of Archbishop Makarios on the Termination of his Exile.' Press conference, Mahé, Seychelles, 29 March 1957 (4 April 1957). Stencilled.
'Archbishop Makarios: Statement on the UN Decision and Cease-Fire Appeal, Seychelles, 22 March 1957.' (Athens, 30 March 1957). Stencilled.
Papagos, Field-Marshal Alexander, Cyprus statement (DNB, 8 February 1955).
Pissas, Michael, allegations against British troops (DNB, 30 December 1956).
Some Notes on Cyprus (15 September 1954). Stencilled.
Text of Verbal Notes Addressed by the Greek to the Turkish Government, 10 and 19 September (11 October 1955).
World Opinion on Cyprus, compiled and edited by George A. Vassiliades (November 1958).

Greek Information Office (Greek Embassy), London:
'American Ambassador's Visit to Foreign Minister' (16 March 1956).
'A Dutchman Looks at Cyprus'. Tr. and reprinted from the *Nieuwe Rotterdamse Courant* (London, 1956).
News from Greece (1954–1960).

Turkish

News from Turkey (later *Turkish News*) 1956–1960.

Turkey and Cyprus. A Survey of the Cyprus Question with official statements of the Turkish Viewpoint (Press Attaché's Office, Turkish Embassy, London, 1956).

Turkish Views on Cyprus (Turkish Information Office, New York, 1955).

Zorlu, Fatin R. (Foreign Minister), 'Cyprus and Turkey: Questions . . . Answers', interview by William Hillman of the North American Newspaper Alliance.

American

Armour, Senator Norman, *Survey No. 1 Greece, Turkey and Iran.* Special Committee to study the Foreign Aid Programme (US Gov. Printing Office, February 1957).

Congressional Record 1947–1959.

State Department, *US Appeals for Cooperation on Cyprus Dispute* (USIS, London, 14 March 1956).

Since Independence
(August 1960)

UNOFFICIAL SOURCES

Adams, T. W. and Cottrell, A. J., *Problems of Communism*, vol. XV/3 (US Information Agency, Washington, D.C. May–June 1956).

Binder, David, 'Turk Minority in Greece Charges Bias' (article on the Komotiní Turks, Greek Thrace), New York Times, 18 Jan 1965.

Calogeropoulos-Stratis, S., 'Le Problème de Chypre', *Politique Étrangère*, no. 4, 1966 (Paris), pp. 344–61.

Clogg, Richard, 'Greece and the Cyprus Crisis', *The World Today* (RIIA, September 1974), pp. 364–8.

Crawshaw, Nancy:
  The World Today (RIIA)
    'Cyprus: the Collapse of the Zurich Agreement', August 1964, pp. 338–47.
    'Cyprus After Kophinou', October 1968, pp. 428–35.
    'Subversion in Cyprus', August 1972, pp. 25–32.
    'Cyprus: Problems of Recovery,' February 1976, pp. 69–74.
  New Society
    'Cyprus: Is Partition Inevitable?', 20 February 1964, pp. 9–10.

Derwinksi, Hon. E. J., 'The Communist Intrigue in Cyprus', *Congressional Record, extensions of remarks E9633*, 15 September 1971.

Economides, Chris, *The Problem Confronting Cyprus* (Nicosia, June 1964).

Ehrlich, Thomas, *Cyprus 1958–1967* (OUP, 1974).

Evdokas, Dr T. [rival candidate for the presidency of Cyprus]:
  Policy Statements, 15 and 22 February 1968.
  Article 'Machiavelli to Makarios' (Greek), *Gnomi*, 29 March 1970.

Hald, Earl C. (UNDP), 'Economic Development in Cyprus – Prospects and Problems' (9 March 1967). Stencilled.

Harbottle, Michael, *The Impartial Soldier* (RIIA/OUP, 1970).

Heinze, Christian, 'Der Zypern-Konflikt eine Bewährungsprobe westlicher Friedenordnung', *Europa-Archiv*, Folge 19/1964, pp. 713–26.

Higgins, Rosalyn, 'Basic Facts on the UN Force in Cyprus', *The World Today* (RIIA), August 1964.

Karayannis, Lt-Gen. G., 'The Cyprus Question' (Greek), 10 articles, *Ethnikos Kyrix* (Athens), 13–24 June 1975.

Kitson, Frank, *Low Intensity Operations. Subversion, Insurgency and Peacekeeping* (Faber, London, 1971).

Kranidiotis, Nikos, *The Cyprus Problem* (C. Michalas, S.A. Press, Athens, 1975).

Kyriakides, Stanley, *Cyprus Constitutionalism and Crisis Government* (University of Pennsylvania Press, 1968).

Lanitis, N. C., *A Consideration of some Problems pertaining to our Destiny* (Nicosia, 1963).

Mackenzie, Kenneth, 'Cyprus – 1968', *The Geographical Magazine* (London, February 1968), pp. 885–908.

Mango, Andrew, *Turkey: A delicately poised ally*, Washington Paper Series, no. 28 (Sage Publications, London, 1975).

Markezinis, Spyros, 'Strong hope of Permanent Solution on Cyprus', special article in The Times, 2 June 1966.

Matthews, J. E., BSc, FRGS, *Cyprus – An Economic and Geographical Outline* (Zavallis Press, Nicosia, 1961 and 1964).

Maulnier, Thierry, 'Espoirs d'une solution pour Chypre – Mgr Makarios m'a dit . . .', *Figaro*, 10 November 1967.

Le Monde, 'Chypre – Carrefour entre l'Occident et l'Orient' (May 1968).

Ortega, *Index: Destruction of Housing in Cyprus* (After the 1963–64 Crisis). Stencilled.

Pan Publishing House, Nicosia:
  Political Review for 1964.
  Political Review for 1965.

Papadopoulos, Tassos, *Cyprus, Developments and Realities* (Nicosia, August 1969).

Parliamentary Group for World Government, *Cyprus School History Textbooks, a study in education for international misunderstanding.*

Pipinellis, Panayotis, 'West will thank Greece one day', *Athens News*, 27 April 1968.

Polyviou, Polyvios G., *Cyprus: The Tragedy and the Challenge* (John Swain, 1975).

Purcell, H. D., Chapter 7, 'Cyprus since Independence', *Cyprus* (Ernest Benn Ltd, London, 1969), pp. 350–402.

Rustem, Kemal, *Cyprus Economy* (Nicosia, 22 July 1966). Stencilled.

Salih, Halil Ibrahim, *Cyprus: An Analysis of Cypriot Political Discord* (Theo Gaus' Sons, Inc., New York, 1968).

Stavrinides, Zenon, *The Cyprus Conflict, National Identity and Statehood* (L. Stavrinides Press, Nicosia, 1976).

Stegenga, James A., *The United Nations Force in Cyprus* (Ohio State University Press, 1968).

Talarides, K., 'L'Affaire de Chypre', *Politique Étrangère*, no. 1, 1964 (Paris), pp. 74–91.

OFFICIAL AND SEMI-OFFICIAL SOURCES

Greek and Greek Cypriot

AKEL:
  Statement of AKEL (Nicosia, 25 April 1964).

Anonymous:
  Turkish Political Aims and the Cyprus Economy (circa 1967–68). Stencilled.

Cyprus Trade Unions:
  Appeal by Cyprus Trade Union Federations & Organisations to their Turkish Colleagues (Nicosia, 20 February 1964).

Government of Greece:
  Kostopoulos, Stavros (Foreign Minister), and Papandreou, George (Prime Minister), *The Cyprus Question and Greek-Turkish Relations, 24 April 1964* (PM's Office, PID, Athens, 27 April 1964).
  Papandreou, George, Statement (PM's Office, PID, 13 April 1964).

Greek Communal Chamber:
  Cyprus Today, years 1964–1976 (After March 1965 published by the Ministry of Education).
  Makarios, 'Proposals to amend the Cyprus Constitution', *Cyprus Today*, vol. 1, no. 6 (November–December 1963).

The Republic of Cyprus:

Makarios, *Five-Year Programme of Economic Development*, address to the House of Representatives on 21 August 1961.

Census of Population and Agriculture 1960, vols. I & VI (Nicosia, 1962 and 1963).

Tornaritis, Criton, QC (Attorney-General), *Legal Aspects of the Problem of Refugees in Cyprus* (Nicosia, 1975).

Turkey Invades Cyprus: The Attila Outrage (Nicosia, September 1974).

The Ministry of Finance:

Economic Review 1962.

Patsalides, A. (Director of Planning Bureau, later Minister of Finance): *Planning for Economic Development in Cyprus* (August 1964). Stencilled.

Patsalides, A: *Budget Address 1969* and for the years 1970–1971.

Patsalides, A: *Economic Repercussions of the Turkish Invasion and Reactivation of the Economy* (April 1975).

Statistical Data by Ethnic Group (Nicosia, March 1964).

Economic Report, years 1966–1970.

Functional Analysis of the 1967 Budget.

The Third Five-Year Plan 1972–1976.

Solomides, R. (Minister of Finance): *Budget Address 1967* and 1968.

Solomides, R.: *Second Five-Year Plan, Address before the House of Representatives* (8 April 1968). Stencilled.

Solomides, R.: *Summary of the Second Five-Year Plan* (Planning Bureau, 8 April 1968). Stencilled.

Reply to: United Nations Questionnaire on Economic Trends, Problems and Policies 1967–1968 (3 May 1968).

Emergency Economic Action Plan, 1975–1976 (Revision of the Third Five-Year Plan).

Public Information Office-PIO:

Facilities granted to Turkish Cypriots: An Analysis of Government Policy (1970).

Plans for Partition and the Constitution of Cyprus (January 1964).

Dr Ishan Ali Addresses Turkish Cypriots (circa 1964).

Their Crime: Moderation, Friendship and Peace (30 April 1965).

The Function of the United Nations Force in Cyprus (April 1967).

Tornaritis, Criton, QC (Attorney-General), *Land Consolidation Bill* (26 August 1967).

Makarios: 'Archbishop's farewell messages to troops from Greece' (6 December 1967). Stencilled.

Makarios: 'The President bids farewell to the Officers and Men from Greece' (7 December 1967). Stencilled.

Note by the Attorney-General of the Republic (6 January 1968) on the Provisional Cyprus Turkish Administration.

Cyprus: The Problem in Perspective (April 1968. Revised June 1969 and May 1971).

The Clearing up of Certain Misconceptions (Nicosia, July 1969).

Makarios, speech at Morphou (3 May 1970). Stencilled.

The Economic Consequences of the Turkish Invasion and the Future Prospects of the Cyprus Economy (Nicosia, April 1975).

The Cyprus Problem: Historical review and analysis of latest developments (Nicosia, June 1975).

Emergency Economic Action Plan, 1975–76 (Nicosia, 1975). Stencilled.

Turkish and Turkish Cypriot

Ajans-Turk Press, Ankara:

Cyprus: Turkish reply to Archbishop Makarios' Proposals (circa 1964).

Anonymous:
Turks say No to Enosis.

Aziz, Matron Turkan:
'Nurse and Patient shot dead in Matron's home', *Special News Bulletin* (Turkish Communal Chamber, 2 January 1964).

Bilge, Suat:
Le Conflit de Chypre et les Chypriotes Turcs (Ankara, Ajans-Matbaasi, 1961).

Cyprus-Turkish Cultural Association, Ankara:
Cyprus. Why? Why? (1964).

Denktash, Rauf R.:
Letter 9 June 1970 to the author (N.C.); security reasons for refusing the Greeks freedom of movement in Turkish-controlled areas.
The Cyprus Problem, Turkish Cypriot Administration (Nicosia 1974).
A Short Discourse on Cyprus.
Chapters IX, X, XI of an unpublished book on the 1963 crisis from the private papers of Mr Denktash, by courtesy of the author.

London Office of the Turkish Community in Cyprus:
Makarios' Mock Justice (11 May 1964).

Ministry of Foreign Affairs, Ankara:
Foreign Policy of Turkey at the United Nations Between the years 1966–1972: Public Interventions, Selected Documents, Official Communiqués, compiled and edited by Yuksel Solemez, deputy director of International Organisations, MFA, vol. 1, pp. 296–301, vol. 2, pp. 832, 912–13.

Provisional Cyprus Turkish Administration:
United Nations aid to Cyprus (Nicosia, March 1970).

Special Committee on Cyprus Affairs under Chairmanship of Prof. Suat Bilge:
Cyprus. Past/Present/Future (Ankara).

Turkish Communal Chamber:
Riza, H. A., *The House of Representatives: The Separate Majority Right* (1963).
Looking Back (Nicosia, 1963).
The Turkish Case 70:30 and the Greek Tactics (1963).
Federation and the Cyprus Economy (November 1964).
History Speaks (1964).
Conspiracy to destroy the Republic of Cyprus (1969).
Statement by Mr R. R. Denktash, President of the Turkish Communal Chamber. Stencilled.

Turkish Cypriot Committee of Human Rights:
Human rights and Cyprus (Nicosia, June 1969).

Turkish Cypriot Information Office (later Public Information Office of The Turkish Cypriot Administration):
Orek, Osman N., *A Legal Exposé on the Main Points of the Land Consolidation Bill* (Nicosia, September 1967).

Cyprus: The Paradox of Enosis (Introduction by Osman Orek).

Cyprus: The Problem in the light of truth (Nicosia, September 1967).

Re-organisation of the Turkish Cypriot Administrative System (29 December 1967).

New Greek Atrocities in Cyprus (photographs) (Circa 1968).

The clearing up of certain misrepresentations (Nicosia, July 1969).

The Cyprus Problem (Akritas Plan) (Nicosia, 1971).

Cyprus: Where Race-Politics alone Determine Human Values (June 1973).

Orek, Osman N., *Injustices in the application of United Nations Development Programme in Cyprus* (1973).

Europe-Cyprus and Turkish Community (circa 1973–74).

The Question of Cyprus: Can Makarios abandon Enosis? (Nicosia, undated).

Rifat, Dr M. (Mufti of Cyprus), *Cyprus: Religious Aspect of the Conflict* (20 February 1973).

Turkish National Party, Cyprus:

Who is at fault? (April 1964).

The Vice-President and Others:

The Cypriot Turkish Case and Greek Atrocities in Cyprus (*Halkin Sesi* Press, Nicosia, January 1964).

Miscellaneous

British Information Services (BIS) British High Commission, Nicosia:

Digest of the Cyprus Press (1960–1971).

Cyprus Press Digest (1964–1976, Nicosia).

House of Commons Select Committee on Cyprus:

Report from the Select Committee on Cyprus. Session 1975–76 (HMSO, April 1976).

Report from the Select Committee on Cyprus – Observations by the Government (HMSO, August 1976).

US Government Printing Office:

Crisis on Cyprus: 1974. A Study Mission Report (14 August 1974).

Crisis on Cyprus: 1975. One Year After the Invasion (20 July 1975).

Crisis on Cyprus: Crucial Year For Peace 1976 (19 January 1976).

A SELECTED LIST OF INTERNATIONAL DOCUMENTS
COLONIAL PERIOD

Council of Europe (Strasbourg) Consultative
  Assembly, Official Reports of Debates
6th Ordinary Session 1954.
7th Ordinary Session 1955.
8th Ordinary Session 1956–1957.
9th Ordinary Session 1957–1958.
10th Ordinary Session 1958–1959.

International Labour Office (ILO)
  Official Bulletin vol. XL, no. 2 (Geneva
    1957), pp. 66–84.
  Official Bulletin vol. XLI, no. 3 (Geneva
    1958), pp. 199–202.

United Nations Documents

General Assembly Records

Sixth Session
  A/C.4/SR 208 22 November 1951.
  A/C.4/194 27 November 1951. Add.
    1, 13 December 1951.
  A/PV 340 12 November 1951, p. 66.

Eighth Session
  A/PV 439 pp. 66–7.

Ninth Session
  A/C.1/PV 749 14 December 1954.
  A/C.1/PV 750 14 December 1954.
  A/C.1/PV 751 15 December 1954.
  A/C.1/PV 752 15 December 1954.
  A/PV 514 17 December 1954, pp. 538–40.
  Report of the First Committee A/2887.

Tenth Session
  A/BUR/SR 102 [General Committee] 21
    September 1955, pp. 2–5.
  A/PV 521 23 September 1955, pp. 1–5.

Eleventh Session
  A/C.1/PV 847 18 February 1957.
  A/C.1/PV 848 18 February 1957.
  A/C.1/PV 849 19 February 1957.
  A/C.1/PV 850 19 February 1957.
  A/C.1/PV 851 23 February 1957.
  A/C.1/PV 852 22 February 1957.
  A/C.1/PV 853 21 February 1957.
  A/C.1/PV 854 21 February 1957.
  A/C.1/PV 855 22 February 1957.
  A/C.1/PV 856 22 February 1957.
  A/PV 660 26 February 1957, p. 1199.
  Report of the First Committee A/3559.

Twelfth Session
  A/C.1/PV 927 9 December 1957.
  A/C.1/PV 928 9 December 1957.
  A/C.1/PV 929 10 December 1957.
  A/C.1/PV 930 11 December 1957.
  A/C.1/PV 931 11 December 1957.
  A/C.1/PV 932 11 December 1957.
  A/C.1/PV 933 12 December 1957.
  A/C.1/PV 934 12 December 1957.
  A/PV 731 14 December 1957, pp. 618–23.
  Report of the First Committee A/3794.

Thirteenth Session
  A/C.1/PV 996 25 November 1958.
  A/C.1/PV 997 25 November 1958.
  A/C.1/PV 998 26 November 1958.
  A/C.1/PV 999 26 November 1958.
  A/C.1/PV 1000 28 November 1958.
  A/C.1/PV 1001 28 November 1958.
  A/C.1/PV 1002 1 December 1958.
  A/C.1/PV 1003 1 December 1958.
  A/C.1/PV 1004 2 December 1958.
  A/C.1/PV 1005 2 December 1958.
  A/C.1/PV 1006 3 December 1958.
  A/C.1/PV 1007 3 December 1958.
  A/C.1/PV 1008 4 December 1958.
  A/C.1/PV 1009 4 December 1958.
  A/C.1/PV 1010 4 December 1958.
  A/PV 782 5 December 1958, pp. 457–9.
  Report of the First Committee A/4029 and
    Addendum I.

SINCE INDEPENDENCE (AUGUST 1960)

United Nations Documents

Security Council Records

1963 S/PV 1085   27 December.

1964 S/PV 1136⎫ 18 June.
     S/PV 1138⎬ 19 June.
     S/PV 1139⎭ 20 June.
     S/PV 1143   9/11 August.
     S/PV 1146⎫ 11 September.
     S/PV 1147⎬ 11 September.
     S/PV 1151⎪ 16 September.
     S/PV 1153⎭ 17 September.

1965 S/PV 1191⎫ 17 March.
     S/PV 1192⎬ 18 March.
     S/PV 1193⎭ 19 March.
     S/PV 1224   15 June.
     S/PV 1234⎫ 3 August.
     S/PV 1235⎬ 5 August.
     S/PV 1236⎭ 10 August.
     S/PV 1252   5 November.
     S/PV 1270   17 December.

1966 S/PV 1286   16 June.

1967 S/PV 1362   19 June.
     S/PV 1383   24/25 November.
     S/PV 1385⎫ 20 December.
     S/PV 1386⎭ 22 December.

1968 S/PV 1398   18 March.
     S/PV 1432   18 June.

1969 S/PV 1474   10 June.
     S/PV 1521   11 December.

1970 S/PV 1543   9 June.
     S/PV 1564   10 December.

1972 S/PV 1646⎫ 15 June.
     S/PV 1647⎭ 15 June.
     S/PV 1683   12 December.

1973 S/PV 1727⎫ 15 June.
     S/PV 1728⎭ 15 June.
     S/PV 1759   14 December.

1974 S/PV 1771⎫ 29 May.
     S/PV 1772⎭ 29 May.
1974 S/PV 1779⎫ 16 July.
     S/PV 1780⎪ 19 July.
     S/PV 1781⎪ 20 July.
     S/PV 1782⎪ 22 July.
     S/PV 1783⎪ 23 July.
     S/PV 1784⎪ 24 July.
     S/PV 1785⎪ 27 July.
     S/PV 1786⎬ 28 July.
     S/PV 1787⎪ 29 July.
     S/PV 1788⎪ 31 July.
     S/PV 1789⎪ 1 August.
     S/PV 1792⎪ 14 August.
     S/PV 1793⎪ 15 August.
     S/PV 1794⎪ 16 August.
     S/PV 1795⎭ 30 August.
     S/PV 1810   13 December.

1975 S/PV 1813⎫ 20 February.
     S/PV 1814⎪ 21 February.
     S/PV 1815⎪ 25 February.
     S/PV 1817⎬ 27 February.
     S/PV 1818⎪ 4 March.
     S/PV 1819⎪ 5 March.
     S/PV 1820⎭ 12 March.
     S/PV 1830⎫ 13 June.
     S/PV 1831⎭ 16 June.
     S/PV 1863   13 December.

1976 S/PV 1925⎫ 11 June.
     S/PV 1926⎬ 14 June.
     S/PV 1927⎭ 15 June.

Note: The above are the verbatim reports of debates in the Security Council on the Cyprus problem.

Reports of the Secretary-General on the United Nations Operation in Cyprus
[United Nations Force in Cyprus – UNFICYP]

S/5671 29 April 1964.
S/5764 (for the period 26 April 1964–8 June 1964).
S/5950 (for the period 8 June 1964–8 September 1964 and Add. 2, 15 September 1964).
S/6102 (for the period 10 September 1964–12 December 1964).
S/6228 (for the period 13 December 1964–10 March 1965).
S/6426 (for the period 10 March 1965–10 June 1965).
S/6253 26 March 1965.
S/7001 (for the period 11 June 1965–8 December 1965).
S/7191 (for the period 9 December 1965–10 March 1966).
S/7350 (for the period 11 March 1966–10 June 1966).
S/7611 (for the period 11 June 1966–5 December 1966).
S/7969 (for the period 6 December 1966–12 June 1967).
S/8286 (for the period 13 June 1967–9 December 1967).
S/8248 16 November 1967.
S/8446 (for the period 9 December 1967–8 March 1968).
S/8622 (for the period 8 March 1968–7 June 1968).
S/8914 (for the period 8 June 1968–2 December 1968).
S/9233 (for the period 3 December 1968–2 June 1969).
S/9521 (for the period 3 June 1969–1 December 1969).
S/9814 (for the period 2 December 1969–1 June 1970).
S/10005 (for the period 2 June 1970–1 December 1970).
S/10199 (for the period 2 December 1970–19 May 1971).
S/10401 (for the period 20 May 1971–30 November 1971).
S/10664 (for the period 1 December 1971–26 May 1972).
S/10842 (for the period 27 May 1972–1 December 1972).
S/10940 (for the period 2 December 1972–31 May 1973).
S/11137 (for the period 31 May 1973–1 December 1973).
S/11294 (for the period 2 December 1973–22 May 1974).
S/11568 (for the period 23 May 1974–5 December 1974).
S/11717 (for the period 7 December 1974–9 June 1975).
S/11624 18 February 1975.
S/11684 4 May 1975.
S/11900 (for the period 10 June 1975–8 December 1975).
S/12093 (for the period 9 December 1975–5 June 1976).

General Assembly Official Records (GAOR)

Twentieth Session

A/C.1/PV 1408 11 December 1965.
A/C.1/PV 1409 13 December 1965.
A/C.1/PV 1410 13 December 1965.
A/C.1/PV 1411 14 December 1965.
A/C.1/PV 1412 14 December 1965.
A/C.1/PV 1413 15 December 1965.
A/C.1/PV 1414 15 December 1965.
A/C.1/PV 1415 16 December 1965.
A/C.1/PV 1416 16 December 1965.
A/C.1/PV 1417 17 December 1965.
A/C.1/PV 1418 17 December 1965.
A/PV 1402 18 December 1965 pp. 1–11.
Report of the First Committee A/6166.

Twenty-ninth Session

A/SPC/SR 922 28 October 1974.
A/SPC/SR 923 29 October 1974.
A/PV 2270   29 October 1974.
A/PV 2271   30 October 1974.
A/PV 2272   31 October 1974.
A/PV 2273   31 October 1974.
A/PV 2274   1 November 1974.
A/PV 2275   1 November 1974.

Thirtieth Session

A/PV 2401   11 November 1975.
A/SPC/SR 975 12 November 1975 pp. 118–24.
A/SPC/SR 976 12 November 1975 pp. 124–6.
A/PV 2404   13 November 1975.
A/PV 2405   13 November 1975.
A/PV 2406   14 November 1975.
A/PV 2407   14 November 1975.
A/PV 2411   19 November 1975.
A/PV 2413   20 November 1975.

Index

Note: * indicates after Independence

Aaland Islands 88, 132

Abdoh, Dr D. (UN del., Iran) 330, 331, 334, 336

Acheson, Dean 60; his plan 371*

Active service: troops put on 147

Adamantos 49; fined for political speech, November 1948 40–1; expelled from AKEL 53

Adelphi Forest 149

Aden 258

Aegean 17; Greek Cypriot descent from colonists 19

Aeolia, SS: smuggled arms etc. landed as 'books' 148

Afro-Asian states 272

Afxentiou, Gregoris 120, 122, 149, 150, 200, 251–2, 348*, 381*; killed in battle with the security forces 232–3

Aghia Arkha 184

Aghia Napa Church 49

Aghios Ambrosios 308 fn.

Aghios Dhometios, 315; Police Station 290

Aghios Epiktikos 122

Aghios Georghios 105, 107, 109, 110, 111, 128, 206, 223, 350; trial of crew 116–18

Aghios Georghios Church (Famagusta), damaged by Turkish rioters 231

Aghios Loukas Church, set alight by the Turks 300

Aghios Mamas 185

Aghios Nicolaos RAF Signals Station, bomb explosions at 138

Aghios Omologhitadhes 309 fn.

Aghios Serghios 387*

Aghios Theodoros 374*, 375*

Aghios Vasilios, 288

Aghoursos 304

Agros 126, 185

Aitken, William. MP 78

AKEL (Reform Party of the Working People): founded 1941 at Skarinou 30; early political activities, tactics of violence 31–3; domination of trade unions 31, 53; record in municipal elections 31, 34, 42; members tried and imprisoned for seditious conspiracy 32–4; replaces the Communist Party 34; campaigns for self-government 37–8, 40; rejects Winster plan 39; drops self-government from

programme after meeting leader of Greek Communist Party 41; contacts with international communism 41, 49, 51 and fn., 381*; pursues Popular Front tactics 41, 49, 51–2, 54, 257; dissension within 41, 53; initiates plebiscite proposals 46–7; opposition to bases 51–4, 140, 151; friction with the Ethnarchy 51, 53–4, *et seq.*; relations with Makarios 51, 53, 151, 308; purge of dissidents, extremists gain control 53; proscribed by British, members arrested 150–2; its opposition to violence in the national struggle 151; clashes with EOKA 151, 256–7, 281–2, 307–9; suspected by Grivas of colluding with the British 152, 281–2; released from detention 256; denounces EOKA's murders of leftists 307; supports Makarios as sole representative in future negotiations 308; opposes passive resistance 311; ban on lifted 355; supports John Klerides in first presidential election 355; switches allegiance to Makarios in first parliamentary election 362; contacts with the USSR 381–2*; *see also* Communists *and* PEO

Akhna 280

'Akritas' 184

Akritas, Loukis, 64

Akritopoula 280

Akrotiri 357–8, 360, 389*, 394*; British base used for bombing Egyptian airfield, 205; French aeroplanes stationed at 205; RAF Hospital 246

Albania, Greek irredentist claims against 57, 61

Alevakaris 117

Algeria 338

Ambushes 122, 126, 129, 146, 148, 149, 152, 175, 176, 177, 188, 202, 203, 205, 315

American Academy, Larnaca 22

American Confederation of Labour 69

AHEPA (American Hellenic Educational Progressive Association) 59

American Radio Station: Cypriot Communists' dynamite attacks on 40

Amery, Julian, Under-Secretary of State for the Colonies 196, 358, 359

Amiandos 121, 122, 140; miners' strike 40

Amiandos Mining Company 205

Amnesty: British terms (February 1956) 164–5, 197

Anatolia 222, 259, 287; attachment of Cyprus to 87

Anatolia Agency 277

Ancient Greece: Cypriot obsession with 18, 23, 279

ANE (Valiant Youth of EOKA) 255–8, 274, 278, 280 and fn., 306 and fn., 310

Angel, Z. (UN del., Colombia) 270

Anglo-Cypriot talks 235

Anglo-Greek relations 84, 86, 96, 124, 130, 238, 273, 279

Anglo-Hellenic Institute, Athens 73

Ankara Radio 239, 276, 286, 294, 354

Ankara University: Turkish Cypriots' political action 45

Ano Panaghia 180

Anti-Greek riots, Istanbul 136, 212; Smyrna 136, 212

Antioch, Patriarchs of: abortive efforts to control Church of Cyprus 19

AON 54

Arabs 8, 326

Araujo, A. (UN del., Colombia) 330

Archbishop of Athens, *see* Dorotheos *and* Spyridon

Archbishops of Cyprus, *see* Kyprianos, Cyril III Basileiou, Leontios Leontiou, Makarios II Myriantheus, Makarios III Mouskos

Archiepiscopal elections 20, 36 50; electoral procedures 402*, App. 3

Argyros 143

Aristotelis, Assistant Superintendent: murdered 175

Armenians 20, 122

Armitage, Sir Robert, Governor 141; examines prospects for a constitution, decides no progress possible unless Enosis campaign is checked 74–5; reports to Cabinet, is instructed to prepare for new constitution 80–1; escapes assassination 127; leaves Cyprus, becomes Governor of Nyasaland 140

Armour, Senator, author of report on Greece and Turkey, his warning on the dangers of the Cyprus problem to Western security 173

Asha: EOKA attack on Mukhtar 257

Asia Minor: the 1921 war in 90, 222, 268

'Asklypios', EOKA's agent at Kykko 183; arrested 184

Assyrians in Cyprus 19

Ataturk, Mustapha Kemal 18, 42 fn., 43, 67, 87, 136, 137, 226

Ataturk's guerrillas 90

Ataturk Square, Nicosia, Turkish riots in 276

Athalassa Farm 177

Athalassa Police Headquarters 384*

'Athanatos' 184

Athenagoras, Archbishop, Head of the Greek Church in Western Europe 190 and fn.

Athenagoras, Ecumenical Patriarch 28, 259

Athens 278, 304, 313, 325, 327, 353, 385*, 388*, 394*; Cyprus riots and demonstrations in 65, 68–9, 82, 169, 216, 238; the centre of Hellenism 385*; EOKA B financed from 388*

Athens Radio 82, 85, 100, 115, 139, 145, 155, 158, 261, 273, 294

Atrocities: alleged British 241, 242, 246, 251–2, 266–7, 269, 282, 293, 316, 317, 320–2; Greek against Greek 257, 267, 351, 359, 387*; Cypriot intercommunal 288–93 (Geunyeli) 367*; Turkish Army 393*

Atrocity campaign against the British 244–55, 282

Attlee, Clement, Prime Minister 196, 197; refusal to see Cypriot delegation 35

Attorney-General, *see* Tornaritis *and* Henry

Australia 333

Austria 260

Averoff, Evanghelos, Greek Foreign Minister 216–19, 225, 254 fn.; argues Greek case at UN 219–21, 223–4, 226–7, 229, 230, 266–7, 270–1, 285, 329–30, 332–6; contacts with Grivas 237, 239, 260 and fn.; reconciliation with Zorlu 337, 338–9, 340, 342–3; role in the Zurich settlement 340–3, 344–6, 357

Avghi: communist newspaper revived 152

Avghousti, Evanghelos: murdered 308

Avgorou 257, 301

Azinas, Andreas 54, 95–7, 101–3, 105–7, 111, 339, 350

Azinas, father of Andreas Azinas 101, 103, 106

Baker, Brigadier (later Field-Marshal Sir Geoffrey) 186, 232

Balkans 68, 260

Ban on 1931 exiles' return lifted 35

Barclay's Bank, Limassol, manager of attacked 181

Baring, Lt 289–90, 292, 293

Barnabas, the Apostle 19

Basic Articles, the 27 of the Cyprus Constitution (1959) 364*, 365*

Bayar, President of Turkey 67, 239

Beckingham, Professor 42 fn.

Beirut 119, 174

Belaunde, Victor (UN del., Peru) 333, 334

Belgian Mines 255

Belgium 260

Belgrade, Eastern Orthodox Patriarch of 172

Bell, Dr, Bishop of Chichester 172

Benites Vinneza, L. (UN del., Ecuador) 87

Berberoglou, A. M. 55
Bevan, Aneurin 76, 79, 171, 191, 196, 201, 300, 318
Bevan, Dr: assassination of 205
Bil, Hikmet 136
Bilge, Suat, Turkish Foreign Office legal adviser 352
Bishops (Cyprus), *see* Kition, Kyrenia, Paphos
Bishops (Cyprus): friction with the British authorities 22
Bitsios, Pandelis 48
'Black Book', compiled by EOKA on alleged tortures 179
Black and Tans 228
Boghaz 121; military camp 120
Bohy, Georges 15
Boland, F. H. (UN del., Ireland) 225
bomb explosions 136, 188, 200, 386*, 387*
Boston Theological College, Makarios's scholarship to 46
'Botsaris' 184
'Bouboulis' 184
Bourke, Sir Paget, Chief Justice 290, 356
Bowker, Sir James, British Ambassador, Ankara 275, 276
Boycott of British goods, EOKA's 287, 310–11; *see also* Passive Resistance
Boyd-Carpenter, John, MP 189
Braiu, Bernard, MP 201
Bridel, Professor (Swiss constitutional lawyer) 351
British colonial rule, merits and failures of 24–7
British Consulate-General, Athens 73, 93, 94, 97, 128, 200
British Consulate (Crete); destroyed by students 214
British Council 75
British Council of Churches 189
British Embassy, Athens 200, 224; attack on 394*
British Forces, *see* Middle East Land Forces (MELF), Middle East Air Force (MEAF), RAF, Regiments, Royal Marines, Royal Marine Commandos, Royal Military Police, Royal Navy
British Institute Nicosia, destruction of 139, 140
British military bases 194, 324, 326; communist opposition to 51–2, 54; Sovereign Base Areas 356–61, 367*, 389*, 393*
British residents in Cyprus, property looted 394
Brockway, Fenner, MP 181, 234, 253
Brosio, Manlio, NATO Secretary-General 376*
Brown, Cpl: killed in gun battle 233
Brown, Irving, ICFTU 215
Brussels 255

Bryn, D. (UN del., Norway) 224
Buddhism 228
Building Workers' Union 309
Bulganin 124
Bulgaria 83; Greek claims against 57
Bunche, Dr Ralph: visit to Paphos 370*
Butler, Brigadier (Parachute Regiment) 182
Butler, R. A., MP (later Lord Butler): criticises Dr Fisher's unhelpful intervention 189
Byronic tradition 58
Byzantine: supremacy 19, 20; practice of poisoning water wells 177
Byzantium 18, 222, 346

Caccia, Sir Harold 160
Cacoyannis, George 53
Callaghan, James 253, 298, 299, 300, 393*
Camp K (Kokkinitrimithia) 247, 282, 285
Canon, Cavendish, American Ambassador, Athens 66, 172–3, 215
Canon Law 28, 385*
Canterbury, Archbishop of (Fisher) 171, 172, 196, 231; his proposals for a settlement 189
Cantons, Turkish Cypriot 371*, 392*
Cardiff, Maurice, director, British Council, Cyprus 75
Casement, Sir Roger 223
Castle, Barbara, MP 261–2, 275, 317–18, 319, 322, 323
Cease-fire 368*, 369*, 390*, 391*, 392*, 395*
Celler, Emmanuel 59
Central Office of Information 63, 65
Chamber of Commerce 35
Charity, HMS 110
Chartas, Andreas 232
Chartas, Christos 149, 150
Chatos 143, 144, 384*
Cherkezos 143
Chichester, Bishop of 191
Chief Justice 117, 118, 141, 145, *see also* Hallinan 248; *see also* Paget Bourke
China 228
Christianity: Cyprus's conversion to 19
Christodoulou, Michael 117
Christodoulou, Phidias 142–4
Christofi, Photis 203
Christoudes, Andreas 143
Chrysafinis, George, QC 50, 111, 142
Chrysorroyiatissa, Abbot of 169, 221, 252; murdered 156
Chrysostomos, Panayotis: inquest 320–1
Church of Cyprus, the Autocephalous Eastern [Greek] Orthodox: its historic independence 19–20; its traditional role in politics 19–20, 21, 22, 28, 34, 37, 41, 52, 90, 108, 172, 252, 310; British tolerance of its activities 22; opposition to

Church of Cyprus (*cont.*)
self-government 26, 163; hostility towards the Communists 31, 41, 46, 163; sponsorship of plebiscite (1950) 46–7, 49; its role criticised by Turkey 87, 132; its sponsorship of EOKA revolt 176, 249, 310; its power as landowner 361–2
Church Laws; repeal of the 1937 35
Churchill, Winston 23, 77, 81 fn., 82, 220
Civil Service: ratio Greeks to Turks in 341
Classics: influences of 23, 25
Clements, Martin, Nicosia District Commissioner: holds enquiry in Metaxas Square 176, 182
Coeur de Lion, Richard 20
Cold War 40, 44; need for Western unity in the face of 135
Colina, de la, R. (UN del., Mexico) 333, 335
Collier, Colonel: killed in Limassol 315
Collins, Canon: called for support for Fisher 189
Colonels, the Greek (Papadopoulos, Makarezos, and Pattakos) 374, 376
Colonial Office 28, 56
Colonies, Secretary of State for: first visit (1955) to Cyprus since 1878 124
Comet, HMS 110
Commercial Lyceum (Larnaca) 109, 148
Committee of Cyprus Autonomy (1957) 28–9
Commonwealth: 1948 Constitutional plan debars discussion of island's status within 38; certain territories within which could never expect full independence (Hopkinson's 'Never') 76–7; newly independent territories' right to contract in or out of 77; members' right to decide future 299; Grivas's ban on imports from 313
Communal Chambers, elections for 362
Communist Party of Cyprus 26
Communists 30, 34, 38, 40, 50–1, 54, 57, 61, 86, 91, 92, 115, 120, 126, 136, 138, 140, 150–1, 215, 279, 306, 315, 342, 348, 352, 364*, 381–2*, 385–6*; *see also* AKEL *and* PEO
Communists: mayor and councillors imprisoned 50
Conscription 370*
Conservative Government: Cyprus policy 123, 218, 298; embarrassment at Council of Europe's intervention 293; right-wingers object to concessions over bases under Zurich settlement 345
Constantine, King of Greece 23
Constantinople 18, 19, 90, 346
Constitution(s): first Legislative Council (1878) 26; suspension of in 1931 27; demand for restoration of, in late thirties 28; of the Republic (Zurich) 341–2, 365*

Constitutional Commissioner 162, 362
Constitutional plans: Labour Government's (1948) 37–8 and fn., 74, 84; of 1954 80–1; Harding-Makarios negotiations 156–7, 160–1, 163–5; Radcliffe's 207–11, 219, 222, 223–5, 237, 242, 244, 264 and fn.; Foot's 274–5; Macmillan's partnership plan 296–300
Consultative Assembly, 37, 39, 44
Coombe, Major Brian: ambushed by EOKA, captures Zakos and Michael 152; awarded George Medal, his press conference in Nicosia 153
Co-ordination Committee for Enosis (ESEA) 384*
Copper: main source of wealth 17
Corfu 18
Cornaro, Catherine 20
Coronation ceremony riots in Paphos 54, 206
Council of Europe 125 fn., 244, 254, 293; Kassimatis's Cyprus speeches 46, 64, 218; *see also* European Commission on Human Rights
Council of Ministers 385*
Court martial of two army officers 179
Courtney, Mr, US Consul, Nicosia 158
Cox, Sir Christopher, Colonial Office's educational adviser 148
Creech Jones, Arthur, Secretary of State for the Colonies 33, 35, 37
Cremer, Mr: kidnapped by EOKA 188 and fn.
Crete: Makarios's visit to 213; cancellation of Sixth Fleet's visit to 216
Crossman, Richard 78, 79, 300
Curium 265
Cutliffe, Mrs: murder of, in Varosha 319, 322
Cypriot Students' Committee 68
Cyprus Army 341, 355, 365*
Cyprus Broadcasting Station 114, 138
Cyprus Conciliation Committee 192
Cyprus Enosis Front (KEM) 353
Cyprus Mail 290
Cyprus Mines Corporation (CMC) 174 fn., 175
Cyprus Regiment 43
Cyprus Turkish Association 55
Cyprus Workers' Confederation, *see* SEK
Cyril III, Archbishop 27
Czech arms 373*, 377*
Czechoslovakia: supplies arms to Cyprus 384*

'Dafnis' 120
Daily Telegraph 170
Dakota aircraft destroyed (Nicosia airport) 176

Daskalakis, Professor, Rector of Athens University: launches campaign of hatred against Britain 82

Davies, Clement 170, 195, 197

Davies, Rodger, US Ambassador: murder of 393*

Davlos 392*

Death penalty 147, 148; made mandatory 206

Decolonisation 365*

Defence White Paper (1957) 259

de Gaulle 327

Demetriou, Andreas 147, 180, 182; execution of 181

Democratic Union (Greece) 213, 354, 355, 362

Demokratis: editor of sentenced to three months' imprisonment 42

Deniz: Turkish vessel caught smuggling ammunition 353–4

Denktash, Rauf 44, 111, 112, 141, 276, 286, 296, 352, 354, 374*, 375*, 377*, 383*, 392*, 393*; joins Foot and Dervis in appeal to end communal strife 303

Deportation 167–8; reactions to 168–73

Dervis, Dr, mayor of Nicosia 265, 303, 314, 352, 353, 354; friction with the Turks 55

De Valera 220

Devonshire, Duke of 25

Dhali 247, Mukhtar of shot dead 257

Dhekelia Base 360, 393*; power station 357, 360

Diamond, HMS 186 fn.

'Dighenis', *see* Grivas 90, 114, 126, 154, 188, 238, 348

Diplis 184

Direkoglou, Fevzi 142, 143, 144

Disraeli, Benjamin 22

Djenghiz, Hussein 142, 143, 144

Dodecanese Islands 57, 71, 72, 239

Dolder Hotel, Zurich 340

Dominion status for Cyprus 76

Donnelly, Desmond, MP 261–2, 299

Dorchester Hotel: Cypriot delegates' meeting, February 1959 344

Dorotheos, Archbishop of Athens 239

Drakos, Markos 114, 152, 184, 187, 232

Driberg, Tom 58, 77, 79, 261

Droullia, Mr 218

Drousiotis 107

Dulles, John Foster, US Secretary of State: intervenes to prevent Karaolis's execution 181; denounced by EOKA 279

Durrell, Lawrence 75, 409*

EAEM (The Solid United National Front) 302, 310

EAM 239

EAS (National Liberal Coalition) 38, 47

Eastern Mediterranean 73, 79, 87, 104, 129, 130, 135, 140, 158, 159, 375*, 389*

Eastern Orthodox Church, *see* Patriarchs

Eastern Roman Empire 222

Eastern Thrace 90

Ecevit, Bulent, Turkish Prime Minister, 389*, 391*, 393*

Ecole de Guerre, France 91

Economic development plan (November 1955) 146

Economist, The 73

Ecumenical Patriarch, *see* Athenagoras

EDA 67, 213, 285

EDEK, Socialist party 387*

Eden, Sir Anthony, Foreign Secretary, Prime Minister 73 fn., 157, 158–9, 160, 171, 189, 195 and fn., 197, 220; meeting with Papagos 70; statement on oil 217

Edinburgh, Duke of 216

EDMA 352, 353, 355

EDON 352

Education: disruption of by EOKA, parents' dislike 307

Education, Ministry of, Athens 23

Efstathiou 233

Egypt 76, 77, 79, 128, 174, 205, acquisition of bases in 22; Greek minority in 88 nationalisation of the Suez Canal 200

Egyptians in Cyprus 19

Eisenhower, President 221, 279

Ekrem, Mr Justice 141

ELAS 92

Elections, Greek parliamentary, *see* Greece

Elections (Cyprus): municipal 31, 34, 42; presidential 377*; parliamentary 382*

Electoral Law 362

Elizabeth, Princess 216

Elliot, Walter 196 and fn.

Ellison, Mr Justice 233

EMAK 111

Emergency, state of 147

Engen, H. (UN del., Norway) 271

English School, Nicosia 22, 141

ENOSIS: origins of 13, 18–19, 100; rise of movement during Greek War of Independence 20–1; Turkish Cypriot objections to 20–1, 24, 43, 48, 54–5, 84, *et seq.*; Gladstone's sympathy for 25; communist opposition to during greater part of British rule 26; agitators destroy Government House in 1931 riots 27; decline in public agitation for 27–8; Secretary of State for Colonies doubts seriousness of 29; nationalist and church obsession with 31, 35; revival of Greek demands for during World War II 31, 43; Greek Parliament's unanimous resolution in favour of, 1947 36; British attempts to establish liberal government precluding

ENOSIS (*cont.*)

38–9; Akelists accused of betraying 39; AKEL switches to supporting 41–2; church holds plebiscite for 45–50; promotion abroad of campaign for 49; Makarios sponsors organisations for furtherance of 52; Greek pressure for 61–3; House of Commons discussion on 77–9; UN discussions on 84, 86–7, 222, 225, 230; demonstrations in Cyprus for 109, British determination to resist 166; Kassimatis recognises lack of support for, at UN 230; Averoff describes independence as transition in struggle for 260 and fn.; TMT warning of possible revival of 274; Denktash brands Macmillan plan as stepping-stone towards, 296; Makarios accepts indefinite deferment of 322–3, 339.

After Independence: modified form of, considered by USA 371*; shelved by Makarios after Kophinou fighting 377*; rival presidential candidate (Evdokas) bases campaign on 377*; adherence of EOKA extremists to 378*; Greek officers in Cyprus encourage 383–4*; ESEA formed for promotion of 384*; Soviet Union's objections to 386*

Enosis (Bulletin) 109, 115

'Enosis and nothing but Enosis', Cypriot policy of 163

Entezam, N. (UN del., Iran) 227

EOKA (National Organisation of Cypriot Fighters): birth of 105; outbreak of the revolt 114; early activities of 114–15; infiltration of government departments 128, 141; early arrests of members 128–9; Poulis's murder 141–5; reverses in Limassol 148; explodes bombs during Lennox-Boyd's visit, destroys Hermes aircraft 166; intensifies hostilities after Makarios's deportation 168, 174–6; routed by the security forces 182–7; documents recovered by British 186; action in England rumoured 190; orders boycott of Radcliffe 195–6; renews violence 200–1; conspires to oust Theotokis 215; first members executed 216; Averoff denies Greece sending arms to 223; losses in spring 1957 231–4; offers to suspend operations on Makarios's release 235; seizes opportunity to rebuild forces during cease-fire 236; keeps issue alive by memorial services and intimidation 243; pursues atrocity campaign 244–55; prepares for the Second Round 255–6; forms anti-Turk groups 255–6; clashes with the leftists 257, 280–2, 306–9; ordered by Grivas to suspend operations 265; plans renewed violence 277, 279, 282; starts passive resistance 282, 306, 310–15; clashes with the Turks 302–5; renews action against security forces and Greek civilians 315; executes Samaras 316–17; murders Mrs Cutliffe 319; intensifies action 328–9; reacts unfavourably to Zurich settlement 342–4; fate of prisoners holds up settlement 346; boycotts Makarios's reception 346; campaign's running costs 349; divided loyalties caused by 350–1; political activity after settlement 351–2; parades Czech weapons 377*; retains positions in police after Independence 378*; links with National Front 378*; *see also* Grivas *and* Guerrilla warfare

EOKA B 386–7*; proscription of 387–8*; US Ambassador's murder attributed to 393; *see also* Grivas

Epalxis 354

EPEK, Liberal coalition 66, 214

Ephesus, the Council of 19

Ephimeris 49–50

Epirus, northern: Greek claims to 66

Episkopi 394*

Erim, Professor Nihat 351

Erkin, F. C., Foreign Minister of Turkey 367*, 382*

ESEA (Co-ordination Committee for the Cyprus Struggle) 384*

Esin, S. (UN del., Turkey) 266

Esmer, Professor Ahmet 194 fn.

Ethnarch: traditional leader of the Greeks in temporal and spiritual matters 20; British refusal to recognise 22; Makarios retains office of 51, 242, 309

Ethnarchy 35, 46, 49, 54, 66, 69, 70, 77, 78, 124, 178, 191, 195, 215, 216, 217, 230, 240, 259, 269, 281; Athens Branch's role in ousting Theotokis 215; members exiled by the British after 1951 riots 216

Ethnarchy Council 51–2, 61, 126, 127, 145, 157, 162–3, 166, 178

Ethnic origins of the Cypriots 19, 20, 21

Ethniki 353, 359

Ethnikos Kyrix 73

European Commission on Human Rights (Council of Europe); Cyprus inquiry 218, 253–4, 274

Evaghelakis, Evanghelos 232

'Evaghoras 100, 101, 103, 104, 107; dismissal of 118–19

Evdokas, Dr, Nicosia psychiatrist 377*, 383*

Evkaf (body administrating Moslem properties): colonial administration's control over 42, 44, 209

Evros, Greece 374*, 390*

Evrykhou 121

Executions 181, 216, 233

Executive Council (EXCO) 36, 37, 75, 100, 139
Ezekiel, Bishop (Greek, USA) 60

Fabian Bureau: study on strategic colonies 34–5, 45
Faik, Sergeant 110
Famagusta 140, 280 fn., 301, 309, 315, 319, 320, 360, 370*, 390*, 391–2*; old Police Station 316; Cutliffe murder (1958) 319–22; Old City 376*
Faringdon, Lord 31
Farouk, King 88
Fascist attacks: Greek resistance to 130
federation, concept of dismissed by Radcliffe 209
Federation of Trade and Industry 178
Finland 88, 132, 260
First World War 23
Fisher, *see* Canterbury
Flags 155–6
Foot, Sir Hugh (Lord Caradon), Governor 267, 279, 294, 298, 359; appointed Governor, his qualities for post 263; influence with the Labour Party 263; reaction in Greece 263; Kutchuk's anxieties concerning 263; distrusted by Grivas 264, 283; statement to journalists after arrival in Cyprus 264–5; calls on Mayor of Nicosia 265, 271; conciliation policy 273, 278, 283; warned by TMT 274; favours unitary self-government, arrives in London with new plan which Cabinet accepts 274–5; visits Ankara, 28 January 1958 276 and fn.; appeals for continuation of peace, 2 February 277; meets Makarios in Athens 13 February 278; communicates with, and attempt to meet Grivas 283–5, 297; reported differences with the Army 283–4; orders island-wide standstill, introduces strong measures 303 and fn.; corresponds with Mayor of Kyrenia on allegations of British brutality 317; visits Famagusta with Kendrew after Cutliffe murder 319; commutes *Deniz* arms smugglers' sentences 354
Foot plan, the 274–9
Forces Broadcasting Services (FBS) 273
Forestry Department 24; soldiers trapped in fire 186
France 325, 327, 390*
Frederika, Queen 67
French troops' arrival in Cyprus during Suez crisis 200
Frydas, Mr, Greek Consul, Nicosia 314
Fuad, Mr, Turkish magistrate 251
Fulbright, Senator 60
Fulton, Senator: pleads for Pallikarides's life 253

Gaitskell, Hugh 170, 195, 197, 318–19
Gatwick, crash of aircraft carrying Turkish delegates 344
Geneva 371*, 391*, 392*
Georghiades, Antonis 184, 185, 187, 347, 350
Georghiou, Nikos 246
Georkatzis, Polykarpos 119 fn., 232, 367*; escapes from prison 200; found dead 381
Geunyeli 367*, 389*; massacre at 288 and fn., 289–95, 303
Geunyeli Report 293
Ghandi, Mahatma 282, 311
Ghaziveran: battle between Greeks and Turks at 368*
Ghazouleas 106
Ghizikis, President of Greece 388*, 390*
Gibraltar 80, 88
Gill, police sergeant 288–9, 292
Gladstone 25, 197
Gleadell, Brigadier (Chief of Staff) 318
Gnomi 383*
Gothic influence 8
Gough, Frederic, MP 253
Government House 131, 177
Governors of Cyprus, *see* Armitage, Foot, Harding, Palmer, Storrs, Winster, Wright
Grammos, Battle of 61
Grand National Assembly, Ankara 345
Great Britain 194, 235, 242, 272, 275, 286, 294, 296, 300, 311, 323, 325, 327; strategic interest in Cyprus 22, 34, 70, 130, 135, 137, 163, 165, 259, 324, 325, 328, 340, 341, 356–7, 360, 364*, 370–1*; educational policy 22, 23, 25, 126; offers Cyprus to Greece 23; relations with Greece 24, 62, 73, 123, 163, 223, 238, 244, 254, 273; attempts to establish self-government 26, 35, 158, 276, 278, 283, 298; tries to stop Cyprus discussion at UN 83, 96; refusal to discuss Cyprus question 124; invites Greece to Tripartite Conference 125; its attitude to self-determination 139, 160, 161, 267, 275, 299; relations with Turkey 194, 267, 276, 323, 324, 394–5*; efforts to reach settlement at international level 297; qualified support for independence 323; its acceptance of the Zurich agreement 342, 344; backs Turkey's appeal to the Security Council 368–9*; negative role as guarantor of Cypriot independence 364*, 372*; refuses Ecevit's request for action under Treaty of Guarantee 389*; authorises Turkish Cypriot refugees to fly from Akrotiri to Turkey 394*; *see also* British Military Bases
'Greater Greece', the 'Great Idea' (*Megali Ellada*, Megali Idea) 18, 90–1, 346
Greece 74, 84, 124, 215, 217, 218, 236, 237, 240, 275, 284, 323, 326, 329, 340, 342, 344,

Greece (*cont.*)

364*, 367*, 374*, 388*; early links with Cyprus 19; relations with Britain 24, 62, 73, 123, 163, 223, 238, 244, 254, 256, 273; relations with Turkey 44, 61–2, 67–8, 69, 73, 85, 89, 134, 136, 212–13, 259, 285, 296, 326, 341, 343, 346, 356, 359, 364*, 371–2*, 375–6*, 381–2*, 385*, 390–2*; pursuit of Enosis 73–4; parliamentary elections 164–6, 214; attitude to Spaak's Cyprus formula 305, 324–7; withdrawal of forces from NATO Hq Izmir 295, 396*; rejects Macmillan plan 305; changes policy from self-determination to Independence 322; Greek Cypriots' dependence on 345; agrees to place Army contingent under UN 370*; *see also* Member States

Greek Americans: role in Cyprus dispute 59, 68, 396*

Greek Army 100, 128, 221, 345, 347, 348, 371*, 373–4*, 376–8*, 381*, 385*, 388–90*; stand against the Italians (1941) 257

Greek Civil War 107

Greek Communists: disclose Grivas's identity 348

Greek Confederation of Labour 61, 63, 64, 69

Greek Consul, Nicosia 104, 121, 237, 311, 342

Greek Consulate-General, Izmir 136

Greek Consulate-General, Nicosia 177

Greek Consul-General, Nicosia 235

Greek Cypriot internecine strife, *see* AKEL and EOKA

Greek Independence Day 105; Lefkoniko disturbances (1945) 32

Greek junta 381*, 384–5*, 386*, 387*, 388*, 389*, 390*, 393*

Greek mines in Cyprus: EOKA's source of dynamite 174

Greek officers: secret landings in Cyprus 371–3*

Greek Orthodox churches: attacked in Istanbul 136

Greek Parliament: adopts unanimous pro-Enosis resolution 36, 58

Greek Press Union, Athens 251

Greek Rally 63, 67

Greek War of Independence 13, 20, 32, 36, 187, 279

'Green Line': cease-fire line set up in 1963 367–8*

Grice, Alan: killed by bomb explosion 205

Griffiths, James, British Colonial Secretary 59, 76, 79, 192, 197

Grivas, Colonel George, alias 'Dighenis', leader of EOKA 42, 99, 114, 146, 154, 186, 191, 197–202, 218, 220, 223, 235, 238, 242, 248–50, 255, 260, 274, 277, 315, 344–5, 365, 378, 388; birth at Trikomo 90; adopts Greek nationality at seventeen, fights Asia Minor campaign gaining life-long interest in guerrilla warfare 90; youthful ambition to join crusade for 'Greater Greece' 90; his service in two world wars 91; forms terrorist organisation X (Khi) 91; takes up cause of Enosis, enters politics 92–3; seeks help in Athens for Cyprus revolt 93; secret visits to Cyprus 93, 94–5; relations with Makarios 93–8, 104–9, 112–13, 174, 202, 239–40, 311, 314, 347, 352–3, 378; sets up Revolutionary Committee, Athens, seeks Archbishop Spyridon's help 94; leaves for Cyprus via Rhodes to organise revolt, lands at Khlorakas 100–1; trains guerrillas and makes all preparations for revolt 101–13, *passim*; his obsession with communism 107–8, 115, 152, 178, 256, 350, uses schoolchildren in guerrilla warfare 108–9, 120–1, 145, 155–6; moves to temporary hq. on eve of revolt 113; sets up extra command at Lefka, orders formation of three new guerrilla groups, chooses site for ambushing Gen. Keightley 121; opens second major offensive 122; moves to Troodos area, prepares for next offensive 127; intensifies action against the police 128–9; escapes capture during Spilia operation 149–50; attitude to Harding-Makarios talks 162–6; reaction to Makarios's deportation 173–4; intensifies attacks 173–5; moves to Stavros Psokos, reorganises mountain groups 179–80; gives orders on treatment of Shilton 180–1; announces execution of two British corporals 181; evades security forces in the mountains, escapes to Limassol 183–5; disbands mountain groups 185; sets up hq. in Panaghides's house and reorganises guerrilla groups 187; suspends operations (August 1956) 188, 305 (Aug. 1958), 305; rejects Greek Government's proposal for a truce 204–5; rejection of Harding's surrender terms 218; reluctance to declare cease-fire 234–5, 237; forms anti-Turkish groups 255–6 and fn., 302–3; hostility to Hugh Foot 264–5 and fn., 273, 283–5, 297; becomes increasingly isolated 279, 338, 347; wages passive resistance and boycott campaign, 282, 310–15; his puritanical outlook 310; orders Elias Samaras's execution 317; rejects independence plan 322–3; dissociates himself from NATO, initiative over Cyprus 326; decides, against Averoff's advice, to continue struggle 338–9; his objections to Zurich settlement and refusal to co-operate 342–3, 346; delays ordering cease-fire 346–7; flies to Greece, promoted

Lt-Gen. in retirement 347–8; his role in the Enosis struggle 348–51; warns Cypriots against ratification of the London agreement 352; (after Independence) his return to Cyprus and attack against Turks in the Mansoura area 371*; leads attack against Turks (Aghios Theodoros/Kophinou) 374–5*; ordered to withdraw and recalled by Greece 375; his permanent removal requested by Turkey 376; secret return to Cyprus 384*; engages in subversion, joins the bishops' conspiracy against Makarios 385–6*; demands amnesty for all political prisoners as condition for releasing Minister of Justice 387*; death from heart attack 387*

Grivas diary, discovery of 200–1

Grivas, Dr Michael 94–5

Guerrilla(s): memorial services for deceased 243

Guerrilla warfare 90, 92–3, 94, 95–6, 98, 101–9, 113–14, 118–22, 140, 149–50, 152, 156, 174–6, 177, 179–81, 182–9, 201, 202–4, 205, 231–4, 348, 349, 378*, 385*, 386*, 387*; unsuitability of Cyprus for 92–3, 95; *see also* Grivas *and* EOKA

Guevara, Che 349

Gunes, T., Turkish Foreign Minister 392* (Gunes plan)

Gunewarden, R. S. S. (UN del., Ceylon) 225

Gyani, General, UNFICYP commander 369*, 370*

Hadjigeorghiou, Nitsa 207

Hadjikharos 54

Hadjimiltis, Limassol District leader, 185

Halifax, Lord 65, 70

Hallinan, Sir Eric, Chief Justice 119, 141

Hammarskjold, Dag 231, 241, 254 fn.

Hammond, Sergeant: killed 315

Hampton, Frederick, British Labour attaché, Athens 69

Hankey, Lord 72

Haravghi 307

Harding, Field-Marshal Sir John, KCB, DSO (Lord Harding of Petherton) 146, 148, 158 fn., 171–2, 177, 179, 192, 211, 274, 338, 355; appointed Governor 139; arrives in Cyprus, meets Makarios 140; assumes responsibility for security 141; orders closure of Samuel School 145; announces £38 million development plan 145; proclaims state of emergency 147; escapes assassination 147, 174–5; policy influenced by strategic priorities 151; allows Mouskos's funeral to take place in Nicosia 152; predicts that EOKA's days are numbered 153; negotiations with Makarios 151, 156–7, 160–2, 164–6, 181,

192–4, 213, 215; statement on deportations 168–9; opposes renewal of talks with Makarios, has consultations in London 193; regrets need for sterner measures 206; commutes Xenophontas's death sentence to life imprisonment 207; warns that self-determination cannot be implemented without Greek and Turkish consent, urges Cypriots to study Radcliffe's proposals 210; decides Makarios's detention is no longer justified, favours new political initiative 234; willingness to grant Grivas and guerrillas a safe-conduct 236; accuses EOKA of organising denigration campaign against the security forces 249; reassesses Cyprus's strategic importance 258–9 and fn.; ends two-year governorship 262; praised by Kutchuk 264; concludes no settlement possible without agreement of Greece and Turkey 275

Harding-Makarios talks, *see* Harding *and* Makarios

Harriman, Averell: invites Makarios to New York 239

Hellenic nationalism, indoctrination in 90, 108, 155

Hellenism 18, 42, 58, 61, 114, 119, 222, 229, 259, 346, 352, 385*

Henry, Sir James, Attorney-General 253

Herrarte, A. (UN del., Guatemala) 334

Highland Light Infantry: soldiers killed and wounded in bomb incident at fountain 204

Hilarion: surprise attack on by Greeks 369–70*

Hill, Corporal, 188 fn.; execution of 181

Hill, Sir George, historian 24

Hiroshima 52

Hirst, Geoffrey, MP 253

Homeric words in Cypriot Greek 19

Hong Kong 80

Hopkinson, Henry (Lord Colyton), formerly First Secretary, British Legation, Athens, later Minister of State for the Colonies 71, 74, 75, 76, 78, 159

Hopkinson's 'Never' 76, 81 and fn., 122, 159, 298

Hotel Grande Bretagne, Athens 238, 278

House of Commons 74, 206, 217 and fn., 252–4, 278, 294, 297, 328 and fn.; Debates 75–80, 159 and fn., 191 and fn., 192, 196, 297–300; Colonial Secretary (Creech Jones) comments on sedition trial 33 and fn.[2]; Labour Government's decision to call a consultative assembly 35; Younger's statement 62 and fn.[3]; Hopkinson's statements 71 and fn.[1] (July 1954) 75–6; Foreign Secretary's statement on the Tripartite Conference 123 and fn.[3]; reaction to Makarios's deportation 170–3

House of Commons (*cont.*)
and fn.[7]; Home Secretary's (Major Lloyd George) statement on Archimandrite Makhereotis's expulsion 190 and fn.[3]; Labour support for Makhereotis, documents concerning his activities placed in Library 191 and fn.; Prime Minister's statement on self-determination 195 and fn.[4]; Colonial Secretary's (Lennox-Boyd) comments on Ismay's mediation offer 235 and fn.[2]; Foreign Secretary's (Selwyn Lloyd) statement after visit to Athens and Ankara 276 fn.[2]; Labour Opposition accuses Government of partiality towards the Turks 294; Colonial Secretary comments on troops' behaviour in Famagusta after Cutliffe murder 320 and fn.[1]; reaction to the Zurich settlement, February 1959 345 and fn.[2]; Foreign Secretary's statement on military bases 356 and fn.[2]; concern for British troops' safety on UNFICYP duties 375 and fn.[1]
House of Lords 25, 71–2, 196 and fn.[6], 206, 217
House of Representatives (Cyprus) 341, 342, 355, 362, 365*, 378*
Hungary 225
Hurriyet 45

Ill-treatment, *see* Atrocities
Illueca, J. (UN del., Panama) 226
Independence (of Cyprus) 346*, 364*, 366*, 373*, 377*, 378*, 387*; Krishna Menon's thesis supporting 322; Makarios's support for 322, 329; Greek Government drops self-determination in favour of 322, 329, 330; Greece's initiative for 325; bid for at UN 328; Cyprus after 364–96*; threatened by coup 389–93*
Indian Ambassador 217
Inonu, Ismet, Turkish President, Prime Minister 370*, 371*; receives Turkish Cypriot delegation (1948) 45
Inspector of Mines' evidence at *Aghios Georghios* trial 116–17
Intercommunal co-operation 26, 153, 269, 303, 351
Intercommunal strife 24, 55, 99, 153, 155, 175, 176, 182, 188, 231–2, 255–6, 265, 287, 288–93, 295, 301–5, 361, 365*, 366–7*, 370*, 373–5*, 377*, 383*, 384*
Intercommunal talks 377*, 381*, 383*, 384*, 386*, 387*
International Congress of Free Trade Unions (ICFTU) 69, 254–5
Ioannides, Evadoras 49
Ioannides, Kostas 382*
Ioannides, Dr Odysseus, mayor of Nicosia 383*

Ioannides, Polykarpos 49–50, 126, 168–9, 382*
Ioannou, Supt. Alexis 110
Ioannou, Nikodemos: murder of 308
Ioannou, Phifis: journeys behind Iron Curtain to seek political guidance, sees Cominform leaders in Bucharest (1948) 41
Ionian Islands: cession of, to Greece in 1864 23, 25
'Ipsilantis' 180, 183, 184; captured 185–6
Irineos, Abbot 232, 251–2
Irredentism, Greek 23, 61, 90, 91, 93, 378*
Ismael, Mehmet 142, 143
Ismay, Lord, Secretary-General of NATO: offers to mediate 234, 235, 236, 242
Israel 102
Istanbul 137, 194, 197, 259, 285, 286; Anti-Greek riots 1955, 132, 136
Italian invasion of Greece, 1940 91
Italy 325, 327
Izmir 295, 324, 353; anti-Greek riots (1955) 136; Greek withdrawal of NATO units from (1958) 324

Jackson, Sir Edward, Chief Justice 37
Jacovides, attends Peking Peace Conference 51 fn.
Jamali, M. F. (UN del., Iraq) 83
James II, King 20
Jeger, Lena 58, 73 fn., 77, 191, 253–4, 261
Jewish immigrants 33
Jewish massacre of Salamis Greeks, AD 115–16 18
John, Mr Justice 247
Johnson, President 376*
Joint Constitutional Commission 351, 354
Joint Council 356
Joint Force 372*
Jordan 78
Justice for Cyprus Association (USA) 68

Kafkallides 185
Kaimakli 147, 301
Kakopetria 107, 127, 150
Kalamai 272
Kalamata: occupation of by X 92
Kalavassos 188 fn.
Kallis 143, 144
Kallithea 101
Kalopsidha 138, 176
Kambou river 180
Kaminaria 185
Kanli 292
Kannavia 150
Kantara Pass: English couple's murder 188
Karadimas 110, 111, 118, 232
Karamanlis 157, 166, 212, 213, 215, 216, 217, 219, 230, 239, 323, 325, 328, 340,

344, 345, 347, 353, 393*; leaves France to become Greek Prime Minister 390*

Karaolis, Michael 142, 146, 180–1, 182; trial of, 141, Supreme Court's dismissal of appeal 145; execution of 181

Karaolis Camp 320–2

Karapattas, Vassos 247

Karavas 188, 257, 391

Karodonitis 143, 144

Karpas the 18, 186, 374*, 392*, 393*, 395*

Kartalis, George 213, 215, 230

Kassimatis, Gregoris, Greek liberal deputy 46, 48, 64, 218, 230

Kastellorizon 371*

Kathikas 317

Kathimerini 124

Katsoulis, Ioannis 121, 127, 128

Katsouri, Despoullia: killed by EOKA 309

Kavouri 217

Keightley, General Sir Charles 121, 258 fn.

Kemal, Mustapha, *see* Ataturk

Kendrew, General 319; differences with Foot on questions of policy 284

Kerber, Dr Karl (biographer of Makarios) 156

Khandria 154

Kharalambous, Hadji 203

Khi, 91; *see also* X

Khlorokas 96, 101, 106, 107

Khoman, T. (UN del., Thailand) 225, 227

Killearn, Lord 72

'Kimon' 122

King Paul 217

Kinonia, Mount 232, 252

Kition, Bishops of: Papadopoulos 27–8; Mouskos (later Archbishop Makarios III) 46, 49–50; Anthimos 59, 102, 104, 170, 178, 238, 264, 309–11, 314, 326, 342–3, 385*; urges Grivas to halt operations 234

Kizya, L. E. (UN del., Ukraine) 226

KKE (Greek Communist Party) 41, 57

Klerides, Glavkos 254, 283, 284, 285, 352, 374*, 377*, 387*, 390*, 392*

Klerides, John, KC, father of Glavkos 35, 42, 354, 355

Knights Templar 20

Kokkina beach-head 371*, 373*

Kokkinitrimithia, *see* Camp K

Komma tou Yialou 280

Komotiní 227

Kondemenos 289

Konya (Turkey): partition demonstration at 286

Kophinou, 373; Greek attack on 374*, 376*, 382*, 385*, 388*

Koprulu, Fuad, Turkish Foreign Minister 63, 73, 74, 161

Kosmas, General 93, 96

Kostopoulos, murder of 129

Kourdhali 149

Koutalianos, Evanghelos Louka 117 fn., 118

Kranidiotis, Nikos, Ethnarchy secretary 102, 103, 158, 192, 193, 238

Krishna Menon, V. (UN del., India): exponent of Cypriot independence 85, 227–30, 272, 322, 331–3, 335, 336

Ktima, destruction of 368

Kuneralp, Z., Turkish Foreign Minister 300, 376*

Kutchuk, Dr Fazil, leader of the Turkish Cypriots, first vice-president of the Republic: forms KATAK 43; warns community of impending dangers after church plebiscite 48; appeals for calm 153; opposes self-determination 194; praises Eden 197; criticises Makarios's release from Seychelles 238; asserts partition the only solution, and that Turkey would claim all territory north of the 35th parallel 244; praises Harding 264; attends London Conference (1959) 344; co-operates with Makarios in appeal to end racial strife 351; supports Makarios against Grivas 352–3; urges Cypriots to surrender arms 354; becomes Republic's vice-President 355; joins Makarios in opposing postponement of Independence 358; threatens to revert to partition if Greeks revive Enosis 358; proposes changes for delineation of base areas 358–9. *After Independence:* vetoes law providing for mixed army units 365*; receives Makarios's thirteen constitutional amendments 366*

Kykko, abbot of 127

Kykko forest 180

Kykko Monastery 46, 179, 183, 184 187

Kykko RAF Camp, Battle of Britain celebrations 139

Kyperounda 121

Kyprianos, Archbishop, executed (1821) 21

Kyprianos, Bishop of Kyrenia 50–1, 59, 94, 126, 163, 168–9, 237, 353, 354, 385*

Kyrenia; detainees escape from castle 139; ambush on pass 202; Turks establish bridgehead 389–91*

Kyrenia, Bishops of, *see* Myriantheus, Kyprianos

Kyrenia Range: operations in 186; set alight by Turkish bombardment 390*

Kyriakides, Renos 122, 149, 150, 254

Kyriakides, Stanley 361 fn.

Kyrou, Achilleus 93

Kyrou, Alexis 27, 70, 82, 83, 86, 87, 88, 92 fn., 103, 105, 259

Kythrea: church murder 175; Georkatzis's body found nearby 381*

Labour Party (GB) 317–18, 328; reluctance to give up Cyprus 34; Cyprus lobby in 37; abortive attempt to introduce liberal regime 39; its Cyprus policy 79, 136, 191, 196, 294; pledge to give Cypriots self-determination 192, 272, 298, 300; Greek Cypriots encouraged by 86, 192, 218, 261, 268, 297, 329; attitude to the Turks 197, 275, 300; Brighton annual conference, Cyprus discussion (1957) 261; Hugh Foot's influence 298; back-pedals on self-determination 299

Lapithos 391*

Larnaca 182, 200, 265, 301, 362*; 'Green Line' set up in 367*

Latin rule in Cyprus 20

Ledra Palace 147

Ledra Street: incidents in 129, 143, 182, 202, 231

Lee, Jennie, MP 252–4

Lefka 115, 121, 183, 187, 392*

Lefkoniko: disturbances in 32, 148; Police Station attacked 140; first collective fine 148; fatal explosion village fountain 204, 209; EOKA murder of left-winger 307

Lefkosiades, Archimandrite 185

Left-wing Nationalists (OAE) 306 and fn., 307

Left-wing Patriots (OAP) 306, 307

Legge-Bourke, Major Harry, MP 79

Legislative Council 24

Lenas, Stylianos 232

Lennox-Boyd, Alan (Lord Boyd of Merton), Secretary of State for the Colonies 124, 125 fn., 132, 159, 162, 164, 166, 170, 171, 200, 211, 219, 223, 235, 236, 253–4, 264, 268, 297, 298, 320, 327; visits Athens and Ankara (December 1956) 210

Leontios, Bishop of Paphos, Archbishop Leontios: prosecuted for sedition 28; becomes Archbishop, reshapes Ethnarchy Council 36; obstructs the British 36, 39; ordains Michael Mouskos (Makarios III) 46

Liatis, Alexis, Greek diplomat 161, 213

Liberal Party (GB): Turkish distrust of 197

Limassol 184, 185, 220, 265, 279, 338, 368*, 378*, 387*, 390*; mayor of 33; riots in 89; customs 183; Central Police Station 382

Lindos Bay 101

Linzee, Captain Robin 179 fn.

Liopetri, battle of 315

Listowel, Lord 72, 196

Lloyd, Lord, Under-Secretary of State for the Colonies 196

Lloyd George, Major Gwilym, Home Secretary 190, 197, 286

Lloyd, Selwyn, Minister of State for Foreign Affairs, Foreign Secretary, 74, 83, 84, 195, 196, 220, 266, 276 and fn., 277, 278, 279 fn., 328, 344, 345, 356, 357

Lodge, H. Cabot (UN delegate, USA), 60, 86, 137, 269, 270, 335

Loizides, Savvas 96, 97, 105, 115, 215, 216, 268–9, 272; deportation of 27

Loizides, Socrates 48, 54, 65, 100, 101, 102, 103, 104, 106, 107, 110, 111, 112, 115, 117, 119, 126

London Agreement, *see* Zurich

London Committee 357–8

London Conference 342, 352, 356, 359; Zurich and London Agreements (1959) concluded 345

Loufti, O. (UN del., Egypt) 226

Louka, Gregoris, bodyguard to Grivas 200

Loukas, Andreas 320–2; inquest on death of 321–2

Lusignan, Guy de, King of Jerusalem 20

Lysi 183, 200, 249, 280

Lyso 234

Lyttelton, Oliver, Secretary of State for the Colonies 74, 79

McCarran, Senator 61

Macdonald, Angus, journalist: murder of 205

MacDonald, Malcolm, Secretary of State for Colonies 29

Macedonia, western 57, 83

McLachlan, Donald 73

Macmillan, Harold, Foreign Secretary, Prime Minister 123, 124, 129, 130, 132, 135–7, 158 fn., 159, 160, 216, 241, 295–6, 300, 304, 305, 329, 345, 355

Macmillan plan 294

Madariaga, Salvador de 147

Maghoub, M. A. (UN del., Sudan) 226

Mahé, Makarios's statement 237

Maitland, Patrick, MP 201

Makarezos, Colonel 374*

Makarios II, Archbishop 41; statue of defiled 307

Makarios III (Michael Mouskos), Archbishop of Cyprus, first President of the Republic 69, 72, 74–5, 82, 95, 97–8, 103, 119, 122, 149, 151–2, 174, 188, 189–93, 200–2, 210–11, 213–15, 219–20, 224, 234, 241, 253–4, 257, 262, 264, 275–6, 279–85, 296, 299, 304, 306–9, 313–15, 328, 333, 335, 337, 343, 348, 352–3, 358, 369*, 371*, 373*, 382*; birth 46; activities in plebiscite as Bishop of Kition 46, 49; Elected Archbishop, undertakes to work for Enosis 50–1; Colonial government's distrust of 51; early political activities 51–6; seeks support in Greece 62, 65–6, 73, 86, 125; communicates with

UN Trusteeship Committee 64; campaigns for Enosis in USA 68; dissuaded by Greek Government from attending UN General Assembly 70; defies British authorities by preaching seditious sermons 81; seeks support in England 86; early meetings with Grivas 93-4, 96, 104-5, 107, 113; considers Grivas's plans for revolt, but bans his return to Cyprus until sent for 94; orders start of armed action 98, 105; orders cease-fire 115; upholds school discipline 121; vetoes plan to assassinate General Keightley 121; meets Lennox-Boyd 124; denounces Tripartite Conference plan 125-7; opposes deployment of guerrillas and large-scale arms build-up 127-8; threatens passive resistance 138; meets Harding 140, 156-7, 161; condemns emergency measures 147; conducts murdered abbot's funeral 156 and fn.; negotiates with Harding 156-67; deportation to Seychelles and reactions to this 167-73; pastoral message from exile 178; statements in Seychelles at time of his release 235-7; return to Athens 237-9; writes to Grivas 239-40; refuses to denounce violence and controls Cypriot politics from Athens 242; accuses the British forces of atrocities 251 and fn.; speech at Kalamai 272-3; meets Hugh Foot 278; accuses the British of Turkish bias 293 fn.; asks Grivas to reconsider boycott 311; meets Barbara Castle and proposes independence 322-3, 325; opposes NATO sponsored talks on Cyprus problem 326-7; urges Grivas to keep truce until the spring 329; informed by Averoff about pending settlement 340; backs up Averoff over Zurich Agreement with reservations 342; interview with Karamanlis 344; meets Cypriot delegates at Dorchester Hotel, later accepts Zurich and London agreements 345; returns to Cyprus 346; asks Grivas to meet him 347; supports Government's call for arms surrender 351, 354; friction with Grivas whom he meets in Rhodes 353; elected President of the Republic 355; bargains over the British military bases and meets Duncan Sandys 356-7; joins London negotiations 357; refuses to resume talks 359-60; offers AKEL five seats in the House of Representatives 362; pursues policy of non-alignment 364, 368*, 381*; tactless treatment of the Turks 365*; submits thirteen constitutional amendments to Kutchuk 366*; agrees to joint truce force 367*; declares wish to terminate the Zurich and London agreements 367*; abrogates the Treaty of Alliance 369*; resists pressure for trial of Denktash 374*; shelves Enosis 376-7; introduces conscription 377-8*; delays action against the National Front 378*; escapes assassination 381*, 387*, 389*; rejects Turkish demands for local autonomy 383*; clashes with the Greek junta and refuses its order to surrender arms to the National Guard 384-5*; friction with the Cyprus bishops 385-6*; condemns violence and forms Tactical Reserve Force for own protection 386-7*; complains to Greek Ambassador about local disorders 387*; accuses the Greek junta of conspiracy against him and requests Greece to replace Greek officers in the National Guard 388*; takes refuge in Akrotiri British Base, London, 389*; returns triumphantly to Cyprus 395*

Makheras, Monastery of 232, 381*

Makhereotis, Archmandrite, priest of the GOC in Camden Town: arrest and deportation 90-1

Makins, Sir Roger, UK Ambassador, Washington 173

Mallalieu, E. L. 74, 77, 78

Malta 37, 78

Mammari 288, 289

Manchester Guardian 170

Mansoura 371

Mao Tse Tung 349

Mari 374

Markezinis, Spyros 214

Markos, General, Commander of the Communist guerrillas in Greece 40; meeting with Ziartides 41

Maronites 20

Martial law declared in Turkey 136, 395*

'Mason-Dixon' Line 231, 265, 288, 295

Matsis, Kyriakos 150

Matthews, Jim 318

Maudling, Reginald 245 fn.

Mavronikolaos, Kyriakos 117

Mavros, George, Greek Foreign Minister (1974) 64, 391-2*, 392*

Mavros Gremnos: command post set up by Grivas 183

Maximos, Demetrios 58

Mayor of Kyrenia 317

Mayor of Nicosia 271, 295, 309, 313

Mediterranean 194, 330, 350

Megali Ellada, Megali Idea, see 'Greater Greece'

Melas, George (NATO perm. del., Greece) 137, 325-7

MELF *see* Middle East Land Forces

Melos, Anarghyros 117, 118

Menakas, Savvas, left-winger beaten to death 307
Menderes, Adnan, Turkish Prime Minister 69, 170, 194, 195, 238, 277, 297, 340, 344, 345, 360
Menderes, Etem, Turkish Foreign Minister 194
Mesaoria 17, 90, 392*
Metaxas, Greek dictator 61, 216
Metaxas Square: Cypriots overturn army jeep in 139; riots in 152
Michael, Christodoulos 141, 142, 144
Michael, Kharilaos 152; execution of 188; reactions to execution 218
Middle East 194, 221, 260, 294, 350; British commitments in 130
Middle East Air Force, RAF 360
Middle East Headquarters 74; bases 258
Middle East Land Forces (MELF) 121
Milia 309
Milikouri 184, 240, 252, 267
Military bases (British) 344; negotiations over after Zurich 356–8, 359–61
Mixed Municipal Commission: failure to agree on municipal boundaries 366*
Mobile Reserve, the 220 fn., 277
Monasteries: security forces search 149
Montgomery, Field-Marshal 65, 70
Moran, Corporal 152
Morgan, Mr Justice 246
Morrison, Private, killed 317
Moscow, Eastern Orthodox Patriarch of 172
Moslems in Greece 172
Mount Troodos, radar installations on 360
Mount Vitsi, northern Greece: meeting between Greek and Cypriot communists 41
Mouskos, Kharalambos (cousin of Makarios III): his funeral 152
Mouskos, Michael: Bishop of Kition 1948, Archbishop Makarios III October 1950, first President of the Republic of Cyprus, August 1960, see Makarios III
Mufti, functions of 22; Colonial Administration abolishes the High Office of 42
Municipal Market, Nicosia 295
Municipalities, separate, see Turkish Cypriots
Munro, Sir Leslie (UN del., New Zealand) 86
Munster, Earl of 72
Myriantheus, Bishop of Kyrenia, Archbishop Makarios II 27, 28, 36, 37, 38, 40, 41, 46, 47–8, 49
Myrianthopoulos 143, 144

NAAFI 177, 205, 328, 358
Nasser, President 371*
National Agrarian Party X 93
National Front, the 378*, 381*, 382*

National Guard 371*, 372*, 373*, 374*, 375*, 377–8*, 384*, 385*, 387*, 388*, 389*, 390*, 391*
National Radical Union (Greece) 213
Nationalism: development of rival Greek and Turkish 22, 364–5*
NATO, see North Atlantic Treaty Alliance
NATO Council 213, 219
Nea, Ta, 261
Near East 132
Nehru, Pandit 217
Neo-Classicism 18
Neos-Demokratis 150
Newton, Captain 233
New York Times 276
Nicosia: Old City under curfew 176, 182, 202, 231, 288; gun battle at General Hospital 200; intercommunal fighting 295; Airfield 360, 390*; Turkish enclave isolated by Greeks 373*, 390*; broadcasting station 389*; Turkish tanks reach outskirts of 393*
Nicosia–Kyrenia road: strategic positions on, taken up by Turkish contingent 367*; comes under Turkish control 369*; Greek contingent's abortive attempt to break through to 390*
Nikitas 185
Nisot, (UN del., Belgium) 331
Noble, Commander (UN del., Britain) 221, 222, 223, 224, 229, 263 fn., 267, 268, 272, 330, 331, 332, 333, 334, 336
Noel-Baker, Francis 58, 162, 164, 171, 191, 192, 193
Noel-Baker, Philip 58, 86, 201
North Atlantic Treaty Alliance (NATO) 65, 67, 73, 74, 78, 129, 130, 157–8, 159, 171, 194, 195, 196, 213, 225, 236, 259, 305, 319, 323, 325, 327, 328, 330, 338, 342, 343, 364, 371, 381, 386; importance of Turkey in 71; Cyprus vital to Britain's discharge of NATO obligations 84, 135; stability of, undermined by Greco-Turkish conflict 136, 383*; Cyprus problem discussed in Council 213; Council's decision to extend terms of reference to political disputes between member states 219; members support Britain and Turkey against Greece at the UN 224; Greek offer in event of Enosis to grant bases under NATO control 225; distrusted by the Greeks as a group of colonial powers 234; offer of mediation 234–5, 237, 242; supports Britain's efforts to call Tripartite Conference 260, 295; requests Britain to postpone policy statement 296; withdrawal of Greek forces from 324, 396*; possibility of Greece leaving 326; Averoff and Zorlu meet at Conference 340;

Makarios rejects suggesstions that members should participate in peace force 367*, 368*

Northern Epirus 214

Norway 327, 328

Notis 100

Nutting, Anthony, MP 64, 65, 87, 88, 137

O'Brien, C. C. (UN del., Ireland) 334

'28 October Street' incident 50

O'Driscoll, Captain 179 fn.

Organisation for European Economic Co-operation (OEEC) 342

Ogmore, Lord 72

OHEN 101, 102, 168–9

Oil, security of British supplies 195, 217, 220, 258

Old Trade Unions, see PEO

Olympus, Mount 95

Omodhos 187

Omorphita 293, 300, 377*; interrogation centre 245

Order in Council, government by 26, 147

Ormsby-Gore (later Lord Harlech), Secretary of State for the Colonies 28

Ortakeuy 367

Osman, PC Kemal 110

Ottoman Empire 20, 22, 43, 329

Ottoman Public Debt 25

Ottoman system of land tenure 21

OXXI Day, 28 October 258

Paget, Reginald, MP 80, 191, 299

Pakhna 187

Palamas, C. Xanthopoulos- (UN del., Greece) 267

Palekhori 142

Palestine 78, 263

Pallikarides, Evaghoras, 206, 267; executed 233–4

Palmer, Sir Richmond 50, 148

Palodhia 185

Panaghia 183, 184

Panaghides, Dafnis: headquarters set up by Grivas in house of 187

Panaghiotou, Andreas 246

Panayotakis, C., Greek Ambassador, Nicosia 385*

Pancyprian Congress 353

Pancyprian Federation of Labour, see PEO

Pancyprian Gymnasium 46, 52, 90, 109, 121, 145, 149, 152, 154, 265, 381*

Pancyprian National Assembly 52, 126

Pancyprian National Organisation: organisation of pupils 307 fn.

Pancyprian Trade Union Committee (PTUC) 30

Pandelis, Modestos 115

Panhellenic Committee for the Cyprus Struggle for Enosis (PEEAK) 58

Panhellenic Committee for the Union of Cyprus with Greece 221

Papadopoulos, Bishop of Kition 27–8

Papadopoulos, Christodoulos 93, 107

Papadopoulos, Colonel George, Greek dictator 374*, 381*

Papadopoulos, Tassos 347, 387*, 388*

Papagos, Field-Marshal, Greek Prime Minister 63, 67, 70, 71, 73, 86, 96, 97, 100, 105, 124, 125, 157, 212

Papaioannou, Ezekiel: replaces Phifis Ioannou as AKEL's Secretary-General 41; campaigns behind Iron Curtain 49; denounces British bases 51–2; escapes from detention 178

Papandreou, George, Greek Prime Minister 215, 216, 217, 230, 374*

Papantoniou, Michael 117

Papapolitis 215

Papathanghelou, Papastavros 168–9

Paphos 317, 350, 370*, 383*, 388*, 390*; its background of lawlessness 120, 182, 301; forest 182, 183, 186, 206

Paphos, Bishop of 385*

Paphos bishopric: discovery of pistols in 189

Paphos Gymnasium 306

Paralimini Police Station, EOKA attack on 138

Paraskeva, Antonis: murder of 308

Paris Peace Conference (1946) 58

Parity, Turkish demand for 209

Parkinson, Sir Cosmo, Perm. Under-Sec. for Colonies: refuses to discuss Enosis 31–2

Partiality: alleged British towards the Turks 293, 294

Partition 225, 230, 238, 260, 267, 275, 278, 282, 285, 286, 301, 305, 328, 331, 334, 335, 345, 376*, 392*; first mention of 196 and fn., Lennox-Boyd's reference to as a possible option in final settlement 210; importance attached by Turkey to Lennox-Boyd's reference to 211, 223, 268; acclaimed by Kutchuk as the only solution 244; Turkish demands for 262, 274, 287–8, 295, 296, 297, 300, 327, 329, 330, 339; Turks move north in order to facilitate 304, 308; India's objections to 333; Turks threaten to revive demand for, if Greeks revive Enosis 358; *de facto* existence of 383*, 395*

Partnership plan (British) 324

Passalides, John (Chairman of EDA) 214, 215

Passive resistance 138, 140, 282, 306, 310–15

Patatsos's execution 188; reactions to 218

Patriarchate, Ecumenical 285–6
Patriarchs of the Eastern Orthodox Church:
of Antioch 19; the Ecumenical (Constantinople), *see* Athenagoras; of Alexandria
28; of Belgrade 172; of Moscow 172
Patriotic Front 362*
Pattakos, Colonel 374*
Paul, the Apostle 19
Paul, King of Greece 58, 65
Pavlides, Sir Paul, resignation from EXCO
138, 142
Pavlides, Stelios, KC 32–3, 50, 142, 143, 293
fn.
Pavlis 184
Peake, Sir Charles, British Ambassador,
Athens 65, 158, 160 fn., 217
Pearson, Derek (Colonial Office): visits
Makarios in Seychelles 211
Pearson, Lester (Canadian Prime Minister)
376*
Peive, Y. V. (UN del., USSR) 270
PEK 54, 111, 112, 118, 128
PEKA 243, 255, 264, 274, 278, 280, 283, 293,
306, 308 and fn.
Peloponnese 8, 92
Pentadaktylos 95, 180
PEO (Pancyprian Federation of Labour) 33,
41, 53, 54, 86, 127, 141, 142, 256, 280 and
fn., 281 and fn., 287, 296, 304, 307 and
fn., 308, 311, 355; formation of 33; strike
after arrest of left-wingers 127
PEOM 307 and fn.
PEON 54, 101, 102, 168–9
Peoples' Democracies 273
Peravassa 184
Perez-Perez, S. (UN del., Venezuela) 226
Peristerona-Pighi: clash between security
forces and villagers 300
Perivolia-tou-Trikomou 106
Persian Gulf 258
Persians in Cyprus 19
Pezmazoglou, George, Greek Ambassador,
Ankara 260
Phaneromeni Church 46, 81, 152, 182, 265,
273
Phantis 178
Pharmakides, Mr: kidnapped by gunmen
359
Philhellene 26, 75, 86, 162
Philhellenism 23, 58, 263, 273
Philia 288, 289
Phoenicians 18
Phos, Nicosia newspaper: urges Grivas to
call a truce 178
Picot, G. Georges- (UN del., France) 224
Pierides, Mr Justice 141
Pighi 280
Pipinellis, Panayotis, Greek Foreign Minister
213, 217, 375*
Pissas, Michael 31, 63, 69, 127, 254–5

Pitsilia 127
Plastiras, General, Greek Prime Minister 64,
66
Platres: interrogation centre 245, 246, 247
Platts-Mills, John 45
Platys (river) 185
Plaza Lasso, Galo (ex-President of Ecuador):
UN mediator in Cyprus 371*, 372*, 373*
Plebiscite 45–50, 71, 77, 82, 83, 222
Poisoning of Army reservoirs considered by
EOKA 177
Police, EOKA's plans to liquidate 122;
Turkish auxiliary killed 153, 188; Maltese
policeman killed 188; British police
sergeant killed 200; two police sergeants
killed 202; condone Turkish attacks 220;
Turkish police sergeant escapes to Turkey
294
Police Gazette (Athens) 74
Polis 317
Politis, John 64
Polykarpou, Polykarpos 382*
Polystipos 150
Pomas-tou, Khloraka 105
Popular Front (EAS): rejects the 1948 constitutional plans 38
Populist Party of Greece 92
Poskotis 115
Potomac Charter 157
Poullis, PC: murder of 129, 141, 143
Privy Council of Great Britain: Karaolis's
appeal to 181
Prodhromos 108
Profumo, John, MP 253
Progressive Party (Greece) 214
Provisional Cyprus Turkish Administration
376*
PTUC 30–1; proscription of 33
Pyla Detention Camp 287 fn., 316; Foot's
visit to 273
Pyroi, Detention Camp 267

Quiroga-Galdo, G. (UN del., Bolivia) 226

Radcliffe, Lord 195, 196, 197, 207–11, 219,
223–4, 225, 237, 238, 242, 244, 264, *see
also* Constitutional plans
Radical Union 216
RAF 252, 289, 329; flies Makarios to
London 389*; *see also* Middle East Air
Force
Raftis, George 206
Ramos, C. (UN del., Argentine) 336
Reddaway, John 242
Redgrave, Major 290
Rees-Davies, William 77
Reform Party of the Working People:
formation of in 1941, *see* AKEL
Refugees 384, 394*, 395*

Regiments: Duke of Wellington's 232; First Suffolk 232; Gordon Highlanders 149, 182; Grenadier Guards 252, 290, 292; Highland Light Infantry 204; King's Own Yorkshire Light Infantry 186 fn.; Parachute 182, 185, 245, 253, 295; RAC 320; RAF 186 fn.; Royal Artillery 206, (29th Field Regiment) 319, 321; Royal Engineers 152, 233, 241; Royal Green Jackets 375; Royal Horse Guards 186 fn., 289, 290, 291, 301; Royal Leicestershire 180; Royal Norfolk 186 fn.; Royal Ulster Rifles 320; South Staffordshire 141, 186 fn., 245

Renaissance 18

Republic of Cyprus 360, 364–7*, 369*, 370*, 372*, 381*, 385*, 394*, 395*; delay in its establishment 357; birth of 362; described by Turkish Foreign Minister as a form of federal state 367*; illegal Greek forces in 371*; breakdown of law and order in 382*; threatened *coup d'état* 389*

Reveille 257

Revolutionary Committee, Athens: establishment of 94

Rhodes 19, 24, 73, 78, 100, 101, 106, 174, 353

Riots: in Cyprus 27, 32, 109, 121, 139, 145, 148–9, 152, 167, 175, 182, 206, 265, 276–7, 288, 294, 295, 301; in Greece 65, 89, 214, 216, 394*; in Turkey 136–7, 213

Riza, Police Sergeant Ali 153

Robinson, Kenneth 58, 171, 191, 253, 264, 299, 320

Rollin, Professor (Belgian lawyer) 218

Roman Catholic Minority, Athens: opposes Makarios's deportation 172

Roman Empire 71

'Romanos' 122

Rooney, PC: murder of 174, 176

Royal Commission, advocated for Cyprus 272

Rossides, Michael 181, 248–9, 382*; death sentence commuted 257

Rossides, Zenon 52, 65, 216

Royal Hellenic Air Force: flies Grivas to Athens 347

Royal Marine Commandos 149, 182, 245

Royal Marines 232

Royal Military Police 321

Royal Navy 27, 107, 116, 174, 183, 223

Russia 343

Russian expansionism in the Eastern Mediterranean 22

St John's Cathedral, Nicosia 126

St Pancras: Cypriots in 77; pro-Cypriot MPs 300

St Spyridon 149

Saitta 185

Sakellarios, Admiral 96, 106

Sakkas, Andreas: murder of in coffee shop 308

Salamis 18, 19

Salisbury, Lord: resigns from the Cabinet 236–7

Salonika: riots in 89, 214; Karamanlis's electoral campaign in 213

Samaras, Elias 315, 317; sent to England 316

Samaras, Xanthos 315, 316

Sampson, Nikos 232, 390; acquitted of murder 246–7; death sentence commuted 257; proclaimed President of the Republic 389*

Samuel, Agathocles 145

Samuel School: unruliness of 109, 145, 146

Sandys, Duncan, Minister of Defence 189, 356–7

Sanerkin, Dr Nedjat 320

Sarper, Selim 84, 85, 87, 88, 137, 222, 226, 227, 229, 268, 270–1

School children: recruitment of by EOKA 108–9, 155

School disorders 54, 109, 121, 145–6, 148–9, 154–6, 175, 182, 206, 265

Schools, new technical, boycotted by EOKA 243

Scotsman, The 170

'Sebastianos' 180; arrested 184, 187, 207

Sedition 32, 49–50, 81, 169

Sedition Law 80, 81, 98

SEK (Cyprus Workers' Confederation) 63, 69, 127; formation of 31

Self-determination 84, 87, 88, 123, 124, 126, 127, 131, 132, 133, 134, 135, 137, 139, 149, 156, 157, 159, 160, 161, 162, 163, 166, 171, 191, 192, 193, 194, 195, 196, 197, 201, 215, 217, 219, 221, 222, 238, 242, 244, 260, 261, 266, 267, 268, 269, 270, 271, 272, 273 fn., 275, 276, 281, 286, 296, 298, 299, 300–1, 311, 322, 323, 363, 383*, 384*; Greek insistence on absolute right to 89

Self-government 26, 37, 38, 39, 76, 77, 85, 125, 130, 134, 135, 137, 151, 157, 158, 162, 163, 164, 165, 173, 193, 194, 195, 207, 209, 259, 274, 276, 287, 296, 300, 322, 334, 335, 336, 365*

Serbia 23

Serfdom, abolition of 30

Servas, Plutis 37; sentenced to three months' imprisonment 41

Seychelles 178, 211, 233, 238, 275, 382*; Makarios's banishment to 168; Makarios's farewell press conference 237

Shaw, Mr Justice 188, 247

Shepilov, Dimitri, Russian Foreign Minister: visit to Athens 217

Sheri Courts 43, 44

Shilton, Private Ronald 181, 188 fn., 248–9; capture of 180; discovery of body 181 fn.
Shuttleworth, Captain 233
Sinda 303
Skylloura, 288, 289, 291, 304
Slavophobia: endemic in Greece 124
Smyrna (Izmir): Greek minority in 259
Snowden, Philip 27 fn.
Soho: Enosis propaganda in 190
Solley, Leslie, MP 33
Sophocleus, Athanasios 174–5, 254
Sophocleus, Neofytos: puts bomb in Harding's bed 174
Sovereignty (British) problems 134, 135, 193, 207, 274, 275, 296, 330, 356, 389*
Soviet bloc 58, 66, 138
Spaak, Paul-Henri, NATO Secretary-General 295, 305, 323, 324, 325, 326, 327, 328; proposes independence 260; intervenes to get settlement 323–4
Spain: attitude to the Cyprus question 88
Spain, International Brigade, Cypriot Communists with 41
Sparrow-hawk, operation in the Pentadaktylos Range 202–4, 249 fn.
Special Assize Court 146–7, 250
Special Branch 129, 141, 223, 250
Spender, Sir Percy (UN del., Australia) 224
Sphongaras, George 247–8
Spilia 149, 150
Spyridakis, Dr 120–1, 145, 149
Spyridon, Archbishop of Athens (Primate of Greece) 58, 65, 66, 82, 214
Stalin 52
State Department: information leakage gives rise to reports that USA favoured Enosis, 1947 36, 60; reaction to Makarios's deportation 172
Statute of Westminster 77
Stavros Psokos 179
Stephanopoulos, Stephan, Greek Foreign Minister 69, 71, 73, 82, 97, 130, 133, 135
Sterling Area 310; exchange controls complicate EOKA's arms purchases 103
Storrs, Sir Ronald, Governor 24, 26, 88, 147 fn.
Strategic importance of Cyprus 17, 33, 34, 37, 45, 54, 131, 132, 135, 136, 156–8, 160, 171, 194–5, 205, 207, 220, 235, 258–9
Stratos, George 94–5
Strovolos 113, 142, 143
Styllis 184
Sudan 88
Suez base 140, 163
Suez Canal: British troops' withdrawal from 163; nationalisation 200; impact on Cyprus situation 205
Suez crisis 206, 221, 232, 258, 326, 335, 337, 350

Sulzberger, Cyrus 34 fn.
Sunay, President of Turkey 375
Sunday Dispatch 269
Sunday Times 170
Sunni Moslems 21
Supreme Court of Cyprus 145, 248; High Court of Justice 341; Constitutional Court 366*
Svolos, Professor, leader of the Greek Socialist Party 63
Switzerland 333, 340, 347
Syria 17, 384*

Tactical Reserve Force 386, 389
Tafall, Osorio, Special Representative of UN Secretary-General 377
Tass, Soviet News Agency 381, 382
Tasvir 45
Taxes, British imposition of 22
Temblos 188
Thant, U, Secretary-General of the UN 369*, 370*, 375*, 376*, 377*
Theoklitos, Archbishop 348
Theotokis, Spyros 157, 158 and fn., 159, 160 fn., 173, 178, 213, 214, 215, 216 218
Thirty-fifth Parallel: Kutchuk threatens to claim all territory north of 244
Thrace, Western 222, 226, 259
Thrassyvoulides, Michael 247
The Times 170, 193
Tinos: Grivas meets Azinas 97
TMT (Turkish Defence Organisation) 256, 274, 277, 287, 303, 304, 305, 353, 369
Tornaritis, Criton, Attorney-General 80, 81, 109, 116, 139 and fn.; visits Seychelles to discuss Radcliffe plan with Makarios 211
Torture, *see* Atrocities
Trade Unions 30–2; division of into right-wing and left-wing groups 31; formation of first exclusively Turkish *TU* 43; *see also* PEO *and* SEK
Trade Unions, New, *see* SEK
Trade Unions, Old, *see* PEO
Trade Unions and Trade Disputes Law 30
Trainor, Mr Justice 307, 321
Transitional Committee 351
Trapeza 203
Treasury's parsimonious policy 25
Treaties and agreements: of Alliance (Greece and Turkey) 342, 354, 358, 366–7*, 369,* 390,* 396*; of Alliance (UK and Hashemite Kingdom of Jordan) 130; Bagdad Pact 130, 224, 259, 276; Balkan Pact 69, 85, 87, 148, 225; Cyprus Convention 22–3; of Establishment 359, 361; of Guarantee 13, 342, 358, 366*, 372*, 389*, 391*, 393*, 396*; Lausanne 24, 42, 44, 87, 129, 132, 133, 134, 194, 195, 219, 222, 226, 227, 297, 329; Sèvres 18; Tripartite

Declaration, 130; Zurich and London 340–2, 362; *see also* NATO

Triandafyllides, Michael 283, 286, 352

Trikomo: Grivas's birthplace 90, 384*

Tripartite Conference on the Eastern Mediterranean 126, 129–36, 137–40, 156, 163

Trooditissa 185

Troodos Forest 182, 223; operation 186

Troodos, Mountains and Forest 182, 185, 186, 223, 389*

Trullan Council, the 20

Trusler, Assist. Superintendent 289, 290, 291

Tsadha 155

Tsaldaris, Constantine (Populist Party leader), 214, 215, 230

Tsangaris, Sotiris 232

Tsatsos, Constantine 230

Tsatsos, Themistocles 230, 351

'Tselingas' 120

Tsiros, Alexis 111

Tuomioja, Sakkari, Foreign Minister of Finland, UN mediator in Cyprus 369*, 371*

Turkey 85, 124, 193, 235, 257, 259, 296, 297, 304, 325, 327, 343, 356, 359, 375*, 377*, 381*, 391*, 394*; relations with Greece 44, 61, 69, 73, 84–5, 89, 134, 136, 260, 262, 264, 285, 326, 341, 342, 346, 360, 364*, 371*, 372*, 374*, 375*, 376*, 381–2*, 385*, 388*, 390–2*; importance of to NATO 71, 79; early warnings 73; diplomatic intervention in Cyprus dispute 73, 74, 89, 279; proximity to Cyprus 87; Turkey's interest in 134, 237; disturbances in 137, 277; relations with Britain 194–5, 267, 276, 323, 324, 394–5*; willingness to abandon partition 275, 328; distrust of British Labour Party 275; supports partition 286, 329; strategic importance of 294; its demand for a military presence in Cyprus 342; right of intervention under Zurich 344; denies approving arms smuggling to Cyprus 354; rejects Makarios's thirteen Constitutional amendments 366*; supports Britain's appeal to Security Council (1964) 368–9*; refusal to place army contingent under UNFICYP 370*; preparations for invasion of Cyprus 375*; Turkish Cypriots' economic dependence on 383*, 395*; lands forces in Cyprus (1974) 389*, 393*; demands autonomous zones 392*; loses opportunity to negotiate settlement 395*; US ban on military aid to 396*

Turkish army 367*, 372*, 389*, 393*, 394*

Turkish conquest of Cyprus 18, 20

Turkish Consul-General, Nicosia 325

Turkish Consulate-General, Salonika: bomb explosion 136

Turkish Cypriot Communal Chamber 366*, 374*, 383

Turkish (Cypriot) Fighters 372*, 374*, 384*

Turkish Cypriots: geographical and racial origins, religion and location 21; relations with Greek Cypriots 20–1, 48, 55; separatist habits 21–2; their secularism, 22; hostility to Enosis and counter-agitation 24, 35, 45, 48; demands for parity 24; relations with colonial government 26–7, 35, 55, 276–7; special enquiry into affairs of 42–5; contribution to British war effort 43; educational disadvantages of 44; activities in stimulating Turkey's interest 45, 55, 285–6; criticise British failure to enforce sedition laws and control Enosis movement 55; issue of separate municipalities 55, 295, 341, 366*; form Cyprus Turkish Association 55; testify against Greeks (trial of Karaolis) 142–4; constitutional safeguards for 208, 341; co-operate in Greek trade unions' appeal for calm 231; demand partition 244, 285–8; distrust of Foot 263, 273–4; opposition to Foot's plan 275–6; clash with British forces 276–7; security forces' dependence on 277; hope for troops from Turkey 287; alleged British bias towards, the Army's natural sympathies with 293–4; obtain veto powers and Communal Chambers (Zurich) 341; gun-running activities (*Deniz* episode) 353–4; reactions to Independence (1960) 362

After Independence:

rise in nationalism 364–5*; friction with the Greeks over Constitution 365–6; enact law setting up own municipalities 366*; major Greek attacks against 366–7*, 368–9*, 371*, 374–5*; 700 taken hostage by Greeks 367*; cede tactical positions to British troops 367*; refugees 368*, 393*; UN withdraws escorts from 370*; hostility towards UN 370*, 373*; increase fortifications 373*; blockaded by the Greeks 373*; form Provisional Cyprus Turkish Administration 376*; Makarios lifts restrictions on, Greeks still debarred from Turkish-held enclaves 377;* on day of Greek coup withdraw into enclaves 389*; enclaves in south surrender 389*; mass migrations to north 394*; *see also* Kutchuk, Intercommunal Strife *and* TMT.

Turkish military base 275, 278

Turkish Minority Association (KATAK) 43

Turkish Tribute 25, 26, 27

Tylliria 187

Tzarapkin, S. K. (UN del., USSR) 226

United Nations (UN) 99, 100, 103, 104, 105, 111, 122, 135, 230, 234, 236, 239, 241, 264, 266–73, 274, 322, 373*; AKEL's memorandum to, requesting plebiscite 46, 48; early Greek Cypriot effort to enlist support 59, 65, 73–4; Greece's appeal to, 73–4, 78, 82, 89, 123, 124–5, 127, 131, 163, 212, 218, 260–1, 263; Cypriot nationalists' expectations of 75, 126; Debates 83–9, 137–8, 219–29, 328–38

　　Member states' stand on Cyprus issue: Afghanistan 60, 269; Afro-Asian states 270; Arab states 85, 224, 270; Argentine 336; Australia 83, 88, 224; Austria 334; Belgium 225, 269, 331; Bolivia 226, 270; Byelo-Russia 226; Canada 271; Ceylon 225, 272, 331; Chile 271; Colombia 83, 88, 270, 330, 333, 334, 336; Commonwealth 224; Czechoslovakia 83, 85, 226, 266; Denmark 271; Egypt 226, 271; El Salvador 87, 88; Ethiopia 332; France 83, 85, 89, 224–5, 269, 338, 376; Ghana 272; Great Britain 83, 84, 87, 88, 221–2, 224, 229, 266, 267, 268, 272, 329, 330, 331, 332, 334–5, 336; Greece 83, 87, 88, 219, 220, 221, 223–4, 226, 227, 229, 230, 266, 267–8, 269, 270–1, 272, 329, 330, 332, 333, 334, 335–6, 337, 338–9; Guatemala 270, 271, 334; Haiti 271, 331; Iceland 83, 331, 337; India 85, 227–9, 230, 272, 331–2, 333, 336; Indonesia 87; Iran 227, 269, 330–1, 332, 333, 334, 335, 336, 337; Iraq 83, 87, 225, 272; Ireland 225–6, 331, 334; Jordan 226; Latin American States 138, 270, 337; Lebanon 271; Liberia 85, 337; Luxembourg 85; Malaya 269, 337; Mexico 272, 333, 335, 337; Morocco 272; Nepal 331; Netherlands 83, 85; New Zealand 85, 86–7, 88, 338; Norway 85, 244, 271; Pakistan 225, 269, 337; Panama 226, 229, 270, 331; Peru 227, 333, 334; Poland 226; Portugal 225, 269; South Africa 85; Soviet bloc 87, 270, 337; Spain 225, 337, 338; Sudan 226; Sweden 85, 87; Syria 83, 85, 87, 226, 270, 271; Thailand 225, 227, 230; Tunisia 271; Turkey 84, 85, 87, 88, 222–3, 226, 227, 229, 266, 267, 268, 270–1, 329, 330, 332, 333, 334, 335, 336, 338; Ukraine 226; United Arab Republic 331, 337; Uruguay 270; USA 83, 85, 86–7, 225, 227, 269, 270, 272, 329, 335, 337; USSR 83, 85, 224, 226, 229, 266, 270; Venezuela 226; West Irian 87; Yemen 87; Yugoslavia 226

Security Council 369*, 376*, 389* and fn.

UNESCO (United Nations Educational, Scientific and Cultural Organisation) 218

UNFICYP (United Nations Force in Cyprus) 369–70*, 373*, 374–6*, 385*, 390*, 392*

UNSCOB (United Nations Special Commission on the Balkans) 58

Ulus 170, 197
Umharam, Tekke of 18
Unified Party 378*
USA 82, 158, 167, 270, 323, 327, 329, 339, 354, 364*; the importance of in the Cyprus struggle 59, 60, 67, 88; waning goodwill towards, on the part of Greece 67; reaction to Makarios's deportation 172–3; abstains from vote at UN 230; departure of the Nationalist delegation for, sounds Turkish Government on possibility of Cypriot independence 260; proposals 368*, 388*; concern at Makarios's foreign policy 371*
United States Information Services (USIS) 89
US military aid: ban on, to Turkey 396*
US Vice-Consul, Nicosia, murder of 188
USSR 52, 63, 214, 217, 219, 224, 350, 364*, 371*, 376*, 381*; 383*, 386*, 388*, 396*; supports Greece at UN 85; penetration of the Mediterranean 195

Valvis, Zafiris 97, 128
Vance, Cyrus, US envoy 376
Varnava, Maria: killed by EOKA 309
Varosha 282 fn., 309, 319
Vasilia: first intercommunal clash 175
Vassiliades, Mr Justice (former President of the Supreme Court) 384
Vatan 45
Vavilas 392
Venetians' military power 18
Venizelos, Eleftherias 23, 87, 132
Venizelos, Sophokles 64, 215, 217, 230, 268
Ventiris, General 97
Vigilance groups 302
Village Improvement Boards 51
Violence: tradition of in Cypriot rural area 99–100; Makarios's refusal to denounce 161–2, 169, 172, 236, 242
Visser't Hooft 172
Vlakhos, Evanghelos, Greek Consul-General, Nicosia 240; suggests Grivas declares a truce 204
Vokolida: attack on leftists by EOKA 257
'Volkan' 139
Votsi's coffee shop, Nicosia, 142
Vretcha 183

Wadsworth, J. J. (UN del., USA) 225
Webb, Sidney (Lord Passfield) 25

Western alliance: role of Greece in 212, 323, 350, 386*; efforts to solve problem within the framework of 261, 335, 337; defence 294, 364*, 396*

Whipping: introduced for offenders under 18; officials' attitude to 147

White, Lincoln (official spokesman of the State Department) 172

Wideson, Odysseus, 175

Williamson, Douglas, Assistant Commissioner, Platres: killed by parcel bomb 205

Winster, Lord 37, 39; condemns municipalities 25; appointed Governor, arrives Cyprus 35–6; reception boycotted by Greeks 36; dismisses four absent Greek members of Advisory Council 36; paves way for Consultative Assembly 36; dissolves Assembly 38; sponsorship of inquiry into Turkish Cypriot affairs 44; initiates Cyprus H.L.Deb. 71–3

Wolseley Barracks 114

Women (EOKA) prisoners 207

Woodhouse, C. M., 91, 261

World Council of Churches 46, 172

Wormwood Scrubs, imprisonment of Cypriot prisoners 250, 253, 254

Wright, Sir Andrew, Governor: arrives in Cyprus 45; Archbishop Myriantheus requests plebiscite 46; discourages plebiscite 47–8; states Enosis issue is closed 47–8, 69

Wyatt, Woodrow 80

'X', right-wing terrorist organisation, Greece 42, 91, 92, 93, 95, 128, 348; X-Party of National Resistance 92

Xanthi, Mufti of 227

Xenophontas, Nikos: death sentence commuted 207

Xeros 106, 384*

Xydis, Stephen 224 fn., 254 fn.

Yalman, editor of *Vatan* 45

Yates, William, MP 192 fn.

Yerakinis, General, Commander of the National Guard 383*

Yerasa 185

Yerolakkos Police Station 289

Yiallouros, Petros: killed in riot 154

Yiangos 184

Yiasoumi 307

Yiolou 317

Young, Major-General: truce force set up under 367*

Younger, Kenneth 62

Yugoslavia 68; defence talks in Athens with Greek and Turkish Chiefs of Staff 85

'Zaimis' 248

Zakharades, Nikos, rift with Markos 41, 57

Zakos, 152; executed 188; reactions to execution 218

Zavros, Special Constable 129

'Zedro', Afxentiou's code name 142, 143

Zeinidine, F. (UN del., Syria) 226, 270

Zekia, Mr Justice 145

Ziartides, Andreas 32, 152, 178, 304, 306, 308, 309; journeys behind the Iron Curtain to seek guidance on future policy 41, 52; warning to Makarios 53; attempt on his life, 138; returns to Cyprus (1957) 256

Zorlu, Fatim, Turkish Foreign Minister 131–2, 133, 134, 276, 330, 332, 333–4, 335, 336, 337, 338, 340, 342, 345, 357

Zurich 342, 346, 351, 362, 365, 366

Zurich and London Agreements 340, 341, 342, 344, 345, 352, 353, 354, 356, 358, 360, 362, 364, 365*, 367*, 371*, 383*, 393–4*